APOSTLE OF THE CRUCIFIED LORD

Apostle of the Crucified Lord

A THEOLOGICAL INTRODUCTION
TO PAUL AND HIS LETTERS

Michael J. Gorman

WILLIAM B. EERDMANS PUBLISHING COMPANY
GRAND RAPIDS, MICHIGAN / CAMBRIDGE, U.K.

Wm. B. Eerdmans Publishing Co.
2140 Oak Industrial Drive N.E., Grand Rapids, Michigan 49505 /
P.O. Box 163, Cambridge CB3 9PU U.K.

Printed in the United States of America

18 17 16 15 14 13   16 15 14 13 12 11 10

Library of Congress Cataloging-in-Publication Data

Apostle of the crucified Lord: a theological introduction
to Paul and his letters / Michael J. Gorman.
p.   cm.
Includes bibliographical references.
ISBN 978-0-8028-3934-3 (pbk.: alk. paper)
1. Bible. N.T. Epistles of Paul — Theology.   I. Title.

BS2651.G64   2004
227′.06 — dc22

2003058383

www.eerdmans.com

Contents

Acknowledgments   vii

List of Maps   ix

Introduction   x

1. PAUL'S WORLD(S)   1
   The Greco-Roman Context of His Mission

2. PAUL'S RÉSUMÉ   40
   The Mission of the Former Persecutor

3. PAUL'S LETTERS   74
   Apostleship in Absentia

4. PAUL'S GOSPEL   98
   The Good News of Christ Crucified and Raised

5. PAUL'S SPIRITUALITY   115
   *Covenantal, Cruciform, and Charismatic; Communal,
   Countercultural, and (New-) Creational*

6. PAUL'S THEOLOGY   131
   A Dozen Fundamental Convictions

7. 1 THESSALONIANS   146
   Holiness and Hope in a Pagan World

CONTENTS

8. 2 THESSALONIANS   167
   Cruciform Faithfulness and Goodness before the Parousia

9. GALATIANS   183
   The Sufficiency of the Cross and Spirit

10. 1 CORINTHIANS   227
    Chaos and the Cross in Corinth

11. 2 CORINTHIANS   287
    Paul's Defense of Cruciform Ministry

12. ROMANS   338
    Gentile and Jew in Cruciform Covenant Community

13. PHILIPPIANS   412
    The Hymn of the Crucified Lord in the Cruciform Community

14. PHILEMON   454
    The Cross and the Status Quo

15. COLOSSIANS   471
    The Cosmic Crucified Christ as the Wisdom of God

16. EPHESIANS   498
    Walking Worthily of the Cosmic Crucified Christ

17. 2 TIMOTHY   532
    Suffering Rather than Shame

18. 1 TIMOTHY   551
    Proper Order and Conduct in God's Household

19. TITUS   571
    Ordering Church Life and Leadership between the Epiphanies

20. EPILOGUE   580
    Paul Our Contemporary

   Scripture Index   593

Acknowledgments

The writing of any book requires the assistance of many people, some of whom may not even realize the help they have provided.

I begin by acknowledging my debt to my teachers and my colleagues in Pauline studies. Some of those colleagues, whom I am privileged to count also as friends, have critically read parts of the manuscript: Warren Carter, Steve Fowl, Beverly Gaventa, Kathy Grieb, Frank Matera, Judy Ryan, Jeff Siker, Marty Soards, Marianne Meye Thompson, Ron Witherup, and Tom Wright. Judy Ryan and Ron Witherup deserve special mention for reading numerous chapters, while Tom Wright did the same and also graciously sent me a copy of the page proofs of his *New Interpreter's Bible* commentary on Romans. Of course, I hold none of them responsible for deficiencies that remain in the text.

I owe a debt of gratitude also to my many students over the last two decades of teaching in various settings; they have helped me to clarify my thinking and my means of expressing the conclusions to which I have been driven. Some of them have also read various versions of the manuscript in whole or in part: my students in classes on Paul, including Matthew Frisoni, who made many helpful suggestions; a former research assistant, Bill Garrison; and another former research assistant, Rev. Pat Keane, then a seminarian, who carefully read several drafts of the book, made numerous valuable suggestions, verified Scripture references, and helped create the index. Most recently, Irene Morin, Zenaida Bench, and Judy Langmead completed the index. Judy Langmead also proofread much of the manuscript.

A sincere word of thanks is due also to my family for their constant support: my wife Nancy, my children, and my father. Special thanks is due my son Mark, a budding historian, who read parts of the manuscript.

ACKNOWLEDGMENTS

I am grateful, as well, to friends who have supported this project, especially George Leiman, for his ongoing interest, and Steffanie Felder, who helped with typing at some crucial moments.

I also express my deep gratitude to those who made the writing of this book possible. The first draft was largely completed during a sabbatical in 2001 from all of my responsibilities at St. Mary's Seminary and University. I thank our President-Rector, Fr. Robert Leavitt, for his generosity, support, and interest; Dr. Chris Dreisbach for taking on my administrative responsibilities in my absence; and the Executive Board, faculty, and staff of the Ecumenical Institute of Theology for their help and encouragement.

I am grateful as well to the group of wonderful people, mostly from Fresno, California, with whom I traveled to Turkey and Greece during my sabbatical. The entire group, and especially its leaders, Dr. Jim Westgate and Rev. Gordon Donaho, made my journey most rewarding. Most of the photos in this book were taken by the author, largely during that experience.

I would also like to acknowledge the sources of several other illustrations: the photgraphs of papyrus on page 80, from the State Museums of Berlin, Papyrus Collection; the photograph of p^{46} on page 94, from the Institute for New Testament Textual Research, Münster, Westphalia; the reconstruction of central Roman Corinth, from N. Papahatzis, *Ancient Corinth: The Museums of Corinth, Isthmia and Sicyon* (Athens: Ekdotike Athenon, 1981); and the map of ancient Philippi on page 416, from C. Bakirtzis and H. Koester, eds., *Philippi at the Time of Paul and after His Death* (Trinity International Press, 1998).

Finally, I wish to thank John Simpson and the entire Wm. B. Eerdmans Publishing Company for their support of this project, and for allowing the printing of several prepublication versions for student use. Those versions were prepared by Wipf and Stock Publishers under the guidance of Jon Stock and Jim Tedrick, to whom I also extend my thanks.

Introduction

This book is offered first of all to those who wish to engage the apostle Paul and his letters because they believe that he and they have something to say to the contemporary Christian church. It is also offered to others who are interested not only in the historical and literary aspects of Paul's letters, but also, and even primarily, in their religious or theological content. The book is designed to be read in conjunction with Paul's letters.

Writing a textbook on the apostle Paul and his letters is a daunting task. The interpretation of every verse, nearly every word, is disputed. The texts have been analyzed by some of the greatest minds of the last two thousand years and continue to be placed under the microscope by thousands of scholars — and millions of lay readers — around the world. Trying to write on the meaning of Paul and his letters is similar to preparing a book on the meaning of life: there are so many points of view on the topic that the author is forced primarily to offer his or her own perspective.

That is what I do in this book. Nevertheless, although this book's perspective is distinctive, it is neither isolated from the interpretations of others nor so distinctive as to be idiosyncratic. In fact, much of what this book says about Paul can and will be found elsewhere, for I have of course learned much from many, and on many Pauline topics there is actually quite a bit of general agreement. Writing about this man and his letters, therefore, is somewhat like conducting a symphony. One repeatedly reads the score carefully, listens to interpretations of it by respected conductors, reads the score again (perhaps while listening to first one interpretation and then another), and so on. For more than two decades I have read and listened, developing my own (ever-evolving) interpretation and occasionally producing recordings myself.

Like listening to music, reading the letters of Paul requires constant attention to both small details and grand themes, and the careful reader is constantly going back to see how the themes inform the details and the details create the themes. This back-and-forth movement — what is sometimes called the 'hermeneutical (interpretive) circle' — eventually yields a framework within which one hears and reads the music, or the text.

Such a framework is seldom, however, simple, reducible to one descriptive word. For this book, six key words describe the frame of reference within which Paul is understood: 'Jewish,' 'covenantal,' 'narrative,' 'countercultural,' 'trinitarian,' and especially 'cruciform.' This list may strike some readers initially as an odd combination of Jewish and Christian (and perhaps even anachronistic Christian) language, but as the book unfolds, it will hopefully become clear that Paul's own experience and his writings are well described by these terms. It may also occur to some readers that the absence of a descriptive term like 'eschatological' or 'apocalyptic' is peculiar. I believe it is best to include that aspect of Paul within the realm of 'narrative,' which refers in part to the story of God from promise to ultimate fulfillment.

As much as possible I have tried both to indicate areas of significant scholarly debate and to justify my own reading of Paul. In a book of this size and scope, however, it is of course impossible to mention every issue or defend every interpretation.

Though I have worked directly with the Greek text of the New Testament, the scriptural quotations, unless otherwise indicated, come from the NRSV (New Revised Standard Version). Many interesting and significant alternative translations from the NIV (New International Version) and NAB (New American Bible) are also provided and noted as such.

There are two distinctive features of this book's format. The first is the set of reflection questions that appears at the end of each chapter. These are included for individual consideration, group discussion, or both as one means of achieving the book's basic goal: engaging Paul and his letters as the pastoral, spiritual, and theological challenge they were intended to be. In the chapters on each letter (chaps. 7–19), the final reflection question is always, "In sum, what does this letter urge the church to believe, to hope for, and to do?" That is the question, in fact, that drives this book.

The second distinctive feature is a brief collection of quotations, from a variety of sources and perspectives, that appears just prior to the reflection questions in chapters 7 to 19. These are also intended to stimulate thought and conversation by engaging the views of others.

A NOTE TO THE READER

This book contains not only an introduction to Paul and his letters, but also a fairly extensive commentary on each of those letters. It is intended for a wide reading audience but with theological students especially in mind. Those who are unable, for whatever reason, to read the entire chapter on a particular letter are advised to read carefully the introduction ("The Story behind the Letter"); the outline of the letter, which appears at the beginning of "The Story within the Letter"; and the summary or summaries of the letter that are provided (at the end of short letters and at two or more junctures in longer letters). And of course, as noted above, Paul's letters themselves should be read in conjunction with this book.

In order not to confuse the reader, throughout this book I have used double quotation marks (". . .") only for direct quotations from Scripture and other sources, and single marks ('. . .') for definitions of words, technical terms, idioms, and figurative or special uses of words and phrases.

FOR FURTHER READING AND STUDY

Following are a few works and web sites on Paul that are either general or comprehensive in scope, and as such are not included in the bibliographies that appear at the end of each chapter.

Becker, Jürgen. *Paul: Apostle to the Gentiles.* Translated by O. C. Dean. Louisville: Westminster John Knox, 1993. An in-depth analysis of each letter on the assumption of various developments in Paul's thought from earlier to later letters.

Brown, Raymond E. *An Introduction to the New Testament.* Part III. New York: Doubleday, 1997. A comprehensive analysis of the critical issues surrounding each letter, plus attention to the letters' theological content.

Donelson, Lewis R. *Colossians, Ephesians, 1 and 2 Timothy, and Titus.* Westminster Bible Companion. Louisville: Westminster John Knox, 1996. A brief but theologically rich exposition of the text on the assumption that although Paul did not write these letters, they remain significant.

Dunn, James D. G., ed. *The Cambridge Companion to St. Paul.* Cambridge, Eng.: Cambridge University Press, 2003. A brief but excellent introduction to Paul's life, letters, theology, and legacy by a group of top-notch Pauline scholars.

Hawthorne, Gerald F., Ralph P. Martin, and Daniel G. Reid, eds. *Dictionary of Paul and His Letters.* Downers Grove, Ill.: InterVarsity, 1993. An encyclopedia of authoritative articles, many of significant length and substance, devoted to specific letters and to related topics.

Horrell, David. *An Introduction to the Study of Paul.* New York: Continuum, 2000.

A brief but insightful survey of issues and trends in Pauline interpretation, with
helpful suggestions for further reading.

Johnson, Luke Timothy, and Todd C. Penner. *The Writings of the New Testament: An
Interpretation.* Part 4. Rev. ed. Minneapolis: Fortress, 1999. A splendid literary
and theological analysis of each of the letters, with arguments for the Pauline
authorship (broadly understood) of all thirteen letters.

Roetzel, Calvin. *The Letters of Paul: Conversations in Context.* 4th ed. Louisville: Westminster John Knox, 1998. A standard introductory text with especially helpful
chapters on Paul's world and on the form and function of the letters.

Sanders, E. P. *Paul.* New York: Oxford University Press, 1991. A basic introduction by
the architect of the 'new perspective' on Paul, stressing certain neglected aspects
of Paul's Jewishness.

See also:

ntgateway.com/paul/
"Paul the Apostle," part of "New Testament Gateway," maintained by Professor Mark
Goodacre, with many links to good sites.

textweek.com/pauline/paul.htm
"Paul and the Pauline Epistles," part of "The Text This Week," with links to articles
and much more.

luthersem.edu/ckoester/Paul/Main.htm
"Journeys of Paul," maintained by Professor Craig Koester, with photographs and
text.

CHAPTER 1

PAUL'S WORLD(S)

The Greco-Roman Context of His Mission

I extended the frontiers of all the provinces of the Roman people, which had as neighbors races not obedient to our empire. I restored peace.

C. Julius Caesar Octavianus (Caesar Augustus)[1]

Appreciating great historical figures requires an understanding of their world: Martin Luther at the dawn of sixteenth-century Europe, or Abraham Lincoln in nineteenth-century America, or Rosa Parks in the middle of the twentieth century, or the apostle Paul in the first. Paul was a man of several worlds — the culture of the hellenized Mediterranean basin, the political reality of the Roman Empire, and the orb of Second Temple Judaism. But of course, these worlds were not really distinct; they constituted one first-century world. Roman citizens (and nearly everyone else) wrote in Greek more often than not; Palestinian Jews were hellenized; and both Greek and Roman gods and goddesses took on the traits of local deities.

A full study of this world would be a book in itself. The purpose of this chapter is simply to introduce some dimensions of Paul's world(s) that will be helpful, and in some cases necessary, for understanding him and his letters. We will briefly consider Paul's Mediterranean culture, the Roman Empire, contemporary Judaism, some pagan religions and philosophies, and the Roman city.

---

1. *Res gestae divi Augusti* (Things accomplished by the divine Augustus).

PAUL'S MEDITERRANEAN CULTURE

In recent decades, due to the influence of the social sciences on biblical studies, it has become popular to speak of 'the culture of the Mediterranean basin' or to use similar language that generalizes about the culture of this vast region. Even today we speak of 'Middle Eastern' or 'Mediterranean' values or culture or cuisine. But some caution is in order; Roman values and customs in Italy and their Jewish counterparts in Palestine were hardly identical. The Mediterranean basin contained a mixture of peoples and cultures, and generalizations may fail to recognize the differences represented by these various groups. Nevertheless, it is helpful — with appropriate caution — to speak of some general characteristics of the Mediterranean culture of Paul's day.

HELLENIZATION

First to be noted is the region's *hellenization*. The triumph of Alexander the Great (d. 323 B.C.) meant the spread of Greek culture throughout the Mediterranean basin and beyond. Greek language, ideas, education, philosophy, religion, politics, and values went wherever Alexander had gone. A somewhat simplified form of classical Greek, *koinē* (common) Greek, became the norm for conducting commercial and business affairs, as well as for most other forms of communication; it is the language of the New Testament.

The Jewish communities that had dispersed throughout the region (the Diaspora) were not immune to this hellenization. They often thought in Greek ways, and they used a Greek translation of the Hebrew Scriptures (the Septuagint, abbreviated LXX). Even Palestine and Palestinian Judaism could not escape its influence. To be sure, Greek culture did not normally replace local culture but rather merged with it, as it did in different ways in the Jewish communities of Jerusalem, on the one hand, and the Jewish communities of Alexandria in Egypt, for example, on the other. The reality of hellenization did not make everyone a Greek philosopher, but it did make everyone a debtor to and participant in the heritage of Greece that permeated and helped shape the region.

SENSE OF GROUP IDENTITY

A second important aspect of ancient Mediterranean culture was its *sense of group identity*. Whereas contemporary Westerners tend to define themselves and their identity first of all as individuals, ancient Mediterranean cultures

2

**Alexander the Great,
Istanbul Museum of Archaeology**

tended to define the self primarily in terms of group membership. This fundamental cultural difference is sometimes referred to as the distinction between a 'monadic' and a 'dyadic' culture. In a monadic culture the self can be defined alone (mono-), with emphasis on the person as an individual. In a dyadic culture, however, the self can never be defined alone but always and only in reference to another (dy-, 'two'), and particularly to the group — the family, the city, etc. In a dyadic culture, value is placed on inheriting and living by the norms and customs of the group, not on the formulation of independent judgment and values. To live is to live as part of a body and to take one's place within that body. To deviate will likely spell disaster.

HONOR AND SHAME

This sense of group identity leads to another generalization about ancient Mediterranean culture: it was a culture of *honor and shame*. Simply defined, honor and shame refer to the ongoing attribution and withdrawal of esteem by peers — one's family, socioeconomic group, city, etc. In Roman society this respect was based primarily on such things as wealth, education, rhetorical skill, family pedigree, and political connections. These were the culture's primary 'status indicators.' In a dyadic culture 'self-esteem' is an oxymoron; the only esteem one has is bestowed not by the self but by the group. To 'lose face' by failing to please the group, by failing to embody the group's values, constitutes both the loss of honor and the loss of self. In this environment peer pressure is not something to avoid, as most Westerners would assert, but is in fact the *appropriate* norm.

HIERARCHY

The culture of Paul's day, despite (and in fact because of) the emphasis on group solidarity, was also very *hierarchical*. Greco-Roman culture exhibited a hierarchy that can be usefully (though not perfectly) compared to the Eiffel Tower: a small pinnacle (the 'elite'), reinforced by a larger but still small support sector (the 'retainers'), all standing on the shoulders of a massive foundation (the 'nonelite').[2] In this hierarchical arrangement, power was concentrated at the top among the elite (no more than 5 percent of the population), but the people were of course concentrated near the bottom. At the pinnacle was the emperor. Beneath him were the senators, the equestrians (a class of high-ranking military and political figures), and the decurions — aristocrats with land and other forms of wealth but only local political power. Supporting this governing class was a network of people sociologists call retainers: political and religious officials (priests, government bureaucrats, etc.) who keep the machinery of power running, attend to the needs of the elite, and derive a measure of power and status from their connection to the elite. Further down were those of some means but little or no political power, including merchants. Still further toward the bottom were the slaves who were 'middle managers' for the elite (see discussion below); then the working lower class of free persons and freedpersons (artisans and the like); lower-level slaves, and the free, working poor (e.g., day laborers). At the very bottom, as in

---

2. A somewhat more precise graphic representation of this reality can be found in the illustration in Gerhard E. Lenski's *Power and Privilege: A Theory of Social Stratification* (New York: McGraw-Hill, 1966), p. 284, reproduced on page 5. It is not focused, however, on the urban context; therefore, 'day-laborers and slaves' has replaced 'peasants' in the illustration.

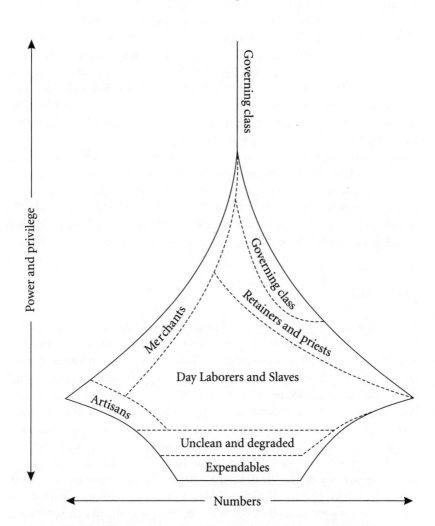

The hierarchical structure of societies such as that of Paul's time
(From Gerhard E. Lenski, *Power and Privilege: A Theory of Social Stratification*
[New York: McGraw-Hill, 1966], 284 — slightly modified)

any society, were the unclean and the 'expendables': those without any wealth, power, or status, such as widows, orphans, and the disabled.

The Jewish communities of the ancient world both participated in the Roman vertical hierarchical culture and constituted a culture of their own. Outside Palestine, in the cities of the Diaspora, Jews frequently lived near one another, practicing their trades as members of the artisan sector of their city. They interacted with Gentiles, of course, including the elite, but very few — even the most educated — were actually part of the elite. In Palestine there was a hierarchy within Jewish society itself: a few Jews participated in the ruling class; others were retainers who supported (and benefited from) either Jewish religious or Roman political powers, or both; still others were artisans and merchants; and many were poor: day laborers, peasants, the unclean, or expendables. Related to this hierarchy was what we might also call a 'horizontal' or 'concentric' hierarchy. Power and purity were in the hands of those closest to the center, whether that center was conceived of as the temple or the Law. Those males who were part of the ritual or legal system constituted the inner circle, followed by other Jewish males with some religious standing, related Jewish women and children, the poor ('the people of the land'), and finally Gentiles. This was symbolized in part by the construction of the temple, with its Holy of Holies and succession of courts, the last being the Court of the Gentiles.

PATRIARCHY

An inherent aspect of the hierarchy of Mediterranean culture was its *patriarchy*. The male head of household governed his own little universe, with his wife, children, and slaves as personal property. This gave free men power and privilege in their own homes, even if nowhere else. For example, men could — and did — 'expose' deformed infants they had fathered (i.e., leave them on the garbage heap outside town, either to die or to be 'adopted' as slaves or prostitutes). Men ruled the empires, provinces, and cities (though rulers' wives could of course exercise considerable power), and in general controlled the temples.

Women were primarily assigned to the home as wives, mothers, and household managers, but this did not mean they had no other role in society. Elite women had more freedom than others, and during the Roman period they might receive a good education. Some women were prominent in business, and some cults gave women considerable leadership and participatory roles. There were, of course, goddesses as role models for the importance of the female gender in the religious sphere. In many temples priestesses attended to the needs of the gods and their devotees, and women often figured prominently in religious processions and other events. Some cults, especially the mystery religions (see below), attracted women exclusively or primarily. In the Diaspora (outside Palestine), Jewish women were likely to be active in their communities and sometimes even in their synagogues, as benefactors and leaders. Nonetheless, throughout the Mediterranean world, much of one's access to education, public life, and religious leadership was determined by gender, and males were clearly the privileged half of the human race.

SLAVERY

Another unavoidable aspect of hierarchical Greco-Roman culture was the institution of *slavery*. In urban areas a significant percentage of all inhabitants were slaves (though firm numbers are unavailable, and scholars' estimates differ); even smaller households often had a few slaves, while the larger households of the very wealthy had many. To be a slave was to belong, not to oneself, but to another (Aristotle, *Politics* 1.1254a.14), and to live to do the other's bidding — without the right to refuse (Seneca, *On Benefits* [*De beneficiis*] 3.19). It was to possess few if any legal rights, and to be in a state of dishonor. Slaves were used and abused; they could be forced to work long hours and could be punished severely. Disobedient, unruly, runaway, or otherwise troublesome slaves could be tortured or even killed, though Roman law in the imperial period required a just cause for the death of a slave. Many slaves, both male and female, were sexually exploited by their masters. Not all slaves did difficult manual labor or suffered mistreatment, however, as some (perhaps many) masters were generally humane.

Unlike the American system of slavery, slavery in the Greco-Roman world was not based on race. Slaves could be made (through conquest or piracy), found (as children 'exposed' at the town dump or otherwise abandoned), or even, though much more rarely, self-made (through selling oneself into slavery). Yet there were similarities to slavery in the United States. By Paul's time most slaves were born into slavery; a slave's children also became the slave owner's property. As property, slaves were bought and sold privately or through 'retailers.' As in the slave era in the United States, they were judged and priced according to their actual or potential usefulness. Domestic slaves contributed to the needs and comforts of the master and his family. It was also possible for a slave to acquire skills in a trade and even to rise to some prominence as, for example, the manager of his master's business. Furthermore, in the first century a small number of slaves throughout the empire constituted the 'imperial household,' functioning as the empire's civil service. But it would be erroneous to think that slavery was generally a means of self-improvement or advancement.

Freedom, the goal of nearly every slave, required the generosity of the master and his willingness to lose the monetary value of his property. But among the elite it could also be a status symbol to release slaves and thus demonstrate to peers the virtue of generosity. There is some evidence that during the Roman period slaves could expect liberation at the age of thirty or so (when life expectancy was not a lot longer), but how often this actually occurred, and why (perhaps to relieve the master of the care of elderly and infirm slaves), is a matter of debate. Manumission could occur while the master was alive, either at his discretion or through the payment of a specified sum by the slave or another person for the slave. Sometimes a god (through the priests) would effect a sacral manumission. Occasionally a master would liberate slave children by legally adopting them as his own. Manumission could also occur at the owner's death according to the provisions of his will.

Freedpersons usually became the clients of their former owners, who, as patrons, often helped their new clients financially. Freedpersons could now travel at will but could not vote. They might find life more difficult and fail (at least economically) in their new status, though some — such as the first-century Stoic teacher Epictetus — succeeded not only economically but also in other important ways. Some freed slaves even became Roman citizens.

PAUL'S ROMAN EMPIRE

Paul lived at a time that had one overriding and unifying reality — the Roman Empire, heir to Alexander's conquered world. A complete discussion of the Roman Empire is of course impossible in this book, though certain aspects of Paul's social, political, and religious world will be mentioned briefly as appropriate in the discussion of specific Pauline texts. Here we highlight just a few aspects of the imperial reality that affected Paul's mission and message: the pax Romana, community in the empire, mobility in the empire, and imperial unity through cult and theology. The last of these is given special emphasis, for it refers to the religious dimension of empire, as Paul's 'pagan competition' (considered later in the chapter) included the cult of the emperor.

PAX ROMANA

No empire in human history is as celebrated as the Roman Empire. This empire is synonymous with the 'Roman peace' — the *pax Romana*. The empire ended an era of civil strife in Rome and unified a huge area of land containing diverse peoples. The systems that built and maintained that peace have been the envy of many for two millennia: government, military, architecture, roads, and so on.

The empire's birth can be dated to 31 or, more properly, 27 B.C., though of course its birth was preceded by years of preparation and followed by centuries

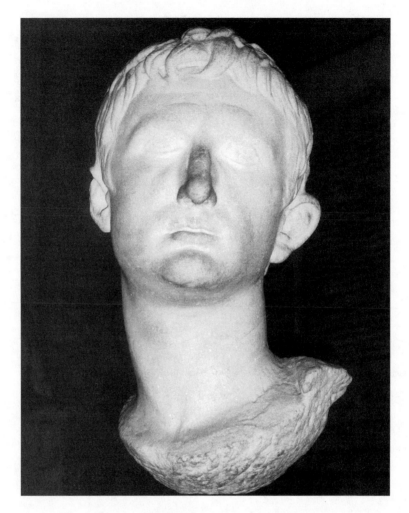

Augustus, Istanbul Museum of Archaeology

of development. In 31 B.C. Octavian, the adopted son of Julius Caesar, defeated
Mark Antony at the Battle of Actium. He subsequently (27 B.C.) received from
the Roman Senate the name Augustus ('revered one,' 'honored by the gods') —
and all succeeding emperors kept the name.[3] He was welcomed as Rome's sav-

3. The term 'emperor' comes from the Latin *imperator* (commander). Julius Caesar called
himself *imperator*, and his successors, beginning with Octavian (Augustus), took it as a *prae-
nomen* (first name). Octavian also kept his adoptive father's name, Caesar, as a *cognomen* ('last
name' — but often the name by which one was known), while later emperors used it as part of
their imperial title.

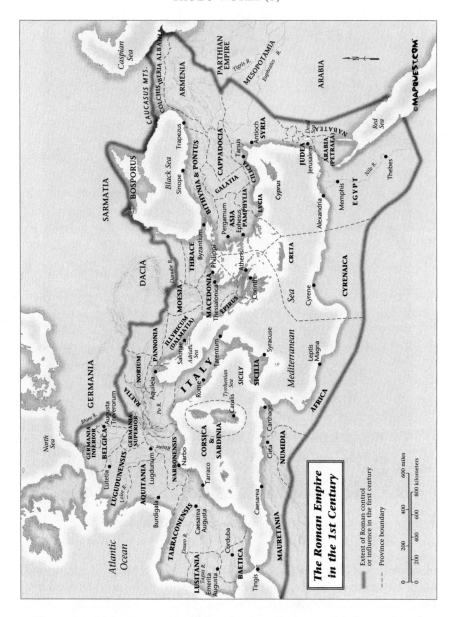

The extent of the Roman Empire at the time Paul wrote his letters (c. 50)

**A first-century sculpture (now in the Louvre, Paris) of the flaying of Marsyas
for insulting Apollo evokes also the humiliation of crucifixion**

ior and the incarnation of divine good news for the whole world. Under him,
major expansion of Rome's power took place in all directions, as Augustus himself boasted in his *Res gestae divi Augusti* (Things accomplished by the divine
Augustus). Roman law, Roman values, Roman gods, Roman roads, and Roman
coins spread everywhere, and the emperors that followed Augustus continued
the work of Rome's first imperial savior.

But there was a dark side to this 'peace' that cannot be forgotten. An empire was born, but a republic simultaneously died. The Romans established and

maintained their empire through conquest, subjugation, and intimidation. It was, in other words, peace through war. The Romans invaded and enslaved; they moved the conquered in and out; they formed new colonies and refounded old cities as their own colonies. They imposed taxes and tributes to maintain the empire (especially the military and the elite) and its pax among the subjugated peoples. And they had a deterrent to make sure those who might threaten the peace understood the consequences: crucifixion.

The Romans did not invent crucifixion, but they did perfect it. With trees, single beams, and variously shaped crosses, they would kill any noncitizen who put the pax in jeopardy. Their own writers knew it was the cruelest of deaths, yet in spite of this — or was it because of this? — a Roman crowd would gather to watch insurrectionists, slaves, and others die in naked shame. There could be nothing more irrational or more un-Roman than to honor — not to mention *deify!* — a man crucified by the imperial authorities.

COMMUNITY: EMPIRE, CITY, FAMILY

The image of a crowd of Romans watching government officials put a group of rebellious slaves or political revolutionaries to death may strike us as odd and even sadistic, but in the first century it was something of a family get-together. For the empire envisioned itself as one large family under the headship of its father, the emperor himself (*pater patriae*, 'father of the country').

The family, or household (Gk. *oikos*; Lat. *domus*), was the fundamental unit of Roman society. That family would include not only the male head of household with his wife and children, but perhaps also extended family and, among those of even moderate means, household slaves.

Many families in the first century lived in cities, some of which (like Rome and Ephesus) were quite large in area and population. Some of these cities, with special obligations and duties to the emperor and the empire, were colonies of Rome. (Further discussion of the city may be found in the last section of this chapter.) Within these cities lived various kinds of people, often within the same household: citizens and noncitizens; slaves, free, and freedpersons (former slaves); poor and wealthy. Everyone was very conscious of these socioeconomic differences.

The engine that ran the empire, the family, and the city was love of honor or status (Lat. *philotimia*), which took on a godlike role. The pursuit of honor — the admiration of one's peers — created a fiercely competitive society, at least among those of means. They strove to outdo one another in accumulating honor for the emperor and for Rome, for their particular city and family, and of course for themselves. A building project financed by a wealthy man, for instance, could accomplish all three. It beautified and served the city while it could be dedicated to the emperor and prominently inscribed with the backer's name.

The elite of a city associated primarily with people of similar status. The men would often spend their time in civic-minded activities (all for honor, and never working with their hands), congregate in the baths, and entertain one another at dinner parties. If the nonelite (artisans, family slaves, etc.) happened to be in attendance at such a dinner, they would be served food of lesser quality in separate rooms.

There was really no middle class in Roman society, at least nothing like the large, relatively well-to-do and independent American middle class.[4] The 'working class' were people of little status even though they constituted a large percentage of the population. Nonelite but free individuals had their own means of community, called collegia, or (loosely) 'clubs' — social organizations with religious overtones and a variety of functions. One kind of collegium was the trade guild, an association of workers (largely male), such as tentmakers or shipbuilders, who met for business and social purposes. Another type was strictly religious, dedicated to the practice of one of the cults. Yet another kind, especially for the poor, was the burial society, a fellowship designed to help defray the high cost of burials. These collegia were sanctioned by Rome, though problematic groups could be banned.

The structure of relationships in Roman society was not, however, a completely horizontal affair. In addition to interaction between masters and slaves, and between the wealthy and the tradespeople who supplied their goods, there was a system of patron-client relations. Starting from the emperor, who was seen as patron of the entire empire, and moving down into the elite strata, people of means and status acted for the benefit (financial and other) of those of lesser means and status. In return, the beneficiaries — the clients — gave the patron their loyalty and honor. Clients might include a man's former slaves, several working poor people, perhaps an artist or teacher dependent on the patron for support, or a group of people, such as a collegium.

MOBILITY: TRAVEL IN THE EMPIRE

Despite the community and stability found in one's household and city — not to mention the availability of most goods and services — some people either desired or were required to travel. Whether for business, pleasure, government or military service, or religious purposes, moving around the empire was quite common.

---

4. 'Retainers' were so dependent on the elite, and such a small percentage of the population, that they did not constitute what we think of as a middle class.

One of the (partially restored) main roads in Ephesus

Rome is justifiably famous for its extensive system of superior roads (a political and military necessity for a smooth-running empire), some of which can still be seen and used. The roads connected cities, making possible the transport of people, goods, mail, ideas, and religions. Road travel (mostly on foot; otherwise on a donkey, in a vehicle drawn by animals, or — for the most powerful — on a mat carried by personal slaves) could take place year-round, though winter travel in the higher elevations would naturally have to be curtailed at certain times. (Both Turkey and Greece are more mountainous than one might think.) Highway travel could still be risky business, however, due to robbers and natural dangers. Inns were notorious for their 'services': bad food, unsafe and unhealthy conditions, shady owners, and prostitutes.

In addition to the highways, the Mediterranean and its adjoining bodies of water provided various routes for travel. Travel was again restricted during the winter months, however. Sea voyages were even more dangerous than inland trips; one storm could be fatal, and despite imperial efforts, pirates sailed the seas hoping to find goods (including people) to steal and sell.

UNITY: IMPERIAL POWER, CULT, AND THEOLOGY

Travelers throughout the empire found a diversity not only of beliefs and rituals but also of landscapes — geographical and otherwise. Yet unifying and dominating the religious, political, civic, recreational, and architectural landscape of the Mediterranean basin in the first century was the cult of the emperor. Devotion to the emperor — including not only the reigning emperor but also his family and his predecessors, especially Julius and Augustus — was a multifaceted affair that permeated the culture. It was a form of religious and nationalistic, or theopolitical, allegiance, both to deified humans (the emperors) and to a cultural and political entity (the Roman Empire). In many respects, therefore, it was one of the most fundamental cohesive elements in the empire, helping to hold its diverse constituencies together.[5]

The cult of the emperor was in some ways a continuation of the Hellenistic ruler cult, which was known in much of the territory that became the Roman Empire. But for Rome it was a very significant change in attitude and behavior from the period of the Roman Republic, and it met with some resistance in Rome itself. Perhaps the change was inevitable, however; after all, as ancients and moderns alike have often assumed, no one but (a) god could subdue and then control a huge portion of the known world. From the time of Julius on, Caesar was not only the top political but also the top religious figure, the chief priest *(pontifex maximus).*[6] Julius was treated in many ways like a god before his posthumous elevation to deity, at which point his (adopted) son Gaius

5. This cohesive element was stronger in certain areas than in others (being especially strong in Asia Minor), and it did not exist in isolation; the cohesion of the empire was established and reinforced also by taxes and tribute, by the military, and so on. But nothing symbolized or unified the Roman Empire more powerfully than the emperor himself, as the object of admiration or fear (or both), and simultaneous devotion to him and to Rome was essential to the empire's stability.

6. The famous inscription at Delphi that names Gallio as proconsul of Achaia in the early 50s (while Paul was in Corinth) has the form of a greeting from the emperor Claudius (ruled 41-54), identified as 'Tiberius Claudius Caesar Augustus Germanicus Pontifex Maximus.'

Remains of the temple of the imperial cult in Corinth

Octavius (Augustus) and successor became, naturally, the son of a god.[7] And even before Augustus was formally deified after his death in A.D. 14, he initiated programs dedicated to himself, Julius, and Rome that would become the imperial cult.

This cult spread like wildfire throughout the empire during the first half of the first century, especially in the cities, and most especially in the colonies (extensions of Rome) in Greece and Asia Minor like Pisidian Antioch, Corinth, and Philippi. (Recent scholarship has demonstrated the falsity of the common notion that the imperial cult did not flourish or impact Christians until the time of Domitian at the end of the first century.) In the provinces Roman citizens were expected to participate in the cult of Rome and the divine Julius, while noncitizens were to be devotees of Rome and Augustus.[8]

7. Gaius Octavius became the adopted son of Julius Caesar upon the latter's death, as prescribed in his will. He was actually the grandson of Julius's sister Julia.

8. Even Palestine was not immune from the imperial cult; before the birth of Paul, Herod the Great had already built (or rebuilt) two cities dedicated to the emperor (Caesarea Maritima and Sebaste [Samaria]), three temples for the imperial cult, and numerous statues of the emperor. He had also dedicated games (even in Jerusalem!) to Augustus. The majority of Jews, of course, opposed the imperial cult, and because of it, in part, many even considered revolt against Rome.

By the time of Paul's ministry as recorded in his letters and Acts, temples for the imperial cult had been erected, or were being erected, in nearly all the major cities of the empire; these temples were often the largest and most central sanctuaries in a city. The huge, elevated imperial temple at Pisidian Antioch was visible for miles. Even more modest temples for the cult, such as the one at Corinth dedicated to Octavia (the sister of Augustus and wife of Mark Antony, who divorced her for Cleopatra), were impressive edifices. In addition to temples, cities erected other buildings and monuments dedicated to the emperors, as well as statues of them. Sometimes imperial statues were placed inside temples devoted to other gods. Coins, which previously bore the images of gods, now also bore the image of the emperor. Cities celebrated the reigning emperor's birthday, accession, conquests, and so on, resulting in a busy calendar of ceremonies, festivals, parades, and contests (athletic, gladiatorial, and other types) in his honor. Cities — and within cities, leading citizens — vied to sponsor the most impressive events and erect the most monumental structures. The emperor was everywhere, all the time — sponsored by his friends.

The imperial cult, then, was in part a form of prestigious civic and patriotic service, a kind of 'God and country' phenomenon. Public oaths of allegiance were part of this theopolitical activity. But the cult also encompassed more explicit forms of religious devotion to the emperor and to Rome. These included ceremonies honoring the 'genius' ('immortal spirit,' but also a kind of guardian deity) of the emperor, sacrifices offered by the imperial priests, the burning of incense, special meals, and so on. The imperial cult was a multifaceted ritual of power — human and divine.

All these cultic activities were, in fact, both religious and political, and devotion to the emperor and devotion to the empire were inseparable. Behind and within the activities was a theology, a set of convictions about Rome as the gods' choice to rule the world, an election proven and displayed in Rome's victories throughout the world, and in the 'peace' those victories achieved. The emperor was the divinely appointed and empowered patron, protector, father, and epitome of Rome and its power. Augustus was the bringer, and his successors the guarantors, of peace and security — in a word, of salvation. This was his 'evangel' or good news *(euangelion/euangelia)*, as an inscription from 9 B.C. at Priene, not far from Ephesus in the province of Asia, asserts about the 'savior' *(sotēr)* Augustus: "[S]ince the Caesar through his appearance [*epiphanein*] has exceeded the hopes of all former good messages [*euangelia*], surpassing not only the benefactors who came before him, but also leaving no hope that anyone in the future would surpass him, and since for the world the birthday of the god was the beginning of his good messages [*euangelia*]. . . ." This inscription echoes the sentiment expressed by Horace, in a poem *(Carmen saeculare)* written in 17 B.C. for games in honor of Augustus: "Already faith and peace and honor and ancient modesty and neglected virtue have courage to come back, and blessed plenty with the full horn is seen." Similarly, a shepherd's speech in Virgil's *Eclogues* (1.6-8) contains this claim about Augustus: "[I]t is a god who wrought for us this peace — for a god he shall ever be to me; often shall a tender lamb from our folds stain his altar."

As magnificent benefactors, Augustus and his imperial successors were given (or took for themselves) titles such as Savior, God, and Lord. The emperor was 'equal to God' (cf. Phil. 2:6, where this is predicated of Christ). Although most emperors did not require the actual worship of themselves as a god (notable exceptions being Caligula [Gaius], who ruled from 37 to 41, and possibly Domitian, who ruled from 81 to 96), the power and might of the imperial office made each of them recipients of godlike honors simply by being emperor of Rome.

Jews (and thus the earliest 'Christians') enjoyed exemption from certain aspects of Roman life, including the imperial cult. Needless to say, however, any movement or message that appeared to displace the emperor from his throne would be understood as counterimperial and anti-Roman (cf. Acts 17:1-9).

PAUL'S JUDAISM(S)

The Judaism of Paul's day is known as early or Second Temple Judaism.[9] It is often said, however, that what existed was in fact a plurality of Judaisms, not one monolithic entity. There is much truth in this view, for there were in fact various groups, but Jews everywhere and of all stripes were still united in several basic convictions, institutions, and practices: monotheism, election/covenant, land, Moses and the Law (Torah), temple and synagogue, circumcision, and hope for the kingdom of God. To be Jewish was to confess and worship the one God YHWH, who had graciously chosen Israel to be God's distinctive people. This God had entered into covenant with Israel, revealing the Law to Moses and thereby calling Israel into a covenantal relationship characterized by love, obedience, and faithfulness toward YHWH, and love, justice, and purity toward others. This covenant was expressed in certain practices of 'piety' and 'virtue' (as Philo summarized it), in good times and bad, whether at home or dispersed, and lived out in hope of a time when Israel's sufferings and subjugation would cease forever.

9. The temple in Jerusalem was destroyed in 587 B.C., rebuilt after the Babylonian exile, and greatly expanded by Herod the Great beginning in 20 B.C., before being destroyed again in A.D. 70 by the Romans.

To understand Paul we must keep in mind not only this general Jewish worldview, but also at least four dimensions of Jewish unity in diversity: subjugation to Rome; some common boundary markers; a theological development that affected many Jews (apocalypticism), including Paul; and some of the different Jewish groups (sometimes called 'schools' or 'parties').

SUBJUGATION TO ROME

As noted above, Jews had some privileges under Roman rule, but they were nonetheless under foreign domination. Though Jews had learned to deal with such a situation, it had not seemed appropriate to certain Jews two centuries earlier when, under Seleucid rule, the Maccabeans had revolted (167-164 B.C.). Nor did it seem right to many Jews under Roman occupation; these feelings led to sporadic acts of defiance against Rome and eventually to a full-scale attempt in A.D. 66-74 to cast the Romans out of Palestine. The unsuccessful revolt brought on the Romans' destruction of the Jerusalem temple in 70 and the famous mass-suicide incident at Masada (climaxing ca. 74).

It is within this political context that we must understand Jewish hopes for the kingdom (reign) of God and for a Messiah, or 'anointed one' (Gk. *christos*). Contrary to popular opinion, however, the evidence suggests that hope for a messianic figure was not the only, and perhaps not even the main, form of Jewish expectation regarding the coming of God's reign. Some Jews who did look for a Messiah thought they could hasten his coming by revolutionary activity; others thought they had to tolerate the Romans and wait for God to act. There was, in other words, a variety of hopes for deliverance and salvation in Second Temple Judaism, but they were always theopolitical in character. No clear evidence exists, however, for any Jewish hope for a *suffering* Messiah, much less a Messiah who would be crucified and then resurrected.

BOUNDARY MARKERS: RITUAL AND RELIGIO-ETHICAL

To be Jewish was, and is, to be different. This is the root meaning of purity or, in biblical language, holiness — to be set apart for God's purposes. To be holy is to be distinctive; the term 'holy,' when applied to people, is shorthand for 'peculiar by virtue of being obedient to God's commandments.' Holiness is the way of life that marks out the covenant people, the expression of the fact that this people is called, or elected, by God.

In the latter part of the twentieth century, under the influence of E. P. Sanders and others, it became commonplace to refer to the basic pattern of the religion of first-century Judaism as 'covenantal nomism.' Covenantal nomism means the keeping of the Law (Gk. *nomos*) not as a way of *getting in* but of *staying in* the covenant: doing the Law is what those chosen by a gracious God do after they are in covenant relationship. It has also become a scholarly convention, under the influence of such scholars as James Dunn, to refer to certain distinctive Jewish practices — especially circumcision, calendar observance (i.e., observing the Sabbath and festivals), and food laws — as 'boundary markers.' One of the significant results of these new understandings in Pauline studies has been the rejection of older notions of Judaism as a religion of 'works righteousness' in which Jews supposedly earned their salvation by doing good works. Rather, says this 'new perspective,' Jews expressed their gracious election by obeying the Law. Another impact on Pauline studies is the notion that Paul's real criticism of Judaism and Judaizers was not Judaism's self-made righteousness but what some have called its 'cultural imperialism,' or ethnic pride.

This new perspective has been an important development in the study of early Judaism and of Paul. Despite its general acceptance and wealth of important insights, it is not without its own problems. One problem is that scholars sometimes now put too much emphasis on the three ethnic boundary markers mentioned above. It is true that Jews (especially those in the Diaspora) felt themselves to be, and in fact usually were, different from their non-Jewish neighbors. But the differences, the boundary markers, that functioned as *ritual signs* of their covenant with God could not be separated from the *substantive religious and ethical* (or *religio-ethical*) distinctives of that covenant with God. While recognizing the close interconnection between these two kinds of boundary markers, we may nonetheless distinguish between *ritual* and *religio-ethical* boundary markers.[10]

Ritual boundary markers would include circumcision, calendar, and food laws. These were clearly important aspects of Jewish life that marked Jews out from Gentiles. Calling them 'ritual boundary markers' does not diminish their importance, for Jews endured ridicule and sometimes even risked death in their stubborn refusal to compromise these practices. However, what the Jewish *Letter of Aristeas* (second century B.C.) says about food laws is true of each of these ritual boundary markers: they point to meatier (no pun intended) dimensions of Jewish life. "The symbolism conveyed by these things [forbidden animals

---

10. The distinction offered here might at first appear to be an arbitrary one, but in fact it attempts to reflect a discriminating impulse within Judaism. This impulse has its roots in the prophetic tradition, where, for example, mercy and justice are preferred to sacrifice (Hos. 6:6; Isa. 1:12-17; Mic. 6:6-8), a preference echoed by Jesus, according to Matthew's Gospel (9:13, contrasting mercy toward sinners with separation from them, and 12:7, contrasting mercy with Sabbath observance). Ideally, all the distinctives belong together; what the prophetic tradition will not tolerate is the presence of ritual markers in the absence of religio-ethical ones.

and food] compels us to make a distinction in the performance of all our acts, with righteousness as our aim" (v. 151).

Although non-Jews certainly noted the odd (to them) ritual boundary markers (such as diet and circumcision), what also struck them, and what Jews repeatedly emphasized in the Diaspora, were the religio-ethical markers. These would include the distinctives of Jewish *monotheistic worship* and *morality*. Non-Jews observed that Jews worshiped only one God, exclusively and without the use of images, and that they abstained from the imperial cult. Furthermore, non-Jews noted that Jews refrained from certain social behaviors, especially such practices as (1) sexual relations with people other than their spouses and (2) exposing their unwanted children on the town garbage heap. Of course, Jews also noted these same distinctives and regularly accused non-Jews of being generally idolatrous and immoral. Even as a Christ-believer, Paul could draw upon these generalizations, as Romans 1:18-32 demonstrates. (At the same time, however, in Romans 2–3 Paul echoes the prophetic tradition in suggesting that although his fellow Jews maintained certain ritual boundary markers, they had abandoned the religio-ethical ones and had thus, in his estimation, committed the same kinds of mistakes as the Gentiles.)

It was precisely the differences of monotheistic worship and morality that generated Jewish concern about Gentile contamination. At the same time, ironically, many Gentiles disdained Jews for their monotheism and consequent refusal to bow to the gods and the emperor. Yet it was also often the substantive religio-ethical distinctives of monotheism and morality that attracted certain Gentiles to Judaism, while the ritual boundary markers (such as circumcision) were more offensive to these same Gentiles. Those who found Jewish monotheism and morality captivating would affiliate loosely with a synagogue but not undergo circumcision to become truly and fully Jewish. These Jewish sympathizers, or 'God-fearers' (cf. Acts 10:2; 13:16, 26; 16:14; 18:7), would have been prime candidates for Paul's circumcision-free gospel.

What Jews could not always agree about in the first century was the precise extent of the distinctiveness (or holiness or Law observance) required to be a 'true Jew.' These disagreements helped create the plurality of Judaisms noted above and described below. The precise definition of Israel was, in many ways, up for grabs.

APOCALYPTICISM

Before we consider some of the various answers to the question of Israel's identity, we must take account of a development that was not one of the Judaisms per se. Rather, it was a worldview that found a home in a variety of Jewish groups, including the Pharisees and the Qumran community, producers of the Dead Sea Scrolls. This very important phenomenon is apocalypticism, or apocalyptic, as it is often called.[11] The term itself derives from the Greek word *apokalypsis,* meaning 'revelation.' Apocalyptic may be defined as a worldview about the meaning and goal of history, understood as a cosmic battle between God and the forces of evil, that is communicated through visions and other forms of unusual revelations. This worldview is often preserved in a kind of writing known as an 'apocalypse' (such as Dan. 7–12 and the entire book of Revelation), a revelation to a human via a supernatural being, or in other writings that contain apocalyptic themes or sections (such as Mark 13 and parallels). In addition to the biblical apocalypses, some half-dozen other early Jewish apocalypses have been preserved. Scholars sometimes divide these apocalypses into two types, 'historical' or 'horizontal' (revealing future events, especially judgment and salvation), and 'cosmic' or 'vertical' (revealing the present heavenly reality through a trip or vision), but in fact the two can be mixed, as they are to some degree in the book of Revelation. Paul himself had an apocalyptic view of history but also claims to have made trips to heaven (see below and chap. 2).

The origins of apocalyptic (as defined above) are debated among scholars. It seems to have arisen out of the prophetic tradition as an answer to the problem of Israel's constant oppression at the hand of foreign rulers, when the situation seemed more grave than ever and hope for divine intervention within the normal historical framework no longer seemed possible. Whatever the precise historical and sociological causes for its birth, apocalyptic functioned fundamentally to give hope — hope that God, in a new way and a new day, would once again deliver Israel and her people (and in some cases, all humanity) from oppression, persecution, and other crises. That coming divine intervention would be cosmic in scope, shaking up and then re-creating the heavens and the earth. It would also be a day of judgment for evildoers and a day of salvation, including resurrection into God's heavenly presence (or into God's kingdom on the renewed earth), for the just.

This worldview envisioned two kinds of unseen realities, then, a present reality of supernatural beings 'up there' (the 'vertical' or 'spatial' dimension of apocalyptic) and a future reality of participation with those beings (the 'horizontal,' 'eschatological,'[12] or 'temporal' dimension of apocalyptic). These two

11. Some scholars distinguish between 'apocalyptic' (or 'apocalyptic eschatology') as the worldview and 'apocalypticism' as the movements and communities that embodied this kind of worldview.

12. The adjective 'eschatological' and the noun 'eschatology' refer to teachings about the 'last things,' or the future of salvation history.

realities were linked by the experience of visions and visits, which served as a foretaste of the future and a means to endure and engage the present.

Apocalypticism was also characterized by a multifaceted dualism, or belief in strong pairs of opposites. Apocalyptic thought was characterized by cosmic, chronological, and ethical dualism.

Cosmic dualism refers to the conviction that the cosmos is the battleground between two opposing sets of forces, those of God and the powers on God's side, and those of Satan and the powers on Satan's side. These powers include angels and demons (who by this time populated the Jewish universe), but also humans who align themselves either with God (e.g., the holy ones of Israel) or with Satan (e.g., the oppressing pagans). Already engaged in spiritual warfare, these two opposing forces will meet at some future and final cataclysmic battle in which God will ultimately defeat the forces of evil.

This cosmic dualism leads naturally to both chronological and ethical dualism. *Chronological* dualism means that history is conceived as divided into two ages, the present age and the age to come. The present age is characterized by evil, injustice, and the oppression of God's people, whereas the coming age will be characterized by righteousness, justice, and the liberation of God's people from bondage to the oppressors. The new age cannot and will not evolve gradually out of current historical circumstances, which are beyond repair, but only by means of a spectacular divine intervention to crush the enemy and establish justice. For this reason apocalyptic, though ultimately hopeful and optimistic, is also rightly described as pessimistic; it has no hope in the normal processes of humans and history to resolve the crisis.

In this situation human beings must choose sides. Will they align themselves with God and the forces of right, or will they take sides with Satan and the demons? Will they prepare appropriately for the final battle and divine victory, or will they betray their allegiance and live as minions of Satan? There is no middle ground, no gray area, but only black and white. This is the *ethical* dualism of apocalyptic.

In various forms the apocalyptic mind-set was expressed in important Jewish writings produced before and during the first century A.D. These include the canonical books of Ezekiel, Zechariah, Daniel, and (to a lesser extent) parts of other prophetic books; the noncanonical books of *1 Enoch, 4 Ezra,* and *2 Baruch;* many of the writings from Qumran (the Dead Sea Scrolls); and much of early Christian literature, including many of the letters of Paul.[13]

---

13. In fact, the great twentieth-century German New Testament scholar Ernst Käsemann once remarked that apocalyptic was the mother of all Christian theology. Even if somewhat exaggerated, the comment underscores the importance of apocalyptic for understanding the New Testament.

JUDAISMS

When we read the New Testament Gospels, we encounter several Jewish parties or groups, and still others are known from other ancient Jewish and pagan sources.

Sadducees, Pharisees, Essenes, Zealots

Among those mentioned in the Gospels, the Sadducees, the group associated with the priestly aristocracy who focused on the Torah alone and denied the resurrection and angels, played little if any role in the life of Paul.[14]

Among the Judaisms of Paul's day, the most important for our purposes is the Pharisees. Unfortunately, our knowledge of the Pharisees comes from non-Pharisaical sources (including the priestly, aristocratic Jewish historian Josephus[15] and the four New Testament Evangelists, who are not too sympathetic) and from one former Pharisee — Paul himself. Nevertheless, the sources agree that the Pharisees were a nonpriestly group zealously dedicated to the protection and promotion of the Law and to the purity of Israel. Experts in the written law, they also put great stock in the unfolding of that written law in various oral laws. The Pharisees developed a series of principles for interpreting Scripture, called midrash, that allowed the ancient texts to speak to new situations. Unlike the Sadducees, they affirmed the resurrection of the dead, final judgment, and the existence of powers or spirits other than God. They embodied an apocalyptic and often nationalistic perspective, but to what degree is debated, as is their actual prominence in the first half of the first century.

Another Jewish group with apocalyptic, nationalistic, and purity commitments was the Qumran community and its parent body, the Essenes. The Essenes rejected the temple priests in Jerusalem, believing them to be impure and unfit. Some Essenes remained in the cities, assembling to interpret and observe Scripture according to their own beliefs. These basic convictions were anti-Sadducean and similar in many respects to those of the Pharisees, but they were even more radically apocalyptic. The Qumran community, located in the wilderness near the Dead Sea south of Jerusalem, separated from Jerusalem and

---

14. According to Acts 23:1-11, Paul had at least one encounter with a group of Jews that included Sadducees. It is possible that Paul defined himself in part (as a Pharisee) in contrast to the Sadducees.

15. For references to the Pharisees in Josephus, see especially his *Jewish Antiquities* 13.171-73, 288, 297-98; 17.41-45; 18.11-25; and his *Jewish War* 119-66.

**The Essene community at Qumran built a settlement in the wilderness near
the Dead Sea and eventually hid its scrolls in the caves nearby.**

the rest of Israel to establish a pure remnant community studying Scripture and
preparing for the coming of God's great final battle. Known for producing the
Dead Sea Scrolls — a collection of biblical texts, commentaries, community
guidelines, and other writings — the community's documents reveal a thoroughly apocalyptic mind-set; they were part of a cosmic struggle between darkness and light, Satan and the God of Israel, that would be consummated in a
battle leading to the defeat of all enemies (including the Romans). Dedicated to
the teachings of their founder, called the 'Teacher of Righteousness,' the members were apparently waiting for two messiahs, one priestly and one royal (who
would be a military victor), and a prophet. Their method of scriptural interpretation, called *pesher,* was based on the assumption that Scripture was fulfilled in
the present experiences of their community as the true Israel.

Even more radical, but moving in a different direction, were the Zealots,
participants in a Jewish liberation movement whose theopolitical zeal led them
to attempt the overthrow of Roman rule. Scholars disagree about the origins of
an organized revolutionary movement (a party of Zealots), some positing their
existence early in the first century, some just before the outbreak of the Jewish
War in the 60s. In either case, there was a spirit of zeal and a desire for revolt in
the air. Like many Second Temple Jews, the Zealots as a group (and zealous Jews

more broadly speaking) counted among their heroes the priest Phinehas, the prophet Elijah, and the Maccabees — all of whom burned with religious and national zeal, even to the point of lethal violence.[16] Unlike most other Jews, groups like the Zealots were prepared to take their zeal to the ultimate level of violent political revolt.

Diaspora Judaism

Outside of Palestine — where the above-mentioned groups flourished — Jews lived among Gentiles, in the Diaspora, or dispersion. Establishing synagogues wherever possible, these Jews continued the worship of the one God without direct benefit of the temple. (An inscription at Corinth, for example, reads "[Syn]agogue of the Hebr[ews].") As noted above, they distinguished themselves with a set of interconnected ritual and religio-ethical boundary markers. Circumcision, dietary practices, and their own calendar were well known among their Gentile peers. So was their covenantal avoidance of certain accepted practices, as noted above, such as frequenting the pagan temples (idolatry) and exposing or killing defective newborns (immorality). The Roman authorities tolerated the Jews, though they found them odd in many ways, and even exempted them from military service and imperial adulation. Occasionally the Jews' Gentile neighbors did not feel kindly toward them, however, and persecutions of various types were not unheard of.

This is not to say that Jews in the Diaspora were unaffected by their environment. On the contrary, life in the Diaspora, which obviously consisted of more interaction with non-Jews than in Palestine, offered unique challenges and opportunities. Though certain Gentile practices repulsed most Jews, causing them to stress their own distinctive ways, there was always a tension between separation and assimilation. Those Jews who chose or were forced to interact regularly with non-Jews (and they were the majority) reacted to their environment along a continuum from antagonism to accommodation. However, the evidence suggests that, despite the variety in Jewish acceptance of non-Jewish culture (education, values, etc.), the great majority of Jews attempted to maintain their essential ritual and religio-ethical boundary markers.

Some Jews were attracted to Hellenism's intellectual values and philosophies. In this connection we must especially note Philo of Alexandria (died ca. A.D. 50), who was known for his allegorical method of scriptural interpretation and a more intellectual approach to Judaism. A prolific writer who blended

---

16. Num. 25:6-13 (Phinehas); 1 Kings 17–19 and Sir. 48:1-12a (Elijah); 1 Macc. 2:23-26 (the Maccabean Mattathias).

Jewish tradition and classical philosophy, he is testimony to a vital Hellenistic Judaism informed by the best of Gentile education.

Mystics and God-Fearers

Mention must also be made of a strand of Judaism that probably does not qualify as a school but as a trans-school movement, namely, *Merkabah* Judaism. The Hebrew word *merkabah* means 'chariot,' referring to Ezekiel's chariot described in Ezekiel 1. *Merkabah* Judaism was a mystical form of Jewish spirituality in which people had ecstatic experiences (including dreams and trancelike states), during which they made journeys to (one of the) heaven(s). There they encountered God and/or other heavenly beings. Although the preponderance of evidence for this movement appears after Paul, there are sufficient earlier sources to suggest that *Merkabah* Judaism existed in the first century. One such source is Paul himself (2 Cor. 12:1-4).

Finally, another group (though again not an organized one) of Jews and semi-Jews, already noted, must be included here: Gentile converts and God-fearers. Although most Jews probably did not actively proselytize, some Gentiles were attracted to Jewish beliefs (e.g., monotheism) and practices (e.g., compassion). Of these, a percentage became full-fledged Jews, but others affiliated informally with the local synagogue without (in the case of males) being circumcised. These were the Gentiles known as God-fearers.

To be sure, however, Judaism held no attraction for most Gentiles, and some non-Jews disdained the members of this cult from the East, with their strange beliefs (only one God!) and strange practices (such as circumcision) that separated them from other peoples.

PAUL'S PAGAN COMPETITION

Paul's Greco-Roman religious world was of course polytheistic. In the first century the cities of Italy, Greece, Anatolia (the 'land of the East,' also known as Asia Minor; modern Turkey), and the rest of the empire were amalgams of "many gods and many lords" (1 Cor. 8:5): Greek and Roman deities, local deities, gods of the 'mystery religions,' Egyptian gods, and even, quite often, the God of Israel. Shrines were scattered throughout the countryside, while large temples — sometimes dozens of temples to as many gods — filled the cities. Although there was a hierarchy of gods — with Jupiter at the top, and older gods generally considered better than newer ones — most people (save Jews and

The base of a column from the Asclepeion at Pergamum
(western Asia Minor), sculpted with the insignia of Asclepius
the healing god — an emblem still used by modern medicine

then Christians) were quite tolerant and could be devoted to many gods. Furthermore, the distinct identities of the gods were often blended together, with Artemis/Diana (for example) taking on the traits of the local Phrygian mother goddess Cybele. Such syncretism went hand in glove with tolerance and with an empire, for accommodating local gods facilitates the subjugation of peoples. But tolerant syncretism created obvious problems for those who acknowledged only one God.

Religion in antiquity offered adherents a number of common rituals and other activities. These included prayers, sacrifices, meals, processions, festivals, and various kinds of contests (athletic, artistic, rhetorical, etc.). Nearly every major public event, and many public buildings, had a religious dimension. In fact, it would be a mistake to think of some activities as 'secular' and others 'religious.' The culture and its varied dimensions were all inherently religious.

Religion, in this sense, met a wide range of individual and corporate human needs. From the deities people sought salvation, defined largely in this-worldly terms: peace and prosperity, guidance and protection, harmony and solidarity, ecstasy and escape, beauty and love, physical health (frequently) and (less often) immortality. Above all, most inhabitants of the empire believed, any and all available gods were needed to bless their emperor/empire and to protect them from enemies, whether military or cosmic. The deities, in turn, required satisfaction through perpetual sacrifices, but they seldom made ethical demands on their adherents. Their relationship with humans was more *contractual* and focused on proper *ritual,* rather than *covenantal* and focused on proper *ethical behavior* (as in Judaism).

Among the religious experiences popular in the first century were several so-called mystery cults, which generally provided access to knowledge and/or a certain experience of the deity — and thus to rebirth, salvation, and even immortality — through an initiation rite. Initiates often shared a sacral meal. The mystery cults could be co-opted for political purposes, but they tended to be more personal than the cults of the traditional gods.

Despite the popularity of the mysteries, with their promise of immortality, it seems that most people were more concerned with surviving life than surviving death. Actual belief in an afterlife was not widespread; a popular gravestone inscription read, "I was not, I am not, I care not." The mysteries therefore must have provided a sense of spiritual satisfaction and emotional release in the present. In addition to joining the mysteries, many people sought to overcome their sense of enslavement to the powers of the universe (especially fate) by using astrology. Some also tried to harness certain of those powers for their own benefit (and often the harm of others) by using magic. As in our own day, such quasi-religious practices were not limited to the masses; even emperors consulted astrologers.

Some of the most important gods and goddesses of Paul's world are noted in the following chart.

Significant Deities in Paul's World

Deity	Description
Aphrodite/Venus	Goddess of love/sex/beauty. Her famous temple on the Corinthian acropolis had been, prior to Paul,

	home to many sacred prostitutes. She was also patroness of seafaring and mother of the imperial family. Main cultic centers included Corinth and Paphos, Cyprus (cf. Acts 13:6).
Apollo	Son of Jupiter and god of music and youthfulness. He was also believed to provide healing and, through the oracles at Delphi, guidance. A large temple at Corinth was probably dedicated to Apollo.
Artemis/Diana	The goddess of the hunt and (perhaps) fertility, transformed into a mother goddess in Asia Minor. She was the patron deity of Ephesus ('Artemis the Great'), where her temple was among the seven wonders of the ancient world. Ephesian Artemis was worshiped throughout the empire. Devotees experienced oracles, epiphanies, and healings at her shrines.
Asclepius	Son of Apollo and a major god of healing who appeared on earth as a snake. The sick would travel to one of the many 'Asclepeia' (campuslike spaces with baths, shrines, sleeping rooms, theaters, and other buildings), hoping Asclepius would appear to them in their sleep to heal them. Corinth, Epidaurus, and Pergamum (Pergamon) were among the several hundred cities with such healing centers. Those healed would mold models of healed body parts and display them at the shrines.
Cybele/Magna Mater	Ancient Phrygian mother goddess expected to provide a fertile earth, and often blended with other similar goddesses. Especially popular in Pisidian Antioch and throughout Phrygia and Galatia, but also even in Rome, she was honored by sacrificing bulls. Priests of the cult, who were self-castrated to identify with Cybele's son and lover Attis (who, after being cut up, was reconstituted by Cybele but without his genitalia), also performed frenzied, masochistic rituals accompanied by flutes and tambourines. Initiates, placed in a pit, were 'washed' in the blood of a bull as it was being sacrificed. Annual rites included a Mardi Gras–type celebration of Attis's revivification.

Demeter	Goddess of vegetation. She was celebrated, together with her daughter Persephone, in the Eleusinian mysteries at Eleusis, outside Athens. A two-stage initiation process of identification with Persephone and sacrifice to Demeter was purported to insure happiness after death.
Dionysus/Bacchus	God of wine, fertility, and ecstasy. Cultic activity (the Bacchanalia) focused on entering a drunken frenzy, to the accompaniment of flutes and various percussion instruments, in order to experience the god's gift of life. Members of this mystery cult believed Dionysus — represented by the phallus — provided them with a rebirth and with immortality. The cult was often the target of restrictions by Roman officials.
Isis and Osiris/Serapis	An Egyptian goddess and her brother-consort who had been cut into pieces and reconstituted through Isis's use of magic. Isis was believed to be full of compassion and the guarantor of immortality, while Osiris/Serapis was known as a healer. This widespread mystery cult was especially popular among women, but it also appealed to men and even to the emperor Caligula, who put the rites for Osiris's revivification on the official Roman calendar.
Tychē/Fortuna	Fate or chance. Many felt that it, rather than Zeus/Jupiter, ruled the universe.
Zeus/Jupiter	The chief god of the pantheon who took on a variety of specific traits at various times. The temple of Zeus in Athens, which can still be seen, was the largest in Greece. Zeus and Hermes (his messenger) had a joint cult in some places (cf. Acts 14:8-18).

In addition to the religious cults and practices, a variety of philosophical schools were influential in Paul's day. These included the following:

- *Cynics* (lit. 'dogs,' the name they were disparagingly given) were a radical, countercultural group known for frugality, inattention to clothing and bodily care and comforts, brash speech, begging, and other offensive public behaviors (e.g., public sex). By wandering about and using an often confrontational style of teaching, they attempted to instruct the masses in the pursuit of freedom. The Cynics influenced the Stoics (see below).

31

Zeus, Istanbul Museum of Archaeology

- *Epicureans* believed that pleasure — understood not as sensuality but as virtue known through the senses — was the goal of human life. They downplayed or denied the existence of the gods and of immortality, and sought to free people from superstition. Some find Epicurean influence at Corinth and among the recipients of the Pastoral Letters.
- *Platonists* did not abound in the time of Paul, but their conviction that the body was the tomb of the soul and thus of little importance seems to have affected many people.
- *Stoics* found the universe to be permeated by reason, *logos,* which is identified with God/Zeus. There is a spark of this universal reason in each human being, constituting the person's true self. The goal of life is to live in harmony with reason/God/the true self and not be affected by the vicissitudes of life. 'Apathy' (*apatheia,* indifference to things that cannot affect the true self), self-sufficiency, and contentment are therefore important Stoic virtues. Originating from the philosophically oriented Zeno (333-264

B.C.), first century A.D. ('late') Stoicism majored on ethics. It included the philosopher Seneca, the ex-slave Epictetus, and the emperor-philosopher Marcus Aurelius.

Some of Paul's possible converts would have been committed to one or another of these philosophical schools, and Paul himself appears to have been affected in various ways by them (how, and to what degree, is a matter of ongoing debate).

PAUL'S CITIES

The array of religious and philosophical options discussed in the previous sections, some mutually compatible and some not, existed especially in the cities, where people and ideas were plentiful and, thanks to transportation networks, portable. Moreover, Paul spent most of his time in cities; he was an urban missionary. It is important, therefore, to have some familiarity with the cities of Paul's world.

THE IMPORTANCE OF CITIES

Many of the cities Paul visited had long histories, dating back to classical or Hellenistic Greek times. The city walls and roads, the temples and other buildings, and the cemeteries were often quite ancient. At the same time, however, some cities had been devastated by war and had been refounded as colonies not long before the birth of Christianity. Such was true, for instance, of both Corinth and Philippi.

The city, whether large (like Rome, Ephesus, Pisidian Antioch, Thessalonica, or Athens) or modest (like Philippi and probably Colossae), was the religious and commercial heart of a region. The larger cities might be as vast as fifty square miles and contain several hundred thousand people. At certain times — for special religious celebrations or athletic competitions — a city's population could swell dramatically, though temporarily, providing opportunities for increased sales of local products and artisan crafts, including tents. Surrounding the city were farmlands and woods that provided the grains, vegetables, and animals needed for everyday life, for religious festivities and sporting events, and for trade.

The web of first-century cities in the Roman Empire was not unlike the network of urban airline hubs today. The cities were connected by roads and shipping routes that provided for the regular and relatively rapid exchange of people and ideas, of philosophies and religions. Many of the cities Paul evangelized, whether for a short or long period, had important harbors, were located on significant trade routes, or both. For example, Corinth, located on a narrow isthmus linking the Aegean and Adriatic Seas, had two satellite ports, one leading to each sea, and was thus a major intersection of east-west trade. Its strategic location was also important for north-south inland trade. In Macedonia, to the north, both Thessalonica and Philippi were on the Via Egnatia, the main road between Rome and Asia Minor. Thessalonica was also the only harbor city located directly on the Via Egnatia in Greece, while Philippi used nearby Neapolis as its port. In the province of Asia, Ephesus, where Paul spent a considerable amount of time, was a major port in the apostle's day (though eventually silting from its rivers resulted in the separation of the sea from the city).

THE PLAN OF THE CITY

Nearly every city was built around an acropolis ('high city'), or peak, often a buttelike natural formation. Whether located inland or overlooking some body of water, the acropolis was the city's focal point, visible for miles in all directions. On this peak were located one or more temples, usually to the city's chief deity or deities, and gradually also to Augustus or another emperor, as well as other public buildings. In Athens, for example, stood the Parthenon, the most prominent of several edifices, housing Athena's statue. Athena also protected the coastal city of Assos (see Acts 20:13) in western Asia Minor, from within an impressive temple overlooking the sea. In Philippi there are inscriptions from the cult of Artemis on the acropolis. And in Corinth the extraordinarily lofty Acrocorinth (rising nearly two thousand feet) was home to the temple of Aphrodite, among others.

Usually the major edifices and activities of the city were to be found on flatter ground below the acropolis. Here were situated the following kinds of structures:

- **the agora** — the marketplace/forum, a large rectangular, columned area ringed by temples, public buildings, shops, and other structures.
- **colonnades** — covered outdoor sidewalks, especially popular in larger cities.
- **temples and shrines** — dedicated to deities, past rulers, and, increasingly in the first century, emperors, with small markets and restaurants attached to some.

The Acrocorinth dominated the city of Corinth.

- **synagogue(s)** — in some cities but not others, where Jews might meet in homes or outside (as in Philippi, according to Acts 16).
- **shops** — small structures where merchants would sell their wares or produce and artisans would ply their trades.
- **public buildings** — structures for various municipal or provincial activities, including those known as **basilicas.**
- **the *bouleutērion*** — a small, semicircular, theater-like structure for meetings of city officials.
- **the bema** — a bench in the agora used for official public announcements and speech making, and for public hearings.
- **fountains and monuments** — often dedicated to a god or emperor, and sometimes inscribed with the name of the benefactor.
- **one or more theaters and arenas** — semicircular, round, or elliptical structures, often built into a hillside to blend into nature and/or take advantage of natural acoustics, and used for drama, athletic events (games, races, etc.), religious and political ceremonies, and music, often on one of the many public holidays. Among these were the round **amphitheater,** which was more common in the western part of the empire and more prominent after Paul's time; the elliptical **circus,** such as at Rome and Laodicea; and the *odeion,* used exclusively for music. Gladiator fights, which took place in such arenas, grew in popularity after Paul's time.

The ancient theater of Pergamum, built into one of the steepest inclines
used for such purposes in the ancient world

- **baths** — a series of rooms with cold, warm, and hot water for relaxation
  (bathing, sauna, etc.), sometimes open to both sexes, sometimes restricted
  to single-sex use.
- **residences** — small homes and apartments, sometimes next to or above
  the shops on the agora, and larger homes outside the central district.

Most impressive of all these structures were the various temples, both up
above, on the acropolis, and down below, adjacent to the agora and beyond.
The temple of Artemis at Ephesus, for example, was among the seven wonders
of the ancient world, attracting both worshipers and tourists to the great city.
The size and grandeur of the buildings and of the statues they housed were
constant reminders of the power and patronage of the gods and the emperor.
As omnipresent as McDonald's golden arches in the contemporary landscape,
the temples reminded everyone that the gods and the emperor were to be both
admired and feared, petitioned and thanked.

It is ironic, then, that the movement associated with Paul's gospel did not
build new temples but met in houses. Some of these meetings may have been in
the small apartments *(insulae)* and other relatively small dwellings in the city
centers, often next to or above a shop; such homes may have only accommodated a dozen people or fewer. Larger homes would have had a separate dining

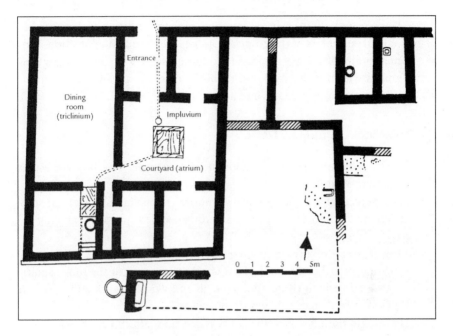

Floor plan of a Roman house typical of the elite

room (the triclinium, or room for three couches), an atrium (reception/salon) and other public spaces of varying sizes, and an open interior courtyard — all of which could welcome guests. A large house-church might have had space for a gathering of fifty to one hundred people, but not necessarily all in one area. Some very large houses with expansive courtyards might have accommodated several hundred people.

Much of a city's land was public space of one sort or another. It appears that city neighborhoods were often naturally organized according to ethnicity or trade. While the elite lived in larger houses in the main part of the city or farther outside, the nonelite lived on top of one another in the apartment buildings and smaller houses that lined the urban streets. Urban life along these narrow corridors, which were not particularly clean or sanitary, was crowded and not very private; it was a 'face-to-face' experience, and people knew who the local troublemakers were. This situation created an interesting paradoxical dynamic. On the one hand, any activity that was perceived to threaten the welfare of the polis or the empire might very well be met with ostracism, mob violence, or eventually formal legal and political action. On the other hand, any message and community offering salvation, equality, and power to all, irrespective of status, would certainly create interest among the nonelite in the cities.

These cosmopolitan, urban centers of idolatry and imperial power became for Paul epicenters of the gospel, despite rather frequent opposition. People from all strata of the city responded to the apostolic message, creating new communities within their city. From them the message spread into the countryside, down the Roman roads, and across the seas.

QUESTIONS FOR REFLECTION

1. What major similarities and differences do you perceive between Paul's world and yours?
2. What aspects of the political, social, cultural, and religious life of our society are most important for understanding people's spiritual searching today?
3. Identify some of the contemporary forms of 'competition' facing the Christian gospel and church. That is, what are some of the most significant ways in which contemporary men and women express their search for God, rebirth/renewal, and immortality?
4. How might the answers to the last two questions affect the way the church interprets the Christian gospel to others?
5. What are the indicators of honor or status in the culture and church as you have experienced them? Why is it important to understand these indicators?
6. What do you think of the claim made by many Christians that 'the West' and/or the Northern Hemisphere has moved into a post-Christian or even pagan era? What is the significance of this claim for the life and mission of the church?
7. What are the gods and goddesses of our own day, and where are their temples?
8. Is Christianity still an urban faith? What lessons might the church learn from the urban setting of Paul's mission work?

FOR FURTHER READING AND STUDY

General

Bell, Albert A., Jr. *Exploring the New Testament World: An Illustrated Guide to the World of Jesus and the First Christians.* Nashville: Nelson, 1998. A basic, readable guide, illustrated and containing bibliographies.

Cohen, Shaye J. D. *From the Maccabees to the Mishnah.* Philadelphia: Westminster, 1987. A superb introduction to the unity and diversity of belief and practice within ancient Judaism.

Ferguson, Everett. *Backgrounds of Early Christianity*. 3rd ed. Grand Rapids: Eerdmans, 2003. A standard and splendid account of the world in which Paul lived.

Jeffers, James S. *The Greco-Roman World of the New Testament Era: Exploring the Background of Early Christianity*. Downers Grove, Ill.: InterVarsity, 1999. A thorough but readable social history of the first century, with numerous illustrations.

Shelton, Jo-Ann. *As the Romans Did: A Sourcebook in Roman Social History*. 2nd ed. New York: Oxford University Press, 1998. A collection of nearly 500 excerpts from primary sources revealing the social life of the early empire, organized by topics (patronage, families, education, slaves, religion, etc.).

Technical

Barclay, John M. G. *Jews in the Mediterranean Diaspora from Alexander to Trajan (323 BCE–117 CE)*. Edinburgh: T. & T. Clark, 1996. A fascinating analysis of the range of Jewish assimilation, acculturation, and accommodation — and yet common practical distinctives — throughout the Diaspora, including a chapter on Paul himself.

Barrett, C. K., ed. *The New Testament Background: Selected Documents*. Rev. ed. San Francisco: Harper and Row, 1987. Nearly 300 excerpts from ancient documents illustrating political, philosophical, and religious (especially Jewish) beliefs and practices.

Koester, Helmut. *History, Culture, and Religion of the Hellenistic Age*. 2nd ed. Vol. 1 of *Introduction to the New Testament*. New York and Berlin: Walter de Gruyter, 1995. A classic analysis of the Hellenistic age and its influence on Roman culture.

Kraemer, Ross Shephard, and Mary Rose D'Angelo. *Women and Christian Origins*. New York: Oxford University Press, 1999. A collection of insightful and provocative essays, with several on the Greco-Roman and Jewish context.

Meeks, Wayne A. *The First Urban Christians: The Social World of the Apostle Paul*. New Haven: Yale University Press, 1983. A groundbreaking and now classic social description of Paul's environment and of the churches he started within it.

Murphy-O'Connor, Jerome, and James H. Charlesworth, eds. *Paul and the Dead Sea Scrolls*. New York: Crossroad, 1990. A collection of essays on the similarities and differences between the convictions of those who produced the Dead Seas Scrolls and the apostle Paul.

Price, S. R. F. *Rituals and Power: The Roman Imperial Cult in Asia Minor*. Cambridge: Cambridge University Press, 1984. A very significant study that has become the basis for much New Testament scholarship.

Sampley, J. Paul, ed. *Paul in the Greco-Roman World: A Handbook*. Harrisburg, Pa.: Trinity Press International, 2001. A collection of authoritative essays from various scholars.

Sanders, E. P. *Paul and Palestinian Judaism*. Philadelphia: Fortress, 1977. A modern classic that revolutionized Pauline studies, arguing for 'covenantal nomism' as the basic pattern of Palestinian Judaism.

CHAPTER 2

PAUL'S RÉSUMÉ

The Mission of the Former Persecutor

I have seen the truth and the truth has made me odd.

Flannery O'Connor

Paul was born a Jew, lived a Jew, and died a Jew. It was therefore obviously as a Jew that he experienced the once-crucified Jesus as the resurrected and exalted Lord. Paul did not set out to found a new religion but to call Jews and especially Gentiles to confess the Jewish Messiah (Gk. *christos,* hence English 'Christ'), sent by the one true God YHWH, as the Lord. In retrospect, we can of course say that Paul was a 'Christian' — one who confesses and follows Jesus as Christ and Lord. But we must do so without forgetting the inherent Jewishness of this very term ('Christian') and of the great Christian apostle Paul.[1]

Our goal in this chapter is not to provide a full biography of Paul. Rather, we will briefly highlight some key aspects of the life of this lifelong Jew, from his early years in Diaspora Judaism, to his life as a Pharisee in Palestine, to his zealous commitment to extinguish the early Jesus movement, to his encounter with the resurrected Jesus, to his subsequent life as apostle of the Jewish God and his crucified Messiah among the Gentiles. It is of course from this last phase that his letters ap-

---

1. It is interesting that the word 'Christian' appears twice in the book of Acts and once in a New Testament letter that might have been influenced by the Pauline tradition (Acts 11:26; 26:28; 1 Pet. 4:16), but it is completely absent from the Pauline correspondence. Since, according to Acts 11:26, believers were first called 'Christians' *(christianoi)* at Antioch, while Paul was there, he may have known the word, but his own terms for believers are especially 'saints/holy ones' *(hagioi)* and 'brothers [and sisters]' *(adelphoi).*

pear. In them we find the thoughts of a man on a mission: *to create a vast network of multicultural communities obeying and glorifying the one true God of Israel by living lives of faith, hope, and love in Christ Jesus the Lord by the power of the Spirit.*

SOURCES FOR THE LIFE OF PAUL

What can we know about the life of Paul, and how can we know it? There are basically four kinds of sources:

- the seven letters bearing Paul's name that are undisputed as to their authorship by Paul (Romans, 1 and 2 Corinthians, Galatians, Philippians, 1 Thessalonians, Philemon)[2]
- the six letters bearing Paul's name that are disputed as to their authorship (2 Thessalonians, Colossians, Ephesians, 1 and 2 Timothy, Titus)
- the book of Acts
- other documents, inscriptions, archaeological evidence, coins, etc., from Paul's era

Of these four types of sources, all historians naturally rely heavily on Paul's own (undisputed) letters. They are divided on the use of the disputed letters and Acts, depending on their assessment of the date, authorship, and historical value of these writings. For example, some scholars believe Acts was written by, or contains documents from, a former companion of Paul named Luke, while others believe that 'Luke' — whoever he was — wrote several decades later, was not Paul's companion, and artificially created passages that sound like journal entries from trips with the apostle. Similarly, some scholars believe the disputed Pauline letters come from Paul's hand and faithfully reflect his life and thought, while others believe they are later writings from the hand of well-meaning but not completely faithful disciples. As for other sources, every historian must and does rely on them, but each scholar interprets the meaning and importance of the considerable amount of historical data provided by such sources in different ways.

The task of constructing a life of Paul — or even figuring out when and where he wrote a particular letter — is an extraordinarily difficult one. For example, even someone who believes that the book of Acts is quite historically reliable must raise certain questions. What do we do with the conflicts between Acts and

---

2. On the issues surrounding Pauline authorship of the letters attributed to him, see chap. 3. To summarize later discussions, the position of this book is that Paul is more or less directly responsible for eleven of the thirteen letters — all but 1 Timothy and Titus.

Paul's own writings? Was Acts intended primarily to provide a 'history' of Paul's activities, or an interpretation of them? Does Acts have a particular perspective on Paul (and on other people and subjects) that affects its telling of the story?

The 'Paul of Acts,' the 'Paul of the undisputed letters,' and the 'Paul of the disputed letters' constitute at least three different figures. Do they present the same person from different angles? Can their perspectives be understood in complementary fashion, or is there unresolvable conflict? Why, for instance, does Acts never have Paul writing a letter? Why does it appear to narrate three missionary journeys when Paul expresses no parallel segmentation of his mission work? Why do we hear little or nothing about Paul's trademark teaching on justification, or the centrality of the cross, in Acts? Why does Paul himself never mention his Roman citizenship or his studies with the teacher Gamaliel, even though Acts does? Why are none of the details of his Damascus road experience narrated in the letters as they are in Acts? And so on.

These issues are further complicated by the lack of hard data from secular history to corroborate the letters and Acts, or even to provide some 'pegs' on which to hang the information we can glean from the New Testament. (The most important is likely the date of Gallio's proconsulship of the province of Achaia in Corinth, before whom Paul appeared, according to Acts 18:12-17. But even this date — probably 50-51 or 51-52 — has been debated.) Writing 'New Testament history' is a difficult task indeed.

All is not lost, however. Most scholars today acknowledge these kinds of difficulties and try to find a compromise between using Acts uncritically and dismissing it as useless for constructing Paul's life. In fact, there is something of a trend toward placing greater trust in the historical reliability of Acts even while recognizing that it has a 'theological axe to grind' in telling the story of Paul — as does Paul himself in writing autobiographically.

The end result of all these phenomena contains both good news and bad. The bad news is that there are many questions that cannot be answered with certainty, and there is therefore quite a spectrum of opinion on certain subjects. The good news is more important. First, there is some general agreement on the basic framework of Paul's life and ministry. Second, many of the most debated historical questions do not prevent an intelligent reading of Paul's letters. And third, some of the different interpretations of Paul can be seen as mutually complementary rather than contradictory.[3]

3. The approach of the present writer is to do everything possible to allow the witness of both Paul and Acts to stand. As noted in the excursus on pages 43-44, I have become increasingly impressed with the value of Acts as a reflection of first-century realities, which in turn augments my appreciation of the reliability of its story of Paul. The important series The Book of Acts in Its First-Century Setting, edited by Bruce Winter (see bibliography), has become rightly influential in this regard.

Excursus: More on the Issue of Sources

The book of Acts and Paul's letters contain differences in perspective and in details about Paul's life and ministry. Some of these kinds of differences are reconcilable, while others may not be, at least with our limited knowledge, for neither Acts nor the Pauline correspondence has the history of Paul's mission as its primary agenda.

In fact, both Acts and the letters present their narratives of Paul's activities (and other data) for certain theological and rhetorical purposes. Nevertheless, biblical scholars generally agree that Paul's undisputed letters are the primary sources for constructing a chronology or narrative of Paul's life and ministry, since they are written by the apostle himself. But scholars differ markedly in their assessment of the disputed Pauline letters and Acts. Of these two sources, Acts is particularly important to consider, since it purports, at least, to present a coherent narrative of Paul's missionary activity following his Damascus road experience.

There are three major approaches to the value of Acts in writing the story of Paul. The maximalist approach takes Acts to be a more or less reliable account of Paul's activities and correlates its narrative with the letters. The minimalist approach, on the other hand, views the narrative of Acts with suspicion and uses very little of it for constructing an account of Paul's life and ministry. But even proponents of this approach generally grant Acts accuracy in certain key matters, such as Paul's eighteen-month stay in Corinth (18:11), a ministry of some two or three years in Ephesus (19:8, 10; 20:31), and a mission to 'north Galatia' (16:6; 18:23). A moderating approach, which is probably the one employed by most scholars, uses the undisputed letters as the main source for knowledge about Paul but supplements such knowledge with information from Acts, to the extent that it does not contradict the letters or clearly represent Luke's alleged distortion of history for theological purposes. These three approaches should not be viewed as precisely defined methodologies but as key points along a spectrum.

The issues involved in determining the most appropriate use of Acts are complex and certainly cannot be settled here. The present writer has become convinced in recent years that Acts is a much more reliable guide to the first-century world and to the history of early Christianity than many scholars recognize. This conviction leads one to a critical approach that leans toward the maximalist, rather than the minimalist, end of the spectrum. That is, Acts should be given the benefit of the doubt on the general veracity of its narratives. This position should still be held, however, with due moderation and caution, with an admission that there remain difficulties in the use of Acts and in the correlation of it with the letters. However, perceived differences between Paul's letters and Acts that appear to be irreconcilable should be labeled as such with great caution in light of the quantity and character of the data we possess.

No matter what one's position on the historical reliability of Acts, one must recognize that neither Acts nor the letters supply us with all the information we would like to have to engage in historical reconstruction, especially the most important kind of historical reconstruction for this book: to discern and describe the situations that occasioned the various letters. In the discussion of the letters, we will present summaries of the data from Acts that might be relevant along with the information that can be mined from the letters. However, little or no clearly relevant data from Acts exist for many letters, so the interpretation of those letters is not significantly affected by one's approach to Acts. Moreover, even those who differ somewhat on the circumstances that led to the writing of a particular letter may agree on the most significant aspects of its interpretation.

In the present chapter we attempt to outline Paul's life and mission generally, making use of both the letters and, more cautiously, Acts.

A GENERAL CHRONOLOGY OF PAUL'S LIFE

Despite all the challenges mentioned in the previous section, Acts and the letters agree on a number of key points about Paul: that he was a persecutor of the early followers of Jesus as Messiah; that he had an about-face; that he preached the gospel among the Gentiles, especially in Asia Minor and Greece; and that he suffered for his witness. Very little from these canonical sources (or from other early Christian sources) can be said with much certainty about his early life or about the end of his life. For example, Paul's martyrdom under Nero is based on a later, believable tradition, but it does not appear in the New Testament.

What follows is a very general and tentative chronology of Paul's life. Since we have very few pieces of hard data, and many of those we do have designate periods of time (e.g., 'for three years' or 'after three years'), some of which may be approximations, any particular Pauline chronology is not only approximate but is also interdependent — one date is relative to another. Because of the range of dates given, most scholarly reconstructions fit within this framework. (It should be noted that a range of dates [e.g., ca. 33-39] may exceed the period of time described [e.g., 'three years in Arabia and Damascus'] because of the broad range of possible historical reconstructions.)

Approximate Dates	Event
ca. 5 B.C.–A.D. 10	Birth in Tarsus, followed by education in Tarsus, then Jerusalem
ca. 30-36	Persecution (1 Cor. 15:9; Gal. 1:13-14; Phil. 3:6; Acts 8:1-3; 9:1-2)

ca. 33-36	Call/conversion (Gal. 1:15-16; Acts 9; 22; 26; cf. Phil. 3:3-11)
ca. 33-39	Three years in Arabia and Damascus (Gal. 1:17)
ca. 36-39	First Jerusalem visit: two weeks with Cephas and James (Gal. 1:18-19)
ca. 37-48	Early missionary work in Syria and Cilicia and possibly elsewhere (Gal. 1:21; cf. Acts 9:30)
ca. 46-58	Period of mission work in Asia Minor, Greece, etc., and writing of most extant letters
ca. 47-51	Jerusalem meeting/'council' (Gal. 2:1-10 = Acts 11:27-30? Acts 15?)[4]
ca. 50-52	Corinth stay of eighteen months (Acts 18)
ca. 52-57	Ephesus stay of two-to-three years (Acts 19; see Acts 19:8, 10; 20:31), including possible imprisonment
ca. 54-58	Arrest in Jerusalem (Acts 21:27-36)
ca. 60-63	Imprisonment in Rome (Acts 28)
ca. 62-68	Possible release from Rome and further mission work/letter writing
ca. 62-68	Death

Additional imprisonments occurred throughout this span of years. If *1 Clement* 5 (ca. A.D. 96) and later sources are correct, Paul died a martyr, probably in Rome.

Within the general time frame of the major mission activity circa 46-58, Acts presents us with three mission trips, which are followed by a final (unsought) trip to Rome. We cannot be certain that Paul's mission work followed exactly the routes outlined in these trips as they are narrated in Acts, nor can we be certain that Paul himself would have perceived his ministry as a series of such trips. Nevertheless, the trips outlined in Acts do provide a framework for Paul's mission that accurately highlights the general geographical extent of his work as reflected in the letters. Moreover, rightly or wrongly, this framework of mission trips has become a convention in the study of Paul, and it is foolish to pretend otherwise. The itinerary of each trip follows.

---

4. There is significant scholarly debate about the relationship between the narrative of the (private? cf. Gal. 2:2) meeting in Gal. 2 and the narratives in Acts that might refer to the same event. Many scholars connect Gal. 2 to Acts 15 despite discrepancies, while a minority of scholars connects Gal. 2 with Acts 11:27-30. Neither solution is without difficulties, and some scholars suggest that we should not attempt to link Luke and Paul here.

Paul's 1st Journey
△ = Starting point

Paul's 2nd Journey
△ = Starting point

Paul's 3rd Journey
△ = Starting point

Maps of Paul's three missionary journeys according to Acts

The Hellenistic city gates of the city of Perga (southern Asia Minor),
through which Paul would have walked

FIRST TRIP (ACTS 13–14: CYPRUS,
PAMPHYLIA, SOUTH GALATIA)

Departure from Syrian Antioch for the port of Seleucia and on to Salamis, on
the east coast of the island of **Cyprus**. From Salamis to Paphos, on the southwest coast of Cyprus. Departure from Paphos in a northwest direction for the
port of Perga, in the province of **Pamphylia** in Asia Minor. From Perga north to
Pisidian Antioch, the provincial capital of **Galatia**. From Pisidian Antioch

Remains of the important port of Troas,
a Roman colony on the Aegean Sea in northwest Asia Minor

southeast to Iconium, then southwest to Lystra, then southeast to Derbe. Back through Lystra, Iconium, and Antioch, and then through the region of Pisidia (southwest Galatia) to the province of Pamphylia and south to Perga. West to Attalia to set sail for Syrian Antioch.

SECOND TRIP (ACTS 15:36–18:22: SYRIA, CILICIA, GALATIA, PHRYGIA, ASIA, MACEDONIA, ACHAIA)

From Syrian Antioch on land through **Syria** to the province of **Cilicia**, in southeastern Asia Minor. Departure for **Galatia** and the cities of Derbe, Lystra, and (probably) Iconium. Then west and north through the provinces of **Phrygia** and **Galatia** (avoiding Asia), approaching the province of Bithynia to the north. Without entering Bithynia, west to the port of Troas in Mysia, in the northwest part of the province of **Asia**. Departure by ship for the island of Samothrace, then to the port of Neapolis, in the province of **Macedonia** (first European visit). On to Philippi, then southwest along the coast through Amphipolis and Apollonia to Thessalonica. From there to Beroea and then south into the province of **Achaia** and the city of Athens. From Athens west to Corinth and then

A mosaic, located in the town of Beroea, of Paul in Troas
receiving the call to evangelize Macedonia

the port of Cenchreae. Departure from Cenchreae by ship to Ephesus, then on
to Caesarea, and then by land to Syrian Antioch.

THIRD TRIP (ACTS 18:23–21:16: GALATIA, PHRYGIA, ASIA, MACEDONIA, CYPRUS)

From Syrian Antioch to **Galatia** and **Phrygia** and then to Ephesus, the provincial
capital of **Asia**. From Ephesus to the province of **Macedonia**. South to "Greece"
(Achaia; probably Athens and Corinth) and then back to Macedonia. Departure
from Philippi by ship to Troas in Asia Minor, and then down the **Asia** coast to
the ports of Assos, Mitylene, Samos, and Miletus, bypassing Ephesus. From
Miletus to Cos, Rhodes, and Patara; then past **Cyprus** and to Tyre, in Syria. From
Tyre to Ptolemais and then Caesarea, and finally on to Jerusalem.

TRIP TO ROME (ACTS 21:15–28:31: JERUSALEM, CYPRUS, ASIA, CRETE, MALTA, ITALY)

Arrest in **Jerusalem**, followed by various procedures there. To Antipatris and
then Caesarea, for a hearing with Felix. From Caesarea to Sidon, around north-

eastern **Cyprus**, to Myra in Lycia, the southernmost region of **Asia**. Then to Fair Havens near Lasea, on the island of **Crete**. Shipwreck, and escape to the island of **Malta**, south of Italy. From Malta to Syracuse, Sicily, then to Rhegium, up the western coast of **Italy** to Puteoli, and finally to Rome for two years.

This activity, whether understood as four trips (as Acts has it) or not, reflects Paul's mission work in approximately the years 48-62.

Into this overall framework scholars locate some or all of the thirteen letters that bear Paul's name. (As we will see in the next chapter, the genuineness of some of these letters is debated.) The earliest are likely 1 Thessalonians (and 2 Thessalonians, if genuine) and Galatians, written between 48 and 51; then 1 and 2 Corinthians, in the mid-50s; then Romans in the middle to late 50s. The 'Prison Epistles' — Philippians and Philemon, as well as Colossians and Ephesians, if the latter two are genuine — may have been written during one or more imprisonments in the middle to late 50s, or from Rome in the early 60s. If the 'Pastoral Epistles' (1 and 2 Timothy, Titus) are genuine, they may have been written in the 60s after Paul's captivity in Rome (assuming he was eventually released), though recent defenders of authenticity sometimes locate two of the Pastorals (1 Timothy and Titus) earlier in Paul's ministry. 2 Timothy, if genuine, could have been written during the Roman imprisonment mentioned in Acts or during a possible later imprisonment in Rome that is not mentioned in Acts.

We now examine briefly various aspects of Paul's résumé that are the main concern of this chapter.

DIASPORA JEW

According to Acts — and there is little reason to doubt this claim — Paul was born in and influenced by the city of Tarsus in the province of Cilicia, in the eastern part of modern Turkey (22:3; cf. 9:11; 21:39). The exact date of his birth is unknown, though it was possibly about the same time as Jesus' birth; the evidence can be interpreted to yield a date between about 5 B.C. and about A.D. 10. Paul's Jewish parents were members of the tribe of Benjamin (Phil. 3:5) living in the Diaspora. Not much else is known of his family or of their socioeconomic situation. His father may have become a Roman citizen (which would result in Paul's Roman citizenship; see Acts 22:27-28; 16:37; 23:27),[5] perhaps by perform-

---

5. As noted above, Paul's letters never confirm or disconfirm his Roman citizenship. "Rods" (2 Cor. 11:25), a Roman form of punishment, were not usually used on citizens, but officials eager to punish those perceived as troublemakers did not always ask questions before acting.

ing some civic good to earn his citizenship, but he may also have been a slave who was liberated by a generous fellow Jew. Some have suggested that his father was an artisan who taught Paul his tentmaking craft, but it is also possible that Paul chose to learn the craft later in life, even after his call/conversion. Finally, we do not know whether Paul's father was a Pharisee (as Acts 23:6 may imply) or if Paul became a Pharisee after moving to Palestine.

In any event, as Jewish residents of the Diaspora, Paul's parents would probably have given their son two names. The first, Saul (Gk. *Saulos*), was the name of the tribe's most famous ancestor, King Saul, transliterated from the Hebrew. The second, Paul (Lat. *Paullus*), was a common Roman name, perhaps chosen for their son because of its similarity to Saul. There is no evidence that Saul changed his name after the Damascus road experience. Luke, however, calls him Saul until his commissioning in Antioch (see Acts 13), after which he refers to the Apostle to the Gentiles exclusively by his Gentile name, Paul.[6]

Tarsus was a thriving, cosmopolitan university town. The first-century geographer Strabo records the presence of numerous 'schools of rhetoric,' the ancient equivalent of liberal arts colleges, in Tarsus. Strabo tells us that the city was also a center for Stoicism, and there was a Jewish presence throughout the region. All these aspects of Paul's early environment appear in Paul's letters.

As a Jew of the Diaspora, Paul would have studied the Scriptures of Israel in Greek, using the Septuagint and other versions of the translated sacred writings. His self-designation as a "Hebrew of Hebrews" (Phil. 3:5 NIV) may imply his knowledge of Hebrew and/or Aramaic (see also Acts 22:2), which he could have learned as a child or later in Jerusalem. Direct quotations and allusions to the Scriptures abound in his letters (often from the LXX, but also from the Hebrew), and they reveal knowledge of many typical Jewish methods of scriptural interpretation. Paul was probably also exposed to various contemporary Jewish writings and leading ideas of the day, but it is impossible to know whether he (or his father) had an explicitly apocalyptic perspective in the early years.

His letters also suggest that Paul was a product of the non-Jewish Hellenistic school system, or at least of its subject matter. Like Philo in Alexandria, as a youth he may have followed the standard curriculum of literature, mathematics, music, and philosophy, and then proceeded to rhetoric, the art of eloquence and persuasion. In the schools of rhetoric, students learned the art of argument and its application to speech writing, public speaking, and letter writing. Paul's letters reveal a thorough acquaintance with the substance and the tricks of the

---

6. Three additional occurrences of the apostle's name Saul appear in Acts, but all in accounts of his conversion (22:7, 13; 26:14).

rhetor's trade, even though he formally distances himself from rhetoric, or at least rhetorical showmanship (1 Cor. 2:1-5, Paul's own words; cf. 2 Cor. 10:10, the words of his detractors). Paul was a brilliant letter-writer, even if his public-speaking presence was less than impressive.

As part of his Hellenistic education, or perhaps merely by breathing the intellectual air in Tarsus (and/or in his family), Paul was also exposed to Stoicism. First-century Stoicism was much more interested in ethics and in daily life than in the more speculative philosophy of its earlier days. Stoic methods of argument, ideas, and terms appear in the letters. Paul can either adopt, adapt, or refute certain Stoic notions, depending on his understanding of their correspondence to the Scriptures or to his gospel. According to some scholars, an analysis of the deep structure of Paul's thinking suggests his ongoing interaction, not only with Judaism, but also with Stoicism.

Paul, then, came under three major influences associated with Tarsus: Diaspora Judaism, Hellenistic education and rhetoric, and first-century Stoicism. The effect of these formative forces was permanent, though Paul would scrutinize and reinterpret each of them in light, first, of the teaching of the Pharisees, and second, of God's revelation in the crucified Messiah.

PHARISEE AND PERSECUTOR

At some point in his youth Paul, probably with his family, moved to Palestine (Jerusalem is implied by Acts 22:3). The Paul of Acts claims that he studied in Jerusalem under the great rabbi Gamaliel (22:3), a claim disputed by some scholars, since Paul himself never mentions it in his letters (though some scholars argue that his largely Gentile audience would not likely know or care about a Palestinian rabbi). There is, however, no other historical reason to dispute the claim, and its accuracy would help explain Paul's knowledge of rabbinic argumentation. Moreover, Acts 26:4 can be interpreted to mean that Paul spent part of his educational years in both Tarsus and Jerusalem. It is also possible, though not as likely, that Paul received some education in non-Jewish Hellenistic rhetoric and literature in a city like Jerusalem, which was itself quite hellenized. Whatever the precise circumstances of his coming to Palestine, the Diaspora Jew (by birth) was becoming a Palestinian Jew.

It may have been in Jerusalem that Paul adopted an apocalyptic view of history as constituting two ages (see chap. 1). It is clear from his letters that he had an apocalyptic perspective similar to that of other apocalyptic Jews, though it is radically reworked in light of God's intervention in history through the death and resurrection of the Messiah.

PAUL THE PHARISEE

Whatever else happened to Paul in Jerusalem, he became, or became more deeply, a Pharisee. Both Acts and Paul himself attest to his being a Pharisee (Acts 23:6; 26:5; Phil. 3:5). In his letters this affiliation is recalled as a onetime badge of pride (explicitly in Phil. 3:3-6 and implicitly in Gal. 1:13-14). As noted in chapter 1, however, our evidence for early-first-century Pharisaism is very sparse. Still, it can be fairly safely said that the Pharisees were distinguished by three major concerns: zeal for the Law, both written and oral; commitment to the purity of Israel; and belief in the bodily resurrection of the dead. This belief in resurrection was likely part of a broader apocalyptic worldview that believed God was about to transform history.

The first two concerns were closely connected and could lead to extreme beliefs and action. As protectors and promoters of the Law, the Pharisees believed they were protecting Israel from divine judgment. Keeping Israel holy and pure, by keeping her in line with the Law of Moses, meant opposing any and all perceived threats to the proper doing of the Law and thus to Jewish ethnic and religious purity. One significant dimension of this protective activity would be to keep Jews free of Gentile contamination. This could mean insisting on separation from Gentiles at meals, requiring male Gentiles associated with the synagogue to be circumcised, or opposing the Roman occupation of the land. Paul could later summarize his attitude in terms like "preaching circumcision" (Gal. 5:11) — maintaining Israel's purity, as embodied and symbolized in this God-given boundary marker — and "zealous" (Gal. 1:14; Phil. 3:6).

For some Pharisees, including Paul, this ardor meant the possibility of intimidation and even violence toward fellow Jews who violated the Law, or toward anyone who endangered Israel's purity or otherwise opposed God. Paul also refers to his zeal as part of his "earlier life in Judaism" (Gal. 1:13-14). This does not mean he later abandoned Judaism for Christianity. Rather, he is using a technical term, developed during the time of the Maccabean revolt in the second century B.C., for extreme nationalistic Judaism. For first-century Jews, politics and religion were inseparable. Although there is no hard evidence that Paul planned revolutionary violence against Rome, it is not at all impossible that he would have supported such activity.

PAUL THE PERSECUTOR

Nothing, however, is more certain about Paul (or Saul) the zealous Pharisee than his intense disdain for and persecution of the earliest church, or assembly of believers in Jesus as Israel's Messiah. Both Acts and Paul's own letters attest to this grim reality.[7] His reputation was such as to make his supposed change of heart suspect.

The precise nature of this persecution cannot be known with certainty. It is not impossible that Paul's angry zeal grew to the point of planning punishment (Acts 26:11), and possibly even lethal violence. Acts says he approved of the stoning of Stephen (8:1) and 'voted' for the deaths of others (26:10), but that his trip to Damascus was intended to apprehend believers and bring them to the officials in Jerusalem (9:1-2), presumably for a severe religious reprimand. It is likely that his pattern of opposition consisted first of scriptural argument and private reprimand, then of intimidation and public renunciation, and finally of threats to hand people over to the authorities, whether Jewish or secular. Handing Christ-believers over to Jewish officials could result in their being beaten, as Paul himself later was (2 Cor. 11:24: "forty lashes minus one"). Paul may also have sometimes followed the strategy of those who arranged Jesus' crucifixion by accusing him of treason. As a threat to Israel, the Christ-believers had to be stopped, and the Romans could perhaps once again come in handy.

In any case, by whatever precise means, Paul "was violently persecuting the church of God and was trying to destroy it" (Gal. 1:13). This activity was, for Paul, the manifestation of his zeal for the traditions of his ancestors (Gal. 1:14; Phil. 3:6). Rather than revolting against pagan Rome, Paul seems to have seen his own nationalistic role, at least initially, as more internally focused. His heroes and role models may well have been three zealots from the past: the biblical grandson of Aaron, Phinehas; the prophet Elijah; and the more recent priestly hero Mattathias. These three men, full of violent zeal for YHWH and his law, inspired many first-century Jews. Phinehas and Mattathias in particular were likely especially important for Paul, since each killed his own countrymen out of zeal for God before going to war against pagan enemies.[8]

Acting on a general order from Moses, Phinehas acted with "zeal" (Num. 25:11, 13) and killed Zimri, together with Zimri's Midianite consort, to stop "the plague [of idolatry and immorality] . . . among the people of Israel" (25:7-9). According to Psalm 106:30-31, his act was not only celebrated but also "reckoned to him as righteousness / from generation to generation forever." According to the book of Numbers itself, God rewarded this violent zeal because it brought salvation to Israel: "The LORD spoke to Moses, saying: 'Phinehas son of Eleazar, son of Aaron the priest, has turned back my wrath from the Israelites

---

7. See Acts 7:54–8:3; 9:1-2; 22:4-5; 26:9-11; Gal. 1:13-14; 1 Cor. 15:9; Phil. 3:6.

8. Additional, but somewhat less parallel, zealous inspiration may have come from Moses' ordering the deaths of 3,000 Israelites following the golden-calf incident (Exod. 32:25-29). The use of the term 'zealot' here does not mean that Paul was part of an organized resistance movement. Paul was a zealot, but not a Zealot.

by manifesting such zeal among them on my behalf that in my jealousy I did not consume the Israelites. Therefore say, "I hereby grant him my covenant of peace. It shall be for him and for his descendants after him a covenant of perpetual priesthood, because he was zealous for his God, and made atonement for the Israelites"'" (25:10-13).

Elijah the prophet, in one of the most dramatic stories in the Bible, also exhibited his zeal for God (1 Kings 19:10) by challenging the prophets of Baal in a contest to show who was the one and true powerful God, YHWH or Baal, and then having them killed when he and YHWH won the contest (18:17-40).[9] Hundreds of years later, following in the spirit of Elijah and the footsteps of Phinehas, Mattathias "burned with zeal for the law" and killed an unnamed Jew as the latter offered a pagan sacrifice at the command of Antiochus IV (1 Macc. 2:23-28). This incident unleashed the famous Maccabean revolt under the leadership of Mattathias and his sons, including Judas Maccabeus. Phinehas, Mattathias, and Paul had a common zeal for God, Israel, and the Law that expressed itself first of all in violence toward apostate Jews. Paul, it would appear, sought his righteousness and justification (divine approval) in such zeal (though he would later certainly call it 'unenlightened'; cf. Rom. 10:2-3).

But why? Why did Paul perceive this band of fellow Jews in his day as a threat to Israel? Why did his zeal for God lead to persecution? What was wrong with the Christ-believers that led Paul to conclude that they were polluting Israel? Several reasons have been suggested, all of which have a significant degree of plausibility. The Christ-believers:

- had a relaxed attitude toward the Law;
- had a critical stance toward the temple;
- accepted Gentiles into their (Jewish) community and to their table, without circumcision;
- contradicted the Law by their outrageous and near blasphemous confession of a defeated, cursed criminal (see Deut. 21:23) as raised from the dead to be Israel's Messiah;
- foolishly put Israel at risk of political reprisals from the Roman authorities by proclaiming the advent of (a false) Messiah;
- blasphemed by identifying a human being with God by referring to Jesus as 'Lord.'

9. This contest followed the prophet's accurate prediction of a drought on the land as a divine punishment for Israel's worship of Baal (17:1-7), a cult promoted by King Ahab and his non-Jewish wife Jezebel (16:31-34), who also killed the Lord's prophets (18:4, 13). Although Elijah did not kill any Israelites (who immediately confessed YHWH as God when Baal lost the contest), his violent zeal for God in killing the false prophets became legendary (cf. Sir. 48:1-4).

Although one or another of these reasons may have been the most important, it is likely that their cumulative effect drove Paul over the edge. He opposed everything the Christ-believers stood for: their convictions, their conduct, the composition of their community. His was a comprehensive zeal that could not be contained or arrested.

Or so it seemed.

THE TRANSFORMING EXPERIENCE: APPEARANCE, CALL, COMMISSION, CONVERSION

Whether on his own initiative or, as Acts has it, with official sanction (9:2), Paul set out for Damascus to try to stop the cancer that had metastasized to that region from Jerusalem. The churches were still very young; although the year cannot be specified with certainty, it was within a few years of Jesus' execution, sometime between A.D. 32 and 35.

And then it happened: Paul was turned around. But what was it, exactly, that happened? Acts has Paul tell the story three times (9:1-31; 22:1-21; 26:2-23), each version a bit different from the others.[10] What concerns us first of all, however, is Paul's own understanding of what occurred as expressed in his letters.

APPEARANCE

First, Paul says, Jesus appeared to him, as he had appeared to the original apostles and believers (1 Cor. 15:5-8). Paul had seen Jesus, the Lord (9:1). It was a divinely granted revelation (Gal. 1:16; Gk. *apokalypsis*). This would mean at least the following (though Paul would not necessarily have understood all the implications of his experience the moment it happened):

- Jesus was no longer dead but alive.
- God had raised Jesus and thereby both vindicated and exalted him.
- The crucified Jesus was indeed exalted as the Messiah (God's anointed one) of Israel and thereby the royal Son of God and Lord.

---

10. For example, in Acts 9 Saul (Paul) alone sees the light, but all hear the voice; in Acts 22 Saul alone hears the voice, but all see the light; and in both accounts Saul alone specifically falls to the ground. In Acts 26, nothing is said about what the companions saw or heard, but they all fall to the ground with Saul. Moreover, in Acts 26 Jesus issues Saul a full-blown commission, whereas in Acts 9 and 22 he simply instructs Saul to go to Damascus to receive his commission.

- Jesus' death was not merely a curse on him but an efficacious death "for [others'] sins."
- The eschatological resurrection of the dead, and thus the last days, had begun.
- Jesus could be encountered as a living presence.
- The encounter with Jesus was an experience of undeserved mercy.
- Violent zeal for the Law was misguided, and persecuting the church was a grave error.
- The significance of the Law, temple, and circumcision needed to be reevaluated in light of God's vindication of Jesus.
- Gentiles, who were to come to God in the last days, must somehow be part of God's unfolding plan in the death and exaltation of Jesus.

As astonishingly comprehensive as this list sounds, every item follows from Paul's transformative experience if in fact it was, as Paul believed, a revelation of the resurrected Jesus.

CALL AND COMMISSION

Second, Paul says, God graciously called him, in the same way he had called the prophets Isaiah and Jeremiah.[11] Though neither prophet is mentioned by name, Paul's claim that God "set me apart before I was born and called me through his grace" (Gal. 1:15) echoes the declarations of the prophets:

> And now the LORD says,
>   who formed me in the womb to be his servant,
> to bring Jacob back to him,
>   and that Israel might be gathered to him,
> for I am honored in the sight of the LORD,
>   and my God has become my strength —
> he says,
> "It is too light a thing that you should be my servant
>   to raise up the tribes of Jacob

---

11. Paul never claims the title 'prophet,' though he clearly sees himself in continuity with the biblical prophets and appears to exercise the gift of prophecy (inspired speech). This is likely because he sees the title 'prophet' in the church as a reference to someone who speaks inspired oracles but, unlike an 'apostle,' has not seen (or been commissioned by) the resurrected Lord as Paul, Peter, and James have (cf. 1 Cor. 12:28 with 9:1-2 and 15:3-10). Acts, on the other hand, expresses Paul's continuity with the biblical prophets by repeatedly showing the similarity of his function and fate to theirs.

and to restore the survivors of Israel;
I will give you as a light to the nations [Gk. *ethnōn*, meaning
    also 'Gentiles'],
  that my salvation may reach to the end of the earth." (Isa. 49:5-6)[12]

Now the word of the LORD came to me saying, "Before I formed you in the womb I knew you, / and before you were born I consecrated you; / I appointed you a prophet to the nations [*ethnē*]." Then I said, "Ah, Lord GOD! Truly I do not know how to speak, for I am only a boy." But the LORD said to me, "Do not say, 'I am only a boy'; / for you shall go to all to whom I send you, / and you shall speak whatever I command you. / Do not be afraid of them, / for I am with you to deliver you, says the LORD." (Jer. 1:4-8)

Furthermore, like the call of the prophets, Paul's call carried with it a commission. Paul's specific commission was to "proclaim him [God's Son] among the Gentiles" (Gal. 1:16; see also the accounts in Acts). The words 'appearance' ("he [Christ] appeared also to me" [1 Cor. 15:8]) and 'call/commission' ("God . . . called me" [Gal. 1:15]) together suggest both something seen (the resurrected Lord) and something heard (a divine summons); although Acts and the letters disagree on the details, they agree on these two sensory aspects of the experience.

But why the Gentiles? It is difficult to resist the conclusion that the focus of Paul's commission was directly related to the focus of his persecution: Gentile participation in the community of Christ-believing Jews. Paul's encounter with the resurrected Christ signaled for him that the last days had been inaugurated. And Paul knew that the prophetic hope was that the Gentiles would come to Israel's God in the last days. This hope, not coincidentally, was powerfully expressed in one of the very texts to which Paul alludes in Galatians 1:15:

I will give you as a light to the nations [Gk. *ethnōn*, 'nations'],
  that my salvation may reach to the end of the earth. (Isa. 49:6)[13]

Paul interpreted his vocation to be not merely to *allow* but to *urge* the Gentiles to turn to the true God by acknowledging his Messiah, the Lord, Jesus. Those who formerly were excluded were now to be included.

Although Paul's awareness and understanding of his commission may have developed over time, he seems to have seen it in retrospect as an essential dimension of his initial encounter with the risen Jesus.

12. Paul, of course, had no way of knowing what most biblical scholars believe: that the prophet referred to in Isa. 49 is the so-called second Isaiah, the exilic author of Isa. 40–55, not Isaiah of Jerusalem, the eighth-century prophet responsible for Isa. 1–39.

13. The call of Jeremiah also contains a mission to the nations/Gentiles, though for Jeremiah it principally meant a call to prophesy *against* the nations (see esp. Jer. 46–51).

It is difficult also to resist the conclusion that Paul's later suffering for Christ, which was such an integral part of his apostolic identity and mission, also grew directly out of the experience of being divinely called while being a violent persecutor (1 Cor. 15:9). (This is certainly part of what the powerful story of Acts 9 seeks to convey when it narrates Paul's encounter with Jesus as including the question, "Saul, Saul, why do you persecute me?" [Acts 9:4; 22:7; 26:14].) The experience also impressed on Paul God's faithfulness and grace (mentioned in both 1 Cor. 15:9-10 and Gal. 1:15), which would become central to his mission and message.

The word 'grace' must especially be stressed. There is absolutely no evidence that prior to his call Paul felt any guilt for his persecuting zeal; he had no self-doubt about his mission. Nor is there any concrete evidence that he had previously engaged in missionary activity toward Gentiles, urging them to convert and be circumcised (as some scholars have argued). No, the letters testify that Paul was 'surprised by grace.' They also strongly suggest that any disdain for Gentile impurity he had became a zeal for Gentile inclusion, not that one form of zeal for Gentile inclusion (by circumcision) was transformed into another form of zeal for Gentile inclusion (apart from circumcision).

In summary, the experience of a revelation and appearance of Jesus as a divine call and commission meant at least the following to Paul:

- He was the recipient of unexpected and unmerited grace.
- He had a mission to proclaim Jesus as God's Son among the Gentiles.
- He would, more than likely, suffer in the execution of his commission, even as he had previously inflicted suffering.

CONVERSION

Paul's Damascus road experience is often referred to as his 'conversion.' That designation, however, fell on hard times in the later part of the twentieth century. Some interpreters of Paul feared that it implied either that Paul underwent something like a Christian conversion experience of remorse and repentance or, more erroneously, a change of religions from Judaism to Christianity. A few words from the pen of Lutheran bishop and Harvard professor Krister Stendahl capture the essence of the argument: Paul should be understood as "the called — not the converted — Apostle."[14]

But Paul's experience of the resurrected Jesus was not merely a prophetic

---

14. Krister Stendahl, *Paul among Jews and Gentiles* (Philadelphia: Fortress, 1976), p. 23. The entire treatment (pp. 7-23) of Paul's "call rather than conversion" (p. 12) is provocative.

call and commissioning; it was a religious conversion. "No historical prophet came around on his experience as Paul did when called to his task," comments one Jewish scholar of Paul, Alan Segal.[15] From the perspective of modern sociology, argue Segal and others, a religious conversion does not necessarily mean a change of *religions* but a change of *religious identity and community.* A conversion may be defined, more fully, as a radical reorientation of one's fundamental commitment that is expressed in three things:

- convictions, or belief
- conduct, or behavior
- community affiliation, or belonging

By this definition, Paul certainly experienced a conversion: a radical change in belief, behavior, and belonging. We might equally say that he experienced a death and resurrection, even a participation in the death and resurrection of his new Lord. This language will, in fact, become central to Paul's understanding of believers' existence (see esp. Rom. 6, and the discussion of Paul's spirituality below, in chap. 5).

On the way to destroy the church of God, then, Paul became convinced that Jesus was alive and was indeed the Messiah and Lord (conviction). He consequently stopped persecuting the Christ-believers and began preparing to proclaim the one he had opposed; he would no longer imitate people like Phinehas and Mattathias, seeking his own justification through violent zeal for the Law (conduct). And he left the Pharisees[16] to join the growing community of Jews and Gentiles committed to Jesus (community affiliation). In so doing, however, he remained a Jew; he shifted parties, so to speak, changing from zealot for Torah to zealot for Messiah — the exalted, crucified Messiah Jesus.

APOSTLE AMONG THE GENTILES

As we have seen, Paul's encounter with the resurrected Jesus led him to the deep conviction that he had been called by God to be an apostle among the nations. Having experienced an appearance of the Lord, and having been commis-

---

15. Alan F. Segal, *Paul the Convert: The Apostolate and Apostasy of Saul the Pharisee* (New Haven: Yale University Press, 1990), p. 6.

16. Paul's claim to be a Pharisee, according to Acts 23:6, is meant to show his long-standing (and ongoing) Pharisaic belief in the resurrection of the dead, not to imply his continued affiliation with the Pharisees as a group.

sioned, he, no less than Peter and those who had been with the earthly Jesus, was now the authoritative messenger of God (1 Cor. 9:1; 15:7-11; Gal. 1). Such is the basic meaning of 'apostle' (Gk. *apostolos*) — one sent with the message and authority of the sender, and in the sender's stead.

THE NATURE OF APOSTLESHIP

Forms of the word 'apostle' (including 'apostleship') appear more than twenty times in the undisputed letters of Paul, and another ten times in the disputed letters. Paul identifies himself as an apostle in the opening of four of the seven undisputed letters (Romans, 1 and 2 Corinthians, and Galatians), and five of the six disputed letters also open with the self-descriptor "apostle" (Colossians, Ephesians, 1 and 2 Timothy, and Titus). Paul considers apostleship to be a gift — the most important gift in the church (1 Cor. 12:28). With the gift come certain responsibilities and rights. The chief responsibility, of course, is to preach the gospel and form communities of those who believe that gospel and are thus reconciled to God through Christ; Paul acts as Christ's ambassador and God's spokesperson (2 Cor. 5:16-21). Apostles are stewards, accountable to God for the quality of their ministry (1 Cor. 3:10-15; 4:1-5). They are also parents who give birth to, nurture, and discipline their children (1 Cor. 4:14-21; Gal. 4:19-20; 1 Thess. 2:7b-12).

Associated with the gift of apostleship are the rights of financial support and companionship by a "believing wife," as well as the expectation of (if not the outright right to) respect (1 Cor. 9:1-12; 1 Thess. 2:7). In addition, inasmuch as apostleship means authoritative representation and parental responsibility, Paul expects the believers in his churches to heed his advice, and he can exert his apostolic power in various ways, even from a distance (1 Cor. 5:1-5). If he is uncertain that those he has spiritually fathered will comply, he can threaten (explicitly or implicitly) a paternal disciplinary visit (1 Cor. 4:14-20; 2 Cor. 12:11–13:10; Philem. 22).

But for Paul, apostleship is not primarily about power or authority as they are normally understood. To be an apostle is not merely to preach, but also to live, the gospel. This means for Paul that his life (and those of his colleagues) will especially reflect the reality of Christ crucified. As he writes to the Corinthians with a touch of sarcasm:

> For I think that God has exhibited us apostles as last of all, as though sentenced to death, because we have become a spectacle to the world, to angels and to mortals. We are fools for the sake of Christ, but you are wise in Christ. We are weak, but you are strong. You are held in honor, but we in dis-

repute. To the present hour we are hungry and thirsty, we are poorly clothed and beaten and homeless, and we grow weary from the work of our own hands. When reviled, we bless; when persecuted, we endure; when slandered, we speak kindly. We have become like the rubbish of the world, the dregs of all things, to this very day. (1 Cor. 4:9-13)

As this passage indicates, and many others confirm, for Paul the essential mark of apostleship is conformity to Christ crucified in sacrifice, weakness, and suffering (see further below under "Suffering Servant"). There are other "signs" of an apostle — "signs and wonders and mighty works" (2 Cor. 12:12) — but for Paul at least, these are not the primary indicators of apostleship.

It is Paul's commitment to living the gospel, in fact, that leads him not to use the very rights he has as an apostle (1 Cor. 9:12b, 15; 1 Thess. 2:1-12). This lends an unusual dimension to his apostolic power: it is characterized by sacrifice, the renunciation of power, and intimate nurturing, so much so that he draws on maternal as well as paternal images to convey the character of his ministry (1 Thess. 2:7; Gal. 4:19). Paul will do anything necessary to bring the gospel to Jews and, especially, Gentiles (1 Cor. 9:19-23).

Paul saw himself primarily as the apostle for the Gentiles (Rom. 1:5; 11:13). According to Galatians 2, the "pillars" (2:9) of the church (Peter, James, and John) agreed that Paul and his colleague Barnabas would be sent to the uncircumcised (non-Jews), Peter and the others to the circumcised (2:8). (It should be noted, however, that this 'decision' was made after Paul had probably been evangelizing Gentiles for a decade or more [see Gal. 2:1-2]. Unfortunately, we simply do not know much about this early period of his mission work.)

Despite the 'division of labor' that occurred at the Jerusalem meeting, it is very important that we not think that Paul's apostleship to the Gentiles meant that he excluded Jews from his concern or efforts. Several facts demonstrate Paul's ongoing efforts to evangelize Jews as part of his mission:

- Paul's gospel is about the crucified Jewish Messiah who manifests God's faithfulness to Israel, not merely some divine envoy who reveals God's concern for non-Jews.
- Paul specifically declares that the gospel is the power of salvation for all, Jews and Gentiles (Rom. 1:16-17).
- Throughout his letters Paul understands the church to be a unified community of Gentiles and Jews who acknowledge Jesus as the Messiah of Israel ("Christ") and Lord of the nations (Gal. 3:28; 5:6; 6:15-16; 1 Cor. 7:17-20; 12:13; cf. Col. 3:11).
- Attempting to be sensitive to cultural differences without compromising basic principles, Paul claims that he deliberately accommodates himself

differently to Jews and to Gentiles in order to bring the gospel to each group (1 Cor. 9:19-23).

- Some of Paul's most important coworkers in the proclamation of the gospel were Jewish (e.g., Timothy, Barnabas, Prisca/Priscilla and Aquila).
- On five occasions (by the mid-50s) Paul received an official flogging of thirty-nine lashes at the hands of Jews (i.e., synagogue leaders doling out an official punishment; 2 Cor. 11:24), suggesting that he regularly initiated contact with the Jewish community and sought, not its approval (which he did not need), but its favorable response to the gospel, at great risk to his own safety.[17]

All of this means that the pattern in Acts of Paul's going first to the Jews is historically plausible, reflecting Paul's own understanding of the gospel and of his mission, as well as the actual results of his efforts (the composition of his churches) and his experience of persecution.

A small — but vocal and influential — number of scholars believes Paul held to salvation or justification by two tracks, belief in Christ for Gentiles and adherence to the Jewish Law for Jews. This interpretation, sometimes called the 'two-covenant theory,' contradicts everything we know about Paul's convictions, behavior, and communities. His gospel was "to the Jew first and also to the Greek [Gentile]" (Rom. 1:16). The proponents of this theory, though well intentioned, are guided less by historical than by ideological concerns. (For further discussion, see the introductory section of the chapter on Romans.)

Paul's primary mission, then, was to preach the gospel *among* the nations and thereby *to* the uncircumcised. But because his mission was part of a larger divine plan of bringing all peoples to recognize Jesus as Lord, he was happy to proclaim the good news to Diaspora Jews, and was grief-stricken when only a relatively few responded (Rom. 9:1-5). In fact, *Paul's concrete goal was to build multicultural communities of Christ-believers consisting of Jews and Gentiles alike.* If this were not true, then texts like Galatians 3:28 would make no sense whatsoever ("There is no longer Jew or Greek . . . for all of you are one in Christ Jesus").

PAUL, ISAIAH, AND THE GENTILES

Still, Paul's major concern, as we have seen, was the Gentiles. Paul's confidence that the end had begun in Jesus' death and resurrection meant that the Gentiles,

17. It is also of course possible that Paul was pursued by zealots on a mission like his own former mission, but the frequency of encounters, plus the corroborating evidence of Acts, makes it more likely that Paul regularly evangelized among Jews and thereby sometimes generated serious negative reactions.

as well as the Jews, were being summoned to covenant relationship with the God of Israel. At some point very early on, perhaps under the influence of preaching and worship that interpreted Jesus and the church in light of Israel's Scriptures, Paul seems to have developed his notion of apostleship especially in light of the book of Isaiah, chapters 40–66.[18]

Each of the two major sections of Isaiah 40–66 (chaps. 40–55 and 56–66), though addressing different circumstances, attempts to reassure Israel regarding God's salvation. The goal of 40–55 is to comfort the people (40:1-2), for, despite their predicament, YHWH is sovereign and is about to bring them back from Babylon in a new exodus. The purpose of 56–66 is to reassure the people that the promised salvation, though not yet fully present, will arrive as a new creation.

Several themes in Isaiah 40–66 (with different nuances in 40–55 and 56–66) seem to have captured Paul's imagination and shaped his vision:

- *Monotheism and the reign of God:* YHWH the God of Israel is the one true God, the only and sovereign Lord of the world (43:10-13; 44:6-20; 45:5–46:13).
- *Good news of redemption:* YHWH is about to act in faithfulness and compassion to redeem and restore Israel (43:1-7, 14-21; 44:21-28; 51:12-16; 52:1-12; 54:1-17; 57:14-21; 59:15b-21; 61:1-11; "good news" in 52:7 and 61:1).
- *Universality:* the salvation of Israel will also result in the acknowledgment of the one true God by the nations of the earth and even the formation of one multinational community worshiping the one God (51:5; 52:7-10; 56:1-8; 60:1-22; 65:1-2; 66:20-23).
- *Newness:* God's salvation will be a new exodus, a new covenant, and a new creation, yielding a new song (42:9-10; 43:14-21; 62:2; 65:17-25; 66:22).
- *National servanthood and mission:* YHWH has called Israel to be his servant and a light (witness) to the nations (42:6-7; 43:8-13; 49:6; 51:4; 55:5; 60:1-3).
- *Personal servanthood and mission:* YHWH has called not only Israel, but also the prophet, the unidentified suffering figure of 52:13–53:12 (Israel? the prophet? another figure?), and even Cyrus (45:1-8) to be his servant (for Israel/the prophet, see also 42:1-9; 49:1-6; 50:4-11; 61:1-3).

18. This part of the canonical book of Isaiah is often called Deutero-, or Second, Isaiah (chaps. 40–55) and Trito-, or Third, Isaiah (chaps. 56–66). Most scholars believe that these chapters were not written by Isaiah of Jerusalem, during the eighth century, but by a 'second' Isaiah, during Israel's sixth-century Babylonian exile, and by a 'third' Isaiah after the return from exile. Paul, of course, was not aware of all the historical issues, but he seems to have read this second half of Isaiah as a unit. In addition to Isa. 40–66, Paul's sense of vocation was also informed by other scriptural books, such as portions of Exodus, Deuteronomy, the Psalms, 'First' Isaiah (chaps. 1–39), and other prophetic books.

Paul reads these themes under the influence of the early church's (including his own) experience of God in Jesus, and he comes to some significant conclusions. The mission of the suffering servant has been taken up by Jesus, who died for the sins of all and was vindicated by God in resurrection. His vindication meant his exaltation to universal lordship and thus (in some sense) equality with God (compare Phil. 2:9-11 with Isa. 45:23). Therefore, in Jesus God is bringing about the new creation, exodus, and covenant — the deliverance from sin that will redeem Israel and bring the Gentiles to God. Like the writer of Isaiah 40–55 ('the second Isaiah'), Paul sees himself as called to represent Israel by bringing the light of the gospel to the nations and by suffering, like Jesus, while doing so.

TRAVELING PREACHER, COMMUNITY BUILDER, AND SUFFERING SERVANT

The apostolic vocation we have just considered, cast in the mold of Isaiah 40–66 (and especially the servant of chaps. 40–55) but reshaped in light of Jesus, led Paul to three fundamental activities: proclaiming the good news, forming communities of Jews and especially Gentiles who believe the good news, and suffering for the good news. Each of these was constitutive of his apostleship, which took him out of Palestine (for the most part) and back into the Diaspora, though far beyond his native Tarsus. We turn now to these three dimensions of his apostleship: how he proclaimed the gospel and started communities, plus how — and how much — he suffered.

TRAVELING PREACHER

Paul covered a lot of territory; if the journeys outlined in Acts even approximate his actual activity, he may have walked and sailed some ten thousand miles.[19] He traveled by foot and by ship, constantly risking life and limb both on land and at sea. The dangers of land travel were no less real than the threat of shipwreck.

As noted in chapter 1, the topography of Anatolia (modern Turkey) and Greece would have been a challenge to the ancient traveler. Both countries are mountainous and home to numerous lakes and rivers. Even travelers following the main Roman roads would be forced to go through hilly and mountainous regions, avoiding travel to and through certain areas during the winter months,

19. Estimates vary and are, of course, based on incomplete sources.

The Tauros (or Taurus) mountains in southern Asia Minor

when snow and ice made travel treacherous or impossible. In 2 Corinthians 11:26 Paul himself witnesses to the "danger from rivers," possibly those that cut through the mountain canyons of southern Anatolia, as well as to "danger in the wilderness," the deserted areas far from the cities. Other dangers were posed by humans rather than by nature: mentioned in the same Corinthian text are "bandits." During all these land voyages, it appears, Paul traveled modestly on an artisan's budget by walking rather than riding on animals or in carts at extra expense to himself, his team, and (ultimately) his supporters. When he traveled by ship, there would also have been expenses (unless Paul found a sympathetic owner of a commercial ship) and "danger at sea" (11:26 again) from storms that could cause shipwrecks (11:25) and from pirates (though neither Paul nor Luke mentions the latter).

COMMUNITY BUILDER

Although he may have evangelized in the countryside as he walked, Paul's primary objective was to establish communities of Christ-believers in the cities of Asia Minor and Greece; he was an urban missionary, as we noted in chapter 1. In some cities he may have stayed only for weeks, but in others he remained for long periods of time, some two years or so in Ephesus and eighteen months in Corinth.

Paul did not travel or engage in mission work alone but with coworkers. His coworkers varied in number and abilities over the years, but their number is quite impressive: some three dozen are named in the letters. They served as fellow evangelists and community builders, cosenders of letters, messengers, and secretaries; they also provided emotional support, visited him in prison, and (no doubt) helped him think through his mission and message. Paul clearly saw them as close associates; he gave them titles like coworker and partner, as well as fellow slave, fellow soldier, and fellow prisoner. Among the most important of these teammates were:[20]

- **Timothy** (see Rom. 16:21; 1 Cor. 4:17; 16:10; 2 Cor. 1:1, 19; Phil. 1:1; 2:19; Col. 1:1; 1 Thess. 1:1; 3:2, 6; 2 Thess. 1:1; 1 Timothy; 2 Timothy; Acts 16:1-3; 17:14-15; 18:5; 19:22; 20:4)
- **Titus** (see 2 Cor. 2:13; 7:6, 13-14; 8:6, 16, 23; 12:18; Gal. 2:1, 3; 2 Tim. 4:10; Titus)
- **Barnabas** (see 1 Cor. 9:6; Gal. 2:1-13; Acts 9:27; 11:22-30; 12:25; 13:1-12, 42-50; 14:1-20; 15:1-39)
- **Silvanus/Silas**[21] (see 2 Cor. 1:19; 1 Thess. 1:1; 2 Thess. 1:1; Acts 15:22-41; 16:16-32; 17:1-15; 18:5)
- **Priscilla (Prisca) and Aquila**[22] (see Rom. 16:3; 1 Cor. 16:19; 2 Tim. 4:19; Acts 18:1-4, 18-28)
- **Sosthenes** (see 1 Cor. 1:1; Acts 18:17)

This was not an inexpensive operation: travel expenses, room and board, rental of occasional facilities, and so on. Paul decided early on not to be a financial burden to any community in which he worked (1 Thess. 2:9). The ministry was self-supporting; Paul worked night and day with his hands, specifically in the tentmaking trade (Acts 18:2-3). He would have made tents of either leather or, more likely, linen, which were then sold to market owners and shop owners, home owners, spectators at games (such as the biennial Isthmian Games held near Corinth), and others. We do not know if others generally worked as well, though Priscilla and Aquila shared the same craft (Acts 18:2-3). Paul and his team did accept financial support from communities they had founded and then left; the Philippians were especially generous.

---

20. References include texts from undisputed letters, disputed letters, and Acts.

21. The Latin form "Silvanus" appears in the letters, while the Semitic or Greek form "Silas" is used in Acts.

22. "Prisca" appears only in the letters, the diminutive "Priscilla" only in Acts.

Manual work was the labor of the lower class and slaves, and the elite disdained such work. Moreover, people expected teachers who were 'worth their salt' to charge for their services and/or be supported by a well-to-do patron. Doing neither opened Paul to accusations of inferiority as a teacher and apostle, and to derision for associating with the riffraff.

As 1 Corinthians 9 demonstrates, Paul could — and did — cite Scripture and the teaching of Jesus to justify his right to be supported by his converts. Refusing to exercise this right and working with his hands, however, were apparently absolutely essential to his self-understanding as an apostle. It was a concrete way of being an imitator of Christ: [x] possessing a right, associated with a certain privileged status, that would be advantageous to oneself; yet [y] freely choosing not to use the right; but rather [z] lowering oneself to the status of a slave for the benefit of others. This apostolic pattern was grounded in the master story of Christ that Paul narrates in Philippians 2:6-11, which we will consider in chapter 4. The following parallels between it and 1 Corinthians 9 clearly show this relationship:

Parallels between Philippians 2:6-11 (Christ) and 1 Corinthians 9 (Paul)

Possession of privileged status/right [x]

Philippians 2:6a	**1 Corinthians 9:1-12a, 13-14, 19a (excerpts)**
Though he [Christ Jesus] was in the *form of God,*	Am I not *free?* Am I not an *apostle?* . . . Do we not have the *right* to our food and drink? . . . Or is it only Barnabas and I who have no *right to refrain from working for a living?* . . . Do I say this on human authority? Does not the law also say the same? For it is written in the law of Moses, "You shall not muzzle an ox while it is treading out the grain." . . . If we have sown spiritual good among you, is it too much if we reap your material benefits? If others share this *rightful claim on you,* do not we still more? . . . [T]he Lord commanded that those who proclaim the gospel should get their living by the gospel. . . . For *though I am free* with respect to all. . . .

Decision not to exercise the right [y]

Philippians 2:6b	**1 Corinthians 9:12b, 15, 18**
[he] *did not regard equality with God as something to be exploited,*	Nevertheless, *we have not made use of this right.* . . . But *I have made no use of any of these rights,* nor am I writing this so that they may be

68

applied in my case. Indeed, I would rather die than that — no one will deprive me of my ground for boasting! . . . What then is my reward? Just this: that in my proclamation I may make the gospel free of charge, so as *not to make full use of my rights* in the gospel.

Self-lowering to slave status [z]

Philippians 2:7-8	1 Corinthians 9:12c, 19b
but *emptied himself,* taking the form of a *slave,* being born in human likeness. And being found in human form, he *humbled himself* and became obedient *to the point of death* — even death on a cross.	. . . but we *endure anything* rather than put an obstacle in the way of the gospel of Christ. . . . I have made myself a *slave* to all, so that I might win more of them.

Paul, then, saw himself as a kind of little Christ (to borrow an expression from Martin Luther). His life was his first evangelistic and pastoral message, which is why he thought he could invite others to be imitators of him — that is, of Christ (1 Cor. 11:1).

Upon entering a city, Paul and his team would probably have sought out the local Jewish community, where he might find lodging and a place to set up shop. He and his team apparently normally attempted to establish a nucleus of Jewish believers before, or while also, seeking out Gentiles. If possible, they would speak in the synagogue or wherever else Jews gathered. If there were no Jews, or if the mission to them was unsuccessful, Paul focused exclusively on the Gentiles. This evangelistic activity occurred occasionally in public — in the open air or in rented halls — but more often in the workshop, as Paul "worked night and day" (1 Thess. 2:9; cf. 2 Thess. 3:8).

Accompanying Paul's preaching, though this aspect is not often stressed, were deeds of power, as both Acts (e.g., 15:12) and the letters (Rom. 15:14-21; 2 Cor. 12:12; Gal. 3:1-5) attest. Paul can even summarize his Spirit-empowered ministry as one that took place "by word and deed" (Rom. 15:18). This ministry of powerful deeds would certainly have included healings and possibly also exorcisms. These miraculous events — "signs and wonders and mighty works" (2 Cor. 12:12) — were evidence, both for Paul and apparently for his audiences and then his communities, of his apostleship and of the presence of God's power in him and his message. No less miraculous for Paul was the regular departure from pagan worship and ways of living that accompanied the response to his message. This too was the work of the Spirit, who, after all, is the *Holy* Spirit. Ironically, however, it was the message of the *cross* that brought about the outpouring of the Spirit through Paul and on his hearers (Gal. 3:1-5). The defeat of sin and evil powers on the cross was being translated into the defeat of sin and evil powers in people's real lives.

As success ensued and a community was formed, Paul and the new believers would need a place to meet. They depended on the hospitality of one or more of the believers. The free poor living in very modest urban tenements (Latin *insulae*) would have been able to accommodate only a very small group. Nevertheless, some house churches probably met in such homes. More often a house church or, later, a group of house churches would meet in the home of one of the wealthier believers. Depending on the size of the house and how many spaces (e.g., dining room[s], courtyard[s], etc.) were used, these gatherings may have been as small as twenty-five or thirty or possibly as large as several hundred. This situation had inherent problems, as the networks of hierarchy, patronage, and friendship involving the householder encountered a new set of relationships in which everyone was part of God's family or household (see, e.g., 1 Cor. 11:17-34; Philemon; cf. Col. 3:18–4:1; Eph. 5:21–6:9). In addition to houses, some scholars think, the believers would have occasionally rented halls for their meetings, as the various guilds did.[23]

The house churches were not incidental to Paul's mission but central to it. Paul did not envision his mission merely as the accumulation of converts but as the creation of communities — (relatively) small alternatives to the various other religious and political communities. Paul envisions the church as a body (1 Cor. 12) and a family (addressing his letters to "brothers" [and "sisters"]), both corporate images.

SUFFERING SERVANT

Evangelistic success, however, was a two-edged sword. While it brought salvation to Jews and especially Gentiles, it also frequently brought opposition and suffering, both to the converts and to Paul himself. Nearly one-third of Acts recounts Paul on trial or in prison, and in five of the thirteen letters he is identified as a prisoner (Philippians and Philemon, whose authorship is undisputed, and Colossians, Ephesians, and 2 Timothy, whose authorship is disputed).

For Paul, suffering was one way of identifying with his Lord, of reliving his story in the present. His suffering was also, therefore, like Jesus' death, an act of

---

23. It is possible that there was a precedent for house churches in the Jewish community ('house synagogues'), though Jews normally built separate structures.

love for those to whom he preached — those who had responded, those who might yet respond, and even those who opposed his gospel. Paul is, indeed, honored to suffer in love for Christ and for others (2 Cor. 1:5-6; 12:15; Phil. 1:12-14). In weakness he finds strength and effectiveness (2 Cor. 12:10); in suffering he sees the manifestation of the power of God for the salvation of Gentiles and Jews (2 Cor. 4:7-12).

This suffering is so important for Paul that he 'catalogs,' or lists, his trials on numerous occasions.[24] These catalogs account for some of the most rhetorically powerful texts in Paul's letters. For instance, in 2 Corinthians 11:23-28, comparing himself to his 'opponents,' he says he has undergone

> far greater labors, far more imprisonments, with countless floggings, and often near death. Five times I have received from the Jews the forty lashes minus one. Three times I was beaten with rods. Once I received a stoning. Three times I was shipwrecked; for a night and a day I was adrift at sea; on frequent journeys, in danger from rivers, danger from bandits, danger from my own people, danger from Gentiles, danger in the city, danger in the wilderness, danger at sea, danger from false brothers and sisters; in toil and hardship, through many a sleepless night, hungry and thirsty, often without food, cold and naked. And, besides other things, I am under daily pressure because of my anxiety for all the churches.

The frequency, scope, and painfulness of these experiences, and those listed elsewhere, are quite astonishing. They include public disgrace, psychological pain, physical deprivation and pain, fatigue from physical labor, political and religious punishment and torture (including flogging and imprisonment), and general suffering. There were trials caused by the forces of nature and by human beings, by his fellow Jews and by Gentiles, and even by fellow followers of Jesus as the Messiah. Ultimately this was the cost of apostleship.

CONCLUSION

Paul left us letters, not a journal or an autobiography. Every attempt to write about his life is fraught with difficulties. As one scholar has said, "The definitive biography of the man [Paul] is yet to be written and may never be written. But were the apostle to have written an autobiography, without doubt he would have stressed the cruciform and Christocentric pattern of his life."[25]

24. Rom. 8:35; 1 Cor. 4:8-13; 2 Cor. 4:7-12; 6:3-10; 11:23-33; 12:10.
25. Ben Witherington III, *The Paul Quest: The Renewed Search for the Jew of Tarsus* (Downers Grove, Ill.: InterVarsity, 1998), p. 303.

It has sometimes been said that Jesus was a teaching, healing, and suffering/dying Messiah. As the Messiah's representative, Paul fulfilled each of these roles as well. He preached and taught, healed (assuming that healing was among the "mighty works" he performed), and suffered. He saw these aspects of his ministry as absolutely constitutive of his apostolic call. In that sense he carried on the mission of Jesus, finding in his identification with Jesus the purpose of his zeal. These various dimensions of his mission grew out of his gospel, found expression in his letters, and created a spirituality for himself, his co-workers, and his churches. To these subjects we turn in the following chapters.

QUESTIONS FOR REFLECTION

1. What is the meaning and importance of the claims that open this chapter: "Paul was born a Jew, lived a Jew, and died a Jew. It was therefore obviously as a Jew that he experienced the once-crucified Jesus as the resurrected and exalted Lord. Paul did not set out to found a new religion . . ."?
2. What is the historical and theological importance of understanding Paul's transformative experience as an appearance of Jesus? as a call and commission? as a conversion?
3. How might Paul's understanding of apostleship inform, and perhaps even correct, contemporary notions of 'apostleship' and ministry more generally?
4. What are some of the contemporary parallels to Paul's apostolic roles of traveling preacher, community builder, and suffering servant?
5. What do you consider to be the significance of community and partnership in ministry and in the church more generally?

FOR FURTHER READING AND STUDY

General

Bruce, F. F. *The Pauline Circle.* Grand Rapids: Eerdmans, 1985. A study of Paul's colleagues.

Roetzel, Calvin. *Paul: The Man and the Myth.* Minneapolis: Fortress, 1999. A careful study by one of the leading interpreters of Paul's life and letters in their historical context.

Stendahl, Krister. *Paul among Jews and Gentiles.* Philadelphia: Fortress, 1976. A short collection of essays, of which the two main pieces, on Paul's 'conversion' and on the West's 'introspective conscience' in interpreting Paul, are classics.

Witherington, Ben, III. *The Paul Quest: The Renewed Search for the Jew of Tarsus.* Downers Grove, Ill.: InterVarsity, 1998. A very helpful analysis of Paul in his various 'roles': writer, rhetor, prophet, apostle, storyteller, ethicist, etc.

Technical

Bolt, Peter, and Mark Thompson, eds. *The Gospel to the Nations: Perspectives on Paul's Mission.* Downers Grove, Ill.: InterVarsity, 2000. A collection of essays (in honor of Pauline scholar Peter T. O'Brien) on various historical and theological aspects of Paul's mission activity.

Donaldson, Terence L. *Paul and the Gentiles: Remapping the Apostle's Convictional World.* Minneapolis: Fortress, 1997. An analysis of how Paul's convictions about Gentile membership in the people of God changed from Torah to Christ as a result of his encounter with the resurrected Lord.

Hengel, Martin. *The Pre-Christian Paul.* London and Philadelphia: Trinity Press International, 1991. A reconstruction, relying on Acts and other historical sources, of Paul's citizenship, education, and persecution of Christians.

Hengel, Martin, and Anna Maria Schwemer. *Paul between Damascus and Antioch: The Unknown Years.* Louisville: Westminster John Knox, 1997. A massive history of Paul's activity from his conversion to the first missionary journey (ca. 33-47 or 49), arguing for the reliability of Acts.

Kim, Seyoon. *The Origin of Paul's Gospel.* Grand Rapids: Eerdmans, 1982. An analysis of the Damascus road experience as the source of Paul's high Christology and hence mission.

Longenecker, Richard N., ed. *The Road from Damascus: The Impact of Paul's Conversion on His Life, Thought, and Ministry.* Grand Rapids: Eerdmans, 1997. A collection of essays exploring various aspects of the impact of Paul's conversion/call on his life and thought.

Malina, Bruce J., and Jerome H. Neyrey. *Portraits of Paul: An Archaeology of Ancient Personality.* Louisville: Westminster John Knox, 1996. A study of the way Paul was perceived and described in his time, using the insights of cultural anthropology.

Murphy-O'Connor, Jerome. *Paul: A Critical Life.* Oxford and New York: Oxford University Press, 1996. A carefully researched, detailed reconstruction of Paul's life and ministry that is helpful even when one disagrees with a particular interpretation of the evidence.

Riesner, Rainer. *Paul's Early Period: Chronology, Mission Strategy, Theology.* Translated by Doug Stott. Grand Rapids: Eerdmans, 1998. A reconstruction of Paul's activity and theology using Acts (arguing for its reliability), other historical sources, and the letters, with emphasis on 1 Thessalonians as a test case.

Segal, Alan F. *Paul the Convert: The Apostolate and Apostasy of Saul the Pharisee.* New Haven: Yale University Press, 1990. A significant sociological study of Paul as a 'convert' (defined sociologically) by a leading Jewish interpreter.

Winter, Bruce W., gen. ed. The Book of Acts in Its First-Century Setting. 6 vols. Grand Rapids: Eerdmans, 1993-. A monumental examination of Acts in its ancient literary, historical, and theological settings that demonstrates the usefulness of Acts for the interpretation of the first-century world and of Paul.

CHAPTER 3

PAUL'S LETTERS

Apostleship in Absentia

Our beloved brother Paul wrote to you according to the wisdom given him, speaking of this as he does in all his letters. There are some things in them hard to understand, which the ignorant and unstable twist to their own destruction, as they do the other scriptures.

2 Pet. 3:15b-16

Letters have an inherent appeal to us as readers. They are intimate, revealing, and frequently full of life's experiences and wisdom. Letters have been extraordinarily important in the history of the church. In the twentieth century, for example, we can think of the correspondence of people like the Reverend Dr. Martin Luther King, Jr.; C. S. Lewis; and Dietrich Bonhoeffer. Especially in the early centuries of Christianity, many important theological issues were discussed in letters.

Paul was an avid and eloquent correspondent. His preserved letters — or at least those attributed to him — constitute nearly half the New Testament documents (thirteen of twenty-seven). Although they vary in form, style, purpose, and content, they also share many important features. Looking at them as a whole, we can say with some confidence that Paul invented a new genre of letters; indeed, it was a new genre of literature. This genre is the apostolic — or perhaps, more generally, the pastoral — letter. Its basic function was to speak for the apostle in his absence.

In this chapter we consider Paul's letters: their character and purpose; their literary and rhetorical form; their content and sources; the question of their authorship; and their dissemination, collection, and order.

APOSTLESHIP IN ABSENTIA

A quick reading of Paul's letters reveals the following kinds of contents within them:

- personal greetings
- thanksgivings, blessings, and other prayers
- reviews of the relationship between Paul and the recipients, and of their experience of the gospel
- summaries of basic beliefs
- quotations and explanations of Scripture texts
- practical explanations of theological concepts
- moral instructions and admonitions, sometimes with reasoned argument
- criticisms and warnings
- autobiographical statements
- travel plans

This summary list suggests something of the character of a Pauline letter: it is a surrogate for Paul himself. It says what the apostle would say in person. It is a communication designed to accomplish Paul's apostolic goals in absentia and to make the presence of the absent apostle felt among the letter's recipients.[1] Not only that, it is designed to remind them of their experience of God in Christ by the presence of the Spirit. It is, therefore, a tool of Paul's apostleship. As such, it may be described as narrative, occasional, pastoral, and authoritative in character.

A NARRATIVE LETTER: A STORY BEHIND AND WITHIN

Referring to a letter as 'narrative' in character may at first seem odd. But a close inspection of Paul's letters reveals that he is always telling stories, no matter how brief they may be — stories about God in Christ, about himself, about his relationship with the recipients and their reception of the gospel, about the life within the community, and so on. In his letters there is a three-way intersection of God's story, Paul's story, and the recipients' story. Indeed, the intent of a Pauline letter seems to be both to rehearse the past and to guide the future of this 'triangular relationship,' this three-way intersection of personal narratives.

---

1. The notion of the presence of a person via personal correspondence is found, of course, in other musings about letters, both ancient (e.g., Seneca, *Epistle* 40.1) and modern.

This confluence of narratives is, to be sure, really one narrative — the story of God's saving power experienced in one particular community with the assistance of one particular apostle and his coworkers. A letter from Paul says, 'This story is not over.' As we examine the various Pauline letters, therefore, we need always to be attentive to both the past and the (hoped-for) future of this triangular narrative relationship. There is always a story behind the letter, as well as one taking shape within it.

AN OCCASIONAL LETTER: A 'WORD ON TARGET'

It follows, then, that each of Paul's letters is occasional in nature — occasioned, or elicited, by a specific set of circumstances within the 'triangular' narrative relationship that exists among Paul, the letter's recipients, and God. This fact is neatly summed up in the phrase coined by the late J. Christiaan Beker: a letter from Paul is a "word on target."[2] In most cases these circumstances include one or more problems (at least from Paul's perspective) that have arisen in the apostle's absence. What ensues, in some form, is a "conversation in context," to borrow Calvin Roetzel's apt description of a Pauline letter.[3] There is only one problem, of course: we have the 'transcript' of only one side of the conversation.

Reading a Pauline letter, therefore, is something like being in a room with someone on the telephone and listening only to that one end of the two-way conversation. As we listen, we try our best to imagine what the other party is saying that causes the various reactions and comments from the person in our presence. This can be a frustrating, misleading, and potentially dangerous endeavor. If we draw erroneous inferences, we may misjudge the character and convictions of the other party, not to mention the responses of the person in the same room.

So, too, with a letter from Paul. We are forced to try to reconstruct the other end of the conversation. Some interpreters of Paul carry this to a precarious extreme, however, believing they can deduce very much about Paul's explicit recipients, and even his implicit opponents, from the letters. This process is sometimes known as 'mirror reading,' and it has rightly received some rather harsh criticism in recent years. If one assumes, for instance, that every time Paul says, 'Don't do x,' there has been a problem regarding x, one may be assuming

---

2. J. Christiaan Beker, *Paul the Apostle: The Triumph of God in Life and Thought* (Philadelphia: Fortress, 1980), p. 12.

3. Calvin J. Roetzel, *The Letters of Paul: Conversations in Context,* 4th ed. (Louisville: Westminster John Knox, 1998).

the existence of a problem that Paul wants only to preempt. Or again, if one assumes that every affirmation Paul makes is a negation of some opponent's position, one may be creating opponents, or at least positions, that never existed. Nevertheless, in spite of these concerns, we must still proceed — though with due caution — in our attempts to understand the community, possible opponents and critics of Paul, and issues Paul is addressing if we are going to understand Paul himself.

A PASTORAL LETTER: COMMUNITY FORMATION

As an apostle, Paul's primary mission was to found churches, or multicultural communities of Christ-believers. As we noted in the last chapter, Paul saw himself as the spiritual parent of these communities, and also of individuals who had come to faith. He cared for them like a father, even like a mother or nurse (1 Thess. 2:7), and he longed for their maturation in Christ (1 Cor. 3:1-3; Gal. 4:12-20). Thus his relationship with these communities and individuals continued after their conversion and after his departure from them. The letter became, for Paul, a way to exercise his parental responsibility and engage in the ongoing spiritual formation of his converts. In effect, then, as noted above and others have also said, Paul invented a new letter genre, the 'pastoral letter.'

Paul directed these letters almost exclusively to entire communities, not individuals. Even the so-called letter to Philemon is really written "to Philemon our dear friend and co-worker, to Apphia our sister, to Archippus our fellow soldier, and to the church in your [Philemon's] house" (Philem. 1b-2). And two of the three Pastoral Letters (1 Timothy and Titus, not 2 Timothy) concern the life of the whole church, even though they are written to one individual.

This pastoral work of spiritual formation by letter may be summarized in the Greek noun *paraklēsis,* from the verb *parakaleō,* often translated 'urge,' 'exhort,' or 'encourage.' This word has two related but distinct connotations; depending on the context, it can mean either to comfort or to correct, to give a boost or to give a kick. Paul's letters seek to do both: to encourage continued faithfulness and/or to urge a return to the right path. The most explicit example of this difference, in a text where the verb *parakaleō* is used in these two different senses, is 1 Thessalonians 4:13–5:11. Paul urges the Thessalonians to comfort one another with words of the gospel's eschatological hope (4:13-18, with *parakaleō* in v. 18), and to exhort one another to holy living with words of the gospel's moral urgency (5:1-11, with *parakaleō* in v. 11). Paul's goal is always to guide those to whom he writes toward a way of life, an ongoing personal narrative, that is more congruent with the gospel narrative of the death and resurrection of God's Messiah.

AN AUTHORITATIVE LETTER: CONFORMITY TO CHRIST

In some respects a letter from Paul was not really a letter at all. Although it was written in the form of a letter, as we will see below, it was intended for oral reading to a community of believers gathered, almost certainly, for worship. This circumstance alone elevated the status of the letter to near scriptural standing, since the Scriptures of Israel would have been the primary source for readings in the assembly.[4] To be sure, Paul's letters were sometimes disputed and perhaps even rejected by contentious communities or factions within them. Nevertheless, they were read in worship, and they themselves have a liturgical quality to them. Paul utilizes various devices, from beginning to end, both formally and materially, to place his letter recipients in the presence and grace of God.

Writing a letter that is to be read in the assembly at worship means that Paul is exercising the authoritative side of his apostolic calling as well as the pastoral side (not that the two are separable). He is an ambassador for Christ, a commissioned spokesperson. His role is like that of the prophets, to speak (or, in this case, to write) the 'word of the Lord.' Paul knows that sometimes he has a direct word from Jesus (i.e., spoken by the earthly Jesus and passed on to the church) on a given subject, and that sometimes he does not have such a word but must speak his own word (see 1 Cor. 7:10, 12). Paul understands the difference between these two forms of authority, yet even in making this kind of distinction he believes himself to have "the Spirit of God" (1 Cor. 7:40), the "mind of Christ" (1 Cor. 2:16). His words are not offered as take-it-or-leave-it advice, but as Spirit-inspired prophecy. This is because his gospel has been revealed to him by God (Gal. 1:11), and this gospel is incarnated in the life and message of the apostle — at least in Paul's own estimation.

Which brings us to the ultimate nature of Paul's authority and that of his letters. It is not merely that Paul says 'Obey my words,' but rather "Be imitators of me, as I am of Christ" (1 Cor. 11:1). In his letters Paul above all seeks to represent Christ crucified, to proclaim once again the gospel of God's faithfulness in the death and resurrection of his Messiah. The letters reveal Paul's interpretation of what it means for specific believers in specific situations to live faithfully in Christ the Lord, conformed to him and thereby fulfilling the righteous demand of the divine covenant by the power of the Spirit.

---

4. In fact, by the time of 2 Peter, Paul's letters were compared to "the other scriptures" (2 Pet. 3:15b-16, quoted at the beginning of this chapter).

ANCIENT LETTERS AND RHETORIC

It is often said that form follows function. Paul adopted and adapted ancient epistolary and rhetorical forms and techniques to advance his apostolic purposes. In the Greco-Roman world, letter writing could be a commoner's means of everyday communication or the vehicle of an expert rhetor's persuasive speech-making. Paul's letters contain a little of both. He could be down to earth and practical, but almost always with a rhetorical flair (whether deliberate or not) that communicated with the utmost effectiveness. The body of his letters is, in that sense, the text of a speech — we might even say a sermon — written for delivery by another. All parts of the letter — from greetings and benedictions, to autobiographical narratives and travel plans, to short maxims and longer discourses that constitute the body — serve the overarching rhetorical and pastoral function of the letter.

PAUL'S USE OF THE ANCIENT LETTER

As in our day, there was in antiquity a variety of types of letters: business letters, official letters, love letters, letters of friendship, recommendation and introduction letters, letters of advice (Gk. *parainesis*),[5] discursive letters (speeches or essays in letter form), and so on. Some ancient lists of letter types contain twenty or more varieties. Paul's letters, like many in antiquity, seem to contain elements of various letter types, though sometimes scholars insist on calling this or that letter a 'letter of friendship' (e.g., Philippians) or a 'parenetic letter' (e.g., 2 Timothy). Such classifications may be helpful, but what matters most is determining the character and function of the various parts of each letter, and of the letter as a whole.

These various kinds of letters all followed a similar pattern, just as most modern letters follow a predictable pattern such as the following (with bracketed words more commonly used only in business letters):

- Date
- [Recipient's address]
- Salutation (Dear . . .)
- Greeting
- Body
- Closing paragraph
- Sentiment (Love, Sincerely, etc.)

5. Rendered into English as 'parenesis' or 'paraenesis'; the adjective form is 'parenetic.'

**Example of an ancient letter written on papyrus,
rolled, and sealed for delivery**

- Signature
- [Title]

This pattern, though not inflexible, allows both writer and reader to acknowledge a relationship appropriate to the character of the correspondence. Significant additions or revisions to the pattern by the writer may be deliberate or not, but they will often be noticed by the recipient — the lack of a date, the peculiar wording (or the absence) of a closing sentiment, the abnormal length of a greeting, the inclusion of attachments, and so on.

In Paul's day letters also had a standard basic format, as follows:

- Opening
  - Identification of sender and addressee, normally in the form of 'Person X to Person Y'
  - Greeting, often a simple 'Hello' (Gk. *chairein*)
- Thanksgiving or other prayer
- Body
- Final wishes/exhortations/greetings
- Closing, sometimes a simple 'Farewell'

See page 81 for an example of a letter (dated 168 B.C.) from an Egyptian wife to her absent husband (called "brother"), imploring him to return home immediately when she learns that he has been permitted to depart from a distant temple of Serapis, perhaps following a religious pilgrimage:[6] Paul both adopts this basic letter format and adapts it to his purposes. At the risk of anachronism, we may say he 'Christianizes' the ancient letter. Some general aspects of this adaptation are important to note.

Paul creatively embellishes the letter's opening to establish in clear theo-

---

6. Found in C. K. Barrett, ed., *The New Testament Background: Selected Documents*, rev. ed. (San Francisco: Harper and Row, 1987), pp. 28-29.

An Ancient Letter Illustrating the Typical Letter Format

Format	*Letter Content*
Opening	
— Identification of sender and addressee	Isias to her brother Hephaestion
— Greeting	greeting.
Thanksgiving or other prayer	If you are well and other things are going right, it would accord with the prayer which I make continually to the gods. I myself and the child and all the household are in good health and think of you always.
Body	When I received your letter from Horus, in which you announce that you are in detention in the Serapeum [temple of Serapis], at Memphis, for the news that you are well I straightway thanked the gods, but about your not coming home, when all the others who had been secluded there have come, I am ill-pleased. . . . I was in want of everything while you were still here, not to mention this long lapse of time and these critical days, during which you have sent us nothing. As, moreover, Horus who delivered the letter has brought news of your having been released from detention, I am thoroughly ill-pleased. Notwithstanding, as your mother also is annoyed, for her sake as well as for mine please return to the city, if nothing more pressing holds you back.
Final wishes/exhortations, including often a wish for health and greetings to mutual acquaintances	You will do me a favor by taking care of your bodily health. [no greeting]
Closing	Good-bye. Year 2, Epeiph 30.[7]

7. Epeiph was a summer month in the Egyptian calendar; this date corresponds to August 29, 168 B.C.

logical terms the identity of the sender(s) and recipient(s) as well as their relationship. For example, in 2 Corinthians he writes: "Paul, an apostle of Christ Jesus by the will of God, and Timothy our brother, To the church of God that is in Corinth, including all the saints throughout Achaia" (1:1). The identification of the sender(s) and addressee(s) also sometimes foreshadows the body of the letter, hinting at its purpose, as in 1 Corinthians: "To the church of God that is in Corinth, to those who are sanctified in Christ Jesus, called to be saints" (1:2a).

The greeting is also theologically embellished. Paul is fond of saying "grace and peace." The word "grace" (Gk. *charis*) is a play on words of the standard greeting *chairein* ('greetings,' 'hello'), while "peace" echoes the Semitic salutation *shalom*. What Paul offers is not merely a greeting but a fresh taste of the gifts of the covenant God offered in Christ.

The letter's opening may also contain traditional or liturgical language from the church's life. This kind of language places the letter in its appropriate context — the presence of God. It may also add weight to Paul's apostolic claim and introduce the letter's theme: "Paul an apostle — sent neither by human commission nor from human authorities, but through Jesus Christ and God the Father, who raised him from the dead — and all the members of God's family who are with me, To the churches of Galatia: Grace to you and peace from God our Father and the Lord Jesus Christ, who gave himself for our sins to set us free from the present evil age, according to the will of our God and Father, to whom be the glory forever and ever. Amen" (Gal. 1:1-5; cf. Rom. 1:1-7).

Paul's thanksgivings are particularly important, often anticipating the thrust and intent of the letter body; 1 Corinthians is a prime example, with Paul mentioning the touchy matters of spiritual gifts and eschatology (end-time matters):

> I give thanks to my God always for you because of the grace of God that has been given you in Christ Jesus, for in every way you have been enriched in him, in speech and knowledge of every kind — just as the testimony of Christ has been strengthened among you — so that you are not lacking in any spiritual gift as you wait for the revealing of our Lord Jesus Christ. He will also strengthen you to the end, so that you may be blameless on the day of our Lord Jesus Christ. God is faithful; by him you were called into the fellowship of his Son, Jesus Christ our Lord. (1:4-9)

When a letter has no thanksgiving, its absence is quite noticeable, as in Galatians, where it appears that Paul is so angry and anxious to get to the topic at hand that he has no use for a word of thanks but only for an expression of astonishment (see 1:6-10). The thanksgiving, when present, concludes the letter's preliminaries, all of which have placed the recipients in the presence of God and reminded them of God's grace that comes in the gospel and through the ministry of the apostle.

The body of the letter is, of course, the most peculiarly Pauline adaptation of the ancient letter format. Here Paul combines epistolary form, scriptural exegesis, Hellenistic rhetoric, and more (see below) to produce the heart of his pastoral correspondence. As noted in the list at the beginning of this chapter, the body of a Pauline letter contains various kinds of materials, but especially three major types: autobiographical review (usually with a hortatory purpose); pastoral instruction, or parenesis; and future plans. Unfortunately, some interpreters of Paul relegate much of the parenesis to a separate, less central collection of 'closing exhortations.' This should be resisted, for much of a Pauline letter is naturally parenetic, or hortatory; after all, he is a pastor giving spiritual direction.

Paul does sometimes appear, nonetheless, to pull together a hodgepodge of closing exhortations about believers' behavior in general, or in the assembly, before signing off. The best example may be in 1 Thessalonians: "Respect those who labor among you. . . . admonish the idlers, encourage the faint hearted, help the weak. . . . See that none of you repays evil for evil, but always seek to do good to one another and to all. Rejoice always, pray without ceasing. . . . Do not quench the Spirit. . . . abstain from every form of evil" (5:12-22). But a close reading of the letter suggests that even these exhortations are carefully related to the community and to the letter as a whole.

Such final words of advice precede, or are sometimes mixed with, several elements of the letter's formal closing. Though these are not consistent in every letter, they include a doxology and/or benediction, greetings, an invitation to share the holy kiss, warnings, and a signature or other sign of apostolic authority. Each of these elements reinforces the apostolic and liturgical character of the event of the letter itself, and especially of its being read in the assembly.

PAUL'S USE OF ANCIENT RHETORIC

The letter format depicted above was followed, more or less, by writers of informal as well as formal correspondence. More formal letters, written by those who had studied the art of letter writing in the schools of rhetoric, might embody an argument about some philosophical, religious, and political topic — all three fields being quite interconnected for the ancients.

That Paul was skilled in rhetoric — the art of effective and persuasive communication — is undeniable. This is a bit ironic, since Paul himself has suspicions about rhetoric as antithetical to the power of the gospel, though he is primarily critical of the flashy rhetoric that had become popular in his day and with which certain Corinthian believers were enamored (1 Cor. 1:18-25; 2:1-5). He was accused of lacking the charismatic personal presence often associated with good public speakers — an accusation he never denied (2 Cor. 10:10). Nevertheless, his letters attest his great rhetorical skill, and even those critical of his speaking ability acknowledged the power of his written words.

Greco-Roman rhetoric is a vast field of study, about which only a few things can be said here. It is generally held that there were three kinds of ancient rhetoric, each with a different basic objective: forensic, deliberative, and epideictic. Forensic rhetoric was intended to defend or criticize some past action. Deliberative rhetoric was designed to urge, persuade, or dissuade the audience about some possible future action. Epideictic rhetoric was intended to praise or blame, often a present or ongoing action or quality, or as a reflection on past actions (like a eulogy).

One might assume, given the pastoral character of Paul's letters, that most of them are primarily examples of deliberative rhetoric, and this is probably true. However, ancient speeches, and Paul's letters, could combine two or more kinds of rhetoric. For example, 1 Corinthians 9 contains some lines of forensic rhetoric (self-defense), and chapter 13 is a specimen of epideictic rhetoric (in praise of love), while the overall purpose of the letter is clearly deliberative, seeking to alter the Corinthians' behavior. Moreover, it is certainly possible that certain letters contain dimensions of deliberative rhetoric but have a substantial forensic (Galatians?) or epideictic (1 Thessalonians?) function.

One particular rhetorical form that occasionally appears in Paul's letters is the diatribe. Often used by ancient teachers (such as the first-century Stoic Epictetus, in his *Discourses*), the diatribe did not consist primarily of a lengthy rebuke, as it often does today, but of a creative dialogical mode of instruction and exhortation. It employs such rhetorical devices as imaginary conversation partners, rhetorical questions, exaggeration, hypothetical objections, and erroneous conclusions. The real speaker refutes the interlocutor's errors (sometimes beginning with the famous phrase, "May it never be!"),[8] using them as a springboard for teaching. Examples of the diatribal mode may be found scattered throughout Romans 1–11 (e.g., chaps. 2 and 6), in Galatians 2 and 3, and perhaps elsewhere in Paul.

More generally, the principles of rhetoric included guidelines for the construction of a speech (and, as noted above, the body of a letter was largely a speech in writing). The speech, which focused on a particular issue, or *stasis*, normally had several parts, including:

---

8. Gk. *mē genoito*. Translations include 'By no means!'; 'Of course not!'; 'Absolutely not!'; etc. See Rom. 3:4, 6 (plus a similar phrase in 3:9); 6:2, 15; 7:7, 13; 9:14; 11:1, 11; 1 Cor. 6:15; Gal. 2:17; 3:21; 6:14.

- *exordium,* an introduction to the character and the issue
- *narratio,* a narrative of the events central to the issue
- *propositio,* or thesis
- *probatio,* or arguments in support of the thesis
- *refutatio,* or refutation of the opponents' real or imagined position or potential rebuttal
- *exhortatio,* or exhortation
- *peroratio,* or recapitulation and elicitation of agreement, with a final (often emotional) appeal

Some interpreters of Paul have attempted to divide many of his letters into these main rhetorical parts, arguing about the precise beginning of each section. Others are more cautious, questioning the possibility and value of such rhetorical analysis. There is also considerable debate about how both rhetorical analysis and epistolary analysis (according to the letter format described above) can be simultaneously applied to Paul's letters.

Although it is sometimes true that Paul seems to follow the standard rhetorical sequence quite carefully (for instance, in Galatians), it seems equally true that Paul can alter or mix the sequence. For example, if he is dealing with more than one issue in a letter, he may well need more than one set of arguments (as in 1 Corinthians) or refutations (as in Romans). An obsession with form (whether epistolary or rhetorical) over substance is not wise. What is important for readers of Paul's letters to realize is that Paul both adopts and adapts ancient conventions. Attention to aspects of rhetorical structure can assist in interpreting a letter's content.

Within the various parts of the rhetorical speech or letter, ancient writers and orators, including Paul, tried to make their cases by three general types of appeals, or proofs:

- *ethos,* an appeal to the moral character of the speaker (e.g., 1 Thess. 2:1-12; 2 Cor. 11:7-11)
- *pathos,* an appeal to the emotions (e.g., Gal. 3:1)
- *logos,* an appeal to logic (e.g., Rom. 6)

As the examples suggest, we find all these types of appeals in Paul's letters.

Ancients could also appeal to various kinds of authorities in the course of their argument, and Paul is no exception. But this topic takes us back to the actual content of Paul's letters, for his most obvious authorities are going to be religious ones. We find in Paul's letters a creative use of tradition and precedent, blended with his own creativity.

LETTER CONTENTS AND SOURCES

We have already briefly noted the various contents of a typical Pauline letter. The variety is quite remarkable, given the relative brevity of the Pauline corpus. Much of this material is original to Paul, but much is not. His originality lies in large measure in his ability to exploit a scriptural text, an early Christian hymn, or an image for all its worth. He makes whatever he uses his own and uses it to explain and support his convictions concerning the crucified Lord and believers' existence in him.

Among the contents of Paul's letters we find non-Jewish material, common Jewish material, and specifically messianic Jewish (i.e., early Christian) material. The following lists are not meant to be complete but representative:

- Non-Jewish
  - Stoic terms (e.g., *autarkēs*, 'content,' Phil. 4:11)
  - Occasional quotes from pagan writers (e.g., 1 Cor. 15:32)
- Common Jewish
  - Citations of, and allusions to, Scripture (e.g., Rom. 3:9-20; Rom. 9–11)
  - Jewish midrashic (interpretive) techniques (e.g., Gal. 4:21-31)
  - Appeals to leading Jewish figures such as Moses (e.g., 2 Cor. 3) and Abraham (e.g., Gal. 3; Rom. 4)
- Messianic Jewish (early Christian)
  - Words of Jesus and allusions to his teaching (e.g., 1 Cor. 7:10; Rom. 12:14, 17)
  - Creeds, summaries of the gospel, and confessions of faith (e.g., Rom. 1:3-4; 1 Cor. 15:3ff.)
  - Hymns or poetic texts (e.g., Phil. 2:6-11)
  - Prayers in Aramaic: *Abba* (= "Father," Gal. 4:6; Rom. 8:15); *Maranatha* (= "Our Lord, come," 1 Cor. 16:22)
  - Other liturgical excerpts: the Lord's Supper (eucharistic) rite (1 Cor. 11:23-26), perhaps the baptismal rite (Rom. 6:1-11?; Gal. 3:27-28?)
  - Apocalyptic tradition (e.g., 1 Thess. 4:15-17)
  - Lists of virtues, vices, and common exhortations (e.g., Gal. 5:19-23)

Paul's genius, as noted above, is his ability to weave all these elements into a coherent whole governed by the image of Jesus as the crucified but now exalted Messiah and Lord. His letters are thus specimens of what we may call *focused intertextuality* — a woven fabric of variegated threads with a dominant thematic color, to which all the threads seem destined to pay homage.

AUTHORSHIP AND AUTHENTICITY

We turn next to the issue of the authorship of the Pauline letters, for according to most scholars, not all of the thirteen can be said with certainty to stem directly from the apostle's hand. But this statement — 'directly from the apostle's hand' — immediately raises the question of what we mean by the word 'authorship.' More than half the letters attributed to Paul were cosent by one or more named associates (1 and 2 Corinthians, Philippians, Colossians, 1 and 2 Thessalonians, Philemon), and another one (Galatians) mentions "all the members of God's family who are with me" as the cosenders.[9] These cosenders or, more often, other associates would also deliver the mail and, following ancient custom, probably interpret its contents. (Although the empire had a postal delivery system modeled on the famous Persian system of couriers, it was not available to the general public, which had to rely on traveling family members [including slaves] and friends, or pay someone to deliver correspondence.)

The question that arises, of course, is to what degree a co*sender* of a letter was also a co*author*. From the perspective of the recipients, the mention of a cosender would at least imply that the person(s) named agreed with and stood behind the letter's contents. It seems unlikely that Paul would mention cosenders unless he knew, at least by consulting with them, that they did in fact agree with him. In some cases this consultation — and thus the input of the cosenders — may have been substantive, while in other cases Paul may simply have sent the letter with the approval of the cosenders and with the addition of their names to add weight or familiarity to a letter. We certainly cannot, however, rule out the possibility that the person(s) named as cosenders contributed to its contents and ought, therefore, also to be called coauthors.

Furthermore, most if not all of Paul's letters were actually composed by a secretary (e.g., Tertius, named in Rom. 16:22), perhaps at Paul's dictation — or perhaps not.[10] Such assistance in letter writing was common in antiquity, and a secretary could sometimes be allowed not merely to transcribe, but also to edit or even compose letters. How much leeway did Paul's secretaries and associates have in the production of his letters? How much influence did they have on the style or substance of his letters? The answers to these questions are, frankly, unknown. Also unknown is the degree to which certain of Paul's ideas may have circulated and evolved before being finally put down into writing. The core of a

9. Thus all of Paul's letters except Romans, Ephesians, and the Pastoral Epistles (1 and 2 Timothy and Titus) claim cosenders.

10. The technical term for such a secretary is 'amanuensis.' Although only Tertius is named in Paul's letters, the use of a secretary is implied in the presence of greetings or other words written in Paul's own hand at the end of several letters: 1 Cor. 16:21; Gal. 6:11; Col. 4:18; 2 Thess. 3:17; Philem. 19.

letter from Paul himself may have grown into a larger document that was not published until some time later. All this is to say that if we define Pauline authorship to include greater, rather than lesser, input from minds other than Paul's, then some of the perceived differences between the so-called authentic and inauthentic letters may be explained.

But we are getting ahead of ourselves. Using several criteria, scholars generally divide the Pauline letters into two categories, either 'authentic' and 'inauthentic' or, more objectively, 'disputed' or 'contested' (as to authorship) and 'undisputed' or 'uncontested.' The criteria that are used include:

- the language (vocabulary and style) of the letters
- the thought (theology) of the letters
- the historical situations reflected in the letters

Just as two friends, two preachers in the same religious tradition but from different places or times, or two people in a teacher-pupil relationship exhibit both similarities and also differences in their writings, so it may also be with Paul and those who are sometimes called 'Paulinists.' If there is a gap in time (say between the [now deceased] teacher and the student), then historical developments may be reflected in the later writings.

Which of Paul's letters are questioned on the issue of authorship? Nearly everyone, without hesitation, acknowledges Paul's authorship of seven letters: Romans, 1 and 2 Corinthians, Galatians, Philippians, 1 Thessalonians, and Philemon. (In fact, five of these, as noted above, are actually cosent and perhaps coauthored.) These letters can be dated and located within a time frame that covers, more or less, the decade of the 50s. They are written in a fairly common vocabulary and style, and they have a similar perspective on many topics, though they hardly reveal a monochromatic apostle. Furthermore, they say little or nothing that seems out of place for the early churches in the 50s.

Other letters are then judged against these. The eschatological perspective of 2 Thessalonians, it is claimed, conflicts with that of 1 Thessalonians, while the theology and ethics of Colossians and Ephesians conflict with those of Galatians and Romans. Furthermore, the Pastoral Epistles — 1 and 2 Timothy and Titus — reflect a later kind of institutionalization of creed and ministry that is foreign to Paul, many argue. Moreover, it is frequently said, these letters generally embody a tone and spirit that cannot be fit into the ministry and message of the historical Paul as we know it from undisputed sources. Letters that bear Paul's name but are judged to have been written by others are called *pseudonymous* ('[bearing a] false name') works.

What follows are estimates of the percentages of biblical scholars who *reject* Paul's authorship of the six books in question: 2 Thessalonians = 50 percent; Colossians = 60 percent; Ephesians = 70 percent; 2 Timothy = 80 percent; 1 Timothy and Titus = 90 percent. The numbers are obviously only approximations, based on an ongoing survey of scholarly publications on the Pauline letters, and they are not intended to suggest that historical scholarship is like an opinion poll. Rather, they give us a rough indication of which of the disputed letters are more or less likely to be from the hand of Paul. Those with the greatest scholarly support for authenticity (2 Thessalonians, Colossians) differ less in theology and style from the undisputed letters, and can be more easily fit into what we know of Paul's ministry, than those with very little scholarly backing on authenticity.

In addition to judgments about entire letters, scholars also question the authorship of certain passages in the undisputed letters, using criteria similar to those listed above. These passages include those judged both pre-Pauline and post-Pauline in origin. Pre-Pauline texts are those known to and used by Paul, such as early creedal or hymnic texts like Philippians 2:6-11 and 1 Corinthians 15:3ff. (as they are believed to be by many scholars). Post-Pauline texts are those alleged to have been inserted into a letter after its composition and are generally called 'interpolations.' Among the passages that some scholars label interpolations are Romans 13:1-7, 1 Corinthians 14:33b-35 or 36, and 1 Thessalonians 2:14-16.

SOME HISTORICAL AND THEOLOGICAL OBSERVATIONS

What are we to make of these matters? Several observations are in order, both historical and theological. First, the question of authorship of the disputed letters is more open than it was a generation ago. Changing definitions of 'authorship,' as noted above, have contributed to the reopening of the question. So has a scholarly willingness, in some quarters, to allow for greater differences among letters due to the contingent circumstances that occasioned them. Furthermore, some interpreters of Paul have noted previously overlooked or underestimated similarities between undisputed and disputed letters (e.g., Philippians and 1 Corinthians vis-à-vis the Pastoral Letters). This does not mean that a trend toward attributing all thirteen letters directly to Paul has developed, only that the final chapter of the story has not yet been written. There are scholars who accept anywhere from seven to all thirteen of the letters as essentially from Paul, written during his lifetime. Perhaps we need to understand authorship as a spectrum or continuum, some letters having the most direct input from Paul himself, others having somewhat less, and still others having much less — if any.

Second, readers of Paul's letters need to recognize the domino effect of recognizing the similarities as well as the differences between undisputed and disputed letters. For example, there are very close connections between

Philemon and Colossians that make it difficult — though not impossible — to accept one as authentic and not the other. Similarly, a recent trend allowing for the authenticity of 2 Timothy, but not of 1 Timothy and Titus, must deal with the very distinctive language that permeates all three documents and no other Pauline letters.

Third, it appears that in antiquity imitation was not only the sincerest form of flattery, it was a permissible way to honor and extend the rightful authority of a leading figure. Early Jews and Christians who did this — and there is plenty of evidence in noncanonical literature that they did do it — were not violating their moral code by lying or bearing false witness. Rather, they were doing what their forebears and contemporaries also seem to have done repeatedly — to acknowledge the ongoing value of past teachers by reusing their basic perspectives in a new setting. Biblical writers constantly recycle the themes of monotheism, exodus, covenant, and so on without crediting sources. To do so in the name of Isaiah or Daniel (as it appears) does not dishonor but rather honors the source. If Paul's friends or 'disciples' wrote in his name, it was to allow him to speak to new situations. Whether they did so faithfully is a different — and difficult — question.

Fourth, it needs to be said that some of the doubt about Paul's authorship of certain letters has sprung from scholarly distaste for certain aspects of the writings in question. This antipathy first developed in Protestant circles, where some smelled 'early Catholicism' — the institutionalization of creed and ministry — in the allegedly later Pauline letters. Although the general dislike of the Pastorals is no longer limited to those with an anti-Catholic bias, it is not impossible that theological preferences have affected historical judgments.

Finally, from a theological perspective, three constructive points need to be made. The first is about inspiration. A fundamental theological axiom ought to be that Scripture's inspiration is independent of its human authorship. If this were not true, we would have confidence in the inspiration of precious little of the Bible — maybe 20 percent: a handful of letters from Paul and a dozen or so prophetic books. The authorship of everything else is unknown or disputed.

The second is about the canon and the process of canonization. Christians affirm that both the composition of the biblical books over time and the process of collecting certain books into an authoritative collection, or canon, were human endeavors guided by the Spirit of God. The church today lives with the results of those processes in the canon. The combining, editing, and supplementing of sources was a normal and natural part of those human activities.

The final point is that fashions change. A case in point: the letter of James. Martin Luther considered it "an epistle of straw," far inferior to the truly evangelical writings like Galatians, Romans, and the Gospel of John. Many Protestants have struggled with the document ever since. But in the late twentieth century many Christians began to take the gospel's demand for social justice much more seriously. James rose to the occasion; the once marginalized letter took center stage, along with books like Luke and Amos.

It is possible that this same phenomenon could happen once again, even with such marginalized writings as 1 Timothy and Titus. These are church documents in which the integrity of the church's witness — in its doctrine, in its behavior, and above all in its ministers — is treated with utmost seriousness. In an age when the norm (in practice, and even sometimes on paper) is quite the contrary, these sidelined Pastoral Epistles may once again have something to say.

My own positions on the question of authorship for each letter are set forth in the various chapters. Like most scholars, I have changed my views over the years, having thought Paul wrote as many as thirteen or as few as seven letters. To summarize later discussions, and as mentioned in chapter 2, I hold now to the view that Paul is more or less directly responsible for eleven of the thirteen letters — all but 1 Timothy and Titus.

The letter to the Hebrews, though included with Paul's epistles in some ancient collections, and frequently thought to be from Paul, does not claim to be from the apostle (unlike the thirteen we have been discussing) and differs markedly in style and substance from the Pauline letters. As to who wrote Hebrews, Origen said already in the third century, only God knows.

THE DISSEMINATION, COLLECTION, AND ORDER OF PAUL'S LETTERS

With the possible exception of Ephesians (if it was not actually written to the Ephesians but as a circular letter summarizing Paul's teachings) and the Pastoral Letters (if not really written by Paul to his delegates), Paul's letters were written for specific communities and/or individuals.[11] Nonetheless, they have been recognized for many centuries as letters that speak to universal concerns as part of a canon, or collection of authoritative writings. How did the process of discrete letters becoming collected and canonized get started?

---

11. These issues concerning Ephesians and the Pastorals will be addressed in the appropriate chapters. Romans is sometimes thought to be a summary of Paul's theology, but is still undeniably addressed to a specific community, the believers in Rome.

THE DISSEMINATION AND
COLLECTION OF THE LETTERS

It is clear that those who received letters from Paul not only read them aloud in their own churches (1 Thess. 5:27), but also eventually shared them with other churches. At least some of these churches also found Paul's words edifying, even if their circumstances were different from those of the intended audience. According to Colossians 4:16, Paul (or one of his associates) encouraged this practice. The combination of (1) reading and interpreting Paul's letters when the community gathered for worship with (2) the sharing of those letters with other communities began the process of Paul's letters becoming part of what would become the Christian canon.

How this process began and developed in the first and second centuries cannot be known with certainty. We know that Paul wrote letters that did not make it into the canon and have not survived (see 1 Cor. 5:9; 2 Cor. 7:8; cf. Col. 4:16). It appears also that sometimes people wrote letters in his name without his permission (cf. 2 Thess. 2:2). Thus, as letters attributed to Paul emerged and circulated, churches had to discern which ones were genuine and, among them, which were universally applicable and authoritative. At some point someone decided to collect some or all of Paul's known and valued letters together. Who might have started the ball rolling? Again, we do not know, but suggestions have included Paul himself, Timothy, Luke (the author of Acts), Onesimus (the slave of Philemon who, according to some traditions and interpretations, became bishop of Ephesus), or one of Paul's disciples.

Already by the end of the first century, many of Paul's extant letters were known and quoted by the author of 1 *Clement,* a document from the church in Rome to the church in Corinth (ca. 96). This suggests the existence of a collection. The New Testament letter called 2 Peter, often dated in the early second century (though perhaps several decades earlier), refers to "all" of Paul's letters (3:16), probably implying a collection. References to Pauline letters in other second-century writings similarly suggest the existence of Pauline collections. One important factor, not only for the Pauline letters but also for the overall development of the canon, was the activity of the second-century heretical presbyter Marcion. His love for Paul but disdain for things Jewish led him to construct a canon that removed all Jewish writings and references. A heavily edited Paul (erroneously) survived the cut, and ten of his letters — the thirteen we know, minus the Pastoral Epistles — were abridged into Marcion's canon. (It has been said that the only one who ever understood Paul was Marcion, and he misunderstood him.)

In response to Marcion and other heretics, the famous bishop-theologian of Lyon, Irenaeus (d. ca. 200), claimed it was erroneous to remove the Pastoral

Epistles from the Pauline corpus, and he used them frequently in his own work. Also, by the end of the second century in Rome (if the conventional dating is correct), there appeared an annotated list of the New Testament books now known as the Muratorian Canon. This list refers to thirteen letters of Paul, the same thirteen we recognize today, divided into two groups: letters to churches and letters to individuals. The latter group must have been the subject of some debate, since the Muratorian Canon asserts their universal value. (Some scholars have even spoken of a 'battle' for Paul among various parties.) The Muratorian Canon also recognizes the existence of two heretical forgeries of Pauline letters furthering the cause of Marcion. It does not, however, mention Hebrews, which sometimes was associated with Paul.

If this important list from circa 200 is representative, then the Pauline canon was more or less settled by the end of the second century, though disputes about the four letters to individuals and especially about Hebrews persisted in some quarters. This conclusion is confirmed by the oldest surviving manuscript of Paul's letters, p^{46} (papyrus 46), which dates from about 200. Although the outer pages of both ends of the manuscript are missing, it apparently contained the nine letters to churches and Hebrews, but not all the letters to individuals, though this may have been accidental rather than deliberate.[12] Clement of Alexandria (d. ca. 215) mentions thirteen Pauline letters (minus Philemon, plus Hebrews), while Origen (d. 254) states that the thirteen are universally accepted but that Hebrews (which Origen, as noted above, did not ascribe to Paul) is disputed. Eusebius of Caesarea (d. ca. 339) includes the thirteen plus Hebrews. The several canonical lists that were affirmed by bishops or approved by church councils in the fourth century contain the twenty-seven books of the New Testament still deemed sacred Scripture today, including, of course, the thirteen letters that bear Paul's name. (The most important of these lists appeared in a letter of Athanasius, the bishop-theologian of Alexandria, circa 367.) Nonetheless, several spurious letters were occasionally recognized by certain churches, including one called 'Third Corinthians' and a letter to the Laodiceans.

THE ORDER OF THE LETTERS

The earliest collections of Paul's letters were probably not all arranged in the same order. Some scholars believe that Ephesians, as a sort of summary of the

12. The manuscript p^{46} contains the following letters: Romans (beginning at 5:17), Hebrews, 1 Corinthians, 2 Corinthians, Ephesians, Galatians, Philippians, Colossians, and 1 Thessalonians. The missing outer leaves would have had room for 2 Thessalonians and some (but probably not all) of the letters to individuals. There is some evidence that the compiler was working with a fixed number of bound leaves and simply ran out of room.

Portions of Romans 15–16 from the oldest manuscript
of Paul's letters, p⁴⁶ (ca. 200)

Pauline corpus (whether or not from the hand of Paul), may have once stood at
the head of the collection as an introduction to it. However, since Ephesians is
longer than Galatians but follows it in the canon, it has also been suggested that
Ephesians was a later letter inserted out of order (according to length) into a
very early collection of Paul's genuine letters, arranged in descending order according to length. Another scholarly theory is that, like the seven letters of Revelation 2–3, Paul's letters were originally collected into a group of letters to
seven churches according to total length for each church (Corinth [two long

letters], Rome, Ephesus, Thessalonica [two short letters], Galatia, Philippi, Colossae).[13] Any of these theories is certainly possible, but we cannot determine their validity with any certainty.

Early manuscripts of the Pauline letters and of the entire New Testament (which date from about the early third to the fifth century) present Paul's letters in one basic sequence with minor variations: letters to churches, followed by letters to individuals, each group presented from longest to shortest. Manuscript p[46] (ca. 200) presents the letters to churches basically in descending order according to length (see note above), though Hebrews should actually follow rather than precede 1 Corinthians. (Two letters to one church, however, would not be separated.)[14]

This pattern, with minor variations, became the norm for the nine letters of Paul to churches that were accepted as authoritative. The inclusion of a group of four letters to individuals (1 and 2 Timothy, Titus, Philemon), also arranged according to length, meant that the two categories (to churches, to individuals) recognized by the Muratorian Canon were maintained.[15]

The important fourth- and fifth-century manuscripts B (Vaticanus, fourth century), ℵ (Sinaiticus, fourth century), A (Alexandrinus, fifth century), and C (Ephraemi Rescriptus, fifth century), as well as the roughly contemporary letter of Athanasius (ca. 367) mentioned above, list the Pauline letters in the sequence we know them today, except that in each case Hebrews is inserted into the lineup between 2 Thessalonians and 1 Timothy — that is, between the letters to churches and to individuals. (Hebrews actually appears in several different locations in other manuscripts.)

Certain very early collections of Paul's letters may have been ordered according to their perceived theological or pastoral importance. In more recent times four of the Pauline letters have been called the *Hauptbriefe,* or 'chief letters': Romans, 1 and 2 Corinthians, and Galatians. Whatever truth there may be in the theological assessment indicated by this collection within the collection,

---

13. The Muratorian Canon supports the idea of early Christian interest in seven churches addressed by Paul. For both Revelation and the Pauline letters, seven was connected with completeness and universality. The Muratorian Canon presents the letters in a distinct order, however, which appears to represent the compilers' understanding of their chronology (at least for the letters to churches): Corinthians (2), Ephesians, Philippians, Colossians, Galatians, Thessalonians (2), Romans; Philemon, Titus, Timothy (2).

14. We can assume that whatever letters to individuals the manuscript contained were arranged in similar fashion.

15. In what eventually became the standard sequence, Ephesians is technically out of order by being placed after Galatians. The length of ancient documents was generally measured in lines *(stichoi),* and document lengths could vary depending on a scribe's lettering habits. Galatians and Ephesians are actually quite comparable in length, as are Philippians and Colossians. Both Ephesians and Colossians occasionally appear out of order in the manuscripts.

we would err to neglect the supposedly lesser lights. And no one today seriously suggests a rearranging of the accepted canonical sequence.[16]

In this book the letters are presented, not in canonical order, nor in a presumed order of theological importance, but in a chronological order that approximates the order in which they were written, at least as far as I can determine that chronology. There is no consensus on this matter among New Testament scholars, but many would agree that:

- 1 Thessalonians is probably the earliest.
- 1 and 2 Corinthians, as well as Romans, can be dated with some specificity.
- Galatians is probably rather early and precedes Romans.
- Colossians should be dated as late as possible if from the hand of Paul, and as early as possible if not.
- Ephesians clearly builds on Colossians.
- The Pastoral Epistles are the latest Pauline letters if not authentic, and possibly still the latest if authentic.[17]

The undisputed Captivity Letters (Philippians and Philemon) are difficult to date, though Philippians has much in common with the so-called chief letters, and Philemon is probably closely related to Colossians. 2 Thessalonians is generally thought to be later than 1 Thessalonians, but that may be by a matter of months or decades, depending on its authenticity. To a growing number of scholars, 2 Timothy seems different from 1 Timothy and Titus, more like the undisputed letters, and thus perhaps earlier than the other two Pastoral Epistles.

Thus the order of presentation in this book is a reasonable chronological one: 1 Thessalonians, 2 Thessalonians, Galatians, 1 Corinthians, 2 Corinthians, Romans, Philippians, Philemon, Colossians, Ephesians, 2 Timothy, 1 Timothy, Titus.

QUESTIONS FOR REFLECTION

1. What are some of the advantages and disadvantages of communicating about sensitive issues, whether in the church or elsewhere, by letter?
2. Identify some of the possible assets and liabilities for the church in having authoritative, canonical writings that were such 'occasional' documents as Paul's letters.

16. The current sequence is that of many manuscripts from the early medieval period on and was used by Erasmus in 1516 when he prepared the first printed Greek New Testament.

17. Traditionally, defenders of authenticity have placed the Pastorals late in Paul's career, but a recent trend has been to locate them earlier.

3. What aspects of Paul as a communicator in his particular context — as ancient letter writer and rhetor — might be instructive to communicators of the gospel today?

4. Discuss the proposed theological axiom "Scripture's inspiration is independent of its human authorship." Does this negate the need for careful historical scholarship?

5. What are the possible assets and liabilities involved in assessing the value of Pauline letters according to their supposed date of composition? the character of their original audience (church or individual)? their supposed theological weightiness?

FOR FURTHER READING AND STUDY

Doty, William G. *Letters in Primitive Christianity.* Philadelphia: Fortress, 1973. A basic guide to letters in antiquity, Paul's letters, and the smaller formal elements within early Christian letters.

Murphy-O'Connor, Jerome. *St. Paul the Letter-Writer: His World, His Options, His Skill.* Collegeville, Minn.: Liturgical Press, 1995. An insightful study of the ancient letter-writing process, the letter form, and the collecting of Paul's letters.

Roetzel, Calvin J. *The Letters of Paul: Conversations in Context.* 4th ed. Louisville: Westminster John Knox, 1998. A classic, helpful text focusing on the form and occasional nature of Paul's letters, with an excellent survey of the world in which he wrote them.

Stirewalt, M. Luther, Jr. *Paul, the Letter Writer.* Grand Rapids: Eerdmans, 2003. A study of the influence of official letters on Paul's correspondence.

Stowers, Stanley K. *Letter-Writing in Greco-Roman Antiquity.* Philadelphia: Westminster, 1986. A first-rate analysis of Jewish and non-Jewish letter forms and their relationship to NT letters.

Trobisch, David. *Paul's Letter Collection: Tracing the Origins.* Minneapolis: Fortress, 1994. An original exploration of the origin of the process of collecting Paul's letters that attributes it to Paul himself, who is thought to have assembled four of his letters that treat the financial collection for the Jerusalem church.

White, John L. *Light from Ancient Letters.* Philadelphia: Fortress, 1986. A collection of texts, with discussion.

CHAPTER 4

PAUL'S GOSPEL

The Good News of Christ Crucified and Raised

The cross is the signature of the one who is risen.

Ernst Käsemann[1]

Paul is rightly associated with the word 'gospel' *(euangelion)*, a term meaning 'good news' that appears in the Pauline correspondence some sixty times, forty-eight of those in the undisputed letters. For Paul the gospel is not, however, just words; it is *power* — "the power of God for salvation" (Rom. 1:16; cf. 1 Thess. 2:13). It is God's efficacious utterance, the new divine word that does not return empty but accomplishes God's purpose (Isa. 55:11).

The nature of this power and the substance of this good news must be carefully analyzed. In this chapter we consider the content of Paul's gospel according to summary statements in his letters, the larger story these statements embody and infer, the religious and political ('theopolitical') character of the Pauline gospel, and the benefits of the gospel for those who respond to it in faith.

CHRIST CRUCIFIED AND RAISED

Paul can say with utmost conviction and honesty that his mission was to "know" — to experience and to proclaim in both word and deed — nothing but "Jesus

---

1. Ernst Käsemann, "The Saving Significance of the Death of Jesus," in *Perspectives on Paul*, trans. Margaret Kohl (Philadelphia: Fortress, 1971; reprint, Mifflintown, Pa.: Sigler, 1996), p. 56.

Christ, that is Jesus Christ *crucified*" (1 Cor. 2:2, author's translation and emphasis). This fixation on a 'dead criminal' or even a dead Messiah sounds narrow, if not morbid. Where is the 'good news' without the resurrection?

To be sure, Paul's gospel was not good news to him, and would not be good news to anyone else, without the resurrection (see, e.g., 1 Cor. 15). Indeed, it was the risen Lord whom Paul first encountered in the vicinity of Damascus. Nevertheless, it is absolutely crucial for Paul that his gospel be understood as centered on Christ crucified; the resurrected Lord is continuous with the crucified Messiah. In the famous and eloquent words of Ernst Käsemann quoted above, the cross is the "signature of the one who is risen." This means that although the cross must be narrated and understood in connection with other events in the story of Christ and the larger story of Israel's God, those stories are themselves, for Paul, to be understood through the interpretive lens of the cross. The resurrection makes that perspective both *possible* and *necessary*.

THE GOSPEL IN CREED AND HYMN

Paul affirms that the source of his gospel is not human beings but God alone (Gal. 1:1, 11-12). Ironically, however, it appears that Paul often cites (or perhaps paraphrases) portions of creeds, hymns, and other short confessions of faith from the early churches to summarize his own gospel. In citing such material, Paul both affirms it and (frequently) creatively reuses it for his own particular purposes. These early liturgical fragments provide us with a sketch of the early Christian, and of the Pauline, gospel. Some of these fragments (or allusions to such fragments) include the following texts, listed in canonical order, in which certain key words and phrases are highlighted:[2]

> . . . the gospel of God, which he *promised beforehand* through his prophets in
> the holy scriptures, the gospel concerning his Son,
>> who was *descended from David* according to the flesh and was *declared*
>> *to be Son of God with power* according to the spirit of holiness by *resur-*
>> *rection from the dead,* Jesus Christ our Lord.
>
>> (Rom. 1:1-4; the indented words from vv. 3-4
>> are generally considered to predate Paul)

---

2. It must be noted that there is scholarly consensus on the pre-Pauline, liturgical character of most of these texts, but there is ongoing debate about some of them, including one of the most important, Phil. 2:6-11, which is partially cited below. It must also be noted that some of the NRSV translations provided are debated, but that discussion lies outside our present purposes.

They are now justified by his grace as a gift, through the *redemption* that is in Christ Jesus, *whom God put forward as a sacrifice of atonement by his blood,* effective through faith. (Rom. 3:24-25a)

It will be reckoned to us [as righteousness] who believe in him who raised Jesus our Lord from the dead, *who was handed over to death for our trespasses* and *was raised for our justification.* (Rom. 4:24-25)

He who did not withhold his own Son, but gave him up for all of us, will he not with him also give us everything else? (Rom. 8:32)

If you *confess* with your lips that Jesus is Lord and *believe* in your heart that God raised him from the dead, *you will be saved.* (Rom. 10:9)

No one can say *"Jesus is Lord"* except by the *Holy Spirit.* (1 Cor. 12:3)

. . . Jesus Christ, *who gave himself for our sins to set us free from the present evil age,* according to the will of our God and Father. (Gal. 1:4)

And it is no longer I who live, but it is Christ who lives in me. And the life I now live in the flesh I live by faith in the Son of God, *who loved me and gave himself for me.* (Gal. 2:20)

But when the *fullness of time* had come, God sent his *Son,* born of a woman, born under the law, in order to *redeem* those who were under the law, so that we might receive *adoption* as children. (Gal. 4:4-5)

And being found in *human form,*
    he humbled himself
    and became obedient to the point of death —
    even *death on a cross.* (Phil. 2:7d-8)

. . . how you *turned to God* from idols, *to serve* a living and true God, and to *wait for his Son* from heaven, *whom he raised from the dead* — Jesus, *who rescues us* from the wrath that is coming. (1 Thess. 1:9b-10)[3]

Taken together, these texts indicate that a rough outline of the Pauline gospel would highlight certain key points in the story of Jesus and in its significance:

- the divine promise issued through the prophets
- Jesus' coming as the fulfillment of the divine promise

3. To this list from the undisputed letters could be added several texts from the disputed letters, including Col. 1:15-20; Eph. 1:3-14; 1 Tim. 3:16; 2 Tim. 2:8; 2:11-13.

- Jesus' status as son of David and Son of God (which implies royal and messianic status)
- Jesus' death by crucifixion as both God's gift and Jesus' self-giving
- God's raising of Jesus
- Jesus' status as Lord
- the return of Jesus, and a future day of salvation and wrath
- the requirement of a human response: faith, confession of Jesus' lordship, service to God
- the effects of Jesus' death and resurrection for those who believe: the outpouring of the Spirit, forgiveness of sins, liberation from sin and from the present evil age, justification, redemption, deliverance from the coming wrath[4]

In addition to scattered fragments testifying to various elements of the gospel, more fully developed accounts of it that appear to be traditional (i.e., handed down) and perhaps also liturgical in character may also be found in Paul's letters. For instance, in 1 Corinthians 15:3-8 Paul refreshes the Corinthians' memory about the gospel he had preached (v. 1):

> For I handed on to you as of first importance what I in turn had received: that *Christ died for our sins in accordance with the scriptures,* and that *he was buried,* and that *he was raised on the third day in accordance with the scriptures,* and that *he appeared* to Cephas, then to the twelve. Then *he appeared* to more than five hundred brothers and sisters at one time, most of whom are still alive, though some have died. Then *he appeared* to James, then to all the apostles. Last of all, as to one untimely born, *he appeared* also to me. (emphasis added)

Here we have a basic creed, or statement of the gospel, with four chief affirmations, or 'articles,' three of which include some interpretation and/or elaboration:

Gospel Affirmations and Elaborations in 1 Corinthians 15:3-8

Affirmation/Article	Interpretation/Elaboration
Christ [the Messiah] died	— for our sins — according to the Scriptures
he was buried	

4. A fairly comprehensive summary of this gospel in Paul's own words may be found in both Rom. 5:1-11 and 2 Cor. 5:11-21.

he was raised	— on the third day
	— according to the Scriptures
he appeared	— to . . . then to . . .
	— Then . . . to . . .
	— Then . . . to . . . , then to . . .
	— Last of all . . . to . . .

It is crucial to note that these four articles, like the majority of the bulleted points collected from the shorter statements of the gospel, are not speculative theological or philosophical assertions but *narrative* statements. Paul's gospel is a story, a narrative about what God and Christ have done "for us." His good news has, therefore, a twofold character. It is good news *about* God and his Messiah and, therefore, good news *for* "us."

This means that the theological and the soteriological (salvific) dimensions of Paul's gospel are inseparable. So, when Paul summarizes his gospel proclamation as the revelation of the righteousness of God (Rom. 1:16-17) or as Christ crucified (1 Cor. 2:2), he is saying something about God and Christ, but also about the possibility and even the necessity of participating in this event. When Paul, in Romans 3:21-26, summarizes his gospel in terms of the righteousness of God (in all likelihood once again drawing on earlier tradition), he writes not only of God's gracious activity of redemption and atonement, but also of the need for appropriation of the gift by faith; his gospel is about "the righteousness of God . . . for all who believe" (3:22). Divine initiative requires human response.

PAUL'S MASTER STORY

One implicit but very important dimension of the creed preserved in 1 Corinthians 15 is the assertion that Jesus is both the crucified Messiah (for all knew the manner in which he died) and the living, exalted Lord whose resurrection by God ("he was raised," not 'he rose') was his vindication. Elsewhere, therefore, Paul cites the early acclamation "Jesus is Lord" as the corollary of God's raising him from the dead (1 Cor. 12:3; 2 Cor. 4:5; Rom. 10:9; Phil. 2:11); reciting the acclamation means believing in the vindication, and vice versa. Believers, therefore, implicitly affirm the entire gospel simply by confessing "Jesus is Lord." When they do so, they mean that the crucified but resurrected and exalted Jesus is God's Messiah and Lord. As such, this Jesus rightly shares in the honor due the one true God, the God of Israel, and is the proper recipient of the homage wrongly paid to any and all other so-called lords and gods, including Zeus, Apollo, and of course, the emperor.

Nowhere in Paul's letters is this portrayed more graphically than in Philippians 2:6-11, which is possibly an early hymn fragment, a creed sung in worship indicating two main 'acts' (humiliation and exaltation) in the drama of Christ's story, each divided into 'scenes.' The translation is my own.

The Drama of Christ's Story in Philippians 2:6-11

1. Humiliation

[x] Possession of status	2:6a	Although Jesus the Messiah was in the form of God,
[y] Renunciation of status	2:6b	he did not regard this equality with God as something to exploit for his own advantage,
[z] Self-abasement/self-enslavement	2:7-8	
(i) incarnation		but he emptied himself by taking the form of a slave — that is, by being born as a human being.
(ii) death		And being found in human form, he humbled himself by becoming obedient to the point of death — even death on a cross.

2. Exaltation

[a] Divine vindication	2:9	For this reason God superexalted him and bestowed on him the name that is above every name,
[b] Universal acknowledgment	2:10-11	so that at the name of Jesus every knee will bend — in heaven, on earth, and under the earth — and every tongue will confess, "Jesus the Messiah is Lord," to the glory of God the Father.

Although most scholars believe Paul probably did not compose this text himself (though he certainly could have), it too embodies his gospel in masterful form.[5] Consisting of two basic parts ([1] humiliation — [2] exaltation), it re-

---

5. The unending debate about the character and history of this text cannot be explored here. Earlier scholarship both insisted on and focused on its pre-Pauline origins as a creed or hymn; current scholarship is divided on the question of origins, but generally united on the im-

cites the story of Christ in stages that are followed by a response from God. Christ moves from [x] a position of preincarnation equality with God (status),[6] which [y] he does not exploit for selfish advantage, through his [z] self-emptying incarnation and self-humbling obedient death on the cross. This renunciation of status and two-part self-abasement lead to his consequent [a] exaltation by God to the position of Lord (vindication) and [b] acknowledgment by all creation. Here we find, then, the explicit rationale for the confession "Jesus is Lord" (Gk. *kyrios*). The conclusion of this hymn borrows the language of Israel's devotion to YHWH as the one true God and Lord:

> Turn to me and be saved,
>> all the ends of the earth!
>> For I am God, and there is no other.
> By myself I have sworn,
>> from my mouth has gone forth in righteousness
>> a word that shall not return:
> "To me every knee shall bow,
>> every tongue shall swear." (Isa. 45:22-23)

Hearing in Philippians 2 the echo of the Scripture text that reserves such confession and adoration for YHWH alone, we also find that the exalted Jesus is on the divine side of the great divide between deity and humanity. For those who sing this hymn, including Paul, Jesus is an integral part of the divine identity. As N. T. Wright has shown, Paul interprets Israel's Shema — its fundamental statement of faith in and allegiance to YHWH alone — as an affirmation of one God the Father and one Lord Jesus:

> Hear, O Israel: The LORD [Heb. YHWH; LXX *kyrios*] is our God, the LORD [Heb. YHWH; LXX *kyrios*] alone. (Deut. 6:4)

> We know that "no idol in the world really exists," and that "there is no God but one." Indeed, even though there may be so-called gods in heaven or on earth — as in fact there are many gods and many lords — yet for us there is one God, the Father, from whom are all things and for whom we exist, and one Lord [Gk. *kyrios*], Jesus Christ, through whom are all things and through whom we exist. (1 Cor. 8:4b-6)

---

portance of the text to Paul and on the necessity of focusing on its meaning in its Pauline (rather than pre-Pauline) context.

6. Though this interpretation of the opening lines as depicting the preincarnate Christ is still debated, it is now held by the majority of Pauline scholars.

Only if that is true does another summary of the Pauline gospel ultimately make sense: "in Christ God was reconciling the world to himself" (2 Cor. 5:19).

Much more could be said about the well-known and extraordinarily rich hymnic (or at least poetic) text from Philippians 2, though space permits only a few comments. First, it contains allusions to a number of important figures, including especially Adam (with whom Christ is contrasted; cf. Gen. 3) and the suffering servant of Isaiah 52:13–53:12 (to whom Christ is compared). It would also have been heard in cities like Philippi, where the imperial cult was omnipresent, as a contrast with and challenge to the misplaced honor given to the emperor as universal lord, or *kyrios*. Second, like 1 Corinthians 15:3ff., it also is a narrative. Unlike the Corinthians text, however, it contains nothing explicit about the salvific effect of the story — the events of the story occurring 'for us.' In itself the text is theological and christological only, not soteriological ('for us') or ethical ('as an example'). Nevertheless, again and again in his letters, Paul mines this narrative to interpret not only Christ's coming, death, and exaltation ('the Christ event,' as some have called it), but also his own ministry and the life of believers. That is, Paul uses the text ethically.[7]

In fact, both in Philippians and elsewhere Paul reads the narrative found in this hymn as a story of obedient faith, self-giving love, and unwavering hope, even in the face of suffering and death.[8] As such, this hymnic story sets forth both the *source* of believers' salvation in Christ's incarnation, death, and exaltation, and its *shape* as participation in that Christ event. Paul, in other words, finds in the story of Christ Jesus also the story of the church, as we will see in the next chapter. So often and so creatively does Paul exploit this hymn, that we would not be in error if we recognized it as his most important telling of the gospel. It is, we might say, his *master* story. It tells his gospel story more fully, yet succinctly, than any other single text. (An example of a shortened version of the story is 2 Corinthians 8:9.)

Yet even this story is placed by Paul within a larger narrative framework, namely, the story of God's salvation, a story told by God's covenant partner, Israel. The gospel is the story of Israel's God restoring Israel, and then also the nations, to a right, covenantal relationship. To this story we now turn briefly.

---

7. This process was a natural outgrowth of Paul's vision of the inseparability of theology (including Christology) and soteriology (including ethics) noted above.

8. See, e.g., Phil. 1:27–2:5; Rom. 15:1-3; 1 Cor. 9; 10:23–11:1; 2 Cor. 8:9; 1 Thess. 2:7-8.

THE STORY OF GOD'S
FAITHFULNESS AND SALVATION

For Paul the gospel was no human invention and no 'new idea.' Although it had only recently been revealed, it was the culmination of God's plan and activity in and through Israel. The "fullness of time" (Gal. 4:4) refers not to the opportune moment created by the Roman Empire, but to the will and timing of God, to the turning point of history. Paul's dependence on Scripture to interpret the meaning and progress of the gospel reveals that he was absolutely convinced that what had transpired in Christ, and what was transpiring in the mission of the churches, was the focus of God's activity of salvation for all the world.

One of the major theological issues the revelation of the gospel posed for Paul was the question of the faithfulness of God, for in his experience more Gentiles than Jews were responding to the gospel message (see Rom. 9–11). Paul knew, however, that the Scriptures had announced good news about the coming reign of God (Rom. 1:2; Gal. 3:8). The Greek translation (the LXX) of Isaiah even uses the verb related to *euangelion* — *euangelizomai* — in several key portions of chapters 40–66.[9] As we noted in chapter 2, this entire section of Scripture had a profound influence on Paul. Paul believes that in Christ the promises of God are being fulfilled, yet in new and unexpected ways. In Christ the prophetically promised new exodus, new covenant, new heart, and new creation are all coming to fruition. God is being faithful and is saving Israel (despite evidence — the disbelief of many Jews — to the contrary), even as Israel's psalmists and prophets repeatedly said God would.

An essential part of this new thing is really not so new — the inclusion of the Gentiles. For Paul their part in God's plan is not an afterthought but goes back to God's original intention in calling Abraham to form a distinct people of God (Gal. 3:14-29). The good news is for both Israel and the nations, as the great prophetic text had claimed:

> How beautiful upon the mountains
>   are the feet of the messenger who announces [*euangelizomenou*] peace,
> who brings good news [*euangelizomenos agatha*],
>   who announces salvation,
>   who says to Zion, "Your God reigns."
> Listen! Your sentinels lift up their voices,
>   together they sing for joy;
> for in plain sight they see
>   the return of the LORD to Zion.

---

9. Isa. 40:9 (two times); 52:7; 60:6; 61:1-2.

Break forth together into singing,
 you ruins of Jerusalem;
for the LORD has comforted his people,
 he has redeemed Jerusalem.
The LORD has bared his holy arm
 before the eyes of all the nations;
and all the ends of the earth shall see
 the salvation of our God. (Isa. 52:7-10)

The distinctive character of the language of this text, promising salvation, must not be missed. It is not merely 'religious' language, but also political: "Your God reigns!" Even God's name or title is a political term: "Lord" (Gk. *kyrios*). This union of the religious and the political was natural for Jews (including Paul), and for ancients generally, for whom politics and religion were inseparable, being two sides of one coin (see chap. 1). The question for them was not *whether* politics and religion would mix, but only *whose* politics would shape religion and be shaped by it. For Paul the answer was the strange politics of God manifested in the crucifixion and resurrection of Jesus.

A THEOPOLITICAL GOSPEL

The term 'gospel' did not originally refer to a kind of writing but to a piece of news — good news. In Paul's day it was a term known both in the Jewish community and in the wider Greco-Roman world.

As we have just seen, Jews who knew the text of Isaiah 40–66 would have associated the announcement of good news with the onset of God's salvation and reign. They would have understood this in social and political as well as 'spiritual' terms; God's salvation would bring not only the renewal of the people's hearts, but also the liberation of Israel from foreign oppression and the establishment of God's peace, or *shalom.* For non-Jews the word *euangelion* and related terms had a variety of connotations. Perhaps the most important was the use of 'good news' to refer to the onset of an emperor's rule. As noted in chapter 1, the sentiment expressed in the famous Priene inscription of 9 B.C. was taken for granted: "Caesar [Augustus] through his appearance [*epiphanein*] has exceeded the hopes of all former good messages [*euangelia*], surpassing not only the benefactors who came before him, but also leaving no hope that anyone in the future would surpass him, and since for the world the birthday of the god was the beginning of his good messages [*euangelia*]. . . ."

Not surprisingly, therefore, both Paul's gospel and the language in which it is proclaimed are political as well as religious. His gospel, we might say, is a *theopolitical* gospel. It announces an event that has to do with God's intervention in history, something that must be both a 'theological' and a 'political' event. Attempting to separate politics and religion is a very modern effort; the term 'theopolitical' tries to show their interconnection. The following chart indicates how much of Paul's basic vocabulary has this theopolitical character, drawing from the word banks of both the Jewish and the non-Jewish worlds:

The Vocabulary of Paul's Theopolitical Gospel[10]

Greek Term(s)	Common English Translation(s)	Meaning in Jewish Context	Meaning in Broader Greco-Roman Context
euangelion; euangelizomai	good news/gospel; proclaim good news	good news of God's salvation; announce the good news of God's salvation	good news of military victory or of the emperor's birth/reign; announce the emperor's beneficence
kyrios	Lord	YHWH (God)	master; ruler, emperor (imperial title)
sotēr; sotēria	savior; salvation	God as deliverer/savior; God's deliverance/salvation	emperor as political savior; imperial age or results of military victory
basileia	kingdom, reign	God's kingdom, reign	kingdom; empire; imperial rule, age
eirēnē	peace	right relations among humans and between humans and God	imperial rule and cessation of internal and external conflict; Lat. *pax (pax Romana)*
pistis	faith	covenant faithfulness, fidelity	loyalty (reciprocal between Rome and its citizenry); Lat. *fides*

10. Adapted from Michael J. Gorman, *Cruciformity: Paul's Narrative Spirituality of the Cross* (Grand Rapids: Eerdmans, 2001). Other terms (e.g., *politeuma*, "commonwealth," Phil. 3:20) from Paul's letters could be added to this list, but those in the list are frequent in occurrence and/or central to the expression of his gospel.

Greek Term(s)	Common English Translation(s)	Meaning in Jewish Context	Meaning in Broader Greco-Roman Context
eleutheria	freedom	liberation from oppressive political powers	political or ethical autonomy
dikaios; dikaiosynē	just, righteous; justice, justification, righteousness	just, righteous; covenant faithfulness and righteousness	just; (Roman) justice
ekklēsia	church	the assembly of God's people	the local assembly of citizens in a city *(polis)*, or the business meeting of a club *(collegium)*
parousia	[second] coming	presence of God	imperial or other official arrival, visit, presence; presence/ revelation of a deity

Like Jesus, Paul was announcing a new, divinely established political order. Whereas Jesus preached the coming of the reign (or 'kingdom') of God, beginning in his own ministry of teaching, healing, and dying, Paul heralded the lordship of the crucified but now resurrected Jesus whose reign anticipated the final and complete reign of God the Father over a renewed Israel, inclusive of Gentiles, and a restored creation. In each case the language is theopolitical because the event announced is at once religious and political. For Paul, no less than for Jesus, the good news summons people to make a decision for or against YHWH. To whom will Israel and the nations give allegiance? Whom will they acknowledge as Lord? For both Paul and Jesus the good news is a divine intervention that brings salvation by shaking the religious, political, and even cosmic status quo.

In Paul's case, what else could his gospel do? For it centered on a crucified Messiah — an executed, humiliated, cursed criminal. As religious event, this divine intervention was a new divine revelation and thus a summons to know God anew and afresh. As political event, it was a mandate to acknowledge the lordship of Jesus in continuity with Israel's faith and in contrast to the claims of the emperor. As cosmic event, this divine intervention was indeed an apocalyptic occurrence, God's invasion of the current age in order to inaugurate the age to come (see Gal. 1:4). As such, the gospel offers the promises and benefits of that age.

THE BENEFITS OF THE GOSPEL

So far in this chapter we have stressed the narrative character of Paul's gospel as the announcement of good news with social and political dimensions as well as 'spiritual' or (narrowly construed) 'religious' ones. This emphasis has been necessary in part because many people who read the New Testament in general, and Paul in particular, do so without realizing these fundamental dimensions of the gospel; they often think of the gospel in individual, private terms: a message for and about me.

For Paul, of course, the gospel is a personal word. This is especially clear when he says, "I have been crucified with Christ; and it is no longer I who live, but it is Christ who lives in me. And the life I now live in the flesh I live by faith in the Son of God, who loved me and gave himself for me" (Gal. 2:19-20) — though even here Paul is speaking representatively for all believers. But for Paul the gospel, though *personal,* is not *private.* It is the announcement of God's good news for all humanity, for all creation. A theopolitical announcement hardly lends itself to a merely private religious experience.

This personal but not private word is both an invitation and a challenge:

But what does it [Scripture; or perhaps better translated 'he' = God] say? "The word is near you, / on your lips and in your heart" (that is, the word of faith that we proclaim); because if you confess with your lips that Jesus is Lord and believe in your heart that God raised him from the dead, you will be saved. For one believes with the heart and so is justified, and one confesses with the mouth and so is saved. The scripture says, "No one who believes in him will be put to shame." For there is no distinction between Jew and Greek; the same Lord is Lord of all and is generous to all who call on him. For, "Everyone who calls on the name of the Lord shall be saved." (Rom. 10:8-13)

Two of the key words in this text indicate why the good news is in fact good news: people may be "justified" and "saved." For many people, these are two of the first words that come to mind when they think of Paul — and rightly so. They are two of the great 'benefits' of the gospel; or, as we said above, the gospel is both good news *about* Christ and good news *for* us. Even here, however, we must always remember that the good news for us is that we can now participate in the grand story of God; 'personal' benefit and experience (which we will explore in the next chapter) must be placed in the larger context of God's salvific activity. In other words, for Paul, realities like 'justification' and 'salvation' are social or corporate realities; we experience them with other people.

In a nutshell, the gospel of Christ crucified is "God for us" (Rom. 8:31).

The specific benefits that flow from that divine disposition are available to all who have faith, who believe the gospel — all who affirm its truths, trust in the divine mercy it reveals, and die to themselves in order to begin life with God. (More on 'faith' may be found in the next chapter.) These benefits are often portrayed in Paul's letters in vivid images; they combine to create a kind of kaleidoscope of grace — a set of distinct yet interrelated pieces of a grand reality that can be viewed from an almost endless variety of perspectives. Although in essence this reality is one, it is helpful to consider some of the various images Paul uses to depict the polyvalent experience of grace offered in the gospel. These benefits include:

- **Justification:** Paul's use of the words "just/righteous" and "justify," which are so central to his lexicon, reveals his appreciation of justification as a complex reality. The word and its cognates come from the vocabulary of (divine) character, covenant, and courtroom. To be justified is to be in a right covenant relationship with the righteous God now, with the certain hope of acquittal by God on the future day of judgment. Christ is believers' source of *righteousness*. See Romans 3:21-31; 5:1-11; 5:12-21; Galatians 2:15-21.
- **Reconciliation and peace:** This benefit implies for Paul a prior condition of enmity between people and God that God has taken the initiative to repair. Christ is believers' *mediator* and their *peace*. See Romans 5:1-11; 2 Corinthians 5:18-21.
- **Forgiveness:** This benefit takes seriously the Jewish perspective that sins and trespasses against God require atonement as a means of forgiveness. Although Paul does not use the words 'forgive' or 'forgiveness' frequently, he cites with approval early interpretations of Jesus' death as a death for sins (plural), with the implication of forgiveness/remission. Christ is believers' *sacrifice*. See Romans 3:21-26; 4:7-8 (citing Ps. 32:1-2 on forgiveness), 24-25; 1 Corinthians 5:7; 15:3, 17; 2 Corinthians 5:18-19.
- **Redemption or liberation:** One of Paul's unique contributions is to understand the human condition as one of bondage, both to sin as a force within and around us and to hostile cosmic powers in the universe. Through Christ we are redeemed or liberated — the language is that of the slave market — from these slave masters in order to be "slaves" of God in Christ. This redemption is completed with the redemption, or resurrection, of the body (see 'bodily resurrection and eternal life' below). Christ is believers' *liberation* and their *freedom*. See Romans 6:12-23; 1 Corinthians 6:19-20; Galatians 1:4; 4:1-11.
- **(Present) resurrection:** Though some interpreters of Paul deny it, Paul clearly affirms that believers participate in Christ's resurrection by being

raised to a new life. Ironically, however, this resurrection life conforms to Christ's cross (see chap. 5). Christ is believers' *life*. See Romans 6:1-14, especially verses 11, 13.

- **Incorporation into the people of God:** Through a variety of images — body of Christ, new creation, Israel of God, temple of the Holy Spirit, etc. — Paul expresses the reality that believers constitute the covenant people of God. Christ is believers' *community*. See Galatians 6:16; 1 Corinthians 3:9-17; 12:1-31; 2 Corinthians 5:17.
- **The gift of the Spirit:** The Spirit — the personal presence of God and Christ in the individual and community — is given to all who believe. The Spirit makes known the love of God and makes possible the life of faith, hope, and love. Christ, by the Spirit, is believers' indwelling *power*. See Romans 5:1-5; 8:1-27.
- **The certainty of God's love:** For Paul, God's gift of Christ is the proof and manifestation of divine love in the past, present, and future. The certainty and presence of this love is communicated now, as noted above, by the Spirit. Christ is believers' *demonstration of divine agapē*. See Romans 5:6-8; 8:28-39; Galatians 2:20.
- **Sanctification:** Christ, for Paul, enables believers to embody the sanctified ("holy") — i.e., distinctive or countercultural — lifestyle appropriate for the people of the covenant. Christ is believers' *holiness*. See Romans 12:1; 1 Corinthians 1:30; 1 Thessalonians 3:13; 4:1-8.
- **Deliverance from wrath:** Paul inherits the Jewish belief in accountability on a future day of judgment, with divine wrath the fate of the unbelieving/ disobedient. God's love manifested in the death of Christ insures protection from this coming wrath. Christ is believers' *security*. See 1 Thessalonians 1:10; 5:9; Romans 5:6-11.
- **Salvation:** For Paul "salvation" refers especially to the future experience of God's grace and glory that results from justification. It is the positive flip side of deliverance from wrath, as well as from all other enemies, most especially sin and death. It includes bodily resurrection, glorification, and eternal life (see below). Christ is believers' *salvation*. See Romans 1:16; 8:18-25; 10:1-21; 1 Corinthians 15:1-2; Philippians 3:20-21.
- **Bodily resurrection and eternal life:** Paul retains his Jewish (Pharisaic) conviction that human life is 'embodied' life both in this life as we know it (before death) and in the life to come (after resurrection). Thus the future hope of believers is for a transformed bodily existence in the presence of God. Christ is believers' *hope*. See Romans 6:20-23; 8:18-25; 1 Corinthians 15:1-58; 2 Corinthians 4:16–5:10; Philippians 3:11, 21.
- **Glorification:** Because Paul believes that humans have failed fully to embody the image of God apart from Christ, in Christ they begin in this life a

process of transformation into the likeness of Christ — the image of God — that is completed in the life to come. Christ is believers' *goal*, their telos. See Romans 5:1-2 (contrast 3:23); 8:12-39; 2 Corinthians 3:12–4:6; Philippians 3:12-21.

A message that effects all these things is indeed powerful, and indeed good news. Once again, however, we must stress that the benefits of the gospel are not matters of 'private religion' but aspects of participation in God's invasion of grace for the salvation of Israel and the nations. To experience these benefits in their fullness requires an acknowledgment of the totality of God's claim on humanity in Christ, and an attachment to the place where that claim is preached and practiced — the church.

It is absolutely crucial, in conclusion, to recognize that each of the benefits of the gospel is ultimately derived from God's grace manifested in Christ, centered in the cross, confirmed by the resurrection, made effective by the Spirit, and experienced in community. The gospel is therefore a trinitarian event for Paul, and a story of death and resurrection both for Christ and for believers, individually and corporately.[11] To believe this gospel is to enter into a relationship with the triune God of the cross and resurrection, and with God's people. That is the subject of the next chapter.

QUESTIONS FOR REFLECTION

1. What is the significance of understanding the gospel as divine power, as efficacious word?
2. Evaluate the meaning and aptness of Ernst Käsemann's claim that for Paul "the cross is the signature of the one who is risen."
3. In what ways has the contemporary church appreciated and/or neglected the (a) narrative, (b) Jewish, and (c) theopolitical dimensions of the gospel?
4. Evaluate the claim that "for Paul the gospel, though *personal*, is not *private*."
5. Which of the 'benefits' of the gospel according to Paul are most and least fully understood and experienced in the church today? Are there other benefits of the gospel that Paul does not highlight?

---

11. As discussed in the next chapter, trinitarian language is used here in recognition that although Paul does not have a fully developed theology of the Trinity, such language is nonetheless appropriate.

FOR FURTHER READING AND STUDY

Few books are devoted to this topic alone. We may single out the following, however:

General

Georgi, Dieter. *Theocracy in Paul's Praxis and Theology*. Translated by David E. Green. Minneapolis: Fortress, 1991. A groundbreaking study of the political ('theocratic') character of Paul's gospel as revealed in his various letters.

Wright, N. T. *What Saint Paul Really Said: Was Paul of Tarsus the Real Founder of Christianity?* Grand Rapids: Eerdmans, 1997. A brief but lucid introduction stressing both the Jewish and the 'political' character of Paul's gospel, mission, and theology for Jews and Gentiles.

Technical

Horsley, Richard A., ed. *Paul and Empire: Religion and Power in Roman Imperial Society*. Harrisburg, Pa.: Trinity Press International, 1997. A superb collection of essays contrasting Paul's counterimperial gospel with the imperial gospel of salvation.

Jervis, L. Ann, and Peter Richardson. *Gospel in Paul: Studies on Corinthians, Galatians, and Romans for Richard N. Longenecker*. Journal for the Study of the New Testament — Supplement Series 108. Sheffield: Sheffield Academic Press, 1994. A collection of very fine essays (in honor of a Pauline scholar) that provides challenging but rewarding reading.

CHAPTER 5

PAUL'S SPIRITUALITY

Covenantal, Cruciform, and Charismatic; Communal,
Countercultural, and (New-) Creational

I have been crucified with Christ; and it is no longer I who live, but
Christ who lives in me. And the life I now live in the flesh I live by the
faith of the Son of God, who loved me by giving himself for me.

Gal. 2:19b-20[1]

Many introductions to Paul will have a chapter on Paul's ethics; this text has one on his spirituality. In this book we wish to stress the inseparability of gospel and life, of believing and living, of relations with God and with others, for the apostle. Thus the term 'spirituality' is intended as a more comprehensive term than 'ethics,' which is nonetheless included within 'spirituality.' For the moment, however, we are less interested in what Paul thought about certain 'ethical issues' — these topics will arise in due course in the discussion of the letters — than in the general shape of life in Christ that he envisioned.

A common and helpful definition of spirituality, from a Christian perspective, is that it is the 'lived experience' of believers — those who affirm that "Jesus is Lord." *Spirit*uality may also be rightly understood as life in the Spirit. In considering the lived experience of Paul, as well as the experience he wanted those in his churches to have, we must remember once again that he was a Jew who believed that the Jewish Messiah had come for the whole world. Thus his spirituality has to do with being part of a community in covenant relation with God — that is, absolutely devoted to the one true creator God — through

1. Author's translation.

God's crucified and now exalted Messiah, who is Lord. This is all made possible by God's grace and the power of God's Spirit.

What follows is a brief look at Paul's lived experience from several overlapping angles. There is no completely neat, clean way to divide up the various dimensions of Paul's spirituality, because they are all intimately interrelated. Our discussion follows a trinitarian structure because the God Paul experiences is, so to speak, 'multidimensional' — known as Father, Son, and Spirit.[2] The distinctive character of Paul's spirituality is that it is *covenantal* (in relation to God the Father, the God of Israel), *cruciform* (shaped in accord with the cross of Christ), *charismatic* (empowered by the Spirit), *communal* (lived out in the company of other believers), and therefore *countercultural* (formed in contrast to the dominant socio-political values of the pagan Hellenistic world). Furthermore, since Paul's experience of God in Christ, by the power of the Spirit in the countercultural community, takes place within the larger work of the creator God redeeming the entire creation, his spirituality is also a *creational,* or better, *new-creational,* spirituality (experienced as part of God's reconciliation of the cosmos to himself).[3] Finally, this spirituality, like Paul's gospel, letters, and (as we will see in chap. 6) theology, has a narrative shape to it. Paul and his churches are called to tell a story with their individual and corporate lives, a story of self-giving faith, hope, and love as the means to embody the story of God renewing covenant and redeeming the world through the crucified Christ.

COVENANTAL: LIVING FOR GOD

Any discussion of Paul's spirituality must begin with the recognition that the purpose of Christ's coming and death was the restoration (for Jews) or establishment (for Gentiles) of right covenantal relations between human beings and God. For Jews, whose story began with God's liberating grace in the exodus, covenantal relations were always initiated by God, and they always entailed a response from Israel of both love for God and love for neighbor. So too with Paul. In the next section we shall see how Paul's experience of the exalted crucified Messiah affected his understanding of this interrelated, two-dimensional

2. Trinitarian language is used here in recognition that although Paul does not have a fully developed theology of the Trinity, such language is nonetheless appropriate, as the following discussion will suggest.

3. Although I have articulated this perspective elsewhere (*Cruciformity: Paul's Narrative Spirituality of the Cross* [Grand Rapids: Eerdmans, 2001], chap. 12 [pp. 304-48]), I am indebted to N. T. Wright for the terms used here ('creational,' 'new-creational') and for his reminder that Paul's spirituality cannot be adequately described without reference to this dimension.

response to God and neighbor. First, however, we must briefly see how the cross affected Paul's understanding and experience of God, for in Christ the covenant is made new, as promised by the prophets. In Paul's experience, to be in covenant relation with God is to know God — or better, to be known by God (Gal. 4:9; cf. 1 Cor. 8:3). For Paul, what is distinctive about this God known in Christ (who is, of course, still the God of Israel)?

Four main things need briefly to be said. First, for Paul God is faithful yet surprising in his mercy. Second, this God of the covenant is trinitarian. Third, the God of the covenant is cruciform. And fourth, God is Father.

GOD IS FAITHFUL AND MERCIFUL

As noted in chapter 2, Paul's moment of conversion and call was for him an experience of undeserved favor, of unmerited grace (Gal. 1:15; 1 Cor. 15:9-10). This became the theme of Paul's lifelong celebration of God's mercy in Christ: he had been surprised by grace, and he wanted others to know and appreciate that grace. The centerpiece of God's grace, of course, was the gift of the Son (Gal. 4:4-5), culminating on the cross. This was the manifestation of God's gracious love, not to the righteous but to sinners, even to God's enemies (Rom. 5:6-8, 20; 2 Cor. 8:9). This grace is now a power unleashed in the world (Rom. 5:21) that bestows life — life with God (6:1-14). No wonder Paul begins and ends his letters blessing his readers with that fundamental gift of God's grace.[4]

But the paradox of grace is, in part, that it is also the manifestation of God's faithfulness. Paul sees God's gracious gift as *mercy* because it is God's love for *undeserving sinners,* and as *faithfulness* because it is *God's* love for such undeserving sinners. God has now kept promises made long ago, even if they have been fulfilled in surprising ways. That is especially the driving force of Romans 9–11, Paul's lengthy, impassioned speech on Israel's faithlessness and God's faithfulness. As we will see below, this faithfulness encompasses God's activity not only as Israel's God but also as creator of the cosmos.

GOD IS TRINITARIAN

The love of God Paul experiences in the cross comes from three sources — and yet the three are one. This reality is expressed most succinctly in the benedic-

---

4. Rom. 1:7; 16:20; 1 Cor. 1:3; 16:23; 2 Cor. 1:2; 13:13; Gal. 1:3; 6:18; Eph. 1:2; 6:24; Phil. 1:2; 4:23; Col. 1:2; 4:18; 1 Thess. 1:1; 5:28; 2 Thess. 1:2; 3:18; 1 Tim. 1:2; 6:21; 2 Tim. 1:2; 4:22; Titus 1:4; 3:15; Philem. 3, 25.

tion in 2 Corinthians 13:13: "The grace of the Lord Jesus Christ, the love of God, and the communion of the Holy Spirit be with all of you." It is unpacked more fully, yet still concisely, in the theologically dense center of Romans, 5:1-11. There Paul explains that *God's* love is seen in *Christ's* sacrificial death (5:8) and is "poured into our hearts" (5:5) through the *Holy Spirit.*

Although it is true that the Christian church took several hundred years to hammer out a theology of the Trinity, the grace-filled experience of Paul and his churches can only be described adequately as trinitarian. Throughout his letters Paul writes of an ongoing encounter with the one God of Israel (YHWH, the Lord) that is an experience of God as "Abba," or Father; an experience of the crucified (but now living) Jesus as the resurrected Messiah, Son of God, and Lord; and an experience of the Spirit of God (who is also called "Lord," 2 Cor. 3:17) promised long ago by the prophets. None of these experiences is of an impersonal force but of a personal being, and none is independent of the other. Paul encounters God as Father, Son, and Spirit; they are distinct yet inseparable; they are three yet one.

The trinitarian character of Paul's experience of God, and thus of God, is manifested in various ways in the Pauline corpus. In addition to the trinitarian character of the cross, the three-in-one God appears in texts about confession of faith and baptism (e.g., 1 Cor. 6:11; 12:3, 13), spiritual gifts and ministry (e.g., 1 Cor. 12:4-6; Rom. 15:16), prayer (1 Thess. 5:16-19), and the life of faith and the experience of grace more generally (Gal. 4:4-6; 2 Cor. 3:3; 13:13; 1 Thess. 1:1-5).[5]

All of this means that to be in covenantal relationship with God is to be in relationship with Father, Son, and Spirit, who are in relationship to one another. The Father is the father of the Lord Jesus, who has now adopted believers and made them his children. Believers relate to this Father just as the earthly Jesus did, by calling out "Abba" (= 'Father'; Rom. 8:15; Gal. 4:6; cf. Mark 14:36). Yet they confess Jesus as "Lord," acknowledging him with the title once reserved for YHWH, or God the Father, alone, as we noted in the previous chapter (e.g., Isa. 45:23 as applied to Jesus in Phil. 2:9-11). And they experience the Spirit as the Spirit of God (e.g., Rom. 8:11, 14; 1 Cor. 3:16) as well as the Spirit of the Son (e.g., Gal. 4:6); in fact, in Romans 8:9 Paul identifies the Spirit in both ways.

GOD IS CRUCIFORM

The inseparable interconnections of Father, Son, and Spirit in Paul's experience lead to (or perhaps derive from) an important, and distinctively Pauline, claim: that God is cruciform, or crosslike. (The word 'cruciform' literally means 'in the

---

5. For further exploration of this topic, see my *Cruciformity*, chap. 4.

shape of a cross,' but it can be used metaphorically.) That is, we learn from Paul that the cross of Christ is not only *initiated* by God, it *reveals* God. Christ crucified is the power and wisdom of God (1 Cor. 1:18-25).

The revelatory character of the cross means that when we see it we are shown something not only about Christ but about God; we discover that God is vulnerable, powerful in weakness. We discover that God is faithful and loving beyond measure, even toward enemies (Rom. 5:6-8).

Furthermore, the revelatory character of the cross means that we are shown something not only about the 'historical Jesus' but also about the living Lord, and therefore about the Spirit. We discover that the same Jesus who went to the cross in faith and love (Gal. 2:15-21) continues by the Spirit to create a community of crosslike faith and love (5:6, esp. in light of 2:19-20). (More on this below.)

GOD IS FATHER

One of the distinctive features of Jesus', Paul's, and (it appears) most early Christians' relationship with God was their practice of calling God "Father," often using the Aramaic word *Abba* to do so (for Paul, as noted above, see Rom. 8:15 and Gal. 4:6). Although not prominent in the Hebrew Scriptures or in Judaism, the title "Father" for God was sometimes used in Jewish communities. For Jews, including Jesus and Paul, "Father" in reference to God was not merely a term of endearment. As Father, God is worthy of honor and obedience, and he provides his children with their needs and with an inheritance.

For Paul, God's fatherhood is experienced as in adoption — those who come to faith are brought into the family of God (Rom. 8:12-17; Gal. 4:4-7). As adopted children, believers are heirs of their Father and coheirs with Christ (Rom. 8:17); they will inherit God's glory. In the meantime, they know God intimately and obediently as children, joyfully but respectfully calling out, "Abba! Father!"

ALIVE TO GOD

Paul characterizes the life of knowing the God of Israel, revealed in Christ, as being alive to God (Rom. 6:11). This means being fully open to the gracious and peculiar power, wisdom, and love of God the Father manifested in the cross. It necessitates first of all a kind of death to everything else in order to have this life with God (Rom. 6:1-11; Gal. 2:19-20; 5:24; 6:14). Which brings us to the next aspect of Paul's spirituality: the basic shape of daily existence, the life of conformity to Christ.

CRUCIFORM: FAITH, HOPE, AND LOVE

To be a believer in covenant relationship with God through Christ is also, of course, to have a relationship with Christ. Paul attempts to describe this relationship in a variety of ways. For example, according to Galatians 3:27, believers have already "put on Christ" (RSV), while Romans 13:14 exhorts them to do so, indicating that dressing oneself with Christ — a vivid metaphor — is not a onetime experience. It is a way of life.

IN CHRIST AND CHRIST WITHIN

The metaphor of 'putting on' Christ points to an intimate relationship. One of Paul's basic and favorite phrases to describe the life of faith, therefore, is being "in Christ." This means being 'surrounded' by him as by clothing, under his power and influence, shaped into the pattern, or story, of his sacrificial love.[6] It is also, as we will see in more detail below, to be in his body, the community of those who confess him as Lord and together seek to be shaped by him.

While Paul speaks frequently of being in Christ, he also speaks of believers having the risen Christ living within them. "It is no longer I who live, but it is Christ who lives in me" (Gal. 2:20; cf. Rom. 8:10). Christ is not merely outside, but within; he permeates the life of the individual believer and of the community.

This relationship of being in Christ and Christ being within may be called one of *mutual indwelling*. It means that Christ (or the Spirit of Christ — Gal. 4:6) is not an external model but an internal power. Outside of Christ, people are indwelt by sin — a powerful anti-God force (Rom. 7:17).[7] In Christ a person is indwelt by him (Christ), who replaces sin as the determinative power in the believer's life and thereby, with the assent and cooperation of the believer, moves him or her toward the goal of the divine call: conformity to the Son of God (Rom. 8:29). One of the chief hallmarks, then, of Paul's spirituality is this life of 'mutual indwelling' between Christ and believers that results in conformity to Christ.

DYING AND RISING WITH CHRIST

Paul expresses this overall goal of conformity to Christ in a variety of ways, but the most powerful involves the language of death, of crucifixion. He speaks of

6. E.g., Rom. 6:11; 8:1; 1 Cor. 1:30; 2 Cor. 1:21; 2:17; 5:17; Gal. 3:26, 28; 5:6; Phil. 1:1; 2:1; 4:2, 4, 7, 19; 1 Thess. 2:14; 3:8.
7. It should be noted that Rom. 7 is often thought to be a description of believers' existence; for reasons why this is probably in error, see the discussion in the chapter on Romans.

baptism as an experience of dying and rising with Christ that means the 'crucifixion' of the old self (Rom. 6). Elsewhere, speaking for all believers, he says he has been cocrucified with Christ (Gal. 2:19), and he asserts that believers have crucified the "flesh" — not their bodies, but their sin-induced anti-God propensity — with its "passions and desires" (5:24). He introduces his hymnic master story by telling the Philippian believers to allow their corporate life — their story — to take the shape of Christ's story of obedient self-emptying and self-giving in his death on the cross (Phil. 2:1-5).

We may refer to this conformity to Christ crucified as *cruciformity* (from 'cruciform,' meaning, as noted above, 'cross-shaped' — literally or metaphorically). It is clear from the texts cited above that this is not a onetime experience but an ongoing reality. It begins at the first moment of faith, expressed in baptism, and continues throughout life. Believers both die and rise with Christ in baptism (Rom. 6:1-11); the paradox is that the new or 'resurrection' life to which they rise is a life of ongoing 'death' — ongoing conformity to the death of Jesus.

THE MEANING OF CONFORMITY TO CHRIST CRUCIFIED

One way to summarize Paul's understanding of believers' existence can be found in the imperative "Be[come] imitators of me, as I am of Christ" (1 Cor. 11:1). Here Paul offers himself as a model for living, but only inasmuch as he is conformed to Christ; the ultimate similarity he desires is between believers and Christ. This text should not be misunderstood as a call for a spirituality of imitation, if imitation is understood as copying an external model. For as we noted above, Paul's experience of Christ is of one who lives within him, and within whom he lives. To become an imitator of him is, paradoxically, to pursue a spirituality, not of imitation, but of indwelling.

All the talk of dying with Christ sounds well and good, but what does it mean? Fortunately Paul sheds some light on the term by taking some more common terms, 'faith' and 'love,' and interpreting them in light of the cross. This can happen, and indeed must happen, because Paul finds in Christ's death on the cross the definitive and paradigmatic revelation of faith and love, of right relations with God and with others. Paul, in fact, "live[s] by the *faith* of the Son of God who *loved* me by giving himself for me" (Gal. 2:20). For this reason, what matters ultimately for believers is *"faith* expressing itself in *love"* (5:6).[8]

Appearing immediately before Galatians 5:6 is a reference also to hope: "For through the Spirit, by faith, we eagerly wait for the hope of righteousness"

---

8. Author's translation and emphasis for this and the previous text; for a full discussion, see the comments on these passages in the chapter on Galatians.

(5:5). Similarly, at the end of one of his more well known texts, Paul claims that "faith, hope, and love abide, these three; and the greatest of these is love" (1 Cor. 13:13). This 'triad of virtues,' as it has sometimes been called, is clearly very important to Paul.[9] The fundamental shape of the cruciform life is the life of faith, hope, and love. That is to say, therefore, that Paul's spirituality is a spirituality of *cruciform* faith, hope, and love. Faith and hope refer primarily to the believer's appropriate relationship with God, while love refers primarily to one's relationship to others — to fellow believers, to outsiders, and even to enemies. We will explore each of these three very briefly.

FAITH

Faith for Paul is the appropriate response to the gospel (Rom. 10:5-17), the subjective basis (i.e., the required human response) for justification (3:21-31; Gal. 2:15-21), the objective basis (i.e., the effective act to which humans respond) being Christ's faithful, obedient death.[10] It is a comprehensive response, having both cognitive (belief) and relational (trust) dimensions. But it is more than either of these or both together; faith is more like a posture of surrender and commitment to God. It is, in fact, a covenantal term, what the Scriptures of Israel refer to as *love* for God. This kind of love — with one's whole heart, soul, mind, and strength — is really *fidelity* or *loyalty*. That is why Paul can speak of the "obedience of faith" (Rom. 1:5; 16:26).

To 'obey' God is to become God's 'servant' or 'slave' (1 Thess. 1:9; Rom. 6:22), but that requires a disconnection or liberation from sin, humanity's slave master apart from Christ (6:12-23). In other words, faith is an experience of death and resurrection — a death to the old self, to the flesh and its passions, and to the world, in order to live to God in Christ (Rom. 6:11; 2 Cor. 5:15). This kind of faith can very well be costly, as Paul himself knew all too well. This is because Jesus himself demonstrated his faith — his loyalty to God — by becoming "obedient to the point of death — even death on a cross" (Phil. 2:8).

Faith is cruciform, then, because Jesus' life of faithful obedience toward God was cross-shaped.

HOPE

For Paul, hope is the future tense of faith. It is the assurance that the process of transformation into Christ's likeness will find its completion in the presence of

9. It appears also in 1 Thess. 1:3 and 5:8 and in Rom. 5:1-5; cf. Col. 1:4-5.
10. E.g., Gal. 2:20; Rom. 5:18-19; Phil. 2:6-8.

God after death (Rom. 8:29; Phil. 3:7-14). It is the confidence that the bodily resurrection and eternal life (1 Cor. 15; Rom. 6:23) offered through Christ's death will come to pass as part of the redemption of the entire universe (8:19-25). In a word, hope is the assurance of glory — of sharing in the fullness of humanity in God's presence.

But glory, for believers, is not attained now. It is preceded by a time of suffering, of tribulation. Many Jews expected such a time of suffering (the 'messianic woes') before the arrival of the Messiah and God's kingdom. For Paul, this suffering does not create despair but builds hope (Rom. 5:3-5) because, as in the story of Christ, suffering precedes resurrection. Moreover, without suffering there will be no glory (Rom. 8:17), yet the "weight" of eternal glory far outweighs the momentary suffering believers experience now (2 Cor. 5:16-18; Rom. 8:18).

Hope, then, is also cruciform, because suffering preceded Christ's own glorification. But the conformity to the cross that believers are called to experience does not always entail physical suffering. The life of faith and hope is always also a life of love — and love can also be a way of embracing the cross.

LOVE

Love has a very specific meaning for Paul — conformity to the pattern of Christ's self-giving, sacrificial love on the cross: "who loved me by giving himself for me" (Gal. 2:20, author's translation).[11] Love is therefore less a feeling than an action. Negatively, love does not "insist on its own way" or "seek its own interests" (1 Cor. 13:5, NRSV and NAB). Positively, it seeks the welfare of others and builds them up (1 Cor. 8:1).[12] In effect, love is the edification of the other. It is the gift of self to others, the willingness to "spend and be spent" for them (2 Cor. 12:15).

Faith and love are inseparable for Paul. Love is faith in action (Gal. 5:6). It is the 'horizontal' (people-to-people) dimension of covenant faithfulness, of which fidelity to God is the 'vertical' aspect. Because Paul catches up in one word ('love') all the demands of covenant fidelity toward others, we must understand love for Paul to encompass more than narrowly defined personal relations. In fact, the love of which he speaks overlaps with the Hebrew Scriptures' notion of justice: special, concrete attention to the weaker or needier members

11. Paul occasionally speaks of love for God (Rom. 8:28; 1 Cor. 2:9; 8:3), but his preferred terms for the human relationship with God are faith, obedience, and hope. In the triad of faith, hope, and love, the term 'love' always refers to love for others, not for God.

12. Cf. Phil. 2:4 for both aspects in one text.

of the local or wider community (see 1 Cor. 11:17-34; 12:12-26; 2 Cor. 8:1-15). Furthermore, the love of God in Christ does not neglect outsiders and even enemies (e.g., 1 Thess. 5:15; Rom. 12:9-21; Gal. 6:10). After all, Christ's death was God's gift for those at enmity with God (Rom. 5:6-8).

Like faith, love can be costly; it cost Christ his life, and it often cost Paul his time (not to mention his sleep! — 2 Cor. 6:5; 11:27), his money, and his status. And it almost certainly finally cost him his own life, too. Love, like faith and hope, is cruciform.

CHARISMATIC: LIFE IN THE SPIRIT

As noted above, life in Christ is simultaneously life in the Spirit of God, the Spirit of Christ. Paul specifically relates the Spirit to several key aspects of the believer's life — and to the cross.

THE PRESENCE OF THE SPIRIT

For Paul the Spirit is not an optional supplement to life with God in Christ; when the gospel rains on people, it pours down the Spirit upon them (Gal. 3:1-5; cf. Rom. 5:5). Everyone in Christ possesses the Spirit and is possessed by the Spirit; life in Christ without the Spirit is impossible (1 Cor. 12:1-7; Rom. 8:9b). Possessing the gift of the Spirit is the proof of being in Christ, of being part of God's covenant people.

The twofold gift of Christ and the Spirit (see Gal. 4:4, 6) inaugurated, in Paul's view, the new age and thus the 'eschatological' people of God. As the prophets had said, this new time and its people would be marked by an outpouring of the Spirit — the real presence — of God. The Spirit believers receive is this "promised Spirit." Moreover, the Spirit is the "first installment" (NRSV, NAB) of, or "deposit" (NIV) on, believers' future glory (2 Cor. 1:22; cf. Eph. 1:14). The Spirit connects believers both to God's past and to God's future, as well as to God's present.

Paul's main designations for the Spirit reveal something of believers' experience of that Spirit:

- Because the Spirit is the Spirit of *God,* the Spirit forms believers into a community of God's people marked by God's presence, like a temple (1 Cor. 3:16).
- Because the Spirit is the *Holy* Spirit, the Spirit forms believers into a dis-

tinctive ("holy") covenant community whose patterns of living differ from those of their pagan neighbors and fulfill the will of God (e.g., 1 Thess. 4:1-8). Paul's favorite designation for believers is "saints" or "holy ones" (Gk. *hagioi*).

- Because the Spirit is the Spirit of *Christ* (Rom. 8:9-10; Gal. 4:6), the Spirit molds believers into a community that lives in accord with the pattern of Christ (e.g., Phil. 2:5). To live according to the Spirit is to live according to Christ.

This last point brings us to the really distinctive feature of the Spirit in Paul's thinking and experience: the primary indication of the presence of God's Holy Spirit is not ecstatic manifestations or mystical journeys to heaven — both of which Paul, and no doubt other first-century believers, experienced (e.g., 1 Cor. 14:18; 2 Cor. 12:1-10). Rather, the primary work and sign of the Spirit is to keep believers connected to the cross of Christ. The Spirit is the Spirit of cruciformity, enabling fidelity to God rather than the flesh or the world, sustaining hope in the midst of suffering, and empowering people for self-giving love.

Paradoxically, this life of serving others is a life of freedom; the Spirit indeed spells "freedom" for Paul. This freedom is not libertinism to do as one pleases, but it is freedom *from* bondage either to the self (in the absence of law) or to law (as a means of self-righteousness or ethnic pride) and *for* the service of God and others (Gal. 5:1-15).

One way Paul describes this cruciform life of freedom in the Spirit is with the metaphor of walking — though, unfortunately, many translations render the Greek verb 'walk' *(peripateō)* as "live" (e.g., Gal. 5:16). Life in the Spirit is a journey toward the future with God; in the present, believers 'move in step with' the Spirit by allowing the Spirit, rather than the flesh (humans' anti-God propensity), to direct them. Within this 'walk,' Paul asserts, the Spirit has a multidimensional 'ministry' in the church. Here we mention two aspects, fruit and gifts.

THE FRUIT AND GIFTS OF THE SPIRIT

The "fruit" of the Spirit is listed by Paul in Galatians 5:22-23: love, joy, peace, patience, kindness, generosity, faithfulness, gentleness, and self-control. The agricultural image suggests the natural product of the Spirit's presence, while the singular noun ("fruit" not "fruits") may suggest the inseparability of the nine 'virtues' listed. Love is listed first because without it, nothing else has any value (cf. 1 Cor. 13:1-3) — especially not the gifts of the Spirit.

The gifts (1 Cor. 12; Rom. 12:3-8; cf. Eph. 4:7-16), unlike the fruit, are given not in bulk but individually, according to the Spirit's own best judgment (1 Cor. 12:7, 11). The purpose of the gifts is to edify others (12:7; 14:1-5); they are concrete expressions of the fruit that begins with love.

SOME ADDITIONAL DISPOSITIONS OF FAITH

To walk in, or according to, Christ and the Spirit is to live in faith, hope, and love; it is to use one's gifts in the service of others. Many other things grow from these basic elements, of course, but space permits us to mention only three: humility, joy in suffering, and continuous prayer.

For Paul, Christ was a man of humility and meekness (2 Cor. 10:1); these were not qualities that the Roman Empire celebrated. But because Christ humbled himself, believers are also called to live in humility and meekness. This means lovingly counting others as more important than oneself and trying to *show* honor rather than *receive* it (Phil. 2:1-4; Rom. 12:10).

One of the paradoxes of Paul's experience is that despite his life of suffering, he 'rejoiced in the Lord' no matter what he was experiencing or where he was experiencing it. His letter to the Philippians — written from jail — is full of joy (1:3-4, 18-19, etc.). Paul's secret was, in part, the knowledge that Christ had been delivered out of his suffering through resurrection and exaltation, and thereby vindicated by God the Father; in part, the certainty that his sufferings benefited the gospel and thereby others; and in part, the ongoing experience of the presence of Christ's comforting Spirit — which came in some measure through the grace and generosity of others.

Finally, Paul was a person of prayer — constant prayer. He does not tell us much about his prayer habits or methods except that he claims never to stop (e.g., Rom. 1:9; Phil. 1:3-4; 1 Thess. 1:2, referring to the frequency and regularity of his prayers, perhaps following Jewish patterns of prayer throughout the day), and sometimes prayed in "tongues" (1 Cor. 14:14, 18). He gave thanks for the good that was happening among his communities; he prayed for their growth in areas of concern; and he interceded for their endurance in the face of opposition. He invited others to pray for his ministry, and generally to pray with thanksgiving and joy at all times (e.g., 1 Thess. 5:16-18; Phil. 4:4-7).

COMMUNAL AND COUNTERCULTURAL

As we noted in previous chapters, Paul's experience of God in Christ is personal but not private. The work of the Spirit is not to bring disconnected individuals into a private experience of God, but to create a multicultural community of people who live in distinction to their pagan neighbors — neighbors who worship false gods (not the one God), confess the emperor (rather than Jesus) as Lord, and are intoxicated with the spirit of the age (instead of the Holy Spirit) — and to bear witness to God's reconciling activity in the cross of Christ. As such, they are a kind of 'counterculture,' an alternative community, a sort of 'colony of heaven' (see Phil. 1:27; 3:20). In the tradition of the book of Leviticus and the literature of Jewish piety more generally (especially that of the Diaspora), Paul views those gathered to be God's people as "holy" *(hagios)* — set apart for God's purposes, and therefore different from others.[13]

Paul draws on a variety of other images to express the character of this Spirit-formed, holy community: Israel of God (e.g., Gal. 6:16), body of Christ (e.g., 1 Cor. 12), temple of the Holy Spirit (e.g., 1 Cor. 3:16). The church is also constantly depicted as a fellowship — a community with common concerns and a common mission — and as a family of brothers and sisters.

As a community, the church has both internal and external responsibilities. Internally the members are to love one another, edify one another, bear one another's burdens (summaries in Rom. 12:3-21; Gal. 5:13–6:10). If one suffers, all suffer, and if one rejoices, all rejoice. Externally they are to bear witness to their neighbors and to love all — even their enemies. If persecuted, they — like Paul — would be expected neither to be surprised nor to retaliate (Rom. 12:14-21; cf. 1 Cor. 4:12-13). They are, in other words, to share their faith, express their love, and remain secure in their hope as they interact with the world around them (Phil. 2:12-16).

EQUALITY IN CHRIST

Much more could of course be said about the church as an integral part of Paul's spirituality. Space permits only one final comment: the church is where people of all genders, races, and socioeconomic conditions are *equal* (Gal. 3:28). This means, for Paul, that men and women are both gifted (note the number of women he worked with [see, e.g., Rom. 16]); that all races and ethnic groups are on equal footing in Christ; and that the honor the rich and powerful typically bestow on one another has no importance — and no place — in the church.

---

13. One scholar has rightly referred to holiness as a "neglected feature of Paul's theological grammar" (Calvin Roetzel, *Paul: The Man and the Myth* [Minneapolis: Fortress, 1999], p. 36). Unfortunately, some English translations obscure the significance of holiness for Paul by translating one of his most important designations for believers, "holy ones" *(hagioi)*, as "saints" (consistently in the NRSV and regularly in the NIV, though not at all in the NAB).

Even slaves and masters are brothers under the one Lord (see Philemon). The Spirit does not make all the *same,* only *equal.* The church is God's community of unity in diversity (1 Cor. 12).

LIVING THE STORY

Such a church of equals in Christ, called to holiness, is where the one God of Israel is served, the death of Christ celebrated by all, and the presence of God in Christ through the Spirit experienced in worship and in daily life. It is where the story of Christ crucified as God's wisdom and power is told in the power of the Spirit, not merely with words but with a living story — the faithful narrative of all the "saints" or "holy ones," one of Paul's favorite designations for believers. The story of Christ is 'performed' in real life. It is a story of forsaking status; spending and being spent; loving enemies, including the excluded; and even suffering — but always in hope of the glory of God. Embracing this cruciform existence is what it means to live in the power of the resurrection now — to live in the new age inaugurated by Christ's death and resurrection and by the gift of the Spirit.

To live such a life is to live in continuity with the story of Israel but in marked discontinuity with the Roman polis with its gods and values. It is to confess Jesus rather than Caesar as Lord, and therefore to live by the story of Jesus' cross and resurrection rather than by the pseudogospel of imperial salvation. The *ekklēsia* interrupts the empire's story of idolatry, immorality, injustice, violence, and the pursuit of honor with its own story — told in word and life — of the Spirit of God's Son alive in the world for the salvation of all.

(NEW-) CREATIONAL: THE LARGER STORY

In the history of the interpretation of Paul, the apostle's spirituality has often been understood as focused on a private experience of God. In recent times that has been corrected, as we have noted, as the communal character of Paul's spirituality has been increasingly recognized. We would be remiss, however, to end the story there, for Paul's vision of God's work is more than personal, more than communal; it is universal and cosmic: "in Christ God was reconciling the world to himself" (2 Cor. 5:19a). To be reconciled to God is to be part of this universal and cosmic activity; it is to experience the "new creation" (5:17).

This new creation refers not merely to the individual believer (so NIV and NAB in 2 Cor. 5:17), but to the great act of re-creation in which individuals participate. As the book of the prophet Isaiah had promised, God would one day renew not only the people of Israel but the whole creation:

> For I am about to create new heavens
>   and a new earth. (Isa. 65:17a; cf. 66:22)

For Paul that new (meaning 'renewed') creation is occurring now, though of course it is still incomplete and will be finished only in the future. The proof that the new creation is under way is the existence of a community of reconciled people, Jews and Gentiles, living in covenantal relationship with God in Christ by the power of the Spirit (cf. Gal. 6:15).

This present life together, then, is part of the greater plan of God, which is to liberate the creation itself from "its bondage to decay" (Rom. 8:21). The community of those in Christ, given the "first fruits of the Spirit" (8:23), is a sign of hope for the cosmos that God will indeed be faithful and will redeem it, too. In the meantime, the experience of believers, especially their suffering and groaning in anticipation of full redemption, is a kind of fellowship of suffering and hope with the created order (8:22-23).

To be part of this fellowship is to know the sufferings of Christ and to be conformed to him in contrast to the surrounding culture, to be comforted and empowered by the Spirit, and to have the hope that the God of Israel, who is the Father of the Lord Jesus, will complete the new creation that has already begun. The church is the fellowship that speaks and lives that personal, communal, and cosmic story.

QUESTIONS FOR REFLECTION

1. How is the term 'spirituality' understood today, both within and outside the church? How is this understanding similar to or different from Paul's?
2. Do you agree that Paul's experience of God is 'trinitarian'? Why is this claim important?
3. How might everyday Christian believers appropriate Paul's notion of 'cruciformity'?
4. The Holy Spirit has sometimes been labeled the 'silent partner' in the Trinity. How might Paul's experience of the Trinity be instructive for the contemporary church?
5. Reflect on the claim that for Paul the Spirit "connects believers both to God's past and to God's future, as well as to God's present."
6. How would Paul respond to the claims made by some that his doctrine of justification by faith makes ethics unimportant?
7. How does the following statement reflect — or not reflect — the realities

of the church today: "the honor the rich and powerful typically bestow on one another has no importance — and no place — in the church"?

8. How ought Paul's 'cosmic' perspective affect Christian spirituality today?

9. What are the implications of thinking of spirituality in narrative terms — the church as telling a story in deeds as well as words?

FOR FURTHER READING AND STUDY

General

Fee, Gordon D. *Paul, the Spirit, and the People of God*. Peabody, Mass.: Hendrickson, 1996. The condensation of key conclusions from *God's Empowering Presence* (see below), with careful attention to the Spirit's identity, activity, and gifts.

Meye, Robert P. "Spirituality." In *Dictionary of Paul and His Letters*, edited by Gerald F. Hawthorne, Ralph P. Martin, and Daniel G. Reid, pp. 906-16. Downers Grove, Ill.: InterVarsity, 1993. A succinct but wide-ranging survey of Paul's understanding of life in the Spirit/in Christ.

Sampley, J. Paul. *Walking between the Times: Paul's Moral Reasoning*. Minneapolis: Fortress, 1991. A basic introduction to Pauline 'ethics' as life between the cross-resurrection and the parousia.

Tobin, Thomas H. *The Spirituality of Paul*. Message of Biblical Spirituality 4. Collegeville, Minn.: Liturgical Press, 1991. A basic but helpful discussion of the major aspects of Paul's spirituality, with attention to Paul's experience of power.

Technical

Dunn, James D. G. *Jesus and the Spirit: A Study of the Religious and Charismatic Experience of Jesus and the First Christians as Reflected in the New Testament*. London: SCM Press, 1975. Reprint, Grand Rapids: Eerdmans, 1997. A groundbreaking study on the experience of the Spirit by both Jesus and Paul.

Fee, Gordon D. *God's Empowering Presence: The Holy Spirit in the Letters of Paul*. Peabody, Mass.: Hendrickson, 1994. A comprehensive exegetical study of the Spirit in Paul, with important theological (including trinitarian) conclusions.

Gorman, Michael J. *Cruciformity: Paul's Narrative Spirituality of the Cross*. Grand Rapids: Eerdmans, 2001. A study of the central role of the cross in Paul's experience of God (Father, Son, and Spirit) and in the life of faith, love, power, and hope.

Schweitzer, Albert. *The Mysticism of Paul the Apostle*. London: Black; New York: H. Holt, 1931. A classic investigation of Paul's religious experience, stressing 'participation in Christ' rather than justification by faith as the central feature of Paul's theology and life.

CHAPTER 6

PAUL'S THEOLOGY

A Dozen Fundamental Convictions

One is sometimes (not often) glad not to be a great theologian; one might so easily mistake it for being a good Christian.

C. S. Lewis[1]

For some people a theologian is someone who writes learned, theoretical tomes and is out of touch with the daily life of real people (and perhaps even with God). Paul was certainly not a theologian in that sense; he was an evangelist, a pastor, a spiritual director, a community builder, a person deeply in communion with God. Thus we have looked first at his gospel and his spirituality before considering his theology, or his 'thoughts' about God. Paul did, however, operate with a set of clear convictions, and he was much more consistent (though always creatively so) in the articulation and application of these convictions than he is often given credit for. His task was to set forth, as clearly and persuasively as possible, the significance of these convictions for himself and his communities. That is precisely what a theologian's true task always has been, as recent theological discussion has suggested in speaking, for example, of the "pastoral function of Christian doctrine."[2] Paul was indeed a theologian in this sense; we might today call him a 'pastoral theologian.'

As a pastoral theologian, Paul was very sensitive to the peculiar circum-

---

1. C. S. Lewis, *Reflections on the Psalms* (New York: Harcourt, Brace and World, 1958), p. 57.

2. See Ellen T. Charry, *By the Renewing of Your Minds: The Pastoral Function of Christian Doctrine* (New York: Oxford University Press, 1997).

stances of his communities. This book proceeds on the assumption that much of what Paul said in his letters was contingent upon the situations that prompted those letters. Furthermore, in developing an understanding of Paul, it is helpful to proceed letter by letter, as we will do in the second part of this book. Nevertheless, it also makes no sense to approach Paul's letters as if he were always 'shooting from the hip,' or as if they had never before been read. It will not harm us — in fact, it will help us — to read his letters through some lenses, that is, with some advance appreciation of his mind.

What follows is a brief description of twelve fundamental Pauline convictions. They are what some would call his basic theological tenets, so we might also refer to them as Paul's 'big ideas.' But even these big ideas are largely narrative statements, or claims made within a narrative framework. They lurk within and behind nearly every text of every page of every letter. Since many have already been mentioned or discussed as aspects of his gospel or his spirituality, they serve not only as an overview but also as a summary, especially of the previous two chapters.

Some may object that searching for consistencies across contingent letters, or within a corpus of letters that may reflect developments in Paul's thought, is inappropriate. But the contingency factor, while very important — as we will see in subsequent chapters — does not eliminate a general coherence to Paul's thought. The same is true for development; although certain situations may have prompted the evolution or fine-tuning of convictions, the evidence of Paul's letters does not suggest (at least not to me) either his general lack of coherence or the 'lateness' of any of the following points, even those most carefully articulated in the (relatively late) letter to the Romans.

Here, then, are Paul's big ideas, or at least the twelve that I find most crucial. (Note: Since these ideas do not always come to expression in one succinct place, the illustrative texts are meant to highlight key dimensions of the topic, not necessarily the topic in its entirety. All texts are chosen from the undisputed letters.)

1. THE COVENANT GOD OF ISRAEL

The one true God who created the world chose and covenanted with Israel to be the people of God and thus the vehicle of divine blessing among the nations (Gentiles). This God is an impartial judge who expects obedience from all people, whether to the Law of Moses or the unwritten law inscribed on the human heart. (The term that some recent scholars [especially E. P. Sanders and James D. G. Dunn] have used to describe Judaism's understanding of its obedience to the law of God within the context of this covenant relationship is 'covenantal nomism.') However, like the prophets, Paul believes that God finds Israel faithless and disobedient, and the Gentiles idolatrous and immoral (Rom. 1:18–3:20). God has therefore planned since the times of the prophets to effect a new covenant with Israel (Jer. 31:31-34; cf. 2 Cor. 3:6), and thus with and for all the nations.

Illustrative texts:

For us there is one God, the Father, from whom are all things and for whom we exist, and one Lord, Jesus Christ, through whom are all things and through whom we exist. (1 Cor. 8:6)

Or is God the God of Jews only? Is he not the God of Gentiles also? Yes, of Gentiles also, since God is one. (Rom. 3:29-30a)

There will be anguish and distress for everyone who does evil, the Jew first and also the Greek, but glory and honor and peace for everyone who does good, the Jew first and also the Greek. For God shows no partiality. All who have sinned apart from the law will also perish apart from the law, and all who have sinned under the law will be judged by the law. For it is not the hearers of the law who are righteous in God's sight, but the doers of the law who will be justified. (Rom. 2:9-13)

And the scripture, foreseeing that God would justify the Gentiles by faith, declared the gospel beforehand to Abraham, saying, "All the Gentiles shall be blessed in you." (Gal. 3:8)

2. THE POWER OF SIN AND THE POWERLESSNESS OF THE LAW

Paul believes that the fundamental human problem, experienced by Jews and Gentiles alike, is not merely sins (plural) but sin (singular). Sin operates as a kind of power within and upon the human race. It manifests itself in sins, or inappropriate ways of relating both to God (idolatry rather than faith) and to other humans (immorality and injustice rather than love). Being under the power of sin is like having an addiction; addicts are enslaved to their addiction as if to a master. Human beings are thus *covenantally* (morally and spiritually) *dysfunctional.* Since the human problem is both sin and sins, human beings need a solution that deals with both — liberation or redemption from sin, and forgiveness for sins — and that restores them to appropriate relations with both God (faith) and others (love). The Law of Moses, despite its positive value, cannot deliver people from sin or effect righteousness and life.

Illustrative texts:

Is the law then opposed to the promises of God? Certainly not! For if a law had been given that could make alive, then righteousness would indeed come through the law. But the scripture has imprisoned all things under the power of sin, so that what was promised through the faith of Jesus Christ [NRSV mg.; NRSV, "faith in"] might be given to those who believe.

(Gal. 3:21-22, NRSV, altered)

We have already charged that all, both Jews and Greeks, are under the power of sin. (Rom. 3:9)

For God has done what the law, weakened by the flesh, could not do.

(Rom. 8:3a)

3. THE RIGHTEOUSNESS OF GOD: FAITHFULNESS TO ISRAEL AND MERCY TO THE GENTILES

This phrase, "the righteousness of God," has been interpreted in a variety of ways, but it is probably best understood primarily as God's covenant faithfulness and saving power. (Some argue for one of these two against the other, but it is impossible for Paul to separate them; see Romans 1:16-17.) For Paul, God manifests faithfulness in the face of human (Gentile as well as Jewish) faithlessness, particularly in the sending of the Son to effect salvation — to die for humanity's sins and to liberate humanity (Gentile and Jew alike) from sin. In so doing God keeps the promise made to Abraham that through him all the nations would be blessed.

Illustrative texts:

What if some were unfaithful? Will their faithlessness nullify the faithfulness of God? By no means! (Rom. 3:3-4a)

But now, apart from law, the righteousness of God has been disclosed, and is attested by the law and the prophets, the righteousness of God through the faith of Jesus Christ [NRSV mg.; NRSV, "faith in"] for all who believe. For there is no distinction [between Jew and Gentile], since all have sinned and fall short of the glory of God; they are now justified by his grace as a gift, through the redemption that is in Christ Jesus, whom God put forward as a sacrifice of atonement by his blood, effective through faith. He did this to show his righteousness, because in his divine forbearance he had passed over the sins previously committed; it was to prove at the present time that he himself is righteous and that he justifies the one who has the faith of [NRSV mg.; NRSV, "has faith in"] Jesus.   (Rom. 3:21-26, NRSV, altered)

And if you belong to Christ, then you are Abraham's offspring, heirs according to the promise.   (Gal. 3:29)

4. THE REVELATORY, REPRESENTATIVE, AND RECONCILING CRUCIFIXION OF JESUS THE MESSIAH

For Paul, the death by crucifixion of Jesus the Messiah has a rich, polyvalent, almost inexhaustible significance. Three of the most important dimensions of this death need to be constantly recalled. (a) Jesus' death on the cross *reveals* the faithfulness, love, and (paradoxically) power of God. (b) As Messiah, Jesus dies as the faithful, obedient *representative* of Israel, God's covenant people, and also as the representative of all human beings; he is a kind of second Adam whose actions contrast with and counteract those of Adam (Rom. 5:12-21). His death is the quintessential covenantal Jewish and human act of faith toward God and love toward others. (c) This death, as an act of both God and God's Messiah, brings about human *reconciliation* with God: forgiveness for sins and redemption from sin.

Illustrative texts:

For Jews demand signs and Greeks desire wisdom, but we proclaim Christ crucified, a stumbling block to Jews and foolishness to Gentiles, but to those who are the called, both Jews and Greeks, Christ the power of God and the wisdom of God. For God's foolishness is wiser than human wisdom, and God's weakness is stronger than human strength.   (1 Cor. 1:22-25)

God proves his love for us in that while we still were sinners Christ died for us.   (Rom. 5:8)

But the free gift is not like the trespass. For if the many died through the one man's trespass, much more surely have the grace of God and the free gift in the grace of the one man, Jesus Christ, abounded for the many.   (Rom. 5:15)

The Son of God . . . loved me and gave himself for me.   (Gal. 2:20)

We are convinced that one has died for all; therefore all have died. . . . In Christ God was reconciling the world to himself, not counting their trespasses against them.   (2 Cor. 5:14b, 19)

5. THE LORDSHIP OF JESUS

It is virtually certain, despite some scholarly objections, that Paul affirms the preexistence and divine status of Jesus (Gal. 4:4; Rom. 8:3; Phil. 2:6). But when he speaks of Jesus as Lord, he is thinking primarily of the exalted status bestowed on Jesus as a consequence of his obedient, faithful, human death. God's resurrection and exaltation vindicate the crucified Jesus as indeed the Messiah of Israel and Lord of all. If Jesus is Lord, then Caesar is not, and neither is any other Greco-Roman deity. As "Lord," Jesus shares in the honor otherwise due only to God (compare Phil. 2:9-11 with Isa. 45:23). Therefore he is to be not only confessed but also obeyed; those who live "in him" live within the sphere of his beneficent, grace-filled sovereignty.

Illustrative texts:

Therefore I want you to understand that no one speaking by the Spirit of God ever says "Let Jesus be cursed!" and no one can say "Jesus is Lord" except by the Holy Spirit.   (1 Cor. 12:3)

Therefore God also highly exalted him
 and gave him the name
 that is above every name,
so that at the name of Jesus
 every knee should bend,
 in heaven and on earth and under the earth,
and every tongue should confess
 that Jesus Christ is Lord,
 to the glory of God the Father.   (Phil. 2:9-11)

6. THE CLIMAX OF THE COVENANT
AND THE OVERLAP OF THE AGES[3]

Paul believes that in Christ, all the promises of God are fulfilled, are "Yes" (2 Cor. 1:20). The new covenant, promised by the prophets for the last days, has been established through the coming, death, and resurrection of Jesus. Thus Christ becomes for Paul the lens through which he reads the Scriptures of Israel. Christ is indeed the goal, the focus of the Law (Rom. 10:4), and of the Prophets and Writings as well. His coming and death mean that the 'new age' or 'new creation' that Judaism anticipated has been inaugurated, even as 'this age' continues. The new covenant communities of believers, then, exist during the 'overlap' of the two ages. This is an 'in-between' time, during which believers live a bifocal existence, with one eye on the past (Christ's death and resurrection) and the other on the future (Christ's return and our resurrection). The following graphic represents this basic Pauline perspective, which is a revision of the typical Jewish apocalyptic view of the linear procession of the two ages from this (present) age to the (future) age to come:

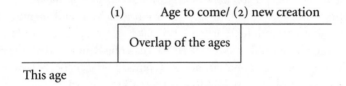

(1)   Age to come/ (2) new creation

Overlap of the ages

This age

Here (1) represents the first coming of Christ ('incarnation,' death, and resurrection) and (2) represents his 'second coming,' or parousia, and believers' resurrection, at which time the new age arrives in its fullness (see also #12 below).

Illustrative texts:

For in him [the Son of God, Jesus Christ] every one of God's promises is a "Yes." For this reason it is through him that we say the "Amen," to the glory of God.   (2 Cor. 1:20)

These things happened to them to serve as an example, and they were written down to instruct us, on whom the overlapping of the ages has arrived.
                                                      (1 Cor. 10:11, author's translation)

---

3. The very helpful summary phrase "the climax of the covenant" comes from N. T. Wright's book, *The Climax of the Covenant: Christ and the Law in Pauline Theology* (Edinburgh: T. & T. Clark, 1991; Minneapolis: Fortress, 1993).

If anyone is in Christ, there is a new creation: everything old has passed away; see, everything has become new! (2 Cor. 5:17)

In the same way he [Jesus] took the cup also, after supper, saying, "This cup is the new covenant in my blood. Do this, as often as you drink it, in remembrance of me." (1 Cor. 11:25)

7. JUSTIFICATION BY GRACE THROUGH FAITH

The term 'justification' is part of the same word family as the word 'righteousness' (Gk. *dikaiosynē*). As used by Paul, this rich term draws on three primary spheres of meaning for its significance: (a) God's character and activity (righteousness, holiness, fidelity, salvation); (b) the covenant (the expectation of just or righteous conduct); and (c) the law court (the notion of a verdict of acquittal). Justification for Paul may be defined as follows: *the establishment or restoration of right covenantal relations with God, including fidelity to God and love for neighbor, with the certain hope of acquittal on the day of judgment.*

Justification, then, is about reconciliation with God and membership in God's covenant community. For Paul, this takes place by God's initiative and grace, to which humans respond in faith — trust, obedience, and public confession. Faith is not merely a onetime act of response to the gospel but an ongoing covenantal relationship with God that is itself a kind of crucifixion and resurrection, so that the covenantal obligations can now be fulfilled.

Illustrative texts:

. . . not having a righteousness of my own that comes from the law, but one that comes through faith in [or "the faith of"] Christ, the righteousness from God based on faith. (Phil. 3:9)

We hold that a person is justified by faith apart from works prescribed by the law. Or is God the God of Jews only? Is he not the God of Gentiles also? Yes, of Gentiles also, since God is one; and he will justify the circumcised on the ground of faith and the uncircumcised through that same faith. (Rom. 3:28-30)

Therefore, since we are justified by faith, we have peace with God through our Lord Jesus Christ, through whom we have obtained access to this grace in which we stand. (Rom. 5:1-2a)

So you also must consider yourselves dead to sin and alive to God in Christ Jesus. (Rom. 6:11)

By sending his own Son in the likeness of sinful flesh, and to deal with sin, he [God] condemned sin in the flesh, so that the just requirement of the law might be fulfilled in us, who walk not according to the flesh but according to the Spirit. (Rom. 8:3b-4)

8. THE TRINITARIAN EXPERIENCE OF GOD

It has been out of fashion in some circles to use the words 'Trinity' and 'Paul' in the same sentence, though that has been changing of late. There can be little doubt, however, that Paul's experience of God can best be described as trinitarian — he knows one God in three realities: Abba/Father, Messiah/Son of God/ Lord Jesus, and Holy Spirit/Spirit of God/Spirit of Christ.[4] Believers know and are known by God the Father, who has adopted them. They live "in" the crucified but now exalted Christ, who also lives in them. They are empowered to live in Christ, as God's children, by the Spirit.

Illustrative texts:

And because you are children, God has sent the Spirit of his Son into our hearts, crying, "Abba! Father!" (Gal. 4:6)

Now there are varieties of gifts, but the same Spirit; and there are varieties of services, but the same Lord; and there are varieties of activities, but it is the same God who activates all of them in everyone. (1 Cor. 12:4-6)

The grace of the Lord Jesus Christ, the love of God, and the communion of the Holy Spirit be with all of you. (2 Cor. 13:13)

But you are not in the flesh; you are in the Spirit, since the Spirit of God dwells in you. Anyone who does not have the Spirit of Christ does not belong to him. But if Christ is in you, though the body is dead because of sin, the Spirit is life because of righteousness. If the Spirit of him who raised Jesus from the dead dwells in you, he who raised Christ from the dead will give life to your mortal bodies also through his Spirit that dwells in you. (Rom. 8:9-11)

4. As in previous and subsequent chapters, trinitarian language is used here in recognition that although Paul does not have a fully developed theology of the Trinity, such language is nonetheless appropriate.

9. CRUCIFORMITY, OR THE LAW OF CHRIST

For Paul the death of Jesus is not only revelatory, representative, and redemptive, as noted above (#4), but also paradigmatic. The essence of believing existence is conformity to the crucified Christ, or cruciformity. Though cruciformity may involve suffering, it is much more comprehensive than that. Paul twice refers to it as the "law of Christ," or the narrative pattern of the crucified Messiah (Gal. 6:2; 1 Cor. 9:21). This narrative pattern refers specifically to the kind of "faith working through love" (Gal. 5:6) that is rooted in the cross, where the Son of God expressed his faith (faithfulness, obedience) by giving himself in love (2:19-20). He did not seek his own welfare but that of others, as Paul's master story tells it (Phil. 2:1-11). This is the pattern of life for all believers: faith toward God, love toward others. Faith oriented toward the future is hope; thus Paul summarizes believing existence as a life of faith, hope, and love.

Illustrative texts:

Through the Spirit, by faith, we eagerly wait for the hope of righteousness. For in Christ Jesus neither circumcision nor uncircumcision counts for anything; the only thing that counts is faith working through love. . . . Bear one another's burdens, and in this way you will fulfill the law of Christ.

(Gal. 5:5-6; 6:2)

If then there is any encouragement in Christ, any consolation from love, any sharing in the Spirit, any compassion and sympathy, make my joy complete: be of the same mind, having the same love, being in full accord and of one mind. Do nothing from selfish ambition or conceit, but in humility regard others as better than yourselves. Let each of you look not to your own interests, but to the interests of others. Let the same mind be in you that was in Christ Jesus,

who, though he was in the form of God,
    did not regard equality with God
    as something to be exploited,
but emptied himself,
    taking the form of a slave,
    being born in human likeness.
And being found in human form,
    he humbled himself
    and became obedient to the point of death —
    even death on a cross.   (Phil. 2:1-8)

I want to know Christ and the power of his resurrection and the sharing of his sufferings by becoming like him in his death, if somehow I may attain the resurrection from the dead. (Phil. 3:10-11)

We always give thanks to God for all of you and mention you in our prayers, constantly remembering before our God and Father your work of faith and labor of love and steadfastness of hope in our Lord Jesus Christ.

(1 Thess. 1:2-3)

10. THE SPIRIT AS PROMISE FULFILLED AND HOPE GUARANTEED

For Paul the outpouring of God's Spirit promised by the prophets for the last days, which would renew Israel and bring the nations to Zion, has occurred. He especially sees the Gentiles' experience of the Spirit as proof that the new age has begun and as promise that it will be consummated in the near future. All believers possess, and are to be guided by, the Spirit.

Illustrative texts:

Christ redeemed us from the curse of the law by becoming a curse for us — for it is written, "Cursed is everyone who hangs on a tree" — in order that in Christ Jesus the blessing of Abraham might come to the Gentiles, so that we might receive the promise of the Spirit through faith. (Gal. 3:13-14)

He who has prepared us for this very thing [life with God beyond death] is God, who has given us the Spirit as a guarantee. (2 Cor. 5:5)

11. THE CHURCH AS ALTERNATIVE COMMUNITY

Paul's vision of the church is of a covenant community of Jews and Gentiles, one set apart and "holy," or distinct from its host culture. It thereby exists in continuity with Israel and in contrast to the pagan Roman Empire and all its religious and social subcultures. Within the church there is to be an ethos of harmony, humility, and above all love — not only toward siblings in the faith but toward outsiders and enemies as well.

Illustrative texts:

Do you not know that wrongdoers will not inherit the kingdom of God? Do not be deceived! Fornicators, idolaters, adulterers, male prostitutes, sodomites, thieves, the greedy, drunkards, revilers, robbers — none of these will inherit the kingdom of God. And this is what some of you used to be. But you were washed, you were sanctified, you were justified in the name of the Lord Jesus Christ and in the Spirit of our God. (1 Cor. 6:9-11)

For this is the will of God, your sanctification: that you abstain from fornication; that each one of you know how to control your own body in holiness and honor, not with lustful passion, like the Gentiles who do not know God. (1 Thess. 4:3-5)

For just as the body is one and has many members, and all the members of the body, though many, are one body, so it is with Christ. (1 Cor. 12:12)

But our citizenship is in heaven, and it is from there that we are expecting a Savior, the Lord Jesus Christ. (Phil. 3:20)

We urge you, beloved, to admonish the idlers, encourage the faint hearted, help the weak, be patient with all of them. See that none of you repays evil for evil, but always seek to do good to one another and to all. Rejoice always, pray without ceasing, give thanks in all circumstances; for this is the will of God in Christ Jesus for you. (1 Thess. 5:14-18)

12. THE PAROUSIA, THE RESURRECTION, AND THE FINAL TRIUMPH OF GOD

As an apocalyptic Jew and a Pharisee, Paul found in the resurrection of the Messiah the beginning of the age-to-come, the invasion of the future into the present. Just as Christ was the representative human in his death, so also was he in his resurrection. Specifically, Paul found in Christ the "first fruits" (1 Cor. 15:20) of the general resurrection, the guarantee of bodily resurrection for all who are in him and share in his cruciform life, as well as the assurance of God's final defeat of sin and death and of the restoration of the entire cosmos. In that restoration God will "be all in all" (1 Cor. 15:28), and the divine intention for this cosmos will be fulfilled.

Illustrative texts:

I want to know Christ and the power of his resurrection and the sharing of his sufferings by becoming like him in his death, if somehow I may attain the resurrection from the dead. (Phil. 3:10-11)

The Lord himself, with a cry of command, with the archangel's call and with the sound of God's trumpet, will descend from heaven, and the dead in Christ will rise first. Then we who are alive, who are left, will be caught up in the clouds together with them to meet the Lord in the air; and so we will be with the Lord forever. (1 Thess. 4:16-17)

But in fact Christ has been raised from the dead, the first fruits of those who have died. For since death came through a human being, the resurrection of the dead has also come through a human being; for as all die in Adam, so all will be made alive in Christ. But each in his own order: Christ the first fruits, then at his coming those who belong to Christ. Then comes the end, when he hands over the kingdom to God the Father, after he has destroyed every ruler and every authority and power. For he must reign until he has put all his enemies under his feet. The last enemy to be destroyed is death. For "God has put all things in subjection under his feet." . . . When all things are subjected to him, then the Son himself will also be subjected to the one who put all things in subjection under him, so that God may be all in all. (1 Cor. 15:20-28)

I consider that the sufferings of this present time are not worth comparing with the glory about to be revealed to us. For the creation waits with eager longing for the revealing of the children of God; for the creation was subjected to futility, not of its own will but by the will of the one who subjected it, in hope that the creation itself will be set free from its bondage to decay and will obtain the freedom of the glory of the children of God. (Rom. 8:18-21)

Although these twelve points are hardly arbitrary, others might shorten the list, stress one aspect over against another, and delete or add certain topics. Even this list could be abbreviated to three overarching and interrelated themes: *covenant, cruciformity,* and *community.*

Whether three or twelve in number, and whatever specific 'big ideas' are enumerated, they must not be separated from Paul's mission, the mission noted in chapter 2: *to create a network of multicultural communities obeying and glorifying the one true God of Israel by living lives of cruciform faith, hope, and love in Christ Jesus the Lord by the power of the Spirit.* Paul's theology expresses and informs that mission; his letters are not deposits of ideas but instruments of his mission.

Before we turn to those letters themselves, we need briefly to address a question that crosses many people's minds and is answered in the twelve points listed above, though not explicitly. The question is, What did Paul think was wrong with Judaism? This is, however, the wrong question. For Paul there is nothing wrong with Judaism. But there is something wrong with *humanity* — Gentiles and Jews, males and females, slave and free — and only the Jewish God, acting in the Jewish Messiah and through the Spirit of the Jewish God and his Messiah, can fix the problem. In fact, Judaism is for Paul the solution — only it is a restored, renewed, inclusive, eschatological, messianic Judaism.[5] His letters attest to this solution and to its embodiment in real people and communities.

As noted in chapter 3, we proceed now to the letters according to the sequence (as I understand it) in which they were most likely written: 1 Thessalonians, 2 Thessalonians, Galatians, 1 Corinthians, 2 Corinthians, Romans, Philippians, Philemon, Colossians, Ephesians, 2 Timothy, 1 Timothy, and Titus. Scholars disagree about this order, and it is of course possible to read the following chapters out of the order in which they are presented.

QUESTIONS FOR REFLECTION

1. In what sense is it appropriate to speak of Paul as a 'theologian'? Are there limits to, or problems with, that label? If Paul has been rightly understood as a theologian, how should that affect our understanding of the theological task?

2. With which 'big ideas' has Paul been associated in your experience and, as far as you know, in the history of the church? Are they similar to or different from those discussed in this chapter?

3. Which of Paul's big ideas do you find most compelling for the church to grasp or grapple with at this time?

4. One of Paul's big ideas that weaves throughout the list is 'covenant.' Why is this notion significant for understanding Paul? for understanding ourselves as Christians?

5. What significance — both for understanding Paul and for doing theology today — do you attach to the fact that Paul's theology has a narrative character?

6. What 'big ideas' operate within the church today as you have experienced it? What might Paul say about these ideas?

---

5. As we will see in our discussion of Galatians, Paul's apparent disassociation from his past life in "Judaism" (Gal. 1:13-14) is in fact an affirmation of his ongoing ministry on behalf of the Jewish God who has acted to bless and unite both Jews and Gentiles.

FOR FURTHER READING AND STUDY

General

Beker, J. Christiaan. *The Triumph of God: The Essence of Paul's Thought.* Minneapolis: Fortress, 1990. A distillation of Beker's larger classic (see below).

Cousar, Charles B. *The Letters of Paul.* Interpreting Biblical Texts. Nashville: Abingdon, 1996. A helpful introduction to Paul's letters and churches followed by a half-dozen succinct, insightful chapters on key theological themes.

―――. *A Theology of the Cross: The Death of Jesus in the Pauline Letters.* Minneapolis: Fortress, 1990. An insightful study of the central role of Jesus' death in various aspects of Paul's theology.

Fitzmyer, Joseph A. *Paul and His Theology: A Brief Sketch.* Englewood Cliffs, N.J.: Prentice Hall, 1989. A classic, compact, but comprehensive analysis. Also printed as chapters 79 and 82 in *The New Jerome Biblical Commentary.*

Wright, N. T. *What Saint Paul Really Said: Was Paul of Tarsus the Real Founder of Christianity?* Grand Rapids: Eerdmans, 1997. A brief but lucid introduction stressing the Jewishness of Paul's gospel, mission, and theology.

Ziesler, J. A. *Pauline Christianity.* Rev. ed. New York: Oxford University Press, 1990. A general, helpful overview of Paul's theology.

Technical

Beker, J. Christiaan. *Paul the Apostle: The Triumph of God in Life and Thought.* Philadelphia: Fortress, 1980. A modern classic emphasizing the apocalyptic and theocentric nature of Paul's gospel in its coherence, or unity, as well as its contingencies, or diverse expression.

Dunn, James D. G. *The Theology of the Apostle Paul.* Grand Rapids: Eerdmans, 1998. A massive, comprehensive study by one of the world's leading experts, organized principally around the structure of Romans.

Sanders, E. P. *Paul and Palestinian Judaism.* Philadelphia: Fortress, 1983. A classic exploration of Paul that revolutionized the study of both Paul and Second Temple Judaism by focusing on Judaism's 'covenantal nomism' and Paul's participation in Christ.

Tamez, Elsa. *The Amnesty of Grace: Justification by Faith from a Latin American Perspective.* Translated by Sharon H. Ringe. Nashville: Abingdon, 1993. A provocative perspective from a liberation theologian, stressing the political and humanizing character of Paul's theology.

Witherington, Ben, III. *Paul's Narrative Thought World.* Louisville: Westminster John Knox, 1994. An interpretation of Paul's theology with emphasis on its narrative character.

Wright, N. T. *The Climax of the Covenant: Christ and the Law in Pauline Theology.* Minneapolis: Fortress, 1992. A collection of significant, carefully argued exegetical essays.

CHAPTER 7

1 THESSALONIANS

Holiness and Hope in a Pagan World

And may he [the Lord] so strengthen your hearts in holiness that you may be blameless before our God and Father at the coming of our Lord Jesus with all his saints.

1 Thess. 3:13

A superficial reading of 1 Thessalonians might suggest that this letter is rather innocuous, but in fact it packs quite a powerful punch. In all likelihood it is Paul's earliest surviving letter (and thus probably the earliest New Testament document), revealing much about his understanding of the gospel for Gentiles even before the great controversy associated with Galatians. In it Paul reminds the Thessalonian believers of the past effects, the present demands, and the future promises of the gospel among them, despite various forms of opposition to both Paul and the young church. In sum, Paul writes about eschatology and ethics, about holiness and hope in a pagan world.

THE STORY BEHIND THE LETTER

THE CITY

The walled city of Thessalonica (modern Thessaloníki, the second-largest city in Greece) was named for Alexander the Great's half sister, Thessaloniki. The

Thessalonica: The second-century two-level Roman agora
which was likely similar to what Paul encountered

city has been in continuous existence at the same location since 316 B.C.; its Roman ruins, unlike those of Philippi or Corinth, are located among and under modern buildings. The capital of the Roman province of Macedonia in northern Greece, it was a natural port city — the only one on the Via Egnatia — of considerable size and economic and political importance. Although Thessalonica was a free city (not a Roman colony, as was Philippi, about 120 miles to the northeast) that had an independent government and maintained its Greek heritage, it was still a center of the imperial cult. And it was also the site, naturally, of many temples to a wide variety of deities, including Isis, Osiris/Serapis, Dionysus, and Cabirus (a god of fertility and protection at sea). Moreover, on a clear day one could (and can) see Mount Olympus, the abode of the gods, rising high into the heavens across the harbor. Reminders of the idols from which the Thessalonians would be called to turn (cf. 1:9) were everywhere.

MISSION AND PERSECUTION

According to Acts 17:1-9, Paul, Silas (Silvanus), and Timothy (implied by 16:1-3; 17:14-15) founded the Thessalonian church during the second (as Acts presents

Map of the province of Macedonia in the first century

it) missionary journey. The visit followed a very difficult experience at Philippi that included flogging and imprisonment (Acts 16:11-40; 1 Thess. 2:2). The brief Acts account is fascinating in several ways. It depicts Paul as preaching in the synagogue but finding most of his converts among non-Jews: "a great many of the devout Greeks [God-fearers?] and not a few of the leading women" (17:4). Paul's preaching of a Jewish Messiah who had to suffer and rise from the dead, identified as Jesus, was interpreted as "turning the world upside down . . . acting contrary to the decrees of the emperor, saying that there is another king [or, better, 'emperor'] named Jesus" (17:6b-7). It led first to mob action instigated by

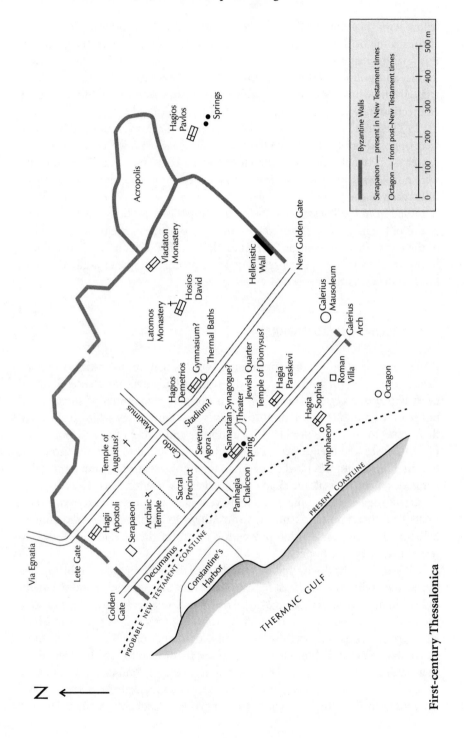

First-century Thessalonica

fellow Jews (beginning in the marketplaces) and then to official proceedings against some of the believers (17:6-7). Clearly, according to Acts, the gospel of this Jewish apostle and his Jewish Messiah was an assault on the religious, economic, and political status quo. During Paul's short visit (only three weeks if 17:2 tells the whole story, but probably longer), someone had rightly made the connection between crucified Messiah and reigning Lord.

1 Thessalonians itself echoes elements of this narrative. Paul and his team were opposed (2:2; 3:4) but nonetheless preached the word with conviction and power — probably meaning miracles of some sort (1:5). The Thessalonians were non-Jews (or mostly non-Jews) who turned from their idols (1:9) and joyfully received the gospel despite persecution (1:6; 2:14). This persecution likely stemmed from the Thessalonian believers' (implicit or explicit) rejection of the claims of the imperial cult, and their refusal to continue participating in the life of the city's cults and collegia. The Thessalonians had become a social and political irritant to their pagan peers, but an inspiring example of faith, love, and hope to believers throughout Greece (1:3, 7-9).

AFFECTION AND CONCERN

Paul's deep affection for this community, which began in the initial visit, permeates the letter (in which he calls the readers "brothers [and sisters]" once every half-dozen verses). He and his team worked "night and day" so as not to burden the church (2:9). With pure motives, he claims, they selflessly devoted themselves to the Thessalonians, like a mother and father (2:1-12). Upon leaving for Beroea and then Athens, Paul desperately wanted to visit his "crown of boasting" again but was blocked by Satan (2:17-20). Meanwhile, apparently, the persecutions in Thessalonica had continued and worsened (3:3). The concerns of 4:13-18 suggest that some of the believers may have been martyred. Eventually Paul therefore sent Timothy from Athens to check on the Thessalonian believers. Had the persecution proven too much for them? Had they forsaken Jesus? Had they lost hope?

What Timothy discovered was good news: the believers were enduring the persecution with such steadfast faith and love that they were an encouragement to Paul in his own sufferings (3:6-10). The Thessalonians also loved and missed their spiritual parent (3:6), though the tone of chapter 2 suggests that some had likely grown critical of the apostle, perhaps for abandoning them in their time of trouble. Now Paul himself wanted to see them face-to-face to strengthen their faith still further (3:10). Until that time, however, Paul could do but two things: pray for them (3:10-13) and send a letter as a substitute for his visit. Having settled in Corinth for a while (Acts 18:1), Paul probably wrote 1 Thessalonians from there, most likely in 50 or 51.[1] The purpose of the letter was, in fact, to be an answer to Paul's own prayer — to strengthen the Thessalonian believers with reassurance and instruction.

THE STORY WITHIN THE LETTER

The purpose and theme of 1 Thessalonians appear twice in the letter, at the end of the long prayerful introduction and in the benediction at the end of the letter:

> And may he [the Lord] so strengthen your hearts in holiness that you may be blameless before our God and Father at the coming of our Lord Jesus with all his saints. (3:13)

> May the God of peace himself sanctify you entirely; and may your spirit and soul and body be kept sound and blameless at the coming of our Lord Jesus Christ. (5:23)

That is to say, the sure hope of the Lord's coming provides the context within which the countercultural ('holy,' 'sanctified,' or 'set apart') life of faith and love that has led to persecution makes sense. Hope makes holiness worthwhile.

To accomplish this purpose, the letter weaves together the stories of the crucified, risen, and coming Lord Jesus; the cruciform apostolic team headed by Paul; and the persecuted Thessalonians. The two stories of the past coming of Paul to the Thessalonians and the future coming of Jesus surround a series of basic teachings on "the will of God, your sanctification" (4:3). In other words, 1 Thessalonians, in the language of the summary of the gospel preserved in 1:9-10, is about what it means to have "turned to God from idols" in response to Paul's preaching (chaps. 1–3), and "to serve a living and true God, and to wait for his Son from heaven" (chaps. 4–5).

The bulk of the letter therefore takes the form of an extended thanksgiving (with details of the story) for the arrival and persistence of the gospel in Thessalonica, followed by a section of parenesis, or instruction. We may therefore outline it as follows:

---

1. There is some scholarly discussion suggesting a later date for 1 Thessalonians as a follow-up to a later visit to Thessalonica (Acts 20:1-2 has Paul in Macedonia for some time), but this is a minority view.

1:1   Opening
1:2–3:13 Thanksgiving — Turning to God: Paul, the Thessalonians, and the
          Gospel
          1:2-10   The Authenticity of the Thessalonians' Conversion
          2:1-12   The Authenticity of Paul's Ministry
          2:13-16   The Common Bond of Suffering
          2:17–3:13 Timothy's Visit: Absence, Concern, and Reassurance
4:1–5:11 Instructions — Serving God and Waiting for the Son
          4:1-12   Serving God: The Call to Holiness
                     4:1-3a   The Call
                     4:3b-8   Sexual Purity
                     4:9-12   Love for One Another and Relations outside
                              the Community
          4:13–5:11 Waiting for the Son: Eschatological Hope and Chal-
                     lenge
                     4:13-18 Hope for the Dead
                     5:1-11   Challenge to the Living
5:12-28   Closing Exhortations and Final Matters

Summaries are provided for chapters 1–3 and 4–5.

1:1. OPENING

The very brief, unornamented opening is noteworthy only for two things. First, it identifies three authors, and although Paul is clearly the principal writer (note "I" in 2:18–3:5), the use of first-person-plural language ("we/us/our") throughout most of the letter indicates the ongoing concern and involvement of Silvanus and Timothy, as Paul's esteemed colleagues. The presence of their names is not merely a rhetorical device. (To avoid awkwardness, however, we will generally refer to Paul as the writer, bearing in mind the inclusive meaning of his authorship.)

Second, the opening identifies the church as being "in" not only Christ (a common Pauline idea) but also God the Father. This pair corresponds to the summary of Paul's gospel in 1:9-10 and of God's guidance in 3:11. The role of the Spirit, though not mentioned in either of these places, is still prominent in the letter (1:5-6; 4:8; 5:19). The Thessalonians' experience of God and the gospel is trinitarian in character.[2]

---

2. As in earlier chapters, trinitarian language is used here in recognition that although Paul does not have a fully developed theology of the Trinity, such language is nonetheless appropriate.

1:2–3:13. THANKSGIVING — TURNING TO GOD: PAUL, THE THESSALONIANS, AND THE GOSPEL

After the very brief opening, the letter launches into a prayer of thanks (1:2) that quickly becomes a telling of (and apologia for) the story of Paul and the Thessalonians. The thanksgiving continues explicitly in 2:13 and again in 3:9, as the language of prayer reappears to conclude this first major section of the letter (3:9-13). Throughout these first three chapters the mood is one of thanksgiving as Paul rejoices in the Thessalonians' conversion and especially in their persistence despite persecution. It is best, therefore, to consider the entire narrative as part of one long prayer. The historical review gives substance to the apologia and reinforces the mutual esteem between Paul's team and the Thessalonians for which Paul gives thanks.

THE AUTHENTICITY OF THE THESSALONIANS' CONVERSION (1:2-10)

The thanksgiving begins with a brief but comprehensive narrative of the Thessalonians' conversion. In noting his constant gratitude (1:2-3) and acknowledging God's gracious choice of the Thessalonian believers, Paul provides a summary of the gospel he preached and highlights several key aspects of the Thessalonians' initial and continuing response. Before looking at that response, we begin with the gospel summary.

As we have already noted, 1:9-10 summarizes Paul's gospel, though the language and careful structure suggest that it may come from an early creed. The gospel summons pagans to do three things: (1) to turn from idols, (2) to serve the (one) living and true God, and (3) to wait for God's Son from heaven. This means the message was about the one God of Israel and about the Son of God (that is, the Messiah) who delivers those who turn to God from the future divine wrath. Thus the message is apocalyptic, but it is also christocentric. The narrative of Jesus is compact; there is no mention of his death, though it may be hinted at in the reference to "rescue" (see also 4:14, "died and rose again") and is alluded to in the earlier reference to imitating the Lord through suffering (1:6; also 2:7-8 [see below] and 2:15). But other parts of the story of Jesus are named: his being raised by God, his exaltation to heaven, and his return from heaven. The import of these may be summed up in the title "Lord" (see 1:1, 3, 6, 8).

The Thessalonians' response to the good news, which Paul and his team preached with "power," "conviction," and integrity (1:5), was joyful (1:6) as they turned from idols to God. Paul describes their conversion as three-dimensional: it consisted of faith, love, and hope (1:3; cf. 5:8). This Pauline triad, made famous by 1 Corinthians 13:13 (where the order is faith, hope, love), re-appears in the same order in 5:8; the letter's focus on the final item, hope, is quite clear. Not only is the Thessalonians' conversion three-dimensional in this sense, but also in a sense that can only adequately be called trinitarian: an experience of God the Father (1:1, 3, 8-9), Jesus the Son/Messiah and Lord (1:1, 3, 6, 8, 10), and the Holy Spirit (1:5-6). They relate to God the Father as the one who chose and loves them, to Jesus as the Lord who rescues them and whom they obey and imitate, and to the Holy Spirit as the one who empowers preachers and inspires those who hear.

The Thessalonians' response to Paul's message was clearly very positive despite persecution (1:6), which may have involved ostracism, mob activity, legal proceedings, and even killings. For this reason — faith in the midst of persecution — the Thessalonians have a well-deserved and widespread reputation of which Paul is quite proud (1:8).

THE AUTHENTICITY OF PAUL'S MINISTRY (2:1-12)

Already in the first few verses the issue of the integrity of Paul's ministry team had been raised (1:5). Now it is addressed head-on. If the gospel was so successful, how could those who delivered it be anything but authentic messengers of God? Paul's words in these verses suggest that some at Thessalonica may have questioned his motives. They may have associated him with certain kinds of wandering teachers, including some Cynics, who preyed on gullible people for financial gain. Paul both rebuffs the false charges and portrays his team's work in three positive images: maternal, paternal, and christological. Not only were they ideal self-giving teachers, but they were imitators of the Lord Jesus. Paul's intention here is probably twofold: to commend (or even defend) his team's ministry and to offer it as an example of Christlike faithfulness and love.

Paul first reminds his readers that his team's previous suffering in Philippi should have been sufficient to discount any charge of base motives (2:1-3). With God as both authorizer of and witness to their ministry, Paul assures the Thessalonians that he and his partners sought neither human approval of, nor financial gain from, their ministry (2:4-6). Moreover, not only did they not take from the Thessalonians, they gave to the utmost — in spite of possessing apostolic privileges (2:7-12).

Here Paul describes the ministry of apostles with three very important images of self-giving that reveal much about his self-understanding. Because the word "apostle" implies authority, one might conclude that apostles could 'throw their weight around' (the idiom in 2:7a that the NRSV translates "might have made demands"; cf. NAB, "impose our weight").[3] In fact, as Paul says in 1 Corinthians 9, apostles do have the right to financial support. Instead, in faithfulness to the gospel and out of love for the Thessalonians, Paul, Silvanus, and Timothy did not exercise their apostolic right but rather poured themselves (literally, their own "souls") out to their dear children (2:8), treating them with the gentleness of a nursing mother (2:7b) and working night and day so as not to burden their children financially (2:9).[4] Neither did they force them to comply with their teaching like a despotic father, but rather urged and encouraged their children (2:11-12).

The language of selfless, accommodating behavior is at the core of Paul's self-understanding of his apostleship, for in relinquishing a right for the welfare of others, he reenacts the story of Christ, who chose not to exploit his equality with God but emptied himself (Phil. 2:6-8). So too, although Paul and his companions had the right to financial support, they chose not to make demands or impose burdens of any kind, but rather emptied themselves in the giving of their gospel and themselves.[5] This theme of being conformed to Christ in this way will appear in every Pauline letter. It is a way of life, not just for apostles, but for the Thessalonians and for all believers.

THE COMMON BOND OF SUFFERING (2:13-16)

Verses 14-16 are thought by some scholars not to be part of Paul's original letter but rather a later addition ('interpolation') that reflects an anti-Jewish polemic that is foreign to Paul. But these verses make complete sense in context as another affirmation of the Thessalonians' reception of the apostolic message as God's word (2:13) in spite of opposition. Paul refers to the suffering of the prophets, Jesus, the churches in Judea, and his own team to assure the Thessalonians that their difficult experience is normal for those who are faithful to God (2:14-16a); it is their common bond. The talk of wrath (2:16b) is not 'anti-Jewish' but thoroughly Jewish and apocalyptic in content: those who oppose God and his word (in this case the gospel for the Gentiles), even from within Israel, will not be delivered from the coming wrath (cf. 1:10). (See also 4:6, where God is portrayed as an avenger even of believers who practice immorality.)

3. The NIV places this clause in 2:6 and translates it "we could have been a burden to you."

4. There is some difficulty in the translation of 2:7b, which refers either to the care of "a nursing mother . . . for her children" (NAB), to that of a "nurse . . . for her *own* children" (NRSV, emphasis added), or (less likely) simply to that of "a mother . . . for her little children" (NIV).

5. The Pauline pattern of ministry described in these verses (esp. 1 Thess. 2:6-8), the same as that found in 1 Cor. 9 and rooted in the pattern of Christ (Phil. 2:6-8), is displayed in a chart in chap. 2, pp. 68-69. It may be summarized as 'although *x*, not *y* but *z*.'

TIMOTHY'S VISIT: ABSENCE, CONCERN, AND REASSURANCE (2:17–3:13)

Having established that his presence among the Thessalonians was a ministry of self-giving love, Paul now needs to remind them that in his absence he continued (and continues) to care for them. This care has taken three forms — eagerness to visit, the sending of an envoy, and prayer. Paul reveals not only his concern but also his worry, yet, reassured, he concludes with thanksgiving and intercession for his beloved children.

Paul creatively shifts metaphors from parents to children — orphans (2:17) — to stress the depth of his feelings while apart from the community. Paul blames Satan, likely referring to the enemy of God's people as the ultimate source of persecution, for his frustrated attempts to visit (2:18). But the outcome of the cosmic battle is decided, and on the day of victory, the Lord's coming, or parousia, the Thessalonians will constitute the apostle's victory crown. They are his success story; their faithfulness is the proof.

The sending of Timothy was the embodiment of Paul's concern. Paul's motive was not merely positive feelings about the Thessalonians, nor concern about their possible negative feelings toward him. Rather, he deeply feared (note "we/I could bear it no longer" in 3:1, 5) that the intense persecutions would "shake" them, and that they had not really understood that suffering was part and parcel of serving the one true God. Had his team's labor "been in vain" (3:5)?

Timothy returned with two pieces of excellent news: the Thessalonians' faith and love were unfailing, and their esteem for the Pauline team was undiminished (3:6). Once again Paul affirms how the Thessalonians' steadfastness encourages and gives life to him and his colleagues (3:7-8). Therefore they are now ecstatic with joy, despite their own persecutions; Paul prays earnestly to see them, not out of fear but in confidence (3:9-11).

Not that the Thessalonians are perfect. They still need the Lord's strength and Paul's pastoral instruction, so he desires to visit them to "restore" whatever their faith might lack (3:10-11). He prays also that the Lord will cause them to grow in love and in holiness as they anticipate the parousia (3:12-13). Fostering such growth, as we have seen, will be the goal of the rest of the letter.

Summary of 1 Thessalonians 1–3

We see in these three chapters some very important dimensions of Paul's view of believers' existence in general and of ministry in particular. These include:

- Finding themselves between the death/resurrection and the parousia of Jesus, believers live lives of faith, love, and hope in relation to God as Father, Son, and Spirit and in relation to other believers.

- Persecution is normal, not only for ministers of the gospel, but for all believers.
- Ministry is always to be done with integrity before God and others, in conformity to the crucified Christ, and in the power of the Spirit.
- Believers strengthen and confirm one another; ministry is a two-way street, even between spiritual parents (evangelists and pastors) on the one hand, and their spiritual children (converts, congregants) on the other.

In sum, we can say that for Paul apocalyptic existence is a cruciform existence that requires mutual assistance and divine strength.

4:1–5:11. INSTRUCTIONS — SERVING GOD AND WAITING FOR THE SON

As we have seen, in 1:9-10 Paul provides a very brief summary of the nature of the Thessalonians' life together following their conversion from idols: "to serve a living and true God, and to wait for his Son from heaven." Having rehearsed in the first three chapters the story of their conversion and their relationship with Paul and his team, Paul now unpacks some of the particulars of the verbs "to serve" and "to wait."

SERVING GOD: THE CALL TO HOLINESS (4:1-12)

The Call (4:1-3a)

As a faithful Jew, Paul preached a message of turning from idolatry to serve God that always meant a conversion also from immorality. In the Scriptures, the Law and covenant always involve right relationships with God and with others, and Jews, as we noted in chapter 1, perceived Gentiles as both idolatrous and immoral. Those who serve God in the Lord Jesus are called therefore to holiness, or "sanctification" (4:3a). This catchall term for the life owed to and pleasing to God means that the Thessalonians are in fundamental ways a countercultural community. Paul taught them this in person (4:1), passing on instructions bearing the authority of Jesus (4:2), and they should now continue to grow in the life of holiness. Two specific aspects of the countercultural mandate — sexual

157

purity and love for others — appear at the beginning of chapter 4, perhaps in response to questions addressed to Paul via Timothy. Other dimensions will be mentioned briefly in the following section on 'waiting' (4:13–5:11) and in the closing exhortations (5:12-28).

Sexual Purity (4:3b-8)

The first topic of the countercultural life addressed by Paul is sexuality, specifically abstention from any kind of "sexual immorality" (NIV; NAB, "immorality"; Gk. *porneia,* which includes but is broader than NRSV's "fornication"). Paul's basic point is that the call of God is to be different from the Gentiles "who do not know God" (4:5) by being pure rather than lustful (4:5, 7). Here Paul continues the general biblical and Jewish tradition of criticizing pagan sexual immorality and stressing that one of the primary distinctives of those in covenant relationship with God is sexual holiness (see Lev. 18:1-3, 24-30). Jews claimed to be, and were known as, those who did not engage in such pagan practices as sex outside marriage, homosexual relations, abortion, infanticide, and the exposure of unwanted newborns. The earliest believers in Jesus followed suit, and Paul follows the Levitical example in treating this matter with the utmost gravity (4:6, 8).

Within this general rubric, one specific activity is mentioned (4:4), though its precise meaning has been debated. A critical Greek word in the text, *skeuos* (lit. 'vessel'), is most likely a reference to the male genitalia ("how to control your/his own body," NRSV/NIV),[6] though it may be a reference to a wife as a vessel ("how to acquire a wife for himself," NAB; cf. NRSV and NIV margins). In either case, the emphasis is on an approach to sex and marriage that is distinct from what Paul perceives as typical Gentile "lustful passion" (4:5).

This perspective is typical of ancient Jewish criticism of Gentile sexual morality, and similar criticism can be found even in pagan moralists. While Paul's view of Gentile sexual behavior is perhaps stereotypical, there can be little doubt that many Gentiles, especially men, had more libertine sexual lifestyles than Jews would permit. Those who know the true God of Israel and of Jesus Christ must have an approach to sexuality that is controlled and pure, one that does not exploit a fellow believer ("brother [or sister]," 4:6). This concern for the other person reveals not only the way Paul wants the Thessalonians to approach sex and marriage, but also his conviction that believers must only marry believers (cf. 1 Cor. 7:39). Paul does not find sex dirty or bad, but it is ap-

---

6. Phallic symbolism was used in many pagan cults, including those of Dionysus and other cults in Thessalonica.

propriate for believers only in purity and in marriage. The modern conviction that the only unethical sexual behavior is exploitative sex would not be echoed by Paul, for whom nonexploitation is a necessary, but not sufficient, criterion for sexual activity.

Love for One Another and Relations outside the Community (4:9-12)

The concern about lust and exploitation in sexual relations leads Paul to the next general topic, mutual love (Gk. *philadelphia*) within the community of believers, those both near and far. Indeed, right conduct regarding sexuality is, for Paul, a dimension of *philadelphia*. As in 4:1, Paul affirms the Thessalonians and urges continued growth (4:9-10a). Some specific manifestations of love are suggested later: encouragement, exhortation, practical help, and nonretaliation (4:18; 5:11, 14-15).

The brief mention of relations with outsiders in 4:11-12 is supplemented with a more general exhortation to "seek to do good . . . to all" in 5:15. Here the emphasis is on a quiet, self-sufficient life that sounds like a blend of Epicurean and Stoic ideals. Paul's instruction is probably to be understood as a warning not to take 'waiting' for the Son (1:10) too literally, a problem that reappears in 2 Thessalonians. When believers deliberately do not work, they fail to love both outsiders and fellow believers by bearing poor witness to outsiders and imposing a burden on those within the church who would feel responsible for them. The church's practical assistance should go only to the truly needy, while idlers should get a job (5:14).

WAITING FOR THE SON: ESCHATOLOGICAL HOPE AND CHALLENGE (4:13–5:11)

If the previous set of instructions was largely about love, the next set, consisting of two short but carefully developed hortatory discourses, is about hope. Each discourse begins with an introductory word ('. . . concerning *x*') and ends with an exhortation using the verb *parakaleō*. This verb can be translated 'encourage,' but it has two different nuances: 'comfort' (its meaning in 4:18; cf. NAB, "console") or 'exhort' (its sense in 5:11; unfortunately, NRSV, NAB, and NIV all use the neutral "encourage"). These two discourses, then, reveal something about the countercultural hope of believers, both in what it promises (4:13-18) and in what it demands (5:1-11).

Hope for the Dead (4:13-18)

Ancient grave markers often bore the words "I was not, I was, I am not, I care not." So popular was this epitaph that, eliminating the second clause, the marker often bore just six letters: n-f-n-s-n-c, for the Latin words *non fui, non sum, non curo,* meaning "I was not, I am not, I care not." Paul's gospel offered hope based on the past resurrection and future return of Jesus (1:10; 3:13), but it is possible that Paul did not explain to the Thessalonians that some of them might die before Jesus' parousia — and if they did, what would happen to them. The death (lit. 'falling asleep,' a common ancient metaphor for death preserved in the NAB and NIV but relegated to the margins of the NRSV) of some members of the community (4:13), whether by natural causes or, more likely, persecution, had shaken people's hope. Paul calls them to return to and better understand their countercultural hope in contrast to those who have none (4:13).

To do so Paul draws on traditional apocalyptic and political language to unpack the significance of Jesus' resurrection and parousia for the very practical pastoral problem of grief. In a nutshell, he says not only that the dead will be raised, but that they will be the first to meet the Lord.

The apocalyptic language includes especially 4:16 and parts of 4:17. Jesus' return is depicted as the victory of God announced by an archangel and a trumpet (cf. Zech. 9:14; 1 Cor. 15:52), originating in heaven, involving the clouds (cf. Dan. 7:13), and culminating in the resurrection of the dead. Similar images appear in other apocalyptic literature. The political language is a bit more subtle. *Parousia* ("coming," 4:15) and *apantēsin* ("to meet"; lit. 'meeting,' 4:17) are terms used to refer to the arrival and reception of imperial and military figures. The apocalyptic sounds therefore announce the coming of the true emperor and victor, Jesus.

The final fate of all believers is to "be with the Lord forever," which are the ultimate words of encouragement (4:17-18). But the precise way this comes about is a bit unclear in the apocalyptic-imperial imagery. As Christ descends, the dead are raised and then the living are "caught up in the clouds together with them to meet the Lord in the air" (4:17). So there is a 'meeting in the air,' but what happens next? *Where* are "we . . . with the Lord forever"? Do believers stay in the air/clouds with Jesus? return to heaven? or come to earth? Although the first two answers (stay in the clouds, return to heaven) are possible apocalyptic scenarios, only the third one sufficiently takes the political imagery of the parousia into account. In this imagery believers, both dead and living, are depicted as the official city delegation that goes out to meet the emperor and escort him back to the city. Believers greet Jesus and return to earth with him, where he rules as Lord, with his servants in his presence. (One may compare the vision of the descent to earth of the city of God in Revelation 21.) Whether or not Paul believed this to be literally true, his emphasis is on the permanent presence of believers with their Lord.

The graves of the wealthy, like this one in Athens,
were marked with elaborate sculptures.

Given this interpretation (and even the other options for the 'meeting in the air'), we should reject as dangerous imaginations the popular scenarios of a devastating 'rapture' in which planes and cars crash due to the disappearance of Christians.[7] Paul is remarkably restrained in his apocalyptic predictions, and he writes not to implant fear, but to extend hope.

7. 'Rapture' is from the Latin word for 'caught up,' *rapiemur,* translating the Greek *harpagēsometha,* in 4:17.

Challenge to the Living (5:1-11)

Whereas 4:13-18 deals with eschatology and those who are asleep, 5:1-11 focuses on the impact of eschatological hope on those who are awake — or who ought to be. The theme of the discourse is watchfulness. Once again Paul mixes apocalyptic and political images, creatively drawing especially on the former to make applications to everyday life.

Paul apparently contrasts the knowledge of the Thessalonians about "the times and the seasons" with their ignorance about the dead (5:1 in contrast to 4:13), but this is probably only a rhetorical device. Paul is in fact instructing them, in order to make sure that apocalyptic vision leads only to appropriate living in faith, love, and hope (5:8). The passage includes an eschatological reminder (5:2-3), imperatives based on the eschatological identity of believers (5:4-10), and an exhortation to mutual edification (5:11).

"The day of the Lord" (5:2) in the prophets was the coming day of YHWH, bringing both judgment and salvation. For those who acknowledged Jesus as Lord, "the day of the Lord" became the day of Jesus' return, his parousia. "Like a thief in the night," referring to the event's unexpected character, must have been a fairly common image in the early churches (Matt. 24:43; 2 Pet. 3:10; Rev. 3:3; 16:15). Paul's own twist on this image is to connect it with the inflated self-importance of Rome, whose motto of *pax et securitas* ("peace and security") Paul mocks (5:3). The "labor pains" that precede the day of the Lord are welcome only to those who know true peace and hope in Christ (cf. Rom. 8:18-25); for those who do not know God, their false security will lead only to unexpected judgment.

This image of the Lord's coming by night sets up for Paul the apocalyptic dichotomy of two groups of people (5:4-5), the children of light (the church) and those in the darkness (pagan Greco-Roman culture). Those who belong to the light will not be surprised by the day of the Lord (5:4), nor will it mean wrath for them, but salvation (5:9). This does not mean, however, that the Thessalonians' future salvation is so guaranteed that they can fall asleep at the wheel. The apocalyptic metaphors of wakefulness and sobriety (added in 5:6) have real-life corollaries. If those who claim to belong to the day act like those who belong to the night, by failing to keep morally vigilant and thereby falling back into the godlessness of their pagan culture, they betray their identity (5:6). Instead, they must let their true identity — their 'sobriety' — be manifested, through a life of faith, love, and hope (5:8). These are all weapons in a serious battle — the apocalyptic struggle between God and those who oppose God, including the idolatrous culture of pagan Rome. The weapons, of course, are not those of Rome or any other human power.

In other words, Paul can say, Jesus died and rose (Paul normally says "was raised") so that believers will "live with him" (5:10) not only when they sleep in death (recall 4:17) but while they are awake and alive now, between Christ's resurrection and theirs. This important statement of the purpose of Christ's death — not merely to forgive people's sins but to reorient and restructure their entire existence (see also 2 Cor. 5:15) — leads to the concluding exhortation to the Thessalonians, so that they will continue to challenge and edify one another in their common life (5:11).

5:12-28. CLOSING EXHORTATIONS AND FINAL MATTERS

Before ending his letter, Paul leaves the Thessalonians with a list of some seventeen relatively unadorned admonitions about life together. The seventeen exhortations divide fairly evenly between what we might call relational and liturgical admonitions, or behavior toward various groups of people and behavior at worship.

Church leaders, who have formational and educational responsibilities, are to be esteemed (5:12-13a). Peace, patience, nonretaliation, and generally doing good are to be the modes of interaction among all believers (5:13b-14, 15), while special, appropriate attention must be shown to those who will not contribute to the community and those who cannot (5:14). The exhortation to nonviolence and doing good is broadened to include outsiders (5:15b).

Eight of the exhortations, in 5:16-22, generally follow a simple syntactical pattern of qualifier (adverb, object, etc.) + verb (e.g., 'Always rejoice') that suggests material intended for memorization. These imperatives (apart from 5:22) are concerned with the community's liturgical life, which appears to be a vibrant one. It is characterized by joy, prayer, and thanksgiving, which are God's will and are to be done without ceasing (5:16-18). It is characterized also by manifestations of God's Spirit, especially in the form of prophetic utterances, which should be welcomed but also carefully discerned (5:19-21).

A final exhortation to "abstain from every form of evil" (5:22), echoing the letter's general call to holiness, leads into the benediction (5:23-24). This benediction summarizes the theme of the letter, holiness and hope, as did the closing of the first half of the letter (3:11-13). It assures the Thessalonians that they will be kept "blameless" at the Lord's parousia, not by their merely human efforts but by the faithful God who has called them to holiness (5:24; cf. 4:3, 7).

Paul ends the letter with four elements. The first two reflect his deep parentlike affection for and close relationship with the Thessalonians: a request for prayer for him and his team, and a request for the sharing of a holy kiss as a greeting from him (5:25-26). The last two express his apostolic authority (a command that "this letter be read to all") and blessing (5:27-28).

Summary of 1 Thessalonians 4–5

In the second part of 1 Thessalonians we have seen several elements of Paul's teaching about the life of serving God and waiting for the Son:

- Holiness — difference from pagan culture — is the norm for believers' lives, especially in light of their eschatological identity as children of the light.
- The promise of Jesus' parousia and the resurrection of the dead provides both a comforting hope and an ethical mandate.
- The church gathers as a community of worshiping and mutually supportive family members who experience God, Christ, and the Spirit together.

THE STORY IN FRONT OF THE LETTER

Some Readings of 1 Thessalonians

"I Thess is the earliest Christian writing to have been preserved; surely Paul was not conscious that he was composing a work that would have that distinction. Nevertheless, the status of I Thess offers interesting reflections. Were this the only Christian work that had survived from the 1st century, what would it tell us of the way Paul worked, of his self-understanding, of his christology, of his conception of the church or Christian community? Given that most Christians claim to adhere to the apostolic faith, it is interesting to imagine being transported back to the year 51 and entering the meeting room at Thessalonica where this letter of the apostle Paul was being read for the first time. Within the opening ten verses one would hear references to God the Father, the Lord Jesus Christ, and the Holy Spirit, and to faith, love, and hope. That is a remarkable testimony to how quickly ideas that became standard in Christianity were already in place."

Raymond E. Brown, *An Introduction to the New Testament*
(New York: Doubleday, 1997), pp. 464-65

"As a political slogan, *eirēnē kai asphaleia* [1 Thess. 5:3a] = *pax et securitas* is best ascribed to the realm of imperial Roman propaganda. If this interpretation of the phrase is correct, it would imply that Paul points to the coming of the day of the Lord as an event that will shatter the false peace and security of the Roman establishment. . . . Paul envisions a role for the eschatological community that presents a utopian alternative to the prevailing eschatological ideology of Rome."

Helmut Koester, "Imperial Ideology and Paul's Eschatology in
1 Thessalonians," in *Paul and Empire: Religion and Power in
Roman Imperial Society,* ed. Richard A. Horsley (Harrisburg,
Pa.: Trinity Press International, 1997), pp. 158-66, here 166

"Paul's apocalyptic diction is not innocuous. It is radical and impinges on the quality of life lived in the present. In many ways, it is reminiscent of the apocalyptic spirit found in the Negro spirituals. Although the spirituals were noted for their otherworldly orientation, they also had this-worldly functions. . . . These songs expressed longing and hope for another world. Among the this-worldly functions, however, were the building up of community solidarity and the practice of a veiled form of critique and communication. . . . Both the future and the present were important for them [the slaves]. In sum, the spirituals confronted the slaves' sordid experience, remythologized the biblical concepts to speak cryptically but encouragingly, and provided a source of comfort and challenge. Their apocalyptic strain, like Paul's apocalyptic vision, read the present reality in the light of future expectation."

Abraham Smith, "The First Letter to the Thessalonians," in
The New Interpreter's Bible, ed. Leander E. Keck et al. (Nashville: Abingdon, 2000), 11:671-737, here 728

QUESTIONS FOR REFLECTION

1. Why would Paul's gospel be perceived as a threat to the religious, economic, and political status quo in an urban context like Thessalonica? In what respects, if any, is the gospel (or should the gospel be) a challenge to the status quo today?

2. What aspects of Paul's ministry in Thessalonica are especially paradigmatic, on the one hand, and possibly problematic, on the other, for ministry today?

3. In what ways might Paul's (admittedly embryonic) theology of sex articulated in 1 Thessalonians contribute to the discussion of this subject in the churches today?

4. How does Christian hope affect, or not affect, the convictions and conduct of contemporary Christians today? How should it?

5. How do you respond to the interpretations of 1 Thessalonians quoted above?

6. In sum, what does this letter urge the church to believe, to hope for, and to do?

FOR FURTHER READING AND STUDY

General

Best, Ernest. *A Commentary on the First and Second Epistles to the Thessalonians.* Harper's New Testament Commentaries. New York: Harper and Row, 1972. A dated but classic commentary that sought to correct certain missteps in past interpretations of the letters.

Gaventa, Beverly. *First and Second Thessalonians.* Interpretation. Louisville: Westminster John Knox, 1998. An exegetically and pastorally insightful reading, especially helpful for preachers and teachers.

Richard, Earl J. *First and Second Thessalonians.* Sacra Pagina. Collegeville, Minn.: Liturgical Press, 1995. A historically and theologically sensitive interpretation of the letter, understood as a composite.

Smith, Abraham. "The First Letter to the Thessalonians." In *The New Interpreter's Bible,* edited by Leander E. Keck et al., 11:671-737. Nashville: Abingdon, 2000. An interpretation of the letter as a call to maintain an 'apocalyptic' way of life, with reflections for today.

Technical

Bruce, F. F. *1 and 2 Thessalonians.* Word Biblical Commentaries 45. Waco, Tex.: Word, 1982. A concise, careful analysis of the letter, showing Paul's debt to both Jewish and Gentile vocabulary and thought.

Malherbe, Abraham J. *The Letters to the Thessalonians.* Anchor Bible 32B. New York: Doubleday, 2000. A careful analysis of the letters, with special attention to the ancient literary and social contexts.

Wanamaker, C. A. *The Epistles to the Thessalonians: A Commentary on the Greek Text.* New International Greek Testament Commentary. Grand Rapids: Eerdmans, 1990. A sociorhetorical interpretation that argues for Paul's writing of 1 Thessalonians after 2 Thessalonians.

CHAPTER 8

2 THESSALONIANS

Cruciform Faithfulness and Goodness before the Parousia

. . . not to be quickly shaken in mind or alarmed, either by spirit or by word or by letter, as though from us, to the effect that the day of the Lord is already here.

2 Thess. 2:2

The second letter of Paul to the Thessalonians will never win a popularity contest; it is infrequently read, and even less frequently preached. But if we wish to appreciate the nuances with which Paul was capable of exercising his pastoral responsibilities, we will do well to pay careful attention to this brief (only forty-seven verses) but strategic note to the Thessalonian believers. In it Paul admonishes them to Christlike faithfulness and goodness as they await the Lord's parousia — which, contrary to the beliefs of some, is still in the future.

THE STORY BEHIND THE LETTER

The document we call 2 Thessalonians has many similarities to, and yet also substantive differences from, 1 Thessalonians. This combination of similarities and differences has led many scholars to question the order of writing of the two letters or, more often, the Pauline authorship of 2 Thessalonians. Nevertheless, the most coherent and plausible explanation for 2 Thessalonians is probably neither a different order of writing nor its authorship by someone other than Paul. Rather, it is a worsening of circumstances in Thessalonica, not long after the sending and receiving of 1 Thessalonians, that prompts Paul to address similar concerns in new, more forceful ways.

A LETTER FROM PAUL?

As noted in chapter 3, Paul's authorship of 2 Thessalonians is affirmed by approximately one-half of Pauline scholars. As noted above, a few attribute both letters to Paul but question the order of their writing, suggesting that Paul actually wrote 2 Thessalonians before 1 Thessalonians. This opinion, which has not gained a large following, is based on the possibility that the circumstances (with respect to persecution, eschatological beliefs, relations with Paul, and other issues) of the Thessalonian church depicted in 1 Thessalonians could be developments from those depicted in 2 Thessalonians. In the end, however, most scholars agree that the circumstances suggested by 2 Thessalonians are more likely a development from (or at least took shape later than) those in 1 Thessalonians.

More common is the view that Paul did not write 2 Thessalonians at all — that it is a later, pseudonymous letter that may have even been intended to correct 1 Thessalonians in light of the delay of the parousia or in response to hyperenthusiasm about it. The arguments for this interpretation have to do with both form and substance, and with both similarities and differences between the letters.

On the one hand, many scholars have argued (correctly) that the structure and language of 2 Thessalonians have much in common with 1 Thessalonians, as if the writer of the second letter had the first in front of him (or, less likely, her). On the other hand, many scholars have also argued that 2 Thessalonians is so different in style, vocabulary, tone, and eschatological conviction that it could not have been written by the author of 1 Thessalonians. Among the (correct) observations of these scholars is that the second letter is less personal and more forceful than the first. More importantly, it is argued that in the first letter Paul expresses hope in an imminent parousia, whereas in the second letter he presents an apocalyptic tableau that seems to push the return of Christ into the more distant future.

Those who argue for pseudonymity contend that 1 Thessalonians is the blueprint for 2 Thessalonians, the first letter having been copied in part but altered for a different audience. But it can be argued that although there exists an interesting combination of similarities and differences, the conclusion of pseudonymity is neither necessary nor probable when another explanation — suggested by the letters themselves — can account for both the similarities and the differences. Before examining this scenario, two observations — one brief, one a bit longer — need to be made.

First, few interpreters have sufficiently stressed the marked differences that occur within the parallel material in the two letters. There is seldom identical quotation, and the combination of similarity and difference points to an author relating to the same group in different situations.

Second, many interpreters have misinterpreted and/or overinterpreted Paul's eschatological words and their pastoral function. Paul always writes about eschatology in order to build up the particular church to which he writes, and the specifics of what he says depend on his perception of the church's needs. Although he has clear, consistent convictions about some basic points (e.g., the return of Christ, the glorification of believers in God's presence), he is also able to draw on a rich variety of apocalyptic themes and images in his various letters. We cannot expect uniformity.

This is not to say, however, that the eschatologies of the two letters are incompatible. Rather, they are different but consistent, addressing distinct needs. As noted above, it is frequently said that in 1 Thessalonians the parousia is imminent, whereas in 2 Thessalonians it is distant. But it is actually something of an exaggeration to claim that Paul envisions an imminent parousia in 1 Thessalonians. Rather, he writes about the coming of the Lord to 'comfort the afflicted' (those who are grieving, 4:13-18) and to 'afflict the comfortable' (those who are dozing, 5:1-11). This leads him to stress both the certainty (4:13-18) and the suddenness (5:1-11) of the parousia; it is not an event so dubious or distant in the future as to permit either despair or apathy. This focus is not, however, the same as a fixation on the event's imminence.

In 2 Thessalonians the needs of the believers have changed, as we will see below, and Paul addresses the fear of some Thessalonians that the day of the Lord has *already* come (2:2). This situation requires a different eschatological emphasis, one (as in 1 Corinthians) that has a more elaborate end-times scenario. Both eschatological perspectives existed in apocalyptic Judaism, and Paul drew first on one and then on the other in the face of changing pastoral needs.

DEVELOPMENTS IN THESSALONICA

Paul wrote 1 Thessalonians to express relief that the Thessalonians had survived persecution, and to remind them to continue in holiness, faith, love, and hope as they awaited the return of their Lord. In 2 Thessalonians we find clues that the situation has evolved:

- Persecution continues (and has perhaps increased in intensity), though so has the Thessalonians' endurance (1:4). Nevertheless, the Thessalonians

Thessalonica: Artisans and shop workers may have labored in places similar to these small, vaulted locations on the (second-century) agora.

may be seeking (or Paul perceives a need for) additional insight about the meaning of this suffering.
- Some believers have claimed apostolic and/or Spirit-inspired authority to proclaim that the day of the Lord has already arrived (2:2). This has caused confusion and anxiety in Thessalonica.
- The problem of idleness has not gone away and has likely worsened (3:6-15; cf. 1 Thess. 5:14).

The question naturally arises whether these are independent or inter-related developments. It has been frequently suggested that the idleness in Thessalonica was due to eschatological fervor (why work if the end is in sight?), though Paul never makes this connection explicitly, and such a rationale makes more sense in the setting of the first rather than the second letter. More recently, Thessalonian idleness has been interpreted simply as a burden on the community that Paul addresses, in part, by appealing to his own example (3:6-9). Thus the various developments may be independent.

Nevertheless, a tentative proposal such as the following is not implausible. The announcement by certain unidentified individuals — claiming the authority of the Spirit and/or of Paul (2:2) — that the day of the Lord had arrived led to increased consternation by some and increased apathy by others. On the one hand, some would have asked, 'If the day of the Lord has come, why are we still being persecuted rather than being with the Lord in glory?' (Some may have even feared that, despite their faithfulness in persecution, they had been 'left behind.') On the other hand, some would have said (or at least thought), 'Why should we work if the day of the Lord has arrived?' They may have added, 'We will soon be leaving this world anyhow,' or 'The judgment is past, and since we have survived it, we do not need to do good,' or 'There is no need to toil in the kingdom of God.' Thus the (erroneous) 'news' of the arrival of the day of the Lord would have caused major problems in Thessalonica for understanding believers' external and internal relationships.

Exactly how Paul has become aware of such developments (whether interconnected or not), we do not know. But he is clearly concerned to relieve unnecessary anxiety by explaining why the day of the Lord could not yet have come, while he himself is anxious to encourage the Thessalonians' endurance and goodness. At the same time, Paul is miffed at the deceit he finds in the eschatological perversion, and in the irresponsibility he identifies in the idleness. This explains the 'harsher' tone of the letter in comparison to the first; he wants all the Thessalonians to obey (2:15; 3:6, 14-15). All in all, nonetheless, Paul still has a positive view of the Thessalonians and expects the church to come around to his way of thinking about the controverted matters.

Like the first letter, the second was cosent by Silvanus and Timothy. It was probably written not too long after 1 Thessalonians, and therefore likely in 51 from Corinth, though a somewhat later date and a different location are possible. (If the letter is pseudonymous, its occasion, date, and audience are up for grabs.) In placing Paul's eschatological perspectives in 1 and 2 Thessalonians side by side, we find a pastor who steers a middle ground between the extremes of viewing the Lord's parousia as an irrelevant event in the distant future and as a fully accomplished event in the past and/or present.

THE STORY WITHIN THE LETTER

Like 1 Thessalonians, 2 Thessalonians is governed by a tone of thanksgiving, even if it is more subdued (1:3; 2:13) and is peppered also with intercessory prayers and benedictions (1:11-12; 2:16; 3:5, 16). The main contents of the letter, however, relate directly to the three interrelated issues identified above: persecution, the parousia, and idleness. Paul calls on the Thessalonians to get the story of Jesus' parousia straight — it is future, not past — and thus to get their own stories straight as well. Specifically they are to continue in cruciform faith and hope — the steadfastness or endurance *(hypomonē)* of Christ — and to demonstrate cruciform goodness and love by working so as not to be a burden to others in the community. The letter unfolds as follows:

1:1-2	**Opening**
1:3-12	**The Meaning of Persecution**
	1:3-4 Thanksgiving for Endurance
	1:5-10 The Future of Believers and Nonbelievers
	1:11-12 Prayer for Faithfulness
2:1–3:5	**Persecution and the Parousia**
	2:1-3a Warning against Error
	2:3b-12 Two Events before the Parousia
	2:13–3:5 Exhortations and Prayers for Faithfulness
3:6-15	**The Error of Idleness and the Obligation to Work**
	3:6-10 Apostolic Example and Teaching
	3:11-15 Dealing with the Idle
3:16-18	**Final Matters**

A summary of the letter appears at the conclusion of the commentary on the text.

1:1-2. OPENING

The letter begins as does 1 Thessalonians, by naming Paul and his two cosenders, Silvanus and Timothy (the only time any personal names appear in the letter), and identifying the church as composed of Thessalonians who exist "in God our Father and the Lord Jesus Christ" (1:1). The greeting differs slightly from the first letter's by specifying that grace and peace come from the Father and Son (1:2).

1:3-12. THE MEANING OF PERSECUTION

The first section of the letter deals with the Thessalonians' ongoing persecution. After an initial thanksgiving for their endurance (1:3-4), Paul outlines the respective final fates of believers and nonbelievers alike (1:5-10) before offering a prayer for the Thessalonians' continued faithfulness (1:11-12). Thus Paul and his cowriters bracket pastoral instruction and encouragement with prayer. Although there are echoes of the opening of the first letter here, there are also differences that reflect the evolving situation.

THANKSGIVING FOR ENDURANCE (1:3-4)

The letter's initial thanksgiving (cf. also 2:13) is reminiscent of 1 Thessalonians 1:3-8 but is quite compact. The specific reason for thanksgiving now is not merely the presence of such qualities as faith and love but especially their increase. Paul's gratitude is due, in part, then, to what he perceives as answered prayers offered in connection with the first letter (e.g., 1 Thess. 3:12; 4:1, 10). But what appears to be missing here is the third item in the Pauline triad of faith, love, and hope (cf. 1 Thess. 1:3). In fact, however, hope surfaces in strengthened form in the word "steadfastness" (1:4, *hypomonē*), which is joined with faith in the face of persecution. Paul clearly views this Thessalonian "perseverance" (NIV) or "endurance" (NAB) — their cruciform faith and hope — as proof of the Thessalonians' part in the future reality that he will now describe.

THE FUTURE OF BELIEVERS AND NONBELIEVERS (1:5-10)

Paul moves on to explain the meaning of the Thessalonians' suffering by focusing on the fate of those who are afflicted by it and of those who inflict it, together with other nonbelievers. He says the persecution is evidence of God's righteous judgment and has the purpose of ensuring the worthiness of believers for God's kingdom (1:5; cf. 1:11). That is, Paul urges the believers to put the present affliction in future perspective, when fortunes will be reversed. Those who are causing the suffering reveal their true character as ignorant of God and disobedient to the good news (1:8). Their future fate is one of affliction from God (1:6, 8-9), that is, the divine wrath promised by the prophets and preached by both Jesus and Paul.[1] This wrath Paul calls "eternal destruction" and defines as separation from the presence and power of Jesus (1:9, echoing Isa. 2:10-21).

---

1. E.g., for Paul, 1 Thess. 1:10; 2:16; 5:9; cf. Rom. 1:18; 2:5, 8; 3:5; 5:9; and esp. Phil. 1:28.

Believers, on the other hand, especially persecuted believers like the Thessalonians, will receive divine "relief" (1:7): they will inherit the kingdom of God (1:5), enjoying the Lord Jesus' presence and glorifying him forever (1:9-10). This reversal or exchange of fates — the "righteous judgment of God" (1:5) — is predicated on the Pauline conviction that just as believers share their Lord's suffering, so also will they share his glory.[2] It will not occur, however, until the Lord Jesus is "revealed" with his fiery angels of judgment (1:7-8, 10).

"That day" (1:10) is clearly still future — which is why the subject of the next chapter is such a grave matter to Paul. The apocalyptic language used in these verses is intensified in chapter 2, but it is all characteristic of Paul specifically and early Christians generally. The day of the Lord God has become the day of the Lord Jesus, with salvation for the faithful and wrath for the disobedient (cf. Phil. 1:28). For this reason, things said about God in the Scriptures (e.g., having a host of angels) are now predicated of the Lord Jesus.

PRAYER FOR FAITHFULNESS (1:11-12)

The opening chapter concludes with a prayer for the Thessalonians' faithfulness in light of the two future destinies described in 1:5-10. To be made "worthy" of God's "call" is simply to remain faithful (1:11; cf. 1 Thess. 1:3), in spite of persecution, and thus eventually to share in the glory of Jesus (1:12). This is accomplished by the power (1:11) and grace (1:12) of God (cf. Phil. 1:6; 2:13).

2:1–3:5. PERSECUTION AND THE PAROUSIA

According to Paul in chapter 1, it is the certainty of Jesus' future parousia, with the judgment and salvation it will entail, that makes enduring persecution worthwhile. Thus we should be able to understand his alarm, and that of the Thessalonians, at the notion that the parousia had occurred but believers' suffering had not ceased! (Though Paul does not mention it explicitly, the message could also create a false hope that the persecution was about to end, and therefore perhaps a complacency about the need for continued faithfulness.) About this 'deceit' (2:3) Paul warns, teaches, admonishes, and prays, connecting the futurity of the parousia with the purposefulness of suffering. That the whole situation is actual and not merely possible seems certain, given the intensity of Paul's response.

2. E.g., Rom. 8:17; Phil. 3:10-11; cf. 1 Thess. 1:6; 4:13-18.

WARNING AGAINST ERROR (2:1-3a)

Paul begins with strong words of warning, asking or even begging (so NRSV) the Thessalonians not to be disturbed (2:2) or deceived (2:3a) by an erroneous message about the "coming" *(parousia)* of Jesus and the gathering of believers with him[3] — subjects about which he had taught them (2:15; cf. 1 Thess. 1:9-10). It is possible that whoever was spreading the message did not speak of parousia and 'gathering together,' but only of the possibly less specific "day of the Lord" (2:2). But to proclaim that "the day of the Lord is already here" (NRSV) or "has already come" (NIV; NAB's "is at hand" almost certainly misses the point) is to imply, as far as Paul is concerned, all kinds of things that are clearly not yet true — glory rather than suffering, judgment of the wicked, and the reunion of all believers with the Lord.

The messengers may have had a 'realized eschatology' that attributed full, spiritual salvation to the present. Or they may have simply misunderstood the biblical and apocalyptic tradition about the day of the Lord as it was given new shape in the early churches. In any event, they claim either the Spirit (NAB, "spirit"; NIV, "prophecy") or Paul or both as the authority for their teaching. Contrary to what some scholars have said, there is no reason that a "letter" from Paul could not have circulated with this misinterpretation of Paul's teaching. It is more likely, however, that some sort of prophetic utterances have been made and associated with Paul's name, perhaps in the context of worship when Paul's teaching or correspondence was being discussed, that claimed the arrival of the day of the Lord. Furthermore, teachers may have reasoned by "word" (logic) from Paul's explicit teachings to his supposed implicit meaning. But any association of this conviction with Paul is not only an error, from the apostle's perspective, it is a deception (2:3a) foisted upon the Thessalonians.

TWO EVENTS BEFORE THE PAROUSIA (2:3b-12)

After concluding his warning, Paul draws heavily on various apocalyptic traditions to inform the Thessalonians that two things must occur before the parousia: (1) the "rebellion" (NRSV, NIV) or, better, "apostasy" (NAB; Gk. *apostasia*), and (2) the revelation of the "lawless one" (NRSV, NAB) or "man of lawlessness" (NIV). About the apostasy Paul says nothing more. In many apocalyptic traditions in the New Testament and elsewhere, an expectation of faithlessness in tribulation and/or departure from the truth appears (e.g., Mark 13:22 and parallels), and that is likely what is envisioned here. Ironically, then, per-

---

3. Cf. 1 Thess. 4:13-18, esp. 4:15, 17, though different Greek words are used.

haps, the failure of any Thessalonians thus far to apostatize is proof that the day has not yet arrived.

Quite fully developed is the picture of the "lawless one." This figure has parallels elsewhere in the New Testament in the perpetrator of the "desolating sacrilege" and false messiahs of the synoptic tradition (Mark 13:14-23 and parallels), the first beast of Revelation 13, and the "antichrist" of the Johannine letters.[4] According to Paul, the lawless one:

- has preliminary influence in the world already (2:7; cf. 1 John 2:18; 4:3), though his impact is lessened by some restraining agent or force (2:6-7; the first reference is neuter for an impersonal force, the second masculine for a person)
- will be revealed (2:3, 8), i.e., will have a coming (*parousia*, 2:9)
- will exalt himself above all deities, take a seat in the temple of God, and declare himself God (2:4)
- is an agent of Satan (cf. Rev. 12:7–13:8), who is by nature a deceiver who successfully traps nonbelievers (2:9-12) and (it seems) attempts also to deceive believers (2:3; cf. 1 John 3:7)
- will (and perhaps already does) deceive people with miracles (2:9; cf. Mark 13:22 and parallels)
- will be destroyed by Jesus — specifically by the "breath of his mouth" — at his (Jesus') own parousia (2:3, 8)

The identity of the restraining force or person (2:6-7) has been much debated, but Paul's intention (the Spirit? the Roman Empire? Paul or his ministry?) eludes us.

The "lawless" figure is something of a composite of various sources and traditions, biblical and otherwise, but it is clear from the parallels in the synoptics, Revelation, and elsewhere that the broad outlines of this figure must have been quite commonplace in the early churches. Of particular importance is the apparent allusion in 2:4 to Antiochus IV (Antiochus Epiphanes), who in 167 B.C. desecrated the Jerusalem temple and proclaimed himself God (see Dan. 11:36). But it is also possible that a more general allusion to exaggerated royal or imperial power is intended. In either case, Paul's language reminds his readers that the "parousia" of any supposed 'lord' or 'god' is but a sham of the real event in which they and he have placed their hope.

Paul claims to have instructed the Thessalonians about this matter (2:5), even though it is not specifically mentioned in 1 Thessalonians (or elsewhere in Paul, for that matter). It is equally clear, however, that Paul's major concern

4. 1 John 2:18, 22; 4:3; 2 John 7.

here is not some dogmatic stance about the 'antichrist,' and even far less about this figure's actual identity. (Suggestions for what Paul had in mind include an emperor, a Roman military figure, or a false prophet and/or miracle worker.) His overriding concern is pastoral — to stress the futurity of the parousia (2:3) and to encourage faithfulness to the Lord when the days of testing arrive. It is the latter part of the pastoral concern that dominates the next few paragraphs.

EXHORTATIONS AND PRAYERS
FOR FAITHFULNESS (2:13–3:5)

Having made his point about the impossibility of the Lord's day having already arrived, Paul returns to his governing concern — the spiritual health of the Thessalonians. He repeats his thanksgiving for them (2:13; cf. 1:3) as a reminder of their special calling to be in relationship with the triune God: God (the Father) who elects, the Lord (Jesus) who loves, and the Spirit who sanctifies (2:13). This call came through the ministry of Paul and his colleagues, a call ultimately to share in the Lord's glory (2:14), as Paul has already said (cf. 1:12). Thus the Thessalonians are to stand firm in conviction and conduct (cf. 1 Thess. 3:8), heeding the oral and written instructions about the parousia — and keeping alive the hope — that Paul and his colleagues have given them (2:15).

This exhortation leads to a prayer, echoing the earlier prayer for God's power (1:11), for God, their gracious and loving Father, and the Lord Jesus (in whom the church exists, 1:1) to comfort them in this persecution and strengthen them to practice goodness in "work and word" (2:16-17). The mention of work anticipates the discussion of 3:6-15 about the obligation of all to work.

In the next breath, and as a conclusion to this section, Paul requests prayer for the evangelistic efforts of his team (3:1), and for rescue from their own persecutors (3:2; cf. Acts 18:5-17). This prayer is short, however, and turns once again into a promise to and prayer for the Thessalonians (3:3-5). The Lord's faithfulness, Paul reassures them yet another time, will strengthen and protect them, even from the evil one who seeks to deceive (3:3; cf. 2:9-12). After expressing his conviction that the church will comply with his admonitions (3:4), Paul concludes with a prayer-wish that the Thessalonians be inspired to stay focused on God's love and Christ's own steadfastness as they seek to live lives of love and patient endurance in their own particular difficult situation. Since they have been Christ's imitators — conformed to his cruciform existence (cf. 1 Thess. 1:6; 2:14-16) — they should continue in the same path of faithfulness.

3:6-15. THE ERROR OF IDLENESS
AND THE OBLIGATION TO WORK

Paul reserves what are perhaps his strongest words of admonition to the community for the subject of work and idleness. (NAB's "disorderly" conduct probably misses the mark in context.) The language is stern ("command," 3:6, 10) and the prescription — ostracism in order to cause shame (3:6, 14) — may appear extreme. But for Paul these idle busybodies are more than just a nuisance; they are not enemies, but they are malformed believers (3:15) who are failing to exercise cruciform love for others. Their refusal to work, no matter the rationale behind it, is an unacceptable burden to the community (cf. Gal. 6:5). No spirituality, not even one related to the parousia, relieves a Thessalonian believer from the responsibility of imitating Paul — and ultimately Christ — in working for the good of others and refraining from self-centeredness.

APOSTOLIC EXAMPLE AND TEACHING (3:6-10)

Paul issues his command as a restatement of the teaching and example that he and his colleagues provided (3:6-10), but he does so "in the name of our Lord Jesus Christ" (3:6; cf. 3:12) — with the authority of Jesus (cf. 1 Cor. 5:3-5). Given the close connection between the imitation of Paul and of Christ in Paul's letters,[5] this authority implies not only that Paul invokes Christ's name but that he grounds his command in the example and teaching of Christ himself. As recalled also in 1 Thessalonians 2:9, Paul and his colleagues worked night and day, taking no free food (3:8, for which there are many ancient parallels), even though they had the apostolic right to refrain from work and be supported (cf. 1 Thess. 2:7-9; 1 Cor. 9). The mention of voluntary denial of rights is an allusion to the selfless love of Christ on the cross,[6] and the standard Pauline formula 'although x, not y but z' lies behind 3:8-9. The hard work of the Pauline team, then, was intended as a general paradigm of Christlike love and, more importantly in this context, a specific model of working (3:7, 9). Accompanying the example was a concrete command: no work, no food (3:10). It was now time to implement consequences for ignoring the example and instruction.

5. E.g., 1 Thess. 1:6; 1 Cor. 11:1.
6. Cf. 1 Thess. 2:7-9; 1 Cor. 9:19; Phil. 2:6-11; etc.

DEALING WITH THE IDLE (3:11-15)

Those guilty of idleness are described in a Greek play on words that might be rendered 'getting out of work instead of into it' (3:11).[7] Paul exhorts these people directly to get to work (3:12; cf. 1 Thess. 4:10-12), backed by a general exhortation not to tire of goodness (3:13; cf. Gal. 6:9). He tells the rest of the community to avoid the idlers (3:6, 14, forming an *inclusio*, or verbal bookends) in the hope that they will be shamed into the honorable, rather than dishonorable, behavior appropriate for believers (3:14-15).

3:16-18. FINAL MATTERS

The letter concludes with a three-part benediction for the peace, presence, and grace of the Lord (3:16, 18), a prayer-wish especially appropriate for a persecuted church. In the middle is a greeting in Paul's own hand, something noted in other letters too (1 Cor. 16:21; Gal. 6:11; Col. 4:18; Philem. 19), but emphasized here because of the problem of impersonation mentioned in 2:2. The reference to Paul's mark being present in "every" letter is not an anachronism; 1 Thessalonians may be the only surviving letter earlier than 2 Thessalonians, but there is no reason to think that Paul had never before written a letter!

Summary of 2 Thessalonians

The three problems addressed in this letter — persecution, parousia, and work — may seem at first to be of different types (experiential, doctrinal, ethical), but whether or not they were all interrelated in Thessalonica, they are clearly interconnected in Paul's mind.

- Before the Lord's parousia and the salvation or destruction it brings, there will be apostasy and the appearance of the lawless one.
- The time between the first and second comings of Jesus is marked by the sign of the cross, both in the mundane responsibilities of daily activities like working in order not to burden others and to contribute to a community, and in the more dangerous, even life-threatening situations of persecution that might lead to apostasy.
- The steadfastness of Christ requires and empowers communities to embody

---

7. Cf. NAB, "not keeping busy but minding the business of others," and NIV, "They are not busy; they are busybodies."

his faithfulness in both the small and the large concerns of life until the future day of the Lord.

THE STORY IN FRONT OF THE LETTER

Some Readings of 2 Thessalonians

"The Thessalonians indeed were then perplexed about these things [the resurrection and the end], but their perplexity has been profitable to us. For not to them only, but to us also are these things useful."

> John Chrysostom, Homily 1 of his *Homilies on the Second Epistle of St. Paul the Apostle to the Thessalonians* (ca. 400)

"2 Thessalonians surprises one with the narrow focus of its thought. All the resources the author uses (past election, christology, tradition, gospel) stress future salvation and are directed to the life of waiting under pressure. There is not a hint of the life of the community in worship, its structure, or its local leadership. . . . The great past events are the call and election of the community by God, not the death and resurrection of Jesus. There is no reference to the creedal confession of Christ, no cultic enactment or memorial of Jesus' death and resurrection. Baptism is nowhere alluded to, unless one reads it into the word 'call.' In short, the community is shapeless, without specific charismata. 2 Thessalonians is essentially a letter with one theme: faithful endurance under persecution. Fidelity is holding on to the tradition(s) presented in the letter itself. The writer ransacks the resources of apocalyptic thought to underscore his theme. His goal is to rouse his readers to steadfast waiting as the apocalyptic calendar unrolls."

> Edgar Krentz, "Through a Lens: Theology and Fidelity in 2 Thessalonians," in *Pauline Theology*, vol. 1, *Thessalonians, Philippians, Galatians, Philemon*, ed. Jouette M. Bassler (Minneapolis: Fortress, 1991), pp. 52-62, here 61

"[Second] Thessalonians is a challenging letter. It forces the hard question of how to preach and teach passages we find difficult. First, the simple act of admitting the difficulties may be freeing to us and to those who hear us. . . . Second, we need to ask what this text has to say, whether we are prepared to hear it or not. . . . Second Thessalonians will continue to trouble preachers and teachers. Few would argue that this letter is pivotal for understanding the New Testament. Yet the harsh, even ominous language that characterizes this text troubles us precisely because it raises significant issues that the church all too often prefers to neglect."

Beverly Gaventa, *First and Second Thessalonians,* Interpretation
(Louisville: Westminster John Knox, 1998), pp. 95-97

QUESTIONS FOR REFLECTION

1. Many readers of 2 Thessalonians have reacted negatively to this letter because of its perceived vindictiveness and its graphic apocalypticism. How might understanding the circumstances of the letter — and the differences from ours — permit us to appreciate these aspects of the letter? Can a church that does not suffer identify fully with a church and its people that do?

2. Why is eschatology always such a volatile issue in the church? Which aspects of Paul's eschatological perspective have enduring value for the contemporary church? Which remain problematic, either in themselves or as they are used (and perhaps abused) in the church?

3. The notion of 'no work, no food' was not unique to Paul, and has found its way into various modern secular as well as religious perspectives. What might be some appropriate — and inappropriate — ways to make use of this principle today?

4. How do you respond to the interpretations of 2 Thessalonians quoted above?

5. In sum, what does this letter urge the church to believe, to hope for, and to do?

FOR FURTHER READING AND STUDY

General

Best, Ernest. *A Commentary on the First and Second Epistles to the Thessalonians.* Harper's New Testament Commentaries. New York: Harper and Row, 1972. A dated but classic commentary that sought to correct certain missteps in past interpretations of the letters.

Gaventa, Beverly. *First and Second Thessalonians.* Interpretation. Louisville: Westminster John Knox, 1998. An exegetically and pastorally insightful reading, especially helpful for preachers and teachers.

Richard, Earl J. *First and Second Thessalonians.* Sacra Pagina. Collegeville, Minn.: Liturgical Press, 1995. A theologically sensitive interpretation of both letters, arguing for 2 Thessalonians as a (pseudonymous) corrective to apocalyptic preachers wrongly causing alarm and unrest in Paul's name.

Technical

Bassler, Jouette M., ed. *Pauline Theology.* Vol. 1, *Thessalonians, Philippians, Galatians, Philemon.* Minneapolis: Fortress, 1991. A collection of essays that includes two on 2 Thessalonians from different understandings of the letter's authorship and theology.

Bruce, F. F. *1 and 2 Thessalonians.* Word Biblical Commentaries. Waco, Tex.: Word, 1982. A succinct analysis of the letter, showing Paul's debt to both Jewish and Gentile vocabulary and thought.

Malherbe, Abraham J. *The Letters to the Thessalonians.* Anchor Bible 32B. New York: Doubleday, 2000. A careful analysis of the letters, with special attention to the ancient literary and social contexts, that argues for Pauline authorship of 2 Thessalonians.

Wanamaker, C. A. *The Epistles to the Thessalonians: A Commentary on the Greek Text.* New International Greek Testament Commentary. Grand Rapids: Eerdmans, 1990. A sociorhetorical interpretation that argues for Paul's writing of 2 Thessalonians before 1 Thessalonians.

CHAPTER 9

GALATIANS

The Sufficiency of the Cross and Spirit

For in Christ Jesus neither circumcision nor uncircumcision counts for anything; the only thing that counts is faith working through love.

Gal. 5:6

It is difficult to imagine a more passionate, angry, and yet caring pastoral letter than Paul's dispatch to the churches of Galatia. Forged in the heat of controversy concerning one issue — whether circumcision is necessary for Gentile believers in the gospel — it yielded some of the most powerful and influential texts of all time. For the Reformer Martin Luther, Galatians was "my epistle; I have betrothed myself to it; it is my wife."[1] Many since the sixteenth century, particularly those who have looked to Luther as their theological and spiritual parent, have found in his 'wife' the source of their own spiritual life and the mother of their theology. The letter has often been called the Magna Carta of Christian freedom — which is a fine epithet, as long as we allow Paul to define the term 'freedom.' In content it resembles Romans; in tone, 2 Corinthians 10–13.

Of particular importance in the reading of Galatians, of course, has been the theme of 'justification by faith' rather than works, which for many is the central concern of this letter. This long-standing interpretation of Galatians via Martin Luther has come under intense scrutiny in recent decades. Very basic

---

1. From the introduction to one of Luther's commentaries on Galatians, cited in C. K. Barrett, *Freedom and Obligation: A Study of the Epistle to the Galatians* (Philadelphia: Westminster, 1985), p. 2.

questions have been raised, such as: What is the meaning of 'justification'? of 'faith'? What exactly is Paul opposing and proposing in this letter? Although we will find that Paul's major concern is not 'faith' versus what some call 'works righteousness,' a new reading of his letter will prove no less radical and challenging than older approaches (which were rightfully prophetic in their own day). Paul claims that there is absolutely nothing that can or should be added to the gospel of the crucified Messiah and the liberating Spirit, a gospel that generates cruciform faith and love.

THE STORY BEHIND THE LETTER

Paul writes this letter to the (unspecified) "churches of Galatia" (1:2). Galatia was first a territory and then an official Roman province. As a region of north-central Asia Minor (Anatolia), Galatia was the land of the Galatian people, a Celtic tribe that relocated to the area around Ancyra (today the capital of Turkey, Ankara) in the third century before Christ. When Augustus created the province of Galatia, he extended the Galatian territory south and a bit west, making Antioch of Pisidia (or Pisidian Antioch, modern Yalvaç) the provincial capital. The city was huge, geographically larger than Ephesus, the capital of the neighboring province of Asia to the west. Its gently rising acropolis afforded a magnificent view of the city and the fertile countryside. The creation of the province also brought into Galatia such smaller cities as Iconium (a Roman colony, like Antioch), Lystra, and Derbe. These were among the cities, according to Acts, that Paul visited during his journeys through Galatia.

We learn something of Paul's relations with the people of Galatia in both Acts and Galatians, though the occasionally differing (and perhaps conflicting) data cause a variety of interpretive problems. We will allude to some of those issues but cannot address, much less attempt to solve, all of them.

GALATIA(S) AND PAUL ACCORDING TO ACTS

On his first journey (as Acts narrates the trips), probably in 48 or 49, Paul moved from the southern coast of Asia Minor inland to Pisidian Antioch (13:13-51). There, with Barnabas at his side, he went to the synagogue to preach a message of forgiveness of sins through Christ and a liberation or justification (*dikaiōthēnai*, 13:39) for those who believe, a restored relationship with God that the Law of Moses could not provide (13:39-40). After opposition from some of the Jews who did not believe their message, they went to the Gentiles until city officials, at the insti-

Pisidian Antioch: **Plan of the excavation**

gation of some Jews, drove them out of town (13:44-51). Paul and Barnabas then proceeded to Iconium (modern Konya) for more preaching to Jews and Gentiles, accompanied by "signs and wonders," and opposition as well as belief, escaping just before a planned stoning (14:1-7); then to Lystra, where healing a crippled man led to their being proclaimed Zeus and Hermes and to Paul's being stoned nearly to death — this time by a crowd instigated by Jews from Antioch and Iconium (14:8-20); and then to Derbe, where they were successful but apparently not persecuted (14:20-21). They then retraced their steps to encourage the churches in the face of persecution and appoint leaders (14:21-23).

Paul's second journey (beginning in 49 or 50) followed his receiving the blessing of the Jerusalem leaders — against some Pharisee agitators (15:1, 5, 24) — to preach to the Gentiles without requiring their circumcision and adherence to the Law of Moses (15:1-29). Paul set out with Silas and, coming through his hometown of Tarsus, visited Derbe and Lystra, where he added Timothy to his team (16:1-5). Perhaps surprisingly, he had this son of a Jewish mother and Greek father circumcised because of the local Jews who knew of the young man's heritage (16:1-5), an act of accommodation to Jewish sensitivities that must have occurred before the writing of Galatians. They also visited other (unnamed) towns in the area (16:4-5) before heading north and then west, ending up finally in Greece. According to many scholars, Acts implies that Paul founded some

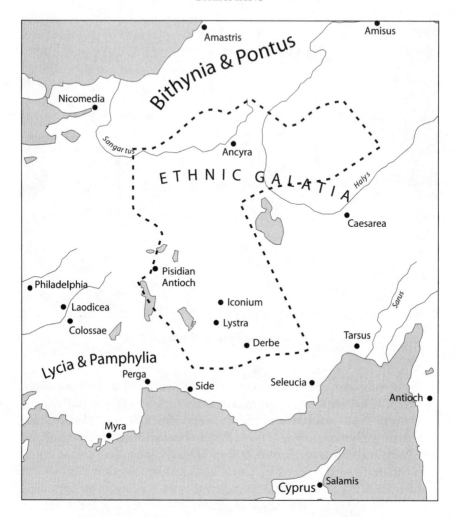

Ethnic Galatia (to the north) and the province of Galatia
(outlined with dotted line) in the first century

churches in central or even northern (ethnic) Galatia during this trip (16:6 in light of 18:23), but the information is ambiguous at best. On his third trip, Paul again visited the region of Galatia, though no towns are named (18:23).

Much ink has been spilled on whether Paul wrote to churches of the more northern region of Galatia (supposedly founded on the second journey) or to churches in the south along the Antioch to Derbe line (founded on the first trip). It is curious that Luke's only two uses of the word "Galatia" (16:6; 18:23) might refer to a region north of the Antioch-Derbe line, but even if this is true, it does not mean that Paul uses the word the same way. This supposed evidence for a northern mission, however, is slim and indefinite. Moreover, the issues that Paul addresses in Galatians — justification and the Law of Moses — echo the stories and concerns Luke connects to the named, southern cities, especially the sermon in Pisidian Antioch. (This point is important whether Paul and Luke write independently or Luke depends on Paul.) Furthermore, the experiences of both persecution and miraculous deeds depicted in Acts in southern Galatia are reflected in Galatians (3:1-5; 6:12). Because Luke says little about what happened in Galatia during Paul's second and third trips, we do not know if he thinks Paul had similar experiences of controversy, persecution, and miracles then, even if Luke has the northern area in mind.

Though there is no consensus on this issue, there is currently a scholarly preference for the north Galatian theory. Without going into more detail about the arguments for and against the north Galatian and south Galatian theories, we may suggest (despite current scholarly leanings) that, on balance, the evidence is stronger for a letter to the southern churches. If the letter is directed to the south, it could have been written as early as 49-51 and from any location; otherwise it was likely written in the years 53-55, probably from Ephesus. Although no firm conclusion is possible within the range of years 49-55, the most likely date, in this writer's estimation, is 50 or 51, after the Jerusalem conference (Acts 15 = Gal. 2:1-10 — though not everyone equates these two meetings). The intended audience was the group of churches in southern Galatia, especially in the vicinity of the Pisidian Antioch–Derbe line.

As for the actual interpretation of the letter, the date and precise target population probably matter very little, though the stories of Acts may provide corroborating evidence for data supplied by Paul in Galatians.

GALATIA AND PAUL ACCORDING TO GALATIANS

Paul's success in Galatia — wherever exactly he was — was largely among pagans, not Jews (4:8-9). In Paul's day the largely pagan population of the province adhered to traditional local deities as well as others from the East and from Greece and Rome, including the emperor. On the acropolis of Pisidian Antioch, for example, there are remains from a temple to Cybele as well as ruins of an impressive imperial temple to Augustus that was being constructed at the time of Paul's visits. Many of the city's columns — including some in the imperial temple — were decorated with the head of a bull — the animal used in sacrifices to Cybele, under the leadership of her self-castrated priests.

Paul had come to Galatia because of a 'weakness of the flesh' (4:13 literally). This may refer to a "physical infirmity" (NRSV) or (physical) "illness" (NAB,

Pisidian Antioch: Among the deities of Galatia were the Anatolian mother goddess Cybele and the Roman emperor Augustus — both worshiped at this spot on the acropolis at Antioch.

NIV), perhaps related to his eyes (cf. 4:15), but it may also refer to his persecution (cf. "thorn . . . in the flesh," 2 Cor. 12:7), which was evidenced in his scars (6:17). He "publicly exhibited" Christ crucified (3:1) — scars and all — and was very well received, like a divine angel or messenger (4:12-15). Many Galatians believed the gospel, were baptized into Christ (3:27), and received the Spirit (3:1-5; 4:6; 5:25). From the beginning of Paul's mission and continuing to the time of the crisis he addresses, the Spirit was evidenced in miracles (3:5), but also in prayer to God as Father (4:6-7) and in right living (5:16-26). From Paul's point of view, until very recently the Galatians "were running well" (5:7). Nevertheless, the letter suggests that the communities were not without normal tensions and moral issues to address (5:13–6:10). And at least some persecution seems to have accompanied the birth of the Galatian churches (3:4 NIV; cf. 6:12; cf. Acts 13–14).

The Advent of the 'Circumcisers'

Following Paul's evangelistic visit (or perhaps a second visit — 4:13), a group of people whom Paul thinks of as troublemakers (1:6-8; 5:10, 12) — "agitators"

(NIV, 5:12) — arrived in Galatia. Like yeast, Paul claims (5:9), they permeated the church, working to challenge and correct Paul's evangelizing efforts. (The frequent designation 'Judaizers' is open to misunderstanding and may be a misuse of the ancient verb 'to Judaize' — i.e., to live like a Jew.) Although some scholars argue that these interlopers or 'influencers' were (non-Christian) Jews interested in converting Gentiles to Judaism, most interpreters of Galatians believe they were Jewish believers (i.e. 'Christians') from outside the Galatian churches. There is no evidence that these outsiders came with the direct approval of any of the apostles in Jerusalem, but Paul clearly sees a precedent for their activity in the "false believers" (2:4) and in the "circumcision faction" (2:12), the "people . . . from James" (2:12) who do not see Gentiles as equals in Christ. The latter group, at Antioch, persuaded Peter and Barnabas not to have table fellowship with Gentile believers (2:11-14) even after James, Peter, and John had agreed in Jerusalem not to require Gentile circumcision (2:1-10).

'Agitators' the visiting preachers certainly were, from Paul's viewpoint; more neutral terms for these people that are commonly used are 'missionaries' or 'teachers,' though neither term conveys their distinctiveness. It is tempting to call them 'zealots,' for they seem quite similar to the zealous Paul of earlier days, devoted to the Law and to the purity of Israel. Their obvious desire to bring Gentiles fully into Israel makes the term 'circumcisers' more appropriate, since their primary mission (at least in Galatia) was to convince Gentile believers to be circumcised and then "live like Jews" (2:14, *ioudaikōs zēn* and *ioudaizein*, borrowing phrases Paul uses in his critique of Peter). That is, the Gentiles were counseled as follows:

- to be circumcised (5:2-12; 6:12-13; cf. 2:3-5; obviously applicable only to males);
- to follow Jewish calendar (4:9-10) and dietary (2:11-14) customs; and (probably)
- to follow the whole Law (see 3:5, 10, 12; 5:2-4).

In doing so, the circumcisers apparently argued, the Gentiles would consummate their new faith in Jesus as Messiah by (1) becoming full members of God's covenant people begun in Abraham and (2) embracing the ritual (circumcision, diet, calendar) and ethical boundary markers of Israel. Otherwise the Gentiles' faith and experience would be incomplete; they would still be outside Israel (4:17) and unable to live the lives of holiness to which the covenant called God's people and in which the Law guided them. In fact, it is likely that the circumcisers taught the Gentiles that without circumcision and Law observance they did not truly possess the Spirit (cf. 3:1-5, 14). Furthermore, while not denying the importance of Christ's death for sins, their Christology was not centered on Christ's cross but, almost certainly, on his role as teacher of the Law.

Because the circumcisers seem to have embraced a comprehensive vision greater than the mere desire for Gentile circumcision, the most apt descriptor of all for them may be the term that some scholars have used of Second Temple Jews more generally — 'covenantal nomists' (*nomos* = 'law'; hence 'nomists'), people who believed that keeping the Law was the way to express and maintain their covenant status. Perhaps we should say more specifically that the circumcisers were *messianic* covenantal nomists, since it is probable that they affirmed Jesus as Messiah. In this chapter, however, we will refer to them by the more restrictive but less cumbersome term 'circumcisers,' understanding that term as pointing to this comprehensive vision. As messianic covenantal nomists, the circumcisers would have believed (1) that through Messiah Jesus the God of Israel was graciously inviting Gentiles to the covenant; (2) that entrance into the covenant was gained by faith in the Messiah followed (for males) by circumcision; and (3) that God expected his covenant people to live distinctive lives of holiness in which they observed the Law of God.

An inevitable corollary — if not the main thrust — of the circumcisers' message was a critique of Paul. They seem to have found his apostleship *dubious,* his message *deficient,* and his ministry *dangerous.* They likely claimed that his message and ministry originated in himself and had the sanction of neither Jerusalem nor heaven. His truncated gospel offered the Gentiles the Jewish Messiah without bringing them into the realm of the covenant and Law that the Messiah embodied. His emphasis on the cross and Spirit without circumcision and the Law had generated unnecessary persecution from Jewish leaders and, through them, from pagan mobs and government officials.

In spite of (or perhaps because of) Paul's vehement reaction to the circumcisers, we would be remiss not to give them the benefit of the doubt, at least initially, on their motives. They were not antichrists opposing Jesus' messiahship. Nor were they 'legalists,' teaching a doctrine of salvation by works, as many traditional interpretations have presented them. They were — like Paul — Jews who affirmed God's gracious election and covenant, Jesus as the Messiah, and the inclusion of the Gentiles in the covenant — only on terms that differed significantly from Paul's. (Designating them 'cultural imperialists' is somewhat appropriate but perhaps a bit too general.)

Paul's Response

After the circumcisers' arrival, the Galatians began seriously to doubt Paul (4:15) and, more importantly, his gospel. For Paul this was abandoning the very

God who had called them (1:6). Paul's reaction to this situation was both visceral and systematic, and both elements are clearly preserved in Galatians. On the emotional side, he replaces the customary thanksgiving with a stern rebuke (1:6); he calls the Galatians foolish (3:1); in intimate and heart-wrenching terms he expresses deep consternation about their departure from him and his ways (4:12-20). He wonders whether he wasted his time (4:11) and feels as if he must start over from scratch, and do so from a distance (4:18-20).

As for the circumcisers, Paul (indirectly but clearly) pronounces a double curse on them and anyone else like them (1:8-9); he accuses them of perverting the gospel (1:7) and of sorcery (3:1); and he even wishes they would castrate themselves (5:12). More substantively, Paul charges them with hypocrisy in failing to keep the Law themselves (6:13). Even more importantly, he accuses them of wanting to circumvent the cross in order to avoid persecution, replacing cross and Spirit with "flesh" (6:12). He, on the other hand, embraces the "offense of the cross" and welcomes the life, and even the persecution, that accompany it (5:11; 6:14, 17).

Paul's emotional outbursts are placed, therefore, within a carefully constructed narrative argument about the meaning of the cross and the experience of the Spirit within the great plan of God for Jews and Gentiles. The bottom line for Paul may be put this way: 'My grace-filled gospel from God about the cross and Spirit is sufficient for entry into, and life within, God's covenant people, so don't get circumcised and follow Jewish custom and Law!' Whereas the circumcisers may be called messianic covenantal nomists, Paul, we may say, is a *cruciform covenantal charismatic*. He is focused on the crucified Messiah whose death unleashes the age of the Spirit, by whom believers fulfill the covenant through cruciform faith and love — apart from circumcision and the Law.

This is clearly for Paul an either-or situation. The "truth of the gospel" (2:5, 14) is at stake. What the circumcisers see as *supplementing* Paul's gospel, Paul sees as *supplanting* it; he can therefore label it nothing other than a different, perverted gospel (1:6-7). If they are right, Christ died for no purpose (2:21); to embrace their message would be to cut oneself off from Christ (5:2, 4). If wrong (as they surely are for Paul), they will be judged (5:10).

This account of the story behind Galatians is a historical reconstruction that cannot be offered without some caution. Its general outline is, however, echoed by many recent commentators. What is often underemphasized, however, is the situation of persecution the letter presupposes. Not only is this situation mentioned in connection with the circumcisers' avoidance of the cross, and Paul's embrace of it, but it appears also in Paul's account of the Galatians' conversion: "Have you suffered [Gk. *epathete*] so much for nothing — if it really was for nothing?" (3:4 NIV). Many translators and commentators simply render the verb "suffer" as "experience" (so NRSV, NAB), but the stories in

Acts and the words of Paul elsewhere in Galatians (esp. 6:12) suggest that in 3:1-5 Paul alludes to the full spectrum of the Galatians' conversion experience: hearing, believing, receiving the Spirit, witnessing miracles, and suffering persecution.

THE STORY WITHIN THE LETTER

Paul responds to the Galatian crisis by telling a series of stories — stories about himself, about Christ, about the Galatians and their experience of the Spirit, about God, about the Law, about biblical characters like Abraham and Hagar and Sarah, and about life together. These stories demonstrate Paul's skill and creativity in interpreting early Christian tradition and Scripture, as well as human experience in light of both. These stories all serve his main purpose of dissuading the Gentile Galatians from being circumcised. They are organized into three main divisions, which are suggested by Paul himself at the beginning of the letter. He says "the Lord Jesus Christ"

1. "gave himself for our sins"
2. "to set us free from the present evil age"
3. "according to the will of our God and Father" (1:4).

These three phrases suggest that Paul will focus on (1) Christ's death on the cross, which is the core of his gospel (chaps. 1–2), and (2) the cross as the means by which people are liberated from the present evil age to live in the realm of the Spirit (chaps. 5–6), all of which (3) is the plan of God the Father promised in Scripture (chaps. 3–4). These stories are enveloped by hard-hitting words that summarize the apostle's passions and convictions (1:1-10; 6:11-18).

This three-stage set of narrative arguments addresses all the circumcisers' charges and claims as the letter unfolds. Paul asserts the divine origin of, and scriptural precedent for, his apostleship and gospel. He interprets Christ's death on the cross as an act of the Son's faithfulness toward God the Father (who sent him) and of love toward us. This death inaugurated the promised new creation, which is the age of the Spirit, who liberates those who believe the gospel in order to be God the Father's adopted children. *To return to the Law would be to return to slavery; it would be to live an anachronism.*

This Spirit is the Spirit of the Son, who was sent, like the Son, by the Father. The Spirit of the Son comes to all — Gentile and Jew, male and female, slave and free — who respond to the gospel and are baptized, enabling them to be crucified with Christ, to live Christlike lives of faith and love, and thus to fulfill the Law. *If Christ the crucified Son of God fulfilled the covenant's demands of faithfulness and love, then those who are crucified with him, and in whom he lives by his Spirit, will also fulfill the covenant's same demands by the work of the Spirit — without subscribing to Jewish custom and Law.* The age of the Law itself is over because it has fulfilled its function of leading all to the Messiah.

All this fulfills the promises made to and through Abraham, that God would include Gentiles in the blessings of (1) covenant membership as God's children and (2) the Spirit — through the Messiah alone (who died a cursed death) and by faith alone. This inclusion of the Gentiles in justification apart from compliance with Jewish custom and Law renders being circumcised irrelevant to the question of inclusion in the covenant, and the pursuit of circumcision as a means to gain inclusion a serious mistake. For Paul the gospel is all about crucifixion (Christ's and ours), not circumcision; about the Spirit, not the Law.

The letter takes shape as follows:

1:1-5	**Opening and Theme**
1:6–2:21	**The Gospel of Christ: Justification through Crucifixion**
	1:6-10 Apostolic Rebuke, Curse, and Claim
	1:11-24 The Divine Origin of Paul's Apostleship and Gospel
	2:1-10 Jerusalem's Initial Approval of Paul's Gospel
	2:11-14 A Betrayal of the Gospel
	2:15-21 The Gospel of Christ
3:1–4:31	**The Promise of the Father: The Testimony of Scripture**
	3:1-5 The Galatians' Initial and Ongoing Experience of the Spirit
	3:6-14 God's Promise of the Spirit to Abraham
	3:15-29 The Law and the Promise
	4:1-7 The Father's Gift of the Son and the Spirit
	4:8-20 Apostolic Appeal
	4:21-31 Freedom and Slavery: The Allegory of Hagar and Sarah
5:1–6:10	**The Freedom of the Spirit: The Life of Faith and Love**
	5:1-12 Christ, the Spirit, and Circumcision
	5:13-15 Freedom, Cruciform Love, and the Fulfillment of the Law
	5:16-26 Walking in the Spirit
	6:1-10 The Law of Christ in the Life of the Community
6:11-18	**Summary and Final Summons**

Summaries of chapters 1–2, 3–4, and 5–6 appear following the commentary on those sections of the letter.

1:1-5. OPENING AND THEME

Paul begins his letter "to the churches of Galatia" by emphatically identifying himself as an apostle from God rather than humans (1:1). This is a key theme of the entire opening chapter, almost certainly because it was disputed by the circumcisers. The first verse appears to be constructed chiastically (in *abb'a'* form) to stress the nonhuman source and agency of Paul's apostleship. It is not *(a)* from humans or *(b)* through humans but *(b')* through Jesus Christ and *(a')* from God the Father. Yet Paul does not stand alone as he writes; he is joined by "all the members of God's family" (1:2; lit. 'brothers'), an implicit claim that all true believers agree with his gospel and with what he is about to write. The universal church joins Paul in welcoming Gentile believers without circumcision.

It is important early on for Paul to link Christ with God the Father, as he does in both 1:1 and 1:3, for his christocentric gospel, which he thinks is being challenged, is both the will and the work of the Father in fulfillment of promises made long ago. The ultimate proof of Christ's connection to God the Father is the resurrection, itself an act of the Father (1:1).

Paul's grace-peace wish comes, like his apostleship, from both God the Father and the Lord Jesus (1:3). Having already identified the Father as one who raised Jesus, Paul now employs three phrases to identify the Lord Jesus, referring to Christ's death, its purpose, and its divine sanction (1:4). As noted above, this provides the basic content and structure of the entire letter. It will be unpacked throughout the letter, with a somewhat polemical summary in 2:15-21.

The phrase "gave himself for our sins" is a common New Testament idiom that likely predates Paul and that Paul reuses in 2:20, giving it his own significant twist. Even here Paul takes this 'self-giving/dying formula,' with its traditional Jewish emphasis on the death as a sacrifice for sins, and makes it part of a larger vision of Christ's death by connecting it to the second phrase, "to set us free [NAB, NIV: 'rescue us'] from the present evil age." This phrase introduces another Jewish framework for the interpretation of Christ's death, that of apocalyptic hope in the imminent end of this age and the beginning of the age-to-come: the age of righteousness and justice that will be marked by the knowledge of God and the presence of God's Spirit throughout the world. According to Paul, that age has begun in the death of Jesus, which was therefore an — no, *the* — apocalyptic event. Although the present evil age still exists, it is overlapped by this invasion of the future in Jesus' death, thus allowing people to escape the grip of the present age and all its powers (including, as Paul will later say, the "flesh").

Thus for Paul, Christ's death is not merely a *sacrificial* but also an *apocalyptic* event that offers liberation as well as forgiveness. Implied here, and stated explicitly in chapters 5 and 6, is that the gift of the Spirit, unleashed by God after Christ's death and resurrection, continues the liberating work of Christ in his death. This death and its effect on human beings was willed (and promised) by the Father (according to the third phrase of 1:4), who is therefore to be glorified forever (1:5). It turns out, then, that Paul's vision of liberation is trinitarian, willed by the Father, effected by the Son, and empowered by the Spirit.[2] What more could the Galatians — or the circumcisers — want?

1:6–2:21. THE GOSPEL OF CHRIST: JUSTIFICATION THROUGH CRUCIFIXION

The brief summary of Paul's gospel in 1:4, together with his self-defense in 1:1, becomes the focus of the series of narratives that Paul relates in the first major section of the letter. Before presenting the content of the gospel itself in the letter's thesis (2:15-21), Paul rehearses the gospel's origin, progress, and current threatened status — without the normal thanksgiving that introduces most Pauline letters.

APOSTOLIC REBUKE, CURSE, AND CLAIM (1:6-10)

Paul issues a series of very negative words beginning with "I am astonished" instead of 'I am thankful' (1:6). The whole paragraph constitutes a substitute for, and parody of, the traditional thanksgiving.

First is a rebuke of the Galatians for 'deserting' the one — God, not Paul — who graciously called them in Christ (1:6). They have turned to a "gospel" that is no gospel at all, for the circumcisers have stirred up confusion and perverted the gospel of Christ — that is, Christ crucified (1:4; 2:20; 3:1), embraced by faith (2:16; 3:2) — that Paul preached. There follows in 1:8-9 a double curse (let them "be accursed" [NRSV, NAB] or "eternally condemned" [NIV]; Gk. *anathema*) pronounced on anyone who would contradict the original Pauline gospel the Galatians "received." Paul's curse targets anyone who preaches contrary to his (which is in fact God's) gospel: someone claiming an angelic revelation, Paul himself, and — by implication — the circumcisers.

Paul's words seem harsh, but he uses them as proof that no matter what anyone says, he is not a people-pleaser in any way whatsoever; he is Christ's ser-

---

2. As in previous chapters, trinitarian language is used here in recognition that although Paul does not have a fully developed theology of the Trinity, such language is nonetheless appropriate.

vant (*doulos*, 'slave'), aiming to please him — the corollary of being an apostle (1:10; cf. 1:1). For this reason he will stand up to the circumcisers just as he stood up to the false brothers (2:4-5) and to Peter (2:11-14). He is absolutely confident in the truth of his message.

THE DIVINE ORIGIN OF PAUL'S APOSTLESHIP AND GOSPEL (1:11-24)

Paul's confidence in his apostleship and gospel do not, however, stem from himself but from their origin in God's revelation and call; that is the central claim narrated in the next few verses, which are critical to understanding Paul's mission and message. Paul seeks especially to show that his apostleship is independent of Jerusalem, even though the churches of Judea and (later) the Jerusalem officials approved of it.

Paul begins by picking up the claim of 1:1, now with emphasis on the gospel itself — the one the circumcisers are 'perverting.' They should know whose message they are tampering with — it is not something that some humans "made up" (1:11 NIV) or even taught Paul. Rather, his gospel came directly via a revelation (*apokalypsis*) of Christ by God (1:12). Paul then proceeds to narrate this "revelation" and its aftermath.

Much ink has been spilled on the subject of Paul's initial encounter with Christ, which occurred according to Acts on the 'Damascus road' (narrated three times in Acts;[3] implied also in the reference to Damascus in Gal. 1:17). Here we will not attempt to compare Galatians with Acts but simply note the significance of the encounter as Paul narrates it. In chapter 2 (and elsewhere[4]) I suggested that the terms 'conversion,' 'call,' and 'commission' are all appropriate descriptions of this revelatory event.

Paul clearly describes a conversion experience (1:13-16), from his "earlier life in Judaism" (1:13 — a story with which the Galatians were familiar) to his current life (in Christ/in the church). He has radically changed, from persecutor (1:13) to proclaimer, from zeal "for the traditions of my ancestors" (1:14) to zeal for the good news of Christ (cf. Phil. 3:2-11). But we must be careful not to confuse this 'conversion' for a change of religions. Paul is still a Jew (cf. 2:15). The term "Judaism" in 1:13-14 probably refers specifically to the kind of zealous Judaism that sought its purity at any cost, even the cost of violence. Its heroes were people like the high priest Phinehas (Num. 25:6-13) and the Maccabean

---

3. Acts 9:1-31; 22:1-21; 26:2-23.
4. In my *Cruciformity: Paul's Narrative Spirituality of the Cross* (Grand Rapids: Eerdmans, 2001), chap. 2.

Mattathias (1 Macc. 2:23-26), whose zeal led them to kill their fellow Jews in order to wipe out impurity and avoid God's wrath.[5] Paul's desire to "destroy" the church of God (1:13) manifested just such a zeal. In his conversion, then, he has changed his 'brand' of Judaism, from an exclusive, Torah-centered Judaism to an inclusive, Messiah-centered Judaism. The violent perpetrator of punishment (perhaps with the Jewish thirty-nine lashes), opposed to a sect that preached a crucified Messiah and welcomed Gentiles, was now willing to suffer on behalf of the same Messiah and his people, especially his Gentile people.[6] No wonder Paul could not tolerate the circumcisers!

Paul's conversion is also a story of prophetic call and commission (1:15-16). Borrowing the language of the prophets Jeremiah and (Second) Isaiah, Paul claims that God graciously called him and appointed him to "proclaim him [God's Son] among the Gentiles":

> Before I formed you in the womb I knew you,
> and before you were born I consecrated you;
> I appointed you a prophet to the nations. (Jer. 1:5)

> The LORD called me before I was born,
>   while I was in my mother's womb he named me.
> He made my mouth like a sharp sword. . . .
> And he said to me, "You are my servant,
>   Israel, in whom I will be glorified." . . .
> "I will give you as a light to the nations,
>   that my salvation may reach to the end of the earth."
>   (Isa. 49:1b-2a, 3, 6b)

God's grace and pleasure resulted in the revealing of the Son, not merely *to* Paul (1:16 NAB, NRSV) but *in* him (correctly NIV, NRSV mg.). That is, Paul's mission, message, and person would be inseparable; he would proclaim Christ crucified — the faith and love of God's Son (2:20) — to the nations, not only with his mouth but with his life (cf. again 6:17).

Paul highlights the importance of this call and commission being directly from God by telling the Galatians that for a long time he did not set foot in Jerusalem to confer with the previously appointed apostles (1:17). He spent those years in Arabia (the area south of Damascus or, possibly, where Mount Sinai is located) and then Damascus. Whether preaching, praying, or whatever, he was not conferring with church authorities. When he did finally go to Jerusalem, three years after his conversion/call (or after his return to Damascus), it was

---

5. Similar zeal was associated also with Elijah (1 Kings 17–19; Sir. 48:1-2).

6. E.g., 6:17; cf. 2 Cor. 11:23-29, where the thirty-nine lashes are mentioned in v. 24.

only for two weeks in order to confer with Cephas (Peter) and James (1:18-20). What transpired there is unknown (the passing on of church traditions or teachings about the earthly Jesus?), but afterward Paul headed north to preach around the cities of Syrian Antioch and his hometown of Tarsus in Cilicia (1:21). Developing a reputation as the persecutor-turned-proclaimer, he still was unknown personally among the Judean churches — though they rejoiced in his mission work (1:22-24). Paul had developed quite a reputation.

The point of this last part of the narrative is to stress Paul's independence from, but approval by, the Jewish believers, including the apostles themselves. They recognized in him the grace of God at work — a grace being extended through his preaching, as his commission demanded, beyond the walls of Israel to the Gentiles.

JERUSALEM'S INITIAL APPROVAL
OF PAUL'S GOSPEL (2:1-10)

In 2:1-10 Paul moves from the unofficial approval of his work narrated at the end of chapter 1 to the official support of the "pillars" (2:9) — James, Cephas (Peter), and John — of the Jerusalem church. It was apparently years later — fourteen years after either his call/conversion or his first Jerusalem visit — that Paul again visited Jerusalem. There he encountered both significant, official support and his first opposition from believers (though Paul in 2:4 calls them "false believers" or "false brothers"; Gk. *pseudadelphous*). Paul mentions this opposition first of all to contrast it with the support of the Jerusalem apostles, and secondly to connect it with the circumcisers who have come to Galatia. The narrative informs the Galatians that although Paul may not *need* Jerusalem's approval, he *has* it (or at least had it), and that he has never tolerated, nor ever will tolerate, opposition to the gospel he has received from God. This second theme will continue in 2:11-14 in even bolder terms.

The Jerusalem meeting narrated in 2:1-10 is equated, by most scholars, with the 'Jerusalem Council' recounted in Acts 15:1-29. There are, however, several differences in the two accounts that have led some scholars to suggest that in Acts 15 Luke has condensed two or more meetings into one, or that our passage refers not to Acts 15 but to the brief 'famine relief' meeting in Jerusalem mentioned in Acts 11:27-30. The latter (minority) group of scholars would generally date Galatians quite early (ca. 49) and contend that the Jerusalem Council of Acts 15 followed, and was intended in part to resolve, the Galatian crisis. For our purposes we note only that the majority view (Galatians 2:1-10 = Acts 15:1-29) probably possesses the preponderance of weighty evidence.

According to Paul, the meeting was largely a three-on-three, or even one-on-three, event (a "private meeting," 2:2). Paul's attitude toward the Jerusalem leaders borders on cavalier (2:6); he has gone to them because it has been revealed as God's will (2:2), not out of deference to the "pillars." (He is not really disrespectful but, following the biblical principle of God's impartiality, respects only their consistency with the gospel, not their status.) As living symbols of the reality of the gospel and the success of his ministry, Paul took with him two people: his Jewish coworker Barnabas (2:1), his companion on the first mission trip and thus in Galatia, and the uncircumcised Gentile Titus (2:1, 3), who would figure prominently later in Paul's ministry.[7] In a private meeting Paul explained to the "acknowledged leaders" (the "pillars") his gospel for uncircumcised Gentiles so that his work would not have been "in vain" — probably meaning in danger of being opposed or undone by leading Jewish believers (2:2). The response of the three "pillars" was threefold:

- not to circumcise Titus (Paul's test case, as it were), in effect admitting Gentiles to the church fully, without circumcision (2:3);
- to approve of Paul's evangelistic ministry to the Gentiles as the working of God's grace, in parallel to Peter's among Jews (2:7), by extending to Paul and Barnabas the "right hand of fellowship" (2:9); and
- to require Paul and Barnabas to remember the poor, which they were happy to do (2:10).[8]

In stark contrast to the pillars, a group of false brothers slipped in, observing Paul's team's 'freedom' and trying to enslave them (2:4), probably a reference to their criticism of Paul's law-free, circumcision-free gospel and its social manifestation in the unity of Gentile and Jew. To these Paul paid not a moment's attention, ultimately in the interest of the "truth of the gospel" for people like the Galatians (2:5). The subtext here is self-evident; the circumcisers, like the false brothers, oppose the truth of the gospel and should not be heeded in any way whatsoever.

---

7. Barnabas was a Levite, if Acts 4:36 is correct. The first mission trip is narrated in Acts 13–14. Barnabas, though not Titus, was present at the Jerusalem Council according to Acts 15. Titus was particularly involved in Paul's ministry in Greece (see 2 Cor. 2:13; 7:6, 13-14; 8:6, 16, 23; 12:18).

8. It is sometimes said that the presence of this last requirement (and no more) contradicts the account in Acts 15, which essentially prohibits the Gentiles from idolatry and immorality (Acts 15:19-20, 28-29). There is, however, no contradiction because Acts reports the requirements placed on Gentile believers, while Galatians reports the obligation placed on Jewish evangelists.

A BETRAYAL OF THE GOSPEL (2:11-14)

In 2:11-14 Paul recounts a very unpleasant but significant incident at (Syrian) Antioch, a prominent center of the early church and, according to Acts, the home base for Paul's early mission work. Cephas (Peter) and Barnabas had apparently understood the Jerusalem decision to mean that Gentile and Jewish believers could and should have table fellowship together. The arrival of "people . . . from James," who are probably also "the circumcision faction" (2:12), caused a radical change of heart in Peter, the Jewish believers in Antioch, and even Barnabas. Peter (followed by the others) now refused to eat with the Gentiles (2:12) and apparently wanted to compel them to be circumcised and follow the Law ("live like Jews," 2:14).

Paul interprets this about-face as cowardly, hypocritical, reprehensible, and — above all — contrary to the "truth of the gospel" (2:14). Paul sees Peter and the others as traitors, the functional equivalent of the "false believers" at Jerusalem (2:4). But Peter is an apostle, and Paul cannot tolerate either apostolic hypocrisy (for Peter himself was apparently no longer following all Jewish customs, 2:14) or opposition to the gospel of God's unconditional grace for Gentiles without their becoming Jews. Fearlessly Paul "opposed him [Peter] to his face" (2:11), starting with the rhetorical accusation in 2:14 and continuing with the speech that summarizes his gospel (2:15-21, or at least part of it). Both the boldness and the content of Paul's encounter with Peter are, of course, intended for the Galatians and the circumcisers.

THE GOSPEL OF CHRIST (2:15-21)

Few passages in the Pauline letters are more dense, or more important for understanding the apostle Paul and his gospel, than this one. For Paul himself, it is a speech with an original audience (Cephas) and a new audience — all those in Galatia. Most interpreters of Galatians have correctly identified it as the thesis, or *propositio*, of the letter.

It has also been seen by many readers as a key passage containing Paul's 'doctrine' of justification by faith rather than works, and understandably so, for forms of the words 'justify/justification' (*dikaioō* and *dikaiosynē*, the latter sometimes translated 'righteousness'), 'faith/believe' (*pistis* and *pisteuō*), and 'works' (of the Law, *erga nomou*) appear five, four, and three times, respectively. Just as important are two other sets of words, 'live,' which like 'justify' occurs five times, and 'die/crucify,' which together appear a total of three times. Also significant is the very frequent mention of 'Christ (Jesus)/Jesus Christ/the Son of God' — a total of nine times. Finally, it is important to note words for 'sin/sinner/transgressor' (four times), and the word 'grace,' which appears only once but nonetheless provides a kind of heading for the entire passage: "the grace of God" (2:21).

This text, then, is about the grace of God in the death of Christ, by which sinners who believe and thus share in Christ's death are justified and find life. In fact — and this is a crucial pair of observations — it appears that 'justification' is virtually synonymous with 'life,' and 'faith' is virtually synonymous with 'crucifixion.' Ironically, life comes through death, and only through death — Christ's death for us, and our death with him. This is the substance of God's grace, and the heart of Paul's gospel.

Defining Some Key Terms

Before looking at the flow of Paul's argument, we must make a few comments about the first three key words noted above: 'justification,' 'faith,' and 'works.' Recent study of Paul has significantly advanced our understanding of the realities to which these terms point, and has also raised some difficult questions about them.

1. 'Justification' (and related words like 'righteousness,' all of which come from the same Greek root) has often been understood as a legal (judicial, forensic) concept. It is associated with the image of God as a judge rendering a 'not guilty' verdict to the guilty. However, although there is certainly a judicial dimension to justification, as we noted in chapter 6, it is now generally understood as a much more relational and especially covenantal concept than previously recognized (cf. Rom. 5:1-11, where it is paired with 'reconciliation'). To be justified is to be restored to right covenantal relations now, with certain hope of acquittal on the future day of judgment (Rom. 5:9-10; Gal. 5:5).

2. 'Faith' is likewise a covenantal term that implies not merely intellectual assent, but faithfulness — a total commitment of the self from the heart that is more akin to loyalty, obedience, and devotion (as in 'love of God') than to 'belief' or even 'trust' (though each of these must still be understood to be part of faith). A growing number of scholars — approaching a consensus — believe Galatians 2:15-21, like Romans 3:21-26 and Philippians 3:2-11, speaks not only of *our* faith but of *Christ's* faith, understood in this covenantal way as his faithfulness. Space does not permit an argument for this interpretation, but it is recognized in the NRSV margin and will be adopted as the basis for the commentary below. Specifically, it affects two verses (see page 202 — the phrases in question are in italics). The NRSV marginal translation (our interpretation) means that Paul understands Christ's death as his faithfulness to God in giving himself on the cross "for me" (us — Paul speaks representatively), and that it, rather than our performance of the works of the Law, is the basis of our right relationship with God.

The Faith of Christ in Galatians 2:15-21

Text	NRSV	NRSV margin
2:16	yet we know that a person is justified not by the works of the law but *through faith in Jesus Christ.* And we have come to believe in Christ Jesus, so that we might be justified *by faith in Christ,* and not by doing the works of the law, because no one will be justified by the works of the law.	yet we know that a person is justified not by the works of the law but *through the faith of Jesus Christ.* And we have come to believe in Christ Jesus, so that we might be justified *by the faith of Christ,* and not by doing the works of the law, because no one will be justified by the works of the law.
2:20	and it is no longer I who live, but it is Christ who lives in me. And the life I now live in the flesh I live *by faith in the Son of God,* who loved me and gave himself for me.	and it is no longer I who live, but it is Christ who lives in me. And the life I now live in the flesh I live *by the faith of the Son of God,* who loved me and gave himself for me.

3. Finally, the phrase "works of the law" has been the subject of much disputation. Earlier interpretations of Paul stressed that Paul was pitting any kind of human effort, including attempts to 'be moral' or obey the commandments, against "faith" (usually understood as 'belief' or 'trust') as the basis of justification (usually understood forensically). Although it is true that Paul dismisses any human effort as the basis of justification, this traditional interpretation has sometimes included the erroneous conclusion that Paul also dismissed 'good works' as unnecessary or unimportant. Furthermore, recent research suggests that the term "works of the law" may refer more to the ritual boundary markers of circumcision, calendar, and diet, rather than, say, the Ten Commandments — though this is by no means a settled question. In either case, two things are clear in 2:15-21 and elsewhere in Paul: justification is only by God's grace, not by human effort or status, and justification has a serious and thorough ethical dimension.

The Text

With these remarks in hand, we may proceed to the text itself. It is helpful to keep in mind the last verse (2:21), which both summarizes and serves as a key to the overall meaning of the passage. Paul begins with an emphatic affirmation, intended to include all Jewish believers ("We . . . Jews by birth [NAB, 'nature']"), that it is not their status as Jews who possess (or even perform) the Law that justifies them (2:15-16). While tipping his hat to the commonly held Jewish perspective distinguishing Jews from Gentile "sinners," Paul speaks as a Jewish believer who knows (as surely Peter and the circumcisers ought to know) that this distinction was not the basis for their justification. In 2:16, and again in 2:21, Paul asserts repeatedly and emphatically that the source of their justification is not possessing or performing the Law or any of the works of the Law. This is an impossibility both in principle and in experience, as Scripture itself asserts (Ps. 143:2 [142:2 LXX], quoted in 2:16). If it were possible, "Christ died for nothing" (2:21).

Rather, the source of all believers' justification is Christ's death, at God's initiative and as the expression of God's grace, as 2:21 clearly asserts.[9] The pair of antithetical grounds for justification — the Law versus Christ's death — appears also in 2:16, but now Paul twice refers to Christ's death as his faith(fulness), each time in opposition to the works of the Law. The faith of Christ, expressed in his death, is therefore the *objective* ground of believers' justification. Does this mean that justification is a 'done deal' for all because Christ has died? Not at all; Paul absolutely stresses the need for faith as the proper response to God's grace in Christ's death, and faith is therefore the *subjective* ground of justification. Paul says clearly that the purpose/result of faith is justification (2:16). It is possible, however, that even here Paul does not speak of faith *in* Christ but faith *into* (Gk. *eis*), a faith response that 'moves' people from outside of Christ into him (as the parallel text about baptism in 3:26-27 also suggests). Shortly (2:19-21) the nature of this faith will be more fully described.

In 2:17-18 Paul links his claims about justification in 2:15-16 to the social situation of Gentiles and Jews in Antioch and Galatia. First, he rejects the idea (perhaps suggested by the circumcisers) that if this experience of justification in Christ brings Jewish believers into contact with Gentiles and pollutes them with sin, then Christ is a "servant of sin." Next, he says he cannot go back and rebuild what he has torn down (that is, the requirement that Gentile believers observe the Law)[10] without admitting to, or else committing, serious transgression. Paul is adamant about the social implications of this new life/justification in Christ (cf. 3:28).

Paul then returns to the subject of faith, although the word itself does not

9. For the initiative of God, note the occurrence of the verb 'justify' in the passive voice, implying God as the actor, three times in 2:16.

10. There may also be an allusion here to the temple wall of Jew-Gentile separation (cf. Eph. 2:11-22, esp. v. 14).

appear, and to the character of the life that justification by faith has brought about in him (speaking representatively for all believers). In two potent images Paul depicts the response of faith as a death experience that generates life. First, the response of faith is a death "to the law, so that I might live to God" (2:19a). It is a severance from the Law as one's hope for justification and life — the very things most Jews found in the Law. How this death happened *through* the Law is unclear, but the purpose/result of it is life in relation to God (the parallel with the middle of 2:16 is unmistakable: faith in order to be justified, death to the Law in order to gain life with God).

Second, the response of faith is a death inasmuch as it is an act of such complete identification with Christ's death as to be a participation in it, a 'cocrucifixion' (*synestaurōmai*, 2:19b). The perfect tense of the Greek verb (= 'I have been crucified') suggests a past act with ongoing consequences; believers remain in a constant state of being crucified and thus dead (2:20a). The old life and old self are gone, together with their passions (5:24; cf. 6:14b; Rom. 6:1-14). This too engenders life, because the crucified but resurrected and living Christ now lives in believers (2:20a) — who likewise exist in him (3:26). Naturally this does not mean a literal death, for believers do go on living "in the flesh" (NIV, "body"), but not in their own strength. Rather they live 'in' or 'by' the faith of the Son of God (2:20b). But what does that mean?

The clue is in the last phrase of 2:20, where the Son of God's death, understood as the expression of his faith, is described in the phrase "loved me and gave himself for me" (cf. 1:4). Because this phrase clearly refers to the one act of death on the cross, we render it better as 'loved me by giving himself for me.' So for Paul, Christ's death on the cross was simultaneously his act of self-giving faith(fulness) toward God (2:16, 20) and self-giving love toward humanity (2:20). It was a unified act of covenant fulfillment, of love for God and for neighbor. It was the epoch-altering and paradigmatic performance of what Paul, referring to the essence of the believer's life, will later call "faith working through love" (5:6 NRSV, NAB), or (better) "faith expressing itself through love" (NIV). To live by the faithfulness of the Son of God, then, is to live in such wholehearted devotion to God that it expresses itself in sacrificial, or cruciform, love for others. And this is possible only by means of the Spirit of the Son given by God (4:6; cf. 5:16-25, esp. v. 25); that is, "Christ . . . lives in me" (2:20).

To look for justification and life anywhere other than in the faithful death of Christ and in our cocrucifixion with him voids the grace of God and the death of Christ (2:16). *For Paul, any attempt to supplement crucifixion supplants it.*

Summary of Galatians 1–2

Thus far Galatians has been largely an autobiographical presentation of the essence of the gospel, and Paul has chosen each aspect of the material to be instructive and exemplary. The first two chapters of the letter have affirmed, in sum, that:

- Paul's apostleship and gospel have their source in God's call and revelation, not in any human person (even the Jerusalem apostles) or teaching.
- Paul's apostleship began in an unexpected experience of conversion, call, and commission that changed the zealot persecutor of the church into an unstoppable proclaimer of God's universally available grace, especially among the Gentiles.
- His missionary activity among the Gentiles was unofficially appreciated by Jewish believers, and then, years later, formally approved by the Jerusalem leadership.
- The influence of Jewish believers who thought Gentiles should be circumcised did not deter Paul, who publicly opposed Peter on the matter after Peter succumbed to their influence.
- The gospel is about the grace of God that justifies Jews and Gentiles who respond in faith to the proclamation of Christ crucified.
- The source of this justification, therefore, is not possession or performance of the Jewish Law and its customs, but the covenant-fulfilling, faithful and loving death of God's Son, who now lives in believers.

3:1–4:31. THE PROMISE OF THE FATHER: THE TESTIMONY OF SCRIPTURE

Shifting his attention from Peter and those of like mind (the circumcisers), Paul now addresses the Galatians directly. Beginning with their experience of the Spirit (3:1-5), he interweaves their story and his (3:1-5; 3:23-29; 4:1-20) within a series of scriptural interpretations (3:6–4:7; 4:21-31) with one goal, one thesis: to show that their liberating experience of the Spirit, which has made them God's children and which began and continues through faith, is the fulfillment of God's ancient promise to Abraham to bless all nations/Gentiles. To seek circumcision would be a return to slavery, as 5:1 will state explicitly.

THE GALATIANS' INITIAL AND ONGOING
EXPERIENCE OF ṬHE SPIRIT (3:1-5)

Paul now connects the faith of which he has just spoken (in 2:1-21) to the Galatians' initial and ongoing experience of the Spirit. As noted in the introduction, he calls them foolish (3:1, 3) for even thinking about trading the bewitching message of the circumcisers for the powerful message of Christ crucified (3:1). This message was clearly and publicly delivered by Paul, not only through his words about Christ but also through his story (1:13) and his persona, symbolized by the scars (6:17) that mark his own grace-filled conversion. The Galatians possessed or performed no "works of the law" but simply responded in faith to the gospel, and thereby received the Spirit (3:2). The Spirit continues with them as God's gracious gift received in faith — manifested, for example, in the working of miracles (3:5). To abandon "faith" for "works of the law" would be to abandon the "Spirit" for the "flesh" — both literally (bodily circumcision) and figuratively (the anti-God impulse that leads people to value humanly defined status).

Furthermore, to make this foolish move would be also to abandon the cross, something the circumcisers appear at least to want to de-emphasize (6:12). For Paul the Spirit is intimately connected to the cross: one responds to the message of the cross and receives the Spirit (3:1-2); one experiences Christ living within (by his Spirit) by being cocrucified with him (2:19-20). Moreover, the presence of the Spirit in Galatia, especially at the churches' birth, was characterized by suffering (3:4 NIV, correctly, against NRSV and NAB; cf. Acts 13–14), another form of identification with the cross.[11] If the Galatians abandon faith, the Spirit, and the cross, that suffering — and indeed their entire experience of Christ — will have been "for nothing" (NRSV, NIV), "in vain" (NAB).

Paul's main point in all this is not stated explicitly but becomes clear as the rest of chapter 3 unfolds: that the Galatians' experience of the Spirit by faith is evidence of their being fully incorporated into the Messiah and the messianic (eschatological) age as Gentile recipients of the Spirit who was promised by God. Nothing more is needed or possible. To change would be to regress, to live as if the new age had not begun.

GOD'S PROMISE OF THE SPIRIT TO ABRAHAM (3:6-14)

The compact and complex scriptural argument in these verses builds to 3:14 and the thesis that Paul wants to drive home: "in Christ Jesus the blessing of

---

11. For the confluence of the Spirit and suffering, see also Rom. 8.

Abraham [has] come to the Gentiles, so that we might receive the promise of the Spirit through faith." This summarizes both Paul's gospel (see 3:8) and the Galatians' experience. Paul focuses on Abraham because Abraham was understood as the proselyte par excellence, and was almost certainly the focus of the circumcisers' arguments for Gentile circumcision. After all, according to Genesis 17 Abraham and his male family members received circumcision as the sign of God's covenant with him, an everlasting covenant with both him and his descendants, who would be members of the covenant only if they too were circumcised (Gen. 17:9-14). At stake, then, is the definition of Abraham's descendants or children, that is, members of the covenant people and recipients of the blessing (originally the land) promised to Abraham.

Quoting Genesis 15:6, one of his favorite texts, Paul first shows that Abraham's righteousness or justification came from faith (3:6), thus making faith (not circumcision) the defining characteristic of Abraham and his children (3:7). Paul then connects Genesis 15:6 with Genesis 12:3 to demonstrate that Abraham's righteousness, children, and blessing would extend to include Gentiles (or nations, Gk. *ethnē*) who believe (3:8-9). For Paul, these texts recorded the gospel announced in advance (3:8). It is a gospel of faith, righteousness, and blessing — not the blessing of the land, but the blessing of the Spirit, for the prophetic tradition (assumed but not named by Paul) had interpreted God's eschatological blessing as the presence of God's Spirit throughout the land.[12] Inasmuch as the prophets also believed that the Gentiles would eventually come to Zion and participate in the true worship of God, they implicitly acknowledged the eschatological gift of the Spirit to the Gentiles, too; Paul makes that belief explicit.

Paul's complex scriptural argumentation continues in 3:10-14 with citations from Deuteronomy and Habakkuk.[13] This passage has been much disputed, but three points of Paul's argument are clear: (1) fundamentally the Law carries with it a curse rather than the blessing of life; (2) justification (and thus life) derive from faith, not the Law; and (3) Christ redeemed "us" (Jews/Jewish believers) from the Law's curse in order to open the blessing of Abraham — the Spirit — to Jews and Gentiles alike. This important third point rests on two images that appear in 3:13. The first is the image of a figure hanging on a tree, which was for Jews an image of a person cursed by God: "anyone hung on a tree is under God's curse" (Deut. 21:23). The second is Paul's creative image of Christ's death as an act of slave redemption (cf. 1 Cor. 6:19-20). This redemption is effected by an exchange — Christ was cursed for us (on the cross) so that we might be blessed in him (cf. 2 Cor. 5:21). God's promised blessing comes, ironi-

---

12. Ezek. 36:22-32; Joel 2:28-29.
13. Deut. 27:26 and 28:58-59 in 3:10; 21:23 in 3:13; Hab. 2:4 in 3:11.

cally, by a divine curse, which explains in part how the gospel could be a "stumbling block to Jews" (1 Cor. 1:23). It is quite possible, in fact, that Paul had earlier used Deuteronomy 21:23 as a proof text for his opposition to the fledgling church.[14]

As far as Paul is now concerned, however, Christ's cross has inaugurated the age of the Spirit, in which Jews and Gentiles alike inherit Abraham's blessing and are justified by believing the gospel of Christ crucified and thereby being incorporated into the covenant people who exist now in Christ.

THE LAW AND THE PROMISE (3:15-29)

A natural question arising from Paul's apparent dismissal of the Law as the source of blessing and life is, What about the Law? Was it no good? Did it have no purpose? Paul answers this kind of question in three main parts: (1) the Law was later than the promise and thus cannot alter it (3:15-18); (2) the Law was not opposed to the promise but, because of sin, could not deliver life (3:21-22); and (3) the Law had an important but temporary role until the promise was fulfilled (3:19-20, 23-25). This leads to a dramatic affirmation of the equality of all who are in Christ as Abraham's offspring or "seed" (3:26-29).

Paul begins his discussion of the relationship between the Law and the promise with an analogy from everyday life: a person's "will" (3:15 NRSV, NAB) — though the term Paul suggestively uses *(diathēkē)* also means "covenant" (so NIV). His point seems to be that a will and the promises it contains, once ratified, cannot be supplemented or canceled by a third party, even a mediator of the covenant maker or testator (cf. 3:20). In the case of the (Mosaic) Law, since it arrived 430 years (according to standard Jewish chronology; cf. Exod. 12:40) after the divinely ratified covenant *(diathēkē)* with, and promise to, Abraham, it cannot void the Abrahamic promise (3:17). The 'inheritance' associated with the will/covenant — the Gentiles' reception of the Spirit — can therefore come only from (and on the terms of) the promise, not the later Law.

In the middle of this analogy is Paul's significant interpretation of the promise to Abraham and his "seed" with a singular, rather than a collective, sense: to Abraham and his *one* descendant, Christ (3:16). This almost parenthetical remark is significant because it allows Paul later (3:26-29) to redefine Abraham's descendants as all those who are in Christ, the one "seed" (3:29; cf. 3:14). Ironically, then, Paul's singular interpretation actually turns out to be collective.

The subject of the Law's function continues in 3:19-25, though Paul's vari-

14. Interestingly, several texts from the Dead Sea Scrolls apply Deut. 21:23 specifically to crucifixion.

ous images are not completely transparent. The main point is that the Law, in addition to being late, was also temporary and limited in scope. It was *not* an alteration of the original covenant because it did not come directly from God but through a mediator, Moses (3:19b-20). It was intended to function only until Christ the (singular) offspring (NIV, "the Seed") arrived (3:19). And it was added "because of transgressions" (3:19) — which might mean to increase, reveal, or restrain them, since Paul in Romans seems to attribute all three functions to the Law. Here the context suggests both a revealing and a restraining function.

Paul emphatically denies that his argument pits the Law of Moses against the promise to Abraham (3:21). The Law, he implies, bears witness to the need for the promise because the Law itself cannot give life (3:21b) but rather reveals that another life-giving power is needed to liberate those "under the power of sin" — that is, enslaved to sin (3:22a). This power is not our faith (so NRSV, NAB, NIV) but the faith(fulness) of Jesus Christ (NRSV mg.; cf. 1:4; 2:15-21), the benefits of which are appropriated by the response of faith. (The appearance of both kinds of faith in 3:22 — Christ's and ours — is very significant.)

The restraining function of the Law appears in the provocative image of the *paidagōgos* (3:23-25). Variously interpreted as "disciplinarian" (NRSV, NAB), "supervisor" (NIV, implied), and "custodian" (RSV), this term refers to an ancient household slave whose job was to guide a family's (male) children back and forth to school, protecting them from harm and providing some basic moral guidelines. Paul employs the image here to highlight the temporary function of the Law, since the function of the *paidagōgos* was exhausted when the child reached adulthood. Since Christ (3:24) and faith (either ours or, more likely, his; 3:23, 25) have now come, the Law's function has ceased and we are liberated from its rule (3:24-25). Why? Because "in Christ" (NRSV, NAB) believers have reached adulthood, paradoxically, by becoming children of God through faith (3:26; again, either our faith or, more likely, Christ's, but not "faith in Christ" [NIV]).

The important concept 'in/into Christ' dominates the conclusion of this section (occurring three times in 3:26-29). Since Christ is the one Seed or offspring, those who are in him are God's children, Abraham's offspring ("seed," 3:29), and "heirs according to the promise" (3:29). To be "in Christ" means to have responded in faith to the gospel of Christ's faithful death and to have moved in baptism from outside of Christ "into" Christ (3:27; cf. 3:16). Furthermore, Paul continues, it is to 'clothe' oneself with Christ (3:27) — so to identify with him and his death as to be conformed to it (cf. Rom. 13:14; Eph. 4:24). It is likely that this was symbolized in baptism by the donning of new garments. The Pauline experience of faith-baptism-dressing is clearly one of total attachment to and participation in Christ.

As the sole defining criterion of God's children, being "in Christ" erases all distinctions among human beings that are used to identify and separate them (3:28): ethnic/racial (Jew-Gentile), socioeconomic (slave-free), and gender (male-female). This is not to say that these distinctions actually disappear, but that they no longer matter and must not be allowed to divide communities in Christ. What does matter is that these disparate groups are unified in a new creation (6:15) to live in faith, hope, and love (5:5-6). Of particular importance in the context of Galatians is the unity of Gentile and Jew, but the other pairs should not be ignored. It is certainly within the realm of possibility, for instance, that Paul's opposition to circumcision is at least partially motivated (or confirmed) by its exclusion of women. The patriarchies of antiquity gave great status and preference to free males. Paul — or rather Christ, according to Paul — undermines all such patriarchies and, indeed, every system of subjugation based on ethnicity, race, class, status, or gender.

What Paul does not say in these verses is that *all* things are matters of indifference in Christ. He does not, for instance, say 'there is neither moral nor immoral.' The fruit of the Spirit, the evidence of liberation from the "flesh" (5:16-26), remains crucial to the meaning of life in Christ.

THE FATHER'S GIFT OF THE SON AND THE SPIRIT (4:1-7)

Paul now uses the analogies of inheritance, slavery, and majority/minority status introduced in the previous section to depict the radical change that has occurred because of the triune activity of Father, Son, and Spirit that has inaugurated the new age. This will set the stage for an impassioned appeal to the Galatians not to turn back (4:8-20).

Paul begins with the legal principle that because minor children cannot receive an inheritance from their father but are "under" guardians and trustees until the father takes action to change their status, they are "no better than" their father's slaves — who cannot inherit either (4:1-2). The slavery of which Paul speaks is "to the elemental spirits" (*ta stoicheia*, 4:3). The term often means something like 'the elemental principles of the universe' (earth, air, water, fire), though here in Galatians 4 (cf. also 4:9) it appears to indicate a set of hostile cosmic powers behind everything that promises to deliver life to people — both Gentiles and Jews — but enslaves them instead.[15] Humanity before and outside of Christ, says Paul, is in a state of slavery (cf. 3:22).

The analogy is clear: God (the Father) has now taken action that radically alters people's status from minors to legal heirs, and from slaves to free chil-

15. Cf. 4:8-9, as well as Col. 1:16; 2:8, 20; Eph. 1:21; 3:10; 6:12.

dren. This took place "when the fullness of time had come," when it was time (from the Father's perspective) to end humanity's age of minority and make "us" (those who believe the gospel) God's children. Paul depicts God's dramatic action in two parallel, interrelated stages: the sending of the Son (4:4-5) and the sending of the Spirit (4:6-7).

Paul's description of the sending of the Son echoes 3:14. Born to a Jewish woman and fully human, the Son was sent not fundamentally to teach, but to identify with and "redeem" those "under" (i.e., enslaved by) the Law (Jews) and thereby to open up adoption as God's children to a wider group ("we," 4:5) that includes also Gentiles. This redemption was accomplished by the Son's death (1:4); those who identify with the death of the Son become God's children and receive God's Spirit, as the Galatian believers have done (4:6; cf. 3:1-5).

Paul's words about the sending of the Spirit into believers' hearts reveal that he sees the Spirit as a continuation of the gift and ministry of the Son (cf. Rom. 5:5-8). The Spirit is the Spirit of the Son, continuing the Son's pattern of life within the community of God's adopted children (cf. 2:19-20) and enabling them to experience God as Jesus the Son did, calling out "Abba! Father!" (4:6; cf. Rom. 8:15). For believers slavery has ended, and they have received all the privileges of adoption — a Roman custom in which the adopted children were treated like those born to the parents. Being no longer slaves or minors but mature children, believers are "heir[s]" (4:7) — recipients of the Spirit now, and of the fullness of righteousness in the future (5:5).

APOSTOLIC APPEAL (4:8-20)

Having concluded his first of two major scriptural arguments for understanding believers' (especially Gentiles') experience of the Spirit as liberation from slavery, and having applied this directly to the Galatians' experience of the Spirit (3:23-29; 4:1-7), Paul now wears his heart on his sleeve.

He begins by reminding the Galatians that they have in fact been liberated from the pseudogods and "weak and beggarly elemental spirits" (4:8-9; cf. 4:3). Their slavery to the gods and powers that are not God has given way to knowledge of, and by, the true God (4:9a; cf. 1 Cor. 8:3), the God of Abraham. But if, ironically, they turn to Jewish Law — here especially calendar laws (4:10) — they will in effect be abandoning the true God of Abraham revealed in Christ and returning to slavery. In that case Paul will have wasted his evangelistic efforts (4:11).

Appealing now to his initial, warm relationship with the Galatians, Paul begs them not to allow his work to have been in vain (4:12-20). His tone is one of confusion as well as scolding (4:20) as he complains — in creative and compelling imagery — that he has to go through the process of pregnancy/fetal development and the pains of childbirth with them all over again (4:19). What does this developmental process mean for them?

First, it means imitating their parent and teacher, who himself has become like them (4:12a). Paul is referring to his principle of accommodation to the culture in which he ministers (1 Cor. 9:19-23). The Galatians, then, should live as Gentiles (as Paul did among them) and not attempt to live like Jews. Second, they should renew their esteem for Paul. When he was first among them, they did him no wrong (4:12b; so NAB, correctly), for even though Paul had come to Galatia because of a weakness in the flesh (probably meaning as a result of persecution) that 'tested' the Galatians (4:13-14), they received him with "goodwill" (4:15a), like a divine messenger or angel — even as Christ himself (4:14). They would have done anything for Paul, as Paul graphically reminds them (4:15b).

Paul wonders now, however, whether his honesty about the gospel has made him their enemy (4:16). This leads to his third wish: that they will abandon their new 'friends' whose attention to them is not really for their good but for their alienation (4:17 NIV) or isolation/exclusion (NAB/NRSV). The one who really has their best interest at heart — their full inclusion in Christ — is Paul (4:18), their founder and 'mother.'

FREEDOM AND SLAVERY: THE ALLEGORY OF HAGAR AND SARAH (4:21-31)

To illustrate his central thesis about the liberating activity of the Spirit over against an enslaving regression to life under the Law, Paul turns to the ancient and revered rhetorical technique of allegory (4:24). Practiced by Jews and non-Jews alike, this technique was one way of contemporizing an ancient narrative for a new audience. It demonstrates deep respect for both the old story and the new situation, on the assumption that the former can somehow speak to the latter. Paul urges the Galatians, anxious to be "under" or enslaved by (NRSV, "subject to") the Law, to learn a lesson from the Law (here meaning the books of Moses [Gen. 16–18; 21]) itself (4:21).[16] Paul's claim is that the Law itself supports the promises of God (cf. 4:21) and Paul's gospel.

The allegory is an interpretation of the story of the two women, Hagar and Sarah, who bore sons to Abraham. "These women are two covenants" (4:24a), and various dimensions of the story correspond to aspects of the religious situation in Paul's day and especially in the Galatian churches. The major features of the allegory may be seen in the following chart:

16. "Under" (*hypo*) is used in this sense in 3:23, 25; 4:4, 5; 5:18.

Paul's Allegory of Hagar and Sarah

Hagar and Her Child(ren)	*Sarah and Her Child(ren)*
slave woman	free woman
bears children for slavery	[implied: bears children for freedom]
in slavery with her children	free, mother of believers [= her free children]
from Mount Sinai, corresponding to Jerusalem of Paul's day (associated with the circumcisers)	corresponds to Jerusalem above (whose children will be more numerous than the children of the earthly Jerusalem [4:27 = Isa. 54:1])
son Ishmael born according to the flesh [implied: circumcisers are according to the flesh]	son Isaac born through the promise and according to the Spirit = believers being children of the promise and the Spirit
Ishmael persecuted Sarah's son Isaac = circumcisers persecuting Gentile believers	son Isaac was persecuted by Hagar's son Ishmael = Gentile believers being persecuted by circumcisers
= covenant based on law and associated with the circumcisers	= covenant based on promise, Christ, and Spirit, and associated with Paul

Paul's creative hand is evident throughout the allegory. The normal Jewish interpretation of Isaac and Ishmael as father of Jews and of Gentiles, respectively, is revised so that Ishmael is the father of (certain) Jews (Jewish believers who cling to the Law) while Isaac is the father of (certain) Gentiles (Gentile believers). Much emphasis is placed on the contrast between Hagar the slave (Gen. 16:2) and Sarah the free woman, and on the character of Isaac as the child of promise (cf. Gen. 17:15–18:15), to corroborate Paul's own convictions about slavery under the Law and the promise now fulfilled for the Gentiles.

It must be stressed that the point of the allegory is not to disparage the Law and the covenant based on the Law themselves, but the Law and its covenant *as interpreted and practiced by the circumcisers in Galatia.* As we saw in chapter 3, Paul believes that the Law had an important, if temporary, role. *The covenant based on the Law is a covenant of 'slavery' only once the covenant of promise has arrived.*

From this allegory Paul draws two interrelated practical conclusions:

213

(1) drive out the circumcisers, the children of the slave woman, who will not share the inheritance of the free woman's child (4:30, quoting Gen. 21:10; cf. 5:10); and (2) recognize and remain in the freedom all believers have, and do not return to slavery by being circumcised (4:31). The full implications of the second conclusion, implicit in the allegory itself, become explicit at the head of the next section.

Summary of Galatians 3–4

The thrust of Paul's argument in these chapters is that the Galatians are already fully descendants of Abraham (3:6, 29; 4:31), children of the promise as recipients of the Spirit in accord with God's plan and will. Nothing more is needed, and anything else will reverse and annul their freedom. Specifically:

- The Galatians already possess the Spirit by responding in faith to the gospel of Christ crucified.
- God promised to and through Abraham — and his "Seed" (Christ) — to bless, justify, and give the Spirit to all Gentiles who have faith like his.
- The Law postdated the covenant and had a temporary revealing and restraining function for the time between Moses and the Messiah.
- Christ's death as a curse for us redeems believers from that which enslaves them, including the Law and the cosmic powers.
- Ethnic/racial, socioeconomic, and gender distinctions have no importance in Christ.
- God's sending of the Son and Spirit has radically altered believers' situation and must not be undone by returning to the Law, and thus to slavery, through circumcision.

5:1–6:10. THE FREEDOM OF THE SPIRIT: THE LIFE OF FAITH AND LOVE

In the first four chapters Paul has argued for the truth of his gospel: that Christ's cross has inaugurated the age of the Spirit promised by the Father, and that Gentiles receive that Spirit and all attendant blessings without doing the works of the Law. The word 'circumcision' itself has barely been mentioned, but it will appear explicitly at the beginning and end of this last third of the letter (5:2-12; 6:11-18). The real focus of these last two chapters, however, is the ethical implications of Paul's Law-free gospel of cross and Spirit.

Over the years some interpreters have found Galatians 5–6 to be unconnected to the first four chapters, suggesting (1) that a new group of people is being addressed (perhaps Gentile 'libertines' who saw no connection between justification, or the Spirit, and righteous living), or (2) that Paul simply does not do a good job of showing the relationship between the 'theology' of chapters 1–4 and the 'ethics' of chapters 5–6.

Both suggestions are misguided. About the first, it is much more likely that in raising concrete issues of behavior Paul is addressing the concerns of the circumcisers, and of those they have influenced, about the possible dangers of a Law-free gospel of freedom in the Spirit. How can such 'good news' produce a righteous life? What would its criteria be? As for the second suggestion, a careful reading of chapters 5 and 6 will reveal that Paul actually connects them very closely to what precedes, as we have already observed in comparing 2:20 with 5:6 on the topic of faith and love.

To cut, then, to the chase and to put the issue in appropriately Jewish terms: *Is Paul's gospel of cross, faith, and Spirit capable of enabling people to keep the covenant into which they have supposedly been incorporated?* Or, on the other hand, *Is the Law necessary after all to counteract the twin realities of sin and the flesh?* These last two chapters constitute Paul's emphatic yes to the first question and no to the second. They present an overview of life in the Spirit as a life lived according to the cross. It is a life, paradoxically, of both radical freedom and radical 'slavery' — not freedom from responsibility, and not slavery to the Law, but the freedom of death to the "flesh" and cruciform love for others in the Spirit. Ironically, such a life in fact fulfills the Law.

CHRIST, THE SPIRIT, AND CIRCUMCISION (5:1-12)

In these verses Paul spells out very clearly the basic twofold aim of his letter: (1) to warn against Gentile circumcision in principle (5:1-6) and therefore also against the circumcisers themselves (5:7-12), and (2) to affirm Christ and the cluster of realities associated with him (grace, faith, the Spirit, etc.). His warnings and affirmations are grounded in his absolute conviction that Christ and the Spirit are sufficient for justification and righteousness. Christ by his death has liberated those who believe (5:1a; cf. 1:4); they are therefore to remain in that freedom and not allow themselves to be reenslaved by submitting to the Law via the entry point of circumcision (5:1b).

Paul writes emphatically — "Stand firm. . . . Mark my words!" (5:1-2 NIV) — as he will also at the beginning of the similar letter summary (6:11). Superficially there is a contradiction in what he then says. On the one hand, circumcision is antithetical to Christ (5:2-4); that is, circumcision and Christ are mutu-

Pisidian Antioch: **A column carved with the bull of the cult of Cybele**

ally exclusive. On the other hand, circumcision is irrelevant in Christ (5:6); that is, circumcision and Christ are mutually compatible, even if circumcision is insignificant. How do we explain this apparent contradiction?

For Paul, Christ is everything or nothing. Either God has inaugurated the new, eschatological age of the Spirit through Christ, or not. Either justification, or life in the Spirit, is received by faith, or not. Either cruciform faith expressing itself through cruciform love is the essence of covenantal existence, or not. Either this is all of grace, or not. *Whereas for the circumcisers Christ is necessary but not sufficient, for Paul Christ is either sufficient or else not necessary.* Any Gentile Galatians in Christ who are circumcised become an anachronism, returning to their former state of slavery (4:9; 5:1), losing any benefit from Christ (5:2) and removing themselves from him and from grace (5:4). Circumcision is a gate into a way of life — obedience to the entire Law (5:3) — that has had its day but has ended with the coming of the Messiah and his Spirit (3:24). Now anyone — Gentile or Jew — who is in Christ, by faith, shares in the hope of future righteousness (5:5) and expresses that faith, as Christ did (2:20), in love (5:6).[17] Circumcision counts for nothing because 'having' it (or not) neither enables nor prevents entry into the realm of Christ and the Spirit. Seeking it, however, betrays a lack

---

17. On faith, hope, and love, see also 1 Thess. 1:3; 5:8; 1 Cor. 13:13; Rom. 5:1-5.

of confidence in the power of grace and faith, the sufficiency of Christ and the Spirit. That is why circumcision before being in Christ is irrelevant and compatible with Christ, but after being in Christ it is inappropriate and incompatible.

For this reason Paul warns explicitly against the circumcisers. They have "cut in" (5:7 NIV) on the Galatians' spiritual race, tripping them up. Their activity is not from God (5:8) but is like a cancer, or a yeast (5:9), spreading throughout the Galatian churches (cf. 1 Cor. 5:6-8). While Paul expresses confidence that the Galatians will heed him and (he implies) deport the circumcisers (5:10a), he also leaves no doubt about his feelings toward the circumcisers themselves. They will ultimately be punished by God (5:10b), but in the meantime Paul hopes their circumcising knives will slip, inflict a bit of temporal pain and bodily injury (5:12), and (perhaps) put them where they belong — in company with the self-castrated pagan priests of Cybele. As with the biblical writers who preceded him, for Paul the enemies of God and God's people are his enemies, though he would never now pick up the knife himself.

It must be stressed that Paul's message of the sufficiency of grace and faith, of Christ and Spirit, is no formula for 'easy believism' or cheap grace. Paul does not advocate keeping the Law, but he does describe the life of faith as "obeying the truth" (5:7).[18] And as the following passages will show, life in the Spirit of Christ is one of costly grace. Paul himself knew this; his focus on the cross instead of circumcision (part and parcel of his earlier zeal, 1:13-14) had created for him a life of constant persecution that the circumcisers, he is sure, want to avoid (6:12).

FREEDOM, CRUCIFORM LOVE, AND THE
FULFILLMENT OF THE LAW (5:13-15)

Paul saw these circumcisers as attempting to steal believers' freedom and return them to slavery. 'Freedom' was one of Paul's watchwords. In one breath it summarized for him believers' situation in Christ (2:4; 5:1). This freedom provided by Christ and the Spirit was comprehensive: redemption (3:13; 4:5) and liberation from false gods and "elemental spirits" (4:8-9), from sin (3:22), from the flesh (5:16), and from the Law (5:18) — that is, from "the present evil age" (1:4). But a message that focuses on freedom can be misunderstood, as Paul learned also in his dealings with the Corinthians. The circumcisers had good reason to be concerned, as they surely were, about so much emphasis on faith and grace — on 'freedom.' What exactly does it mean for Paul?

In just a few words here (expanded in 1 Cor. 8:1–11:1), Paul provides his an-

---

18. Cf. 2:5, 14; see also, e.g., Rom. 1:5 for the faith-obedience connection.

swer. Freedom is a *communal reality* for him, as the following verses indicate. Negatively, freedom is not an excuse for "self-indulgence" (NRSV) or "the flesh" (literally; so NAB) — the anticovenantal (anti-God, antihuman, and anticommunity) impulse within human beings and communities that seeks to exercise control over them.[19] For Paul the opposite of the flesh is not some immaterial human spirit, but the Spirit of God, the Spirit of the Son. Thus not giving opportunity to the flesh means, by implication, giving opportunity to the Spirit (cf. the same contrast, explicitly, in 5:16-26). Positively, then, freedom means allowing the Spirit to produce the fruit of love (5:13; cf. 5:22), and specifically the kind of radical, sacrificial love that can only be pictured in the image of mutual 'slavery' (NRSV, correctly, translating *douleuete,* related to *doulos,* in 5:13), a more powerful image than simply "service" (NAB, NIV). This is the kind of love found in the story of Christ, the love that issues from faith(fulness) toward God (5:6; cf. 2:20), the love that took the form of slavery (Phil. 2:6-8).

Why is this kind of love necessary for those who by faith now have freedom in Christ? Because the entire Law is "fulfilled" (NAB, correctly rendering *peplērōtai*) — not merely "summed up" (NRSV, NIV) — in one divine word: "You shall love your neighbor as yourself" (5:14, quoting Lev. 19:18). To those who fear that Paul's gospel completely dismisses the Law, Paul echoes Jesus (Mark 12:28-31) in affirming that in loving one's neighbor one fulfills the Law — meaning one's covenantal responsibilities toward other people (so also Rom. 13:8-10; cf. 8:3-4).

Verse 15 is not a word of caution (i.e., 'Bite and devour one another carefully lest you consume one another') but a graphic, if deliberately understated, proscription of unloving, community-destructive behavior. It is the polar opposite of neighbor love (5:14) and burden bearing (6:2), whatever its source — including especially disputes between Gentile and Jewish believers. Love, as Paul says elsewhere (1 Cor. 8:1), builds up; it does not tear down. Paul may well be hinting that some Galatians, and all the circumcisers, reveal their lack of faith and their failure to fulfill or obey the Law (6:13) by their community-damaging activity. To be free is to love and serve others.

WALKING IN THE SPIRIT (5:16-26)

Paul proceeds now to depict in somewhat more detail the life of faith expressing itself in love, in the Spirit, that fulfills the Law. He uses three images to convey the character of this life: walking, warring, and fruit bearing.

---

19. By "flesh" Paul does not here mean 'the body,' as he does in 2:20 and 4:13, as if the body were somehow inherently evil.

In three places the passage contains the imagery of a walk within the Spirit's sphere of influence, being led and guided by that Spirit (5:16, 18, 25). Unfortunately this image is partially hidden in the NRSV, NAB, and NIV, which all render the first verb in the passage "live" instead of 'walk' (*peripateite*, 5:16).[20] The image comes through, however, in 5:18 (NRSV, NIV: "led"; NAB, "guided") and 5:25 (NRSV, "be guided"; NAB, "follow"; NIV, "keep in step with"). Paul reminds the Galatians that "if" (meaning 'since') they live (are justified and in covenant relation with God) by the Spirit, they are obliged also to do the Spirit's bidding (5:25). The 'indicative mood' of justification, so to speak, contains an inherent imperative that cannot be ignored.

The image of life with God as a journey, of course, has a long history before and after Paul. Part of this history may explain the second image: warfare between the "Spirit" and the "flesh" (NRSV, NAB; NIV's "sinful nature" is probably a misleading translation of *sarx*). Jewish tradition, going back to Deuteronomy 30 (esp. 30:15), depicted life as a choice between two paths. These 'two ways' were the choice of God, covenant, blessing, and life, or the choice of other gods, infidelity, adversity, and death. For Paul these choices are between the Spirit and the flesh, two forces in opposition to each other (5:16-17, 24-25). He implicitly associates the flesh with the Law (5:18), and thus with sin as a power (3:22) — a set of connections that becomes more explicit in Romans. Believers have "crucified the flesh" (5:24) by their death with Christ and to the Law (2:19); they have severed their relationship with the flesh, but it still exists and exercises power, even within the community of those in Christ. It must therefore be actively resisted (5:16, 25).

This warfare between the flesh and the Spirit leads to the third image — fruit bearing. Both the flesh and the Spirit are active agents, the former producing "works" (5:19, using a term that echoes, perhaps deliberately, "works of the law"), the latter "fruit" (5:22). Paul includes a list of the "works" and "fruit" of each, respectively, similar to the common ancient genres of vice lists and virtue lists. But Paul's lists have a substantial theological twist. The vice list (5:19-21a) is not simply an inventory of bad habits; the activities listed are covenant violations, actions contrary to faith ("idolatry") and love (the rest). Those whose lives are characterized by such behavior demonstrate that they do not have the Spirit, are outside the covenant and not justified, and hence will not inherit God's kingdom (5:21; cf. 1 Cor. 6:9-10).

In contrast to the works of the flesh is the fruit of the Spirit (5:22-23). This multifaceted fruit differs from the 'gifts' of the Spirit (1 Cor. 12; cf. Rom. 12 and Eph. 4), of which each believer apparently receives at least one, but not all, in that the Spirit imparts the fruit in its entirety to all believers, rather than just

---

20. The same problem reappears, more dramatically, in the translations of Ephesians.

one aspect of the fruit (e.g., joy but not self-control). Once again the list reflects covenant obligations (e.g., love, appropriately listed first in this context, and faith[fulness]), but with clear echoes of that covenant as embodied in Christ (cf. 2:20; 2 Cor. 10:1) and experienced by Paul (e.g., "joy").

The image of fruit bearing might imply a passive and/or individualistic approach to ethics, but that is clearly not Paul's intent (e.g., 5:26). The activity of the Spirit requires the cooperation and effort of believers. This occurs not in isolation but in community and in relationships — where either strife or kindness, envy or generosity can prevail. This communal focus continues in the following section.

THE LAW OF CHRIST IN THE LIFE
OF THE COMMUNITY (6:1-10)

Getting down to some more specifics before concluding with a general admonition, Paul concludes his discourse on life in the Spirit by naming three concrete areas of responsibility and offering one final image of this life. The three responsibilities are for others, for self, and for teachers. The image, like fruit bearing, is agricultural: sowing with abandon.

The first responsibility believers have is for others (6:1-3), and it is twofold: 'restoration' and 'burden bearing' more generally. Those addressed in verse 1 *(hoi pneumatikoi)* are probably *all* the Galatians by virtue of their being recipients of the Spirit (NRSV is close to this reading), rather than a select set of "spiritual" people (so NAB, NIV). They are gently and carefully to "restore" those who have transgressed (in context, meaning returned to the works of the flesh listed in 5:19-21a), lest they also be led astray. This is not optional behavior, because the onetime transgressor may eventually become the regular practitioner, who will then forfeit the kingdom of God (5:21). Neither is bearing one another's burdens optional, whatever they may be — temptation, economic hardship, grief, other forms of loss, etc. (cf. Rom. 12:15).

Such concern for others is faith in action, love like that of Christ on the cross. For this reason Paul calls it fulfilling (cf. 5:14) the "law of Christ." In the context this "law of Christ" is not something he issued but something he lived. It is the covenant "law" — or principle — of faith expressing itself in love (2:20; 5:6). If for Paul Jesus is a teacher (responding perhaps to the circumcisers), he is a teacher inasmuch as the story of his faithful, loving death is his lesson. The law of Christ is the narrative pattern of cruciform love that true faith engenders. Any who think themselves too important to love others in this way deceive themselves about possessing the Spirit (6:3). The Spirit is the Spirit of cruciform love.

The second responsibility is for oneself (6:4-5). Being part of a loving, 'burden-bearing' community does not excuse laziness or irresponsibility. Believers therefore bear both their own burdens and, as the need arises, the burdens of others. The third responsibility, which is an expression of the first two, is to share — probably financially — one's resources ("good things") with the teachers in the community (6:6).

Paul closes out his reflections on life in the Spirit with a traditional biblical image that contains both a warning and an admonition (6:7-10): we "reap" what we "sow." Connecting this to the imagery of 'two ways' and two 'forces' (flesh, Spirit) from 5:16-26, Paul offers the Galatians the option of sowing to the flesh and reaping death, or sowing to the Spirit and reaping eternal life. Life in the Spirit requires ongoing attention; the attaining of righteousness is a hope (5:5), predicated on maintaining one's life in the Spirit (6:9). This means, in a nutshell, constantly "work[ing] for the good of all," believers and nonbelievers alike (6:10).

6:11-18. SUMMARY AND FINAL SUMMONS

The conclusion, or rhetorical *peroratio,* of Galatians echoes several parts of the letter and drives home Paul's basic message: negatively, to avoid circumcision and the circumcisers; positively, to stay focused, with Paul, on the cross.

Paul begins by taking the pen from his secretary to emphasize his personal involvement in the contents and passion of the letter (6:11). Beginning with the circumcisers themselves, he accuses them of having a 'fleshly' but hypocritical pride, and of avoiding persecution "for the cross of Christ" (6:12-13). Throughout Galatians Paul has associated circumcision with the Law, and both with the "flesh," while he has held all three in opposition to the Spirit. Here those associations and antitheses continue. Circumcision, for Paul, has to do with human values and standards that do not matter to God and that create an inappropriate sense of pride among those who are circumcised. Moreover, circumcision does not even lead to obedience of the Law, Paul says (6:13), making another rhetorical stab at the circumcisers. Furthermore, and most importantly, Paul sees in the circumcisers' focus on circumcision an opposition to the cross and its consequences.

It is, in fact, quite possible the circumcisers believed that making Gentiles fully into Jews (through circumcision) would lessen persecution of the messianic Jesus movement by the synagogue. For Paul this was of course an unacceptable compromise. His focus, his only 'boast,' is the cross, which has been the centerpiece of the entire letter. Through the cross, Paul writes, "the world has been crucified to me, and I to the world" (6:14). This is the third of three interconnected affirmations about Paul's own crucifixion — his cocrucifixion with Christ (2:19), the crucifixion of his flesh (5:24), and now his crucifixion to "the world." To die with Christ is so to identify with his cross as to sever all interest in the values and standards of this world and age (cf. 1:4), which repudiates the cross. It is also to affirm, once again, that circumcision and uncircumcision do not matter (cf. 5:6), but the effects of the cross do matter — the inauguration of the new creation promised by the prophets (6:15; cf. Isa. 65:17; 2 Cor. 5:17), which itself is the era in which faith is expressed through love, as the parallel text in 5:6 puts it.

To those who "follow this rule" — the rule of the new creation begun in the cross of Christ and carried on by his Spirit — Paul offers a Jewish blessing of peace and mercy, defining the recipients as the "Israel of God" (6:16). In the new age, what marks Israel as Israel is not circumcision but a new creation of Gentiles and Jews, women and men, slave and free (3:28) who exist together in Christ as Abraham's offspring, as God's own children, distinguished by the sign of the cross. Paul himself, in fact, has been marked — literally. He bears "the marks [*stigmata*] of Jesus branded" on his body (6:17). Paul refers to the scars that he has received in various forms of persecution, perhaps especially the thirty-nine lashes at the hands of synagogue officials (2 Cor. 11:24). But these scars function for Paul as the marks of his master, the Lord Jesus Christ. Like all slaves in antiquity, Paul has been branded as the slave of his owner and Lord. He is Christ's slave (*doulos,* 1:10), cocrucified with him even to the point of physical suffering. Those who question his gospel or apostleship need only look at the correspondence between him and the Lord Jesus.

It is that Lord Jesus Christ, preached in word and deed by his slave and apostle, Paul, who is sufficient to bring grace — and all that this grace includes — to the Galatians (6:18).

Summary of Galatians 5–6

The Pauline gospel experience of cross, faith, and Spirit is sufficient to counteract the powers of sin and the flesh, and also therefore sufficient for justification and righteousness.

- Circumcision is irrelevant in Christ and, if sought by believers, displaces and invalidates Christ as the sole and sufficient means of freedom.
- 'Freedom' is not an excuse for 'the flesh,' for license, for immorality, or for irresponsibility.
- Freedom is a communal reality and a paradoxical reality, experienced only as 'slavery' to others.

- What matters in Christ is the Christlike life of faith expressing itself in love, which is true freedom and which fulfills the Law; it is the mark of those who live in the new creation as the Israel of God.
- Life in Christ is one of 'walking' or 'keeping in step with' the Spirit: crucifying the desires of the flesh and allowing the fruit of the Spirit to be produced.
- Those who 'walk' by the Spirit bear others' burdens and thereby fulfill the 'law,' or narrative pattern, of Christ.

THE STORY IN FRONT OF THE LETTER

Some Readings of Galatians

"Do you see his parental compassion? Do you see the anguish that is fitting for an apostle? Do you see how he has lamented more bitterly than women giving birth? 'You have ruined the image of God,' he is saying. 'You have lost the kinship, you have exchanged the likeness. You need a rebirth and reformation.'"

> John Chrysostom, *Homilies on Galatians* (ca. 390), quoted in
> Mark J. Edwards, ed., *Galatians, Ephesians, Philippians,* vol. 8
> in *Ancient Christian Commentary on Scripture,* ed. Thomas C.
> Oden (Downers Grove, Ill.: InterVarsity, 1999), p. 66

"The Apostle therefore writes the Galatians this epistle in which he shows that with the coming of the grace of the New Testament, the Old Testament should be cast out, so that with the fulfillment of the truth, the figure may be abandoned, and with the attainment of these two, namely grace and truth, one may arrive at the truth of justice and glory. And these two are acquired, if, abandoning the observance of the 'legalia' [i.e., the ceremonial precepts of the Old Law], we concentrate fervently on observing the Gospel of Christ."

> Thomas Aquinas, *Commentary on St. Paul's Epistle to the
> Galatians,* Lecture 1 (thirteenth century), trans.
> F. R. Larcher (Albany: Magi, 1966), p. 3

"St. Paul therefore in this Epistle goes about diligently to instruct us, to comfort us, to hold us in the perfect knowledge of this most Christian and excellent righteousness. For if the article of justification is once lost, then all true Christian doctrine is lost. And however many there are in the world who do not hold this doctrine are either Jews, Turks, Papists or heretics. For between the righteousness of the law and the righteousness of Christ, or between active and passive righteousness, there is no mean. Thus the one who strays from this Christian righteousness must of necessity fall into the active righteousness; that is to say, when one has lost Christ, one must fall into the confidence of one's own works."

> Martin Luther, *A Commentary on St. Paul's Epistle to the Galatians*, in *Martin Luther: Selections from His Writings*, ed. John Dillenberger (Garden City, N.Y.: Doubleday, 1961), p. 106 (1531; translation slightly modernized)

"Paul's message of 'freedom in Christ' must have found attentive ears among people interested in political, social, cultural and religious emancipation. . . . [F]reedom in Christ . . . was not only a 'religious' and 'theological' notion, but pointed at the same time to a political and social experience."

> Hans Dieter Betz, *Galatians: A Commentary on Paul's Letter to the Churches in Galatia*, Hermeneia (Philadelphia: Fortress, 1979), pp. 2-3

"[Galatians is] one of the most important religious documents of mankind."

> Hans Dieter Betz, quoted in James D. G. Dunn, *The Epistle to the Galatians*, Black's New Testament Commentaries (London: A. & C. Black, 1993), p. 2

"Paul's argument against circumcision, which is an argument against identifying with a certain religious disposition and a particular nation, speaks to our current struggles to be shaped by Christ apart from inherited standards of behavior or national allegiance."

> L. Ann Jervis, *Galatians*, New International Biblical Commentary (Peabody, Mass.: Hendrickson, 1999), p. 23

"Paul's chief objection to the Missionaries' message was that it sought to superimpose their Jewish religious culture upon Gentiles who had already encountered the gospel through Paul's Law-free preaching. . . . This sort of cultural imperialism was anathema to Paul. . . . As we reflect on Galatians as Scripture, we must ask ourselves at what points we are in danger of superimposing our religious culture — even the cultures of particular church traditions — on communities that are responding to the gospel in fresh, indigenous ways under the guidance of the Spirit. . . . After reading Galatians carefully we will find ourselves prompted to scrutinize our churches to see whether we may be unintentionally nullifying the grace of God through explicit or implicit membership requirements unrelated to the heart of the gospel."

> Richard B. Hays, "The Letter to the Galatians," in *The New Interpreter's Bible*, ed. Leander E. Keck et al. (Nashville: Abingdon, 2000), 11:347-48

QUESTIONS FOR REFLECTION

1. In Galatians Paul expresses significant passion — anger, disappointment, confidence, etc. What kinds of criteria might be necessary for the appropriate expression of such emotions in the context of church life?
2. What kinds of 'supplements' to the gospel of Christ crucified and the gift of the Spirit have been, or are currently being, introduced into the church? What causes people and movements to try to supplement the gospel? In what ways might Galatians help in identifying and addressing such supplements?
3. How can Galatians contribute to a contemporary theology and experience of the cross? of the Spirit? of their interrelatedness?
4. What is, and what should be, the contemporary significance of Paul's claim that in Christ there is "no longer Jew or Greek, there is no longer slave or free, there is no longer male and female"?
5. What contributions does Galatians make to, and what questions might it raise about, a contemporary understanding of Christian freedom?
6. In what ways do contemporary Christians separate faith and love, or theology and ethics, from each other? How might Galatians assist the church in the theory and practice of keeping them together?
7. How does the tension between individual and communal responsibility ('burden bearing') manifest itself in the contemporary life of the church?
8. Some readers have charged Paul with anti-Semitism in Galatians. What might be the basis for their accusations? What possible rejoinders could be offered to such charges?
9. How do you respond to the interpretations of Galatians quoted above?
10. In sum, what does this letter urge the church to believe, to hope for, and to do?

FOR FURTHER READING AND STUDY

General

Cousar, Charles B. *Galatians*. Interpretation. Louisville: Westminster John Knox, 1982. A brief commentary for preaching and teaching, with emphasis on God's grace as the letter's theme.

Hays, Richard B. "Galatians." In *The New Interpreter's Bible,* edited by Leander E. Keck et al., 11:181-348. Nashville: Abingdon, 2000. A rich interpretation of the letter as an argumentative sermon, stressing Paul's apocalyptic and cross-centered gospel.

Matera, Frank J. *Galatians.* Sacra Pagina. Collegeville, Minn.: Liturgical Press, 1992. An excellent analysis from within the 'new perspective' on Paul, stressing the social and ethical, as well as individual, dimensions of justification.

Williams, Sam K. *Galatians.* Abingdon New Testament Commentaries. Nashville: Abingdon, 1997. A careful exposition stressing the way the letter would be heard in Galatia and balancing exegetical and theological concerns.

Technical

Barclay, John M. G. *Obeying the Truth: Paul's Ethics in Galatians.* Minneapolis: Fortress, 1988. A significant analysis of the theological character of Paul's Spirit-generated ethics in Galatians, and its integral relationship to the rest of the letter.

Betz, Hans Dieter. *Galatians: A Commentary on Paul's Letter to the Churches in Galatia.* Hermeneia. Philadelphia: Fortress, 1979. A classic work attempting to situate the letter in its ancient rhetorical and social context.

Bruce, F. F. *The Epistle to the Galatians: A Commentary on the Greek Text.* New International Greek Testament Commentary. Grand Rapids: Eerdmans, 1982. A solid, learned commentary from a traditional perspective.

Dunn, James D. G. *A Commentary on the Epistle to the Galatians.* Peabody, Mass.: Hendrickson, 1993. A provocative commentary from the 'new perspective' on Paul.

Longenecker, Richard N. *Galatians.* Word Biblical Commentary 41. Waco, Tex.: Word, 1990. A detailed commentary on the Greek text, with attention to both Jewish and non-Jewish contexts.

Martyn, J. Louis. *Galatians.* Anchor Bible 33A. New York: Doubleday, 1998. A major work highlighting the theological and especially apocalyptic character of the letter.

Nanos, Mark D. *The Irony of Galatians: Paul's Letter in First-Century Context.* Minneapolis: Augsburg Fortress, 2002. A provocative treatment of Paul's rhetoric by a first-rate Jewish scholar of Paul who contends that the 'influencers' are Galatian Jews, not 'Christians.'

Witherington, Ben, III. *Grace in Galatia: A Commentary on Paul's Letter to the Galatians.* Grand Rapids: Eerdmans, 1998. A detailed rhetorical analysis of the letter, emphasizing the theme in the title.

CHAPTER 10

1 CORINTHIANS

Chaos and the Cross in Corinth

We proclaim Christ crucified . . . the power of God and the wisdom of God.

1 Cor. 1:23-24

The Corinthian community was Paul's problem child. The believers in Corinth managed to misunderstand just about everything Paul said and did, to their own detriment and Paul's utter astonishment. By the time Paul wrote the letter we call 1 Corinthians, the church, from the apostle's perspective, was in utter chaos. The letter has the appearance of a laundry list of problems, but these are in many respects the presenting symptoms of a more significant disease. What had infected the Corinthians was a divisiveness based on social and spiritual status. But even that, from Paul's perspective, was symptomatic of a more fundamental problem: a failure to understand the real-life consequences of the gospel of "Jesus Christ, and him crucified" (2:2). His goal became to convince the Corinthians to embody the cross in daily life in light of the past resurrection and soon return of their crucified Lord.

In this letter we have more (relatively) clear windows into an early Christian community than in any other New Testament writing. It is also, perhaps, Paul's most practical and contemporary letter.

THE STORY BEHIND THE LETTER

"The trip to Corinth is not for every man," observed several ancient travelers. Corinth had a reputation for trouble, and it was even the namesake for a verb. 'To become Corinthianized' (Gk. *korinthianazesthai*) meant something like 'to become thoroughly immoral and materialistic.' Corinth had the reputation that some U.S. cities have, especially in non-Western cultures. Among its thriving industries was a fairly lively sex trade, some of which may have been connected with, or at least inspired by, the temples of gods such as Aphrodite. (In the Roman period Aphrodite had several functions, including mother of the imperial family, and not merely a sex deity.) Among the ruins of Corinth are also more than two dozen temples, statues, and monuments to Apollo, Asclepius, Athena, Demeter and Kore, Serapis, the emperor, and other gods. At nearby Isthmia are the remains of a large temple to Poseidon.

But Corinth was of considerable strategic importance for the spread of the gospel. Located in the province of Achaia, on the isthmus that connects mainland Greece with the southern section, the Peloponnese, Corinth was a thriving, cosmopolitan, commercial metropolis. It was situated in an impressive spot, dominated by the massive Acrocorinth (site of the temple of Aphrodite), which rose some 1,800 feet into the southern sky. It was the "master of two harbors" (Strabo, *Geography* 8.6.20) — Lechaion (also spelled Lechaeon or Lechaeum), about two miles to the northwest on the Gulf of Corinth, leading to the Adriatic Sea; and Cenchreae (or Cenchrae), about six miles to the southeast on the Saronic Gulf, leading to the Aegean Sea. The two towns were connected by the Diolkos Road, by which goods and even small ships could be transported between the two ports. (Today a canal, conceived by Julius Caesar but not completed until 1893, links the two gulfs.) By these ports Corinth controlled the Asia Minor–Italy trade traffic. And the ports also permitted the east-west flow of religious ideas and their messengers.

Once a powerful Greek city-state, Corinth had been destroyed by Rome in 146 B.C. and left dormant until 44 B.C., when Julius Caesar refounded it as a colony of Rome and populated it with freed slaves and other poor folks, especially from the East. It would not be inaccurate to describe much of the population as 'upwardly mobile,' attempting to better themselves on the socioeconomic ladder. Indeed, Roman Corinth — Paul's Corinth — quickly became the chief city of Achaia, and within the Roman Empire not far behind Rome and Alexandria in significance. Yet the city was not full of the wealthy (and the wealth was not generally old, cultured, Roman money), but rather had a preponderance of hardworking nonelite people who took advantage of their location. An artisan like Paul would have found plenty of opportunities for employment from normal requests for tentmaking work, and perhaps also from special requests for such events as the bi-

Corinth: Remains of the temple of Apollo

ennial Isthmian Games. Second only to the Olympiad, these games held at nearby Isthmia were dedicated to Poseidon, god of the sea, and showcased talent not only in athletics but also in music, drama, and speech (rhetoric).

PAUL'S MISSION

It may have been this combination of the city's features — the challenge of idolatry and immorality, the strategic location, and the opportunity for work —

229

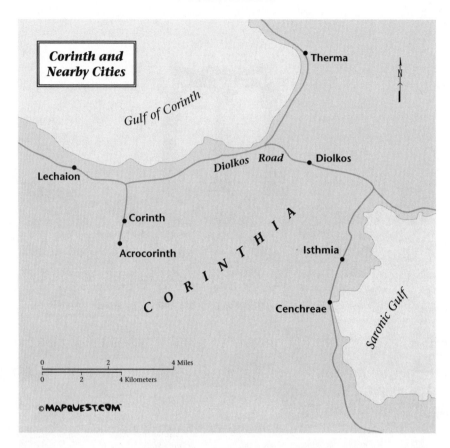

First-century Corinth and vicinity

that led Paul, according to Acts 18:11, to spend eighteen months of his second mission trip in Corinth, during the years 50-51 or 51-52. (Fairly precise dating is possible because of a reference in Acts 18:12-17 to the proconsul of Achaia, Gallio, who is mentioned in an inscription at Delphi that dates from circa 52.) What follows is a summary of Paul's mission according to Acts.

Paul arrived alone in Corinth after little success in Athens (though that may have been more pleasant than the trouble he had encountered immediately before in Beroea, Thessalonica, and Philippi). He met up with a man named Aquila and his wife Priscilla, two Jewish believers who had left Rome when Claudius expelled all Jews, and who were also tentmakers (18:1-4). As per usual, Paul preached in the synagogue, had minimal or no success, and then, joined again by Silas and Timothy, directed his efforts at the Gentiles (18:5-6). Acts tells us that a God-fearer named Titius Justus, a synagogue official named Crispus

Isthmia: Ritual basin from the temple of Poseidon

(and perhaps his replacement, Sosthenes), and many (Gentile) Corinthians "became believers and were baptized" (18:7-8, 17; cf. 1 Cor. 1:1, 14). As in earlier locations, Paul was again opposed by certain Jews, who took the matter to Gallio the proconsul, but he dismissed the case (Acts 18:12-17).

1 Corinthians testifies also to Paul's success. A vibrant, charismatic community developed that included mostly Gentiles (see 12:2) but also Jews, men and women, slaves and free. Some were people of means, intellect, and culture, though most were from various strata of the nonelite, lacking in such 'status indicators' (1:26), to use the language of the social sciences. Together they constituted for Paul the one church of God in Corinth (1:2). It is quite possible that there were actually several different house churches in the city (see the references to households in 1:16; 16:15), perhaps of different sizes and character. Whether one house church or several, they met as a single body (14:23) for regular or occasional celebration of the Lord's Supper and worship together in the house of a wealthy believer (chaps. 11–14), who for at least some time was a man named Gaius, whom Paul himself had baptized (1:14; Rom. 16:23).

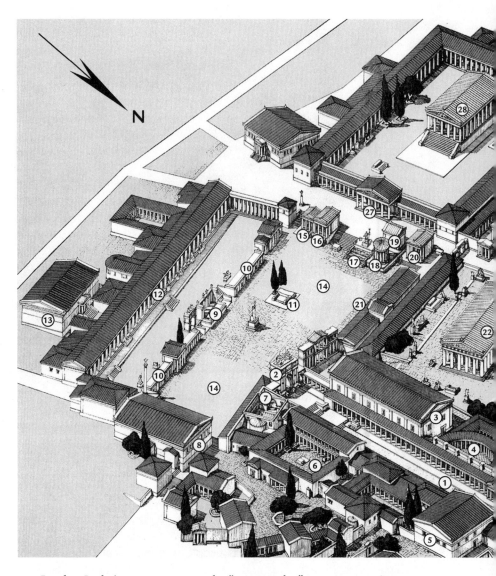

1. Road to Lechaion
2. Monumental Arch
3. Basilica
4. Market
5. Baths
6. Peribolos of Apollo (built in the late first century CE; before that, a possible location of the "meat market" of 1 Cor. 10:25)
7. Pirene Fountain
8. Julian Basilica
9. Bēma (the "tribunal" of Acts 18:12)
10. Market
11. Altar
12. Stoa
13. Basilica
14. Forum
15. Temple of Venus Victrix
16. Temple of the Cults of Rome, the Emperor, and the Senate
17. Fountain of Poseidon

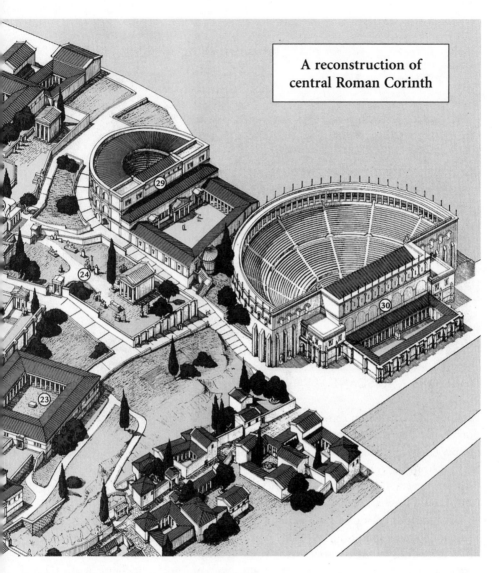

A reconstruction of central Roman Corinth

8. Monument of
   Cn(aeus) Babbius
   Philinus
9. Temple
0. Temple of Tyche
21. Market
2. Temple of Apollo
   (sixth century BCE)
3. Market

24. Shrine of Athena
    Chalinitis
25. Temple
26. Glauke Fountain
27. Market
28. Temple
29. Odeion (built after
    Paul's time)
30. Theater

Corinth: The famous *bēma* where, according to Acts 18,
the proconsul Gallio examined Paul

DIVISIONS AND SCANDALS

Paul probably wished in retrospect that he had baptized no one, for the question of who baptized whom became one of the causes for division in the community (1:13-14). Paul's departure from Corinth was followed by a very successful visit from the Alexandrian Jew Apollos, a bright and rhetorically powerful preacher (1:12; 3:4-6, 22; 4:6; 16:12; cf. Acts 18:24–19:1), and perhaps also a visit from Peter ("Cephas," 1:12; 3:22) — though this is by no means certain.

For various reasons several sorts of divisions ensued along various lines. Some individuals and groups, possibly corresponding to house churches organized according to their respective spiritual fathers (the preacher who converted and baptized them), aligned themselves with one apostolic figure or another — Paul, Apollos, or Peter (1:12). They considered themselves in some sense to 'belong' to their leader and to be that leader's 'servant' (1:12; 3:4-5), perhaps in a client-patron relationship. In addition to baptism, cultural and socioeconomic factors may have drawn people to one or another preacher; perhaps observant Jewish believers claimed Peter while the intellectually sophisticated rallied around Apollos. Some may have been critical of Paul while others joined his 'party.' Still others may have rejected all human allegiances ("I belong to Christ"?) but nonetheless contributed to the factionalism.

Corinth: The road into town from the port of Lechaion
on the Gulf of Corinth, heading toward the Acrocorinth

Other divisions, perhaps related to these, also appeared. Some Corinthians took fellow believers to court (6:1-11). Some avoided the idol temples completely, while others ate within their precincts and may have mocked the scruples of others (8:1-13). Some treated the gatherings for the Lord's Supper like a dinner party for the wealthy and neglected the poor latecomers (11:17-34). Still others (or was it the same people?) looked down on certain members of the community, especially those who did not possess the more spectacular endowments of the Spirit like glossolalia, or speaking in tongues (12:1–14:40).

At the same time, moral scandals had arisen. In addition to the lawsuits, a believer having sexual relations with his stepmother was tolerated, if not celebrated, by the community (5:1-8), and some believers were engaging the services of prostitutes (6:12-20). Many were confused about sex and marriage (7:1-40). An earlier letter from Paul, at least partly on sexual immorality, had confused the Corinthians still further when they mistakenly interpreted his admonition to avoid sexually immoral persons (i.e., believers) as a call to avoid contact with their nonbelieving friends (5:9-13).[1] Added to all this, some Corinthians were de-

---

1. This letter is often called letter A (i.e., Paul's first letter to the Corinthians), with our

nying the resurrection of the dead (15:12), which, for Paul, had profound moral implications about sexuality and about life more generally.

Furthermore, a significant number of the believers appeared to be, in Paul's apt metaphor, "puffed up" (4:6, 18, 19; 5:2; 8:1; 13:4) about whatever conviction or behavior they were flaunting. Though we cannot know with certainty, it appears that many of these attitudes and actions were interconnected. A relatively small group of people, possessing significant status both socially and spiritually, were likely exercising a disproportionate influence on the church as a whole. It is generally thought that these people were self-styled Spirit-filled people, sometimes called pneumatics, enthusiasts, or elitists, who were enamored of displays of powerful speech, whether in preaching or in glossolalia. They felt themselves enlightened and were apparently prone to a kind of moral libertinism in bodily matters such as food and sex ("all things are lawful": 6:12; 10:23) that was coupled with disdain for those of supposedly lesser spiritual and/or socioeconomic status. It is likely that their spirituality focused on the present possession of the glory and power of the Spirit, not on the Pauline pattern of present suffering and humility (cross) followed by future glory (resurrection). This attitude may well have given rise to their critique, not only of 'inferiors' in the community, but of Paul as well.

Thus the situation at Corinth was a complex set of interrelated social, sexual, and spiritual problems that frequently pitted the supposedly enlightened or elite against the supposedly unenlightened or nonelite. Paul found out about these problems — this chaos — through both oral and written communications (1:11; 7:1; 16:17) from the church. From his new base of Ephesus (16:8), he responded by sending Timothy, who had helped him in Corinth, either ahead of or with the letter (4:17; 16:10-11). Paul wished also to send Apollos, who (wisely) refused or discerned it not to be God's will (16:12). But Paul's major response was, of course, the letter, written from Ephesus, probably in 54 (give or take about a year). It is the second of at least four letters Paul wrote to the Corinthians.[2]

THE STORY WITHIN THE LETTER

1 Corinthians is a well-crafted piece of deliberative rhetoric intended above all to strengthen, sanctify, and unify the community (1:8, 10) by urging all its mem-

---

1 Corinthians then being labeled letter B. A few scholars believe that a part of letter A is preserved in 2 Cor. 6:14–7:1, but the evidence does not favor this view.

  2. See further discussion in the introduction to 2 Corinthians.

bers to "let all that you do be done in love" (16:14). These two clues to the purpose of the letter, which serve as bookends to the whole collection of short, carefully crafted discourses within it, suggest also that its famous 'love chapter' (chap. 13) is a crucial piece of Paul's argument. In its immediate context, chapter 13 addresses the problem of disunity through disregard for "weaker" (today we might say 'differently gifted'; see chap. 12, esp. vv. 22-24) believers, but it also alludes to other problems addressed elsewhere in the letter. Indeed, Paul seems to see many of the church's problems as a failure to love, especially a failure by those who possess certain status indicators to love those who lack them.

At the heart of 1 Corinthians 13 and Paul's understanding of love is the part of verse 5 that reads "[love] does not insist on its own way," which is better translated 'love does not seek its own welfare or interests.' This Greek idiom has already appeared in 10:24 and 10:33, where it explains what it means to be an imitator of Paul and, ultimately, of Christ (11:1). Similarly, in Philippians 2 basically the same idiom appears (2:4), as a summary both of the kinds of humility and love that produce unity and of the master story of Christ, who emptied and humbled himself (Phil. 2:7-8).

All this means that when Paul calls the Corinthians to unity through the holiness of humility and love, he is telling them to live out the story of Christ crucified in their community. After all, he had "decided to know nothing among you except Jesus Christ, and him crucified" (2:2). In fact, it was his preaching of the story of Christ crucified, "the power of God and the wisdom of God" (1:24), that had brought the Corinthians to faith and God's Spirit — with whom they were so enamored — to them. Their previous personal and corporate stories had been rearranged by their encounter with God, Jesus, and the Spirit (6:11) in the message of Christ crucified, through whichever minister happened to be the agent.

Now their lives needed to be rearranged once again. Their resocialization, as sociologists would say, had been incomplete. We might more appropriately say their stories, ideologies, and spiritualities of wisdom and power needed to be deconstructed and reconstructed — reshaped by the story of Christ crucified. In this sense 1 Corinthians is not merely deliberative but *subversive* — subversive of the status quo even within the church, whose values are being turned topsy-turvy. Yet the result of the reconstruction process would be a fuller partnership or "fellowship" with God's Son (1:9), in anticipation of the conclusion of the divine story — the revelation and day of the Lord Jesus (1:7-8) and the resurrection of believers that day will bring (chap. 15). This is what holiness is for Paul: countercultural cruciformity in expectation of the coming day of judgment and salvation.

An outline of the way Paul addresses the chaos at Corinth with the cross of Christ in 1 Corinthians follows:

1:1-9   Opening and Thanksgiving
1:10–4:21   Addressing Ecclesiological Chaos:
            The Wisdom and Power of the Cross
            1:10-17   Divisions
            1:18–2:5   The Word of the Cross
            2:6–3:4   Cruciform Spirituality and Corinthian Immaturity
            3:5–4:13   Ministers as Cruciform Servants
            4:14-21   Concluding Warning
5:1–7:40   Addressing Moral Chaos:
            Life between Cross and Parousia
            5:1-13   Incest
            6:1-11   Lawsuits
            6:12-20   Sex with Prostitutes
            7:1-40   Confusion about Marriage
8:1–14:40   Addressing Liturgical Chaos:
            The Cross and Worship
            8:1–11:1   Meat Associated with Idols
                        8:1-13   The Problem and Paul's Solution
                        9:1-27   The Example of Apostolic Cruciformity
                        10:1–11:1 Fellowship with and Imitation of Christ
            11:2-16   Disorderly Women and Men in the Assembly
            11:17-34   Abuse of the Lord's Supper
            12:1–14:40 Spiritual Gifts
                        12:1-31   The Church as Christ's Body
                        13:1-13   The Rule of Cruciform Love
                        14:1-40   The Use of Gifts in Worship
15:1-58   Addressing Theological Chaos:
            Resurrection as Vindication of the Cross
            15:1-11   The Common Creed
            15:12-34   The Consequences of Disbelief and Belief
            15:35-50   Questions about Bodily Resurrection
            15:51-57   The Final Victory
            15:58   Concluding Exhortation
16:1-24   Closing

Summaries may be found after the comments on chapters 1–4, chapters 5–7, 8:1–11:1, chapters 11–14, and chapter 15.

1:1-9. OPENING AND THANKSGIVING

The rich opening of this letter sets the stage and the mood for what is to follow. Paul focuses particularly on the identity of the church, both in the salutation and the thanksgiving, in the hope that the church will live up to its high calling.

Paul begins by identifying himself, with emphasis on his divinely ordained apostleship, and Sosthenes as the letter writers (1:1). If Sosthenes is the (now believing) Corinthian synagogue official mentioned in Acts 18:17, his coauthorship would perhaps strengthen Paul's hearing in a city where his credibility had diminished.

In 1:2 the Corinthian recipients are identified as a local manifestation of a widespread movement of communities that name Jesus as Lord. As such, Paul says twice, they are called to be countercultural ("sanctified," "saints"). After a typical greeting (1:3), Paul resumes this theme in the thanksgiving (1:4-9), even as he expands it. Certain key themes of the letter appear: grace *(charis)*, wealth in speech and knowledge, spiritual gifts *(charismata)*, blamelessness (= holiness), the day of the Lord, and fellowship *(koinōnia)*.

What Paul implies here is quite clever: he affirms the Corinthians' spiritual prowess inasmuch as it is the work of God's grace, yet he reminds them that God's work does not end with spiritual gifts; it continues with the faithful work of establishing the church as a blameless, or holy, people ready for the judgment coming on the day of the Lord (1:8; cf. 1 Thess. 5:23-24). This is what constitutes true fellowship with Jesus (1:9). The focus of the letter, then, will be on how a *charismatic* community must live in order to be true to its identity as God's *countercultural* community.

1:10–4:21. ADDRESSING ECCLESIOLOGICAL CHAOS: THE WISDOM AND POWER OF THE CROSS

The theme of the first four chapters is quite clear: unity, unity, unity (to which Paul actually refers three times in 1:10). Although many interpreters take this verse also as the theme of the entire letter, it is formally separate from the announcement of the broader theme, holiness, of which unity is a (major) part. Paul takes the divisions *very* seriously, suggesting in 3:17 that they may result in the destruction of the church, in which case God would destroy the perpetrators. Paul's desire is that the Corinthians surrender their secular person-centered party spirit and refocus their boasting only in the crucified Lord (1:29, 31; 3:21). It is crucial also to note what Paul does *not* want — that is, for all the Corinthians to say "I belong to Paul" (see 1:12; 3:4-5, 22), for even if they should imitate him (4:16) as their father and as an imitator of Christ, he is their servant, not their 'lord.'

One dimension of this extended discourse on unity is its account of the intersection of three stories: Christ crucified as the power-in-weakness of God; Paul's rhetorically unimpressive, cruciform ministry; and the conversion of the Corinthians — who were generally a group of nobodies (1:28). Based on these stories, the other dimension of these chapters is a careful delineation of the nature of ministry.

DIVISIONS (1:10-17)

Paul has learned of the divisions from a visiting team (slaves? family members? colleagues?) related to one Chloe. The 'slogans' (1:12) he hears from them, whether verbatim or not, represent a spirit of divisiveness and allegiance that was typical among disciples of competing teachers in antiquity but contradicts the gospel. The idiom "I belong to" — literally, 'I am of' — could be used to identify both slaves and devotees of a god, which is why Paul will later stress that he and Apollos are the Corinthians' servants, not the other way around (3:5, 9; 4:1), and that they also are servants of the Lord (3:5-9; 4:1). For now, he uses a trio of rhetorical questions (1:13) to put preachers in their place and Christ in his. Christ is one person/body; Christ, not one of the preachers, was crucified for the Corinthians' redemption; and the Corinthians, though baptized *by* one preacher or another, were baptized *into* Christ — not into one of them. Paul then recalls (with some difficulty) those he baptized (1:14-16), not to give them any special status but to stress that the real work of an apostle is to preach rather than to baptize, and to preach in such an unobtrusive way that the power of Christ crucified — not some human "power" — might be unleashed (1:17). The critique of "eloquent wisdom" (which might be better translated 'showy rhetoric'), and its opposition to the power of the cross, is continued in the next section.

THE WORD OF THE CROSS (1:18–2:5)

"Wisdom" and "power" may very well have been key elements of the specialized vocabulary of the Corinthian elitists/enthusiasts. In 1:18–2:5, which is one of the most important texts in all of Paul's letters, Paul seeks to deconstruct the Corinthians' ideology of wisdom and power and to replace it with the 'word of the cross' (1:18, literally), that is, with Christ crucified as God's wisdom and power (1:23-24). Paul presents his redefinition of these realities (1:18-25) and then offers two corroborations of it: the social makeup of the Corinthian community (1:26-31) and the shape of his own ministry (2:1-5).

Perspective is everything; only those who are called (1:24) and "are being saved" (1:18) can perceive the foolishness and weakness of Christ crucified as the revelation of God's wisdom and power (1:23-24). This has been called the 'kerygmatic paradox,' and it is the most fundamental claim Paul makes in 1 Corinthians. This wisdom is decidedly not the wisdom of Jewish scribes or Gentile philosophers, teachers, and orators, whose purported wisdom does not truly reveal God and is therefore in fact foolishness (1:19-21). Those who are perishing, whether Jew or Gentile, can only stumble over or laugh at the oxymoron — the "stumbling block" — of a crucified Messiah, god, or lord (1:22-23). They desire instead the conventional proofs of power and wisdom such as miraculous signs or philosophical acumen. That humans would fail to see God's wisdom and power is nothing new, Paul avers, and God has been in the business of subverting human understanding since at least the time of Isaiah, whom Paul quotes in 1:19 (Isa. 29:14). God continues such subversive activity in the present, through the cross (cf. 1:20 — Paul again relying on rhetorical questions — and 1:25).

The first demonstration of Paul's radical thesis about the nature of God's wisdom and power is the complexion of the Corinthian church itself (1:26-31). God is clearly not impressed by status-quo wisdom and power, since God has called so few wise, rich, and noble but so many who are "low and despised" (1:26-28). The God revealed in Christ's cross and the Corinthian church has a 'preferential option' for the poor, the bottom rung of society, and is again in the business of subverting the status quo by making somebodies out of nobodies — and vice versa (1:28). Paul combines his description of the majority of the Corinthian believers with another prophetic text, this time from Jeremiah (Jer. 9:23-24), to stress that the only proper kind of 'boasting' is in the Lord, not in oneself or any other human, nor in human wisdom. For Paul, to boast in the Lord is to celebrate Christ as the wisdom from God (1:30), by which of course he means Christ crucified (1:23-24; 2:2). The crucified Christ is true wisdom, because through him come God's righteousness, sanctification, and redemption — a summary of Paul's unique interpretation of Christ's death (1:30).

The second demonstration of the thesis in 1:18-25 is Paul's modus operandi as a preacher among the Corinthians (2:1-5). Not only did God not *choose* the wise and powerful, God did not *use* the wise and powerful. Paul shunned "lofty words or wisdom" (showy rhetoric) and, by his own admission, was weak and fearful in public (2:1, 3-4). These features of his ministry (which were in stark contrast to those of most teachers, including his successor Apollos, and which were probably under criticism), Paul claims, expressed his decision to "know" — to portray in speech and action — nothing but the crucified Christ

(2:2). The inspired result of his weakness and lack of wisdom was a "demonstration of the Spirit and of power," meaning both charismatic manifestations and conversions.

CRUCIFORM SPIRITUALITY AND CORINTHIAN IMMATURITY (2:6–3:4)

If the stories of Christ, the Corinthian community, and the Pauline modus operandi all share a cruciform plot, what does that say to the problem at hand? Paul turns next to answer that question, moving from the general (2:6-16) to the specific (3:1-4).

1 Corinthians 2:6-16 is one of the more puzzling passages in the Pauline corpus. Careful attention to its context, however, helps. The upshot of 1:18–2:5 is the rejection of human wisdom and power (the status quo) and the affirmation of Christ crucified as divine wisdom and power. Keeping this in mind, and recalling that Paul is still primarily concerned about divisions generated by infatuation with human wisdom (3:1-4), will assist in the interpretation of this puzzle. (It is easy to lose the forest for the trees here.) Paul's goal in 2:6-16 is to affirm the reality of Spirit-inspired wisdom but to stress once again its connection to Christ crucified. It is likely that Paul is picking up on the language and claims of the spiritually and socially elite at Corinth, who basked in their own version of 'spiritual maturity' — a supposedly Spirit-inspired wisdom that had, as far as Paul could see, no connection to the cross.

The danger in disconnecting Spirit from cross, Paul asserts, can be seen, ironically, in the crucifixion of "the Lord of glory" by "the rulers of this age," who are "doomed to perish" (2:6, 8). Although Christ crucified truly is the revelation of God's wisdom, the Lord's crucifixion itself could be perpetrated only by those whose "wisdom" failed to enlighten them about the identity of the one they crucified. Now, for believers, failure to identify Christ crucified as the wisdom of God — with all the implications of that identification — reveals the *absence* of wisdom and of the Spirit, despite any and all claims to the contrary.

The inability, therefore, to connect Spirit and cross in theory and in practice reveals one's character as immature and "unspiritual" or "fleshly" (NAB), rather than Spirit-filled (2:14; 3:1). The reason for this is quite simple, and Paul expresses it in an analogy. Only a person's "spirit" knows and reveals the essence of that person (2:11a). So too the "spirit" (Spirit) of God understands and reveals God (2:10-13). If, as Paul has repeatedly asserted, God's wisdom (once "secret and hidden," 2:7) is revealed in Christ crucified, then God's Spirit and everything associated with the Spirit (e.g., charismatic gifts, including wisdom, 2:12-13) must also reflect and point to Christ crucified. The truly spiritual person is the one who makes the connection between cross and Spirit; this kind of person (and Paul claims to be one) has "the mind of Christ" (2:16) and can anticipate the incredible future that God has planned for those who love God (2:9).

Having established in 2:6-16 the connection between cross and wisdom, Paul returns to his main point: that the divisions at Corinth, which effectively negate the cross (1:13), reveal the Corinthians' spiritual immaturity (3:1). They are not 'Spirit people' but 'flesh people,' governed by the opposite of the cruci-form Spirit of God (3:1, 3). Spiritual infancy and mother's milk might have been appropriate when Paul first preached to them, but no longer. Allegiance to Paul or Apollos, rather than to Christ crucified, is a sure mark of spiritual infancy, if not stillbirth. "Still of the flesh" (3:3) implies a precarious position far from Christ and the Spirit; yet Paul still calls this community "the church of God" (1:2).

MINISTERS AS CRUCIFORM SERVANTS (3:5–4:13)

Paul now undertakes to re-form the Corinthians' understanding of apostles/ministers of the gospel and thereby their understanding of the church. Those who minister are servants of God and (by extension) of the church (3:5-9, 18-23), which is God's possession and project (3:9-15), and which, if destroyed, will be avenged (3:16-17). These servants are ultimately answerable only to their Lord, who both equips and judges them (3:12-15; 4:1-7). Because the gospel of Christ crucified must be both preached and lived as the church's foundation (3:11), apostles live a cruciform existence (4:8-13).

In 3:5-9 Paul offers an alternative to the Corinthians' misdirected zeal for human leaders, further developing his prophetic notion that believers should boast only in the Lord (1:31; 3:21). The theocentric tone of this passage is a star-tling contrast to the Corinthian attitude. Paul and Apollos are God's servants whom God assigned and through whom God worked; God caused the growth where one "planted" and another "watered," so all credit goes to God alone (3:5-7). God's servants are not in competition but have a "common purpose" (3:8) for which they will give account. They serve God as "coworkers"[3] in what Paul refers to as God's field and building — the church (3:9).

Having developed the agricultural metaphor in the previous verses, Paul runs for a while with the architectural image (3:10-15). Just as he planted and Apollos watered, so also he "laid a foundation" and another is (and still others may be) building on it (3:10). The remainder of the text is clearly meant not merely to describe and defend the ministry of Paul (or Apollos), but to warn

---

3. It is not clear whether Paul means working with God or with one another (so NRSV).

any and all who "build" in Corinth. Paul was an example of a "wise" master builder (3:10 NAB; the phrase can mean simply "master builder" [NRSV], but the allusion to Corinthian wisdom should not be missed). Now that the foundation — Jesus Christ and him crucified — has been properly laid, it cannot be altered or replaced (3:11). Those who build on Paul's initial ministry will be evaluated by God, on the coming day of judgment (often depicted as a time of fire in apocalyptic imagery), according to the quality of materials used and the quality and durability of their workmanship (3:12-15). Good work will be recognized, bad work destroyed — and the (foolish) builder himself will escape only by the skin of his teeth the flames that destroy his work (3:14-15).

The implicit threat in these verses becomes explicit in 3:16-17, where Paul transforms the general architectural image into a sacred one — the church as God's temple. Now God not only *owns* the church, God *inhabits* the church. By the Spirit's being among them, as the "wise" were fond of saying, the Corinthians as a body ("you" plural in the Greek of each verse) constitute God's temple. Paul has upped the ante, so to speak. If the building is destroyed — which could well be the outcome of the divisions — the supposed builders will have become desecrators, and they will suffer the ultimate loss on the coming day.

The warning continues in 3:18-23 with a word to the self-styled wise and a general admonition to the community. The "wise" must become fools by reconnecting to the cross and taking their place as servants, for God sees through and subverts their human wisdom (3:18-20). The community is not to boast in human leaders, for the leaders "belong" to them (as servants), not the other way around (3:21-22). And ultimately, what matters is that the Corinthians are servants of Christ, who in turn is the servant of God (3:23).

To reinforce what he has said, and to answer his critics, Paul further develops the notion of minister as servant by using the image of "steward" in 4:1-5. Stewards must "be found trustworthy" (4:2), and Paul desires nothing more than approval from God. But any human judgment of Paul's ministry, even by the apostle himself, is inappropriate, for the only verdict that matters is the Lord's future judgment (4:3-5). This attitude does not necessarily make Paul arrogant, for he clearly has examined himself and would try to correct any wrong he discovered (4:4). Rather, what he means is not that he is perfect but that, as far as he knows, he has never strayed from "Jesus Christ crucified."

Returning to the issue at hand more concretely, Paul begins his summary by telling the Corinthians that everything he has said has been intended to apply to himself and Apollos (4:6). Whatever the precise meaning of "the saying" (source also unknown), Paul's bottom line is clear: no more divisive arrogance (4:6b). Those who recognize their own gifts, and the gifts of others, as gifts from God, will not boast (4:7).

But just in case that point is not clear, Paul turns finally to a massive rhetorical attack on the arrogance of elitist Corinthian spirituality by a spirited account of his own cruciform life. The twice-repeated "already," together with the sarcastic imagery of wealth and royalty (4:8), suggests a here-and-now spirituality, a kind of gospel of success. The source of this Corinthian attitude has been debated. Does it derive from a rejection of future resurrection (see 15:12) that leads to a spirituality of present glory? Or does it reflect an Epicurean mind-set? In either case, Paul counters with his own narrative. This is what it means to know only Christ crucified (2:2): to live like criminals awaiting the death penalty or prisoners of war paraded in public (4:9); to be foolish and weak rather than wise and strong (4:10); to suffer physically, whether by circumstance or choice (4:11-12a); to bless and endure when mistreated (4:12b-13, echoing the teaching of Jesus preserved in Matthew's Sermon on the Mount); to be treated like so much garbage (4:13).

Paul is not seeking pity. On the contrary, he is establishing his apostolic authenticity and authority. If his lifestyle is what is appropriate for ministers of the gospel, he should succeed at both. In that case the wise in Corinth — indeed the entire community — should both cease their arrogant divisions and renew their respect for Paul, who not only preaches but also lives the gospel of Christ crucified.

CONCLUDING WARNING (4:14-21)

The somewhat surprising warning that concludes chapters 1–4 makes sense only if read in the context of Paul's sense of apostolic authority as the Corinthians' spiritual father and as an imitator of Christ (4:14-16). Furthermore, it makes sense only if we recognize the gravity of the situation, at least from Paul's perspective. Paul had sent (or perhaps is sending; cf. 16:10-11) Timothy as a (gentle) reminder of Paul's "ways in Christ Jesus" (4:17-18). Since some Corinthians, however, interpreted this as Paul's decision not to visit, he warns them that his absence is temporary and is no excuse for noncompliance. He is coming (the tone is reminiscent of the earlier talk of coming judgment), and he would prefer to do so gently in love. But the other side of his fatherly personality will appear if his children disobey him — and ultimately God — in this crucial matter of church unity.

Summary of 1 Corinthians 1–4

In these four chapters we see some of Paul's basic perspectives on Christ, church, spirituality, and ministry:

- Proud allegiance to human leaders within the church, rather than to Christ, is divisive and destructive.
- The crucified Christ is, paradoxically, the wisdom and power of God.
- Possession of the Spirit and spiritual maturity consist not in having and displaying humanly valued indicators of social or spiritual status, but in living a life connected to the cross.
- The mark of apostleship (or of ministry in general) is faithfulness to God's call in word and deed through conformity to the crucified Christ and service to God's people.
- God's servants are accountable to God for the quality of their labor.
- The church does not belong to human leaders but to God.

5:1–7:40. ADDRESSING MORAL CHAOS: LIFE BETWEEN CROSS AND PAROUSIA

Having dealt at length with Corinthian factionalism, Paul moves on to a new set of issues — the moral chaos and confusion within the church. Not that Paul leaves the issue of divisions behind, for even in these matters, and especially in the topics addressed in chapters 8 to 14, factionalism is very much part of the problem. Certain behaviors are causing other rifts and alignments within the church. And yet, at least from Paul's perspective, the church seems to possess a certain unity in its disunity — a certain common ability to misunderstand (or to be misled by those who misunderstand) the meaning of the gospel in daily life.

In chapters 5 to 7 Paul addresses issues brought to his attention in oral (chaps. 5 and 6) or written (chap. 7) communications. What unifies his responses to these problems is his underlying conviction that believers have a 'bifocal' existence. That is, they live with one eye fixed on Christ's past death and resurrection, and another on his future parousia, with the bodily resurrection and judgment that day will entail. To live between these two events, and to be shaped by both of them, requires a process of careful community discernment guided by the Spirit and, of course, the apostle.

INCEST (5:1-13)

The first situation Paul confronts is, to him, a real shock since it involves a kind of sexual immorality (*porneia*) even the Corinthians' unconverted Gentile ('pagan') friends would not practice or condone. One of the believers is "living with [lit. 'having' (sexually)] his father's wife" — that is, his stepmother (5:1). Such behavior was prohibited by both Roman law and Jewish Scripture (Lev. 20:11; Deut. 22:30; 27:20). What is more, rather than appropriately grieving about this believer's regression to and even beyond pagan practices, the church has become "arrogant" (NRSV) or "inflated with pride" (NAB, closer to the vivid Greek imagery of being 'puffed up') about it (5:2a). Paul's remedy — issued four times — likely seems drastic at first: expulsion of the offending member from the church (5:2b, 5, 7, 13b).

Paul certainly believes that his authoritative apostolic judgment has the approval of the Lord Jesus (5:3-4). What are his motives? First, he is concerned with the offending man's salvation on the day of judgment. The man's behavior is a betrayal of his identity in Christ, and those who live in such a way, no matter their verbal confession or community affiliation, "will not inherit the kingdom of God" (6:9-10). Paul hopes that removing this man from the sphere of the Lord Jesus and remitting him to the sphere of Satan will eventually terminate his behavior so that he will finally be saved (5:5). The stakes are clearly high.

Second, Paul is concerned about the community's spirit of 'toleration,' though in fact they are more than tolerant; they are proud (5:6). Their pride would likely stem from belief in an extreme libertinism (after all, Paul preached a gospel of freedom) that held that what one does sexually, with one's body, has no impact on one's relationship with God (see 6:12-20). In this man they had living proof of their liberation. Paul's Jewish version of 'one bad apple spoils the whole barrel' (5:6), using the image of yeast, assumes both that the behavior is wrong and that it is dangerous to the church. Yet unlike the book of Deuteronomy, Paul's call to purge the community of this evil does not require the death of the evildoer.[4] In fact, as we have seen, it intends his salvation.

The yeast analogy serves not only to illustrate the spread of impurity, but also to connect the whole issue to Christ crucified as "our paschal lamb [who] . . . has been sacrificed" (5:7). Believers, Paul suggests, live in a permanent state of Passover, during which time only unleavened bread may be eaten (Exod. 12). The "yeast" to be removed for the proper ongoing communal celebration of Christ's death is "malice and evil" (5:8).

Here Paul inserts a parenthetical comment to clarify an important and relevant principle from a previous letter: "not to associate with sexually immoral persons" *(pornoi)* or with other kinds of evildoers, idolaters, and so on (5:9-10). What Paul meant was that the community was to disassociate itself (symbolized in the termination of fellowship) from hypocrites, professing believers who were still living as idolatrous and/or immoral pagans — like the man with

---

4. See Deut. 13:1-5; 17:1-7, 8-13; 19:15-21; 21:18-21; 22:20-24; 24:7.

his stepmother (5:11). This is an appropriate form of community discernment, or judgment (5:12). Whether Paul truly thought any Corinthians really believed that he meant they should "go out of the world" (5:10) is highly unlikely. The whole paragraph is a rhetorical device to drive home the importance of the principle of holiness — separation from evil — and its application to the issue at hand (5:13).

LAWSUITS (6:1-11)

The theme of judging (5:12-13) continues in 6:1-11; now, however, Paul writes about inappropriate judging. Some members of the community are suing other members in the pagan courts (6:1, 4, 6). Some scholars believe the elite were taking the nonelite (and legally more vulnerable) to court, but whether or not that is true, Paul's concerns would apply to anyone in the community taking legal action. For Paul this kind of action is a three-dimensional failure: of wisdom (6:2-6), of cruciform love (6:2-8), and ultimately of conversion and sanctification (6:9-11).

Paul calls upon the Jewish (and then early Christian) apocalyptic belief that God's people assist God on the judgment day (6:2-3), and on the Corinthians' self-designation as a community of the "wise" (6:5), to make his first point. How, he asks, can the Corinthians expect to participate in the final judgment of the world if they cannot judge "trivial cases" (6:2) among their own members? A community endowed with wisdom should be ashamed (6:5) of this failure to adjudicate wrongs by an internal (church) 'court' presided over by some of the wise.

But then Paul turns to the lawsuits themselves. Their very existence — no matter who wins or loses — is a "defeat" for the community (6:7; "for you," plural). They, Paul says, "wrong [adikeite, 'do an injustice to'] and defraud" a brother or sister (cf. 8:11; NRSV mistranslates "brother" as "believers" in each place). Why? The heart of his point is expressed in two powerful rhetorical questions: "Why not rather be wronged [adikeisthe]? Why not rather be defrauded?" (6:7b). Paul portrays a common, legal activity (litigation) as injustice and fraud. He does so because he knows the nonretaliatory teaching and example of Jesus, to which he has already alluded in this letter as the inspiration for his cruciform lifestyle (4:12-13), and to which he will return in chapter 13. Love does not seek its own interest (13:5) or rejoice in wrongdoing (adikia, 13:6). Cruciform love does not pursue self-interest in the courts or anywhere else; it does not inflict but rather absorbs injustice.

This failure of love points ultimately, for Paul, to a more fundamental question. Do those who engage in this adikia realize that the adikoi — the unjust — are excluded from the kingdom of God (6:9)? This is because such people, like the others named in 6:9-10, have not been "washed . . . sanctified . . . justified" (6:11). Their behavior is a sign of nonconversion, of being pagans still embroiled in injustice who will not survive the day of judgment. When believers act unjustly, betraying their identity and forsaking the cross of their Lord, they engage in a dangerous anachronism that reveals them to be more like pre-Christ than post-Christ people: "this is what some of you used to be" (6:11a). Those who have believed the gospel and been put into right covenantal relationship with God, who have been baptized and set apart for God, cannot continue in their old ways. Those who claim the presence of the Spirit of God must live the countercultural cruciform love seen in Jesus that is an essential part of leaving idolatry and injustice behind to pursue love of God and neighbor; otherwise the falsity of their claim to justification and sanctification will be revealed on the coming day.

SEX WITH PROSTITUTES (6:12-20)

The list of the immoral in 6:9-10 may have prompted Paul to return to another specific problem of sexual immorality: having sex with prostitutes. Whether these were ordinary or sacral harlots (associated with a temple, such as Aphrodite's), or perhaps 'after-dinner guests' at the homes of some of Corinth's elite, is debated. In any case, the ancient activity seems quite clearly to have been the fruit of a libertine ethic summarized in a 'slogan' of sorts that Paul quotes back to the church: "All things are lawful for me" (6:12, twice). Indeed, most scholars believe that a good deal of this passage consists of Corinthian slogans (perhaps perversions of Paul's own teachings) and Paul's rebuttals (though there is debate over some of the phrases that might represent the Corinthian position — or at least the position of those who used the services of prostitutes). The Corinthians' position also reveals a kind of dualism in which the activities of the body carry no spiritual significance.

Paul's negative response to the libertinism and dualism, though it has the tone of a scolding ("Do you not know?" occurs three times: 6:15, 16, 19), is a carefully structured piece that draws on the diatribe's rhetorical devices to make some very significant theological points. This passage is absolutely crucial to understanding Paul's 'ethic' generally and his sexual ethic specifically. The text appears to be composed as two consecutive but parallel arguments (6:12-18a and 6:18b-20), each consisting of slogans, counterslogans, theological correction and claims, and exhortation. The following chart, which uses the NRSV text but has minor alterations in the punctuation to indicate quotations, shows these parallel elements:

Parallels in 1 Corinthians 6:12-18a and 6:18b-20

	6:12-18a	6:18b-20
Corinthian Slogans	12a — "All things are lawful for me." 12c — "All things are lawful for me." 13a — "Food is meant for the stomach and the stomach for food, and God will destroy both one and the other."	18b — "Every sin that a person commits is outside the body." *Note: failing to recognize this sentence as a Corinthian slogan, many translations render this "Every* other *sin . . . ," inserting a word ("other") that is absent from the Greek text to try to make some sense of it as Paul's idea.*
Paul's Counter-slogans	12b — "But not all things are beneficial." 12d — "But I will not be dominated by anything." 13b — "The body is meant not for fornication but for the Lord, and the Lord for the body." 14 — "And God raised the Lord and will also raise us by his power."	18c — "But the fornicator sins against the body itself." *Note: "the fornicator" is better translated "the sexually immoral person."*
Theological Correction and Claims	15 — *Do you not know* that your bodies are members of Christ? Should I therefore take the members of Christ and make them members of a prostitute? Never! 16 — *Do you not know* that whoever is united to a prostitute becomes one body with her? For it is said, "The two shall be one flesh." 17 — But anyone united to the Lord becomes one spirit with him.	19 — Or *do you not know* that your body is a temple of the Holy Spirit within you, which you have from God, and that you are not your own? 20a — For you were bought with a price.

Exhortation
18a — Shun fornication!
Note: 'sexual immorality' (more generally) better translates porneia.

20b — Therefore glorify God in your body.

The first argument (6:12-18a) focuses on the misunderstanding of sex as an unrestricted activity that is similar to eating. Paul answers the slogan of absolute libertinism, "All things are lawful for me" (NRSV) or "Everything is permissible for me" (NIV), with two criteria of authentic freedom: the 'free' action must be beneficial (probably here to the self, but in 10:23 to others), and it must not enslave or rule over the individual (6:12). He next answers the implicit analogy of sex to food[5] and the belief that the entire body will one day be destroyed (thus permitting sexual indulgence without moral or spiritual consequences). Paul rebuffs the notion that sexual indulgence, which is really immorality *(porneia),* is what the body is intended for, saying instead that the body is intended "for the Lord, and the Lord for the body" (6:13). In developing this idea he relies on the notion of believers as members of Christ's body (see chap. 12) and on the Genesis narrative that says sex makes two people one flesh (6:15-16). Bodily union with a prostitute — sexual immorality — subverts not a physical but an existing spiritual union between Christ and the believer (6:17). Moreover, the believer's body is not destined for destruction but for resurrection (6:14). In other words, whether in life or death, the believer is in a relationship with the Lord that is expressed through the body. For these reasons believers must flee from sexual immorality (6:18a); it derails them from the goal of their existence.

The second (parallel but briefer) argument further develops Paul's perspective on the significance of the body. The corollary of erroneous disregard for the body's spiritual significance is that sin does not involve the body and that no bodily activity can be a sin (6:18b). As shown in the chart, the idea of "every other sin" (NAB; cf. NIV) being outside the body is not something Paul did or would say; his point is that lots of bodily actions, including especially some sexual ones, can be sins — indeed, sins "against the body" (6:18c). But how can one sin against the body? Only if the body is associated with God, which is precisely the point of 6:19-20. One's body is God's temple, filled with God's Spirit, and it does not belong to oneself (6:19). Here Paul refers to the cross as the act of God's purchasing the believer, like the redemption of a slave (6:20a). Henceforth the purchased person belongs not to self, but to the redeemer. For these reasons believers are not only, negatively, to flee immorality (6:18a), but also, positively, to

5. The analogy being as follows: *eating : stomach :: sex : body;* or, 'eating is to the stomach as sex is to the body.'

glorify God in God's temple — their bodies (6:20b). (Thus for Paul both the individual and the community [3:16] are God's temple.)

It turns out, then, that bodily activity *does* matter and *does* have spiritual consequences because of both the present and the future status of the body in relation to God. The body is the locus of spirituality (cf. Rom. 6:12-23; 12:1) and the focus of redemption (cf. Rom. 8:23). Bodily freedom, therefore, cannot be understood as anything less than belonging to the right Lord (God, not self) and honoring that Lord in and through the Lord's temple. Human bodies, to summarize, have both a present purpose and a future destiny that some Corinthians' sexual behavior betrays.

CONFUSION ABOUT MARRIAGE (7:1-40)

It appears that the believers in Corinth were generally confused about the place of sexuality in the lives of those who belong to Christ. Paul's own teachings may have generated some questions about the propriety of sexual activity, even in marriage, and also about marriage itself. It also appears that some of the believers in Corinth concluded not that sex was permissible for anyone with anyone (e.g., even with relatives or prostitutes), but that it was not permissible *at all* for brothers and sisters in Christ, even in marriage. This may have been the sense of the words in 7:1, "It is well for a man not to touch [have sex with] a woman," which are to be attributed not to Paul but to (some of) the Corinthians, as the quotation marks in the NRSV and the NAB indicate.[6] Paul's rather long response in chapter 7 seeks to set out some general principles about marriage and also to address the specific situations of certain groups within the church.

In 7:2-6 Paul rejects the notion that sexual abstinence is appropriate for married believers, except perhaps occasionally for special periods of prayer (7:5-6). He clearly, if a bit clumsily, sees marriage — and sex within it — as an exclusive relationship of mutuality (7:3-4). He realistically sees abstinence from sex within marriage as an invitation to temptation (7:2, 5-6). Paul not only expects husbands (as well as wives) to fulfill the appropriate conjugal needs of their spouses, but — in contrast to much of the pagan world — he also expects them not to engage in sex with other people. Thus, although the word 'love' does not appear in these verses, Paul is describing one aspect of the other-centered love he extols in chapter 13.

6. NIV's rendering of "touch" as "marry" is a complete mistranslation; the NIV margin, "have sexual relations with a woman," is right. Furthermore, the NIV's failure to put these words in quotation marks perpetuates the erroneous impression that they belong to Paul rather than the Corinthians.

Having clarified his position on sex in marriage, Paul makes his preference known in 7:7. The problem, it turns out, is not sex but marriage itself. Although singleness (celibacy) and marriage are both gifts (*charisma*, 7:7), Paul's way of celibate singleness is preferable, he believes. Why? Later he will write that it allows for undistracted devotion to the Lord's work (7:22-36). Paul is not an opponent of sex but a proponent of dedication to Christ. For this reason Paul counsels the unmarried and widows (or perhaps specifically widowers and widows) to stay that way, unless their passion is out of control (7:8-9). Celibacy is a gift of the Spirit, and not all have it.

Returning to the subject of married people in 7:10-16, Paul first commands believers who are married to believers (7:10-11) not to initiate a divorce, basing his strong word on the teachings of Jesus ("not I but the Lord"; see Matt. 5:31-32; 19:3-9; Mark 10:2-12; Luke 16:18). If a woman (and one presumes also a man) seeks a separation, it may lead to reconciliation but not to remarriage (see also 7:39). As for the spouses of nonbelievers (7:12-16), Paul has no direct word from Jesus, who of course addressed a different situation. But especially as Gentiles became believers and (often) their spouses did not, surely some must have wondered if the marriage was detrimental or impure. Paul advises not to seek divorce (7:12-13) because the effect of the unbalanced union is from unholiness toward holiness, and not vice versa, thereby positively affecting children as well as the unbelieving spouse (7:14), who may actually become a believer (7:16). If, however, the unbelieving spouse initiates divorce, the believer is not bound to maintain the union — and may, in fact, be free to remarry, though Paul is not completely clear (7:15). Once again, Paul holds men and women to the same standards.

Paul next shifts gears to explain the general rubric of what we might call 'positive apathy' within which he views marriage and all other 'stations' in life (7:17-24). His bottom line is basically: 'Stay as you were when God called you' (7:17, 20, 24; see also 7:27). As he will say more clearly in 7:29-31, there is a fundamental eschatological perspective underlying this 'apathy' about station. Here, however, the emphasis is on the irrelevance (see esp. 7:19) of all social distinctions for a community that encompasses people from all stations — Gentile and Jew, slave and free, male and female, married and single. What matters is obedience to God, not status or station (7:19; cf. Gal. 5:6; 6:15).

The one sticky point here is Paul's word about slaves, particularly 7:21, in which the main Greek verbal construction is unclear. Does Paul want them to remain slaves even if they can obtain freedom (so NRSV; NAB) or use the opportunity and become free (so NRSV mg.; NIV)? The scholarly debate is endless, though some have declared the problem insoluble. In light of Paul's letter to Philemon (see discussion in chap. 14), an argument can be made that Paul would want slaves to be free.[7] Whatever the answer, ultimately even this does not matter to Paul, for all slaves are free in Christ and all free persons are Christ's slaves (7:22-23). Like husbands and wives, slaves and masters are equal in Christ.

Returning momentarily to a specific group in the church before continuing with more general principles, Paul offers his personal advice to "virgins" (unmarried women), which is, as we would expect, to remain single (7:25-26), though marrying would not be a sin (7:28). We now see clearly what really drives Paul's passion for singleness. There are two things, as we have already observed: eschatology and devotion. Marriage *is* a distraction from total devotion to the Lord, for a married person — whether male or female — is (appropriately) distracted in a way that is not true of single folks (7:32-35). Marriage can also cause no little distress, Paul realistically notes in 7:28. More importantly, Paul believes that because in Christ the new age has begun, "the present form of this world" — with all its institutions like marriage and slavery — "is passing away" (7:31). The result should be a profound relativizing of all human commitments and relationships (7:29b-31b), not only because the time before the parousia is short (7:29), but also because in Christ the future has already invaded the present. That is to say, Paul's perspective on the social structures of this age is indebted as much to the *quality* of the present time as to the *quantity* of time remaining.

Paul wraps up this chapter with advice to two more groups of unmarried people, unmarried but betrothed men (probably; 7:36-38) and widows (7:39-40). Once again, in each instance he permits marriage — especially if strong youthful passions are involved (7:36) — but prefers singleness (7:38, 40). His condition that widows remarry only believers ("only in the Lord," 7:39) simply makes explicit his assumption about believers marrying only believers that permeates the chapter.[8] He closes with the suggestion that his advice here and elsewhere, even when not based on the teachings of the earthly Jesus, derives from his Spirit-inspired apostolic wisdom (7:40; cf. 7:25).

---

7. It is important to note that in Philemon Paul addresses a master; here he addresses slaves. (If Ephesians and/or Colossians is genuine, the matter becomes still more complicated, since nothing is said in either of those letters about slaves seeking, or masters granting, freedom.) For Paul the 'morality of slavery' may ultimately have less to do with the system than with the equality of slave and master in Christ and with the obligations of each.

8. It should be noted that encouraging widows to remain single probably implies the existence of a support system within the church such that remarriage is not a financial necessity or expectation.

Summary of 1 Corinthians 5–7

In these three chapters Paul has articulated some basic principles for life between the first and second comings of Christ. These include:

- Belonging to God's new community entails leaving the immoralities and injustices of one's former life and the pagan world behind.
- Life in Christ means having a bifocal vision: shaping one's existence in light of the past (teachings, death, and resurrection of Jesus) and the future (parousia, bodily resurrection, and judgment).
- The selfish pursuit of avenging wrong in pagan courts — or anywhere else, including the church — is itself an act of wrongdoing and a betrayal of the gospel.
- Sexual behavior in particular is a matter in which sanctification must be expressed; sexual immorality endangers both the individual believer and the community.
- Believers' bodies, which will one day be raised, do not belong to believers for their indulgence but to God for God's glory, and, within marriage (in a narrower sense), to their spouses.
- Marriage, for believers, is a permanent bond of mutuality in Christ. It is not a sin but a gift (as is celibate singleness), though it is also a distraction from total devotion to the Lord and an institution that will end with the passing of this age.

8:1–14:40. ADDRESSING LITURGICAL CHAOS: THE CROSS AND WORSHIP

If pagan culture provided many opportunities for immorality and injustice, it provided no fewer for idolatry and related practices. As the temple of the one true God (3:16-17) located in the midst of many other temples and their various activities, the church found itself interacting, both directly and indirectly, with the explicitly 'religious' dimension of Greco-Roman culture. Problems arising from some dimensions of that interaction, and of the general worship life of the Corinthian community, are addressed in chapters 8 through 14. The most influential Corinthians are all in favor of freedom, as we would expect. In these chapters Paul seeks a kind of order and unity to the liturgical life that is fully open to the Spirit and therefore fully grounded in the cross. Speaking as one charismatic (Spirit-filled person) to others, Paul can argue not only that freedom and *order* are compatible, but also that freedom and *love* are compatible. In fact, freedom and love are not only compatible, they are two sides of the same coin.

1 Corinthians 8–14 is the crossroads of Paul's ecclesiology and his ethics. Twice in these chapters Paul structures his argument in an *aba'*, or 'chiastic,' pattern: chapters 8–10 (actually 8:1–11:1) and chapters 12–14. This pattern suggests that Paul grants special pride of place to the fulcrum of each of these arguments, namely, chapters 9 and 13, to which special attention must be paid.

MEAT ASSOCIATED WITH IDOLS (8:1–11:1)

Once again in these chapters Paul addresses Corinthian factionalism. These divisions may correspond to the 'parties' described in chapter 1, but especially to the overarching divide between the socially/spiritually elite and the nonelite. The issue this time is not allegiance to leaders or sexuality, but the eating of meat (NRSV, "food") offered to (or perhaps generally associated with) idols, either in the precincts of pagan temples (the primary issue, 8:10) or (of lesser importance) in private homes (10:23-30). Jews abhorred the practice as idolatrous and were forbidden from eating this meat in any form anywhere: not at a sacral meal in the pagan temple; not in the restaurant in the temple precincts, where 'leftovers' from the god's meal might be on the menu; and not at home, where additional leftovers, purchased at the temple market, might also be prepared.

The Corinthians are split. There is a group of self-styled possessors of knowledge (8:1, 10), brandishing their knowledge that idols do not really exist and their consequent freedom and right to eat whatever, whenever — even in the temple (8:1-6, 9-11). There is also a group that Paul himself labels "weak" (8:9), people with a 'weak conscience' (8:7, 12) who lack the knowledge of the other group. The believers in this group associate such meat eating with actual idolatry (8:7a). Seeing other believers consume this kind of meat, they might be tempted also to eat and thus (from their own perspective) to commit idolatry (8:7b-10). We will refer to the two groups neutrally as the meat-eaters and the non-meat-eaters.

Paul's response to the situation is as complex as it is creative. He packs a kind of one-two punch. His first move is to affirm the meat-eaters' monotheistic theology but challenge their knowledge-based ethic of personal rights, calling instead for an ethic of others-oriented love (chap. 8). After offering himself as an example of the alternative ethic he proposes (chap. 9), he returns to the theological issue, warning the meat-eaters that participation in a pagan sacral meal is in fact a kind of idolatry, a fellowship with the demonic (10:1-22). The chapters conclude with reiterations of his ethical principles and with permission (though not blanket permission) to eat meat bought at the temple market in private homes (10:23–11:1). The great importance Paul attaches to the principles and arguments developed in these chapters is evident from their reuse in Romans 14.

The Problem and Paul's Solution (8:1-13)

Following the pattern devised in chapter 6, Paul begins chapter 8 by quoting a Corinthian slogan, "All of us possess knowledge," and refuting it with a counterslogan, "Knowledge puffs up, but love builds up" (8:1). Paul claims that he actually agrees with the knowledge the meat-eaters possess. Alluding to (and reinterpreting, in light of Christ) the basic Jewish affirmation of YHWH as the one God (see esp. Deut. 6:4, a portion of the Shema), Paul agrees that the many pagan gods and lords do not really exist, for there is only "one God, the Father," the source and goal of all creation, and "one Lord, Jesus Christ," the agent of creation (8:4-6). Paul also agrees that because all meat is the creation of the one God, it is itself good (10:26), and he does not believe that eating or abstaining from food per se affects one's relationship with God (8:8, which may also contain a Corinthian slogan; cf. Rom. 14 to see that this is Paul's view). So far, so good.

But the counterslogan in 8:1 summarizes Paul's whole attitude toward the *behavior,* or ethic, of the Corinthian knowledgeable meat-eaters. The "necessary knowledge" the Corinthians must have is that the appropriate motto for those who love and are known by this one God (8:2) — the one revealed in the crucified Christ — is not "knowledge" but "love." An ethic grounded in "knowledge" focuses on individual *freedom* and the exercise of one's *right* (8:9; Gk. *exousia,* mistranslated "liberty" in the NRSV), thought to derive from that freedom. An ethic of cruciform love, on the other hand, seeks to edify the other, taking account of the impact of one's behavior on fellow believers (8:11-12) and being willing to forgo the exercise of a right for the welfare of the other (8:13).

The meat-eaters' current behavior, as Paul sees it, is totally and inappropriately self-centered. It shows no concern for the conscience of other brothers or sisters (the non-meat-eaters) and for the grave temptation ("stumbling block") that the behavior poses to these weaker believers (8:9-10). In fact, the exercise of this knowledge and right becomes *sin.* It is sin against the brother or sister, who may be destroyed (severed from Christ) by idolatry (8:11-12a), and also against Christ, who died for that person and whose body is constituted by all believers (8:12; cf. chap. 12).

The gravity of this situation leads Paul to issue a challenge in the form of a claim — to prevent another's falling, he would permanently abandon eating meat of any sort (8:13). And he demonstrates the credibility of his claim, while offering a living example of this kind of love, in the autobiographical chapter that follows.

The Example of Apostolic Cruciformity (9:1-27)

When Paul writes autobiographically, he writes paradigmatically. On the surface 1 Corinthians 9 sounds like a self-defense of apostolic rights, which in part it is. But the whole purpose of Paul's assertion of rights is to show that he, like the Corinthian elite, had legitimate rights that could be deliberately suppressed as an act of cruciform love and, ultimately, of true freedom. In this chapter Paul establishes his apostolic rights (9:1-12a, 13-14); narrates his renunciation of them as a fundamental part of his apostolic identity and modus operandi (9:12b, 15-18); and explains his two motives for doing so — to 'win others' through Christlike freedom and love (9:19-23), and to insure his own participation in the eschatological victory (9:24-27).

Paul cleverly begins by asserting his own freedom — a freedom he never renounces — and thereby identifies his common status with the meat-eaters (9:1). But his freedom is also unique, because it is apostolic freedom. The two proofs of his apostleship offered here are his having seen the resurrected Jesus and his having fathered the Corinthian church (9:1-2). With apostleship come certain rights, for which Paul gives a brief apologia ("defense," 9:3) in 9:3-14 (minus the parenthesis in 9:12b).

Paul asserts two basic rights, to financial support (9:4, 7-12a, 13-14) and to spousal companionship on mission trips (9:5-6). The latter right is of little relevance here and is probably offered only to make it plain that he is equal to other apostles (cf. 9:12a) and that his apostolic rights extend beyond economics. Paul offers three warrants for his right to financial support for meals and other expenses: "human authority" (9:8) or common practice, both secular and religious; the Law (9:8); and the command of Jesus (9:14).

Like a soldier, an apostle does not pay his own way, and like a farmer or shepherd, he benefits from his labor (9:7-8). This principle is enunciated also in Deuteronomy 25:4, Paul says, interpreting (in good rabbinic fashion) the prohibition of ox muzzling as a word about apostolic rights (9:8-12a). Sowing "spiritual good" should reap some "material benefits" (9:11). A further illustration of this is provided by the priests in the Jewish temple (9:13), and the final word comes from Jesus himself (9:14, an echo of the teaching preserved in Matt. 10:10 and Luke 10:7).

"Nevertheless . . ." — Paul's great interruption to all the assertions about his apostolic right to support appears twice (9:12b, 15). He has not used this right and is not seeking to exercise it now. Rather, Paul (with his colleagues, 9:12b) has refrained from using the right so as not to create any obstacle for the spread of the gospel (9:12b; cf. 8:9). Any potential critics, as well as the meat-eaters, need to know his motive: for the good of the gospel and the salvation of others. This decision and its consequent lifestyle have now become Paul's

258

Corinth: Small shops, places to eat, and artisans' workshops
lined the agora and main streets of the city.

"ground for boasting" (9:15) and his "reward" (9:18). As an apostle, he has no
choice but to proclaim the gospel, but to do so free of charge, when he has the
right to be paid, is an admirable sacrifice, something to be proud of. Or is it?

Repeatedly in this letter Paul has condemned pride and counseled boasting
only in the Lord. Has he now contradicted himself? No! Verses 9-23 demonstrate
that Paul's renunciation of financial support is his way of embodying Jesus' cruciform faith and love; it is his way of "boasting in the Lord." It is therefore a free
but also necessary choice. Verses 24-27 confirm that Paul is convinced that only
in embodying such cruciformity will he be guaranteed salvation.

The concrete meaning of such cruciformity is provided in 9:19. In this
verse, read with 9:12 and 9:15, we see Paul succinctly telling his own story in
three stages that parallel the story of Jesus, as narrated in the pre-Pauline hymn
found in Philippians 2, Paul's 'master story.'[9] Like Jesus, Paul possessed a particular status, and thus certain rights associated with that status, but rather than
exploiting them for his own advantage, he took the form of a slave for the benefit of others.

9. For more discussion of Phil. 2, see chap. 4 on Paul's gospel and chap. 13 on Philippians
itself.

Parallels between Philippians 2 and 1 Corinthians 9

	Philippians 2	1 Corinthians 9
[*x*] Possession of status and rights	6a — though he [Christ Jesus] was in the form of God	19a — For though I am free with respect to all
[*y*] Decision not to use the status and rights for self-benefit	6b — [he] did not regard equality with God as something to be exploited	12b — Nevertheless, we have not made use of this right 15a — But I have made no use of any of these rights
[*z*] Self-abasement/self-enslavement	7 — but emptied himself, taking the form of a slave, being born in human likeness. And being found in human form, 8 — he humbled himself and became obedient to the point of death — even death on a cross.	19b-c — I have made myself a slave to all, so that I might win more of them. 12c — but we endure anything rather than put an obstacle in the way of the gospel of Christ.

Manual labor was associated with slaves and disdained by the Greco-Roman elite. Paul's working with his hands and renouncing financial support from the whole church or from some wealthy patron(s) no doubt engendered criticism, especially from the elite Corinthians. Paul, however, sees his refusal of financial support, and his self-lowering to the point of menial labor, as analogous to the self-abasement of Christ from equality with God to the 'slavery' of human life and a shameful death on the cross. Like Christ (though the hymn does not say this explicitly, only in its Pauline context in Philippians), Paul acted for the salvation of all, motivated ultimately by love. He accommodated himself to any and all — Jew, Gentile, and especially the *weak* (9:22; cf. 8:11). His becoming "all things to all people" (9:22), however, does not mean that he had a disingenuous or chameleon-like ministry. Rather, his 'inconsistency' was in fact his consistency, his constant self-emptying his way of fulfilling God's law by coming "under Christ's law" (9:21). In context this "law" of Christ refers to the pattern demonstrated in the chart above and is best translated 'Christ's narrative pattern [i.e., paradigmatic story] of self-enslavement' or 'Christ's narrative pattern of faith [= obedience] and love.' As noted in chapter 4 and indicated in the chart, this pattern can be summarized as 'although *x* (possession of status and rights), not *y* (use of status and rights) but *z* (self-abasement/self-enslavement).'

Consistently embodying this pattern — "do[ing] it all" (9:23) — is Paul's way of *really* sharing in the blessings of the gospel: not the "material benefits" (9:11) he is due as an apostle, but the "imperishable" wreath of final salvation (9:25). Like an athlete who practices self-control and bodily 'enslavement' (9:27), as one would witness at the nearby Isthmian Games, Paul enslaves himself as Christ Jesus enslaved himself. In doing so, Paul does not *renounce* his freedom but *exercises* it in acts of love. Otherwise he would be "disqualified" from the main event (9:27); *he would not be saved.* Let those who have ears (like the meat-eaters) hear.

Fellowship with and Imitation of Christ (10:1–11:1)

Paul's unmistakable (but still only implicit) warning to the meat-eaters about their self-centered exercise of rights will be stated more positively in the form of summary slogans or maxims in 10:23-24 and 10:31–11:1. The warning, however, is not yet complete, for Paul wants the Corinthians now to reconsider the issue of idolatry. Perhaps he thinks they will be open to careful self-examination now that he has shown them the ethical error of their ways. (But perhaps not; maybe the elite Corinthians, at least, still despise him, not only for acting like a slave but for admitting, in effect, to disobeying Jesus [9:14].) In any case, he wants them not to "test" Christ (10:9) by flirting with demon-inspired idolatry, but rather to be Christ's new-covenant partners and imitators.

In 10:1-22 Paul draws on Israel's past as a lesson (10:6, 11) for the Corinthian church: even those who are baptized and participate in the Lord's Supper are not immune from idolatry. Paul's use of the exodus–wilderness–golden calf narrative suggests that even former pagans in the Corinthian church, who are now the Israelites' descendants (10:1), had been taught these biblical stories. For Paul the Scripture narratives not only speak to, but also prefigure, the church.

The church's Israelite ancestors had every spiritual experience imaginable (10:1-4), like the Corinthians themselves: rescued, baptized, and even 'eucharistized' with spiritual food and drink. In fact, they "drank from . . . Christ" (10:4). None of that mattered (or matters, Paul implies), for "God was not pleased with most of them, and they were struck down" (10:5). Their error, from which their spiritual and 'sacramental' experiences did not protect them, was to "desire evil" and to become both idolatrous and sexually immoral (10:6-8). Such immorality was common in pagan temples, and even in private homes. Paul has already shown that the Corinthians, or at least some (most? — 10:5) of them, are immoral in sexual and other respects. They must therefore take care so as not to fall (10:12), and must rely on God, who is faithful (cf. 1:9), to deliver them from this temptation.

But the Corinthians must play their part in God's act of faithfulness: "Flee from idolatry!" (10:14 NIV), which is parallel to "Flee from sexual immorality!" (6:18 NIV). These are the two great temptations to break covenantal relations with God, to test Christ, to reenact the wrong story of one's ancestors. Paul does not now contradict his earlier claim in chapter 8 that idols do not exist (10:19). Rather, he claims that there is something real behind an idol, namely, a demon (10:20-21). Idolatry is not evil because the gods exist, but because the worship of them is part of the great cosmic battle against the worship of the one true God. Moreover, as a general principle, Paul says that whenever one participates in any kind of worship, particularly a sacral meal, one becomes an intimate part-ner *(koinōnos)* with the deity (10:18) — or, if the deity does not exist, with the demonic power behind it (10:20-21). This was true of Israel's sacred meals, it is true of meals in pagan temples (called the 'god's suppers'), and it is true of "the table of the Lord" or "the Lord's supper" (10:17, 21; cf. 11:20).

The conviction driving Paul's argument here is that, unlike the idols but like YHWH, Christ exercises an exclusive and total claim over his body, his community, as expressed in the sharing *(koinōnia:* partnership, fellowship) which is the Lord's Supper (10:16-17, 21). The Lord is still a "jealous" God (Deut. 4:24; 5:9; 6:15; 32:16-21); the Corinthians cannot partake of the Lord's Supper and the suppers of the gods.

Returning finally to the place where he began, Paul now summarizes his main points in two short, proverblike sections (10:23-24; 10:31–11:1) that sur-round a brief discussion of the one subject not addressed so far — eating meat that had been offered to idols not at the temple, but at home. The summaries themselves are quite clear and emphatic. Paul in effect answers the Corinthian slogan "All things are lawful" (10:23, twice) with two rebuttals and then replaces it with four maxims of his own. The rebuttals are "Not all things are beneficial" and "Not all things build up." That is to say, not all deeds are acts of *love,* which seeks the benefit of others and builds them up (8:1; cf. 13:4-7). The substitute maxims that Paul provides stress this criterion of other-centeredness for judg-ing all activity:

- "Do not seek your own advantage [NIV, "good"], but that of the other [NAB, "neighbor"]." (10:24)
- "So, whether you eat or drink, or whatever you do, do everything for the glory of God." (10:31)
- "Give no offense to Jews or to Greeks or to the church of God, just as I try to please everyone in everything I do, not seeking my own advantage [NIV, "good"; NAB, "benefit"], but that of many, so that they may be saved." (10:32-33)
- "Be imitators of me, as I am of Christ." (11:1)

In sum, these maxims call on the Corinthians to glorify God in their eating (or noneating) by living a life dedicated to the welfare of the other, even to the point of renouncing the exercise of status and rights, as an imitator of their spiritual father and, ultimately, of their Lord.

In between these two sets of maxims (10:25-30), Paul may appear to be confusing or self-contradictory, though he actually is not. The issue here is the eating of meat *sold* in the temple precincts (market) but *consumed* in a private home. The Corinthian believers are free to eat such meat as part of God's good creation (10:25-26; implicitly, in their own homes). If at the home of an unbeliever for a meal, they may still eat meat, without asking questions, since the affair is not in the temple and is not (again, Paul assumes) a sacral meal (10:27). If, however, someone identifies the source of the meat, the Corinthians should seek not to be a stumbling block (for believer or unbeliever) by abstaining, thus disassociating themselves from any hint of idolatry (10:28-29a, patterned on the maxims in 10:24 and 10:32-33).

This leaves, however, 10:29b-30. If 10:28-29a is read as a kind of parenthesis, Paul may be reasserting his own position from 10:25-27 that one's freedom should not unnecessarily be curtailed. That is, in a private home, when no questions are raised, there is no reason to hesitate for anyone's sake. On the other hand, 10:29b may be the beginning of Paul's (final) summary, and he may again be quoting the libertine Corinthian position, only finally to refute it with the string of maxims in 10:31-33. In either case, Paul preserves liberty by exercising it through either the use of rights or the renunciation of rights, whichever befits the gospel by serving others and glorifying God.

Summary of 1 Corinthians 8:1–11:1

Since 1 Corinthians 8:1–11:1 is such an important and substantive unit, some summary words are in order:

- Those who live in Christ cannot order their lives according to an ethic of freedom based on knowledge — even correct theological knowledge — that stresses self-interest and rights without regard for the impact of behavior on others.
- The truest expression of freedom is not the exercise of rights but the free decision, out of loving concern for others, not to exercise even legitimate rights. True freedom, in other words, is freedom from the tyranny of the self; it is self-giving love. For those who pattern their lives after Christ, such freedom may also, paradoxically, be an obligation.
- Even apparently correct theological knowledge can be destructive and dangerous when used carelessly or selfishly.

- Allegiance to the Lord Jesus is an exclusive devotion that leaves no room for association with idolatry.

DISORDERLY WOMEN AND MEN IN THE ASSEMBLY (11:2-16)

Few passages in the Pauline letters are as vexing for the interpreter as this one. The difficulty of certain words, the complicated (some would say tortured or inconsistent) logic of thought and interrelationship of sentences, and the veiled (no pun intended) references to ancient social phenomena are just some of the interpretive issues. The result is a complex set of variables that has given rise to numerous reconstructions of the social setting and thus various overall interpretations. Some people find Paul's statements offensive; others conclude that the passage must be a later interpolation similar in spirit to 1 Timothy 2:9-15.

Within this exegetical morass, one very important aspect of the text, about which all interpreters should be able to agree, is often overlooked: Paul assumes without hesitation or discussion that women, like men, may pray and prophesy — speak both *to* God and *for* God — in the gathered church (11:4-5). No matter what else we conclude, we must stress that in this respect men and women are equal in Christ.

The text does raise many specific questions, among which we may note the following:

- Does the text describe male-female or husband-wife relationships — or a little of both? (The Greek words for 'man' and 'woman' can also mean 'husband' and 'wife.')
- What does the word "head" mean in these verses? Does it have multiple meanings in the text? (Some possible nonliteral meanings include 'authority,' 'source,' 'most prominent figure,' and 'contrast or complement to the body.')
- Does the text refer to the practice of wearing some article of clothing (hood, veil, head covering), to hairstyles (loose or bound), or to both?
- Does the passage interpret male-female or husband-wife relationships as hierarchical, reciprocal, or both?

How are we to put together all these variables and answer these difficult questions? Any interpretation must be offered with due humility and tentativeness. However, despite differences in detail, something of a scholarly 'majority opinion' has emerged. It appears that some women in Corinth felt that the gospel (i.e., life in Christ and the Spirit) emancipated them, at least when they were at worship, from their culture's normal public expressions of (a) female distinctiveness from men and/or (b) sexual modesty. These women expressed this evangelical emancipation in the assembly by uncovering their heads and/or letting their hair down, thereby emitting cultural signals of maleness and/or sexual looseness.

Paul seeks to redress this practice, not by 'putting women in their place' (i.e., under the authority of men), but by reminding male and female believers alike of the ongoing need for culturally appropriate signs of gender identity and/or modesty, as well as the reality of equality and interdependence in the church. Interpreters are still divided over whether this gender identity by virtue of creation should be understood as gender hierarchy (i.e., male superiority or prominence) or simply differentiation. In either case, the creative tension in Paul's mind between the two realities of creation/culture and redemption/Christ produces the difficulties and near inconsistencies in the passage.

Paul opens and closes the passage (11:2, 16) by appealing to the importance of apostolic tradition and universal custom in certain matters (cf. also 11:23-26; 15:3-7), including this one. The affirmation of three relationships of 'headship' (11:3) can be understood in either specifically hierarchical (head as authority) or in more generally relational (head as source or contrast/complement) terms. In either case the relationship implies that the "head" can be shamed or disgraced by the behavior of the other (11:4-5), who is the "reflection" (NRSV) or "glory" (NAB, NIV) of the corresponding head (11:7).

These somewhat confusing remarks about headship and glory envelop the concrete practice at issue: the appropriate head covering or hairstyle for men and women at worship. (The context includes but is also broader than just husband-wife relations.) If a man prays or prophesies with his head covered (11:4) — as contemporary males with sufficient social status to lead rites in pagan temples often did (as ancient statues and coins bear witness) — he shames his head (probably meaning Christ; cf. 11:3) by treating Christ like a pagan deity, drawing attention to himself, and dressing in an inappropriately effeminate way.[10] On the other hand, a woman who prays or prophesies with her head uncovered (and/or her hair unbound)[11] disgraces her head (her husband), perhaps by failing to maintain her gender identity and/or her sexual modesty; she has become a 'loose woman,' so to speak, and she might as well adopt the most culturally radical sign of rejecting her femaleness and modesty, a shaven head (11:5-6). The head covering and/or bound hair, then, is a sign of chastity, a sym-

---

10. It should also be noted that in some cults men did not cover their heads, so the precise reference and analogy cannot be discerned with certainty.

11. Although neither NRSV, NIV, or NAB translates the phrase this way, many interpreters have suggested it.

bolic barrier to sexual advances. It is possible that a woman's uncovered head or loose hair in worship would be associated also with the frenzied activity of women in certain pagan cults.

At first glance, the next few verses (11:7-10), which appeal to the Genesis creation narrative, sound like the most hierarchical and patriarchal sentences in the passage, and they well may be. But modern translations can actually create more forceful impressions along these lines than what the text actually says. For example, "*but* woman is the reflection/glory of man" (11:7b) can be translated "*and* woman . . . ," while woman's creation "*for* man" (11:9 NAB, NIV) or "*for the sake of* man" (NRSV) is better rendered "*on account of* man." These nuances may suggest that the relationship of man to woman is not primarily one of superiority but rather of source, as 11:8 states. The enigmatic references to a sign of "authority" and to "angels" (11:10) are probably intended to reinforce the need for order in the assembly, where angels were apparently thought to join with humans in the worship of God. (Another possibility is that women must not sexually tempt angels, like those in Genesis 6:1-4, according to Jewish tradition.)

Whether or not hierarchical tendencies are present in 11:7-10, the ultimate significance of any such tendencies is countered by the reciprocity and equality affirmed in 11:11-12. In the Lord (Christ) men and women are thoroughly interdependent (11:11); the gospel makes them equals (cf. Gal. 3:28) who build one another up through prayer and prophecy. This evangelical affirmation is supplemented by a reminder that even in the ongoing creation of humanity through childbirth, man comes from woman, and both from God (11:12) — an explicit egalitarian affirmation.

The conclusion of the passage is a final admonition in the form of an invitation (11:13), grounded in an appeal to nature (11:14-15) and church custom (11:16). In sum, Paul in this passage affirms both culturally appropriate expressions of gender identity (distinctiveness and sexual modesty), grounded in creation, and gender equality and interdependence, grounded in both creation and Christ. Truly Spirit-filled worship respects these principles and embodies the order that is appropriate to the worship of God and the edification of the community (cf. 14:33, 40).

ABUSE OF THE LORD'S SUPPER (11:17-34)

This passage is of particular importance because it is the only discussion (in conjunction with some verses in chap. 10) of "the Lord's supper" (11:20) in the Pauline letters. It is quite likely that the Corinthian believers, naturally using the models of the ancient religious collegium and the dinner party *(sympo-*

Corinth: A mosaic from the house of a well-to-do
Corinthian family, now in the site's museum

sium), gathered for a meal that included certain ritual elements and was followed by a time of worship, including praise and prophecy (cf. chaps. 12–14). In this passage, however, Paul construes this supper not as a typical Greco-Roman meal, but as an event of solidarity *(koinōnia),* commemoration, and proclamation that brings spiritual blessing in anticipation of the eschatological banquet of salvation. From his perspective, however, the Corinthians have created an event of division, amnesia, and betrayal that warrants divine wrath. They are *not* celebrating the supper of the crucified, present, and coming Lord.

Problem and Solution

Paul begins by contrasting his commendation regarding the previous topic (11:2) with his criticism on this one (11:17, 22), for something that ought to benefit the community is actually harming it (11:17, 34). Paul's understated reaction (for rhetorical effect) to another variation on the Corinthian theme of factions (11:18) actually expresses, in context, his very deep concern (11:18), yet also his hope that something good may yet come from this chaos (11:19).

The concrete problem seems to be something like the following (11:20-22): all the believers, representing a variety of socioeconomic groups, are assembling at the large house of one wealthier member-patron. Those with more wealth, leisure, and status — perhaps the home owner's friends and associates — are arriving early for the evening gathering, which includes a meal, while those lower on the socioeconomic ladder are arriving much later after working into the evening. The 'early birds' are not waiting for the latecomers but joining the patron for what amounts to a private meal, with some overindulging in alcohol and no one showing concern about the needs of the poor who must come late.

Even a very large house would normally have only one or two dining rooms *(triclinia)*, which would not accommodate everyone, so the poorer latecomers are forced to eat separately from the wealthier members, perhaps in the atrium or in other rooms, and to scrounge for leftovers. This event has therefore lost all connection with the teaching Paul had given the Corinthians (11:20, 23) and has come to resemble a typical dinner party of the Corinthian elite. It is possible, in fact, that the Corinthians have completely abandoned the 'ritual' dimension of the Lord's Supper, the special cup and bread that were supposed to be the heart of the experience.

Paul's solution to this problem is multifaceted. In a word, however, it is 'Wait!' (11:33; or perhaps 'Welcome [all]!') — wait for and welcome all in order to eat the *Lord's* supper. But what is this Lord's supper?

The Significance of the Supper

1. First of all, "the Lord's supper" is not a sequence of private meals but an *experience of solidarity,* or fellowship *(koinōnia)*. This fellowship is with Christ (10:16-21) and therefore with one another, for the people are Christ's body (cf. 8:12 and chap. 12) and God's church (11:22). There is to be a special solidarity with "those who have nothing" (11:22), for they are the special object of God's calling in Corinth (1:26-31). Paul believes the 'real presence' of Jesus in this meal is in the members of his body; Christ and church (= people) are inseparable for

him. Thus the warning against eating and drinking "without discerning the body" (11:29) is about discerning and honoring the church members as the body of Christ, and has nothing to do (for Paul) with the 'communion elements' per se. There is one cup and one loaf (10:16-21, 11:24-26), however, which both create and symbolize one body. The Lord's Supper must correspond to this reality and these symbols.

2. Second, the supper is an *event of memory*. Paul reminds the Corinthians of the 'words of institution' — the words of the Lord handed first to him from Jesus (perhaps via the other apostles in Jerusalem) and then passed on to the Corinthian converts (11:23). These words, which echo Luke (22:15-20) more closely than Mark and Matthew, focus on the phrase "in remembrance of me" (11:24, 25), that is, recalling the significance of the death and experiencing its significance once again. 'Remembering' for Jews was never merely recollecting; it meant faithfully responding to God and God's past saving actions, which are made present and effective once again in the act of faithful remembrance. In his death Christ gave himself for sins to establish the new covenant in which the Corinthians now live. To remember Christ's self-giving in death is to participate in it as a present reality, to live faithfully and appropriately in the shadow of the cross.

3. Thus, thirdly, for Paul the ritual is an *act of proclamation* — a parabolic sermon on the heart of Jesus' mission and of Paul's gospel (cf. 15:3-5). This means that for Paul, not only unbelievers but also (especially?) believers need to have the cross proclaimed to them. A community that forgets the cross forgets its identity — its origin as well as its present shape. A community de-centered from the cross will inevitably marginalize the weak. It is only by constantly repreaching the cross in tangible ways (with bread and cup) that the Corinthians will be reminded and enabled to embody the cruciform love that the cross proclaims (11:1; chap. 13).

4. This leads to a fourth dimension for Paul, his emphasis on the forward-looking character of the meal; it is a *foretaste of the future messianic banquet,* a present experience of blessing and spiritual sustenance (10:3-4, 16-21).

In sum, the supper reminds the church that both its life and its preaching must be cross-centered until the parousia.

In 11:27-34 the Corinthian church receives strong words of condemnation, warning, and instruction on their behavior. Communing "in an unworthy manner" (11:27) and "without discerning the body" (11:29) means without seeing the interconnections among Christ, cross, and community. This renders the community 'answerable' for the cross (11:27) and judged by the Lord; Paul explains Corinthian debilitation and death as a consequence of their grave misbehavior — they are like the Israelites in the wilderness (10:3-5). Ultimately, however, the Lord's discipline is always for the community's good (11:32), so if the

Corinthians can really examine themselves to discern their true identity (11:28), and then act as the body of the crucified Christ that they are, they will not ultimately be condemned (11:32, 34). Otherwise they will share the final fate of the unbelieving world (11:32).

SPIRITUAL GIFTS (12:1–14:40)

The theme of the oneness of the community centered on the cross that Paul articulates in 11:17-34 provides the springboard into the next topic, "spiritual gifts." This topic spans three chapters, the first two providing a framework within which the problem of glossolalia in the gathered assembly can be specifically addressed in the last. Gifts, Paul says, are given by God to unify and edify the church, and must always therefore be publicly exercised in constructive cruciform love and with an appropriate degree of order. The apparently uncontrolled charismatic worship in Corinth did not measure up, in Paul's view, to the God, Christ, and Spirit of his gospel.

The Church as Christ's Body (12:1-31)

Chapter 12 carries on the theme of the church as one diverse body formed by the cross, developed first in 1:18–2:5 and then in 11:17-34. In it Paul describes the church as a paradoxical combination of equality and hierarchy. On the one hand are an equality of gifts and a corollary interdependent unity in diversity. On the other hand is a hierarchy of gifts — based on their ability to edify others, not to enhance the self — as well as a hierarchy of members in the body — based on their weakness, not their power. Language about the body was commonly used in antiquity as a metaphor for community. That is not unique to Paul; neither is his focus on interdependence. What is unique is his denigration of power and status, and his prioritizing of the weak members of the body, both of which amount to an inversion of the Greco-Roman (and the Corinthians') status quo. In each case the hierarchy Paul constructs reflects the cross: the values of love and weakness.

Paul uses two different terms to refer to "spiritual gifts," each indicating their origin: *pneumatika* (12:1; 14:1) and *charismata* (12:4, 9, 28, 30, 31), or 'gifts of the Spirit' and 'gifts of grace.' Before addressing their divine source and community-oriented purpose in some detail through the body metaphor, Paul introduces the most basic criterion of all believing existence: the common early Christian confession "Jesus is Lord" (12:2-3). For Paul, of course, this means that the *crucified* Jesus is Lord. This confession, and the reality to which it at-

Corinth: The museum houses the replicas of body parts
made to invoke or celebrate healing by Asclepius at his temple.

tests, is the most basic and essential characteristic of the community, distinguishing it from all forms of paganism. No speech or behavior (such as cursing Jesus, or perhaps using Jesus' name to pronounce a curse — 12:3) that contradicts this confession can be inspired by the Spirit, no matter what the claims of the speaker might be. Conversely, all who utter the claim — no matter what other gift (including gifts of speech) they do or do not possess — are Spirit-filled members of the body of Christ.

Paul's specific take on this early acclamation of Jesus' lordship is actually trinitarian: 'the crucified Jesus who was raised from the dead to the position of Lord by God the Father is present with us through the Spirit.'[12] The import of this perspective becomes clear in 12:4-11, where Paul indicates that the work of the Spirit is actually the work of the triune God, who determines the distribu-

---

12. As in previous chapters, trinitarian language is used here in recognition that although Paul does not have a fully developed theology of the Trinity, such language is nonetheless appropriate.

tion and purpose of the gifts. The Spirit gives the gifts to the various members of the community (12:4, 7-11); Jesus, as the Lord and as the one whose body is constituted by the church, is served (12:5); and God (the Father) activates the gifts (12:6). Every believer has a gift ("to each," 12:7), though not all have the same gift (some of the possibilities are listed for the first time in 12:8-11). Every gift is given as a "manifestation of the Spirit for the common good" (12:7) — a bedrock principle of Paul's perspective on this topic, and one of the main points of the chapter.

This reality of the diversity of gifts but unity of source (God) and purpose (edification of the community) creates a fundamental equality in the church, which Paul now addresses with the language of a "body." After announcing the main point of his comparison between the human body and the body of Christ (12:12-13) as Spirit-generated unity in diversity, Paul first gives an extended description of the human body (12:14-26), which is obviously an implicit description of the church. He then gives a partial explicit application of it to the church (12:27-31).

It is especially interesting that although Paul's focus in these chapters is spiritual gifts, the unity-in-diversity to which he points encompasses ethnic and socioeconomic distinctions (12:13, possibly taken from an early baptismal liturgy). The absence of a word about gender distinctions (unlike the parallel in Gal. 3:26-28 but like Col. 3:11) may be accidental, or it may be related to the issues in 11:2-16 and 14:34b-36 (if authentic). In any case, it is clear that Paul included women among the gifted (11:5).

The image of the body conveys four interconnected main points, three conventional and one not. The conventional points are bodily unity in diversity (12:14, 20), the necessity of all parts (12:15-19, 21), and the solidarity, or mutual interdependence, of all parts (12:26). Feet, hands, ears, eyes, the nose — all are necessary; there can be no body without diverse bodily parts. So, too, Paul implies, the church consists of people with various backgrounds and gifts, all of whom are necessary for the activity of the body (12:19), and all of whom need one another and should care for one another (12:25-26). No one should feel inferior ('I'm not needed,' 12:15-16) or superior ('you're not needed,' 12:21).

The unconventional point in 12:14-26 appears at this juncture and constitutes Paul's first cruciform hierarchy. Not only are feelings of inferiority or superiority inappropriate, but in the church the apparently "weaker" members are actually "indispensable," and the "less honorable . . . less respectable" ones are treated with greater honor and respect (12:22-24a). This is by divine arrangement (12:24b), just as Paul said in 1:26-31, and is intended to preempt dissension by counterculturally showering *more* attention on those of *less* status so that all will receive equal care (12:25). Moreover, when one member of the church suffers either ill or good fortune, the entire church stands with that member, irrespective of that member's status in worldly terms (12:25-26). The God of the cross mixes things up in a radical way, but the Corinthians, it would seem, have not gotten it so far.

Paul follows his discussion of this first cruciform hierarchy (greater honor to the weak) with a second, this one quite explicitly mentioning the church as the body of Christ: greater importance to the gifts that edify (12:27-31). Although there is a diversity of gifts, and not all have the gifts that might signal greater status, there are for Paul "greater gifts" (12:31a). The hierarchy he envisions is reflected in 12:28-29, where apostles, prophets, and teachers clearly rank higher than those who possess the more 'spectacular' gifts (such as healing), including — at the very bottom — those who speak in tongues. This is a direct attack by Paul, not on the gifts (for they are, after all, from God), but on the Corinthians' inappropriate overvaluing of the less valuable gifts, especially tongues. As Paul will say explicitly in chapter 14, the greater gifts are those that edify others (e.g., 14:4-5), thereby most exhibiting love (8:1) and most conforming to the cross. In fact, every gift is to be exercised in love — which is the point of chapter 13.

The Rule of Cruciform Love (13:1-13)

Few passages of the Bible are as often read, or as often read out of context, as 1 Corinthians 13. This encomium, or discourse in praise of a virtue, is intended by Paul as a description of the "more excellent way" to exercise spiritual gifts — and to live as believers more generally — in light of the cross. It contains both an antidescription of the Corinthians and an antidote for their self-centered and self-destructive behavior. In this chapter Paul addresses love's necessity (13:1-3), character (13:4-7), permanence (13:8-12), and superiority (13:13). Despite the absence of any explicit reference to God, Christ, or the Spirit, the agape described in this chapter is clearly the fruit of the Spirit (cf. Gal. 5:22), the kind of love that God has for the world (Rom. 5:6-8) and Christ demonstrated in his death on the cross (Gal. 2:20).

Paul's first words get right to the main point: the use of tongues, or any other spiritual gift, that is not done in love erases any status the person might have and makes him or her "nothing" (13:2). The glossolalia is nothing but noise (perhaps like that of frenzied worshipers in the cult of Cybele) that has no benefit whatsoever (13:1). The possession of prophetic powers and even the absolute self-surrender of one's possessions or one's body,[13] apart from love, mer-

---

13. Whether to "boast" (NRSV, NAB, NIV mg.) or "to be burned" (NRSV mg., NIV ["to the flames"]) does not affect the main point.

its nothing (13:2-3). Love is the hallmark of all believers' activity at all times; it is absolutely necessary.

This agape is described in 13:4-7. But English translations are normally unable to represent the fact that Paul's description is a narrative. The verses have no adjectives ('love is *x*') but only a series of verbal phrases, seven positive and eight negative: 'love does *x*, but does not do *y*,' etc. Love is an action word for Paul, and in these verses love clearly does the opposite of what the Corinthians do. Throughout the entire paragraph there are allusions to various parts of the letter — some phrases explicitly repeating words, others referring more implicitly to situations — that show that Paul thinks of the Corinthians essentially as an unloving bunch. At the supper they act impatiently; they are envious of one another's leaders, status, and gifts; they are arrogant about their own spiritual and social status, and even about some of their immorality; some act rudely and shamefully in legal and sexual matters; some are resentful and do wrong (practice injustice, *adikeō* in 13:6 as in 6:1, 7-9). Few if any are marked fundamentally by the kind of faith, hope, and endurance that God's love generates (13:7). Their story, from Paul's perspective, is not yet one of cruciform love.

Above all, the Corinthians are a people, in contrast to love, that "insist[s] on its own way" (*zētei ta heautēs*; 13:5). This is expressed in an idiom (NAB: "seek[ing] its own interests"; also cf. NIV: "self-seeking") that Paul has already described and denounced in 8:1–11:1, beginning and ending with the slogans and counterslogans that contrast the Corinthian way of life with conformity to Paul's gospel of Christ's cross:

- "Knowledge puffs up, but love builds up." (8:1b)
- "'All things are lawful,' but not all things are beneficial. 'All things are lawful,' but not all things build up. Do not seek your own advantage [*mēdeis to heautou zēteitō*], but that of the other." (10:23-24)
- ". . . just as I try to please everyone in everything I do, not seeking my own advantage [*mē zētōn to emautou symphoron*], but that of many, so that they may be saved. Be imitators of me, as I am of Christ." (10:33–11:1)

This suggests that Paul intends for us to read his description of love, in essence, to mean 'love edifies'; it seeks the good of the other. This is precisely what he will say in chapter 14.

To show the importance of love from another angle, Paul moves on to its permanence vis-à-vis the spiritual gifts, particularly prophecy, tongues, and knowledge (13:8-12). These gifts, no matter their value, are temporary because they provide only a partial revelation of God (13:8-10). They are meant temporarily for the church now, in its immaturity, but not for the time after the parousia and resurrection — "when the complete comes" (13:10). This will be when the church — represented by the "I" of the brief soliloquy in 13:11 — reaches its maturity. This will also be when the church (now the "we" of 13:12) will see God fully, not as if looking into a poor ancient mirror in which the reality and the image (knowledge) do not correspond perfectly. The continuity between the experience of already being fully known by God and fully knowing God is found in the pursuit, not of knowledge, but of cruciform love (cf. 8:1-3).

This connection leads, at last, to Paul's final claim, which is that love is the greatest of the three things that do "abide" (either 'survive into the age to come' or 'matter in the long run in this age') — the Pauline triad of faith, hope, and love (cf. 1 Thess. 1:3; 5:8; Gal. 5:5-6). For the Corinthians especially, Paul can say no more and no less (cf. also the end of the letter: 16:14, 22, 24). Cruciform love is the enduring pattern — the rule — of life in the church.

The Use of Gifts in Worship (14:1-40)

If cruciform love is the church's rule of life, that rule must be embodied when the church assembles for worship, as Paul has said already in 11:17-34 and as he says again in chapter 14. This chapter applies the principles of chapters 12 and 13 to the concrete issue of the exercise of gifts, especially glossolalia, in the public assembly. Corinthian worship, in Paul's estimation, was chaotic and self-indulgent, certainly anything but cruciform. His basic perspective on the situation can be summarized quite briefly: the church gathers to worship God and to be edified, so its members must pursue gifts, and then exercise them publicly, in a way that is worshipful and edifying for others — that is, in love.

On the basis of the principles enunciated in chapters 12–13, Paul reminds the Corinthians that they should all pursue both love and gifts, and therefore the gifts that best express love by building up the church (14:3-5, 12, 17). These are the "greater gifts" (12:31), especially prophecy (second only to apostleship [12:28], which cannot be pursued). Unlike tongues, which is "speaking mysteries in the Spirit" (14:2) and which edifies only the speaker (14:4) unless it is interpreted (14:5), prophecy edifies, encourages, and consoles (14:3). We must conclude, then, that prophecy is an inspired word of instruction and/or exhortation that addresses the community in the language of the people — like the 'discourses' or 'speeches' in Paul's letters. Paul groups several other gifts with prophecy in the category of 'inherently edifying': revelation, knowledge, teaching, and interpreted tongues (14:5b-6).

Paul draws on analogies from everyday life — the less than distinct sounds of some musical instruments, the quality of a military bugler's call to battle, and the experience of hearing an unknown foreign language (14:7-11) — to stress the need for comprehension when people listen to sounds; so too with gifts in worship (14:12). For this reason tongues speakers should pray "for the power to interpret" (14:13), which is a distinct gift. Paul compares tongues without and with interpretation to prayer and praise with the spirit alone or also with the mind (14:15); he may know two forms of tongues, speech *from* God and speech *to* (self and) God (14:16; cf. 14:28). In any event, Paul does not disparage or dismiss tongues, which he himself uses frequently but to which he prefers 'plain English,' so to speak — out of cruciform love for the community's edification — in the assembly (14:18-19; cf. 14:39).

There follows in 14:20-25 a confusing section that has, ironically, some major translation problems. The gist of the passage, however confusing in itself, is in line with Paul's basic concern: whatever is done should be done to edify whoever is present, whether believer or outsider. Then come Paul's practical directives more clearly articulated: since the purpose of the assembly is edification (14:26), the use of gifts cannot be chaotic or unhelpful. Therefore people are to do their various kinds of gifted speaking in an orderly fashion, one at a time (14:26, 30-31); tongues speakers may speak only if someone can interpret (14:28-29); and prophets as a group are to be mutually discerning and self-correcting (14:29, 32-33). Paul summarizes his main point in a theological assertion that is, for him, axiomatic: God is a God of peace, not chaos (14:33).

Before concluding, Paul (or someone else, later, many scholars think) inserts another confusing text (14:33b-35 or 36) requiring women to be silent. If Paul himself wrote this, however, he cannot mean that women should be absolutely silent in the assembly, for they are allowed to speak to and for God (cf. 11:5). Some have suggested that Paul is nonetheless attempting to silence a group of female prophets, or to remind women (specifically wives) of their appropriate public role (submission), or to prevent frenzied speech. Still others have suggested that in 14:34-35 Paul is quoting, and in 14:36 rebuking, misguided Corinthians who wish to suppress women's voices in the assembly. But the evidence for something like slogans and counterslogans (as in 6:12-20 and 8:1-13) here is meager at best.

The gist of 14:33b-36 in context, if Paul did in fact write it, is probably to keep women from adding to the chaos by calling out for explanations of prophecies or interpretations of tongues. For Paul's major concern, reiterated in 14:37-40, is that the church's assembly be a time when the community's various sounds, which are all gifts of the Spirit, are manifested in an orderly way so that all the members, and any outsiders, are built up in faith, hope, and love. This requires a certain self-discipline, even a cruciform relinquishing of 'the right to speak,' on the part of some of the gifted. The result, however, would be a marked contrast from the frenzied pagan ceremonies with which most Corinthians would have been familiar (12:1-3) and to which their own worship had become too comparable.

Summary of 1 Corinthians 11–14

In chapters 11–14 we have seen Paul express several major concerns (see also the summary of 8:1–11:1 above):

- The community's worship requires an appropriate combination of freedom, or spontaneity, and order, so that it follows the customs of the churches and ensures the edification of its members.
- The church is the body of Christ, a community of unity in diversity that remembers, proclaims, and embodies the cross of its Lord by giving special attention to its poorer and weaker members.
- Cruciform love — love that is patient and kind but not rude or arrogant, not seeking its own interest but bearing and enduring all things — is the most fundamental and distinguishing feature of the church's life.
- The modus operandi of the church is always cruciform love, which gives meaning and shape to its worship life, especially its exercise of spiritual gifts for the edification of the body.

15:1-58. ADDRESSING THEOLOGICAL CHAOS: RESURRECTION AS VINDICATION OF THE CROSS

Few books of Scripture culminate as dramatically as does 1 Corinthians with its majestic chapter 15. Together perhaps with Romans 8, it represents the pinnacle of Pauline rhetoric and theological argument, and yet (like Rom. 8) it does not contain the musings of an armchair theologian. Rather, it embodies the deepest and most practical convictions of a man who believes that what he has to say is a matter of life and death for himself and his readers/hearers.

Paul is not so sure that the Corinthians grasp the full meaning of resurrection; he finds them 'eschatologically challenged,' as we might say idiomatically. A number of issues already addressed in the letter relate to eschatology: the question of judging apostles and their work (chaps. 3, 4, and 9); the man to be delivered to Satan (5:1-13); the lawsuits (6:1-11); the problem with prostitutes (6:12-20); the passing away of this age (chap. 7); the threat of condemnation for not discerning the body (11:17-34); and the permanence of love versus gifts (chap. 13). Moreover, the dominant Corinthian spirituality seems to be one in which the present experience of believers, particularly in ecstatic worship, in a sense of freedom from future judgment, and in apathy about the physical body, is one of glory and power — something that Paul himself reserves for the future. This kind of 'realized' or 'collapsed' eschatology by the Corinthians is one plausible meaning of the phrases "already you have all you want . . . have become rich . . . have become kings" (4:8). Although this is debated, the most compelling explanation for the Corinthians' behavior is a belief in present spiritual resurrection coupled with a denial of future, bodily resurrection (15:12). But even if the Corinthians had no sense of a present resurrection, some of them, likely the most influential, denied the resurrection in any meaningful sense, including Paul's belief in its future, bodily character. Theologically, then, they were functionally pagans in their denial of bodily resurrection, following in the footsteps of Plato, the Epicureans, and the man on the street.

Chapter 15 is Paul's exposition of the implications, for this life and the next, of Christ's bodily resurrection as the "first fruits" of believers' bodily resurrection. Jesus' resurrection vindicates his death and guarantees the ultimate defeat of the powers of sin and death; it therefore also insures the validity and value of believers' cruciform existence until the parousia and/or their own resurrection. This chapter, in other words, is the foundation of the entire letter.

THE COMMON CREED (15:1-11)

Paul begins by reminding the Corinthians of the content of the gospel that he received and preached, and that they received and still affirm (15:1, 3, 11). This gospel is the means of their salvation, but only if they hold on firmly to it, for if they do not, their faith will have been in vain (15:2). The possibility of vain labor and belief is one of the chapter's themes (see 15:10, 14, 58).

The contents of Paul's gospel — what he received and preached — have the appearance of an early creedal statement consisting of four main points, or 'articles' (15:3-8): (1) that Christ died for our sins in accordance with the Scriptures; (2) that he was buried; (3) that he was raised on the third day in accordance with the Scriptures; and (4) that he appeared to Cephas, then to the Twelve, to more than 500, to James, to all of the apostles, and finally to Paul. In context the main point of this fascinating text is that from the very beginning the Corinthians have affirmed that the same Christ who died and was buried also "was raised on the third day." How, then, could some now deny the resurrection of the dead?

Paul's short autobiographical and self-revelatory remarks (15:8-11) serve not merely to stress the apostle's sense of his own unworthiness and of divine grace, but also to indicate his overarching concern: that if there is no resurrection, if he did not really encounter the living Christ, then the whole Jesus-as-Messiah project has been in vain — literally, 'empty' (15:10). Paul, however, is certain that God has raised Jesus and that all is not in vain (15:10).

THE CONSEQUENCES OF DISBELIEF AND BELIEF (15:12-34)

The denial of the resurrection of the dead by some Corinthians leads Paul to explore the consequences of both denying and affirming the resurrection of the dead. It is important to note both his and their different starting points. Paul, as a former Pharisee, begins with the conviction that God will one day raise the dead. In his worldview resurrection is a *possibility* (in fact, it is a certainty) that has become a *reality* in the resurrection of the crucified Messiah Jesus from the dead. He interprets his encounter with the resurrected Lord in the light of his Pharisaic understanding of a future bodily resurrection of the dead. On the other hand, as former pagans steeped in anything but belief in bodily resurrection, some Corinthians (at least) deny the resurrection of the dead in principle. They begin, in other words, with the *impossibility* of the bodily resurrection of the dead, which forces them to interpret Christ's experience and their own in certain ways that have nothing to do with the bodily resurrection of the dead. The fundamental issue and starting point, then, is the possibility or impossibility of the resurrection of the dead (15:16), the affirmation or denial of which affects one's understanding both of Christ and of believers' existence.

For Paul the implications ("if . . . then," 15:13) of denying the resurrection of the dead are grave indeed (15:12-19):

- Christ has not been raised (15:13, 16).
- Paul's preaching and the Corinthians' faith have been in vain (15:14, 17).
- Paul's preaching misrepresents God (15:15).
- Believers are still in their sins because (it is implied) Jesus' death was really just a brutal crucifixion and not a death for sins (15:17).
- Believers who have died have perished; they are permanently dead and will not be raised (15:18).
- Apostles and believers alike are the most pitiable souls, for they (implied) have endured much cost for what amounts to a hoax full of empty claims and promises (15:19).
- The Corinthian ritual of baptism on behalf of the dead (which Paul chooses not to condone or condemn but to exploit for his argument) is pointless (15:29).
- Paul's daily danger and suffering (including literal or, more likely, figurative fighting with "wild animals") — his apostolic lifestyle and boast — are absurd and of no gain (15:30-32a).
- Hedonism is the logical lifestyle (15:32b).

In other words, without the resurrection of the dead there is no reason for faith, hope, or love — the kind of love that endures suffering. Death is the ultimate enemy, life nothing other than a meaningless trip to experience, like an orgy.

"But in fact," writes Paul, "Christ has been raised from the dead" (15:20a) — as he knows by personal experience and they know by his witness. Therefore all the implications of denying the resurrection of the dead are reversed. Paul focuses on the fundamental reality of Christ's parousia (15:23), which signals the future resurrection of the dead and God's ultimate victory over death:

• Christ is the "first fruits" of believers who have died, i.e., the first of many (15:20, 23).
• Christ is the second Adam, who undoes the reign of death initiated by the first Adam (15:21-22).
• Christ is alive and reigning now as Lord, in the process of defeating all enemies, not with Roman imperial power, but with the power of God evidenced in resurrection (15:24-28).
• In God's future, death — humanity's most powerful enemy — will finally be destroyed, and God will "be all in all" (15:24-28).

In light of these truths — and the lifestyle implications they imply — Paul counsels the Corinthians in general to separate themselves from the bad influence of those who deny the resurrection of the dead (15:33), and he warns the deniers in particular to 'sober up' and end this ignorance of God, this 'sin' (15:34).

QUESTIONS ABOUT BODILY RESURRECTION (15:35-50)

In good rhetorical form, Paul next addresses questions (or perhaps objections), either known or anticipated, to his doctrine of bodily resurrection. Specifically he considers two issues (15:35) — the process of resurrection *(how)* and the nature of the resurrection body *(what)* — by providing an analogy from nature (15:36-41) that is then applied to the questions (15:42-49).

The analogy Paul offers is the ancient belief that a seed that is sown must die in order to come to life (15:36, the how), plus the observation that the resulting plant is a transformation of the original seed: "you do not sow the body that is to be" (15:37, the what). Echoing Genesis 1, he expands the latter part of the analogy by remarking that there is a wide variety of "bodies" in the universe (plant, animal, human, and heavenly), each of which has its distinctive "glory," or divinely given splendor (15:38-41). Thus the analogy indicates that (1) there is both continuity and discontinuity in the death that effects the transformation from seed to body, and (2) there are different kinds of bodies, each with its own glory.

So too with the resurrection of the dead (15:42a). There is continuity, for that which is sown ("it," 15:43-44, meaning the body that dies) is also that which is raised, yet there is also discontinuity. Death and resurrection mean transformation: from a body that is perishable, dishonorable, weak, and "physical" into a body that is imperishable, honorable, powerful, and spiritual (15:42b-44). By "spiritual" body Paul clearly does not mean the absence of the body (as in a 'free-floating' spirit) — which would ruin his analogy — but rather a transformed body. This transformed body is not merely "flesh and blood" (15:50) because it has been changed from one kind of glory to another. It has been transformed from the glory ("image") of Adam, representing mortal earthly existence, into the glory ("image") of Christ, "the man of heaven," representing immortal existence (15:45-49). *But both forms of existence are bodily* — each with its own splendor, the "spiritual" greater than the "physical."

THE FINAL VICTORY (15:51-57)

Having explained the how and what of bodily resurrection, Paul shifts from rhetorical analogy to triumphant apocalyptic proclamation. The theme of the first few verses is again transformation ("we will all be changed," 15:52; "put on [clothes]," 15:53-54). Yet there is still the emphasis on continuity, too: the subjects of each sentence — "we" and "this body" — indicate continuity of the self in embodied, though transformed, existence. This transformation affects both living and dead believers (15:51b); when the trumpet, a standard feature of apocalyptic literature that announces the triumph of God (e.g., Zech. 9:14; cf. 1 Thess. 4:16), suddenly sounds, the dead will be raised and transformed, and the living will likewise be changed (15:52). This is all God's doing,[14] for it indicates the time of God's final defeat of "the last enemy" (15:26). This victory is the conclusion to the victory of God begun in Christ's death (alluded to in 15:57), through whom believers have been freed from the power of sin and the law (15:56). Now, at the climax of God's salvation in the bodily resurrection of believers, the final enemy is defeated, the final victory won.

CONCLUDING EXHORTATION (15:58)

For this reason, and this reason alone, Paul writes in conclusion, the Corinthians should be steadfast and faithful in the Lord. They can live the life of cruciform

---

14. God's agency is expressed in the passive voice of 15:52, "the dead will be raised [by God] imperishable, and we will be changed [by God]," meaning that God will raise the dead and change us.

love they find in Christ Jesus, see modeled in Paul, and hear about throughout the letter. Why? Because their labor in the body, like Paul's, "is not in vain" since Christ has been raised as the first fruits of their bodily resurrection.

Summary of 1 Corinthians 15

According to Paul in 1 Corinthians 15:
- Christ's resurrection is an original and integral part of the gospel.
- If there is no resurrection of the dead, Christ was not raised, the gospel is not good news, and believers' life of faith, hope, and love is in vain.
- Since Christ was raised, however, he is the first fruits and guarantor of believers' bodily resurrection.
- At the parousia, all believers will experience a transformation from a perishable to an imperishable body following the resurrection of the dead; there is thus continuity and discontinuity between pre- and postparousia embodied existence.
- The parousia will lead to the final defeat of all the enemies of God and humanity, including the last enemy, death itself.

16:1-24. CLOSING

Having completed the body of his letter, Paul addresses briefly a few additional matters regarding his relationship with the Corinthian church.

Paul first invites the church to participate in the collection for the (poor) believers in Jerusalem (16:1-4), in fulfillment of an agreement made with the Jerusalem leaders (Gal. 2:10). Paul repeats the invitation at length in 2 Corinthians 8 and 9, and eventually delivers the gift himself (Rom. 15:25-29).

He then informs them of his travel hopes, which include the possibility of an extended stay in Corinth after he leaves Ephesus via Macedonia (16:5-7). In the meantime, however, the opposition and thus also the opportunity in Ephesus are too great to leave (16:8-9; cf. 15:32).

Paul next writes about two colleagues well known to the Corinthians, his coworker and his successor in Corinth, Timothy and Apollos (16:10-12). Paul seems to expect some hostility toward Timothy, who is either on the way to Corinth or about to go, no doubt because he represents the now controversial Paul. So Paul requests a safe and hospitable welcome and send-off for Timothy. As for Apollos, Paul seems to want the Corinthians to know that the absence of

Apollos during these controversies was his own decision, not Paul's, for Paul had urged Apollos to make a visit.

Further personal business will follow, but first Paul recapitulates his letter in five brief exhortations, which can perhaps be summarized as an appeal to be firm (in faith and hope) and to do everything in love (16:13-14).

Finally, Paul commends to the Corinthians three of their number who have visited him, reconnecting them to him in his absence. He also commends others who serve in the church and are worthy of assistance and recognition (16:15-18).

The last words of greeting and grace begin with a message from Aquila and Prisca (Priscilla), the tentmaking Jewish believers originally from Rome who had also worked with Paul in Corinth. In addition, the church in their house, and all the believers, send greetings — a symbol of the universality of the church (16:19-20a). Paul concludes with instructions for the holy kiss, his signature, a curse for those who lack love for the Lord, a common early Christian prayer for the parousia ("Our Lord, come" = Aram. *maranatha*), a benediction, and a final offer of apostolic love (16:20b-24).

THE STORY IN FRONT OF THE LETTER

Some Readings of 1 Corinthians

"Let us observe that entire first epistle, written I should say not with ink, but with bile, swelling indignant, disdainful, threatening, invidious. . . . [Paul] smites them [the Corinthians] on the face."

> Tertullian (d. ca. 225), *De pudicitia* 14.4, 10, cited in Robert D. Sider, "Literary Artifice and the Figure of Paul in the Writings of Tertullian," in *Paul and the Legacies of Paul*, ed. William S. Babcock (Dallas: Southern Methodist University Press, 1990), pp. 99-120, here 113

"Paul was right to add the name of Christ here [to his appeal for unity in 1:10], because that is what the Corinthians were really rejecting."

> Theodoret of Cyr, *Commentary on the First Epistle to the Corinthians* 167 (fifth century), cited in Gerald Bray, ed., *1-2 Corinthians*, Ancient Christian Commentary on Scripture, vol. 7 (Downers Grove, Ill.: InterVarsity, 1999), p. 9

"Since the Corinthians had a liking for teaching that was clever rather than benefi-cial, they had no relish for the Gospel. Since they were eager for new things, Christ was already out of date to them. At any rate, if they had not yet already fallen into those errors, they were already naturally inclined towards seductive things of that sort. So it was easy for the false apostles to get a hearing among them, and to adul-terate the teaching of Christ. For it certainly is adulterated, when its natural purity is so spoiled, and, as it were, painted a different colour, that it is on a level with any worldly philosophy. Therefore, in order to suit the Corinthians' taste, they added seasoning to their teaching, with the result that the true flavour of the Gospel was ruined. We are now in a position to understand why Paul was induced to write this letter."

John Calvin, *The First Epistle of Paul the Apostle to the Corin-thians* [ca. 1556], Calvin's Commentaries, trans. John W. Fraser (Grand Rapids: Eerdmans, 1960), p. 9

"1 Corinthians is more than a practical letter aimed at telling the readers what to do and what not to do. The letter in fact primarily seeks to influence the minds, dispo-sitions, intuitions of the audience in line with the message Paul had initially preached in the community (2:2), to confront readers with the critical nature of God's saving action in the crucified Christ in such a fashion that it becomes the glasses to refocus their vision of God, their own community, and the future. The advancing of such an epistemology gives the letter a theological purpose that uni-fies its otherwise unconnected structure."

Charles B. Cousar, "The Theological Task of 1 Corinthians," in *Pauline Theology,* vol. 2, *1 & 2 Corinthians,* ed. David M. Hay (Minneapolis: Fortress, 1993), pp. 90-102, here 102

"The disturbed state of the Christians at Corinth explains the need for so much at-tention. Paradoxically, the range of their problems (rival 'theologians,' factions, problematic sexual practices, marital obligations, liturgy, church roles) makes the correspondence exceptionally instructive for troubled Christians and churches of our times. Attempts to live according to the gospel in the multiethnic and crosscultural society at Corinth raised issues still encountered in multiethnic, multiracial, and crosscultural societies today. . . . For those studying Paul seriously for the first time, if limitations mean that only one of the thirteen letters can be ex-amined in depth, I Cor may well be the most rewarding."

Raymond E. Brown, *An Introduction to the New Testament* (New York: Doubleday, 1997), p. 511

"In order to form a Christian community identity within a pluralistic pagan world, Paul repeatedly calls his readers to a 'conversion of the imagination.' He invites them to see the world in dramatically new ways, in light of values shaped by the Christian story."

Richard B. Hays, *First Corinthians,* Interpretation (Louisville: Westminster John Knox, 1997), p. 11

QUESTIONS FOR REFLECTION

1. What might Paul's experience with the 'less than fully resocialized' Corinthians, most of whom were from a pagan background, say about the needs for instruction and spiritual formation in the contemporary church?
2. In what ways do the current divisions within Christianity resemble and/or differ from those that Paul observed and criticized in Corinth?
3. How well or poorly does the church, in your experience, both minister to and learn from the 'nobodies' (persons without status indicators) in its midst?
4. What contributions can the early chapters of 1 Corinthians make to contemporary Christian understandings of spirituality and ministry?
5. In what ways does Corinthian sexual and law-court activity resemble that of the contemporary church? What ethical principles and practical applications can be drawn from these situations and Paul's responses to them?
6. How might Paul's response to the issue of eating meat associated with idols inform a contemporary theological understanding of such topics as freedom, rights, and the meaning of love?
7. What are some of the possible implications of Paul's understanding of the Lord's Supper for contemporary liturgy, ethics, and ecumenism?
8. In what ways do problems of unity and diversity manifest themselves in the contemporary church? What insights does Paul's discussion of this topic offer?
9. What are the implications of being the body of Christ for Christian theology and practice today?
10. What are some of the contemporary challenges to, and implications of, a doctrine of bodily resurrection, whether Christ's or believers'?
11. What are the most common social and spiritual 'status indicators' in the church today? What forms of a gospel of 'glory' or 'success' exist today? How pervasive and influential are they?
12. Are there contemporary theological and ethical issues that are not sufficiently considered in the church in light of the cross, resurrection, and/or parousia? How might Paul's 'bifocal' vision illumine these issues?

13. Many of the problems at Corinth focus on the tension between appropriate engagement with and appropriate withdrawal from the structures and practices of 'the world.' How is that tension manifested today, and how might Paul's letter be useful in addressing the tension?
14. How do you respond to the interpretations of 1 Corinthians quoted above?
15. In sum, what does this letter urge the church to believe, hope for, and do?

FOR FURTHER READING AND STUDY

General

Collins, Raymond F. *First Corinthians.* Sacra Pagina. Collegeville, Minn.: Liturgical Press, 1999. A massive, theologically and rhetorically astute analysis of the letter.

Hays, Richard B. *First Corinthians.* Interpretation. Louisville: Westminster John Knox, 1997. A very thoughtful commentary on the letter, with provocative insights on its contemporary message.

Murphy-O'Connor, Jerome. *St. Paul's Corinth: Texts and Archaeology.* Wilmington, Del.: Michael Glazier, 1983. A fascinating study of ancient Corinth, with helpful diagrams.

Sampley, J. Paul. "The First Letter to the Corinthians." In *The New Interpreter's Bible,* edited by Leander E. Keck et al., 10:771-1003. Nashville: Abingdon, 2002. An insightful commentary with attention to the letter's cultural conventions as well as its central convictions.

Soards, Marion. *1 Corinthians.* New International Biblical Commentary. Peabody, Mass.: Hendrickson, 1999. A clear, concise exposition of the NIV text.

Witherington, Ben. *Conflict and Community at Corinth: A Socio-Rhetorical Commentary on 1 and 2 Corinthians.* Grand Rapids: Eerdmans, 1995. A significant, learned (but readable) commentary on the letter in its social context.

gbgm-umc.org/umw/corinthians
  "Conflict and Community in the Corinthian Church," a superb site sponsored by the United Methodist Church, with photos, text, maps, links, etc.

Technical

Conzelmann, Hans. *1 Corinthians.* Translated by J. W. Leitch. Hermeneia. Philadelphia: Fortress, 1975. A gold mine of data on historical context and parallels.

Fee, Gordon D. *The First Epistle to the Corinthians.* New International Commentary on the New Testament. Grand Rapids: Eerdmans, 1987. A detailed analysis of all aspects of the text, highlighting the division between the community and Paul.

Hay, David M., ed. *Pauline Theology.* Vol. 2, *1 and 2 Corinthians.* Minneapolis: Fortress, 1993. A collection of insightful scholarly essays from various perspectives.

Thiselton, Anthony C. *The First Epistle to the Corinthians: A Commentary on the Greek Text.* Grand Rapids: Eerdmans, 2000. An exhaustive commentary that highlights not only the letter's social context and theological message, but also its interpretation through the centuries.

CHAPTER 11

2 CORINTHIANS

Paul's Defense of Cruciform Ministry

Whenever I am weak, then I am strong.

2 Cor. 12:10

Paul's second letter to the Corinthians is the sleeper among the four traditional 'chief letters' of the apostle: Romans, Galatians, and the Corinthian correspondence. It does not have the contemporary feel of 1 Corinthians, with its issues of unity, sex, lawsuits, women in the church, and tongues, or the theological profundity of Romans, or the nearly uncontrollable passion of Galatians. But 2 Corinthians is actually more than a sleeper; it is something of a sleeping giant.

In this letter (or, as some think, collection of letters) Paul bares his soul, and the soul of his gospel, to the Corinthian community of believers he 'fathered.' He does this in order to effect reconciliation between them and him and ultimately, he believes, between them and God. In doing so Paul takes the considerable risk of sounding entirely self-promotional and of alienating the church. However, what Paul is really up to in explaining and defending his apostleship — and also in asking the Corinthians to fulfill a financial commitment to the Jerusalem church — is a defense of the cruciform shape of ministry, whether his or theirs.

THE STORY BEHIND THE LETTER

Reconstructing the events that occurred in the relationship between Paul and the Corinthians leading to the writing of 2 Corinthians is a complex task. The challenge is especially complicated by the contents of the letter itself, since various parts seem to have distinct agendas and tones, referring to different past events and reflecting different contemporary situations. Many scholars have therefore concluded that 2 Corinthians is a composite of several letters. They suggest that a later editor pieced together fragments of several communications from Paul to the Corinthians. Their theories range from the simple, to the moderately complex, to the unwieldy.[1] Some have said, without too much hyperbole, that there are as many 'partition theories' as there are interpreters of 2 Corinthians.

Most interpreters do agree, however, that there are three distinct components to 2 Corinthians: chapters 1–7, 8–9, and 10–13. We shall return to the question of how these components are connected, but for now we can offer a brief, tentative summary of the events behind each of these sections. On almost any reconstruction these events and the letter(s) they generated are to be dated to the mid-50s (54-57), and the correspondence was almost certainly sent from Macedonia (see 7:5).

2 CORINTHIANS 1–7

According to Acts 18–20, after Paul evangelized in Corinth he returned to his home base of Antioch (stopping first in Ephesus, Caesarea, and Jerusalem) and then took up another voyage. This 'third' trip brought him back through the provinces of Galatia, Phrygia, Asia (Ephesus again), Macedonia, and Achaia ("Greece" in 20:2). He headed back toward Jerusalem after stops in the western Asia cities of Troas, Miletus, and Ephesus. Of course, Corinth was not sitting still during Paul's travels and visits elsewhere.

According to the first seven chapters of the letter, 2 Corinthians was actually not Paul's second letter to Corinth. Indeed, already in 1 Corinthians 5:9 Paul had mentioned a letter written prior to 1 Corinthians itself. In addition, 2 Corinthians mentions a harsh letter (2:3-4; 7:8) written after a 'painful' visit by

---

1. A simple theory would posit two letters, chaps. 1–9 and 10–13. An example of a moderately complex theory would posit chaps. 1–7 as one letter, but with 6:14–7:1 as a later addition; chaps. 8–9 as one or two separate letters; and chaps. 10–13 as a distinct letter. A still more complex theory, to the point of being unwieldy, would posit several letter fragments throughout chaps. 1–7, broken up and out of order, plus separate letters in chaps. 8, 9, and 10–13.

Paul to Corinth, during which someone caused him distress (2:1, 5). This correspondence is sometimes designated letters A, B, and C, as follows:

Letter A   the letter mentioned in 1 Corinthians 5:9[2]
Letter B   1 Corinthians
Letter C   the harsh letter mentioned in 2:3-4 and 7:8 (sometimes identified with 1 Corinthians or, somewhat more plausibly, 2 Corinthians 10–13)

The harsh letter (now lost, unless one of the unlikely theories noted above is correct) was sent, probably from Ephesus or Macedonia via Titus, as an alternative to another visit (2:1). It resulted in the community's expressing deep regret, dealing with the offender, and renewing their affection for and obedience to Paul (2:5-11; 7:5-16), as Paul's envoy Titus reported to him in Macedonia (7:6, 13).

If 2 Corinthians is one unified letter, then it can be termed letter D according to this sequence of events. If not, then chapters 1–7 (or 1–8 or 1–9) are likely letter D, and 10–13 letter E. In any event, the theme of the first seven chapters, sparked by this sequence of events, is reconciliation. Even 6:14–7:1 contributes to this theme.

2 CORINTHIANS 8–9

The subject of chapters 8 and 9, Paul's collection from the (largely) Gentile churches of the Diaspora, especially Greece, for the impoverished Jewish 'mother' church in Jerusalem, was an important aspect of his ministry in the 50s (cf. Rom. 15:22-33). The Corinthians, or Achaians, had expressed strong interest (8:11) a year earlier (9:2), to the point of inspiring the relatively poor Macedonians (9:2). But the Macedonians had followed through on their zeal (8:1-2) while the Corinthians had not (8:6-7, 10-12; 9:3). Paul was contemplating a return to Achaia with some Macedonians and was sending Titus and other envoys to collect the gift in advance (8:6-7, 16-24; 9:4-5). Although some interpreters separate chapters 8 and 9 into two distinct letters, they form a coherent whole reflecting one situation.

2 CORINTHIANS 10–13

This last section of the letter presupposes that some Corinthians have (further?) criticized Paul and that a group of self-proclaimed apostles has visited

2. A minority of scholars finds part of this letter in 2 Cor. 6:14–7:1.

Corinth, impressing many, if not all, of the Corinthians. These two developments are almost certainly related to each other, and it is possible that similar problems hinted at in chapters 1–7 have now worsened, or else Paul's understanding of their significance has increased.

The identity of this group of Paul's 'opponents,' as they are generally called, has been hotly debated, with many proposals forthcoming. Some have said they were gnostics, others proponents of Jewish practices for Gentiles (as in Galatia), others Hellenistic 'divine men' (powerful miracle-workers), and still others Spirit people or pneumatics. Paul has his own words for them: "super-apostles" (11:5; 12:11); "boasters . . . false apostles, deceitful workers, disguising themselves as apostles of Christ . . . his [Satan's] ministers" (11:13, 15); people who proclaim "another Jesus . . . a different spirit [or, better, 'Spirit'] . . . a different gospel" (11:4). Somewhat more objectively, he suggests that they are Jewish (11:22) preachers who call themselves apostles and ministers (11:23) of Christ and who focus on ("boast of") their powerful experiences of God's Spirit, probably including rhetorically ornate speech, visions and revelations, and miracles.[3] They are therefore probably best called Jewish Christian pneumatics, or 'Spirit people.' From Paul's perspective, it is not their claim of being Jewish but their claim of having a Spirit-filled ministry of Christ that is problematic.

This group of (supposedly) Spirit-filled preachers apparently fueled earlier criticisms of Paul by some Corinthians themselves that their founding apostle was a weak preacher (10:10; 11:6; cf. 1 Cor. 2:1-5) who insulted them by supporting himself and refusing their patronage (11:7-11; cf. 1 Cor. 9). Thus Paul's modus operandi as an apostle both lies behind, and is at stake in, 2 Corinthians 10–13.

THE STORY WITHIN THE LETTER

The three situations reflected in the three main components of 2 Corinthians raise the question of how these situations, and their corresponding chapters, are interrelated. As noted above, proponents of partition theories find at least two letters, and often more. But there have also been strong advocates of the literary unity of 2 Corinthians, especially among recent proponents of rhetorical criticism. Any plausible theory must explain how the shifts in tone and subject matter relate to one another.

Even defenders of literary unity acknowledge the difference in tone be-

3. See 10:10, 12, 18; 11:6, 18; 12:1, 11-12.

tween chapters 10–13 and the earlier chapters. Traditional arguments for unity have suggested that 10–13 may have been composed a little later than chapters 1–7, reflecting a worsening of the relationship between the Corinthians and Paul, and were included with the earlier chapters rather than sent separately later. Some rhetorical-critical arguments have suggested that chapters 10–13 deal more directly with the most explosive issue that Paul has to address after reconciliation has been established more coolly in the opening chapters. All theories of unity (whether of the whole letter or of just chapters 1–9) have some trouble explaining the presence of chapters 8 and 9.

Without committing definitively to a position, we may offer the following observations and make a suggestion based on them. Clearly the three parts of the letter differ not only in subject but in tone and purpose:

- Chapters 1–7 are largely *conciliatory* in tone and *explanatory* in purpose, an example of *forensic* rhetoric, though not without an appeal to (continued) reconciliation (6:1-2, 11-13; 7:1).
- Chapters 8–9 are *hortatory* in tone and *motivational* in purpose, an example of *deliberative* rhetoric with a clear appeal (8:7, 24; 9:5, 13; etc.).
- Chapters 10–13 are *polemical* in tone and both *dissuasive* and *persuasive* in purpose, a blend of *forensic* and *deliberative* rhetoric, the ultimate goal of which is to edify the readers (12:19) through their own self-examination (13:5).

If this is one unified letter, then we see a rhetorical strategy at work of moving from issues of lesser to greater sensitivity and volatility, and of moving, correspondingly, from less combative to more combative forms of persuasion. If 2 Corinthians is one complex communication, then Paul's strategy is (1) to celebrate a reconciliation that the Corinthians need to embrace fully (chaps. 1–7) by (2) following through on their financial pledge (chaps. 8–9) and (3) separating from the false apostles (chaps. 10–13).

What unifies the shifting rhetoric of 2 Corinthians is its ultimate focus on the cruciform shape of life in Christ. Whether Paul is explaining himself and his gospel, calling the Corinthians to generosity, or lambasting the self-centered power trip of the pseudoapostles (as he sees it), he grounds all that he claims — for himself and his gospel, about his expectations of the Corinthians, and against his opponents — in the cross. As he had decided when he first visited Corinth, he desires to know nothing except Jesus Christ crucified (1 Cor. 2:2). In 2 Corinthians he argues — sometimes gently and politely, sometimes aggressively and acerbically, but always compellingly — that cruciformity is the mark of apostleship, grace, and the Spirit.

The letter unfolds as follows:

1:1-2   **Opening**

1:3–7:16   **The Cruciform Apostleship of Reconciliation**

       1:3–2:13   Paul, the Corinthians, and the God of Consolation

           1:3-11   The God Who Consoles the Afflicted

           1:12–2:13   Paul's Integrity and His Love for the Corinthians

               1:12–2:4   Paul's Integrity and the Canceled Visit

               2:5-13   Paul's Love for the Offender and the Community

       2:14–6:10   Cruciformity and Reconciliation: The Character of Paul's Ministry

           2:14-17   The Fundamental Metaphors of Apostolic Life

           3:1-18   The Ministry of the New Covenant

           4:1–5:10   Courage and Confidence in Cruciform Ministry

           5:11–6:10   The Message of Reconciliation

       6:11–7:16   The Final Appeal for Reconciliation

           6:11-13   A Summary of the Appeal

           6:14–7:1   A Corollary Appeal

           7:2-16   Paul's Consolation and Confidence

8:1–9:15   **The Cruciform Grace of Generosity**

       8:1-24   Christ, the Macedonians, and the Corinthians

       9:1-15   God, the Macedonians, and the Corinthians

10:1–13:13   **The Cruciform Power-in-Weakness of the Spirit**

       10:1-6   Paul's Declaration of War

       10:7-18   The Terms of the Campaign: Edification and Boasting

       11:1-15   Paul's First Speech of Foolish Boasting: Paul's Self-Support

           11:1-4   The Grounds for Boasting

           11:5-11   The Content of the Boasting

           11:12-15   True versus False Boasting

       11:16–12:10 Paul's Second Speech of Foolish Boasting: Paul's Various Weaknesses

           11:16-21a   Introduction

           11:21b-33   The Weaknesses of the Warrior-Minister

           12:1-10   Power in Weakness

       12:11-13   Conclusion to the Speeches

       12:14–13:13 Final Summary, Warnings, Appeals, and Greetings

Summaries of chapters 1–7, 8–9, and 10–13 appear following the commentary on those sections of the letter.

1:1-2. OPENING

The letter begins in typical Pauline fashion. Paul's identification as "apostle" is never in question in his mind, but it had been and still was in Corinth. From one perspective this whole letter is about what it means to be an apostle. The cosender, Timothy, had been with Paul and Silvanus (Silas) when the church at Corinth was founded (1:19; Acts 18:5) and had later been sent by Paul to remind the Corinthians of the meaning of imitating Paul, as their apostle and spiritual father, in their life together.[4] Thus the combination of these two names at the head of a letter would remind the Corinthians of the birth and maturation of their church as a specifically Pauline community, privileged and obligated to honor and imitate the (cruciform) example of their founders.

It is interesting that the letter is addressed not only to "the church of God that is in Corinth" but also to all the "saints" in Achaia (1:1). Corinth was not only the provincial capital, but also the epicenter of the early Christian movement in southern Greece.

1:3–7:16. THE CRUCIFORM APOSTLESHIP OF RECONCILIATION

In the first seven chapters of this letter, Paul sets out to bring closure to the process of reconciliation (described above) that has occasioned the letter.

PAUL, THE CORINTHIANS, AND THE GOD OF CONSOLATION (1:3–2:13)

Using the rhetorical device of *narratio* and the epistolary device of an opening prayer, in 1:3–2:13 Paul seeks to set his relationship with the Corinthians in the larger context of their common relationship with God in Christ.

4. 1 Cor. 4:14-17; 16:10-11; cf. Acts 19:22.

The God Who Consoles the Afflicted (1:3-11)

Paul begins the letter proper not with a typical thanksgiving but with a Jewish blessing, or *berakah* (cf. Eph. 1:3-14). This blessing, which quickly turns into a brief treatise on consolation in suffering, sets the tone for the entire letter: life in Christ is about suffering and endurance, affliction and comfort, partnership and mutual care. It is about an 'abundant life': experiencing the abundant presence of God in the midst of abundant tribulation. Forms of the word "console" (NRSV), "comfort" (NIV), or "encourage" (NAB) appear ten times in these five verses (Gk. *parakaleō* and *paraklēsis*).

The blessing itself extols God as merciful and consoling by nature (1:3). Paul and his colleagues have experienced God's consolation, but the apostle stresses that recipients of this divine comfort are to be conduits rather than containers (1:4). Both affliction and consolation, Paul asserts, are experiences of participation — in God, in Christ, and in community. Believers — apostolic or not — share in Christ's sufferings (1:5, 6) ultimately for the benefit and salvation of others (1:6); they share in God's consolation also for the benefit of others (1:4, 6); and this entire life of affliction and comfort is a fellowship, a *koinōnia* (cf. *koinōnoi*, lit. 'sharers,' 1:7). The point of Paul's emphasizing this fellowship at the beginning of the letter is to renew the bond between himself and the Corinthians and to acknowledge its essential character as a fellowship of the coafflicted and the cocomforted.

Paul continues with a concrete example of what he has been describing: an unbearable affliction in (the province of) Asia, during which he and his colleagues had assumed that death would be their fate (1:8-10). Although Paul provides no more details, the experience could have been an imprisonment, a mob attack, an unusually severe flogging, a literal or figurative battle "with wild animals at Ephesus" (cf. 1 Cor. 15:32), or some other form of persecution. No matter the affliction, God comforted as only God can do, by bringing life out of death (1:9). This not only renewed Paul's trust and hope in God, but also his sense of dependency on the prayers, and thus the comfort, of other believers (1:11). He expects that his future sufferings will also yield similar results, aided especially by the Corinthians' prayers, all to God's praise.

Paul's Integrity and His Love for the Corinthians (1:12–2:13)

Having reestablished the mutuality of the relationship between himself and the Corinthians, Paul takes up the sensitive issue of his failure to pay them a third visit as planned, and of the debacle connected with his second, painful visit and subsequent harsh letter. He continues the theme of reconciliation by explaining his own actions as grounded in integrity and love, and by offering forgiveness and comfort to the one who offended him during that distressing visit.

Paul's Integrity and the Canceled Visit (1:12–2:4)

Paul begins with a short preface in which he 'boasts' about his (and his whole team's) "frankness"[5] and "sincerity" (1:12). This apparent self-praise is really, for Paul, an example of boasting in the Lord ("by the grace of God," 1:12; cf. 1 Cor. 1:31). His forthrightness (even if occasionally painful) and integrity are crucial aspects of the truthfulness of his ministry of proclaiming the gospel. As a result of his sincere proclamation, as well as the Corinthians' sincere response, each will be the other's "boast," or source of pride, at the parousia (1:14). Once again Paul stresses the interdependence of his apostolic team and the Corinthian church.

This prefatory claim to integrity leads directly into Paul's analysis of the shaky relations between himself (note the frequent use of "I" rather than "we" in 1:15–2:13) and the Corinthians due to an actual visit, a subsequent planned but postponed visit, and a substitute letter.

Paul had planned an itinerary, it appears, from Ephesus to Corinth to Macedonia, and then back through Corinth to Judea (Jerusalem), a route that included two stops (a "double favor" or double grace, 1:15) in Corinth, the latter including a send-off with financial support for the trip to Jerusalem (1:16). Paul (no doubt rightly) heard the Corinthian accusation of vacillation (1:17) as a charge of insincerity and, more importantly, as a threat to the integrity of his gospel and, ultimately, to the faithfulness of God. His response, therefore, is passionate. His plans are not made "in a worldly manner" (1:17 NIV; cf. 1:12) with a simultaneous "Yes" and "No" (1:17-19), but in a manner consistent with the gospel that his team preached (1:19). That is, Paul sees God's faithfulness as both the basis and the motive for his own truthfulness and faithfulness. In Christ God does not utter "Yes" and "No" but only "Yes": "in him every one of God's promises is a 'Yes'" (1:20).

This sweeping claim, while primarily addressing the correspondence between divine and Pauline integrity, also reveals Paul's governing hermeneutic, his way of reading Scripture and history. All the promises of God offered to and through Israel, and recorded in Israel's Scriptures, are fulfilled in Christ (cf. Eph. 1:3). This does not mean all the promises have already been brought to fruition, for Christ's death and resurrection are still to be completed on the future day of the Lord. But for Paul and the Corinthians — *together* (1:21) — their ex-

---

5. NRSV; NAB's "simplicity" is weak, and NIV's "holiness" translates a textual variant.

perience of the Spirit is the seal of their belonging to God and a "first install-ment"[6] on that future (1:22; cf. 5:5; Eph. 1:14).

Returning to the urgent matter of the present crisis, Paul calls on the faith-ful God as a witness to his own integrity; the specific motivation for not visiting the Corinthians was to "spare" them (1:23). His goal in ministry is not to cause distress — as if they were not his partners in Christ — but "joy" (1:24). Paul had — unintentionally — caused pain to the people he loved with one visit, which was no source of gladness for him (2:1-2). Rather than inflicting more pain with another visit, and yet also to avoid suffering additional pain himself, he wrote a letter. The purpose of the letter, which was no doubt frank, was reconciliation expressed in shared joy (2:3). Though it was written "out of much distress and anguish of heart and with many tears," its ultimate source was Paul's love for the Corinthians (2:4). Paul, in other words, had been "speaking the truth in love" (Eph. 4:15).

Paul's Love for the Offender and the Community (2:5-13)

The extension of that love is now offered (2:5-11) to the guilty party from that painful visit. Apparently the tearful letter had succeeded in convincing the ma-jority of the Corinthians to punish the offender (2:6). Though some interpret-ers have tried to identify this person with the incestuous man excommunicated by Paul (1 Cor. 5:1-13), the context argues against that interpretation; the of-fender has caused deep pain to Paul and, according to Paul himself, to the whole church (2:5). The Corinthians' decision is rather remarkable, given Paul's disputed status in the community, so his letter must have been persuasive in spite of being painful. Now, however, is the time to extend grace and comfort (*charisasthai kai parakalesai*, 2:7; NRSV, "forgive and console"), that is, love (2:8). The Corinthians have passed their test of obedience (2:9), so if they for-give the offender, Paul forgives him, too (2:10; cf. Matt. 16:19). Paul extends this forgiveness not only out of love for the individual, but especially out of concern for the community (2:10). He fears that prolonged sorrow would permit Satan to score a victory in the church (2:11).

Paul's claims to integrity, love, and occasionally counterintuitive criteria for decision making are given one final expression in 2:12-13. Paul had arrived in Troas, an important port in northwest Asia, and found a great opportunity to spread the gospel there (2:12). Nevertheless, he did not stay there — almost be-traying his apostolic calling — because another part of his apostolic calling left him so uneasy. Unable to find Titus, the bearer of his painful letter to the Co-rinthians, he returned to Macedonia, where he hoped to find Titus and gain

---

6. NRSV, NAB; NIV, "deposit"; all translating *arrabōn*.

Troas: A view of the Aegean Sea from the shores of this ancient port,
where Paul left behind an 'open door' for evangelism
out of concern for the Corinthians

news of the Corinthians' reception of the letter — which he eventually did (2:13;
7:5-16). This, for Paul, was a decision born of love. Although he could have —
and some might say should have — stayed in Troas to preach the gospel of the
cross, the gospel of the cross would not let him stay. He cared for the Corinthians with too much cruciform love to wait in Troas. His anxiety for the Corinthians (cf. 11:28) was a manifestation of this love.

CRUCIFORMITY AND RECONCILIATION:
THE CHARACTER OF PAUL'S MINISTRY (2:14–6:10)

Having established his integrity and love, and having recalled both the history of
the pain and his steps toward reconciliation (1:12–2:13), Paul now puts the concrete topic of his reconciliation with the Corinthians on hold. Instead of continuing the story, he shifts into an extended explanation of his own ministry as a
ministry of cross-centered reconciliation. The story of the Corinthians, the offender, Titus, and Paul will not be lost; rather, it will be placed into a larger story,
the story of God's reconciling work in Christ and through the ministry of Paul.

The Fundamental Metaphors of Apostolic Life (2:14-17)

Paul begins the extended explanation of his apostolic ministry with two governing metaphors that set the tone for, and provide the thesis of, the entire exposition. First, he depicts what he and his colleagues are, and then what they are not.

The first image is the Roman imperial or military 'triumphal procession,' in which the spoils of war, including captive human beings on their way to death, were publicly displayed (2:14). The Romans, who sponsored hundreds of these processions, displayed their captives as a sign of Rome's power and the captives' weakness. So too, Paul and his colleagues are being led throughout the world like weak captives sentenced to death (cf. 4:7-12). Their procession is the spread of the gospel, not only in word, but more especially in their cruciform existence.

This dispersion of the gospel through them is the "fragrance" or "aroma" of (the knowledge of) Christ (2:14-15) — a second and perhaps related image. Whether this aroma refers to the incense that accompanied such processions or to something else (such as sacrifices), Paul claims that his life and message impact both those being saved and those perishing, functioning as confirmation of their life or their death, respectively (2:15-16; cf. 1 Cor. 1:18; Phil. 1:28). This, Paul realizes, is an awesome responsibility, such that "Who is sufficient?" (NRSV) or "Who is qualified?" (NAB) is certainly an appropriate question (2:16). The answer — those called and empowered by God — will be given shortly, but for now Paul uses yet another metaphor to depict his human responsibility as a preacher. Unlike certain unnamed parties, he and his colleagues are not "peddlers" or hucksters but "persons of sincerity" (2:17; cf. 1:12) with a divine commission and corresponding accountability.

The combination of images is striking and significant: prisoner and preacher, aroma and ambassador. It is hard to imagine that someone being paraded around like a captive under a death sentence could be fraudulent in any way whatsoever — and that is precisely Paul's point here and throughout the rest of 2 Corinthians.

The Ministry of the New Covenant (3:1-18)

Mentioning his sincerity reminds Paul of his earlier words of self-commendation (1:12-14) that lead him to yet another metaphor — this one for the Corinthians — that will become a segue into a discussion of the new covenant. Paul and his team need no words of recommendation from anyone, since the Corinthians themselves are their "letters of recommendation" — the proof of his team's value as the "fragrance" (2:14-15) and proclaimers of Christ (3:1-3).

This image of a human letter, which reinforces the theme of mutuality in Christ, includes the following significant elements:

- The Corinthian community is the letter (3:1).
- The letter is a visible, public entity (3:2).
- The subject of the letter is Christ ("a letter of Christ," 3:3).
- Paul and his team prepared the letter with the 'ink' of the Spirit of God (3:3).
- The ink that is God's Spirit is inscribed on/in the Corinthians' hearts (3:3; cf. 1:22).

Apart from the interesting trinitarian (God, Christ, Spirit)[7] character of this description, what is striking is the allusion to the contrast between the "old covenant" written on stone tablets — the Ten Commandments — and the "new covenant" written on human hearts. Such a new covenant was promised by the prophets (Jer. 31:33-34; Ezek. 36:26-27) and is now fulfilled, Paul claims, in Christ. The reality of this covenant, and of God's call to be "ministers" of it, is what generates confidence in Paul and his coworkers (3:4-6), a confidence inspired by the life-giving character of the new covenant, over against the death-dealing "letter" of the old (3:6).

Some caution is necessary here to avoid an inappropriate view of Paul's estimation of the Law and of the old covenant. In 3:7-18 Paul is engaging in a kind of rabbinic interpretation of Moses' "glory" — his shining appearance — upon receiving the two stone tablets of the commandments for a second time (Exod. 34:29-35), after he angrily destroyed the first set subsequent to seeing the golden-calf orgy (32:1-20). Paul is *not* denigrating the Law and the covenant it represents; rather, he is praising the new covenant because of its surpassing greatness and glory vis-à-vis the already glorious first covenant, comparing the greater with the lesser (*not* the worthless). Moreover, despite the emphasis on the end of the old covenant, there is for Paul still continuity between the word of God then and now, since all the promises of God are "Yes" in Christ.

It is important, therefore, to see Paul at work *as a Jew* describing the realization of his Jewish hopes for a new covenant that would remake the old, a covenant that would be different from and superior in effect to the old — as the prophet Jeremiah himself had said (Jer. 31:32). It would be a covenant in which the laws of God would be internalized by the presence of the Spirit and would therefore actually be observed (Ezek. 36:26-27; Jer. 31:33-34). *Thus for Paul, de-*

---

7. As in previous chapters, trinitarian language is used here in recognition that although Paul does not have a fully developed theology of the Trinity, such language is nonetheless appropriate.

pending especially on the prophets Jeremiah and Ezekiel, the old covenant was never intended to be permanent but to be renewed by a covenant involving God's Spirit, which for Paul came into effect with the death and resurrection of the Messiah (3:11; cf. Gal. 3:1–5:1, esp. 3:23-25).

Paul portrays the contrast between the old and new covenants as follows:

The Old Covenant	The New Covenant
of (the) letter (3:6)	of (the) Spirit (3:6)
ministry of death (3:6, 7)	gives life (3:6)
chiseled on stone tablets (3:3, 7)	written on human hearts (3:3)
came in glory (3:7)	came in greater glory (3:10-11)
ministry of condemnation (3:9)	ministry of justification (3:9)
it and its glory now set aside (3:7, 10-11)	permanent (3:11)

The contrasts are similar to those that appear in Romans 5:12-21, in which Adam and Christ are differentiated, though the two passages differ in focus. Of central and ironic significance here, however, is what Paul will say repeatedly throughout 2 Corinthians: that this glorious ministry of life comes through suffering and death — Christ's death on the cross, and the ongoing suffering and even dying of Paul and his team that are an extension of the death of Jesus himself (4:10).

The key word in this passage, then, is "glory" — the mighty radiance and presence of God and of things associated with God. The more glorious new covenant means that those who proclaim it do so "with great boldness" (3:12), in contrast to Moses, who kept the reflected glory of God (in his face) veiled (3:13; Exod. 34:29-35). For Paul this veil represents the inability of the majority of his Jewish brothers and sisters (with "hardened" minds [and hearts], 3:14) to experience fully the glory of God, which occurs only in Christ, who reveals God's glory fully (3:14-16). Reading the old covenant, symbolized by (the books of) Moses (3:15), does not remove the veil; only turning to "the Lord" does (3:16).

But who is this "Lord"? Now Paul becomes complex and borders on incoherency. The parallelism between 3:16 and 3:14 ("through Christ"/"turns to the Lord") suggests that the Lord is Jesus. But Paul explicitly equates the Lord with the Spirit (3:17). Does that mean that the Lord is neither YHWH (God the Father) nor Jesus? Ironically, Paul's point is almost certainly that the Spirit is the Spirit of *both* YHWH and Jesus. The glory of Israel's God is perceived only by seeing the glory of his "image," the (crucified) Lord Jesus (4:4), like an image reflected in a mirror. In line with much ancient thought about God, Paul believes those who so 'gaze upon' the image and glory of God are transformed into the divine image (i.e., Christ; cf. Rom. 8:29), into greater and greater "glory," or resemblance to Christ. This is what Paul means by both "life" (3:6) and freedom (3:17) — transformation into the likeness of Christ. The source of this life is a God whom Paul experiences as triune. His seeming confusion of titles and categories derives from deep convictions, generated and confirmed by experience. These convictions are (1) that the God of Israel is fully revealed and known in the Son, the crucified Messiah (cf. 1 Cor. 1:18-25); (2) that the Spirit of the Son is also the Spirit of God the Father (cf. Rom. 8:9; Gal. 4:6); and (3) that to have the Spirit of God within is also to have the Spirit of the Son (cf. Rom. 8:10-11).

Paul's real interest, of course, lies neither in the fine points of trinitarian theology nor even in the comparison of old and new covenants. Rather, it lies in the privilege and responsibility he feels as a "minister" (3:6) of this new Spirit-centered covenant. As such he is free in Christ to speak and live with the boldness of the Spirit.

Courage and Confidence in Cruciform Ministry (4:1–5:10)

Having reflected on the splendor of the ministry of the new covenant, Paul now blends images from those reflections with themes announced by the metaphors of 2:14-17: he and his colleagues (the use of "we" continues) are engaged in a ministry characterized by weakness (captives in God's triumphal procession) and integrity (preachers accountable to God). He also introduces a new image — treasure in clay jars (NRSV, NIV) or earthen vessels (NAB) — to stress the inestimable value of the gospel and the weakness of its human ministers (4:7). But the focus of this section is that despite the afflictions of the present, Paul and his coworkers "do not lose heart" (4:1, 16) but remain confident because of the presence of the Spirit and the certainty of future glory (5:6). Some of Paul's most powerful rhetoric — in this consistently rhetorically powerful letter — appears in this passage.

"We do not lose heart" (NRSV, NIV) or "we are not discouraged" (NAB), Paul writes, because his ministry is about the glory of God in Christ and by the mercy (4:1) and word (4:6) of that God (4:1-6). Paul had plenty of reason to be discouraged — the continuing criticisms of his ministry (4:2), the rejection of his gospel by some (4:3), and of course all the various forms of tribulation (4:8). But the apostle and his coworkers can hold their heads high, Paul claims, since they have acted with all integrity and spoken with complete honesty, for which reasons they "commend" themselves (4:2). "We do not," however, "proclaim ourselves" (4:5), Paul stresses. Any bit of necessary self-commendation should not be mistaken for a 'gospel' about Paul. The gospel — which is veiled to those who do not believe and are therefore "perishing" because of Satan's activity in the world ("the god of this world," 4:3-4) — is about Christ. Paul and his colleagues preach Jesus Christ as Lord (4:5), the Christ who is the image of God (4:4) and whose glory (4:4) is the glory of God (4:6). Paul and other ministers are therefore not 'lords' but 'slaves' — indeed, the Corinthians' ("your") slaves "for Jesus' sake" (4:5).[8] That is, they take on the form of slaves in conformity to their Lord, who "emptied himself, taking the form of a slave" (Phil. 2:7).

The images of slavery and glory propel the rest of this section of 2 Corinthians. Paul senses the tension between a gospel of glory and a life of slavery and affliction. He resolves it by finding in the pattern of Jesus' death and resurrection the pattern of his own life.

The new metaphor mentioned above is introduced in 4:7-12. Paul and his team have "this treasure" (4:7), the "gospel of the glory of Christ" (4:4), in the fragile pottery of human lives that display weakness (4:7). This reality, described with uncommon eloquence in 4:8-12, makes it plain that the "extraordinary power" (4:7) of the gospel among the Corinthians and others has its source in God, not in any humans. Describing the ministerial experience of himself and his colleagues (4:8-9), Paul says they are:

- "afflicted in every way, but not crushed";
- "perplexed, but not driven to despair";
- "persecuted, but not forsaken";
- "struck down, but not destroyed."

These four rather general descriptive phrases (for more specific catalogs of sufferings, see 6:4-10; 11:23-29) lead to the heart of the matter for Paul — a triple interpretation of these afflictions as a continuation of the death and resurrection of Jesus (4:10-12), that is, a death that paradoxically engenders life:

	Death		Life
4:10	always carrying in the body the death [or perhaps 'dying'] of Jesus,	→	so that the life of Jesus may also be made visible in our bodies;
4:11	For while we live, we are always being given up to death for Jesus' sake,	→	so that the life of Jesus may be made visible in our mortal flesh.
4:12	So death is at work in us,	→	but life [is at work] in you.

The paradox of this arrangement is that as Paul experiences the death of Jesus, he manifests the (resurrection) life of Jesus for the sake of the Corinthians. Cruciform ministry, Paul claims, makes visible (4:10, 11) the life of Jesus — the

8. Cf. 1 Cor. 3:5-9, 21-23; 4:1.

power of God by the Spirit to bring life (cf. 3:6). There are not two things oper-ating, death *and* life, but rather death *in* life, power *in* weakness (cf. 12:9-10).

This is indeed a strange kind of power and glory: in the ongoing death of Jesus that occurs in the concrete lives ("bodies" and "mortal flesh," 4:10-11) of the apostolic ministers, the resurrection power of Jesus is manifested. But it raises the serious question, Do apostolic ministers share only in the suffering and death of Jesus and never in his resurrection and glory? Paul's reflections in the next several paragraphs address precisely this concern.

Paul's initial answer is brief and to the point (4:13-15): the faith (i.e., in the gospel) he has agrees with the Scriptures (4:13) and includes, therefore, hope in the resurrection. He believes for himself what he preaches: that Jesus' resurrec-tion insures believers' future resurrection, including his own and that of all his coworkers, which will mean resurrection with the Corinthians into God's pres-ence (4:14; cf. 1 Thess. 4:14-17). Paul had earlier written to the Corinthians: "If for this life only we have hoped in Christ, we are of all people most to be pitied" (1 Cor. 15:19). Participation in Christ's death now is but a prelude to sharing in his resurrection later. This vision, and the desire to share it with others, keeps Paul going in the life of doing "everything" (especially his enduring afflictions) for the sake of the Corinthians (4:15; cf. 1:6; 2:10). In fact, to be the Corinthians' slave is simultaneously to do everything for the sake of Jesus (4:5, 11) and for the sake of the Corinthians (4:15; cf. Phil. 2:19-21).

This brief affirmation of final resurrection into God's presence leads Paul to a more extended comparative meditation on suffering and glory, on the tem-porary and the permanent (4:16–5:10). He begins by reaffirming that "we do not lose heart" (4:16), which carries even more weight in light of the life of trib-ulation just narrated. This self-revelation is followed by a series of contrasts about the present and the future. It is important for contemporary readers of Paul not to interject either ancient or modern understandings of death and the 'afterlife' into Paul's words; the apostle's fundamental affirmations are two: (1) that the believer's temporary, mortal body will be replaced with a perma-nent one; and (2) that present suffering will be replaced by future glory. These affirmations are presented through a series of images.

The first affirmation means that Paul does not accept the ancient notion that a body is simply a tomb for the soul, which awaits its escape at death. The second affirmation means that although suffering is inevitable, it is not final. The chart on page 304 summarizes the images that convey these two affirma-tions. It reveals that Paul envisions the life of believers in general, and ministers in particular, in two stages (their commonality being affirmed in 4:13). Both stages are "clothed," that is, constituted as a form of bodily existence, as op-posed to being "naked." The body of the first stage is like a tent, temporary and fragile, mortal and subject to destruction (5:1-4). It is characterized by afflic-

Present and Future in 2 Corinthians 4:16–5:10

Present	Future
outer nature wasting away, inner nature being renewed day by day (4:16)	
slight momentary affliction (4:17)	eternal weight of glory beyond all measure (4:17)
what can be seen is temporary (4:18)	what cannot be seen is eternal (4:18)
earthly tent [to be] . . . destroyed (5:1)	building from God, a house not made with hands, eternal in the heavens (5:1)
in this tent we groan, longing to be clothed with our heavenly dwelling . . . we wish not to be unclothed (5:2-4)	further clothed (5:4)
mortal (5:4)	what is mortal may be swallowed up by life (5:4)
Spirit as a guarantee (5:5)	life (5:4)
at home in the body, away from the Lord (5:6)	away from the body, at home with the Lord (5:8)
walk by faith, not by sight (5:7)	[walk by sight?] (5:7)
please the Lord (5:9)	please the Lord (5:9)
[deeds] done in the body (5:10)	appear before the judgment seat of Christ (5:10)

---

tion, but this affliction is also temporary, as well as slight (no matter how severe), in comparison to what is to come (4:17). To be at home in this tent is to be away from the Lord, who is of course in heaven (5:6). But believers possess the Spirit as the guarantee/deposit/first installment (5:5; cf. 1:22) of future life and glory. Therefore, even though their bodies waste away due to natural causes or persecution, they experience a renewal of the inner nature (4:16) — likely a reference to transformation into Christ's likeness (3:18). During this time believers walk by faith rather than sight (5:7), striving to please the Lord and to do good rather than evil (5:9-10; cf. 5:15).

The second stage begins with the resurrection of the dead (4:14). Believers are "further clothed" with a permanent, eternal "building" (5:1, 4; the metaphors are mixed, but the mixture works). The image can suggest either a brand-new or a transformed "dwelling." (This dwelling is sometimes interpreted as the corporate body of Christ in heaven, though it is more likely the individual's transformed body.) Believers appear before the judgment seat *(bēma)* of Christ to be judged and rewarded for their deeds done in the body (5:10). They are then permanently with the Lord (5:8) and, perhaps, walk henceforth by sight (5:7). They have inherited the immeasurable glory and life (4:17; 5:4) of which the Spirit was the down payment and guarantee. Their bodily 'home' undergoes no decay and does not die.

What both stages have in common is a covenantal relationship with the Lord that involves pleasing him (5:9). In fact, the purpose of Paul's comments here is not only to assure believers (himself included) of their future glory, but also to motivate them to good deeds in the present. For Paul, this can only mean an ongoing life of cruciform apostleship. For the Corinthians, as we will see in chapters 8–9, it must include analogous acts of Christlike love.

The Message of Reconciliation (5:11–6:10)

In light of what he has just affirmed about the future of believers and especially of cruciform ministry, Paul now sets out the shape and substance of his message of reconciliation in considerable detail. As he has already hinted several times, for Paul this message is proclaimed not just in word, but also in corresponding deeds. The apostolic ministry of Paul and his coworkers must — and does, Paul asserts — correspond to the message of God's reconciliation in Christ's cross (6:3-4). For this reason the Corinthians should be reconciled to Paul and his ministry — which is the implicit goal of this section and the explicit one of the following passage (6:11–7:16).

Paul links what he is about to say about his own ministry to his previous words on the coming judgment of believers, especially ministers (5:10; cf. 1 Cor. 3:10-15; 4:1-5). Paul and his colleagues act in the "fear" of the Lord (5:11) — recognizing their accountability to God. He claims they are transparent before God and, he hopes, also before the Corinthians (5:11), so that the Corinthians will recognize and honor their integrity and substance (5:12). Simultaneously engaging in and denying this self-commendation, Paul is preparing for the substance of his claims, articulated in the following verses, which mix together the shape of apostolic life and the substance of the apostolic gospel.

What matters to Paul is not "outward appearance" but the "heart" (5:12). His actions may appear odd or insane to some, but whatever their appearance to others, Paul does everything for God and for the Corinthians (5:13), as he has claimed again and again. This is because he and his ministerial colleagues are under the influence of Christ's love (5:14; not their love for Christ, as some have understood the phrase "the love of Christ"). It "urges us on" (NRSV), "compels us" (NIV). Paul is motivated by, consumed by Christ's love, which was expressed in his death — hence the connection of cross and love in Paul's mind (cf., e.g., Gal. 2:19-21).

The Cross of Love

At this juncture it will be useful to build a list of what Paul says about Christ's death in 5:14-21, one of the fullest expositions of this event in all of Paul's writings:

- Its *motive:* Christ's death was an act of love (5:14).
- Its *scope:* Christ died for all (5:14).
- Its *purpose:* he died for (the benefit of) all (5:14), in order that people would no longer live for themselves but for Christ (5:15), so that they would become the righteousness of God (5:21).
- Its *effects:* all have died (5:14), people are no longer to be regarded from a human point of view (5:16), a new creation has begun (5:17), and there is reconciliation with God and forgiveness (5:18-19).
- Its *ultimate source:* God was in Christ (5:19).
- Its *mode:* the sinless Christ became sin for our sake (5:21).

If space permitted, we could devote considerable attention to each of these affirmations; a few critical and synthetic comments will have to suffice.

Paul writes, of course, from the perspective of the believer, and specifically that of an apostle. His references to "all" must be read carefully. Surely Paul is not a universalist (one who affirms the salvation of all people without respect to their confession of faith), as we have seen in 2:15 and 4:3-4. Though it is true that Christ died for "all" (people), the claim that "all have died" must mean that all believers (i.e., all you Corinthians), all who have responded to and benefited from this death, have shared in the cross (cf. Rom. 6:1-11; Gal. 2:19-20). Otherwise Paul's ministry becomes nothing more than what some theologians have called 'accepting your acceptance' — a strange concept for an apostle who believes some people are currently perishing (2:15; 4:3; cf. 1 Cor. 1:18) and who, in the role of ambassador, seeks to effect people's reconciliation with God (5:20).

This interpretation squares with the picture of humanity outside of Christ that emerges in 5:14-21: living for self, at enmity with God (cf. Rom. 5:1-11), guilty of trespasses, and identified with sin rather than righteousness. Into this story comes the gracious initiative of God in Christ, effecting reconciliation and not counting trespasses (5:18-21; cf. Rom. 3:21-26). Christ's death, as the substance of both his love and the Father's love, was an act *for* (5:15) others, the sense of which is probably both for their benefit and in their place (cf. 5:21). This 'exchange,' as it has been called, of the righteous for sinners, means also that the once sinful must now "become" (the embodiment of) God's "righteousness" (5:21). *The purpose of Christ's death was not merely to offer forgiveness of sins so that people could go on their merry way.* Rather, its purpose was to completely reorient human existence toward God (reconciliation), expressed in living for Christ rather than for self (5:15). This is the language of covenant renewal, similar in spirit to 3:1-11, where in 3:9 Paul uses the same word, *dikaiosynē* (righteousness), that appears in 5:21[9] and dominates Romans. The death of Christ, via the ministry of the Spirit, creates people who are the righteousness of God and who are, therefore, part of the "new creation" (5:17; cf. Gal. 6:15) that Christ's death has inaugurated.

This makes Christ's death an apocalyptic, or cosmic, event; it is God's way of bringing about a seismic shift in the story of the world. The new creation that the 'in-Christ' community constitutes is the beginning of the fulfillment of the prophetic promise (e.g., Isa. 40–66) for creation's renewal. There is also, according to Paul, a corresponding seismic shift in the way those in Christ regard others (5:16). Just as "we" (Paul, his colleagues, and anyone else who was once outside Christ) used to regard Christ "from a human point of view" but do so no longer, so also we no longer look at and evaluate others with merely human eyes (NIV, "from a worldly point of view"; NAB, more literally, "according to the flesh"). Paul does not specify the new way of evaluating people, but for him the opposite of "flesh" is "Spirit," and the Spirit of God is associated with the glory of God manifested in the crucified Christ. In other words, the new criterion of evaluation is the cross.

The Cross as Criterion

That Paul expects the recipients of his letter to grasp this criterion and to apply it to him, and to any other claimants to the title "apostle" or "ambassador," is clear from 6:1-10. Paul has already summarized the function of his ministry in the term "ambassador," a term of authoritative, representative speech (5:20). The divine message spoken through Paul is "Be reconciled to God" (5:20). These words certainly constitute both a general summary of Paul's preaching and a word on target for the Corinthians, whose flirtations with rejecting Paul — the one who embodies the message of cross and reconciliation — are proof (in Paul's mind) of their need for reconciliation with God. The Corinthians

9. NRSV, unlike NIV and NAB, renders the term "justification" in 3:9.

might otherwise be guilty of "accept[ing] the grace of God in vain" (6:1), for the time of salvation is now (6:2).

The specific Corinthian focus of that appeal becomes evident in the (now less subtle) self-commendation of 6:3-10. Paul again claims full integrity for his ministry and engages in self-commendation only as God's servant (6:3-4). That is, Paul and his coworkers are once again 'commending' themselves only insofar as they are cruciform slaves of God in Christ for the sake of others (cf. "your slaves for Jesus' sake" in 4:5). Marshaling another rhetorical tour de force (like 4:7-12), Paul now describes the difficult (6:4-5), virtuous (6:6-7), and paradoxical (6:8-10) character of his ministry. These categories recall earlier images of cruciformity (being afflicted), integrity (not peddling the word of God), and paradox (life in death):

- *tribulations* (6:4-5): in great endurance, afflictions, hardships, calamities, beatings, imprisonments, riots, labors, sleepless nights, and hunger;
- *virtues* (6:6-7): in purity, knowledge, patience, kindness, holiness of spirit, genuine love, truthful speech, and the power of God with the weapons of righteousness;
- *paradoxes* (6:8-10): in honor and dishonor, in ill repute and good repute, treated as impostors and yet true, unknown and yet well known, dying and yet alive, punished but not killed, sorrowful yet always rejoicing, poor yet making many rich, having nothing and yet possessing everything.

Paul, in other words, claims in these (nearly thirty) phrases that he and his colleagues in ministry have met the ultimate test of integrity — conformity to Christ. Whether in affliction, or love, or "making many rich" (cf. 8:9), Paul and his team have become, in Christ, the righteousness of God (5:21) by "carrying in the body the death of Jesus" and thereby also making visible "the life of Jesus" in their bodies (4:10).

Paul hopes the Corinthians will not only embrace him fully for embracing this way of life, but also that they, too, will embrace this life for themselves by giving generously to the collection for Jerusalem. Such generosity would be a symbolic gesture of many things, including the Corinthians' reconciliation with Paul and his ministry. But before Paul can get to that subject, he must conclude, at least from his point of view, the process of reconciliation itself.

THE FINAL APPEAL FOR RECONCILIATION (6:11–7:16)

For four chapters, since 2:14, Paul has explained to the Corinthians the nature of his ministry. This has hardly been a digression from the concrete details of his relationship with the Corinthians outlined in 1:1–2:13. Still less should we conclude, as many have, that these chapters are part of another letter that interrupts the flow of 2:13 into 6:11, 7:2, or 7:5. Rather, Paul has used these chapters to demonstrate that his relationship with the Corinthians has been a microcosm of his consistently aboveboard and cruciform modus operandi. This self-presentation constitutes the basis for the appeal for reconciliation that begins in 6:11. The appeal itself (6:11-13 and 7:2-16) brackets a short, puzzling passage (6:14–7:1) that seems, once again, to interrupt the flow of Paul's thought. In reality, however, this apparent 'interpolation' may well be part of the appeal for reconciliation.

A Summary of the Appeal (6:11-13)

Paul's creative use of images in 2 Corinthians has already been noted. In this short summary of his appeal for full reconciliation, Paul again uses vivid word pictures to tell the Corinthians that he fully accepts and loves them, as his children (6:13), and that he hopes they will reciprocate. In other words, the ball is placed — lovingly — in their court.

English translations do not capture well the images Paul employs. Three body parts are mentioned in these verses: mouth, heart, and bowels (*ta splanchna,* one of the sources of affection in antiquity), each referred to as either 'open' or 'constricted.' According to 6:11, Paul and his team have an open mouth and an open heart toward the Corinthians; that is, they have spoken "frankly" (NRSV, NAB) or "freely" (NIV), and they have loved completely. There is therefore no "restriction in our affections," Paul claims (6:12a); any wrongs have been righted, sins forgiven (cf. 2:5-11). As for the Corinthians, however, Paul finds them constricted in the bowels (6:12b; NRSV's bland rendering is "but [there is restriction] only in yours" — i.e., in your affection). The Corinthians have emotional cramps, and it is time for them to 'open up' (6:13; the word "hearts" that appears in NRSV and NIV is absent from the Greek). Paul wants them to express full devotion to him as their father in the faith.

A Corollary Appeal (6:14–7:1)

Unless the compelling, image-rich appeal we just studied was intended to end a letter or a section of a letter, it ought to lead into some additional detail about the way the Corinthians should express their love. But that will have to wait, for instead we find this rather odd text, 6:14–7:1. Its subject matter is relatively clear: a call to radical holiness (7:1) that excludes any kind of 'yoking' (NAB, NIV for *heterozygountes,* 6:14a) or "fellowship" (*koinōnia,* 6:14b) with unbelievers (*apistoi,* 6:14, 15). But what is this doing here?

In popular usage 2 Corinthians 6:14–7:1 has often been cited as an argument against marriage (or, more generally, friendship) between the 'unequally yoked,' i.e., believers and nonbelievers. Whatever the value of this interpretation, there is no evidence from the content or context that the text is focused on this issue. Some of the scholarly suggestions for the interpretation of 6:14–7:1 are listed below; it may be:

- a fragment of Paul's letter mentioned in 1 Corinthians 5:9 that prohibited association with immoral people;
- an additional Pauline word on the problem of those who eat meat offered to idols (1 Cor. 8–10);
- a fragment of another letter or document, perhaps not by Paul and perhaps not even by a Christian (e.g., by a separatist Jewish group), about relations with outsiders; or
- a fragment from an anti-Pauline treatise.

For many interpreters, then, this text is so bizarre as to be either out of place or non-Pauline (there are a number of unusual words, for instance), or both — an 'interpolation' of some sort. But how did it arrive here? And is it really so inappropriate here?

A growing number of interpreters find that this text is thoroughly Pauline, that it has a rhetorical function within the letter as a whole, and that the text belongs where it is because Paul put it there. This interpretation sees the passage as a warning against associating with Paul's opponents, particularly the "false apostles" who will be castigated in chapters 10–13. Though it may seem odd to refer to self-proclaimed ministers as "unbelievers," Paul's assessment of the "super-" or "false" apostles is that they proclaim a different Jesus, Spirit, and gospel (11:4) and are ministers of Satan (11:13-15). Accusing them of unbelief and idolatry (6:16) seems almost tame — but appropriate. A more explicit connection between this passage and the problem of the pseudoapostles appears in the word "Beliar" (6:15), another name for Satan.

If this interpretation is correct, then the point of the passage is to call the Corinthians to disassociate from the false apostles (6:14a) and thus to live in holiness in the fear of God (7:1; cf. 5:11). These admonitions bracket a series of rhetorical questions about the antithesis between the ways of God and the ways of Satan and idolatry (6:14b-16a), followed by a series of Scripture quotes defining the chosen community as God's people who are called to separate themselves from unclean people (6:16b-18). As God's temple (cf. 1 Cor. 3:16), the Corinthian church must reestablish its reconciliation with Paul by severing all ties with his satanic opponents, the false apostles. Though Paul does not dwell on this here, he will return to it, in full force, in chapters 10–13.

Paul's Consolation and Confidence (7:2-16)

The conclusion of the appeal for reconciliation exudes Paul's consolation and confidence regarding the Corinthians. Inviting them to "make room" for himself and his coworkers (7:2), Paul stresses once again his integrity, his love for the Corinthians, and his pride in them (7:2-4). His confidence in them (7:4, 16) means that he is sure (or at least he tells them he is sure!) they will obey him, as they have done before (7:15; cf. 2:9). This consoles him in his affliction (7:4; cf. 1:3-7).

The mention of consolation leads Paul to pick up the narrative of his anxious trip from Troas to Macedonia (7:5; cf. 2:12-13). His arrival there and his anticipation of Titus's visit were traumatic (7:5), but Paul experienced divine consolation and joy when Titus told him of the Corinthians' "mourning" and "zeal" for their apostle (7:5-7). The letter had succeeded in its mission, and the news of its success made Paul both happy for its success and sorry for its pain (7:7-9). Still, he has no regrets about the letter, pleased not that it caused grief but that the grief was "godly" in that it led to repentance and renewed zeal (7:8-11). This was his purpose all along — not the punishment of the offender nor the benefit of the offended (i.e., himself), but the reconciliation of the whole church, before God, with the church's apostle (7:12-13a).

The Corinthians' response was satisfying to Paul in one other respect: his boasting of them to Titus is now confirmed, as the Corinthians welcomed him as Paul's envoy and expressed their obedience via Titus to Paul (7:13b-15). For this magnanimous response to Paul himself, to Titus, and thus to the cruciform Pauline mission and message, Paul rejoices, but he does so with "confidence," undoubtedly because there is still more to do (7:16). Although Paul does not explicitly say what the 'more' might be, the context suggests it will include both disassociating from the false apostles and following through on the pledge to help the Jerusalem church.

Summary of 2 Corinthians 1–7

In the first seven chapters of 2 Corinthians Paul has developed several key, interrelated points:
- Believers participate in a partnership of tribulation and consolation by sharing both in Christ's suffering and in God's comfort.

- Ministerial faithfulness and integrity are founded on and symbolic of God's faithfulness in Christ.
- Ministry is characterized especially by truthfulness/integrity and cruciform love.
- The life of cruciform love — always carrying about the dying of Jesus — is paradoxically also a display of God's resurrection power — the life of Jesus — for the benefit of others.
- The present life of suffering is insignificant in comparison to the immeasurable glory that awaits those who live and die for the Lord.
- God's reconciling love in Christ's death provides the motivation for and shape of ministry as reconciliation in love.
- Ministry with integrity consists of three key elements: difficulty, virtue, and paradox.
- Ministry may be envisioned through a variety of vivid images, including the following: sharing in Christ's sufferings, being led as captives in triumphal procession, not peddling the word of God, making human beings into letters of Christ, carrying in the body the death of Jesus, being Christ's ambassadors, and making people rich.
- Paul's relationship with the Corinthians exemplifies the meaning of reconciliation but also requires ongoing attention and further reconciliation.

8:1–9:15. THE CRUCIFORM GRACE OF GENEROSITY

Paul's desire to collect funds for the support of the church in Jerusalem was a significant concern of his ministry, but not one that normally receives attention equal to the weight he assigned it. Paul mentions it in four of his letters (Romans, Galatians, and 1 and 2 Corinthians); he made extensive efforts to collect funds in at least three regions (Galatia, Macedonia, and Achaia); and it affected both his travel plans and his choice of traveling companions and envoys.[10] Paul's right-hand man in this effort was Titus, who attended the Jerusalem meeting that generated the promise to support the poor (Gal. 2:1, 10; 2 Cor. 8:16-24). It is likely that Paul's preoccupation with this collection carried with it some cost — criticism, lack of support, questions about integrity and consistency — especially in Corinth. And he was not completely sure the gift would be well received (Rom. 15:31).

---

10. Regions: 1 Cor. 16:1; 2 Cor. 8:1-2; Rom. 15:26; travel plans: Rom. 15:22-29; 1 Cor. 16:3-4; 2 Cor. 1:16; 9:3-5; choice of traveling companions and envoys: 2 Cor. 8:16-24.

Paul seems to have had several reasons for this specific mission; some he notes explicitly, while others are implied:

- to fulfill a promise made to the Jerusalem leadership and to express support for the Jerusalem 'mother' church and its authorities (Gal. 2:10);
- to alleviate the suffering of an impoverished community of believers (Rom. 15:26);
- to allow Gentile believers to express tangibly their spiritual debt to Jewish believers (Rom. 15:27);
- to achieve some measure of economic equality among the various churches (2 Cor. 8:13-15);
- to embody the gospel of God's gift and Christ's sacrifice in a concrete way (2 Cor. 8:9; 9:13-15);
- to unify Gentile and Jewish believers, and to express that mission concretely; and
- to create a sense of the universality and interconnectedness of all the communities in Christ.

We know that Paul was successful in his campaign among the Macedonians (8:1-5), but it is unclear how or whether the Galatians responded favorably. The apostle to Achaia does not want to lose the Achaians' support but apparently hopes they will send their own delegates, with representatives from Macedonia, to Jerusalem (8:16-24).

In 2 Corinthians 8–9 Paul calls on the Corinthians to fulfill their commitment to the Jerusalem collection, providing a cluster of reasons for their doing so. Five key words dominate the chapters: 'fellowship,' 'partnership,' or "sharing" (*koinōnia* and *koinōnos*: 8:4, 23; 9:13); "service" or "ministry" (*diakonia* and *diakoneō*: 8:4, 19, 20; 9:1, 12, 13); "overflow" (*perisseuō*: seven times in 8:2, 7; 9:8, 12; plus *hyperballō* in 9:14); "zeal" or "eagerness/earnestness/concern" (*spoudē* and *zēlos*: 8:7, 8, 16; 9:2); and especially "grace" (*charis*: ten times, as noted in the chart on p. 314). These five words carry the weight of Paul's message: that joining in the Jerusalem collection is a way for believers to share in earnest their material abundance as an expression of gratitude for, and participation in, the abundant grace of God offered in Christ. To do so is to prove the reality of God's love and grace in their lives.

Of particular importance is the recurrence of the term *charis*, "grace." Because it has something of a range of meanings, it is difficult to capture its prominence in English translation. Yet it is central to what Paul is about in these chapters: the grace of God, the grace of gratitude, the grace of giving. As the chart on page 314 reveals, the NRSV renders *charis* as grace only twice, whereas the NIV and especially the NAB are more successful at conveying this unifying theme. The grace of God operative in the life of the church both opens and

313

"Grace" *(charis)* in 2 Corinthians 8–9

Verse	NRSV/NAB/NIV
8:1	grace of God/grace of God/grace that God has given
8:4	[begging us earnestly for . . .] the privilege/the favor/the privilege
8:6	[complete this . . .] generous undertaking/gracious act/act of grace
8:7	[excel in this . . .] generous undertaking/gracious act/grace of giving
8:9	[you know . . .] the generous act/gracious act/grace [of our Lord Jesus Christ]
8:16	But thanks be to God/But thanks be to God/I thank God
8:19	[administering] this generous undertaking/this gracious work/the offering
9:8	[God is able to provide you with . . .] every blessing/every grace/all grace
9:14	[the surpassing] grace of God/grace of God/grace God has given you
9:15	Thanks be to God/Thanks be to God/Thanks be to God[11]

closes the two chapters (8:1; 9:14). The focus of the chapters is not precisely the same, however. One difference is the central reference to the graciousness of *Christ* in chapter 8 (8:9) and to the graciousness of *God* in chapter 9 (9:15) — though in fact the two refer, from complementary perspectives, to the same gift of God's reconciling love in Christ (cf. 5:14, 19).

CHRIST, THE MACEDONIANS, AND THE CORINTHIANS (8:1-24)

Paul begins his appeal with a description of the incredible generosity of the Macedonian churches — probably those of Thessalonica, Beroea, and Philippi. He views their largess as an operation of divine grace in their midst (8:1). Paul knows that their generosity was the gracious work of God because their "wealth of generosity" overflowed from their abundant joy and poverty during a time of "severe ordeal" (8:2). Although they were persecuted, they were joyful; although poor, they were generous — beyond their "means" (NRSV, NAB) or "ability" (NIV), as Paul himself has witnessed (8:3). In fact, they begged for the chance to share in the fellowship of such a ministry of God's grace (8:4). They did so

---

11. As in English, the word 'grace' can be used idiomatically in Greek to mean an expression of thanksgiving.

completely as an act of self-dedication to the Lord and to the work of God entrusted to Paul (8:5). The entire experience was a profoundly spiritual exercise for the Macedonians. Who could deny that this is grace at work?

Paul is obviously depicting this overwhelming Macedonian response as an example for the Corinthians, as it has already inspired him to resume, through Titus, his appeal to them (8:5-6). Recalling their abundance of spiritual gifts and such (cf. 1 Cor. 1:7), Paul invites them to abound in this work of God's grace, too (8:7; unfortunately, the image of abundance is missing from NRSV, NAB, and NIV, all of which use "excellence/excel"). Paul will not issue an order to the Corinthians, but he is not ashamed to engage in a bit of rhetorical comparison to motivate them, for he sees this issue as a test of the "genuineness of [their] love" (8:8). They have faith and knowledge, and they have received plenty of love (8:7), but Paul seems to wonder if they are capable of showing love.

Not surprisingly, the mention of genuine love takes Paul to the incarnation and death of Christ, whose love "urges us on" (5:14). The brief narrative of Christ's love (8:9) echoes the famous hymn of Christ in Philippians 2:6-11. In that text, which (as we have seen) functions for Paul as his master story, the one who was in the form of God emptied himself and took the form of a slave by becoming human, completing his self-humbling by dying on a cross (vv. 6-8). The basic narrative pattern of that story is 'although *x*, not *y* but *z*': although Christ was equal with God, he did not exploit that equality for himself but emptied himself in obedience to God and (as Paul interprets the story) for our benefit and salvation.

Here in 2 Corinthians the story line ("although . . .") is similar, but Paul has altered the images to address the specific situation concretely: "[Although] our Lord Jesus Christ . . . was rich, yet for your sakes he became poor, so that by his poverty you might become rich" (8:9).[12] The image is appropriately economic, one of wealth choosing poverty for the enrichment of the poor. It is parallel to another story line that Paul has already recited in 5:21: God made the one who was sinless, sin, so that the sinful might become God's righteousness. The clear reference to Christ's death in 5:21 suggests that Christ's voluntary impoverishment refers at least to his death, while the parallel in Philippians suggests that it also refers to his leaving the 'wealth' or glory of God to become human. This very deliberate act of self-spending for the sake of others, Paul says, is the "grace" of Christ (8:9), the love of Christ, the means of the Corinthians' justification and reconciliation with God. How can one benefit from it without also participating in it? Grace is experienced as grace only when it is extended to others. The Macedonians knew that quite well.

So now, although Paul will not give a command, the Corinthians have two

---

12. This may be classified as an abbreviation of the full narrative pattern to 'although *x, z*.'

examples: the Macedonian churches, who — we now understand — were displaying Christlike grace, and Christ himself. Thus with these two models in hand, Paul can cut to the chase with a word of "advice" (8:10): the Corinthians should follow through on the enthusiastic commitment made the previous year with a correspondingly enthusiastic collection (8:10-11). He is not asking them to bankrupt themselves or to give what they do not have, but merely to give to the needy out of their (relative) abundance, in order that something of a just economic equality might obtain within the churches (8:12-14). The warrant for this practical side of the appeal is a Scripture text (Exod. 16:18) about the daily gathering of manna by the Israelites — some collecting more, some less, but in the end none having too little or too much.

On the assumption that the Corinthians will be won over, and to address some possible concerns they may have, Paul continues with the practical matters of the collection. Paul's equally devoted colleague Titus, accompanied by two additional coworkers (8:18, 22), will handle the collection itself (8:16-24). The two unnamed partners are recognized "apostles" (NAB, translating *apostoloi*, 8:23; NRSV, "messengers"; NIV, "representatives"), one of whom is especially charged by the Macedonian churches for the administration and delivery of the collection (8:19). Thus Paul, by involving others who are respected by the Macedonian and Achaian churches (as Titus clearly is), is attempting to deflect any criticism (8:20; cf. 6:3) of himself regarding the collection. Once again, then, he can say, 'Prove your love! Validate my boasting!' (8:24).

GOD, THE MACEDONIANS, AND THE CORINTHIANS (9:1-15)

The word "boasting" links chapter 8 to chapter 9 (which of course were not two 'chapters' in Paul's mind, unless the proponents of two appeal letters are correct), and creates a shift from 'we' to 'I' language. Paul now continues his appeal on a slightly more personal note, saying more about the collection team and offering biblical principles and promises on giving.

In chapter 8 the Macedonians served as an example to the Corinthians. Now Paul turns the tables and asks that the Corinthians not invalidate the exemplary claims he has made about them to the Macedonians (9:1-5). Paul had successfully used the Corinthian zeal of a year earlier (9:2; cf. 8:10) to motivate the Macedonians. Perhaps he had been called on the carpet with the question, 'When are the Achaians actually going to deliver on their promise?' or perhaps he simply wanted to avoid the shame of answering that question in the words, 'They aren't!' (9:3-4). Thus the sending of the Macedonian emissaries (i.e., with Titus) to the Corinthians was a strategy designed both to reassure the northern churches and to prompt the southern churches before Paul himself, with other Macedonian representatives, appeared in Corinth (9:3-5). Once again Paul wants the actual matter of collection handled at a distance from himself so that the Corinthians feel no pressure — as if Paul were extorting them — but give freely and generously (9:5).

This said, Paul sets out two basic principles for the Corinthians' gift; it should be offered:

- *liberally,* as the ancient image of sowing and reaping suggests (9:6; cf. Prov. 11:24-25); and
- *cheerfully* — willingly and freely (9:7; cf. Prov. 22:8-9, esp. LXX).

Corresponding to these biblical principles of liberality and cheerfulness are biblical promises of God's provision and blessing for those who do give in this way. Specifically, alluding again to biblical texts,[13] Paul asserts that God will both provide for those who are generous and even increase their supply so that they may give all the more (9:8-11). Those who give will always have more to give (cf. Luke 6:38). Furthermore, such generosity is an act of both *diakonia* and *leitourgia,* ministry and worship, the care of those in need and the cause of thanksgiving to God (9:12).

The conclusion of the appeal reverts to the language of testing and obedience. Will the Corinthians demonstrate their true allegiance to the gospel by exercising this ministry (9:13)? Will they be merely a *container* or a *conduit* of God's grace (2:14)? Will they truly experience and, with Paul, 'say grace for' God's "indescribable gift" in Christ? Once again the ball is in the Corinthians' court. Paul can only wait and hope that his efforts have not been in vain. Apparently they were not (Rom. 15:26).

Summary of 2 Corinthians 8–9

In this short section of the letter, Paul has addressed one point — the collection for Jerusalem — but in doing so has offered a brief but comprehensive theology of generosity, of giving with abandon.

- For believers, generous giving is an experience of divine grace, a means of expressing gratitude for grace received from God, and a way of conforming to the generous self-giving of Christ.
- Giving to the needy should be done cheerfully and liberally.
- The generous find that God supplies their own need and more, so that they may give all the more generously.

13. Ps. 112:9 (LXX 111:9); Isa. 55:10; Hos. 10:12 LXX.

- Generosity demonstrates the reality of the experience of grace.
- The Corinthians, while not compelled by Paul to give, ought to feel themselves 'urged on' by grace and love to do so.

10:1–13:13. THE CRUCIFORM POWER-IN-WEAKNESS OF THE SPIRIT

Full of irony and insight, 2 Corinthians 10–13 is one of the most rhetorically and theologically powerful portions of the entire Pauline corpus. It is Paul's no-holds-barred defense of his own ministry and his concurrent attack on his 'opponents.' These opponents or critics find fault with Paul in several respects, feeding on feelings already expressed by some of the Corinthians and addressed by Paul in 1 Corinthians: that he has a weak personal presence and lacks flashy rhetoric (10:10; 11:6), and that he refuses to accept financial support but instead stoops to manual labor (11:7-11; the critics likely accepted money — 11:20). Added to this, it appears, are charges that Paul lacks the signs of authentic apostleship such as miracles, visions, and other displays of power (12:1-12), and perhaps that he is now encroaching on their territory by trying to reestablish relations with the Corinthians (10:15-16). All these criticisms, directly or indirectly, call into question the legitimacy of Paul's apostleship.

From Paul's perspective, however, the fundamental problem of these self-styled ministers of Christ is not that they criticize him. Rather, it is that their criticisms of him belie an understanding of Christ, the Spirit, and the gospel (11:4) that is *so thoroughly antithetical to the message of Christ crucified as to be demonic* (11:13-15). Thus Paul declares war on his opponents (10:1-6).

The issue at stake boils down to this: What is the signature manifestation of God's Spirit in the ministry of Christ's authentic apostles? The answer the Corinthians are hearing from the "super-apostles" (as Paul sarcastically labels them in 11:5 and 12:11) is displays of power — potent speech, visions, revelations, and the like. Paul's response, without denying the validity of such displays of power (in fact, he insists on the abundance of his own mystical experiences and miraculous deeds), is that the hallmark of the Spirit and thus of Christ's apostles is power in weakness. In essence, these chapters constitute an argument, largely from Paul's own experience, that the Spirit of God is the Spirit of Christ, and specifically the Spirit of Christ crucified. This point of view is not at all surprising, given Paul's own commitment, rehearsed for the Corinthians, to "know nothing among you except Jesus Christ, and him crucified"

(1 Cor. 2:2), because for Paul and for all truly called by God, Christ crucified is "the power of God and the wisdom of God" (1 Cor. 1:24).

As suggested in the introductory section of this chapter, the "super-apostles" appear to have been Jewish Christian pneumatic preachers (11:22) who were critical of Paul and proud of their own status and power, claiming that they belonged to Christ as equals with, if not in fact superiors to, Paul and his colleagues (10:7 NIV, NAB; 11:5, 12; 12:11). Paul's strategy in the rhetorical war that unfolds in these chapters is to engage in the kind of self-praise and comparison to others for which he faults the super-apostles. But there is a twist: Paul claims to boast only in the Lord, and specifically only in his self-support, persecution, and other forms of (perceived or actual) weakness. If these four chapters are in fact part of one unified letter, then Paul has prepared the way for this strategy by both criticizing and engaging in self-commendation, and by focusing on his own cruciform style of ministry, in chapters 1–7. As in those chapters and in chapters 8 and 9, so also in chapters 10–13 Paul ultimately desires one thing: the Corinthians' obedience (10:6), by which he really means their obedience to Christ (10:5).

PAUL'S DECLARATION OF WAR (10:1-6)

Paul begins these four chapters with a paradoxical combination of gentle appeal and declaration of war. The tone and substance of the first two verses reveal Paul's heartfelt desire to deal with the Corinthians in Christlike "meekness and gentleness" (10:1). He does not want to show up on their doorstep for a head-to-head confrontation, but as once before, he is prepared to do so if necessary (10:2; 13:1-4; cf. 1 Cor. 4:14-21). In fact, such a confrontation may be unavoidable if the gentle appeal does not succeed and his (actually 'their' — the plural dominates these chapters) opponents continue their accusation of Paul's conduct as unbefitting an apostle — literally 'walking according to the flesh' (see NIV; NRSV mg.) or "by the standards of this world" (10:2 NIV; NRSV, "human standards").

This accusation launches Paul into a sharp rebuttal (appropriate, perhaps, for the one accused of being meek when present and bold when absent, 10:1) in which he characterizes his ministry in general, and his dealing with the Corinthians and their new 'apostles' in particular, as spiritual warfare. Using the vocabulary and imagery of Roman war, Paul claims that his team's combat is not waged according to the flesh (10:3) but rather with divinely empowered weaponry (10:4). These weapons allow them to engage in destruction, captivity, and punishment of resistance (10:4-6).

The stinging analogy to the Corinthian situation is clear. Paul is about to attempt to "destroy" the arguments of the false apostles and 'take captive' the thoughts of the Corinthians — captive to their Lord Christ, whom they are called to obey (10:5). If necessary, any residual resistance will be punished (though how is not explained), presumably upon the next apostolic visit (10:6; cf. 13:1-10). This declaration of war is necessary because the false apostles are leading Paul's beloved Corinthians away from true knowledge of God and surrender to Christ (10:5). Ironically, the very meekness and gentleness of Christ with which this passage begins will become for Paul the criterion by which arguments and thoughts are judged. The ultimate weapon in Paul's arsenal is not his rhetorical ability — though it will now be well displayed — but his Christlike weakness.

It is crucial that we not misunderstand Paul's military imagery here. He is not suddenly adopting a violent, Roman, worldly approach to life in Christ. Rather, ministry that proclaims the cross in word and deed, and that appropriately opposes ministry that contradicts that cross, is the true means to peace and reconciliation of which the Roman imperial movement is but an anemic parody. Paul is ready to wage this kind of war, and only this kind of war, in the name of God's reconciling presence in Christ.

THE TERMS OF THE CAMPAIGN:
EDIFICATION AND BOASTING (10:7-18)

Having declared war on the false apostles — but *not* on the Corinthians — Paul now wishes to make clear his intentions and strategies in this campaign. First, like his ministry in general, this letter (or letter segment) will be an exercise of Paul's authority for the Corinthians' edification, not their destruction (10:8; cf. 12:19). Second, the primary weapon to be used will be that of the opponents, namely, boasting, though in the Lord (10:17).

The NRSV (though not the NIV or NAB) masks the force of 10:7 — if anyone (not "you," NRSV) thinks of himself or herself as belonging to Christ, so does the Pauline team. This is an oblique reference to the rivals' claims to a special, authoritative (apostolic) connection to Christ. Paul cannot and will not back away from his own special apostolic authority (10:8), even if opponents question it on the grounds of its alleged inconsistency (10:10). His letters, more powerful than his personal presence, are not intended to intimidate but to edify (10:8-9). But if his opponents think he cannot be strong in person, they had better be prepared (10:11).

Underlying these words is clearly a rivalry between Paul and the new apostles that has been engineered by them. From Paul's point of view, they are engaging in completely inappropriate self-commendation of themselves and criticism of him. Paul's only recourse is to reaffirm his own authority (10:8), and to do so, more or less, on his opponents' terms — by boasting. Yet for Paul, what he is about to do is radically different from the actions of his rivals. First, Paul will reject self-commendation in favor of boasting in the Lord and being commended by the Lord (10:12-18). Then he will move on to boast, but only in the paradoxical cruciform shape of his life (11:1–12:13).

The first problem Paul has with these ministers is their arrogance, so much so that he would not dare to compare himself with them (10:12). Their self-congratulatory posture, as Paul sees it, proves that they just don't 'get it' (10:12). The second problem Paul has is the location and focus of their boasting, namely, the church in Corinth. This makes them trespassers, crossing the boundaries into an area that God has assigned to Paul — something Paul would never do (10:13-16; cf. Rom. 15:20; Gal. 2:9).

Paul, on the other hand, will boast only in the Lord, a biblical principle (Jer. 9:23-24) that he quotes here (10:17), as he does also in 1 Corinthians 1:31. What Paul means by this crucial principle will gradually become clearer as the two speeches of foolish boasting (which follow) proceed. But at the very least it means to him that no amount of self-praise validates one's ministry or matters in any other way; the only praise that counts comes from the Lord (10:18). In the immediate context, the principle means that ministers should 'stay out' of territory that the Lord has assigned to someone else, for the Lord will not commend interlopers. More broadly, however, the principle means that the only legitimate pride is in obeying the Lord, and specifically (as we will see) in being conformed to the Lord's self-humbling and weakness.

PAUL'S FIRST SPEECH OF FOOLISH BOASTING: PAUL'S SELF-SUPPORT (11:1-15)

Most commentators on 2 Corinthians label the section beginning at 11:16 Paul's 'Fool's Speech,' which it certainly is. But we would misread the letter if we did not acknowledge that, at least from Paul's own perspective, the foolish boasting begins already in 11:1.

The Grounds for Boasting (11:1-4)

Paul feels he has a right to ask the Corinthians to indulge "a little foolishness" (11:1) because he is their father in and for Christ. More specifically, Paul images himself here as the father of the bride-to-be, a role that meant responsibility for the daughter's pure devotion to her betrothed until the wedding day (11:2). This imagery of the church as the bride of Christ is steeped in the biblical tradition of Israel as God's beloved spouse, and of course appears elsewhere in the New Testament (Eph. 5:22-32; Rev. 19:7-9; 21:2, 9). As the spiritual father of the community, Paul shares God's jealousy for the church at Corinth (11:2). His job does not end with the founding of the church, but only with its presentation to Christ (i.e., on the day of the Lord, the eschatological wedding feast), at which time it must be undefiled by the Eve-like deceitfulness of the super-apostles (remembering who employed Eve — cf. 11:14). To submit to their ways would be tantamount to idolatry (often depicted as sexual immorality in the Bible).

But what is so offensive about these "super-apostles"? Much ink has been spilled over this question. Like the fruit in the Garden of Eden, their message was tantalizing to the Corinthians (11:4). But Paul infers that, from his perspective, these people were preaching "another Jesus . . . a different spirit [which should be rendered 'Spirit'] from the one you received . . . a different gospel" (11:4). These three elements — Jesus, Spirit, and gospel — are closely interconnected in Paul's mind and experience. When the gospel of the sending and dying of God's Son is preached and believed, those who believe receive the gift of God's Spirit (e.g., Rom. 5:1-8; Gal. 3:1-5). In fact, the Spirit of God is, for Paul, the Spirit of Christ (e.g., Rom. 8:9); it is "the Spirit of his [God's] Son" whom the Father has sent into believers' hearts (Gal. 4:6). Thus any true experience of the Spirit must be an experience of the Spirit of Christ, which is why Paul can say that both Christ and the Spirit live in believers.

It is highly unlikely that the super-apostles were actually preaching a message with an obviously bizarre understanding of Jesus and the Spirit. What is very likely, however, is that Paul saw a massive incongruence between their gospel and their lifestyle (since for Paul an apostle *was* his or her message, and vice versa), between a message of Christ's death for sin(s) and a preoccupation with powerful manifestations of the Spirit. Is this grounds for a charge of heresy? Yes, it is, at least for Paul, if it amounts to a repudiation of the cross as both the foundation and the form of life in Christ. To disassociate the powerful, resurrected Christ from the crucified Christ is to preach another Jesus; to separate the Spirit of God from the Spirit of cruciformity is to preach a spirit other than the Spirit of the Son given by God; and to abandon the crucified Christ and the God-given Spirit of cruciformity is to offer another gospel.

The Content of the Boasting (11:5-11)

It is this necessary confluence of cruciformity and apostleship that leads Paul immediately to focus on the charges of being "untrained in speech" (11:6) and inappropriately offering his gospel "free of charge" (11:7). He contends that neither of these aspects of his ministry renders him inferior to the super-apostles, however (11:5).

Paul does not fight the charge about his speech; in fact, his lack of showy rhetoric is for him a necessary corollary to his belief in the power of God operating in weakness (cf. 1 Cor. 2:1-5). But what he claims to possess — and (implicitly) what the super-apostles lack — is "knowledge" (11:6). This refers not to esoteric knowledge from special revelations (which both he and the super-apostles claim to have), but to the true "knowledge of God" (10:5), the "knowledge of the glory of God in the face of Jesus Christ" (4:6). In separating the Spirit from Christ crucified, the super-apostles reveal their lack of true knowledge of God.

The charge of offering the gospel free of charge Paul does not resist either. This accusation cuts even more to the heart of his ministry, as 1 Corinthians 9 especially reveals. The super-apostles and some of the (especially wealthier) Corinthians may have felt it shameful for a teacher and supposed apostle not to accept money from those he taught *and* to humiliate himself further by working with his hands. Paul, however, saw his voluntary self-humbling as a way of conforming to his Lord, as both this text and 1 Corinthians 9:19 reveal, each echoing Philippians 2:6-8 and 2 Corinthians 8:9:

> . . . humbling myself [*emauton tapeinōn*] so that you might be exalted.
>
> (2 Cor. 11:7)

> For though I am free with respect to all, I have made myself a slave [*emauton edoulōsa*] to all, so that I might win more of them. (1 Cor. 9:19)

> though he was in the form of God,
>   [Christ Jesus] did not regard equality with God
>   as something to be exploited,
> but emptied himself,
>   taking the form of a slave [*doulou*],
>   being born in human likeness.
> And being found in human form,
>   he humbled himself [*etapeinōsen heauton*]
>   and became obedient to the point of death —
>   even death on a cross. (Phil. 2:6-8)

> Though he [our Lord Jesus Christ] was rich, yet for your sakes he became poor, so that by his poverty you might become rich. (2 Cor. 8:9)

Was this a sin? Paul asks (11:7). He lowered himself for their 'exaltation,' for their enrichment, for their salvation, for their service (11:8), in order not to be a burden (11:9). This modus operandi, which Paul maintained and will continue to maintain as his boast (11:10; cf. 1 Cor. 9:15-18), was motivated solely by love, he claims — that is, by Christ's cruciform love that compels him (5:14). In fact, Paul is so committed to this principle of not being supported by those to whom he is directly ministering, he confesses to the crime of 'robbing' the Macedonian churches (11:8-9; though it is not clear that he actually asked for the gift they gave).

True versus False Boasting (11:12-15)

Thus doing manual labor (and accepting an occasional gift from elsewhere) to offer the gospel freely is Paul's boast, his modus operandi, and he has every intention of keeping the tradition alive despite the criticisms of the super-apostles. In fact, he will continue this approach to ministry precisely *because* of the super-apostles, "in order to deny [them] an opportunity . . . to be recognized as our equals in what they boast about" (11:12). In other words, if Paul were to stop working and start accepting money from those to whom he preaches, he would be stooping to the level of the false apostles and their boast, thereby disassociating himself from the self-humbling of Christ.

It is for this reason that Paul now magnifies the nasty portrait of the rivals that is only hinted at in the sarcastic epithet "super-apostles" (11:5). They are, to borrow a term from Philippians, "enemies of the cross" (Phil. 3:18), boasting in the wrong things, opposing the gospel and the Spirit of Christ crucified. Thus they are "false apostles, deceitful workers" who masquerade (NIV, NAB) as apostles of Christ and agents of righteousness (11:13-15) but are really ministers of Satan, the deceiver. On the one hand, this kind of language is standard fare for ancient rhetoric. On the other, however, Paul intends it to be taken with utmost seriousness; the validity of the Corinthians' relationship with Christ is at stake (13:5). The fate of the false apostles is, of course, already sealed (11:15).

Paul has been blunt, even graphic. But he is not through. There is still much to boast about.

PAUL'S SECOND SPEECH OF FOOLISH BOASTING: PAUL'S VARIOUS WEAKNESSES (11:16–12:10)

This part of 2 Corinthians, often called Paul's 'Fool's Speech,' is the most potent section of these four rhetorically and theologically powerful chapters. Not only that, but his speech is among the best examples of forensic rhetoric in all ancient literature. In it Paul does battle with the super-apostles, and he does so (obviously) right in front of the Corinthians. To engage in this spiritual warfare, Paul produces an amazing rhetorical arsenal: sarcasm and invective, self-praise and self-denigration, irony and paradox, *synkrisis* (comparison) and antithesis, narrative and catalog. The entire speech is a parody of his rivals' foolish, inflated self-praise for the wrong kind of status. In fact, the speech also mocks the entire Roman culture of celebrating power in accomplishments, offering instead a celebration of divine power in human weakness.

Boasting, or self-praise, was a convention of Roman life. The gods, emperors, generals, and city patrons all bragged, publicly listing their glorious achievements (such as the imperial *res gestae*, 'things accomplished') for all to hear or see. So, too, Paul now lists his powerful feats, his military successes; only they turn out — when measured according to human standards — to be weaknesses, defeats, and failures. Thus Paul is following convention only inasmuch as he is challenging it. His real boast is not in himself but in Christ the Lord, whose power is manifested in Paul's weakness, whose life is visible in Paul's dying (12:9; cf. 4:7-12).

The whole speech is dominated by the language of boasting, and weakness, and foolishness. Forms of the Greek words for 'boast/boasting/being elated' appear fifteen times, 'weak/weakness' nine times, and 'fool/foolishness' six times.[14] The *propositio* of the speech, and indeed of the book, appears in the last words: "whenever I am weak, then I am strong" (12:10). It develops, therefore, Paul's claims in 1 Corinthians 1:18–2:5 that God's foolishness and weakness, manifested in Christ's cross, are necessarily and appropriately manifested also in Paul's ministry.

Introduction (11:16-21a)

Paul introduces the speech proper with a plea for the Corinthians' indulgence as he steps out of character (and, in effect, out of Christ, 11:17) and deliberately makes a fool of himself (11:16-21a). His rationale is simple (11:18): to follow the example of others (the super-apostles) who boast, specifically bragging "according to the flesh" (NAB) — according to "human standards" (NRSV). After all, he adds sarcastically, the "wise" Corinthians (1 Cor. 4:10; 10:15) will tolerate any old fool (11:19)! For they have been tolerating these birds of prey (11:20, described in five unflattering images) — so-called apostles who take the Corinthians' money in the name of Christ. But Paul and his team were too "weak" to ex-

---

14. 'Boast/boasting/being elated': 11:16, 17, 18 (twice), 21 (twice), 30 (twice); 12:1, 5 (twice), 6, 7 (twice), 9; 'weak/weakness': 11:21, 29 (twice), 30; 12:5, 9 (twice), 10 (twice); 'fool/foolishness': 11:16 (twice), 17, 19, 21; 12:6.

press such power (11:21a)! These opening words, together with the first speech (11:7-11) and the postscript in 12:13, demonstrate how problematically central was the issue of Paul's refusing the Corinthians' money.

The Weaknesses of the Warrior-Minister (11:21b-33)

Emphasizing once again his playing the fool (11:21b), Paul attacks the super-apostles' proud résumé by taking on two central claims (11:22-23): their Jewish-ness (expressed in three ways) and their status as ministers *(diakonoi)* of the Messiah (Christ). If they are Jewish (perhaps claiming to represent the 'true' faith and/or the Jerusalem apostles), so is Paul (11:22). That settled, Paul moves on to what really matters — the criteria of ministerial status, or apostleship (11:23). Admitting now to speaking as if insane (11:23), Paul launches into his great catalog of tribulations (11:23-29). Though it begins formally as a compari-son to the other 'apostles,' it is clear not only that Paul will win the contest of tribulations by a landslide, but even more importantly that these interlopers are engaged in an entirely different contest, one that does not measure apostolic success in terms of weakness, which is Paul's — and apparently God's — crite-rion (11:30; 12:5, 10).

Paul the 'warrior' now lists his military accomplishments; the servant summarizes his service. The character of the list as a whole sounds very similar to the fate of the Lord he serves. The catalog is carefully structured as follows:

- *uncounted tribulations* (11:23b) — these four general features of Paul's life are so common as to be beyond counting: years of hard labor; imprison-ments; floggings (probably referring to mob, rather than official, action); and various near-death experiences (such as the one narrated in 1:8-11).
- *enumerated adversities* (11:24-26a) — these six items are counted (the last one loosely): five occasions of official synagogue flogging, each of which would have been nearly lethal; three incidents of official Roman beatings (even bothersome citizens were sometimes illegally flogged); one stoning; three shipwrecks; one short adventure adrift at sea; and frequent trips that were tiring and dangerous (see 11:27).
- *dangers* (the rest of 11:26) — most of which are related to the trips, and in-clude various locations and forces (both natural and human): rivers, seas, wilderness regions, and population centers; bandits, Jews, Gentiles, and "false brothers and sisters."
- *difficult conditions* (11:27) — a variety of physical pains and deprivations: hard work (meaning primarily, one suspects, working with his hands); sleeplessness; hunger and thirst; exposure to the elements.

- *anxiety for the churches* (11:28-29) — daily anxiety, including a deep sense of sharing in the weaknesses of, and attacks on, the churches.

While most of these kinds of trials are recounted in Acts and many are listed elsewhere, nowhere else is their quantity or intensity as fully depicted as here.

Before recounting one last incident in some detail, Paul inserts a word about the most important principle of the speech: that he will boast (the future tense sounds like an oath, as 11:31 confirms) only in "the things that show my weakness" (11:30). This leads to a rehearsal of Paul's experience (cf. Acts 9:23-25) of being let down a wall in a basket to escape from Damascus during the reign of King Aretas IV (died A.D. 40). This brief narrative confirms Paul's assertion that God's resurrection power and life appear in situations of weakness and death (cf. 1:8-11; 12:9-10), illustrates the consistency of Paul's cruciform life (over a period of some fifteen years), and contributes to the notion of Paul the warrior. One of the great glories of Roman battle was to be the first to climb the enemy's city wall and thereby enter the city. Such courage and military success were rewarded with a golden crown, the *corona muralis*, or 'crown for the wall.' In a stunning reversal of values, Paul claims that he has experienced the power of God in the weakness of going *down* the wall. That is, for him, a kind of *corona muralis*.

Power in Weakness (12:1-10)

Curiously, Paul next narrates a rather different experience, but also one from the past. In fact, since 2 Corinthians 10–13 was almost certainly written in the mid-50s, and the basket experience occurred shortly before 40, then the heavenly trip of 12:1-4 ("fourteen years ago," 12:2) took place not long after the Damascus escape. As we will see shortly, this chronology may help to explain why Paul tells these two stories back-to-back.

The heavenly trip, a visionary-revelatory experience, has been the focus of intense study for many years, as has the "thorn . . . in the flesh" (12:7) that followed it. It is almost universally agreed that Paul himself is the "person in Christ" (12:2) who had this experience; his use of third-person ('he' not 'I') language to narrate it may be due in part to rhetorical conventions of the day and in part to his hesitation about boasting in what might appear to be 'power' rather than weakness. Nevertheless, it is clear from the context that Paul feels 'forced' to boast about having had "visions and revelations of the Lord" (12:1) in order to demonstrate not only his equality but his superiority to the super-apostles (12:11-12). What ultimately matters to Paul are his weaknesses, for no other boast counts for anything (12:1). Yet he wants the Corinthians to know that no matter what criterion of apostleship the interlopers put forward, he can meet it — visions and revelations, signs and wonders (12:12), or whatever.

The trip itself, though Paul furnishes few details, is not unlike other ancient Jewish (and some non-Jewish) accounts of being "caught up" (12:2, 4) to heaven. Paul's experience may or may not have been a physical journey, he says parenthetically (12:3), but it is reminiscent of other visionary experiences that are referred to as *Merkabah* (from the Hebrew for 'chariot') experiences: mystical encounters with the glory of God in heaven. This is not Paul's call/conversion experience, for he was already in Christ when this took place.

Paul briefly narrates the journey either in two stages or, more likely, twice (v. 2, then vv. 3-4), the second time making it clear that "the third heaven" (12:2) is God's abode of "Paradise" and not merely the third of some seven heavens (as some Jews believed there to be). What, if anything, Paul saw, he does not describe, and what he heard he is not permitted to describe (12:4). But it was obviously an incredible, 'boast-worthy' experience (12:6-7) that would surpass anything the super-apostles had to offer. And it is not unique; he has had others equally stunning (12:7). Paul, however, maintains the principle that he will boast only in his weaknesses — what is seen and heard in him, not in heaven (12:5-7a).

Which is why, he says twice for emphasis, he was given the "thorn": "to keep me from being too elated" (12:7).[15] Its purpose was humility and dependence on God. There are at least three key questions about the phrase "thorn . . . in the [NIV, 'my'] flesh" (12:7; *skolops tē sarki*). What is the thorn? Who gave it? and, Is it "in the flesh" or 'against the flesh'?

The Thorn

Over the centuries the candidates for the identity of the thorn have been numerous: a physical illness (malaria, eye problems, epilepsy, headaches, etc.); a physical defect or disfigurement; a speech impediment; an emotional illness or depression; a spiritual torment or temptation; rejection; suffering and persecution; or his opponents. Drawing on parallels from the Dead Sea Scrolls, a significant number of recent commentators have identified the thorn as Paul's opponents, specifically (at the moment) the super-apostles.

Whatever the answer, Paul terms the thorn "a messenger of Satan," indicating its adversarial character, and yet he also says it "was given to me" (12:7), the phrasing of which suggests its divine origin. (In ancient Jewish theology, it was not impossible, however, for God and Satan to appear to 'work together' in

---

15. The phrase is rendered only once in the NIV, but twice in the NRSV and NAB, because of differences in manuscripts.

adversity; witness Job.) No less confusing is the reference to the flesh, for even though few translations reveal it, the phrase could mean something like 'to guard against the flesh.' That translation is especially attractive in light of the references to false evaluations according to the flesh, or standard human values, in the context (10:2, 3; 11:18; cf. 1:17; 5:16).

As attractive as the 'opponents' thesis is, the context suggests that Paul's 'thorn in the flesh' is the life of tribulation he must face, which is both a gift from God (the gracious gift/privilege of sharing in Christ's sufferings, Phil. 1:29) and the work of the adversary. It is tribulation that will prevent him from being overelated about visions and evaluating things "according to the flesh," as the super-apostles do (11:18). It is tribulation that will teach Paul the sufficiency of God's grace and give him true experiences of Christ's power, the power of power in weakness (12:9-10). Paul's thorn, the thing from which he asked deliverance three times (12:8) but about which he is now content, is identified in context as his "weaknesses" (12:9-10), the broad range of his "weaknesses, insults, hardships, persecutions, and calamities for the sake of Christ" (12:10). About the revelation in heaven, Paul can say nothing, but the revelation that matters to him, and that he passes on to the Corinthians and us, is the one he received after the journey to heaven. Noting Paul's careful choice of interconnected words, we could render his account of this revelation like this (12:9-10):

> The Lord said to me, "My grace is sufficient for you, for [my] power is brought to full expression in weakness." I therefore vow that I will boast all the more gladly in my weaknesses in order that Christ's power may dwell in me as the presence and power of God dwelt in Israel's tabernacle. Therefore I am content in all sorts of weaknesses — insults, hardships, persecutions, and calamities — for Christ, for *whenever* [so, rightly, NRSV] I am weak, then I am strong with the power of Christ.

Paul learned of this power, perhaps for the first time, in the Damascus basket incident. The subsequent trip to Paradise (presumably his first, though not his last) seemed like a radical alternative way of experiencing the power of God. Which would be the norm for Paul's life? The divine answer is the gift of weakness and tribulation; that is the norm for and the essence of apostolic existence, the criterion of authenticity that both transcends and authenticates all other experiences of God's presence and power. The "thorn" therefore certainly includes persecution (and therefore, loosely, 'opponents'), but it is more than that. It is a way of life in conformity to Christ that is intended to keep ministers from being too "elated" — that is, from evaluating things in human terms. The thorn is thus probably to be understood as a thorn *against* the flesh. As such, it is a help *for* the Spirit, enabling the minister to recognize that the Spirit of God is the Spirit of Christ, and that the Spirit who works miracles (12:12; cf. Gal. 3:3-5), the God who lives in Paradise, is revealed in the cross of the Son and in the cruciformity of all "ministers of Christ" (11:23).

Paul, then, knows in experience an unusual power — the power of Christ (12:9), which is the power of the Spirit, the gracious power of God. In Philippians he will say he has learned to cope with anything, even suffering and imprisonment, because of this grace and power: "I can do all things through him who strengthens [lit. 'empowers'] me" (Phil. 4:13). Here, in 2 Corinthians, he says he possesses an "extraordinary power" from God by which "the life of Jesus" is manifested in his affliction and persecution (4:7-12).

Paul's writings contain numerous pithy sayings that could serve as his life motto, but few express himself and his mission better than this: "Whenever I am weak, then I am strong."

CONCLUSION TO THE SPEECHES (12:11-13)

Paul has finished his two speeches of foolish boasting. He confesses to the foolish self-commendation into which he has felt forced because the Corinthians did not stick up for him before the super-apostles (12:11). They have essentially abandoned him, but no matter how much of a 'nobody' ("nothing," 12:11) Paul feels himself to be, or appears to others, he is superior to the super-apostles *by virtue of his conformity to Christ.* Yes, as 12:1-10 has just demonstrated, Paul has the formal credentials of apostles — not only visions and revelations but also all sorts of miracles (12:12). The super-apostles cannot beat him at this power game either.

What really matters now to Paul, however, is the old question of finances and manual labor. The Corinthians do not know how good they have had it. In their apostle they have lacked nothing — no mighty works or other apostolic signs — except the burden of having to support him (12:13). To seal the rhetorical outburst of the past several chapters, Paul now expresses one final word of sarcasm: "Forgive me this wrong!" (12:13; cf. 11:7). Yet even this is offered in love, for Paul, as the next section reveals, has spent himself, and will continue to do so, for the edification of the Corinthians (12:15, 19).

FINAL SUMMARY, WARNINGS, APPEALS, AND GREETINGS (12:14–13:13)

If we imagine 2 Corinthians in part as a piece of forensic rhetoric that has the air of a courtroom drama, then Paul has now rested his case — or so it seems.

He has been both the defense and the prosecution, explaining and defending his own ministry and then (or sometimes simultaneously) attacking that of the pseudoapostles.

It remains for him to give a summation of the entire 'case' — the situation as it stands. Paul does so by relating what he has said to the possibility of yet another visit to Corinth. But in the course of this discussion, it becomes clear that Paul has not really rested his case. Now the focus of his prosecution, however, shifts from the super-apostles to the Corinthians themselves. As in 1 Corinthians 4:14-21, Paul the spiritual father may need to come to discipline his wayward children severely, though that is not his desire.

Talk of a third visit dominates these closing remarks (12:14, 20; 13:1-2, 10). The first mention of it leads once again to the financial question of Paul's support (12:14-18). From several angles Paul reiterates his principled rejection of Corinthian support for his ministry among them (12:14-15; cf. 11:9): (1) he will not burden them; (2) he wants them, not their money; (3) parents save and spend for their children, not vice versa; (4) his self-support is his expression of love — something to be appreciated by the Corinthians (12:15). Taken together, the appropriately financial images of supporting children and 'spending and being spent' are Paul's way of saying that he wants to love the Corinthians in a godlike and Christlike (cf. 8:9; 9:8-10) way.

Even with this claim granted, Paul must return to the subject of the collection, for if he did not burden the Corinthians, perhaps he tricked them (12:16-18). A series of four rhetorical questions and a brief refresher about Paul's sending Titus and a (Macedonian) brother are intended to defend Paul and his team against charges that the collection was intended for their own pockets.

This defensive tone, which dominates not only here but the entire letter, might make the recipients of the letter think Paul is just engaged in self-centered self-justification (12:19a). Paul assures the Corinthians that self-defense is at best a penultimate goal of his ministry and of this letter; as always, Paul claims, whatever he and his team do, it is for the loving edification of the Corinthians (12:19b). He fears, in fact, that their possible rejection of him will mean a rejection of the demands of the gospel — and past experience with the Corinthians renders such concern legitimate. Will they return — or have they already returned — to the errant ways (12:20-21) he dealt with at length in 1 Corinthians? If Paul finds this to be the case when he goes back to Corinth, he will be humiliated (12:21), and as displeasing to them as they will be to him (12:19).

More specifically, this means a third visit could be a visitation of divine judgment executed through Paul (13:1-4). Unrepented sin (13:2), witnessed by the biblically required two or three witnesses (Deut. 19:15) of Paul's visits (and perhaps letters or reports), will hardly result in leniency (13:2) but in a display of apostolic authority hitherto unknown to the Corinthians. Paul will never renege on his commitment to cruciform ministry, but just as he can list his revelations and miracles as part of his apostolic résumé, so also he can and will exercise his divinely granted power to discipline his children (13:2-4; cf. 13:10). Not to do so would be an abdication of his fatherly and ambassadorial duties. The crucified Christ is now the living Christ, and he cannot be repudiated in his church without consequence.

But such a visit is not Paul's preference, so he invites the Corinthians to "examine" and "test" themselves to see if they are truly "in the faith" (13:5 NIV, correctly; NRSV, "living in the faith"; NAB, "living in faith"). In context this phrase seems synonymous with 'in Christ,' for Paul reminds the Corinthians that Christ is in (or among) them unless they fail the test. This is not meant to be a puzzle or a tautology; Paul's point is that the essence of being the church is to be indwelt by Christ, but the only proof of that reality is a life in the faith, a life in conformity to Christ as preached by Paul and his team. If they fail to live faithfully in Christ — accepting Paul as their apostle and forsaking their misdeeds — then Paul and his team will have been failures (13:6) and, more importantly, the Corinthians will have missed the boat (13:7).

Merging themes from both of his extant letters to the Corinthians, Paul closes his remarks with an expression of hope for the Corinthians' 'strength' and 'perfection.' In a word, he wants their obedience, not really to him but to Christ, and not for his sake but for their own. Apostolic authority cuts both ways: to judge and to edify; Paul wants only to do the latter (13:10).

The letter concludes with a series of short appeals summarizing the letter as a whole, with a brief exchange of greetings and a benediction. Here (as throughout this entire last section of the letter) we find that the ultimate goal of 2 Corinthians is not Paul's defense but the Corinthians' edification and coming together (13:11). The series of four short exhortations in 13:11 receives a variety of nuances in the various translations; the point, however, is for the Corinthians to rally around Paul's admonitions in a spirit of peace and unity with the mind of Christ (unity in Paul being connected to Christlikeness; cf. Phil. 2:2; 4:2; Rom. 15:5). Only this response to Paul's letter will guarantee the ongoing presence of the loving, peacemaking God they have encountered in Paul's gospel ministry (13:11).

After the greetings (13:12) appears the well-known trinitarian benediction of 13:13 (v. 14 in NIV). In the context of 2 Corinthians, this is no accident. The Corinthians' experience of God, like that of all of Paul's churches, was an experience of one God known in God the Father, Jesus Christ the Son, and the one Spirit of the Father and the Son. This experience has already been celebrated near the beginning of the letter (1:3-11 and 18-22, esp. 1:21-22), such that the letter's opening and closing constitute an *inclusio* of this trinitarian experience of God.

It is a *koinōnia* — a "fellowship" (NAB, NIV) or "communion" (NRSV) — created by the Spirit among believers that is known most fully in the sharing of suffering and consolation (1:3-7) and in the sharing of resources (8:3-4; 9:13). In such fellowship, believers participate in the Lord's grace of generosity (8:9; 9:14) and in his all-sufficient powerful grace in times of weakness (12:9-10). In these circumstances the love of God in Christ, seen first in the cross and now in the cruciform lives of apostles and ordinary brothers and sisters, makes itself known and urges the community on (5:14).

Summary of Chapters 10–13

In these rhetorically powerful chapters, Paul engages simultaneously in the work of defense and prosecuting attorneys, skillfully arguing that:

- Ministry in Christ can be depicted in terms of being a spiritual warrior (assailing opposition to Christ crucified and taking thoughts captive to him) and the father of the bride (responsible for presenting the church spotless to its husband).
- So-called ministers who practice self-praise, flaunt power, and burden people (especially financially) preach a foreign gospel with a different, nonexistent Jesus and Spirit.
- Paul's ministry to the Corinthians was always done out of love for their edification, including especially his refusal of financial support, which is his perpetual boast and a form of identification with Christ crucified.
- Weaknesses and tribulations are the most fundamental element of Paul's apostolic life and the fundamental means of authenticating any and all apostles.
- Paul has evidence of the other accepted signs of apostleship — visions and miracles — but his apostolic modus operandi is epitomized in the motto "Whenever I am weak, then I am strong."
- Paul's preference for loving edification does not deny the possibility of his exercising judgment on his wayward children if they continue effectively to betray their life in Christ.

THE STORY IN FRONT OF THE LETTER

Some Readings of 2 Corinthians

"What an admirable Epistle is the second to the Corinthians, how full of affections. He [Paul] joys, and he is sorry, he grieves, and he glories. Never was there such care

333

of a flock expressed, save in the great shepherd of the fold, who first shed tears over Jerusalem, and afterwards his blood."

> George Herbert, *The Country Parson*, p. 63, ca. 1630, cited in Ernest Best, *Second Corinthians*, Interpretation (Atlanta: John Knox, 1987), p. 4 (slightly altered)

"[E]xegesis dare not allow itself to be misled into explaining the letter as an essentially biographical document or making its goal a portrait of Paul's personality, for Paul conceives his writing throughout as an apostolic writing. . . . Paul's person is at issue only insofar as he is bearer of the apostolic office, and the theme of the epistle is the apostolic office. . . . An exegesis which intends to pursue the peculiar intention of the letter thus has as its real object of understanding in the apostolic office or, since it is primarily the office of proclamation, in the word of proclamation. What is Christian proclamation, both as to content and execution?"

> Rudolf Bultmann, *The Second Letter to the Corinthians*, trans. Roy A. Harrisville (Minneapolis: Augsburg, 1985), p. 16

"Paul's conviction about the death and resurrection of Christ is used metaphorically to reconstitute his adversity-filled life by means of the death/resurrection life structure; his adversities are to be understood as a dying which brings life. He thus presents the main address of the gospel itself. As the cross will not be fitted into reigning understandings of reality, so also Paul's life will not be fitted into preset understandings of power and value. As an expression of God's actions in the death and resurrection of Christ, Paul's ministry forces a reexamination of the self. . . . Like the gospel, Paul's ministry calls the hearer into question by its very form; and this is what provides its legitimacy."

> Steven J. Kraftchick, "Death in Us, Life in You: The Apostolic Medium," in *Pauline Theology*, vol. 2, *1 and 2 Corinthians*, ed. David M. Hay (Minneapolis: Fortress, 1993), pp. 156-81, here 177

"[T]he greater part of his [Paul's] teachings about ministry stand as a model and an inspiration to subsequent generations of missionaries and pastors. His comments about ministry — that at its heart lie endurance and patience, sacrifice and service, love of the churches, fidelity to the gospel, sincerity before God, and, above all, a rejection of triumphalism with its accompanying pride — remain throughout the aeon to shape and direct the lives of the Lord's servants. Paul's ministry as sufferer and servant is precisely modeled on that of Jesus, and finds it[s] legitimacy in the face of detraction and opposition for just that reason, as also must ours, if that is our calling. Thus 2 Corinthians may be bracketed with the Pastoral Letters in its applicability to the work of those whose vocation it is to serve God as his ministers."

> Paul Barnett, *The Second Epistle to the Corinthians,* New International Commentary on the New Testament (Grand Rapids: Eerdmans, 1997), p. 50

"In . . . 2 Corinthians, personal relations, modest goals and purposes, and even what some might consider rather petty matters are the occasion for grand theological reflections. . . . Throughout 2 Corinthians, and indeed across all his correspondence, he [Paul] has no interest in theological notions for their own sake, but only as they engage life, as they bear on the way people comport themselves. His theologizing, therefore, is never abstract or abstruse; instead it is always engaged, always linked to life as real people — he and his hearers — are experiencing it."

> J. Paul Sampley, "The Second Letter to the Corinthians," in *The New Interpreter's Bible,* ed. Leander E. Keck et al. (Nashville: Abingdon, 2000), 11:1-180, here 3, 21

QUESTIONS FOR REFLECTION

1. In many ways this letter is about ministry. Paul depicts the character of ministry in a series of images (e.g., apostle, one who 'dies' to bring life to others, ambassador, etc.). How might these images inform, or not inform, contemporary ministry?

2. For Paul ministry is a 'two-way street,' a relationship of mutuality in which both parties are conduits of divine blessing (e.g., comfort). In what sense is this still true, or ought it still to be true, today?

3. In what contemporary ways do people claiming to be ministers of Christ display their own obsession with greed and power (spiritual or other)? How does Paul's gospel address this matter?

4. How can a believer or church that does not suffer — such as most in the Western world — fully understand, appreciate, and affirm the promise of glory (resurrection and being with Christ after death)?

5. What does Paul's focus on 'reconciliation' suggest about the nature of contemporary Christian ministry and life together?

6. The subject of money does not always find a welcome home in church circles. What are some of the contemporary issues related to stewardship, and how might Paul's spirituality of cruciform grace and generosity address them?

7. In what ways, if any, do contemporary Christians (laypeople, ministers, theologians) disjoin the Spirit of God and the Spirit of Christ in their theology and/or praxis? How might Paul's perspective contribute to their reunion?

8. What are some of the actual or potential contemporary manifestations of cruciform ministry in parallel to Paul's self-support and general practice of 'spending and being spent' for others? What difficulties and/or potential dangers might exist in a theology and practice of cruciform ministry?

9. Is a spirituality of 'power in weakness' restricted only to 'ministers'? How might it be practiced by ordinary Christians today? What are the challenges of this approach to spirituality in our culture and churches?

10. How do you respond to the interpretations of 2 Corinthians quoted above?

11. In sum, what does this letter urge the church to believe, to hope for, and to do?

FOR FURTHER READING AND STUDY

General

Barrett, C. K. *A Commentary on the Second Epistle to the Corinthians.* Harper's New Testament Commentary. New York: Harper and Row, 1973. A classic exposition, with attention to Corinthian theology and Pauline agony.

Best, Ernest. *Second Corinthians.* Interpretation. Atlanta: John Knox, 1987. A brief treatment focusing on internal church tensions then and now.

Danker, Frederick W. *II Corinthians.* Augsburg Commentary on the New Testament. Minneapolis: Augsburg, 1989. A helpful analysis with emphasis on the letter's cultural context.

Hafemann, Scott J. *2 Corinthians.* NIV Application Commentary. Grand Rapids: Zondervan, 2000. An analysis with special attention to the contemporary meaning of the text.

Lambrecht, Jan. *Second Corinthians.* Sacra Pagina. Collegeville, Minn.: Liturgical Press, 1998. A succinct commentary on the letter as a unified document, attentive to its theological and autobiographical dimensions.

Matera, Frank E. *2 Corinthians.* New Testament Library. Louisville: Westminster John Knox, 2003. An insightful commentary that highlights Paul's theological concerns in context, arguing for the letter's unity.

Sampley, J. Paul. "The Second Letter to the Corinthians." In *The New Interpreter's Bible,* edited by Leander E. Keck et al., 11:1-180. Nashville: Abingdon, 2000. A theologically, exegetically, and homiletically rich commentary with careful consideration of Paul's opponents.

Witherington, Ben. *Conflict and Community at Corinth: A Socio-Rhetorical Commen-*

tary on 1 and 2 Corinthians. Grand Rapids: Eerdmans, 1995. A commentary on the letter in its social context, arguing for the letter's rhetorical unity.

Technical

Barnett, Paul. *The Second Epistle to the Corinthians.* New International Commentary on the New Testament. Grand Rapids: Eerdmans, 1997. A thorough study with a special focus on Paul's understanding of ministry in one unified letter.

Furnish, Victor P. *II Corinthians.* Anchor Bible 32A. Garden City, N.Y.: Doubleday, 1984. A very balanced and insightful commentary, rich in historical and theological interpretation, that supports a two-letter hypothesis.

Hay, David M., ed. *Pauline Theology.* Vol. 2, *1 and 2 Corinthians.* Minneapolis: Fortress, 1993. A collection of insightful scholarly essays from various perspectives.

Martin, Ralph P. *2 Corinthians.* Word Biblical Commentary 40. Waco, Tex.: Word, 1986. A standard, detailed commentary on the Greek text, arguing for two letters focusing on Paul's apostolic ministry.

Thrall, Margaret E. *A Critical and Exegetical Commentary on the Second Epistle to the Corinthians.* International Critical Commentary. 2 vols. Edinburgh: T. & T. Clark, 1994, 1998. A careful, thorough treatment.

CHAPTER 12

ROMANS

Gentile and Jew in Cruciform
Covenant Community

Christ has become a servant of the circumcised on behalf of the truth of
God in order that he might confirm the promises given to the patriarchs,
and in order that the Gentiles might glorify God for his mercy.

Rom. 15:8-9

Romans is arguably the most influential letter ever written. It is certainly the most significant letter in the history of Christianity. Romans has spawned conversions, doctrines, disputations, and even a few reformations, and it has done so quite ecumenically and with a kind of domino effect.

A text from Romans (13:13-14) provoked the conversion of Augustine as he picked up a Bible and opened to that page of Paul's letter. An Augustinian monk named Martin Luther had his theological furniture rearranged by his reading of Romans ("the most important document in the New Testament . . . the gospel in its purest expression" [*Preface to Romans*]; "I was reborn by reading it"). And an Anglican priest called John Wesley, later to become the founder of Methodism, was converted to Christ in a church on Aldersgate Street after hearing a presentation on Luther's *Preface to Romans*.

There is more. A Swiss theologian named Karl Barth in the early twentieth century inaugurated a theological revival by dropping "a bombshell on the playground of the liberal theologians" (as someone has said) — with a commentary on Romans. And the renewal of interest in Paul and Romans has sparked endless ecumenical conversations about 'faith and works,' resulting in significant theological convergence and a joint 1999 Roman Catholic–Lutheran "Declaration on

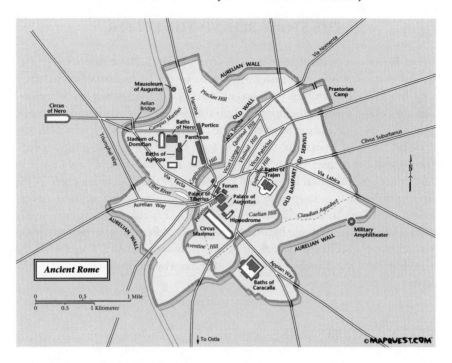

the Doctrine of Justification." The reader and commentator ought, therefore, to approach this document with a mixture of anticipation and trepidation.

How and why has one letter made such an impact? That is a difficult, if not impossible, question to answer. The most obvious answer cites the theological breadth and depth of the document. Luther's colleague Melanchthon called Romans "a compendium of the Christian religion." It has often functioned as such. Nevertheless, this traditional theological approach to Romans has been attacked in recent decades. Augustine and Luther, it is often said, misread Romans, and perhaps, to some extent, they did. But let those who are without sin cast the first stone; who has not misread this very complex document? And while the letter is in fact occasional — the Roman believers were real people with real problems — it is also undeniably Paul's most systematic presentation of his gospel. In fact, as we shall see, its occasional and systematic character are logically interconnected.

Whatever its historical origins and contingencies, Romans is truly a letter for all seasons. It narrates the grace of God toward sinful humanity, both Jews and Gentiles, that creates a multicultural cruciform community of obedient faith issuing in generous love and expectant hope.

THE STORY BEHIND THE LETTER

When Paul wrote to the Roman believers from Corinth, sometime between A.D. 55 and 58 (probably in the winter of 55-56 or 56-57), he had never visited their city despite good intentions to do so (1:8-15; 15:14-33).[1] There had likely been assemblies of believers in the imperial hub that was Rome for a decade or more, perhaps even from the earliest days of the church, as especially Jewish believers traveled between Jerusalem and Rome (see Acts 2:10). As the gospel spread throughout the empire, believers of various backgrounds would have moved in and out of cosmopolitan Rome. Paul knew some of the Roman believers — the list of nearly thirty in chapter 16 is impressive, including Paul's beloved, courageous coworkers from earlier times in Corinth, Priscilla (Prisca) and Aquila (16:3-4). Perhaps (and these figures are just guesses) Paul knew 10 percent of the several hundred believers in various house churches (see 16:5). Nonetheless, he was clearly not the churches' 'spiritual father.' So why did Paul write this lengthy letter?

REASONS FOR ROMANS

The 'reasons for Romans' debate is one of the longest and most complex within modern biblical scholarship. The significance of Rome qua Rome may have been one factor, but certainly not the only or most important one. More substantive answers to the question *Why?* relate obviously to the situation of the churches in Rome, the contents of the letter itself, and Paul's mission work.

One possible key to the letter may be the likelihood of some friction between the Gentile and Jewish believers in Rome. Many scholars believe — though some, it must be mentioned, forcefully disagree — that something like the following scenario occurred in Rome in the years prior to Paul's writing of Romans. In 49 an edict of Claudius expelled the Jews (or at least many of them) from Rome because of their fighting about one "Chrestus" — in all likelihood an allusion to intra-Jewish debate over the identity and role of the Jewish Messiah and, perhaps, whether Jesus was the expected one. (For the edict, see Suetonius, *Claudius* 25.4 and Acts 18:2.) With the lack of Jewish believers for five years, Gentiles constituted the bulk, if not the entirety, of the Roman church,

---

1. The precise date of Romans within this period is disputed but not generally held to be of great consequence. The correlation of Paul's travel plans, people's names (Phoebe, Gaius, Erastus), and related data from Romans (15:25-26; 16:1-2, 23 [cf. 2 Tim. 4:20]), 1 Corinthians (1:14), and Acts (19:22; 20:1-3) makes it virtually certain that Corinth (or its vicinity) was the place of composition.

The emperor Claudius, Istanbul Museum of Archaeology

developing its leadership, mission, and theology. Upon the death of Claudius and the return of the Jews to Rome, the Gentile churches were now poised for multicultural conflict as Jewish believers tried to reconnect with their Gentile siblings in faith. Gentile believers could have developed something of an independent spirit, if not a superiority complex, while Jewish believers could now feel neglected or marginalized. Differences in beliefs and practices would have likely emerged. Was unity possible? necessary? Had the expulsion of the Jews been some sort of divine judgment? The reality of this divergence and resulting tension is described by Paul in chapters 14 and 15: Jewish believers (and perhaps more 'conservative' Gentiles) and Gentile believers (as well as more 'liberal' Jews) judging one another over diet and calendar — matters that Paul finds incidental to the gospel and the kingdom of God. The Stoics called such issues *adiaphora* — neutral, discretionary, nonessential.

If this scenario is close to accurate, then Paul's letter to the house churches in Rome is meant at least to address this situation. The theme of Romans, God's grace to Jew and Gentile alike, embodies Paul's deepest concerns and is therefore systematically unfolded. Indeed, the presentation of his gospel might have been quite different if the churches had consisted only of Gentiles.

One's reading of Romans depends to a significant degree on the part of the letter one sees as most important and as most revealing of the story behind the letter. Some interpreters place most of their emphasis on chapters 1–8 (and maybe some on the exhortations in 12–15, but little on 9–11), seeing Romans as a theological treatise on justification, sanctification, and glorification; there is no particular story behind the letter, only the grand story of salvation. Other interpreters, especially more recently, find the focus of the letter in chapters 9–11 (Paul's concern about God's fidelity and Israel's fate), or in 14:1–15:13 (Paul's concern about factions and judgmentalism), or even in 15:22-33 (Paul's interest in Roman support for his ministry). Whatever their focus, they try to relate the first part of the letter (1–8) to the second (9–16), and the letter as a whole to Paul's ministry. And most interpreters today think the letter must somehow further his missionary and/or pastoral work.

In this book's reading of the story behind the letter, significant emphasis is placed on the second half of Romans (chapters 9–16, esp. 14–15) for understanding the entire letter — even though we will devote more space to the dense theological foundation that Paul provides in the first half (1–8). If there is Jewish-Gentile conflict in the community, then the profound theology about Jew and Gentile must surely have as one of its primary goals the resolution of that conflict. Romans demonstrates, no less than any other Pauline letter, that Paul's theology always had a pastoral function; he had a formational agenda.

This does not mean that Romans has no purpose other than to resolve Jewish-Gentile friction. (In fact, some interpreters do not see conflict management as central to Paul's agenda, while others even doubt the existence of the conflict itself.) Most scholars agree that there is a variety of reasons for Romans. For instance, the letter serves as a splendid introduction to the apostle and his teaching so that the Romans will both accept him when he comes (whether or not there were already some critics of Paul in Rome) and, he no doubt hopes, support him in his mission work, especially as he heads for Spain. In the meantime, he also wants support for the collection for the poor Jewish believers in Jerusalem, and he undoubtedly desires a positive reception of his gospel and ministry when he actually goes to Jerusalem. The moral support of the Roman church would certainly help him in that regard. These goals, too, are part of Paul's commitment to the unity of Gentile and Jew in one covenant community in Christ — whether locally (in Rome) or universally (from Jerusalem to Rome and beyond).

Some interpreters want us to choose between a theological and a pastoral, or between a theological and a rhetorical, reading of Romans. Romans is, however, both pastoral and theological, both rhetorical and theological. The multivalent story behind the letter yields the comprehensive shape of the story within the letter.

THE STORY WITHIN THE LETTER

As noted above, the theme of Romans is God's grace — God's impartial faithfulness and mercy — for Jews and Gentiles that creates the eschatological, or new covenant, community through the "obedience of faith" (1:5; 16:26). This theme is announced at the outset, in what most interpreters agree is the thesis or theme statement of the letter:

> For I am not ashamed of the gospel; it is the power of God for salvation to everyone who has faith, to the Jew first and also to the Greek. For in it the righteousness of God is revealed through faith for faith; as it is written, "The one who is righteous will live by faith." (1:16-17)

Under this banner the letter proceeds to tell the story of God's faithful response to faithless humanity (chaps. 1–4); the resulting new situation for those who are justified by faith, thereby dying and rising with Christ and living in the Spirit (5–8); the question of the future fate of ethnic Israel in light of the failure of most Jews to accept the gospel (9–11); the need for the community at Rome to embody this gospel as they live cruciform lives of holiness and hospitality (12–15); and finally the relationship of all this to God's great story of salvation and Paul's mission within it (15–16).

THE 'TWO-COVENANT' INTERPRETATION

Before proceeding to the letter itself, we must acknowledge but reject one particular reading of Paul in general and Romans in particular. This interpretation, mentioned in chapter 2 on Paul's résumé, has been put forth by a very small but very vocal minority of New Testament scholars (e.g., Lloyd Gaston and John

Gager). These scholars read Paul and Romans as offering a new way for Gentiles, but not Jews, to be justified and to become part of God's people — namely, faith in Christ. Ethnic Jews, they argue, remain God's people and are justified by their keeping the Law.

The concern of these scholars to rescue Paul (and eventually, they hope, Christianity) from 'anti-Judaism' and 'supersessionism' (the idea that Christianity replaces Judaism) may be understandable. It is difficult, nevertheless, to imagine a more tortured reading of Romans, one more driven by ideology than by historical or textual reality. As one *Jewish* scholar of Paul puts it succinctly, "Keeping the Law was for Paul adiaphora [nonessential]; faith in Jesus was most certainly not!"[2]

Nothing could be clearer than the fact that Romans heralds one gospel for Jew and Gentile. It is a tapestry of texts and themes attesting to this reality: from the thematic statement about the gospel as the power of salvation for all (1:16-17), to the impartial criterion of judgment according to deeds (2:9-11), to the theme of the one God of all (e.g., 3:29; 10:12), to the charge of universal enslavement to sin (3:9), to the offer of justification and salvation to all by grace through faith (3:22, 28-30; 10:12), to the multicultural character of the church (9:24, and all of chaps. 9–11 and 14–15), to the need for Jewish and Gentile believers to tolerate cultural differences and welcome one another (14:1–15:13), to the notion of mutual benefit between Gentile and Jewish believers in the Diaspora and in Jerusalem (15:22-23). In all these texts and themes, Romans offers one gospel for all — specifically for both Jews and Gentiles (indeed, says 1:16, Jews first! cf. 2:9-10) — creating one people of God that calls upon the name of the Lord (Jesus) and is saved. Paul's efforts among the Gentiles (primarily) are to ensure that God's promise is extended to them; his gospel, however, in no way excludes Jews.

This does not make either Paul or Romans anti-Jewish or supersessionist, at least not as those terms are normally used. Paul is a Jew participating in first-century Jewish debates about what constitutes real Jewishness, about the true Israel, and about what God is up to in history. He offers a prophetic critique of the Judaism(s) of his day and a simultaneous reinterpretation of the Jewish story to include Gentiles — but that makes him only as 'anti-Jewish' as Isaiah, Hosea, Amos, Jeremiah, and Jesus. Paul is convinced that, in and through Jesus the Jewish Messiah, God has reconstituted Israel as his eschatological people of both Jews and non-Jews who are endowed with the Spirit, circumcised in the heart, and thus able to live in covenant with God and others ('fulfill the Law') — the very blessing to all nations for which Abraham had been chosen and that

2. Daniel Boyarin, *A Radical Jew: Paul and the Politics of Identity* (Berkeley: University of California Press, 1994), p. 42.

the prophets anticipated. Thus Israel is not *replaced* but *reconstituted.* Yet this reconfiguration of Israel as an *eschatologically inclusive* rather than an *ethnically exclusive* people is not fundamentally due, in Paul's mind, to some fatal flaw in Israel (though Israel has in fact "stumbled," according to Romans), but rather to the eternal promises and purposes of God.

The story of Romans — the story of the gospel for Jew and Gentile alike that Romans narrates — may be outlined as follows:

1:1-15	**Opening**	
	1:1-7	Salutation
	1:8-15	Thanksgiving
1:16-17	**Theme: The Gospel as the Power of God for the Salvation of All**	
1:18–4:25	**God's Faithful and Merciful Response to Human Sin**	
	1:18–3:20	Divine Impartiality and Human Accountability
		1:18-32 The Gentile Predicament
		2:1-16 God's Impartial Judgment according to Deeds
		2:17–3:8 The Jewish Predicament
		3:9-20 Humanity under the Power of Sin
	3:21-31	God's Faithfulness and Mercy in Christ
		3:21-26 Justification by Faith: God's, Christ's, Believers'
		3:27-31 The Exclusion of Pride
	4:1-25	The Witness of Scripture in the Example of Abraham
5:1–8:39	**The Cruciform Character of Justification by Faith**	
	5:1-11	Justification as Reconciliation through the Cross
	5:12-21	Free from Sin, under Grace
	6:1–7:6	Dead to Sin, Alive to God
	7:7–8:39	In the Spirit, Not in the Flesh
		7:7-25 Life in the Flesh
		8:1-39 Cruciform Life in the Spirit
		8:1-17 Dying to the Flesh
		8:18-39 Suffering and Glory
9:1–11:36	**God's Faithfulness and the Future of Israel**	
	9:1-29	Jewish Unbelief, Pauline Anguish, and Divine Faithfulness
		9:1-5 Paul's Anguish over Jewish Unbelief
		9:6-29 God's Freedom, Faithfulness, and Mercy
	9:30–10:21	Reaffirmation of Salvation for All through the Gospel
		9:30–10:4 The Current Situation and Paul's Prayer
		10:5-21 The Ongoing Universality of the Gospel

11:1-36   The Mystery of Mercy
    11:1-24   The Remnant and the Olive Tree
    11:25-36   The Logical and Doxological Conclusions
12:1–15:13 Faithful Living before the Faithful God:
Cruciform Holiness and Hospitality
    12:1–13:14   Holiness: A Community of Goodness and Love
        12:1-2   Cruciform Holiness
        12:3-21   Goodness and Love to All
        13:1-7   A Nonrevolutionary Community
        13:8-10   The Rule of Love
        13:11-14   The Eschatological Context
    14:1–15:13   Hospitality: A Community of Jews and Gentiles
        14:1-23   *Adiaphora,* Judgmentalism, and Account-
ability
        15:1-13   Cruciform Hospitality
15:14-33   Paul's Mission and God's Plan
16:1-27   Closing
    16:1-23   Greetings, Commendations, and Final Instructions
    16:25(24)-27 Doxology

Summaries appear after the commentary on chapters 1–4, 5–8, 9–11, and 12–16.

1:1-15. OPENING

Unknown, except by reputation, to many of the Roman believers, Paul uses the salutation and thanksgiving to establish his distinctive apostolic identity but also his commonality with the Romans. He whets their appetite to hear his gospel (1:1, 15), which he will spell out in the following chapters since he has so far "been prevented" from a personal visit (1:13).

SALUTATION (1:1-7)

As in Galatians, where his apostleship is also an issue, Paul writes this letter alone (1:1; unlike the other five undisputed letters). His long self-identification (1:1-5) focuses on both his apostleship and his gospel, while his identification of the Romans centers on their calling.

Paul is a "servant" (*doulos,* 'slave') of Christ, through whom he has received the common believers' experience of grace (cf. 5:2) as well as the particular grace to be an apostle (1:1, 5). Ultimately the source of each aspect of his identity is God, who has called him and set him apart to be an apostle (1:1). The same God has called the Roman believers (1:6-7) to be "beloved" (children), set apart as "saints" who "belong to Jesus Christ" (i.e., also as his slaves), exemplifying the meaning and truth of Paul's gospel (despite his not being their spiritual parent) as "the obedience of faith among all the Gentiles" (1:5).

These key terms — "faith," "obedience," "grace" — are drawn, of course, from Paul's gospel. The phrase "the obedience of faith" is particularly important to Romans, which not only begins but also ends with a reference to it (1:5; 16:26). As the letter unfolds, it will become clear that faith and obedience are not two separate responses to the gospel, one requiring or generating the other, but one unified response of 'obedient faith' or 'faithful obedience.' This is because the gospel is a divine and royal announcement: it is the good news from God (1:1), promised in Scripture (1:2), about God's Son (1:3). This Son was not merely a Davidic *descendant* but is, by God's resurrection of him, the promised Davidic *Messiah*, or Son of God and Lord (1:3-4). The "Spirit of holiness" powerfully at work in Christ's resurrection is the same Spirit at work in all believers, as Paul will discuss at length in chapter 8.

It is likely that in 1:3-4 Paul is citing part of an early Christian creedal tradition that speaks of Christ's exaltation. Neither the tradition nor Paul, however, holds an 'adoptionist' Christology, as some interpreters have suggested.[3] The declaration of (NRSV, NIV, "declared"), or even appointment to (NAB, "established"), messiahship/sonship is a way of describing the resurrection as God's vindication of Christ's death and the commencement of his royal messianic reign. This sort of confession, as Philippians 2:6-11 shows, does not contradict a belief in Christ's preexistent divine status (cf. also Gal. 4:4), even though preexistence is not mentioned in this particular early creed that Paul obviously affirms. The citation of early Christian tradition and the reference to Scripture (1:2) lend authority to Paul's gospel and put him on common ground with the teachers and believers in Rome.

Having identified himself, his gospel, and his readers, Paul offers the Romans grace and peace. In these first seven verses, then, Paul lets his readers know that they and he — despite their different callings — share a common gospel experience of grace understood as the obedience of faith that relates them to God the Father, Jesus the Messiah and Lord, and the Spirit of holiness. The creation of rapport based on this shared experience continues in the thanksgiving.

---

3. The belief that Christ was not the preexistent Son of God but became Son of God through 'adoption' at some later point.

THANKSGIVING (1:8-15)

In these verses Paul does three things. First, he expresses thanks for the Roman believers and the reputation of their faith (1:8). Second, he says he constantly prays for them (1:9). Third, and above all, he expresses his prayer and desire to visit them both as a fellow believer and as an apostle (1:10-15).

As an apostle, Paul is still a fellow believer, so ministry is a two-way street. He anticipates not only imparting a "spiritual gift" *(charisma)* to strengthen the Romans, but also engaging in mutual encouragement *(symparaklēthēnai)* while among them (1:11-12). Nonetheless, he cannot help but also envision an apostolic mission of reaping some "harvest" (or bearing 'fruit') as he does in all the Gentile lands, 'paying his debt' to cultured or uncultured (1:13b-15; cf. 1 Cor. 9:19-23), even though his general mode of operating is only to go to the unevangelized (15:20). Thus preaching the gospel to (or perhaps 'among') those in Rome may here mean teaching the converted as well as converting unbelievers (1:15). In any case, Paul's failure to visit Rome to date has not been due to his lack of desire but to a power outside his control (1:13a), whether satanic (cf. 1 Thess. 2:18) or, more likely here, divine.

With these words written, Paul proceeds to "proclaim the gospel" to those in Rome.

1:16-17. THEME: THE GOSPEL AS THE POWER OF GOD FOR THE SALVATION OF ALL

By most accounts, these dense verses contain the theme or thesis *(propositio)* of Romans and are therefore worthy of careful attention. In them we find a minilexicon of Paul's vocabulary as well as a host of grammatical and other interpretive issues. The key terms include "ashamed," "gospel," "power," "God," "salvation," "believe/faith" (same root, *pist-*, in Greek), "Jew" and "Greek" (Gentile), "righteousness of God," "revealed," "written," "the one who is righteous," and "live." What is noticeably absent, however, has confused some people — no direct reference to Christ. This absence points to at least two of the major interpretive issues. Is this 'justifying faith' oriented to Christ? And is there any implicit, if not explicit, reference to Christ?

The first thing Paul says is that he is "not ashamed of the gospel" because it is "the power of God for salvation to everyone who has faith" (1:16). Quite obviously this gospel can be none other than the one already announced in 1:1-4 and soon to be described in detail over the next fifteen chapters. It must be, therefore, a thoroughly christocentric gospel and 'revelation' (1:3, 17). For Paul, one cannot simply 'have faith' — even faith in the God of Israel — as if the Messiah had never come. The words "ashamed," "power," and "salvation" indicate immediately that Paul is indeed thinking of his gospel of the crucified Messiah. Writing from Corinth to the Romans, he may even be deliberately alluding to his own words sent earlier to, rather than from, Corinth:

> For the message about the cross is *foolishness* to those who are perishing, but to us who are being *saved* it is the *power* of God. . . . God decided, through the *foolishness* of our proclamation, to save those who believe. For Jews demand signs and Greeks desire wisdom, but we proclaim Christ crucified, a stumbling block to Jews and foolishness to Gentiles, but to those who are the called, both Jews and Greeks, Christ the *power* of God and the wisdom of God. . . . "Let the one who *boasts, boast* in the Lord." (1 Cor. 1:18, 21b-24, 31b, emphasis added)

That Paul is not ashamed of the gospel of Christ crucified is a deliberate understatement; he means that he *boasts* in the crucified Lord Christ and therefore in his gospel. The gospel is a power, a "force unleashed" into the world.[4] As such it accomplishes its divine task of salvation, not returning void or empty (cf. Isa. 55:11); it is a "performative utterance."[5]

Paul clearly views God's gospel and salvation as oriented to all, "to the Jew first and also to the Greek" (1:16). He knows that the one God of all humanity (3:29-30) has indeed chosen Israel, to whom and through whom came God's Law, promises, and Messiah (3:2; 9:4-5). But the divine election of Israel was ultimately for the blessing or salvation of all nations (cf. Gal. 3:6-9; Rom. 9–11). Salvation — God's deliverance of Israel, according to the Scriptures — is thus opened universally in this good news, and that is the unique thematic emphasis of Romans. The only condition for the receipt of this salvation is faith. We are wise as readers not to import our own preconceptions of words like "salvation" and "faith" into these texts. The letter itself will unpack their meaning. For now, all we need to say is that both terms are rather comprehensive in scope. Salvation for Paul, though oriented toward the future day of deliverance, is the total experience of being put into right covenantal relationship with God now, being one day raised from the dead, being acquitted on the day of judgment, and therefore having eternal life. Faith, for the hearers, is the total response of obedience to the gospel (1:5). It includes the mind, heart, and body.

The term "faith," however, leads us also to 1:17, and to the possibility that

---

4. Joseph A. Fitzmyer, *Romans*, Anchor Bible 33 (Garden City, N.Y.: Doubleday, 1993), p. 254.

5. Luke Timothy Johnson, *Reading Romans: A Literary and Theological Commentary* (New York: Crossroad, 1997), p. 25.

the notion of faith in Paul's gospel applies to more than just believers. The phrase "the righteousness of God" has been the subject of unending debates. Does it refer to something that *originates in* God (e.g., "righteousness from God," as in the NIV), or something that is *characteristic of* God (e.g., 'God's righteousness'), either a divine quality or a divine activity or both? Despite the long-standing prevalence of the former kind of interpretation, many recent scholars have argued persuasively that the latter interpretation is more often correct, including here in 1:17a. The righteousness of God probably refers to one of the most prominent divine characteristics in the Bible — *God's covenant fidelity to Israel demonstrated in saving power*. Thus the gospel is "the power of God for salvation" because its announcement reveals and makes effective the faithful, saving power of God. We will not be far off the mark if we render "the righteousness of God" as 'God's saving covenant faithfulness.'

Because the terms 'faith' and 'faithfulness' are the same in Greek *(pistis)*, it is quite possible that the very important but compact, cryptic words in 1:17a that are meant to characterize the righteousness of God[6] should be translated as including a reference to *divine* as well as human faith(fulness): 'from/out of/ through [Gk. *ek,* indicating source or agency] God's faithfulness for/toward [Gk. *eis,* indicating goal] the human response of faith.' It is also possible that the faithfulness refers not to God's generally but to Christ's specifically, in which case we could render the whole sentence as follows: 'For in the gospel, God's saving covenant faithfulness is revealed through the faith(fulness) of Christ to generate faith(fulness) among those who hear it.' Even if Paul in 1:17 means to refer to God's (not Christ's) faithfulness, he will later say that God's righteousness/faithfulness is revealed through the faithfulness of Jesus (3:22; see NRSV mg.).

If either reading of 1:17a is correct — and current scholarship suggests that one or the other is — Paul's gospel in Romans is about three forms of faith(fulness): God's, Christ's, and humanity's. Paul will return explicitly to this assertion in two later texts: his restatement of the thesis in 3:21-26 (God's faithfulness revealed in Christ's death, demanding our faith response), and the description of Christ's obedient (and therefore faithful) death in 5:12-21 followed by the response of our obedient participation in that death in 6:1-23.

The central reality of faith for Paul appears also in 1:17b, where he quotes a version of (or perhaps deliberately alters) Habakkuk 2:4. It is not certain whether Paul is saying that the one who is righteous by faith will live, the one who is righteous will live by faith, or the one who is righteous by the faith (as in 'faithfulness') of God (or Christ) will live. Although Paul would not disagree

6. NIV: "by faith from first to last"; NRSV: "through faith for faith"; NAB: "from faith to faith."

with any of these assertions (in fact, as we will see, he affirms the third one in
3:21-26), the third one is probably not the main point here. The first two interpretations are really two sides of the same coin. The life promised in the gospel
is given to those who respond to it in faith. By "faith," as noted above, Paul does
not mean mere intellectual assent, though faith includes assent to the claims of
the gospel — but also much more. Faith means complete trust in and allegiance
to the God of the covenant. It is a term of engagement and commitment.

When people do respond in faith of this kind, they become righteous —
they are justified (the two terms, like 'faith' and 'believe,' derive from one and
the same root — this time *dik-*). To be just, righteous, or justified is not to enter
a 'legal fiction,' as some call it — to be 'counted' as righteous even though one is
not. Rather, to be justified is to be in right covenantal relationship with God,
and this means to live in faith, to live faithfully to the covenant. The end result
will be acquittal on the day of judgment. That — right covenantal relations
with God now, resulting also in acquittal at the judgment — is the goal and the
result of Paul's good news.

1:18–4:25. GOD'S FAITHFUL AND
MERCIFUL RESPONSE TO HUMAN SIN

If the gospel reveals God's covenant faithfulness to save, then there obviously
must be something — in Jewish terms, some enemy — from which Jews and
Gentiles alike need to be, and through faith will be, rescued. That enemy, it
turns out, is a power within and over people that Paul calls "sin," which universally manifests its grip on humanity in all kinds of violations of the covenant
(what we call 'sins') for which people are accountable (1:18–3:20). It is Christ's
death, embodying God's covenant faithfulness and mercy (on the connection
of these in Second Temple Judaism, see, e.g., Luke 1:68-75), that deals both with
the sins and with sin (3:21-26).

But why would Paul need to inform believers — the already converted —
at length about this? His goal is pastoral; the recognition of universal (i.e., Jewish and Gentile) sin, judgment, and mercy for any who believe places Jewish
and Gentile believers alike on equal footing in debt to God's mercy and makes
them equally children of that paradigm of justification by grace through faith,
Abraham (4:1-25). There is therefore no room for arrogance in the church
(3:27-31).

DIVINE IMPARTIALITY AND
HUMAN ACCOUNTABILITY (1:18–3:20)

It is clear, despite some recent scholarly objections, that the whole of 1:18–3:20 moves toward the cluster of conclusions in 3:9-20, that all — Gentiles and Jews alike — are "under the power of sin" (3:9), that none is righteous but all sinful (3:10-18), that "the whole world" is accountable to God (3:19), and that 'works of the law' cannot be the means of justification — of establishing right covenant relations with God (3:20). Paul structures the argument toward that conclusion in *aba'* (chiastic)[7] form: the Gentile predicament (1:18-32), God's impartial judgment according to deeds (2:1-16), and the Jewish predicament (2:17–3:8). His indictment in these chapters is that all human beings are *covenantally dysfunctional,* unwilling and unable to live in covenantal relationship with God and others — and they have no excuse. The entire passage appears to be Paul's reinterpretation of Wisdom of Solomon 11–19 (a popular Jewish document written just before the time of Paul). Paul agrees with Wisdom that Gentiles are evil and God is faithful, but he disagrees with the claim that Jews are preserved from divine judgment.

Underlying this entire negative portrayal of Gentiles and Jews alike *apart from Christ,* with its stress on God's impartial judgment, is Paul's pastoral concern about the behavior of Gentiles and Jews *in* Christ. Implicit in the text is a warning against inhospitable arrogance within the churches at Rome and a reminder that believers, too, are accountable to God's judgment (14:10-12).

The Gentile Predicament (1:18-32)

Paul begins with the bad news, so to speak: what appears in 1:18-32 is both the cause and the manifestation of God's wrath — the righteous response of the holy God of the covenant to human idolatry and immorality/injustice (1:18).[8] It is important that we note that these are two general terms for human sin; they represent the violation of the basic Jewish understanding of the covenant's two great commandments, love of God and love of neighbor. People lack piety and justice, right relations with God and with others, Paul claims.

It was commonplace in Jewish thought and literature (e.g., Wisd. of Sol. 13–14) to charge Gentiles with idolatry and immorality, especially sexual immo-

---

7. 'Chiastic' means 'chi'- (or X-) shaped.
8. Gk. *asebeia* and *adikia:* for the first term NIV's "godlessness" or NAB's "impiety" is better than NRSV's "ungodliness." The NRSV, NAB, and NIV all render the second term "wickedness."

rality. That is, in part, what Paul is doing here. But he also has humanity more generally in mind, and he may in fact also have in view his Jewish readers, who would instantly recognize Gentiles in these verses but not — at least not before reading chapter 2 — themselves (though see the parallels in Jer. 2). Paul does not seem to know about the later rabbinic tradition of seven special ('Noahide,' or related to the time of Noah) commandments for Gentiles; he thinks more in terms of the Jewish covenant, even when describing Gentiles.

Paul repeatedly asserts that the basic Gentile/human problem is idolatry, and that immoralities of various kinds flow from that basic error. He begins with a kind of 'natural theology' — the claim that God's invisible "eternal power and divine nature" are revealed in the creation and can be known, such that those who do not acknowledge God "are without excuse" (1:19-20). "They" in fact knew God but did not honor or thank God as God, which led to their mental 'darkening' (1:21-22, 25, 28), then to blatant idolatry (1:23, 25), and finally to various immoralities (1:24, 26-27, 28b-31). This we may call the 'snowball effect' of covenant breaking; it is like being wrapped further and further inside a situation from which there is no escape.

Three times Paul describes the transition from idolatry to immorality as "God gave them up" (1:24, 26, 28; NAB, "handed them over"; cf. Ps. 81:11-12). Paul is not placing the blame on God for human sin but insisting that God allows human folly to run its natural course without preventing its inevitable consequences; this is part of what Paul means when he speaks of the revelation of the wrath of God (1:18, 32).

The exchange of truth about God (1:25), Paul says, led to the exchange of truth about God's creatures, including fellow humans. One result was that "natural intercourse" was replaced with unnatural (1:26-28). Paul's attack on homosexual relations as "unnatural" means they are contrary to the truth revealed in creation (cf. 1:18). The idea is thoroughly and typically Jewish, part of the stock catalog of vices that Jews (and even some Gentile moralists!) accused Gentiles of practicing, though the language he uses is a Stoic idiom (lit. 'against nature'). This idiom meant contrary to the structure of reality, not contrary to one's 'sexual orientation,' as some today anachronistically argue.

Paul's attention to sexual sin, though the most extended description of human depravity, is neither the main nor the last point in his description of Gentile sin. Although he lists some twenty other sins (in 1:29-31, mostly beginning with 'un' [Gk. *a-*, as in 1:18]), his main concern is the overall predicament, not the individual transgressions. The text of verses 29-31 breaks open the dam and unleashes a flood of evils. The wide variety of evils is symptomatic of a comprehensive cancer that has affected not only the body (1:24) but also the human mind (1:21, 28) and heart (1:24); every dimension of the human person and community needs restoration to health. In this situation of moral chaos —

of people willfully discarding God, suffering the consequences, and all the while applauding (NRSV) or approving (NAB, NIV) one another (1:32) — the wrath of God is experienced now, proleptically, before the actual coming day of judgment and wrath (2:5). It is a situation that leads to death (1:32; cf. 6:23a).

God's Impartial Judgment according to Deeds (2:1-16)

Chapter 2 begins with a direct address, "you have no excuse," that indicates Paul's adoption of a rhetorical strategy called the diatribe, a method of argumentation and instruction using an imaginary conversation partner (the 'interlocutor'). There is considerable debate about the identity of the interlocutor in this diatribe. It is clear that Paul is addressing Jews (in the singular) beginning at 2:17, but does that address go back to 2:1? Or is the person addressed in 2:1 more generic, a sort of 'everyman' or at least every hypocrite? The theme of presumption strongly suggests an implied Jewish interlocutor from 2:1 onward. The answer may not matter, however, because the force of the argument in 2:1-16 is to establish one basic scriptural principle: that God judges impartially on the basis of deeds (summarized in 2:6, 11, 13).[9]

Paul begins the diatribe with a stinging critique of hypocrites who erroneously presume on divine patience and mercy (2:1-5). Such people have no more excuse than blatant sinners; their own actions condemn them with the very judgments they utter against others (2:1-2). A series of three rhetorical questions (2:3-4) reminds the interlocutor that God's patience is not apathy but a call to repentance that, if unheeded, will result in God's wrath on the judgment day (2:3, 5). Thus it becomes clear here that hypocrisy and presumption are as serious as any evil listed in 1:18-32, for what is at stake is the interlocutor's future 'justification' — acquittal at the divine court (2:5, 13, 16).

This leads to the main emphasis of the text: God's impartial judging of Gentiles *and* Jews. As many biblical texts state, God "repay[s] according to each one's deeds" (2:6; cf. Pss. 28:4; 62:12; Prov. 24:12), without partiality (2:11; cf. Deut. 10:17; 2 Chron. 19:7), and therefore justifies only "doers of the law" (2:13). Those who do good, whether in accordance with the written Jewish Law or the divine law written on their hearts (2:12, 14-15), will be rewarded with "glory and honor and immortality" (2:7); evildoers will experience wrath and fury (2:8). Thus Paul wants to establish an absolute connection between the doing of the law now and final justification (leading to eternal life, 2:7) later. This eliminates any Jewish prerogative when it comes to possessing the Law of Moses; as many

---

9. Many of the themes developed in this chapter will also have a pastoral application in chaps. 14–15.

people have said, commenting on 2:13, it is performance, not possession, of the Law that matters. This conclusion becomes a fundamental Pauline principle with wide application in Romans: simply possessing the Law, simply being Jewish, is irrelevant for justification.

At least two questions emerge from this passage. (1) Does all this mean that Paul subscribes to some sort of theory of 'anonymous believers' who have no written law (or gospel) but nevertheless keep God's covenant? The answer is no, for the point of this chapter is to establish divine impartiality, not human success in God's court. In the end, all are sinners (as even 2:12 says) under the power of sin, and none will be justified with or without the law (3:9, 19-20). (2) Does Paul, the apostle of 'justification by faith,' contradict himself by asserting justification on the basis of works? Once again, no, because as a covenant theologian, Paul believes the covenant must be and can be fulfilled. His solution will not be to reject the necessity of covenant keeping but to offer a new means — Christ and the Spirit.

The Jewish Predicament (2:17–3:8)

The stinging diatribe begun in 2:1-5 had lapsed into third-person description in 2:6-16, but the diatribe returns with a vengeance in 2:17-24. In those verses Paul applies the principles of 2:1-16 directly to his Jewish interlocutor before moving on both to redefine the term "Jew" (2:25-29) and yet to reassert the value of being an ethnic Jew (3:1-8). Like the prophet Amos, Paul has surprisingly turned the focus of divine judgment from Israel's enemies to Israel itself, from 'them' to 'you' (cf. Amos 1:2–2:3 with 2:4ff.).

In 2:17-24 Paul first condemns his clearly Jewish (and representative) interlocutor for two significant presenting sins: pride (2:17, 23) and hypocrisy (2:21-23). The pride of which Paul speaks is in having the Jewish name (2:17), law (2:17-18, 20, 23), and mission to instruct the Gentiles — who are blind and in the dark (2:19-21; cf. Isa. 42:6-7). In a word, it is pride in differentness. In fact, however, the Jews are no different from the Gentiles, Paul claims in a series of sharp questions (2:21-23). But even the word 'hypocrisy' does not capture the gravity of the problem. The real error is the Jewish failure to keep covenant, such that Jews, from Paul's perspective, have ironically failed to be God's light to the Gentiles (2:19) and instead have become God's embarrassment — a source of blasphemy — among the Gentiles (2:24). The Jews, unbelievably to Paul, are as guilty of idolatry and all kinds of immorality/injustice as the Gentiles (2:21b-23). No doubt this was a painful conclusion for him to reach.

This situation leads Paul to take the claims of divine impartiality and judgment by deeds one step further in 2:25-29: he redefines the word "Jew." A

Jew is not someone who is physically circumcised but 'inwardly' and 'spiritually' circumcised: "real circumcision is a matter of the heart" (2:29). Here Paul is drawing directly from the books of Deuteronomy and Jeremiah. In Deuteronomy 10:12-22 Israel is called to return to her covenant obligations to God and others and to "circumcise, then, the foreskin of your heart, and do not be stubborn any longer" (10:16) because there is no partiality with God (10:17). Similarly, Jeremiah calls the people to

> circumcise yourselves to the LORD,
>   remove the foreskin of your hearts,

to avoid judgment (Jer. 4:4), and he promises a new covenant when the law will be written on the people's hearts (31:31-34).

Physical circumcision, or lack thereof, is thus (as in Galatians) of no relevance in itself to one's covenant relationship with God. The *ritual* boundary marker of circumcision does not either guarantee or prevent the keeping of the Law, which is the *ethical* boundary marker — and the latter marker is the only thing that matters to God (2:25-27). As in 2:1-16, Paul is not here suggesting that there are countless non-Jews who keep the Law and are therefore inwardly circumcised Jews. What matters here is the principle, which Paul can (and will) use to define all who believe the gospel as true Jews, members of the new covenant, whether circumcised or not.

Objections from the imaginary interlocutor jump immediately from the page beginning at 3:1. Is there no advantage to being Jewish, to being circumcised? Paul suggests there is an advantage (he returns to the subject in 9:4-5), but then turns to the most significant issue the discussion of Israel's faithlessness raises: Does it "nullify the faithfulness of God" (3:3)? To this question Paul offers his first of several 'No way!' rejoinders in Romans (3:4a; NRSV: "By no means!"; lit. 'May it never be!'; also in 3:6) and cites the Psalms to support him (3:4b). Paul here skillfully uses his interlocutor to raise the central theological issue of Romans — the faithfulness of God — to which he will give his most sustained attention in chapters 9–11. In the meantime, the interlocutor's questions serve to dismiss two other false conclusions from Paul's argument thus far: (1) even if Israel's injustice and falsehood *confirm* (rather than nullify) God's justice and truthfulness, God's wrath is not unjust, for God judges righteously and impartially (3:5-7); and (2) even if some good eventually comes out of injustice, that does not mean — as some, bordering on blasphemy, accuse Paul of implying (cf. 5:20; 6:1-2, 15) — that anyone should intentionally do evil (3:8). The most important advantage to being Jewish, then, ought to be knowing that human faithlessness does not compromise divine faithfulness, and that the latter does not excuse the former.

Humanity under the Power of Sin (3:9-20)

Leaving objections behind for now, Paul returns to the main train of his argument in order to sum it up. Although the translation and meaning of 3:9a have been debated, the claims of the rest of 3:9-20 are crystal clear, as already noted. Paul's language is that of the law court as he offers a "jackhammer indictment of human sinfulness":[10]

1. *The charge:* All human beings — Gentiles and Jews alike — are "under the power of sin" (3:9b).

   The conclusion that sin is universal has, of course, been the thrust since 1:18. But how has Paul "already charged" that the problem is being "under" (NIV) or "under the power/domination" (NRSV/NAB) of sin — that is, that sin is humanity's slave master? This is one of Paul's most distinctive perspectives — that human beings are enslaved to a power that is so real that he can call it "sin" (singular). In contemporary idiom we might speak of an addiction, with sin gripping the sinner like a drug, as we say, 'enslaves' the addict. The phrase "already charged" suggests that Paul thinks the evidence presented so far indicates something more sinister and fundamental than sins (plural). But he now returns to the evidence itself.

2. *The evidence:* None is righteous, but all engage in various evil deeds (3:10-18).

   The evidence for human sin so far in Romans has consisted of Paul's own observations and analysis, though certainly rooted in scriptural texts. In 3:10-18, however, he pulls out all the stops by producing a string — a 'catena' (chain) — of scriptural texts (mostly from the Psalms) that demonstrate that his indictment is really God's indictment (see esp. Pss. 14 and 53). Human beings fail to seek or fear God, or to treat other humans with kindness; they are not righteous, not in right covenant relationship with God. The evils they commit involve all parts of their bodies (3:13-18) such that they are literally sinful from head to toe. These sins point to the disease — bondage to sin.

   Taken together, the evidence and the charge suggest that whatever solution Paul proposes will have to deal both with sins (i.e., forgiveness for the misdeeds) and with sin (i.e., redemption or liberation from the power).

3. *The verdict:* "The whole world" stands accountable to (guilty before) God (3:19).

   Since this verdict is based on the Law (Scripture), it includes Jews (those "under the law"), not merely Gentiles, and thus everyone. Everyone is silenced, without excuse or defense.

10. Richard B. Hays, *Echoes of Scripture in the Letters of Paul* (New Haven: Yale University Press, 1989), p. 50.

4. *The logical corollary:* The "deeds prescribed by the law" cannot be the means of justification (3:20).

There is significant scholarly debate as to whether these "deeds" (lit. 'works of [the] law') are what we have called ethical or ritual boundary markers (i.e., moral deeds or circumcision, etc.). In the end this may be a false dichotomy, since Paul clearly believes that (1) the possession of ritual markers does *not* matter, (2) the performance of the ethical markers *does* matter, and yet (3) even those who possess the former are not performing the latter.[11] Paul's point is that neither the actual possession of the Law nor the failed attempt at its performance is going to be the source of anyone's right relationship with God now or acquittal on the day of judgment.

What we have then is a 'no exit' situation, as the late J. Christiaan Beker used to call Paul's assessment of humanity. Although the summary in 3:9-20 is largely a description of humanity apart from Christ, Paul is equally concerned that the believers at Rome — whom he will soon describe as no longer "enslaved to sin" but rather "dead to" it (6:6, 11) — not fall back under sin's power through boasting and its associated evils, or through any other sinful errors.

GOD'S FAITHFULNESS AND MERCY IN CHRIST (3:21-31)

The words "But now" in 3:21 mark a major turning point not only in Paul's letter but in the divine story as he understands it. Paul is about to narrate the revelation of God's righteousness that is manifested in Christ's death and proclaimed in the apostle's gospel. This event inaugurates a new age (cf. 2 Cor. 5:17; Gal. 1:4; 6:15), the age of grace (5:20-21) "in which we [now] stand" (5:2). Thus 3:21-26 unpacks the thesis found in 1:16-17 and leads to the exclusion of any form of pride (3:27-31).

Justification by Faith: God's, Christ's, Believers' (3:21-26)

The bold proclamation of God's faithfulness ("righteousness") in these verses stands over against the dismal portrayal of humanity's faithlessness in 1:18–3:20. Although it appears that Paul is drawing on fragments of early Christian liturgical material (some of which are very difficult to translate), he makes them decisively his own, revealing a distinctively Pauline gospel that is, as 1:17 an-

---

11. As we will see more explicitly later, this is because the Law, weakened by "the flesh," cannot empower people to observe its ethical requirements.

nounced, 'out of faith into faith.' If we follow the majority of the most recent interpretations of Paul, which understand God's righteousness as God's saving covenant faithfulness, and which render phrases normally translated "faith in Christ" as 'the faith/faithfulness of Christ' (3:22, 25), then the faith/faithfulness of God, Christ, and those who respond are all named in this text. This appears most succinctly in 3:22:

1. *What* is manifested: God's righteousness (= saving covenant faithfulness).
2. *Where* or *how* it is manifested: in Christ's faith/faithfulness.
3. *For whom* it is manifested: all who respond in faith.

We will look at each of these aspects of the passage.

What. Paul says several things about God's righteousness or faithfulness. First, it is "apart from [the] law" (3:21a), or distinct from the ethnically specific manifestation of covenant that the Law of Moses constitutes. Yet the Law and prophets (the Scriptures) attest to it (3:21, a claim that becomes the burden of chap. 4). Second, it is "through the faith[fulness]" of Christ (3:22, 26; cf. NRSV mg.) that is manifested in Christ's death. Paul's melding of faith and obedience in 1:5 has prepared the reader to understand Christ's death as his one act of faith (3:25-26) as well as obedience (5:19). Christ's death demonstrates that God's righteousness means neither ultimately ignoring sins nor allowing sin permanently to disturb the relationship between humanity and God, but rather 'justifying' those who have faith (3:22) by sharing in the faith of Jesus (3:26 NRSV mg. [correctly]).

Where/how. Christ's death, then, says Paul, is God's faithful and merciful gift (3:24, 25) as well as Christ's faithful act. This death accomplishes two things: forgiveness for sins and redemption from sin. God "put forward" Christ as "a sacrifice of atonement," referring to the Jewish system of sacrifices for sins (3:25). But this was also an act of "redemption" (3:24) or liberation — the language of deliverance from bondage to Egypt or any other slave master. In other words, Christ's death deals both with sins (the deeds) and with sin (the power) — just as Paul's analysis of the human predicament in 1:18–3:20 requires.

For whom. The benefits of this death are available to Jews and Gentiles, for universal sin — universal failure to live fully as the image ("glory") of God — yields a universal divine response (3:22-23). But this is not automatic; Paul writes to and about "all who believe" (3:22). God's faithfulness in Christ's faithful death is in some very real sense incomplete when it is not met with human faith. When it is met with faith, however, as in the church at Rome, those who respond are justified (3:24, 26) — put into right covenant relationship with God and assured of acquittal at the judgment. This is Paul's good news of God's grace.

The Exclusion of Pride (3:27-31)

It takes no great leap of logic to arrive at Paul's first practical conclusion to the gospel narrative of 3:21-26: there is absolutely no grounds for boasting if justification is by means of faith — God's, Christ's, and believers' (3:27). Boasting is a sign of both Gentile (1:22, 30) and Jewish (2:17) sin. So Paul reminds his readers that the "law" or principle of faith correlates with the "law" of divine impartiality in judgment (3:27-30; cf. 2:1-16). According to 3:28, therefore, those who have or do "works prescribed by the law" — that is, Jews — are justified no differently than are Gentiles. Martin Luther read 3:28 to mean 'faith *alone*': "For we hold that a person is justified by faith ['alone' — Luther] apart from works prescribed by the law." Paul would not disagree with Luther's maxim, as long as he got to define the key terms. Certainly Paul does not think anyone ever could (or ever did) 'earn' right standing with God. But his main point is not so much the exclusion of 'works righteousness' as the exclusion of religious or ethnic pride — Jewish or Gentile. The problem with introducing 'alone' is not that Paul believes something other than faith is needed, but rather that common definitions of faith are often so myopic when compared to Paul's. For Paul, faith is clearly a comprehensive response: trust, absolute surrender, obedience, and commitment to the covenant. The gospel offers grace and demands obedient faith, and thereby opens covenant membership to all on the same terms; that is the point of these verses. And, Paul asserts (3:31), this claim does not "overthrow" but "uphold[s]" the law (the Scriptures) — which leads him to two biblical figures to prove his claim.

THE WITNESS OF SCRIPTURE IN THE EXAMPLE OF ABRAHAM (4:1-25)

In chapter 4 Paul pays tribute to the Jewish principle of "two or three witnesses" (e.g., Deut. 17:6; 19:15), drawing on Abraham, supported by David, in support of his claims in 3:21-31 that (1) justification is through grace by faith, (2) irrespective of circumcision and the Law, and (3) exclusive of pride. Moreover, Abraham is not only the *proof* but also the *paradigm* of justifying faith. In these verses Paul reveals much about his understanding of justification and faith, doing so both in diatribal form with questions that invoke the readers' careful consideration and in midrashic form by rereading the story of Abraham in Genesis 15–17, with special emphasis on 15:6 and 17:5.

What Paul does with Abraham here is quite fascinating. For Jews in Paul's day, Abraham filled a variety of roles. He was seen as the founder of monotheism, as well as the paradigm of virtue and meritorious obedience, especially in the offering of Isaac (Gen. 22, not discussed by Paul here). He was the father of all Jews, the first to be circumcised and thus the first member of the covenant people. Some believed he obeyed the Law even before Moses gave it. And some saw him not only as the father of the Jewish people but as the paradigmatic proselyte (convert). A Jewish argument about who and what constitutes 'a true Jew' (2:28-29) needs Abraham to be convincing.

For Paul, Abraham is a hybrid. He is still "our [Jewish] ancestor according to the flesh" (4:1), but he is clearly not restricted to that role. Paul claims Abraham is "the father of all of us" (4:16), meaning Jewish and Gentile believers in Christ. Abraham is a paradigmatic justified Gentile (like a proselyte) inasmuch as he was justified without either the Law or circumcision, but he is also a paradigmatic justified Jew inasmuch as he was justified not by the Law but by faith (4:9-17a). Paul even implies that Abraham was ungodly, since God justifies the ungodly (4:5; cf. 1:18). Thus Paul reads Abraham's story as the story of a sinner, a Gentile, a Jew, and a 'Christian' — a justified believer. Abraham is Paul's everyman.

The first part of the chapter (4:1-8) focuses on Abraham's justification by faith — supported by the Psalms. Interestingly, Paul dismisses boasting even if justification were by works (4:2), but his main concern is the thesis that Abraham was justified by faith: his faith was "reckoned to him as righteousness" (4:3). An accounting analogy from labor (4:4-5: wages for a worker versus a free gift for a nonworker) provides an initial witness about 'reckoning' that illustrates what David in Psalm 32:1-2 also says (4:6-8). In these verses we learn that justification is a free gift to the ungodly (analogous to the one who does not work) that is received in faith and trust and that brings about a state of 'blessedness' (4:6-9) due to the forgiveness of sins (4:7-8).

The next part of the chapter (4:9-15) establishes Abraham's justification prior to his circumcision and without the Law of Moses. Circumcision was not a prerequisite for justification but a sequel to it, serving as a seal (4:10-11). The promise to Abraham came, moreover, before the Law (4:13-15). All of this means, Paul claims, that Abraham was intended all along to be the father of both Jewish and Gentile believers (4:11, 13).

The final part of the chapter displays Abraham's faith as paradigmatic for all believers, as God's promise was graciously extended to him for all nations (4:16-17), as the Genesis story makes clear to Paul. In these two verses from Romans 4, we learn that for Paul, looking to Abraham, faith is trust in God and the promises of God, particularly in God as the one who "gives life to the dead and calls into existence the things that do not exist" (4:17b). Thus faith is forward-looking — eschatological in orientation, centered on resurrection — and therefore virtually synonymous with hope. It trusts the promises of God (4:18, quoting Gen. 17:5, God's promise that Abraham would have many descendants). Abraham's own good-as-dead body and his wife's barren womb led not to distrust but to greater trust (4:19-21). It was this kind of faith that was reckoned to Abraham as righteousness. The whole scriptural story is told, Paul says, 'for our sakes,' as a foreshadowing of the kind of faith of which Paul speaks — faith in God's raising of the crucified Jesus (4:22-25). Ultimately, then, Abraham bears witness not only to the nature of faith as trust and hope, but also to the nature of justification — receiving the promise of God through faith in God's bringing life from death.

What Abraham found (NRSV, "gained," 4:1), then, was in essence the reality revealed in Paul's gospel: grace, faith, and justification apart from circumcision and Law; he encountered the God who raises the dead. Without ever denying Abraham's Jewishness, Paul universalizes him. That is why the justified are defined as those who "share the faith of Abraham" (4:16). But Paul claims that this universalizing is not original to him: according to Genesis, he reminds us, the covenant with Abraham was for him to be the "father of many nations" (4:17, from Gen. 17:1-8). Paul sees that covenant faithfully fulfilled in the taking of the gospel to the nations.

Summary of Romans 1–4

In the opening chapters of Romans Paul makes the following central claims:
- The gospel is the power of God to save anyone and everyone, both Jews and Gentiles.
- Both Gentiles and Jews have failed to live in proper covenant relationship with God, each group having its distinctive ways of failing to obey God (idolatry) and love others (immorality/injustice); they are covenantally dysfunctional.
- Human beings are judged impartially by God according to their deeds; performance, not possession, of the Law is what matters and what justifies people before God.
- The various kinds of sins people commit, and to which the Scriptures attest, are manifestations of the power of sin, to which humans are enslaved.
- In Christ's faithful (obedient) death, God in saving covenant faithfulness extends both forgiveness from sins and redemption from sin.
- Both Gentiles and Jews who believe the gospel are justified, but they have no grounds for boasting. They have had their hearts circumcised and are therefore members of God's covenant people as 'true Jews.'
- Abraham is the paradigm of such justifying faith, which he had apart from circumcision and the Law; he is Paul's everyman, the example for both Jews and Gentiles.

5:1–8:39. THE CRUCIFORM CHARACTER OF JUSTIFICATION BY FAITH

It would be difficult to imagine any work of more theological depth than Romans 5–8. But what is the purpose of these chapters in the letter? Some have argued that Paul here spells out the normal progress of 'Christian growth,' from justification (chap. 5) to sanctification (chap. 6), and then from despair at one's ongoing sin (chap. 7) to freedom in the Spirit (chap. 8). Although these chapters may describe some development,[12] that is not their main thrust. Principally, Romans 5–8 functions to spell out the meaning and character of justification — a notion Paul has frequently referred to but has, so far, quite meagerly explained.

Paul constructs an extended definition of justification through a series of antithetical narratives that echo the "but now" of 3:21. After a preliminary exposition of justification in 5:1-11, he sets out the story of those who, through justification, have moved from outside Christ into Christ. He tells this story from three narrative perspectives, focusing on three sets of antitheses highlighting three distinct yet interrelated themes. In each narrative, as well as in the initial exposition, the cross figures centrally. The following chart summarizes these chapters:

Summary of Romans 5–8

Text	Narrative Perspective	Antithesis	Theme	Cross
5:1-11	[overview]	enemies vs. friends	justification as reconciliation	the cross as God's love
5:12-21	cosmic, or salvation historical	Adam vs. Christ	free from sin, under grace	Christ's cross as his obedience
6:1–7:6	baptismal	slavery to sin vs. slavery to righteousness	dead to sin, alive to God	crucifixion with Christ
7:7–8:39	existential	flesh vs. Spirit	in the Spirit, not in the flesh	believers' death to the old life, suffering

---

12. E.g., the narrative of Israel's exodus, from slavery to freedom, as suggested by N. T. Wright.

In these three sets of narrative antitheses we find that, in Christ, the human story circumscribed by wrath, sin, the law, and death (1:18-32) is transformed into one of freedom from all these negative aspects of human existence. This is not, then, about the *effects* or *results* of justification (as some set of separable and perhaps optional consequences), but about the very *meaning* of it. Justification means to experience the fullness of the triune God. Just as all who have sinned stand accountable before God, all who are justified live in grace, free to be members of the covenant community that lives under the sign of the cross — those reconciled with God through the death of the Messiah and in the power of the Spirit.

All this lays the foundation for the rest of the letter: for the anguish Paul feels about fellow Jews missing out on the joy of justification, as well as his hope for them (chaps. 9–11); and for Paul's more explicit covenantal stipulations in the new reign of grace (chaps. 12–15).

JUSTIFICATION AS RECONCILIATION
THROUGH THE CROSS (5:1-11)

This multidimensional text contains many key Pauline words and themes that will reappear in the following chapters, culminating in chapter 8. It is artfully constructed in chiastic form as follows:

> 1-2a Justification through Christ
>   2b-5 Hope for future glory
>   6-8 Christ's death as God's love
>   9-10 Hope for future salvation
> 11 Reconciliation through Christ

Noticing this arrangement of the text permits us to make several key observations. First, the way the passage begins and ends in parallel form (a rhetorical technique called *inclusio*) suggests that justification (5:1) is in fact the present experience of reconciliation with God (5:11), or "peace with God" (5:1), which is a condition of "grace" in which believers presently "stand" (5:2). ("Justified" and "reconciled" are used interchangeably also in 5:9-10.) This means there has been a cessation of hostilities, the transformation of God's "enemies" (5:10) into friends. Those who were outside grace — outside the covenant — are now inside it. Second, the center or fulcrum of this text (5:6-8) indicates that the focal point of God's reconciling work is Christ's death, which specifies the meaning of "through our Lord Jesus Christ" (5:2, 11). The passage as a whole contains four explicit and two implicit references to Christ's death. Third, justification has not only past and present aspects but also a future dimension, as the parallel sections between the opening bookends and the fulcrum demonstrate (5:2b-5, 9-10). 'Justification,' in Paul's language, is not the equivalent of 'salvation,' but it does include salvation — which for Paul is future (note the future tense in 5:9, 10) — within its scope.

We may therefore propose a working definition of justification (expanding on the discussion of the topic associated with 1:16-17):

> *reconciliation with God in the present, together with certain hope of salvation (acquittal and glory) in the future, based on the death of Christ in the past, and all known through the gift of the Spirit.*

This definition is borne out by both the structure and the actual content of 5:1-11. A few additional remarks about the content itself still need to be made.

In 5:1-5 Paul depicts a close relationship between believers' past, present, and future experience. The phrase "since we are justified" (NRSV) is better rendered "since we have been justified" (NAB, NIV); justification began in the past (with the response of faith in the gospel) but has an ongoing effect. It is the state of blessedness (cf. 4:6-9) now called 'having peace with God' and 'standing in grace' (5:1-2). It also has a future orientation, the hope of participating in the glory of God that sinful humanity currently lacks (3:23). An echo of Genesis 1:27 ("image of God") suggests a kind of 'paradise restored' theme, and the sure hope of receiving this honor becomes the new grounds of legitimate 'boasting' — in God, not self (cf. 3:27). But the road to glory has a cruciform shape: it includes, or will include, 'sufferings,' as Paul well knew. Although ultimately Paul connects the suffering of believers to Christ's cross, here he stresses not its source but its educative role (frequently acknowledged in antiquity) and its final goal (5:3-4). Suffering begins a chain reaction leading to character, endurance, and hope, a hope that "does not disappoint" (on the last day) — or better, 'will not cause shame' — because the present experience of the Holy Spirit insures believers of God's love (5:5), God's being "for us" (cf. 8:31-39). This experience begins when God's love and the Spirit are "poured out" (5:5, NAB, NIV), which may be a reference to baptism but is more likely a metaphor for the overwhelming experience of the Spirit when the gospel is preached and believed (cf. Gal. 3:1-5). Thus Paul speaks briefly here of a unified experience of the Spirit, suffering, love, and hope that he will develop in chapter 8.

Mention of God's love leads Paul, in the central section (5:6-8), to the ultimate source and manifestation of that love in Christ's death (cf. 8:32). Although the word 'grace' does not appear, it is the best word for what Paul describes — a counterintuitive, sacrificial ("for us," 5:8; cf. "blood," 5:9) death, not for a righteous or good person (5:7), but for people who were "weak" and "ungodly" (5:6) "sinners" (5:8). Paul's use of the first-person plural ("we/us") is important because of its inclusiveness — the death was for himself and all other Jews, as well as Gentiles. In light of 3:21-26, we know that Paul sees this gracious gift also as the display of God's covenant faithfulness and righteousness.

In rabbinic fashion Paul moves on to the logical and 'easier' corollary to justification/reconciliation, namely, 'salvation,' meaning rescue from the (future) wrath of God (5:9-10). Two more references to Christ's death in these verses lead to the conclusion that God's saving love shown in the cross and experienced in the present will, for the justified, remain consistent in the future. The attribution of future salvation to Christ's 'life' at the end of 5:10 may be a reference to the resurrection as the guarantor of hope and salvation, as well as to the current intercessory work of the Son before the Father (8:34). This talk of hope once again returns Paul to the theme of the passage, the present ("now") experience of justification/reconciliation through Christ, which for him is an equal, if not greater, reason to "boast" in God than the future hope (5:11). What unites past, present, and future is the love of God in Christ through the Spirit.

FREE FROM SIN, UNDER GRACE (5:12-21)

Having begun a description of the comprehensive scope of God's gracious transformation, through Christ's death, of sinners and enemies into people who are justified and reconciled, Paul engages in the first of three analyses of the antithetical situations that prevailed before Christ's death and prevail now since it. The contrast in 5:12-21 is obviously between Adam and Christ, between the respective 'deed' and 'age' associated with each, between sin and grace.

Paul first begins, but then aborts, his contrast with the words "just as" (5:12). Paul was about to finish 5:12 with something like, 'so also righteousness came into the world through one man and so grace spread to all.' He gets momentarily sidetracked, however, in a defense of the existence of sin before and without the Law of Moses, probably because he has most recently claimed that "where there is no law, neither is there violation" (4:15).

Paul asserts that the action of one man (Adam) brought sin and thus death (Gen. 2:15-17; 3:1-5, 19) into the world, and indeed to all people "because all have sinned" (5:12). The centuries-long debate about 'original sin' has been in part an interpretation of this verse. Unfortunately, the debate began when Augustine followed the Latin Vulgate's mistranslation of the Greek and read the phrase "because all" (NRSV, NIV) or "inasmuch as all" (NAB) have sinned as "in whom [Adam]" all have sinned. Paul's point is not really to blame Adam, and much less to suggest that original sin is passed on biologically (i.e., through intercourse), but to affirm the universality of sin. We, he says, confirmed and confirm the sin of Adam, acting like little Adams ourselves (cf. the Jewish document 2 *Bar.* 54:17-19). For Paul, Adam is a "type" (5:14) — an antithetical foreshadowing — of Christ, and by extension, sinners are types of the justified. His main point in the digression, however, is that sin existed and that death "exercised dominion" over humanity even before the Law of Moses entered and allowed for violations to be reckoned (5:13-14).

The Adam-Christ contrast continues in 5:15-19, with Paul making one main point in a variety of images and terms: Adam's deed means sin and death, while Christ's means righteousness and life. The following chart, drawing on the language of the NRSV, NAB, and NIV, shows the contrasting parallels:

Adam and Christ

	Adam's Deed	*Consequences*	*Christ's Deed*	*Consequences*
15	trespass	many died	(free/gracious) gift, grace	the grace of God and the free gift abounded/over-flow/have over-flown for the many
16	sin/sinning, one trespass	many trespasses, judgment, condemnation	(free) gift	justification/ acquittal
17	trespass/ transgres-sion	death exercised dominion/came to reign/reigned	abundance/abun-dant provision of grace, free gift of righteousness/ justification	exercise dominion in life/(come to) reign in life
18	trespass	condemnation for all	act of righteousness	justification/ acquittal and life for all
19	disobedience	many were made sinners	obedience	many will be made righteous

The news with respect to Adam is grim; his misdeed set in motion a string of consequences, but only (says 5:12) because all others followed Adam as well. The coming of the Law did nothing to help the situation but only compounded the problems — more trespasses (5:20a). It could not and did not, Paul implies, stop the spread of sin and death, overturn the condemnation, or give righteousness and life. However, in summary, Paul says that "where sin increased, grace

367

abounded all the more" (5:20b), creating the new reign of grace through justification and leading to "eternal life" (5:21). A more powerful force — grace — has "come to reign" (5:17 NAB) through the death of Christ Jesus, a force that liberates believers from the triumvirate of sin, death, and the Law (which is good in itself but has been co-opted by sin: 7:7-12). One gracious act of obedience and righteousness — of faith and faithfulness (cf. 3:21-26) — has changed everything. But just as all had to, in effect, 'share' in Adam's act of disobedient sin to become sinners, so also all who wish to be justified must share in Christ's obedient act of righteousness on the cross — the subject of chapter 6.

DEAD TO SIN, ALIVE TO GOD (6:1–7:6)

In 5:12-21 Paul does not explicitly spell out how believers have moved from the reign of sin to the reign of grace. That he must now do. But he must also dig himself out of a bit of a hole. If more sin resulted in more grace (5:20b), perhaps more sin is in order — as some seem to have thought Paul believed (3:8). Chapter 6 exposes the fallacy of this argument while describing how believers participate in the death of the Messiah that has inaugurated the reign of grace. Through that death they escape from the reign of sin and death (6:1-23) and even the Law (7:1-6).

Many people understandably believe that Romans 6 presents Paul's theology of baptism. But this chapter is not primarily about baptism. It takes baptism as the common starting point for participation in the new covenant community, and it does seek to unpack that common experience. But Paul's major focus is on the contrast between the pre- and postbaptismal life, and especially on the new life "to God" (6:10-11) as a continuation of baptismal crucifixion with Christ. There is above all in the chapter nothing that could be interpreted as giving the baptized any reason for pride or complacency.

The substantive theme of the chapter as a whole is the assertion that life is a type of 'slavery,' either to sin or to God, the master to whom people "present" themselves and their bodies (6:13, 16, 19; cf. 12:1). The chapter divides rather neatly into two parts, signaled by two similar rhetorical questions (6:1, 15), each followed by "By no means!" (NAB: "Of course not!") and "Do you not know . . . ?" These questions are normally translated quite similarly as "Should [or 'Shall'] we [continue/persist in] sin?" But the entire context suggests a more nuanced interpretation: (1) '*Should* we remain in sin that grace may abound?' (6:1, as the logical consequence of 5:20); and (2) '*May* we sin because we are not under law but under grace?' (6:15, as the sequel to the conclusion of 6:1-14 in 6:14).

1. Should the justified remain in sin to increase the flow of grace (6:1-14)? "Of course not!" answers Paul (6:2a NAB), for believers have died to sin in bap-

tism (6:2b-11) and therefore present their bodies to God, not to sin (6:12-14). It is important to see how closely connected baptism and faith are for Paul. People are baptized "into" Christ (6:3; Gal. 3:27; Gk. *eis*) and they believe "into" (Gk. *eis*) Christ (Gal. 2:16). They are two inseparable sides of one coin; the combination of conviction and confession (cf. Rom. 10:5-13) brings about justification (with the promise of future salvation) and entry into the community. What Paul says of baptism can also therefore be predicated of faith: it is a kind of death experience, a cocrucifixion with Christ, as Paul specifically says in Galatians 2:15-20.

Thus the description of 'baptism into Christ' is also a description of 'faith into Christ,' or 'justification by faith.' Justification is therefore an experience of dying and rising. Drawing on already established beliefs and even an early creed, in 6:3-11 Paul outlines several parallels between Christ's death and that of believers. The whole process — death, burial, and resurrection — is summarized in 6:3-4. The resurrection following death and burial in baptism is in order to "walk in newness of life" (6:4). This clearly speaks of a *present* resurrection (6:4, 11). Some interpreters, however, fear that present resurrection smacks of 'triumphalism' or Corinthian 'collapsed eschatology.' What keeps Paul from going down that road, however, is his understanding of "newness of life" as an ongoing state of being dead to sin (6:11) and therefore of sharing in the cross (cf. chap. 8).

Scholars fearful of triumphalism read the future tenses associated with resurrection in 6:5 and 6:8 as temporally future, while others read one or the other only as logically future ('if you do this, then you will . . .'). The key to resolving this problem lies in the connection of 6:5-10 with the end of the reign of sin and death in 5:12-21. In 6:5-10 Paul shows how believers, through participation in Christ's death, experience for themselves the defeat of both sin (now, 6:5-7) and death (later, 6:8-9) accomplished by his death.

In 6:5 Paul continues the thought of 6:4, applying it to sin. According to 6:6-7, being crucified with Christ means liberation from sin as slave master (cf. 3:9, 24) and the death of the "old self" (= the destruction of the "body of [i.e., ruled by] sin"). This is a permanent, irreversible situation, just as Christ died "once for all" (6:10a), a state of being "dead to sin and alive to God" *in* Christ (6:11) and *like* Christ (6:10a). In continuity with this reality, believers are also guaranteed a future resurrection, not to "newness of life" but to "eternal life" (6:23). In 6:8-9 Paul again echoes 6:4 but applies it now to a (literal) future when those who died with Christ "will also live with him" (6:8) and experience that which Christ already has — total freedom from death as slave master (6:9). Thus believers experience Christ's death now, as death to sin (like his), and his resurrection in two stages, as being alive *to* God now (6:11) and as experiencing freedom from death by being *with* Christ in the future (6:8).

The present character of resurrection is reaffirmed in 6:12-14, where Paul draws the ethical consequences of what he has just said. Liberated from sin (6:14), believers are not to allow it to regain its reign over their bodies (6:12) by present-ing their "members" to their old slave master (6:13). To do so would be to reenter the prebaptismal, prefaith sphere of Adam and thereby to live an anachronism. Rather, the justified are to present their members to God since they have been brought from death to life (6:13), or are dead to (= cut off from) sin and alive to God (6:11). As in 1 Corinthians 6:12-20 and Romans 12:1-2 (and in contrast to Rom. 1:18-32), the body is now the place of service to God. Paul also characterizes this state of bodily self-giving to God as "under grace" and not "under law" (6:14) — his own phrases, based on the end of chapter 5, for being part of the post-Christ reign of grace and not the pre-Christ reign of sin, death, and the Law.

2. "Not under law," however, prompts the next rhetorical question: If sin is not *required*, is it *permitted* (6:15)? Is Paul's law-free gospel antinomian, condu-cive to moral chaos? This possibility (or accusation, 3:8) may have caused Jew-ish believers no little consternation and Gentile believers either confusion or glee, depending on their inclinations. Paul explains his negative answer by re-turning to the slavery metaphor with the assumption that everyone is an 'obe-dient slave' to something, either to sin or to righteousness/God (6:16, 18, 20). The justified, as he has already said (6:6-7), were liberated from their old master sin when they obeyed the "teaching" (gospel) from their heart (6:17) and were reenslaved to righteousness/God (6:18, 20). (Paul seems a bit uncomfortable with the slavery analogy [6:19a], but it serves his rhetorical purposes well.) Slav-ery to sin meant freedom from righteousness and growth in iniquity, but now slavery to righteousness means self-presentation to this new master and growth in the countercultural life of holiness (6:19b-20, 22). The results of the two forms of slavery are also antithetical, the "wage" (earned pay), which is death, or the free gift, which is eternal life (6:21-23).

Finally, Paul turns to yet a third topic related to 5:12-20, freedom from the Law (7:1-6). Although he does not see the Law in any sense as evil, it "aroused" humanity's "sinful passions" (7:5; cf. 5:19) and is therefore part of the old regime that ended with Christ's death. Thus believers have also "died to the law through the body of Christ [his death]" (7:4) and are "discharged" from it (7:6), as also from sin.

The legal metaphor Paul chooses to illustrate 'death to the Law' is a bit contorted but very creative (7:1b-4). The principle Paul capitalizes on is that through death (the husband's), the wife is "discharged" or "freed" from the law against 'living with' another man; she can therefore honorably remarry (7:2-3). Paul reads this metaphor as both authorizing believers' freedom from the Law based on a death (not of the former 'spouse' but of the new one) and then per-mitting the liberated believers to "belong to another" (Christ) and "bear fruit for God" through the "new life of the Spirit" (7:4, 6; cf. Gal. 5:22-24).

This whole line of thinking will allow Paul once again to be charged with antinomianism. His final answer to such charges will be the contrast between life in the flesh and in the Spirit (in whom believers actually fulfill the law, 8:3-4; cf. Gal. 5:23b). He alludes to that contrast here (7:5-6), and turns to it at length in 7:7–8:39.

IN THE SPIRIT, NOT IN THE FLESH (7:7–8:39)

Paul's third antithesis about the life of justification is the contrast between life in the flesh and life in the Spirit. As noted earlier, 7:7-25 should be read with 8:1-39, not as descriptions of the 'defeated' and then the 'victorious' justified life, but as contrasting depictions of life before and after justification (inside and outside of Christ), like 5:12-21 and 6:1-23.

Life in the Flesh (7:7-25)

Romans 7:7-25 is one of the most difficult and diversely interpreted texts in the letter. Interpreters agree on a few key points but radically disagree on the main point and function of the text. Agreements include the following: (1) Paul pronounces the Law good and holy; (2) Paul depicts sin as a force or power that makes use of the Law and enslaves people; (3) the "I" of the text experiences a divided self and a resulting moral frustration; (4) Paul presents Christ as the solution to the existential dilemma felt by the "I"; and (5) life in the Spirit (chap. 8) is the alternative to the life depicted in chapter 7. Moreover, most interpreters agree that the use of "I" is significant, as is the shift of verb tenses associated with the "I" and with "sin," from past (7:7-13) to present (7:14-25).

The Identity of the "I"

These rather significant agreements also hint at the major interpretive issue that is debated: the identity of the "I" who is speaking, and the existential situation(s) to which this "I" is referring. Is Paul using the "I" to speak autobiographically, representatively (sometimes called 'in character'), or both? Is he speaking about his own Jewish experience outside Christ, or his own experience in Christ? Is he speaking instead (or also) about all Jews or even all human beings outside Christ, or about all believers in Christ? Or is the situation addressed 'all of the above'? Furthermore, is Paul's main goal to depict some existential plight or to defend either the Law itself or his view of the Law? Or, again, 'all of the above'? The questions are complex.

371

Historically, most readers of Romans 7 have understood Paul to be narrating his own existential situation, either before his conversion or as a believer. Both readings seem plausible, for it is difficult (simply as a human being or specifically as a Christian) not to identify with the inner struggle Paul depicts in such texts as 7:19 and 7:21-23. Nevertheless, the majority of scholars today do not believe Paul is narrating his own preconversion Jewish experience, since elsewhere he indicates no sense of preconversion struggle with the Law but only success and pride in doing it (Gal. 1:14; Phil. 3:4-6). Neither is it likely that he is narrating his current experience as a believer. Despite the existential appeal of this interpretation, the description of the "I" as "sold into slavery under sin" (7:14) is clearly a reference to the person who is "under the power of sin" (3:9) and a slave to sin (6:6, 16, 20, etc.), rather than to someone redeemed from sin, dead to it but alive to God as God's 'slave' (3:24; 6:6, 11, 18, 22, etc.). While believers still must struggle not to allow sin to regain mastery (6:12; cf. 8:13), they do so on the assumption of their current liberation from sin, not their slavery to it.

According to many contemporary interpreters, therefore, Paul is using the "I" to speak representatively as a believer about the experience of those (Jews or all people) who were or are outside the Messiah. It is his perspective on unredeemed humanity seen through the prism of his redemption in Christ. More specifically, we may say that Paul's "I" is Adam, in the sense of 'everyone' living 'in Adam' and thereby under the reign of sin, death, and (eventually) the Law (cf. 5:12-14). Paul even alludes to Genesis 2–3 to tell the story of sin's entry into the human race (past tense, 7:7-13) and the ongoing consequences of its reign (present tense, 7:14-25). This condition of being 'in Adam' and enslaved to sin is also described as being "of the flesh" or 'in my/the flesh' (7:14, 18; 8:8-9). It finds its antithesis in being "in Christ" and therefore "in the Spirit" (8:1, 9-11).

The Meaning of the Text

The significance of this view for understanding Paul's spirituality should not be underestimated. Although Paul clearly expects believers to grow in "sanctification" (6:19, 22), or covenantal countercultural character, he does not believe the experience he narrates in chapter 7 is the 'normal' experience of believers as they constantly lose the existential battle between good and evil. Rather, Paul sees the normal life of believers as one in which they are liberated from sin and empowered by the Spirit to fulfill "the just requirement of the law" (8:4) as they "put to death the deeds of the body" (8:13).

Paul's discussion in 7:7-25 begins with a rhetorical question about the possibility of equating the Law with sin (7:7). This question arises because Paul has said that believers have died both to sin (6:2) and to the Law (7:4). What follows is in part a defense of the goodness of the Law, but is even more a description of the frustrated human (and especially Jewish) condition apart from Christ in spite of the Law. The Law is not the culprit; sin is. But the Law cannot bring life in the presence of such a death-dealing power. It cannot empower its own fulfillment.

In 7:7-13 Paul shows how sin "deceived" and "killed" the human race by "seizing an opportunity in the commandment" (7:11), a commandment that "promised life" (7:10). The allusions to the Genesis account (Gen. 2:15-17; 3:1-24) of God's life-giving commandment (2:16), the serpent's death-inflicting deception of Eve (3:1-5, 13), and the first couple's covetousness (3:6) are unmistakable and explain the many past-tense verbs. In Paul's retelling of the story, the deceiver is not a serpent but a power, sin. Sin "seized an opportunity" (Rom. 7:8, 11) — the issuing of God's good, life-giving commandment — to provoke covetousness, which led (implicitly, through disobedience; cf. 5:12-21) to death. The commandment was, and the Law still is, "holy and just and good" (7:12), but it was (and is) used by sin both to identify and to increase sin in the world (7:13; cf. 5:20).

The shift to the present tense to describe God's commandment/Law (7:12-13) allows Paul to transition from the past, and the beginning of sin's exploitation of the Law, to the present, and the ongoing effects of this sinister arrangement (7:14-25). What Paul finds in human beings is a confused (7:15), divided self, with two 'laws' or 'principles' at war within. "I," he says, "do not do what I want, but [what] . . . I hate" (7:15b, 19). Despite having a delight in the Law and a desire to do good (7:21-22, 25), "I cannot do it" (7:18b). The repetitious character of these verses is deliberate; in 7:14-20 Paul describes the situation twice in careful parallel form ("we know," 7:14-17; "I know," 7:18-20), and then in 7:21-25 he states his conclusion three times for emphasis.

Paul's diagnosis of this situation, as already described in 3:9 and chapter 6, is humanity's enslavement to sin, which he mentions at the beginning and end of this passage (7:14, 25b). What is new now is the idea that sin *indwells* people (7:17, 20) and actually does the evil that humans wish they would not do (7:20). Sin is not merely an external force or master *over* the human race, but an internal power *within* each person. This is life without the indwelling of God's Spirit, or life in the "flesh," determined solely by Adam and not Christ. This does not mean that "the body" is inherently evil; the manifestation of sin in the body's "members" (7:23) has made the self into a "body of [characterized by] death" (7:24), but this situation can be altered (cf. 6:12-23 and chap. 8). Nor does this mean that human beings are exonerated. They have gotten themselves into this predicament and have no excuse (1:18–3:20), but now they are powerless, covenantally dysfunctional. The only solution to the crisis is what God has done through Christ (7:25a) to provide the Spirit, to which Paul turns in chapter 8.

Cruciform Life in the Spirit (8:1-39)

Chapter 8 is in many ways the climax of the section of Romans that begins at 5:1, and also the climax of the letter, *thus far*, as a whole. In this chapter Paul presents a very full discussion of life in Christ as God's children who live in the Spirit, the antithesis of life in the flesh. Although the chapter's focus is life in the Spirit, it is clear from beginning to end that salvation is the work of the triune God and that believers' experience is in fact an experience of that triune God.

For God's children in Christ, the Spirit replaces sin as the indwelling power that determines a person's direction and behavior. Perhaps Paul learned a valuable lesson from his encounters with the Corinthians, for in Romans 8 the Spirit is clearly set out as the Spirit of cruciformity. The effect of the Spirit's presence is cruciform in two major ways: putting to death the deeds of the body, or dying to the flesh (8:13), and suffering with Christ (8:17). These two dimensions of the cruciform Spirit-filled life are discussed in 8:1-17 and 8:18-39, respectively, and they constitute both the proof of the Spirit's presence and the guarantee of eternal life and glory.

Paul expresses the intimacy of believers' identification with Christ and the Spirit in a series of words that begin with the prefix 'co-' (Gk. *syg-, sym-, syn-, sys-;* often rendered 'with'):

- *symmartyrei* (8:16; lit. 'cowitness')
- *sygklēronomoi* (8:17; lit. 'coheirs')
- *sympaschomen* (8:17; lit. 'cosuffer')
- *syndoxasthōmen* (8:17; lit. 'be coglorified')
- *systenazei* (8:22; lit. 'cogroan')
- *synantilambanetai* (8:26; 'co–take hold of'; i.e., 'help')
- *synergei* (8:28; lit. 'coworks')
- *symmorphous* (8:29; lit. 'coformed'; cf. Phil. 3:10, 21)[13]

The main thrust of the entire passage is that death, whether figurative or literal, gives way to life (8:13), that cosuffering with Christ results finally in coglorification with him (8:17). In anticipation of that glory, believers have the presence and love of Father, Son, and Spirit.

Dying to the Flesh (8:1-17)

Paul's emphasis in the first half of chapter 8 is on the stark contrast between believers' situation in the Spirit and their previous situation in the flesh. They are now enabled to please God (8:1-13) and to live as God's adopted children (8:14-17).

---

13. In addition, there is the phrase "with him [Christ]" in 8:32.

Paul begins the chapter by stating a thesis of sorts, which is the undoing of chapter 7: there is no condemnation (cf. 7:24) for those in Christ because they have been liberated from the "law of sin and of death" by the "law of the Spirit of life" (8:1-2); Spirit replaces sin, life replaces death. When enslaved to sin, people's final destination would not be life with God but death (cf. 3:23, 6:23), the natural outcome of their failure to keep covenant with God, a failure that the Law itself could not rectify. Now, however, those in the Spirit are finally able to please God (8:8); their covenantal dysfunctionality has been reversed by the action of God (8:3). Those in Christ, those who have the Spirit inside them, have experienced the prophetic promises of a new heart and a spirit within (e.g., Ezek. 36:26-28; Jer. 31:31-34), and therefore constitute the renewed covenant community as 'true Jews' (cf. Rom. 2:25-29).

In a very significant text, which may incorporate a pre-Pauline formula, Paul says in 8:3-4 that God's sending of the Son both condemned sin (by the Son's lack of sin; cf. 2 Cor. 5:21) and 'dealt with' it. God dealt with sin in Christ by *defeating and disabling* it so that those empowered by the Spirit (also sent by God, 8:15; cf. Gal. 4:4-6) could fulfill the "just requirement of the law," or faithfully keep the covenant in the manner of the Son. (For the Spirit of God is the Spirit of the Son [8:9].) The meaning of this will be unpacked in some detail in chapters 12–15, though it is summarized here in phrases like "live/walk according to the Spirit" and not "according to the flesh" (8:4-5), "please God" (8:8), and "put to death the deeds of the body" (8:13). For Paul, as in Galatians and 1 Corinthians, it will include the cessation of divisions and judgmentalism in the church (cf. Gal. 5:13–6:5; 1 Cor. 3:1-4).

This life is animated and enabled by Christ's own power and presence, experienced as the Spirit of God and of Christ (8:9-13). Paul speaks interchangeably of both Christ and the Spirit being within (8:9-11), replacing sin as the believer's and the church's ruling force. Paul also speaks of believers being in Christ and in the Spirit (8:1, 9). The church and all believers are constantly enveloped and possessed by Christ's Spirit, like the air around and within them.

This life in the Spirit is not, however, automatic; it requires active participation by believers, who must now set their minds on (the things of) the Spirit (8:5-6) and actively oppose the flesh (8:12-13; cf. Gal. 5:16-26). There is the real (though totally anachronistic) possibility that some who are baptized will not make their death to sin an existential reality. For this reason the future of believers is conditional — dependent upon ("if . . . you put to death . . . ," 8:13) their ongoing cruciformity. For those who do live according to the Spirit, the end result is that which the Law promised but could not deliver: resurrection and life (8:11, 13b). This conviction leads Paul to the metaphor of adoption, which is about the creation of heirs.

Believers are those who have received and are now led by the Spirit of God

(8:14-15), who marks them out as people liberated from slavery and fear and as members of God's family by adoption (8:15). The Roman custom of adoption made the adopted children full heirs of the adoptive father's estate. In Jewish tradition, being God's son(s) or children meant intimacy with God and entitlement to the inheritance (cf. 9:4), first of the land and later of eschatological salvation. This eschatological salvation is what Gentiles and Jews alike, in Christ, will inherit as God's adopted children.

The experiential proof (8:16) of believers' adoption is their address to God in the Aramaic of Jesus — "Abba!" or "Father!" (8:15). That churches consisting largely of Gentile believers maintained this custom in prayer, perhaps at baptism (cf. Gal. 4:6, following 3:27) and at other times, attests the power of Jesus' exemplary relationship of both intimacy and obedience toward God. Here, moreover, Paul focuses on the familial status and privilege believers share with Christ: as God's children, they are "joint heirs" or coheirs with Christ the Son (8:17a). That is, they will share in the inheritance of resurrection and life (8:11). However, once again Paul attaches a responsibility, even a condition: "if, in fact, we suffer with him [lit. 'cosuffer'] so that we may also be glorified [lit. 'coglorified'] with him" (8:17b). Sharing the glory of God is humanity's original state (1:23) and final goal,[14] but to be coheirs with Christ in future glory requires cosuffering with Christ now. That is the second dimension of cruciformity, a reality already mentioned in 5:3-4 and now to be developed in 8:18-39.

Suffering and Glory (8:18-39)

The second half of Romans 8 is among the most moving parts of the Bible, culminating in 8:31-39, "one of the most stunning pieces of rhetorical art in the New Testament."[15] Here Paul contends that life in the Spirit — life in Christ, life as God's children — is indeed a life of suffering, but also that no suffering can destroy believers' hope or separate them from God's love in Christ.

The Reality of Suffering

Paul begins by defining the present as an era of suffering, but one that pales in comparison to the coming glory (cf. 2 Cor. 4:17). Paul seems to have adapted a Jewish belief that the age of eschatological salvation would be preceded by a great time of suffering, or 'messianic woes.' For Paul, such suffering is a constitutive part of life in Christ because Christ suffered prior to his glorification (8:17). Life in the Spirit, who is the Spirit of Christ, therefore

14. Rom. 2:7, 10; 3:23; 5:2; 8:18, 21.
15. Johnson, p. 133.

means not the absence but the necessary presence of suffering. At the very end of 8:30 Paul returns to the theme of glory, so assured of this future promise, the inheritance of God's children, that he can speak of it in the past tense: those God justified, God also glorified. Between these references Paul characterizes this age of suffering as creation's "labor pains" (8:22), during which creation (8:19-22), believers (8:23-25), and even the Spirit of God (8:26-27) groan, even as suffering shapes believers into the image of Christ (8:28-30). Apocalyptic writers often used the imagery of labor pains — intense suffering just before intense joy.

The groaning (8:22) of creation is due to its being "subjected to futility" and its "bondage to decay" (8:20-21), an interpretation of the curse of the earth following the first act of disobedience (Gen. 3:17b-19). Just as the earth suffers as a result of humanity's sin, so also it will be liberated and will prosper with humanity's redemption, when God's children are identified, marking the time of salvation (8:19, 21). For Paul, then, salvation is cosmic.

At the same time, believers also participate in the birth pangs as they await the completion of their adoption, bodily resurrection (8:23). Their salvation is not yet complete but is experienced in hope, requiring patience (8:24-25). They already possess, however, the "first fruits" (cf. 2 Cor. 1:22, "first installment") of their salvation, namely, the Spirit (8:23). And for Paul, even the Spirit groans while giving aid to, and interceding for, believers (8:26).[16] This remarkable assertion becomes all the more remarkable in the corollary that God (the Father) and the Spirit of God are of one intercessory mind and will (8:27), thus implying not only fatherly concern but even participation in the children's groans.

The thought of God's love and will leads to the famous claim of 8:28: "all things work together for good for those who love God."[17] This does not mean that God orders all the details of believers' lives into a rose-garden experience, but that all things contribute to the final, or eschatological, good of glorification (8:30), or conformity to the firstborn Son (8:29; cf. 8:17). This is the 'purpose' for which believers have been "called" and "predestined" (8:28, 29). The language is that of Israel's election, now applied to the family of Gentiles and Jews in Christ. Paul's point is not to claim that certain individuals, rather than others, have been predestined to salvation, but to identify the scope, purpose, and dependability of God's call in Christ. But this goal of conformity *(symmorphous)* to "the image of his Son" requires, as Paul has already said, cosuffering *(sympaschomen,* 8:17). Does that mean God and Christ somehow seek believers' harm?

---

16. NRSV's "sighs too deep for words" should be 'groans.'

17. Or perhaps 'God works all things together' — the meaning would be the same for Paul.

Deus Pro Nobis

Paul's answer to that question appears in 8:31-39: No! God is for us, *pro nobis*. No matter what comes, God's love, Christ's love, is certain. Paul formulates this answer with such intensity and passion that only a series of emotionally charged rhetorical questions, borrowed from the courtroom, will suffice (8:31-35). The first declarative sentences do not appear until the second half of 8:33 and 8:34, and even these may be rhetorical questions: Is it God the justifier who brings charges . . . or Christ Jesus the intercessor who condemns? If so, then 8:31-36 consists of nine successive rhetorical questions — all answered only implicitly, but clearly — before the final answer is given in declarative form in 8:37-39.

"These things" (NIV, NAB: "this") in 8:31 refers back to the experiences of cosuffering and groaning that believers in general face, ahead to the apostle's own hardships (8:35b-36),[18] and still further ahead to the general powers in the cosmos that oppose or might oppose humanity (8:38-39a). The present suffering does not mean that God is against us or will fail to bring us to glory, for if God did not withhold but gave his own Son (cf. 8:3),[19] God who justified us (8:33b) will certainly complete the work of salvation (8:32; "everything else" is literally 'all things'; cf. the end of 8:30). Nor does the present suffering mean that Christ Jesus opposes believers, for the love he embodied in his death persists in the present, after resurrection and exaltation, as he intercedes for us at God's right hand (8:34-35a, thus making intercession a trinitarian activity; cf. 8:26-27).[20]

The questions finally bring Paul to his answer, his thesis: "in all these things we are more than conquerors [Gk. *hypernikōmen*] through him who loved us" (8:37). The preceding verse suggests that the subject of the love is Christ, though 8:39 describes it also as "the love of God" in Christ. The Jewish attitude toward suffering was to endure it and, when possible, to resist it and overcome it; the Stoic attitude was to 'conquer' (Gk. *nikaō*) it by recognizing its inability to affect the true, inner self. Paul's attitude was that those in Christ 'hyper-conquer' (Gk. *hypernikaō*) in the midst of suffering because they know God's love and possess a sure hope as they suffer with Christ. Therefore, nothing in all creation — not the vicissitudes of life and death and of present and future, not cosmic or political powers of any sort or in any location — can separate believers from God's love and purpose in Christ for his children.

18. As expected of those devoted to God, according to Ps. 44:22.

19. An allusion to Abraham's offering of Isaac, Gen. 22.

20. As in other chapters, trinitarian language is used here in recognition that although Paul does not have a fully developed theology of the Trinity, such language is nonetheless appropriate.

Summary of Romans 5–8

Chapters 5–8 spell out the meaning of 'justification by faith' with an overview and then three sets of antithetical narratives.

- Justification is reconciliation with God in the present, together with certain hope of salvation (acquittal and glory) in the future, based on the death of Christ in the past, and all known through the gift of the Spirit.
- Adam's one act of disobedience inaugurated the reign of sin and death, while Christ's one act of obedience (on the cross) inaugurated the reign of grace.
- In baptism believers have died to sin and been raised to new life with Christ, liberated from the old self for service ('slavery') to God rather than to sin, the end of which is future resurrection and eternal life.
- The justified are no longer indwelt by sin and captive to the flesh, but experience a mutual indwelling of Christ and the Spirit (in Christ, Christ within; in the Spirit, the Spirit within) so that they may live in covenant relationship with God as adopted children.
- This life has a cruciform shape in two main senses, dying to the flesh and suffering, and culminates in glory: the bodily resurrection, completion of the process of being made into Christ's likeness, and sharing the splendor of God with the entire redeemed creation.

9:1–11:36. GOD'S FAITHFULNESS AND THE FUTURE OF ISRAEL

The gospel Paul preached was for Jews first and also Gentiles (1:16). But his experience was that many Jews — not unlike himself at one time — rejected the gospel about their crucified Messiah. At the same time, many Gentiles were coming to faith, often because of the work of Paul and his associates. This situation caused Paul immense agony; it was his greatest practical, spiritual, and theological challenge. Has God been unfair? unfaithful? Does Paul's gospel of the "righteousness of God" (1:17) ultimately reveal an *unrighteous* God? These questions, briefly raised and addressed in 3:1-9, are now taken up in detail. Paul employs the techniques of diatribe (questions and answers) and midrash (scriptural interpretation), drawing on the bank of Scripture — which he quotes, sometimes with alterations, more than thirty times in these chapters (with nearly half the citations from Isaiah) — for his answers. Dealing with the past, present, and future of God's salvific activity, Paul asserts that God is faithful to Israel even if most Jews are not now confessing the central conviction of his gospel: that Jesus is the Jewish Messiah and universal Lord.

Complicating Paul's situation is the apparent arrogance of (at least some of) the Gentile believers in Rome. This arrogance may have arisen due to the earlier banishment of Jews (including believers) from Rome under the emperor Claudius, as well as the small number of Jewish believers. Both realities may have been interpreted by Gentiles as a sign of divine disapproval and even rejection of the Jews. Paul's sustained theological argument, which focuses on God's great mercy (9:14-29; 11:30-32; cf. 12:1; 15:9) and thus faithfulness, also has a very pastoral aim: to prevent pride and to engender unity and respect. This purpose is later fleshed out in the specific admonitions to the community of Gentile and Jewish believers in 14:1–15:13.

JEWISH UNBELIEF, PAULINE ANGUISH, AND DIVINE FAITHFULNESS (9:1-29)

Paul's discourse begins with a passionate statement of his anguish over the unbelief in the gospel, by and large, of his fellow Jews (9:1-5). This is followed by a narrative defense of God's faithfulness, freedom, and mercy (9:6-29).

Paul's Anguish over Jewish Unbelief (9:1-5)

Paul's claim to "great sorrow and unceasing anguish" (9:2), affirmed three times as a solemn oath (9:1), is one of his most emotional and self-revelatory remarks. He is willing to be cursed (made *anathema*) and cut off from Christ — to forfeit his own salvation — for the sake of his fellow Jews (9:3), who have failed to believe in the Messiah despite all their privileges (9:4-5). Paul's oath is nothing less than an outburst of sacrificial, or cruciform, love, for he knows that Christ became a curse for others (Gal. 3:13). It is also reminiscent of Moses' plea before God to punish him rather than the Israelites who had committed idolatry and immorality before the golden calf (Exod. 32:30-34). The privileges that have not assisted Jews in coming to faith in the gospel of the Messiah include, ironically, the very realities that Paul's gospel affirms as fulfilled now in new ways: for example, "adoption," "the promises," and the Messiah himself (9:4-5). Nevertheless, the thought of God's goodness to Israel leads Paul in 9:5 either to bless God (so NRSV, NAB) as a foretaste of 11:33-36 or to affirm the deity of the Messiah (NIV); the translation of the verse is difficult and debated.

God's Freedom, Mercy, and Faithfulness (9:6-29)

This failure of belief cannot for Paul be the failure of God's performative word (9:6a). Rather, Paul asserts that "not all Israelites truly belong to Israel" (9:6b). This claim leads Paul into a narrative of God's salvific activity (extending to 9:29) that reveals a pattern: that which looks like capricious and unjust divine action is actually part of a larger plan in which God acts freely, mercifully, and faithfully. This (admittedly difficult) passage must be read in context as offering precedents for God's surprisingly merciful activity in and through the gospel. If it is read — as it often is — as a theological treatise on predestination rather than as a testimony to God's mercy and faithfulness, Paul's main concern in chapters 9–11 (and perhaps beyond those chapters) will likely be missed.

Paul begins by recognizing a biblical distinction between descendants of the "flesh" and descendants of the "promise" (9:6b-18). This develops the important contention of 2:28-29 that not all Jews are true Jews (cf. 9:6b) and places it in the framework of divine election rather than human choice or merit. Paul says Abraham's true offspring and thus God's real children are not merely Abraham's physical descendants, but "the children of the promise" made to Abraham and Sarah and fulfilled in the birth of Isaac (rather than Ishmael; cf. Gen. 21:8-14).[21] Similarly, according to 9:10-13, God loved Jacob (= Israel, from whom the twelve tribes of Israel descended) but not Esau (from whom the people of Edom, rejected by God [Mal. 1:3], came). This was due solely to God's call, not anything good or bad done by either of Isaac's sons (9:11-12).

These two examples of God's election at the foundation of Israel as a nation are confirmed for Paul as examples of divine freedom and mercy, not injustice (9:14), in a word spoken to Moses after the exodus (9:15-16; cf. Exod. 33:19) and in the exodus itself (9:17). God is free to show mercy or not to any and all (9:18), but Paul's main point is that God has been (and is) about the business of unexpected, undeserved mercy. This is further affirmed in the scriptural illustration of the potter (9:20-24; cf. Isa. 29:16; Jer. 18:6), which is not intended to defend the predestination of some individuals to salvation and others to damnation, but rather the freedom of God to surprise people with mercy and ultimately to 'glorify' them (cf. 3:23; 5:2; 8:18, 30). Human beings have no right to challenge this divine prerogative, because the same freedom allows God to have mercy on the undeserving, whether Jews or Gentiles (9:24).

The mention of both Jews and Gentiles is an echo of the thematic state-

---

21. Of course, for Paul true Israelites, true children of Abraham, and true children of God are those who share Abraham's faith by acknowledging Jesus as God's resurrected Son/Messiah (4:12-25; 8:12-17). This central conviction is assumed in chap. 9 and reaffirmed in chap. 10.

ment of 1:16-17 that has surfaced repeatedly in the letter. The pattern of God's merciful election is now occurring in the salvation of both Gentiles (9:25-26, applying Hosea's prophetic word spoken about disobedient Israelites [Hos. 1:10; 2:23] to Gentiles contemporary with Paul) and Jews (9:27-29). But the salvation of "the children of Israel" is not always in large numbers — another surprising feature of God's mercy. In fact, Isaiah saw divine mercy in the saving of a small number, a "remnant" (9:27; cf. Isa. 10:20-23), for otherwise Israel would have been destroyed like Sodom and Gomorrah (9:29; cf. Isa. 1:9). This past divine action becomes the paradigm for Paul's own time in his analysis of the Jewish response to the gospel (a "remnant," 11:1-5).

In this section, then, Paul has affirmed God's free exercise of unexpected and undeserved mercy in the past and thus God's faithfulness to Israel and to his promises. This pattern of surprising mercy, according to Paul's reading of Israel's prophets, goes beyond the bounds of ethnic Israel to include even Gentiles, while it simultaneously saves only a remnant of Israel. This practice of Gentile inclusion, paired with the formation of a Jewish remnant, is for Paul the paradigm of God's present activity through the proclamation of the gospel, as we will see in what follows.

REAFFIRMATION OF SALVATION FOR ALL
THROUGH THE GOSPEL (9:30–10:21)

Paul now connects the pattern of the startling mercy of God for Gentiles as well as Jews narrated and defended in 9:6-29 with its present manifestation in the arrival of the Messiah and in the gospel about the Messiah that is spreading throughout the world. Paul begins by noting the contrasting response to the Messiah among Gentiles and Jews (9:30-33) and restates his desire (now a prayer) for the salvation of his fellow Jews (10:1-4). He then reaffirms the availability of the gospel to Jews and Gentiles alike, and thus the necessity of its proclamation (10:5-17), before returning briefly to the themes of contrasting Gentile and Jewish responses to the gospel and God's ceaseless mercy (10:18-21).

The Current Situation and Paul's Prayer (9:30–10:4)

Paul applies the theological observations of 9:7-29 to his own context by noting that Gentiles who were not even looking for righteousness have attained righteousness through faith — the righteousness that derives from the response of faith (in the gospel of the Messiah) — while "Israel" failed to fulfill the Law (i.e., attain righteousness) by means of the Law (9:30-32a). This is a disparagement not of the Law but of misguided zealous attempts to fulfill it apart from the Messiah, as Paul will say in 10:2-4. God's chosen people have by and large missed the boat, so to speak, or in Paul's metaphor (9:32b), "stumbled over the stumbling stone" *(petran skandalou)* — the Messiah (9:33).[22] It appears that many early Christians associated Christ with this stone spoken of by Isaiah.[23] For Paul, at least, the cause of stumbling or 'scandal' among his fellow Jews was the death of the alleged Messiah by crucifixion (1 Cor. 1:23; Gal. 5:11). Those who believe in him, however, "'will not be put to shame'" (9:33; cf. 1:16; 10:11).

Though (most of) his fellow Jews have stumbled, Paul repeats his deep desire for their salvation (10:1), echoing 9:1-5. (In 11:11 we learn that the stumbling is not "so as to fall.") He acts as a court witness, claiming from personal experience (cf. Gal. 1:13-14; Phil. 3:6) that they have a misguided "zeal" by which they attempt to establish right relations with God on their own terms rather than on God's (10:2-3).[24] The means to God's righteousness is not the Law, for the Law points beyond itself to the Messiah, who is the "end" *(telos)* of the Law (10:4). The sense of "end" here has been hotly debated; does Paul mean 'termination,' 'goal,' or both? The context suggests that Paul means both, but with an emphasis on goal. Paul means something like 'the Messiah is the focal point of Scripture, the goal of the salvation history to which Scripture bears witness, and thus the God-given means of righteousness.' The arrival of the Messiah, then, means that the Law ceases to be the means of righteousness, not because it is abrogated, but because only the divine gift of the Messiah and his Spirit makes the fulfillment of the Law, and thus righteousness, possible (see 8:3-4). Righteousness is now available to "everyone who believes" (10:4).

The Ongoing Universality of the Gospel (10:5-21)

To clarify what "righteousness for everyone who believes" means, Paul summarizes for the Roman believers the content and the availability of God's gospel: salvation for all, Gentiles and Jews alike, who believe that God raised the crucified Messiah Jesus and confess that he is Lord (10:5-13). The somewhat confusing text in 10:5-8 is meant principally to affirm the proximity of this divine word of salvation and its character as God's means of covenant renewal (and thus righteousness) through Christ. As in Deuteronomy 30, which supplies the

22. That is, "the stone that causes stumbling" (NAB). This stone has sometimes (mistakenly) been interpreted as the Law or the gospel.

23. Isa. 8:14; 28:16; cf. Matt. 21:42; Acts 4:11; 1 Pet. 2:6.

24. Only the NIV's description of the zeal as "not based on knowledge," rather than NAB's "not discerning" or NRSV's "not enlightened," accurately conveys the Greek.

quotations and key words "mouth" and "heart" in 10:7-10, this invitation to covenant life with God is not something to be searched for hither and yon, for it is present here and now, in the apostolic proclamation. Those who respond in faith, affirming with heart and mouth Jesus' lordship by virtue of God's resurrection of him from the dead, are justified now — part of God's covenant people — and will be saved in the future (10:9-10), as the scriptural citation from Isaiah already cited (9:33) affirms (10:11; cf. Isa. 28:16).[25] Although it is unwise to split hairs about the sequence of human and divine actions named in this verse (belief, confession, justification, salvation), it is important to note Paul's emphasis on both internal conviction and public affirmation.

Because the covenant renewal of Deuteronomy 30 was to take place after exile (Deut. 30:1-5), Paul apparently reads the Deuteronomic text in light of prophetic texts that speak of the postexilic salvation of the nations (Gentiles) as well as Israel. The explicit theological grounding of the universal availability of the gospel, however, is the oneness of the Lord (10:12) — that is, Jesus.[26] As elsewhere (e.g., 1 Cor. 12:3; Phil. 2:11), Paul here applies *kyrios* (lord), the Greek Bible's title for YHWH, to Jesus (10:13, citing Joel 2:32). Salvation is offered to those, and only to those, who "call on" the Lord — on Jesus. Paul knows no other way of salvation — of participation in the covenant — for Jews or for Gentiles.

God's offer of the gospel to all comes through human agents (such as Paul, but also others who are sent, 10:14-16). The rhetorical questions in 10:14-15a and the partial quotation of Isaiah 52:7 in 10:15b forcefully affirm Paul's commitment to the spread of the message about the Messiah (10:17). The word indeed must go out and has gone out (10:17-18). But like Isaiah, the preachers of good news may experience disbelief and disobedience — the two words are synonymous for Paul (1:5; 11:20, 31; 16:26) — to the message (10:16). Nevertheless, Paul sees himself as part of the team of messengers embodying Isaiah's text about announcing good news about the Messiah to the ends of the earth (10:18; cf. Isa. 52:7-10).

With the message having gone out, Paul wonders aloud if perhaps Israel has not heard or understood; the answer is that Israel has indeed heard but has not understood (10:18-19a). Nevertheless, Paul finds in Scripture (specifically in the words of Moses [Deut. 32:21] and Isaiah [Isa. 65:1]) warrant for the belief that God is making Israel jealous by finding (i.e., 'saving') those not looking for God (10:19b-20; cf. 9:25-26, 30) — a clear reference to the believing Gentiles of Paul's day. At the same time, Isaiah bears witness to Paul and his readers that

---

25. The shame referred to is eschatological shame, as in 5:5, where the NRSV translates the same verb as "disappoint."

26. Cf. 3:29-30, where a similar affirmation about God (the Father) and justification is made.

God extends open arms to Israel, ready to welcome back the "disobedient and contrary" covenant people (10:21, quoting from Isa. 65:2; cf. 9:31-33). Paul ends this section where he had begun it, reflecting on the troublesome phenomenon of Gentile belief and Jewish unbelief, but also affirming the fidelity and mercy of God to Israel.

The point of this section as a whole, then, is that justification (covenant relationship with God) and salvation remain available to all, Jew and Gentile alike, who confess Jesus as the (crucified Messiah and) resurrected Lord. The gospel has gone out, and though many Jews have not yet obeyed it, God stands ready to take back the chosen but disobedient people.

THE MYSTERY OF MERCY (11:1-36)

Moving toward his stirring doxological conclusion (11:33-36), in this chapter Paul firmly dismisses any thought of God's rejecting Israel (11:1a), first affirming the existence of a remnant that does believe the gospel (11:1-10) and finally affirming the salvation of "all Israel" (11:25-32). Between these affirmations he describes the role of Gentile belief as (in part) a tool to make Israel jealous (11:11-16) and uses the famous image of the olive tree (11:17-24) to discourage the Gentiles from pride and urge them to faithfulness and kindness.

The Remnant and the Olive Tree (11:1-24)

With a resounding "Of course not!" (11:1a NAB) and a firm declaration (11:2a), Paul answers the burning question of whether Israel's rejection of the gospel means God's rejection of Israel. Returning to the historical pattern of a "remnant" (11:5; cf. 9:27-29), Paul offers himself (11:1b) — and other Jewish believers, implicitly — as tangible proof that once again, as in the time of Elijah (11:2b-4), God has preserved a remnant of faithful, obedient people, "chosen by grace" (11:5). Sometimes, as Scripture observes (11:8-10), in God's mysterious working only a remnant, not the entire people (11:7), perceives what God is up to; the rest trip over a "stumbling block" (*skandalon* in 11:9, citing Ps. 69:22 LXX).

But the good news is that Israel's unbelief is not without purpose in the divine economy, and it is not a fatal fall (i.e., as we will see, it is only partial and temporary). Israel's 'stumbling' (11:11a) over the Messiah (9:32-33; 11:9) has resulted in salvation for Gentiles (11:11b). The Jews' "full inclusion" (11:12; note Paul's confidence!),[27] that is, their eventual salvation (11:26), will bring even

---

27. NAB, "full number"; NIV, "fullness." The Greek is *plērōma*, as of the Gentiles in 11:25.

more blessings (11:12, 15). In the meantime, Paul hopes, through his ministry to the Gentiles, to make Israel "jealous" and thus to bring "some" (11:14) to faith (11:13-16). The existence of a remnant, imaged in 11:16 as holy "dough" related to a large "batch" and as a holy "root" related to multiple "branches," is a sign of the future 'sanctification' (salvation) of the entire batch and all the branches. This reference to a "root" and "branches" leads Paul to the famous analogy of the natural and grafted branches of the olive tree and its root (11:17-24).

It is important to note that Paul addresses this analogy (or allegory) to the Gentiles (11:13; i.e., Gentile believers) as a word of instruction and warning. Israel often understood itself as God's tree, vine, or vineyard.[28] In his use of this traditional image, Paul understands the olive tree not as ethnic Israel but more broadly as God's covenant people rooted in Israel. He says (11:17) that some natural branches of God's olive tree were broken off (= unbelieving Jews) and replaced by a wild olive shoot grafted on (= the contingent of believing Gentiles). The grafted-on branches should not "boast over" (be arrogant toward) the broken-off branches, for they are supported by the tree's root (probably Israel, but perhaps the patriarchs or Abraham) and are even more liable to pruning than were the natural branches (11:18-21). Gentile believers, then, must not be proud about their status or unmerciful toward the natural branches, not even those that have been broken off, for without "awe" (NRSV, NAB; not NIV's reference to 'fear' for *phobos*) at God's mercy, as well as mercy in turn to others, Gentile believers may themselves be cut off (11:20-22). The whole situation has nothing to do with the merits of individuals or of ethnicity but only with the kindness of God and the response of faith.

Moreover, Paul continues in 11:23-24, if God can perform the agriculturally abnormal feat of grafting unnatural branches onto a "cultivated olive tree" (11:24), God surely has the power to graft the broken-off natural branches back on again (11:23). The only thing that must happen for God to do just that is for the broken-off branches — the unbelieving Jews — not to "persist in unbelief" (11:23). Just as the Gentiles who have been grafted on to the tree are there only by God's mercy and their faith (11:20, 22) — that is, their faith in the gospel of the Messiah — so also Jews need only God's mercy and that same faith in the gospel of the Messiah to be reconnected to God's covenant people. This is what Paul has already said repeatedly in chapter 10 and throughout the letter. It is imperative, in other words, to note that Paul does not here change the criterion for inclusion (i.e., salvation). That criterion is, negatively, the end of unbelief, or, positively, faith in the gospel of Christ.

---

28. E.g., Isa. 4:2; 5:1-7; 27:2-6; 60:21; 61:3; Jer. 2:21; 11:16-17; Ezek. 19:10-14; Hos. 10:1; Pss. 80:8-19; 92:12-14; cf. John 15:1-11.

The Logical and Doxological Conclusions (11:25-36)

Everything Paul has said so far in chapters 9–11 now comes to its logical (for him) conclusion (11:25-33), but it is a conclusion that has puzzled interpreters for nearly two thousand years. Paul may have thought of this conclusion as a "mystery" (11:25) in the sense of 'clear revelation,' but for his readers it has been much more confusing than clear. The following paragraphs acknowledge other possible readings of the text but argue for a particular interpretation — with a few loose ends. Whatever Paul's precise conclusion, it was and is meant to lead to the praise of the one all-merciful God (11:33-36).

The first claim Paul makes is relatively clear (note, however, the ongoing tone of correction in 11:25a): Israel's current unbelief ("hardening") is only *partial* and *temporary* (11:25b). It will last only until "the full number [Gk. *plērōma*, as in 11:12 of the Jews] of the Gentiles has come in" (11:25), which some interpreters understand as a fixed number and/or time period (as is common in apocalyptic thought), and others as a general reference to a widespread Gentile response to the gospel. But it may, in parallel with 11:12, mean *all* Gentiles as opposed to some (cf. 11:15, "the reconciliation of the [Gentile] world"). When the Gentiles (in one of these senses) have believed, then "all Israel will be saved" (11:26).

This provocative text — "all Israel will be saved" — is far less clear and elicits three basic questions: *Who? How? When?* Many different answers to these questions have been suggested. We will start in the middle. The basic *how* question seems self-evident: by abandoning unbelief and disobedience, and by believing and obeying the gospel. Both the immediate context (11:23) and the larger context (e.g., 10:5-17, not to mention the letter as a whole) demand this answer, however much it might offend the modern sensibilities of some. In other words, the *how* question must be answered with a firm christological response and not merely a theological one. For Paul, there is no way to salvation (e.g., via the Law) except confession of Jesus as Messiah and Lord. But part of this question involves identifying the agent: Is it Paul through his preaching, a broader group of missioners, or perhaps God acting in some as-yet-unknown future way? We shall return to this issue when considering *when*.

As for the *who* question, it is tempting to import the idea of a spiritual Israel comprised of believing Jews and Gentiles. A few texts in Romans and elsewhere in Paul make this a possibility, for Paul does indeed distinguish between ethnic Israel and a true, or circumcised, Israel (2:28-29; 9:6-7; cf. Gal. 6:16; Phil. 3:3). Once again, however, the whole context and flow of the argument suggest a different answer. Throughout chapters 9–11 Paul's burden is for his fellow Jews, ethnic Israel, the large number of broken-off branches. He has already expressed hope (if not confidence) that the fate of the "batch" and the "branches" will be that of the "dough" and the "root" (11:16). That is, Paul has already implied that God's nonrejection of Israel means more than that *some* nonbelieving Jews will change their minds. Otherwise Paul's argument about a "remnant" of faithful Jews would have been sufficient to demonstrate the fidelity of God. It is difficult, therefore, to resist the conclusion that "all Israel" means 'all Jews' rather than 'all Gentiles and Jews who believe the gospel.'[29]

The oft-quoted text "the gifts and the calling of God are irrevocable" (11:29) confirms this interpretation. If Paul simply meant that Jews are not excluded from the gospel, he would be merely restating the obvious, for there is already a remnant of Jewish believers. But a remnant, however large, hardly seems like a long-term fulfillment of an irrevocable call; it is more a stopgap measure. On the other hand, modern attempts to interpret these words as Paul's affirmation of the salvation of Jews apart from Christ, or by some other means, completely ignore the context and argument of chapters 9–11. Rather, Paul affirms that the stance of *all* Jews will one day be reversed from disobedience to obedience, just as the Gentile believers have received mercy and become obedient (11:30-32). The final statement, "For God has imprisoned all in disobedience so that he may be merciful to all" (11:32), refers, in context, to all Jews and to all Gentiles who believe the gospel. If the "full number" of each (Gentiles and Jews) means "all" in both instances (11:12, 25), then Paul here affirms that eventually all human beings will believe the gospel and be saved. But that cannot be affirmed, or denied, with certainty.

Remaining to be answered is the *when* question. The "will be saved" of 11:26 is linked to two texts from Isaiah (27:9; 59:20-21) that, together, forecast the forgiveness of Jacob's (Israel's) sins, the removal of its ungodliness (cf. 1:18), and the renewal of the covenant when "the Deliverer" comes "out of Zion [Jerusalem]" (11:26-27). This Deliverer could be YHWH but is more likely YHWH's Messiah; the text refers, then, either to the first or, more likely, second advent *(parousia)* of the Messiah. The eschatological coming of Jesus the Deliverer will result in the salvation of all Jews through faith, i.e., through the acknowledgment of his lordship. Specifically, Paul likely means that all his contemporary Jews who have so far disbelieved the gospel and thus been "broken off" from the olive tree (i.e., those alive during and after the time of Jesus' death and resurrection) will believe it, joining the ranks of all faithful Jews who preceded the advent of Jesus and all Gentiles who have believed the gospel.[30] Although the phrase "all Israel" *can*

---

29. There is still the question of whether that means all Jews of all time, Israel as a whole but not every individual Jew, all Jews of Paul's day, or all Jews alive at the parousia; see below.

30. Given Paul's definition of unbelief (rejection of the gospel of Jesus as Messiah and Lord), it seems he either has no concern, or at least expresses none, about Jews who lived before the Messiah and "the end of the law" (10:4). It is also possible, however, that Paul means that at the parousia, when the dead are raised, there will be an acknowledgment of Jesus as Messiah and

mean Israel as a whole but not every individual, and *might* if *plērōma* (fullness) is interpreted narrowly, there is more reason to think that Paul envisages all Jews.

The *logical* conclusion of chapter 11, of chapters 9–11 together, and indeed of the letter to this point yields finally to a *doxological* conclusion. Paul's confidence in God's mercy engenders in Paul praise to God that is expressed in some of the most beautiful language of the New Testament (11:33-36).

Summary of Romans 9–11

In these chapters Paul addresses the problem of Israel's unbelief in the gospel.
- This situation tears Paul's heart, not due to some sentimentality, but to its apparent challenge to his own gospel and especially to God's fidelity to Israel.
- The unbelief is not due to the failure of God's word and is not an example of divine injustice, for God is both free and merciful.
- Israel's lack of faith is due to stumbling over the Messiah in a misguided zeal about the means to righteousness.
- Salvation is available for all those (and only for those) who believe God raised Jesus from the dead and who confess his lordship.
- Israel's unbelief is partial and temporary; a remnant exists, and after a time of the Gentiles coming to faith, the remainder of Israel will also come to faith at the parousia, so that "all Israel will be saved."
- In the meantime, Gentiles should humbly acknowledge their status as "branches" that have been "grafted in" to God's olive tree and should not boast against the Jews.

12:1–15:13. FAITHFUL LIVING BEFORE THE FAITHFUL GOD: CRUCIFORM HOLINESS AND HOSPITALITY

The final word of God and of God's mystery is, as we have seen, "mercy" (11:30-32). This is the good news of God's love in Christ crucified for Jews and Gentiles, the good news of God's faithfulness to the promise made to Abraham that all the world would be blessed through him. This is the gospel that requires, in light of God's mercy, the "obedience of faith" from those in God's new

---

Lord by all Jews. In either case, it is quite possible that Paul believes that an appearance of Jesus, not unlike what Paul himself experienced, is what Jews as a whole will require to acknowledge the crucified Jesus as Messiah and Lord. (I owe this last observation to my colleague Judy Ryan.)

covenant community, and that is the theme of this letter. Although the radical, countercultural character of this obedience has been suggested in chapters 5–8, it is in chapters 12–15 that Paul spells out in some detail what shape this life of obedience should take. The variety of topics in chapters 12 and 13 all relate to the community's general internal life and external relations, while 14:1–15:13 centers on the need for mutual acceptance in the face of factions and judgmentalism. In these chapters Paul calls the Romans to a life of holiness and hospitality that is rooted, not surprisingly (though not always explicitly), in the cross. It should be noted that some of what Paul says to the Romans he has already said to the Corinthians (1 Cor. 8–13).

HOLINESS: A COMMUNITY OF
GOODNESS AND LOVE (12:1–13:14)

Chapters 12 and 13 begin with a general exhortation that governs the entire discussion in 12:1–15:13. They then proceed to more specific words of apostolic counsel, with the themes of goodness and especially love emphasized.

Cruciform Holiness (12:1-2)

These first two verses set the tone and provide the framework for everything that follows. But they begin with a clear link to all that Paul has said thus far, especially in chapters 9–11, for Paul's entire appeal is based on the "mercies of God" (12:1) that he has narrated with passion.

Although the word 'cross' does not appear in the text of 12:1-2, Paul is clearly calling for a cruciform countercultural (i.e., "holy") community. The community address ("brothers [and sisters]") is important; Paul is not writing merely to individuals. The two imperatives — "present your bodies as a living sacrifice" (12:1) and "do not be conformed to this world [lit. 'age'], but be transformed by the renewing of your minds" (12:2) — suggest *death* and *difference*. That is, being a living sacrifice means a constant process of dying yet living, or cruciformity, while being transformed (as a result of this "holy" [12:1] process) means becoming different from the environment that hosts the community. Both minds and bodies are affected, such that believers (Paul implies) are conformed to Christ and take on his mind (cf. 8:29; Phil. 2:1-11). As this occurs, the darkening of minds (1:21) and the degrading of bodies (1:24) associated with life in Adam are gradually undone.

The image of "living sacrifice" suggests an alternative to the temple sacrifices, a sacrifice that Jews and Gentiles can both perform, and perform together as God's temple (cf. 1 Cor. 3:16). It is their spiritual, rational, or reasonable (the term *logikos* can mean any of these) worship. This worship does not occur in specific places or at specific times; it is, rather, the liturgy of life. Building on chapter 6, Paul says believers are constantly in a paradoxical state of dying yet living (cf. Gal. 2:19-20). Dead to sin and alive to God (6:11), with the old self crucified (6:6), believers express their resurrection to new life (6:4) by presenting their bodies and bodily members (6:13, 19) as a living sacrifice to God. The reappearance of the verb "present" reinforces Paul's emphasis on believers' personal responsibility to embody the truth of their situation in Christ. Resurrection and freedom can be experienced only as death to self and slavery to God.

Such a lifestyle is inherently holy, or countercultural, yet again believers must take responsibility by allowing themselves to be transformed and thus to discern God's good will. This transformation describes in part the process of "sanctification" mentioned briefly in 6:19, 22; it is a process of unlearning and learning. Paul's goal in the following paragraphs is to assist the Roman church in that process.

Goodness and Love to All (12:3-21)

Two main topics are addressed in chapter 12, life within the community and proper treatment of those outside it.

Echoing words penned originally for the Corinthians (1 Cor. 12), Paul first counsels the Romans to live "with sober judgment" (12:3) as one unified body of Christ consisting of various "members" (12:4) and gifts (12:6-8). Paul clearly has in mind the factionalism and judgmentalism he will address in 14:1–15:13, as the phrase "according to the measure of faith that God has assigned" reveals (12:3; cf. 14:1, 22-23). The issue is one of attitude and judgment, and a renewed mind (12:2) would lead to humility rather than arrogance (12:3; cf. similar language in Phil. 2:1-5). In a word (which will appear in 12:9), proper self-examination should lead to love.

Paul does not restrict the discussion of Christ's one body to the Romans' factionalism. As in 1 Corinthians, he stresses unity in diversity (12:4-5a), as well as the interdependence and mutual belonging of the various members of the body (12:5b). Moreover, all members have gifts of God's grace (*charismata*, as in 1 Cor. 12:9, 28, 30-31), and prophecy again ranks first.[31]

Here in Romans Paul may be emphasizing the continuity of these gifts with those given throughout salvation history (cf. 11:29). What is also new here is the appearance of five gifts (of the seven named) not specifically listed in

---

31. Technically second in 1 Corinthians, following only apostleship (1 Cor. 12:28-29; 14:1).

1 Corinthians: "ministry" or service *(diakonia),* exhortation (though see 1 Cor. 14:31 [NRSV, "encouraged"]), giving, leading (or having authority), and compassion or mercy. Also distinctive in Romans is the stress on exercising whichever gift one has appropriately and responsibly, as an act of service to God and the church; this seems to be the upshot of the qualifying phrases in 12:6b-8.

The topic of exercising gifts soberly and graciously leads Paul to write next about love and goodness more broadly within and also outside the community (12:9-21). It is tempting to read 12:9-13 as referring only to the treatment of believers and 12:14-21 to unbelievers, but 12:15-16 seems clearly to refer to relations within the church. It has often been remarked that 12:9-21 has the appearance of a collection of maxims or proverbs, a list of (common early Christian?) exhortations (cf. 1 Thess. 5:12-22) offered without development on any one topic, except nonretaliation (12:14, 19-21). Yet the theme of goodness and love, though somewhat general, unites the maxims into a coherent and in fact cruciform shape. Moreover, Paul seems to have done some grouping of the maxims into his own categories.

For example, the first thirteen admonitions (12:9-13) appear to be about love (12:9-10, 13), faith (12:11), and hope (12:12), perhaps once again echoing the substance of 1 Corinthians (chaps. 12–13), in which a discussion of love (linked to faith and hope) follows the topic of gifts in the body. Paul's admonitions speak of a three-dimensional cruciformity:

- *Love.* Love must be "genuine" (NRSV) or "sincere" (NAB, NIV). Believers are to hate what is evil (not evil people) and hold fast to what is good (cf. 1 Thess. 5:21-22). (In 12:14, 21 this principle will be extended to outsiders as conquering evil with good rather than with retaliation.) They are to engage in "brotherly" (NIV) love *(philadelphia, philostorgoi),* or appropriate concern for fellow siblings in God's eschatological family. Practically speaking, this is expressed in outdoing others in showing honor, i.e., anticipating (see NAB) and meeting members' needs as one would those of family members, without selfish interest (12:10). It is also expressed in contributing to fellow believers' material needs and in welcoming travelers, of which there were many in the early churches (12:13). Finally, this love clearly excludes retaliation for evil (12:17), though the focus of that imperative is the treatment of nonbelievers.
- *Faith.* The three admonitions in 12:11 depict the community's relationship to God, possibly enumerating each of the three 'persons': its zeal or eagerness (toward God the Father?), its being aglow with the Spirit,[32] and its service ('enslavement,' as in chap. 6) to the Lord (Jesus).

32. So also many commentators, against most translations' reference to the ardor of the *human* spirit.

• *Hope.* The vocabulary of 12:12 is that of hope in the midst of opposition and is reminiscent of 5:3-5. Believers can be joyful as they endure adversity, with prayer as their means of survival.

These admonitions to cruciformity continue in 12:14-21. Within the community believers are expected to share in one another's sorrow and joy (12:15) and to embody a Christlike humility and concern for others, especially the "lowly" or humble, that creates harmony (12:16). Once again Paul not only amplifies what he has just said (12:3, 10) and echoes sentiments he expresses elsewhere (Phil. 2:1-5; 1 Cor. 12:22-26), but also anticipates the problem of divisiveness that he will address in 14:1–15:13.

This leads to Paul's final exhortation in chapter 12, concerning the treatment of outsiders — especially those who prove to be 'enemies' by their persecution and other evil deeds (12:14, 17-21). A general instruction suggests that believers should attempt to live in harmony with "all" — that is, outsiders — thus preempting trouble (12:18).[33] When evil comes, however, the community must respond as its Lord did and taught; 12:14 is a clear reference to Jesus' teaching preserved in Luke 6:28, and the entire passage here possesses the spirit of Luke 6:27-36 (Jesus' words) and Luke 23:32-43 (Jesus' example on the cross), as well as the entire Sermon on the Plain in Luke and the Sermon on the Mount in Matthew. Persecution is to be met with blessing rather than cursing (12:14). Vengeance, therefore, is not an option, as the Jewish Wisdom tradition itself had said (e.g., Prov. 20:22). For believers, retaliation not only violates their Lord's teaching and example but also usurps the future judgment of God that is central to the Scriptures (12:19, quoting Deut. 32:35).

This certainty of divine wrath — since in biblical thought the enemies of God's people are ultimately God's enemies — frees believers to deal in goodness with enemies. They can offer food and drink (12:20; cf. Prov. 25:21-22) and thereby "overcome [*nikaō*, 'conquer'] evil with good" rather than being "overcome by evil" (12:21). Nonretaliation is an essential part of being "more than conquerors through him who loved us" (8:37). But what about the puzzling phrase "heap burning coals on their heads" (12:20)? Both the present context and the use of this phrase in antiquity suggest, not inflicting some kind of punishment, but something like prompting repentance and turning the enemy into a friend. Repentance is, after all, the ultimate goal of God, who would prefer giving glory rather than inflicting wrath (2:4-11). Moreover, God did not treat enemies with wrath but with love in sending Christ to die (5:6-8). There is, however, no guarantee of success when love seeks to conquer evil, and believers must be prepared (as, for example, Dr.

---

33. "All" means outsiders in similar contexts in Gal. 6:10 and 1 Thess. 5:15.

Martin Luther King, Jr., was) to accept the consequences of the failure of nonretaliation to convert the oppressor.

A Nonrevolutionary Community (13:1-7)

Romans 13:1-7 is among the most difficult and potentially disturbing of all Pauline texts. Over the centuries it has too often been used to support the divine right of kings, blind nationalism, and unquestioned loyalty to rulers — even tyrants.

Some scholars have suggested that this passage is an interpolation, or later insertion, that does not fit the context or represent Paul's own beliefs. This thesis has not generally been accepted, however, and we must proceed on the dual assumption that Paul wrote it and placed it where he did for a reason.

The difficulties of this text suggest that we must approach it carefully, with appropriate exegetical safeguards, in order to avoid the most egregious errors of interpretation. Still, the issues the text raises cannot be fully solved even by careful exegesis, for they extend beyond Romans, Paul, and even the Bible itself into some of the most complex issues of theology and ethics. Exegetically speaking, however, the following set of presuppositions seems appropriate; the text is related to, and should be interpreted in light of:

- its immediate context
- the letter's larger context and overall purpose
- the concrete situation of the Roman church at the time of the letter
- Paul's overarching theological perspectives

These presuppositions hardly solve the interpretive problem, since each of them is itself disputed, but at least the interpretation offered here can be tested on the grounds of the plausibility of various aspects of the text's reconstructed contexts as well as the text itself.

The immediate context of 13:1-7 is the community's call to countercultural cruciformity (12:1-2) as the day of salvation approaches (13:11-14). This is to be expressed especially as loving care for all members and visitors (12:3-13, 15-16; 13:8-10), seeking peace with all outsiders (12:18), and returning good for any evil committed by enemies (12:14, 17-21). Paul's overall purpose in Romans seems to be to proclaim the gospel of God's righteousness for Jews and Gentiles, to apply that gospel to the situation of the church at Rome, and to solicit support for the spread of that gospel. That polyvalent purpose corresponds, we have suggested, to the concrete situation at Rome.

Some of the opposition to the church had likely arisen during the course of synagogue disputes about the truthfulness of Jewish believers' claims that the Messiah *("Chrestus")* was Jesus. Claudius's expulsion of Jews from Rome was clearly a political act designed to break up a perceived political threat. Jewish messianic expectation in general was anti-oppressor, and thus anti-Roman, since Rome was the supreme enemy of God's people at the time. Actual Jewish opposition to Rome did exist at the time, and sometimes took the form of tax protests and threats of revolt, especially in Palestine. It is more likely than not that the earliest churches in Rome included members who were sympathetic to Jewish revolutionary tendencies, and it is possible these tendencies were only increased with their conviction that the Messiah had come.

Since the views expressed in Romans 13 are often labeled 'conservative,' especially in comparison to Revelation 13, it is important at the outset to recall what we noted in the discussion of 1:16-17: that Paul's gospel had an inherently anti-imperial thrust: Jesus and Caesar cannot both rule the universe. This dimension of the gospel will mean that Paul cannot in any way espouse a blind nationalism or patriotism; in this respect he agreed with all Jews that there is but one true Lord, and it is not any earthly political figure. Paul will also agree with his fellow Jews, however, that God poses and deposes human authority (13:1-2).

What does all this mean for the interpretation of 13:1-7? It is clear that the presenting issue at Rome that leads Paul to write these verses is taxation (13:6-7), and specifically the possibility of resistance by Roman believers to Roman taxation (13:2, 4). General statements about authorities (13:1-4) and about submission/subjection to them (13:1, 5) should be understood primarily as providing the Jewish theological foundation for the concrete conclusion. Moreover, the literary context suggests that Paul's overall concern is to apply the principles of believers' cruciform responsibility to this particular situation. If (some of) the Roman believers saw the Roman authorities as enemies, their tax resistance would be for them a form of retaliation, which Paul's gospel prohibits (12:14, 17-20). Enemies the Roman authorities may be, or may one day become, but nevertheless they function as God's "servants" (13:4, 6). As divine servants, they are regarded in the Jewish tradition as accountable and answerable to God for their behavior, a point Paul undoubtedly assumes even if he does not mention it explicitly.[34]

Thus Paul does not see the Roman authorities as enemies, or if he does, he

---

34. See Wisd. of Sol. 6:1-21 (probably written shortly before Romans), where (Roman) rulers are acknowledged as established by God ("your dominion was given you from the Lord," 6:3) and therefore subject to punishment for failing to act with justice ("Because as servants of his kingdom you did not rule rightly, / or keep the law, / or walk according to the purpose of God, / he will come upon you terribly and swiftly, / because severe judgment falls on those in high places," 6:4-5).

treats them according to the gospel, by honoring them. The Romans have re-admitted Jews to Rome and must not be officially persecuting either the church or the Jewish community (though the possibility of such persecution in the future may lie, in part, behind Paul's concerns). Roman officials are not now the objects, but rather the agents, of divine wrath (13:4-5), a point which may be intended to reinforce the reality of God's wrath in the world (1:18) as well as the prohibition of vengeance by believers (12:14-21). This position does not, however, make any Roman rulers — not even the emperor — divine; they are worthy of respect (13:7), but only inasmuch as they are God's servants. Paul's gospel therefore requires that believers in this situation obey the laws and pay the taxes, seeking to live at peace with all.

If Paul has apparently turned an enemy of God's people into God's agent, he has done so in concert with his tradition, in which God's enemies are frequently also divine agents (e.g., Egypt, Assyria, Babylon). Paul does not in any sense idolize Rome but places it in its proper place under God. His advice to the Roman believers does not displace YHWH or Jesus as the true Lord; nor does it create a political theology, especially not one for all times and circumstances, or give blanket approval to any and every state policy and action. What it does, however, is redirect energy from resisting taxes to living in peace — something that may indirectly further the preaching of the gospel.

The Rule of Love (13:8-10)

The mention of obligations in 13:7 ("what is due") leads Paul in 13:8-10 to name the most important debt of all — mutual love. These verses both continue and summarize one of the two great interrelated themes of chapters 12–15 (the other being holiness, to which Paul returns in 13:11-14). They also establish the principle of community love about which Paul speaks at length in 14:1–15:13.

As he does in Galatians 5:14,[35] Paul here summarizes the 'second tablet' of the Law (13:9),[36] in the words "Love your neighbor as yourself." Paul understands love positively as that which edifies and honors (12:9-13; cf. 1 Cor. 8:1), and negatively as that which does no harm (13:10, reflecting the prohibitions in v. 9). Again as in Galatians 5:14, he also asserts that love (and thus the one who loves) 'fulfills' the Law (13:8, 10). This claim echoes 8:3-4, where Paul says God sent the Son so that "the just requirement of the law might be fulfilled" in those who walk according to the Spirit who creates love in the community (cf. Gal. 5:22). Thus for Paul the Son is both the source and the cruciform paradigm (as

35. And like Jesus himself according to Mark 12:31 and parallels.
36. Drawn from Exod. 20 and Deut. 5.

15:3 will make clear) of love, yet only in connection with God as the provider of both the Son and the Spirit. In other words, love is a trinitarian work.

The Eschatological Context (13:11-14)

Underlying all of Paul's exhortations is the conviction that the church is God's eschatological community, called to live in holiness (counterculturally) in anticipation of the coming of Christ and the triumph of God (cf., e.g., 1 Thess. 1:9-10). These verses make that assumption explicit and create an *inclusio* (a set of rhetorical bookends) with 12:1-2. The sacrificial image of holiness in 12:1-2 is transformed into a series of eschatological images in 13:11-14. Paul uses these images in the conviction that the 'salvation' that will arrive on "the day [of the Lord Jesus]" is near (13:12; cf. 13:11).

This conviction means that believers should wake, not sleep (13:11), and live in the light of the coming day, not the darkness of this age (13:12-13). This apocalyptic language for the moral life (13:13; cf. 1 Thess. 5:4-11) is meant to extinguish any remnants of pagan revelry as well as internal dissension (cf. Gal. 5:19-21). Both are instances of providing for, or 'walking according to,' the flesh (13:14; cf. 8:3-17), the latter example ("quarreling and jealousy") being mentioned as a segue into chapter 14. Believers no longer live in the night or in the flesh; immorality is therefore an anachronism. The antidote to such anachronistic behavior is expressed in the language of getting dressed, adopted (ironically) from the conventions of pagan morality as well as from early Christian baptismal liturgies: the Roman believers are constantly to "put on the armor of light" — i.e., "put on the Lord Jesus Christ" (13:12, 14; cf. Gal. 3:27). They are to live out their community story freed from the deeds of the flesh, guided by the Spirit, and clothed in the narrative of cruciform love found in Christ (cf. 15:1-3), into whose death all were immersed in baptism (6:3). This lifestyle, which must be appropriated daily, is their means of spiritual warfare.

HOSPITALITY: A COMMUNITY OF JEWS AND GENTILES (14:1–15:13)

On the surface, Romans 14:1–15:13 might look like a rather anticlimactic conclusion to the substance of this theologically powerful letter: words about a problem, or potential problem, concerning diet and calendar. But nothing could be further from the truth, at least in Paul's mind. This section *is* the climax, the goal toward which the theme of 'Jew and Gentile' has been incessantly driving. The word that matters utterly to Paul is 'hospitality,' or "welcome": "Welcome

397

one another, therefore, just as Christ has welcomed you, for the glory of God"
(15:7). Paul's mission to the Gentiles (15:14-33), to proclaim the Messiah where
he is not known (15:20), in no way excludes Jews, and it certainly is not intended
to give either Gentiles or Jews a superiority or inferiority complex. A community torn by intercultural strife subverts the gospel, as far as Paul is concerned,
and he seeks to unify a fractured, inhospitable multicultural community by
drawing on principles enumerated earlier for the Corinthians (1 Cor. 8:1–11:1).

There have been many attempts to identify the precise makeup and perspectives of the two groups described in these chapters, the "weak"/"weak in
faith" (14:1-2; 15:1) and the "strong" (15:1), or more neutrally, the observant and
nonobservant (of certain food and calendar practices). Although some scholars
deny that there was any concrete problem (making the passage a general admonition to avoid prejudice and practice tolerance, or a general theological statement about Gentile-Jewish relations in the church), and a very few believe the
"weak" are non-Christian Jews, most scholars find a specific problem in relations among two groups of believers at Rome. Paul refers to concrete issues and
addresses the participants as "brothers [and sisters]" (14:10, 13, 15, 21) who serve
the one Lord Christ (14:9) and are called to live in harmony with one another
through Christlike love (15:5).

It seems likely that the first group, the "weak" or observant believers, abstain from meat and wine (14:2, 21) and "judge one day to be better than another" (14:5a), or observe special holidays. The second group eats and drinks
anything (14:2, 21) and does not observe the holidays (14:5b). Although the Judaism of Paul's day did not prohibit the consumption of meat and wine, the
combination of food and calendar observance, together with the naming of the
"circumcised" and Gentiles (15:9-12), strongly suggests that the groups here are
divided along Jewish and Gentile leanings. This is not to say, most scholars
stress, that all the weak were ethnic Jews; it is quite possible that former God-
fearers and even pagan converts felt obliged to completely forsake pagan ways
by observing a strict diet and calendar. Forsaking meat and wine may have been
associated with the rejection of idolatry, in which context much meat and wine
was consumed. It is also possible that some of the "strong" were ethnic Jews
who felt that their freedom in Christ from the Law included especially freedom
from dietary and calendar regulations (probably like Paul himself).

It is important to note what the nature of Paul's exhortation in this situation is not, as well as what it is. Paul does not simply say to the Roman church,
'Anything goes.' *Paul is not the apostle of a modern or postmodern laissez-faire
Christian ethic of absolute tolerance of absolutely everything in the name of freedom and respect for diversity.* What Paul addresses here is a matter that does not
matter, an issue that the Stoics would include as part of the *adiaphora* — the
nonessentials. Diet and calendar do not constitute the kingdom or gospel of

God (14:17). Paul would have — and did have — quite different words for people who tried to impose something contrary to the gospel of Christ crucified (e.g., Galatians) or tried to confuse pagan immorality for the work of the Spirit (e.g., 1 Cor. 5–7).

Neither is this passage an appropriate basis for the modern individualistic mantra of morality, 'That's between me (or you) and God.' Not only is Paul dealing with inconsequential issues, but even on these matters he invokes a necessary concern for the community and for the glory of God that undercuts any self-centered or individualistic program.

What Paul requires in this passage is threefold: multicultural cruciform hospitality that accepts diversity in matters that do not matter; cruciform self-denial for the edification of others; and attention in everything to the praise of God through obedience to Christ. The burden of responsibility is on the strong, but the weak have obligations as well.

Adiaphora, Judgmentalism, and Accountability (14:1-23)

In the first half of this chapter (14:1-12) Paul weaves together a description of the two groups and their mutually judgmental attitudes with his views about service and accountability to the Lord. The weak, calendar-observant vegetarian teetotalers condemn the strong who consume everything but observe nothing, while the strong despise (lit. 'count as nothing') the weak (14:3, 10). On the assumption that the matter at hand is not essential to the gospel message but is something about which deeply held but differing personal convictions are acceptable (14:5; cf. 14:22-23), Paul makes two main points in response.

First, such judgmental behavior does not reflect the welcome of God in Christ (14:3), to which Paul will return in chapter 15, especially 15:7-13. Second, each believer lives for and is accountable to his or her Lord. This point Paul develops at some length and from several angles; it becomes a summary of the fundamentals of believing existence. He is not interested in defending libertinism but in explaining accountability. Believers do not live "to" (NRSV, NIV; or "for," NAB) themselves but to/for the Lord Jesus Christ (14:7-9; cf. 2 Cor. 5:15), which is how they "live to God" (Rom. 6:10-11). Whatever they do, in even the most mundane aspects of life like eating and drinking, they seek to honor God with their behavior (cf. 1 Cor. 10:31). Having this mind-set is absolutely fundamental to life in Christ; it is truly the only life-and-death issue for believers (14:8-9). On nonessential matters, therefore, what matters is that the behavior (e.g., eating or abstaining, observing a day or not) is done to glorify God in Christ. On this basis, and on this basis alone, will each believer one day give account to God as Lord and judge (14:10b-12). Believers are accountable both in life and in death to the Lord who has made them his own and for whom they live, paradoxically, as the Lord's freedpersons and slaves (cf. 1 Cor. 6:19-20; 7:22-23).

The second half of chapter 14 begins with a general admonition to all to refrain from judging others (14:13a), but moves quickly to a word directed to the strong that is an echo of 1 Corinthians 8. Like the meat-eaters in Corinth, the strong in Rome may be putting a "stumbling block" in the way of the weak (14:13b), potentially harming or even ruining them (14:15) by eating meat and drinking wine (14:20-21). Although Paul clearly sides with the strong in their convictions (15:1), stressing that in Christ no food is inherently unclean (14:14, 20), he calls their harmful-to-others actions a failure to embody unifying, edifying love (14:15, 19), and thus also a failure rightly to live out the kingdom through service to the Lord Christ in the peace and joy of the Holy Spirit (14:16-18). *Because the love of the triune God is demonstrated in the death of Christ (14:15), only the community that walks in cruciform love enjoys the presence and blessing of that triune God.* Although the 'liberal' actions that flow from one's convictions about these nonessential matters are not sinful and are accepted by God as long as they are done in faith (i.e., as an expression of loyalty to one's Lord; 14:22-23), they must be curtailed if they do harm to a brother or sister or to the community at large.

Cruciform Hospitality (15:1-13)

Paul's admonition to the strong continues in 15:1-4 before merging back into a general call to harmony and hospitality in 15:5-6 and especially in 15:7-13. 15:1-6 and 7-13 are structured in parallel form, each section beginning with an exhortation (vv. 1-2, 7), followed by an appeal to Christ (vv. 3a, 8-9a), a warrant in Scripture (vv. 3b-4, 9b-12), and a closing prayer-wish (vv. 5-6, 13).

Identifying himself with the strong, Paul calls on them to "put up with the failings of the weak" rather than "please ourselves." This is an obligation to love,[37] and the language is typical of Paul's exhortations to unity through love. Bearing others' burdens fulfills the law, or 'narrative pattern,' of Christ, the crucified Messiah (Gal. 6:2); pleasing others (i.e., acting for their benefit and edification) is how one becomes an imitator of Paul and thus of Christ (1 Cor. 10:33–11:1); a unified, loving community is possible only when, like Christ, believers seek the interests of others rather than their own (Phil. 2:1-11). Paul is clear that 'pleasing' one's neighbors means edifying or loving them (15:2), not placating them or catering to their whims. And as he does elsewhere, Paul once again

---

37. "Ought" in the NRSV is the same verb as "owe" (as in "owe" love) in 13:8.

grounds his exhortation in the narrative of Christ crucified (15:3-4), calling on a text commonly associated with Christ's death in the early churches (Ps. 69) to speak to the Romans (15:3).

Rather than pleasing himself, Christ — as Psalm 69:9 puts it — absorbed the insults of those who had insulted God. By reading this psalm text as an expression of Christ's freely chosen, prayerful attitude toward God, Paul encourages those who are strong to bear the burdens of others. Like Christ, who was 'strong' in position and status with God (2 Cor. 8:9; Phil. 2:6), the strong can — indeed must, if they are to live "in accordance with Christ Jesus" (15:5) — put up with the failings of the weak by abstaining from meat and wine even while believing that their own normal culinary habits are not wrong.

Paul shifts to a prayer for the harmony in life (15:5)[38] and in liturgy (15:6) that will come to the community as they do in fact live according to the narrative pattern of the crucified Messiah. This leads to his final exhortation to hospitality (15:7), grounded in the example of Christ and aimed at the glory of God (a good summary of 15:1-6), which then explodes into a catena of scriptural citations about the plan of God for Gentiles to join Jews in glorifying God. Christ, Paul claims (15:8), became a servant to the Jews both for their own benefit (in fulfilling the patriarchal promises) and also for the benefit of the Gentiles. In other words, all of Romans — its theme, its extended discourse on Jews and Gentiles in chapters 9–11 — is summarized here: God's faithfulness (NRSV, "truth," 15:8) to the Jews and mercy to the Gentiles. The chain of texts witnessing to the inclusion of Gentiles in the worship of God is from all parts (Law, Prophets, Writings) of the Bible: the Greek version of Deuteronomy 32:43 (Rom. 15:10); the Greek version of Isaiah 11:10 (Rom. 15:12); and Psalm 18:49 (Rom. 15:9b) and Psalm 117:1 (Rom. 15:11). If there is now to be a witness to this divine economy, the members of the church at Rome must embody these texts by accepting one another as different but equal participants in God's salvation. Through the Spirit, Paul prays, they will experience faith, joy, peace, and hope (cf. 14:17).

15:14-33. PAUL'S MISSION AND GOD'S PLAN

If it is true that Romans reaches a climax in 14:1–15:13, focusing on the theme of Jews and Gentiles in Christ for the glory of God, then in 15:14-33 Paul describes his own mission and his relationship with Rome as one (significant) aspect of the outworking of God's plan in the world. In 15:14-21 Paul relates his mission to his letter to the Romans, and in 15:22 he relates it to his nonvisit/visit to them.

---

38. Using the same idiom as in Phil. 2:2, 4.

In Romans Paul has occasionally (not least in 14:1–15:13) written "rather boldly" (15:15) to people he, for the most part, does not know. He wants his readers to understand the letter as a "reminder" (15:15), not as an assault on their character (15:14). The letter is part of his ministerial, even "priestly" service — his offering to God being the Gentiles (15:16a). An essential part of his duty is to insure that the Gentiles are an acceptable and holy sacrifice to God (15:16b; cf. 12:1-2). In the case of Rome, apparently, this means gently putting the Gentiles in their place, so to speak. Paul would then have reason to "boast" in the success of his work (15:17), but only in the sense of "what Christ has accomplished" through him to bring about the Gentiles' "obedience" (15:18; cf. 1:5; 16:19, 26). This trinitarian work — it can be attributed to Christ or to the power of God's Spirit (15:19) — includes not only proclamation but also "signs and wonders" (15:18-19; cf. 2 Cor. 12:12). Specifically, Paul sees his gift ("grace," 15:15) to be proclaiming the gospel to those who have not heard (15:20-21), in fulfillment of Isaiah 52:15 (LXX). This Paul has done from his point of origin to the east in Jerusalem all the way westward (from his location in Corinth) to Illyricum.[39]

Thus Paul's general mission to the Gentiles explains his letter to Rome, while his specific mission to unconverted Gentiles explains the lack, thus far, of a personal visit, despite years of trying to go (15:22, 23b; cf. 1:10-14). Feeling that his mission to the region east of Italy was complete, Paul now expresses a desire to pass through Rome on his way to Spain, the western edge of the empire (15:24, 28). His goal is not merely a bit of preaching and fellowship, as 1:11-13 and even 15:32 might suggest, but also a sending by them (15:24), which suggests the provision of a mission base, financial support, and perhaps companions.

This subtle (or not-so-subtle) request for money should not, however, be blown out of proportion and turned into the sole reason for the letter. But generosity to fellow believers and to apostolic work is very important. Because Paul sees his mission as an integral part of God's plan to unite Jews and Gentiles in Christ, he believes that the sharing of resources for the spiritual benefit of Gentile nonbelievers or the material welfare of poor Jewish believers is also integral to God's work (15:25-27). The hard-fought-for collection of funds from churches in Macedonia and Achaia, for the poor believers in Jerusalem, to some extent consumed Paul for years (15:25-28; cf. 1 Cor. 16:1-4; 2 Cor. 8–9). Its imminent delivery to Jerusalem, he thought, was symbolic of the successful completion of his work in those areas, of the unity of Gentile and Jew in Christ, and of the 'debt' Gentiles owe to Jews for their salvation. So, too, Roman believers could one day express their gratitude to God for his mercy by sharing in the proclamation of the gospel in the West. In the meantime, they could pray for

---

39. Illyricum was on the east coast of the Adriatic Sea and across the water from Italy. About Paul's work there nothing specific is known, but see 2 Tim. 4:10 (Dalmatia = Illyricum).

Paul's protection from persecution in Judea[40] and for the acceptance of the Gentiles' offering by the Jewish believers in Jerusalem (15:30-32).

16:1-27. CLOSING

In the final chapter Paul greets the surprising number of believers he knows at Rome, adds some final instructions, and closes with a doxology. It is easy to gloss over these verses, but they reveal some very interesting things about Paul and about the church at Rome.[41]

GREETINGS, COMMENDATIONS, AND FINAL INSTRUCTIONS (16:1-23)

The fascinating list of people and their designations in 16:1-16 is full of tidbits about Paul's relationships, and especially about his positive estimation of the role of women (at least nine are mentioned) in the early churches. Space does not permit an extensive discussion, but a few key points must be highlighted. The following chart is instructive:

People in Romans 16

Name	Designation	Other Biographical Details
Phoebe (vv. 1-2)	deacon of the church at Cenchreae; benefactor (patron) of many, including Paul	Gentile woman; possibly letter-bearer
Prisca and Aquila (vv. 3-4)	coworkers in Christ	Jewish tentmaking couple from Rome who met Paul in Corinth (Acts 18:1-3); risked their necks for Paul; esteemed by Gentile churches; hosted house church in Rome
Epaenetus (v. 5)	Paul's beloved; first convert in Asia (Minor)	Gentile man

---

40. No frivolous request, as the book of Acts attests in 21:27-36; 23:12-35; 25:1-5.

41. Although the manuscript evidence suggests to some that this chapter was not original to the letter, that is not the conclusion of the majority of scholars.

Name	Designation	Other Biographical Details
Mary (v. 6)	hard worker in Rome	Jewish (probably) woman
Andronicus and Junia (not male form Junias) (v. 7)	ethnic "relatives"; fellow prisoners with Paul; prominent apostles; older in Christ than Paul	Jewish couple (?)
Ampliatus (v. 8)	Paul's beloved in the Lord	Gentile man; possibly slave/freedperson
Urbanus (v. 9)	Paul's coworker	Gentile man; possibly slave/freedperson[42]
Stachys (v. 9)	Paul's beloved	Gentile man; possibly slave/freedperson
Apelles (v. 10)	approved (tested?) in Christ	Gentile or Jewish man
those of Aristobulus (v. 10)	—	family or slaves of Gentile male
Herodion (v. 11)	ethnic "relative"	Jewish male
family of Narcissus (v. 11)	those in the Lord	unbelieving Gentile man with believing family
Tryphaena and Tryphosa (v. 12)	workers in the Lord	Gentile or Jewish women; sisters? (freed?) slaves?
Persis (v. 12)	beloved, hard worker in the Lord	Gentile woman; possibly a (freed?) slave
Rufus and his mother (v. 13)	chosen in the Lord also a "mother" to Paul	Gentile man and his mother; possibly the son of Simon of Cyrene (Mark 15:21)
Asyncritus, Phlegon, Hermes, Patrobas, Hermas, and the brothers with them (v. 14)	—	Gentile males, possibly slaves or freedpersons; members of a house church

42 Here and below a number of the names were frequently given to slaves.

Rome: Ruins of the famed forum (agora)

Name	Designation	Other Biographical Details
Philologus, Julia		Gentile couple (?)
Nereus and his sister	—	Gentiles
Olympas		Gentile man
all the saints with them (v. 15)		likely a Gentile house church

This chart illustrates how the several house churches of Rome embody the Pauline vision of an inclusive community: Gentiles and Jews; slave, free, and freedpersons; elite and nonelite; men and women; from all corners of the empire (cf. Gal. 3:28; 1 Cor. 1:26-28). Paul has relations of intimacy, collegiality, gratitude, and admiration with these people. Many are leaders in the spread of the gospel: fellow apostles (the term obviously referring to more than Paul and the Twelve), fellow workers, and even fellow prisoners. They exemplify the cruciform life Paul tries to live and preaches. No wonder he wants the church at Rome to be united in love!

As noted above, especially telling is Paul's esteem for women; of the twenty-six named persons, nine are women. They are among the most hard-working, and they have served in the role of deacon (servant of some kind), benefactor, and even apostle. If Phoebe, the deacon and benefactor of the church at Cenchreae near Corinth (16:1-2), is commended because Paul is sending the letter with her, then it is likely also that he is expecting her to proclaim and interpret it to the church(es) in Rome.

After sending his own personal greetings to individuals, Paul instructs the Romans to greet one another with the holy kiss and, acting as a spokesperson for the church universal, passes on greetings from "all the churches of Christ" (in Achaia? everywhere?).

DOXOLOGY (16:25[24]-27)

Although some ancient manuscripts lack this doxology or locate it elsewhere in the letter, it is a fitting end to Romans and ably sums up the letter's theme in a prayerful spirit. It links the prophets to Paul's apostleship and gospel, and both to the Gentiles. Furthermore, it repeats the purpose of Paul's mission and his letter — "the obedience of faith" — with which the letter opened (1:5). For this grace God is truly worthy of praise through Jesus Christ!

Summary of Romans 12–16

Chapters 12–16 lay out Paul's understanding of faithful living for Gentiles and Jews in the covenant community.

- Believers offer themselves to God as a "living sacrifice."
- The church is a holy and hospitable community in which gifts are appropriately exercised, and where love and honor are offered to all, including outsiders and even enemies.
- The gospel requires Gentiles, Jews, and all 'multicultural' groups within the church to live without mutual judgmentalism concerning matters that do not matter, for the justified live for their Lord in their own distinct ways.
- There is a special burden placed on the "strong," those less scrupulous about nonessential matters, to endure the scruples of the "weak."
- The goal of God's plan and Paul's mission work is the salvation of Jews and Gentiles and the creation of multicultural communities in which they welcome and respect one another as God in Christ has welcomed them; this is symbolized in the collection for Jerusalem.
- Paul is assisted in this work by the financial support of men and women with various gifts.

THE STORY IN FRONT OF THE LETTER

Some Readings of Romans

"[Romans is] a summary of the whole of Christian doctrine [Lat. *caput et summa universae doctrinae christianae*]."

> Philipp Melanchthon, *Commentary on the Epistle of Paul to the Romans* (1532), cited in Joseph A. Fitzmyer, *Romans,* Anchor Bible 33 (Garden City, N.Y.: Doubleday, 1993), p. 74

"This is the book in which each one seeks his own dogmas, and likewise finds each his own [Lat. *Hic liber est in quo quaerit sua dogmata quisque, Invenit et pariter dogmata quisque sua*]."

> Anonymous, quoted in Fitzmyer, *Romans,* p. 103

"This epistle is in truth the most important document in the New Testament, the gospel in its purest expression. Not only is it well worth a Christian's while to know it word for word by heart, but also to meditate on it day by day. It is the soul's daily bread, and can never be read too often or studied too much. . . . Hitherto, this epistle has been smothered with comments and all sorts of irrelevances; yet, in essence, it is a brilliant light, almost enough to illumine the whole Bible. . . . It may therefore be said that this epistle gives the richest possible account of what a Christian ought to know, namely, the meaning of law, gospel, sin, punishment, grace, faith, righteousness, Christ, God, good works, love, hope, and the cross. . . . Moreover, everything is cogently proved from Scripture, and illustrated by Paul's own case or that of the prophets; it leaves nothing to be desired. Therefore, it seems as if St. Paul had intended this epistle to set out, once and for all, the whole of Christian doctrine in brief, and to be an introduction preparatory to the whole of the Old Testament. For there can be no doubt that if we had this epistle well and truly in our hearts, we should possess the light and power found in the Old Testament. Therefore, every Christian ought to study Romans regularly and continuously."

> Martin Luther, "Preface to the Epistle of Saint Paul to the Romans" (1522), in *Martin Luther: Selections from His Writings,* ed. John Dillenberger (Garden City, N.Y.: Doubleday, 1961), pp. 19, 34

"What we have in the letter to the Romans is the exegetical demonstration that Paul's preaching confronts both Judaism and paganism in the proper way with the truth of the Gospel."

> Otto Michel, *The Letter to the Romans* (1955), quoted in
> Fitzmyer, *Romans,* p. 77

"Romans should be read and reread in each new situation. Our suggestions about reading Romans today will be out of date tomorrow."

> William Baird, "On Reading Romans in the Church Today,"
> *Interpretation* 34 (1980): 57

"Its [Romans'] principal message is the justice of God . . . , which includes both judgment and mercy. Because of God's love for the marginalized, who suffer because of sin and the law held captive by it, God's justice is given to make all human beings without exception (whether because of class, ethnicity, or gender) new creatures in Christ. As new creatures they are transformed into subjects related as sisters and brothers, who practice justice in a world where there had not been a single person capable of doing so. These new creatures empowered to do justice are the people justified by faith. . . . Justification cannot be reduced to declaring the one who is guilty to be instead 'just' or 'justified.' There are simply no grounds for affirming that the concern to which Paul granted first priority was the need for the human being to be declared just before God, or for his or her sins to be forgiven. The fundamental problem for Paul was that there is not even one just person *(dikaios)* capable of doing justice in order to transform the reality characterized by injustice."

> Elsa Tamez, *The Amnesty of Grace: Justification by Faith from a
> Latin American Perspective,* trans. Sharon H. Ringe (Nashville:
> Abingdon, 1993), pp. 96, 107

"Romans completely transcends its immediate purpose as a fund-raising letter by providing Paul's most complete and ordered exposition of what he understood his ministry to be about, and therefore what he thought God was up to in the world by using him as an instrument. . . . If theology in the proper sense is the effort of human intelligence to move from the experience of God's work in the world to some small understanding of the character of the God who is at work, then Romans must be called quintessentially theological. As Paul reflects on what the meaning of his mission might be for the salvation of humanity, he is literally trying to catch up with what God is doing. In this sense, Romans is quite rightly designated as Paul's missionary theology. . . . Paul's mind pushes past the traces of God's activity in the experience of his work and the life of his churches, to the boldest sort of conclusions concerning who God might really be. . . . Romans is, as countless minds have perceived before, simply the most powerful argument concerning God in the New Testament. . . . [N]othing in the earliest Christian movement (and little else since) matches Romans for theological profundity, argumentative tensile strength, and, above all, energy. . . . [Paul asserts] in one breath the universality of God's will to save humans and the particularity of God's way of bringing that about. The argument of Romans is, at root, simple. God is one and God is fair."

> Luke Timothy Johnson, *Reading Romans: A Literary and Theological Commentary* (New York: Crossroad, 1997), pp. 8, 10, 16-17

QUESTIONS FOR REFLECTION

1. Why do you think Romans has been such an important part of the life of the church?
2. With what prior understanding of Romans did you approach the reading of this letter? How was your prior understanding confirmed, challenged, or both?
3. In 1973 psychiatrist Karl Menninger wrote a book entitled *Whatever Became of Sin?* What is the status of sin — as deeds or as a power — in the culture today? in the church?
4. What is the significance of understanding justification as being rooted in three expressions of 'faith' (God's, Christ's, and ours)? of understanding it as being defined as dying and rising with Christ?
5. If this chapter's reading of Romans 5–8 is correct, is Paul a believer in 'Christian perfection'? Does he allow any room for mistakes, for sin(s)?
6. What are some of the advantages and possible disadvantages of a theology and spirituality that require suffering as a prerequisite of glory?
7. How do contemporary Christians understand and perhaps misunderstand 'salvation' — such realities as justification, sanctification, resurrection, redemption, and glorification? How should Paul's universal and even cosmic perspective on these affect us today?
8. What are some of the ways Christians understand their relationship to Jews? How should Romans 9–11, if the reading in this chapter is correct, influence us in that relationship?
9. Is there support in Romans 13 for blind nationalistic obedience? If so, how do we justify its place in the canon? If not, how have some people understood it that way?
10. What help might Romans offer for the contemporary church in understanding its mission?

11. What are some of the contemporary versions of judgmentalism ('multicultural' or other) about things that do not matter? Does Paul's perspective ultimately permit any and all beliefs and practices in the church?

12. How should the character of God depicted in Romans inform our theological understanding today?

13. How do you respond to the interpretations of Romans quoted above?

14. In sum, what does this letter urge the church to believe, to hope for, and to do?

FOR FURTHER READING AND STUDY

General

Achtemeier, Paul. *Romans.* Interpretation. Louisville: Westminster John Knox, 1985. A brief but insightful theological exposition focusing on the power of the gospel for salvation.

Barrett, C. K. *Romans.* 2nd ed. London: Black, 1991. A careful, sane analysis by a veteran interpreter.

Byrne, Brendan. *Romans.* Sacra Pagina. Collegeville, Minn.: Liturgical Press, 1996. An excellent rhetorical and theological analysis by a Roman Catholic scholar, stressing divine faithfulness and inclusivity.

Fitzmyer, Joseph A. *Spiritual Exercises Based on Paul's Epistle to the Romans.* New York: Paulist, 1995. A condensation of the insights offered in his full commentary (see below), with questions for reflection.

Grieb, A. Katherine. *The Story of Romans: A Narrative Defense of God's Righteousness.* Louisville: Westminster John Knox, 2002. A compelling interpretation that identifies God's righteousness with Jesus' faithfulness and includes provocative questions for reflection.

Johnson, Luke Timothy. *Reading Romans: A Literary and Theological Commentary.* New York: Crossroad, 1997. A superb interpretation of the letter, highlighting the themes of God's oneness and fairness and Christ's faith(fulness).

Kaylor, R. David. *Paul's Covenant Community: Jew and Gentile in Romans.* Atlanta: John Knox, 1988. A brilliant analysis focusing on the pervasive theme of covenant in Romans.

Meyer, Paul W. "Romans." In *Harper Bible Commentary,* gen. ed. James L. Mays, pp. 1130-67. San Francisco: Harper and Row, 1988. A concise but insightful and influential exposition, focusing on the letter as Paul's refining of convictions expressed in earlier letters so as to defend them in Jerusalem.

Westerholm, Stephen. *Preface to the Study of Paul.* Grand Rapids: Eerdmans, 1997. A beautifully written set of reflections on Romans, written to captivate the intelligent contemporary reader.

Technical

Cranfield, C. E. B. *Romans.* International Critical Commentary. 2 vols. Edinburgh: T. & T. Clark, 1975, 1979. A thorough, if traditional, exposition that presents and evaluates many options for the interpretation of key terms and passages.

Dunn, James D. G. *Romans.* Word Biblical Commentary 38A-B. 2 vols. Waco, Tex.: Word, 1988. A sophisticated, detailed treatment from the 'new perspective' on Paul.

Fitzmyer, Joseph A. *Romans.* Anchor Bible 33. Garden City, N.Y.: Doubleday, 1993. A technically thorough and learned analysis of the letter that takes a fairly traditional (almost traditional Protestant — by a Jesuit!) interpretation.

Käsemann, Ernst. *Commentary on Romans.* Translated by Geoffrey W. Bromiley. Grand Rapids: Eerdmans, 1980. A classic theological analysis stressing the 'righteousness of God' as God's saving power.

Wright, N. T. "Romans." In *The New Interpreter's Bible,* edited by Leander E. Keck et al., 10:393-770. Nashville: Abingdon, 2002. A creative theological analysis that pays close attention to the social and political realities that Paul confronts and challenges.

CHAPTER 13

PHILIPPIANS

The Hymn of the Crucified Lord
in the Cruciform Community

Let the same mind be in you that was in Christ Jesus, who, though he
was in the form of God, did not regard equality with God as something
to be exploited, but emptied himself. . . .

Phil. 2:5-7a

Philippians is one of Paul's shortest but richest and most powerful letters. It has
been called a letter of joy, of friendship, and of thanksgiving — all of which it is.
But at its core lies one of the most famous of all Pauline texts, Philippians 2:6-11,
which many scholars take to be a pre-Pauline hymn creatively used by Paul.[1] In
fact, this text shapes the whole content of the letter; Philippians is Paul's most
sustained exegesis of the story contained in 2:6-11. In this letter Paul calls the
Philippian believers, as citizens of God's counterimperial colony, to perform in
their common life the story of the crucified and exalted Messiah Jesus, the Lord
in whom they live.

THE STORY BEHIND THE LETTER

Paul's letter to the Philippians reflects, in particularly vivid ways, the situation
of the city itself, its believing community, and the apostle.

---

1. The position adopted in this book is that 2:6-11 is most likely a pre-Pauline hymn,
though Paul has thoroughly integrated it into his own spirituality and theology.

Philippi: The remains of the city looking from the Via Egnatia

THE CITY

Philippi was named for Philip of Macedon, the father of Alexander the Great, who had fortified an earlier Greek city. Several military conflicts and many years later, in 31 B.C., Augustus refounded the city — where he and Mark Antony had defeated the assassins of Julius Caesar — as a Roman colony (cf. Acts 16:12) and placed it under his personal patronage. He added army veterans and others to the local population, and citizens of the colony gained many rights and privileges (including exemptions from cocitizenship in the city of Rome and thus from certain taxes) as members of a colony with Italian legal status. Along with these rights came duties, especially the corporate obligation to behave like a loyal imperial outpost. Not all residents of the region would have been citizens of the colony, but all would have felt — and been expected to do obeisance to — the Roman and imperial presence. Official inscriptions in the city's public spaces were mostly in Latin, not Greek, and the city's well-preserved Greek theater was used for gladiator contests during the Roman period.

In addition to its focus on the cult of the emperor and the adulation of Rome, Philippi in the first century seems to have been home to the worship of several local deities; to Silvanus, an otherwise obscure Roman god for males of the lower classes; to Bacchus/Dionysus, the god of wine; to Diana/Artemis

Neapolis: The modern port (Kavála) near Philippi

(hunt, fertility), Apollo (music, youth, health), and Isis (immortality); and of course to Jupiter/Zeus. There is no evidence of a Jewish synagogue, though there appears to have been a very small Jewish community (cf. Acts 16:13, 16).

Protected by mountains and surrounded by fertile river valleys for farming, Philippi was an attractive place in many ways. It was not a large city — its theater held maybe three thousand people — but it was strategically located on the Via Egnatia (remains of which are visible today), the main road between Rome and the East. With the port city of Neapolis ('New City'; modern Kavála) only a dozen miles away, Philippi was a crossroads for both land and sea travel and trade. Among its merchants, inscriptional evidence shows, were traders in purple dye and cloth from the East, including, according to Acts 16, one Lydia of Thyatira.

MISSION AND PARTNERSHIP

According to Acts, Lydia, a "worshiper of God" or Gentile God-fearer, was Paul's first convert in Philippi and thus in Europe (16:11-15, 40). The Acts account has Paul receive the 'Macedonian call' in the port of Troas of Mysia (on the northwestern coast of modern Turkey) during his second missionary jour-

Philippi: **A mosaic adorning the dome of a small Orthodox church commemorating Lydia's conversion**

ney. Acts implies that Timothy (16:1-5) and Silas/Silvanus (16:19, 25) traveled with him to Europe. From Troas they (actually "we," 16:11) set sail for the island of Samothrace and then the port of Neapolis. From there they evangelized Philippi, then Thessalonica, and then Beroea. Acts reports the conversion and baptism of Lydia and her household (16:11-15); the exorcism of a fortune-telling slave girl (16:16-18); conflict with the pagan merchant-owners of the girl and with Roman magistrates, who had Paul and Silas beaten and jailed before learning they were Roman citizens (16:16-39); the conversion and baptism of the Philippian jailer and his family (16:25-34); and, it seems, the conversion of others and the formation of a house church in Lydia's home (16:40).

Whatever value one accords these stories (and the skepticism of some earlier scholars seems to be waning), Paul's letters confirm that he experienced suffering in Philippi (1:29-30; 1 Thess. 2:1-2) and that women played an important role in the church (Phil. 4:2-3).[2] Not only Paul, but also the Philippians themselves endured opposition and suffering, which Paul views as fellowship with

---

2. In passing, it is worth observing that if Luke had wanted to manufacture a story about a Philippian female convert based on Paul's letter, he should have chosen the name of Euodia or Syntyche (Phil. 4:2).

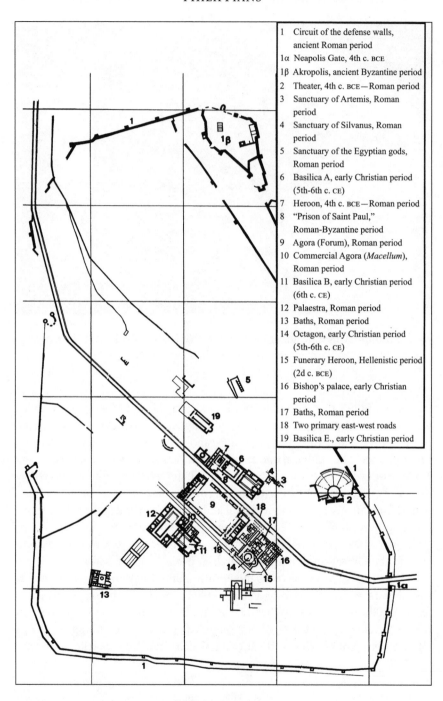

1   Circuit of the defense walls, ancient Roman period
1α Neapolis Gate, 4th c. BCE
1β Akropolis, ancient Byzantine period
2   Theater, 4th c. BCE—Roman period
3   Sanctuary of Artemis, Roman period
4   Sanctuary of Silvanus, Roman period
5   Sanctuary of the Egyptian gods, Roman period
6   Basilica A, early Christian period (5th-6th c. CE)
7   Heroon, 4th c. BCE—Roman period
8   "Prison of Saint Paul," Roman-Byzantine period
9   Agora (Forum), Roman period
10 Commercial Agora (Macellum), Roman period
11 Basilica B, early Christian period (6th c. CE)
12 Palaestra, Roman period
13 Baths, Roman period
14 Octagon, early Christian period (5th-6th c. CE)
15 Funerary Heroon, Hellenistic period (2d c. BCE)
16 Bishop's palace, early Christian period
17 Baths, Roman period
18 Two primary east-west roads
19 Basilica E., early Christian period

Ancient Philippi

him and a gift from God (1:28-30; 2 Cor. 8:2). In fact, this opposition continues in some form even as Paul writes to the Philippians (1:28). Given the fully Roman character of Philippi and the political language Paul uses in Philippians, the cause of this persecution was likely the perception that the gospel Paul first preached, and which the Philippians now passed on to others, was an un-Roman or anti-Roman Jewish message targeting Gentiles (cf. Acts 16:16-24).

In addition to suffering like Paul, the apostle's Philippian converts became cherished partners in his work, supporting him financially and in other ways after he left (1:5; 4:10-20). Their envoy Epaphroditus was the most dramatic of several tangible signs of their sacrificial support for Paul and his mission (2:25-30; 4:18). He had borne gifts from the church during Paul's imprisonment, for which Paul expresses his thanks (2:25-30; 4:10-20). Furthermore, the Macedonian believers who gave from their affliction and poverty to Paul's Jerusalem collection (2 Cor. 8:1-6) would certainly have included especially the Philippians.

The Philippian community, then, was founded in and continued to live in a climate of suffering for the gospel. Yet the Philippian believers were both generous and joyful in their affliction (2 Cor. 8:2). This shared experience between Paul and the Philippians is at the heart of their gospel fellowship, or *koinōnia* (cf. 1:5 and 1:30). Whether in the past or in the present, Paul and the Philippians are united in Christ by their common suffering for him and their common joy in him.[3]

PAUL IN PRISON

Paul's particular form of suffering while writing this letter was imprisonment (1:7, 12-14, 17, 19, 30), in which he continues to bear witness to nonbelievers and believers alike (1:12-14), and from which he expects deliverance rather than death (1:19, 23-26; 2:24). His cosender Timothy (1:1) may be serving as the apostle's secretary and is his soon-to-be-sent envoy (2:19-24).

But where is Paul imprisoned? Theories abound, although we actually cannot know with certainty. We do know that there are believers nearby, some of whom belong to the imperial household (4:21-22), and that there is a *praetorium* (1:13; NRSV translates "imperial guard"). But neither of these hints necessarily locates Paul in Rome, because the *praetorium* and the imperial household could probably refer to imperial contingents in the provinces, too. If Paul is writing from Rome, it may be during the Roman imprisonment noted in Acts 28:16-31, and thus in the early 60s. Another possible place of imprison-

---

3. On joy, often said to be the theme of the letter, see 1:18, 25; 2:2, 17, 18, 28, 29; 3:1; 4:1, 4, 10.

ment is Ephesus, in which case the letter would have been written several years earlier, Paul having spent about three years in Ephesus sometime between 52 and 57. Although there is no hard evidence for an Ephesian imprisonment, Paul speaks of grave dangers in Ephesus (1 Cor. 15:32) and its province, Asia (2 Cor. 1:8). The exchange of envoys between Ephesus and Philippi would have been simpler and faster than between Rome and Philippi or between Caesarea, a third frequently suggested place of imprisonment, and Philippi (see Acts 23:23–26:32). In fact, however, this letter could have been written from any of the several other cities with a *praetorium* (such as Corinth?) where Paul might have been in prison. Uncertainty about the place of composition does not seriously affect the interpretation of the letter.

PAUL'S CONCERNS

It has frequently been suggested that Paul's main purpose in writing this letter is simply to give thanks for the gift received courtesy of Epaphroditus (4:10-20), and in so doing also to update the Philippians on their envoy's situation (by the letter, the return of Epaphroditus, or both), for he had become ill and nearly died (2:25-30). Other issues — possible internal dissension (1:27–2:4; 4:2-3), opposition from outsiders (1:28-29), and threats from Jewish-Christian preachers (3:1–4:1) — are sometimes deemed secondary, or even thought of as parts of other letters combined with this letter of thanks. Many scholars in the past believed that all or part of 3:1–4:1 (plus perhaps some additional verses) was an independent, highly polemical letter, and a good number held that 4:10-20 constituted a separate thank-you note from Paul, distinct from a general hortatory letter identified with chapters 1 and 2 (plus a few additional verses). This would mean that Philippians is an amalgam of three letters. These older 'partition theories,' however, have largely been replaced by arguments for the unity of the letter. But what led to the writing of this letter, and what holds it together?

In recent times scholars have explored the nature of the social relationship — is it a patron-client relationship? a friendship? (and so on) — that existed between Paul and the Philippians by the exchange of gifts. Although this is an important question, we should not allow it to overshadow the material content and major theological theme of the letter. For the letter to the Philippians, while perhaps occasioned by the need to give thanks for a gift, is focused much more on the need for those who are in Christ to live a cruciform life in the face of internal and external challenges to the gospel. The letter is a unified word of exhortation and example grounded in the story of Christ.

THE STORY WITHIN THE LETTER

This characterization of the letter — as a unified word of example and exhortation grounded in the story of Christ — is meant in part to address one of the common questions asked of Philippians: What kind of letter is it? A letter of thanksgiving? of friendship? of exhortation? While Philippians clearly contains elements of all these 'genres' of letters, it is above all an extended meditation on, or exegesis of, the 'Christ hymn' found in 2:6-11. Faced with his own imprisonment, the suffering of the Philippians, their generosity and the self-sacrificial ministry of Epaphroditus, opposition from outside the church and tension within it, Paul composes a letter that relates the story of Christ narrated in 2:6-11 to the ongoing story of the Philippian community. The political language of the hymn (especially the word "Lord"), combined with additional political language at key points throughout the letter, suggests that Paul wants the story of Christ to shape an alternative colony of people governed by a different law, the narrative pattern of Christ. To paraphrase the Greek text of 1:27, the purpose of the letter is to aid the Philippians in living out their 'citizenship' in the divine 'colony' (expressed in the Greek verb *politeuesthe*, related to *polis*) in a manner worthy of the gospel story of Christ, found in 2:6-11, which functions as their 'city charter.' Paul seeks to encourage them faithfully to live the story, to sing the hymn, until the day of Christ (1:6, 10; 3:20).

Philippians 2:6-11, then, is the centerpiece of this letter. It provides the formal structure, material content, and even many of the key vocabulary items for the entire letter. The following chart shows how the words of the hymn reverberate in its preface (2:1-5) and throughout the letter.[4]

Echoes of Philippians 2:6-11 throughout the Letter
(NRSV and Greek Texts)

Phil. 2:6-11	*Elsewhere in Philippians*
2:6 — though he <u>was</u> [lit. 'existing'; *hyparchōn*]	3:20 — our citizenship <u>is</u> [*hyparchei*] in heaven
in the <u>form</u> [*morphē*] of God [see also "form of a slave" in 2:7],	3:10 — becoming <u>like him</u> in his death [*symmorphizomenos;* lit. 'being conformed to his death']

4. The verbal parallels are not always exact; for example, different forms of certain words in 2:6-11 appear elsewhere. Nonetheless, the cumulative effect of these various kinds of echoes is impressive and important. Intertextuality does not always mean precise quotations or repetition.

Phil. 2:6-11	*Elsewhere in Philippians*
	3:21 — that it [the body of our humiliation] may be <u>conformed</u> [*symmorphon*] to the body of his glory
[Christ Jesus] did not <u>regard</u> [*hēgēsato*]	2:3 — <u>regard</u> [*hēgoumenoi*] others as better than yourselves 2:25 — I <u>think</u> [*hēgēsamēn*] it necessary 3:7 — Yet whatever gains I had, these I have come to <u>regard</u> [*hēgēmai*] as loss because of Christ. 3:8 — I <u>regard</u> [*hēgoumai*] everything as loss because of the surpassing value of knowing Christ Jesus my Lord. For his sake I have suffered the loss of all things, and I <u>regard</u> [*hēgoumai*] them as rubbish, in order that I may gain Christ.
equality with God [lit. 'to be <u>equal</u> *(isa)* to God'] as something to be exploited	2:20 — I have no one <u>like</u> [lit. 'equal in soul to' *(isopsychon)*] him [Timothy]
2:7 — but <u>emptied</u> [*ekenōsen*]	2:3 — Do nothing from selfish ambition or conceit [*kenodoxian*; lit. '<u>empty/vain glory</u>'] 2:16 — that I did not run in <u>vain</u> [*eis kenon*] or labor in <u>vain</u> [*eis kenon*]
<u>himself</u> [*heauton*; see also 2:8]	2:3-4 — regard others as better than <u>yourselves</u> [*heautōn*]. Let each of you look not to <u>your own</u> interests [*ta heautōn*], but to the interests of others. 2:12 — work out <u>your own</u> [*heautōn*] salvation 2:21 — All of them are seeking <u>their own</u> interests [*ta heautōn*]
<u>taking</u> [*labōn*]	3:12 — Not that I have already <u>obtained</u> [*elabon*] this
the <u>form</u> [*morphē*; see also "form of God" in 2:6] of a <u>slave</u> [*doulou*], being born in human likeness.	2:22 — [Timothy] has <u>served</u> [*edouleusen*] with me in the work of the gospel 1:1 — Paul and Timothy, <u>servants</u> [*douloi*] of Christ Jesus
And <u>being found</u> [*heuretheis*]	3:8-9 — that I may gain Christ and <u>be found</u> [*heurethō*] in him

Phil. 2:6-11	Elsewhere in Philippians
in human <u>form</u> [*schēmati*]	3:21 — He will <u>transform</u> [*metaschēmatisei*] the body of our humiliation
2:8 — he <u>humbled</u> [*etapeinōsen*] himself [*heauton*; see also 2:7]	2:3 — in <u>humility</u> [*tapeinophrosynē*] regard others as better than yourselves 4:12 — I know what it is to have little [*tapeinousthai*; lit. 'to <u>be humbled</u>']
and became <u>obedient</u> [*hypēkoos*]	2:12 — just as you have always <u>obeyed</u> [*hypēkousate*] me
<u>to the point of</u> [*mechri*] <u>death</u> [*thanatou*] —	2:30 — [Epaphroditus] came <u>close to death</u> [*mechri thanatou*] for the work of Christ 1:20-21 — that . . . Christ will be exalted now as always in my body, whether by life or by <u>death</u> [*thanatou*]. For to me, living is Christ and <u>dying</u> [*apothanein*] is gain. 3:10 — becoming like him in his <u>death</u> [*thanatǭ*]
even death on a <u>cross</u> [*staurou*].	3:18 — many live as enemies of the <u>cross</u> [*staurou*] of Christ
2:9 — Therefore God also highly exalted him and <u>gave</u> [*echarisato*] him	1:29 — he has <u>graciously granted</u> [*echaristhē*] you the privilege . . . of suffering for him as well
the <u>name</u> [*onoma*] that is above every <u>name</u> [*onoma*]	4:3 — whose <u>names</u> [*onomata*] are in the book of life
2:10-11 — so that at the name of Jesus every knee should bend, in heaven and on earth and under the earth, and every tongue should confess that Jesus Christ is Lord, to the <u>glory</u> [*doxan*] of God the Father.	1:11 — the harvest of righteousness that comes through Jesus Christ for the <u>glory</u> [*doxan*] and praise of God 2:3 — Do nothing from selfish ambition or conceit [*kenodoxian*; lit. 'empty/vain <u>glory</u>'] 3:19 — their <u>glory</u> [*doxa*] is in their shame 3:21 — that it [the body of our humiliation] may be conformed to the body of his <u>glory</u> [*doxēs*] 4:19 — according to his riches in <u>glory</u> [*doxē*] in Christ Jesus 4:20 — To our God and Father be <u>glory</u> [*doxa*] forever and ever.

To this chart could be added Paul's frequent use in the letter of the phrase "Christ Jesus" (rather than, say, 'Jesus Christ') from 2:5, as well as the appearance of the verb 'to think, perceive, have the mind' *(phroneō)*, from the same verse, a total of ten times in the letter.[5] In addition, there are allusions to the hymn that employ other terms to express parallel ideas. Paul himself, then, has absorbed both the mind and the language of the hymn and reinforced it throughout all of Philippians.

The significance of 2:6-11 for Paul, not only in Philippians, is such that it deserves to be called his 'master story.'[6] In Philippians the polyvalent character of Christ's story, as Paul reads it, is sufficient to address the multifaceted stories of Paul, his colleagues, his opponents, and especially his readers. Although this text will be discussed in more detail below, some introductory remarks are needed now because of its centrality to the letter.

THE STORY OF CHRIST

Few biblical texts have received as much attention as Philippians 2:6-11. Although (as noted above) many scholars consider it to be an early Christian (pre-Pauline) hymn or hymn fragment, it is clearly owned and loved by Paul even if he did not compose it. We will refer to it as a hymn, on the assumption that its poetic structure suggests that the story it tells could well have been sung.[7]

Modeled on the so-called fourth servant hymn of Isaiah 40–55 (52:13–53:12), the hymnic story has three characters: Christ Jesus (as the suffering servant), God the Father, and the universe of created beings. Verses 6-8 narrate the actions of Christ's self-humbling and self-emptying in spite of possessing equality with God. The result of this servanthood or 'enslavement' is ultimately death on a cross as an expression of obedience to God. The story line, and thus the structure, has its most dramatic shift at verse 9, where the word "therefore" signals the beginning of the narration of God's (the Father's) response to Christ's obedience, as he exalts Christ and bestows on him the divine title "Lord." According to verses 10-11, the story is completed when all created beings acknowledge the lordship of Jesus to the glory of God the Father.

The text, then, is focused on the story of Christ in relation to God and to all creatures, but it does not draw any explicit spiritual or ethical lessons from that story. This is where Paul's creativity enters in. Paul finds in the story of

5. 1:7; 2:2 (twice), 5; 3:15 (twice), 19; 4:2, 10 (twice).

6. See chap. 4 and especially my *Cruciformity: Paul's Narrative Spirituality of the Cross* (Grand Rapids: Eerdmans, 2001), particularly chap. 5.

7. Readers may be familiar with the hymn "At the Name of Jesus," as well as other hymns, based on this text.

Christ told in the hymn a narrative not only of the servant's obedience or faithfulness to God, but also of love for others that is self-sacrificial; of power that is self-emptying rather than self-serving; and of hope that suffering for God is always followed by the promise of divine vindication and exaltation. The hymn thereby becomes for Paul the narrative structure for a life of cruciform service in faith, love, power, and hope as the Philippian community faces the challenges of opposition and discord. To live in this way is to possess what Paul understands to be the "mind" (NRSV) or the 'disposition' (NIV, NAB, "attitude") of Christ (2:5).

The letter unfolds according to the following structure:

1:1-2	**Opening**
1:3-11	**Paul's Prayer and the Hymn**
1:12-26	**Paul's Imprisonment and the Hymn**
	1:12-18a — The Effects of the Imprisonment
	1:18b-26 — The Future of the Imprisonment
1:27–2:18	**A Life Worthy of the Hymn**
	1:27-30 — Unity in Suffering for Christ
	2:1-5 — Unity Within through the Mind of Christ
	2:6-11 — The Hymnic Story of Christ
	2:12-18 — The Faithful Witness of the Community and of Paul
2:19-30	**Two Living Examples of the Hymn**
	2:19-24 — Timothy
	2:25-30 — Epaphroditus
3:1–4:1	**The Hymn and the Enemies of the Cross**
	3:1 — Transition
	3:2-11 — Knowing Christ: The Life of Faith
	3:12–4:1 — Pursuing Christ: The Life of Hope
4:2-9	**Exhortations to Perform the Hymn**
	4:2-3 — Harmony: Euodia and Syntyche
	4:4-7 — Joy and Peace
	4:8-9 — Goodness
4:10-20	**The Fellowship of the Hymn**
	4:10-14 — Paul's Cruciform Contentment
	4:15-20 — The Philippians' Cruciform Gift
4:21-23	**Greetings and Benediction**

1:1-2. OPENING

Philippians begins in customary Pauline letter form — sender(s) to recipients, grace and peace — but with some unusual features in the content. Paul and his cosender, Timothy, identify themselves as "servants" or slaves *(douloi)* of Christ Jesus rather than as apostles or (as in 2 Cor. 1:1; cf. Philem. 1) as apostle and brother.[8] The use of the term *doulos* for both writers places them on equal footing in their fundamental identity as slaves of Christ, continuing the earthly pattern of service (2:7) of their exalted Lord (1:2; 2:11). Later Paul will identify his trusted son (2:22) and coworker Timothy[9] as one who "served [*edouleusen*] with me in the work of the gospel" (2:22). This service consisted in part, like Paul's own service, of looking out for the Philippians' needs and interests rather than his own (2:20-21; cf. 2:23-26).

Also of interest is Paul's use of his common phrase "in Christ Jesus" to express the essential character of the community of saints (NAB, "holy ones") in Philippi. This phrase or its equivalent will reappear at other significant junctures: in 1:13 (though many translations miss it), 2:1, 2:5 (often also missed), 4:2, and 4:21. To be holy, for Paul, is to be in Christ, and vice versa (cf. 1 Cor. 1:2). It is to be called to live in conformity to Christ, specifically Christ crucified.

The appearance of an explicit reference to church leaders, "bishops and deacons" (NRSV), in the address (1:1) is unique in Paul's letters (though see Philem. 2a and, implicitly, the three Pastoral Letters). Translations differ in the rendering of the Greek terms used (*episkopoi* and *diakonoi*, something like 'overseers' and 'servants').[10] The specific terms and the plural form used to designate these two functions or 'offices' suggest shared leadership with a division of labor, perhaps one group focusing on teaching/preaching/spiritual formation and the other on financial/material assistance (like the deacon-patron Phoebe in Cenchreae, Rom. 16:1-2). Not much can be said with certainty, however, about these 'offices.' The overseers or deacons may include the women Euodia and Syntyche as well as Clement, all of whom seem to be identified as Paul's coworkers (4:2-3). If so, then Paul may be singling out the leaders to remind them (especially the two women) of their responsibility to be of one Christlike mind for the service of the whole church (cf. 4:2 and 2:2).

---

8. The opening designation for Paul is "apostle" in nine of the thirteen Pauline letters. In Titus 1:1 he is also *doulos*, while in Philemon he is "prisoner"; in the Thessalonian correspondence no title is used.

9. Who also cosent 2 Corinthians, Philemon, Colossians, and both 1 and 2 Thessalonians (with Silvanus).

10. NAB has "overseers and ministers," while NIV has "overseers and deacons," with a marginal note that the former term is "traditionally" rendered "bishops." The NRSV margin suggests the alternative translation "overseers and helpers."

1:3-11. PAUL'S PRAYER AND THE HYMN

Paul proceeds, in customary fashion, from the salutation to a prayer. This one is in two parts: thanksgiving (1:3-8) and intercession (1:9-11). Each part has an eschatological focus (1:6, 10), and each part reflects Paul's conviction that both his and the Philippians' life ought to embody the hymn text in 2:6-11. This takes the form of Christlike compassion (1:8) or, more generally, righteousness that brings glory to God (1:11).

Paul's evident delight in the Philippian believers, and his claim to constant, joyful intercession for them (1:3-8), are no mere rhetorical flourishes. Both his joy and his prayer are grounded in the Philippians' gospel partnership, or fellowship *(koinōnia)*, with him (1:5). This partnership includes support for Paul's ministry and assistance for him during his imprisonment, but also much more — the fellowship of common holiness or righteousness, witness, and suffering for the gospel, as the first two chapters especially stress. This partnership extends back to the first day of Paul's preaching in Philippi (1:5). Because it was and is the work of God, Paul is sure God will sustain it and complete it at Christ's return (1:6). All this is an intimate fellowship of grace (1:7) — even the suffering that Paul (1:7) and the Philippians (cf. 1:29) are experiencing.

Even in his imprisonment, then, Paul has continued to be concerned both about the spread of the gospel (1:7) and about his converts and friends, particularly those in Philippi — "all of you" (1:4, 7, 8). This concern is a manifestation of Christlike, suffering love, "the compassion [*en splanchnois*] of Christ Jesus" (1:8). Paul uses the same phrase in 2:1 ("if [in Christ] there is any . . . compassion [*splanchna*])" to introduce the expectations for Christlike humility and regard for others that are appropriate for those who live in the Lord who emptied and enslaved himself in incarnation and death (2:6-8). Like Christ in his sufferings, Paul is concerned — deeply concerned — not for his own welfare but for that of the Philippians, even while incarcerated.

This deep concern leads Paul to pray (1:9-11). He prays for the Philippians' life together in the present so that they will be "pure and blameless" in the future, on the day of Christ. Specifically, he prays that they will have an abundance of love, knowledge, and insight or discernment. In the context of Philippians, these can refer only to the cruciform, others-oriented love described in 2:1-4 (and portrayed, in Paul's view, in 2:6-8), and to the general cruciform mind, or perception, required of those who claim Christ as Lord in the face of opposition. In other words, Paul's words about the Philippians' perseverance — a good work being brought to completion (1:6), a harvest of righteousness (1:11) — are not pious platitudes but prayer-dependent and God-dependent promises in a bleak situation, humanly speaking. The Philippians are being persecuted in some form, and the call to remain righteous for the day of divine, rather than human, judgment is a serious one, one that can be accomplished only "through Jesus Christ" (1:11). As Paul prays and the Philippians remain faithful, no matter what comes, they will be ready for that judgment and will participate joyfully, both now and especially then, in glorifying God (1:11; cf. 2:11).

1:12-26. PAUL'S IMPRISONMENT AND THE HYMN

Having completed his prayer for the Philippians and affirmed both their partic-ipation in his 'prison ministry' and his confidence in their faithfulness to the end, Paul proceeds to describe the impact of his current imprisonment on both the gospel and himself. The gospel, contrary to what some might think or fear, has actually been advanced (1:12-18a). And the apostle, despite his own mixed feelings and perhaps again the fears (or even wishes!) of others, is confident of his own deliverance from prison because that would be in the best interest of the Philippians (1:18b-26).

THE EFFECTS OF THE IMPRISONMENT (1:12-18a)

As he begins the body of his letter, Paul wants to assure the Philippians that, un-expectedly and contrary to their concerns, his imprisonment has advanced rather than hindered the gospel (1:12), and this in two main ways. First, Paul's captors (or those in control of his place of imprisonment),[11] as well as everyone else aware of his situation, know that he is imprisoned for Christ (1:13; lit. 'in Christ'). In Paul's view, this means the gospel is making inroads; some may have already come to believe (perhaps some who belong to "the emperor's house-hold," 4:22), and others still may confess Jesus as Lord.

Second, other believers have not, for the most part, been intimidated by Paul's predicament but rather emboldened by it (1:14). Paul certainly wants the Philippians to be similarly empowered to bear witness without fear. That his imprisonment is "in Christ" (NAB) may also suggest to his readers that anyone who lives in Christ may suffer a similar fate. This, too, can be for the advance-ment of the gospel and should therefore be a reason for rejoicing.

---

11. That is, the "imperial guard" (NRSV; NIV, "palace guard") or "praetorium" (NAB; NIV mg., "whole palace"). There is disagreement over the meaning of the Greek word *praitōrion*, translating the Latin *praetorium*, in 1:13. Does it refer to a body of people or to a residence, and was it located only in Rome or also in the provincial capitals?

One minor (to Paul) twist in this very positive picture is the response of some preachers of Christ to Paul's situation. Though most continue to proclaim Christ "from goodwill" and "out of love" (1:15, 16), some are doing so "from envy and rivalry" (1:15), "out of selfish ambition, not sincerely" (1:17). The situation Paul is referring to is difficult to characterize precisely. Apparently some saw his arrest and imprisonment as proof of his demise, his fall from grace and power. Perhaps they saw his imprisonment as being deserved for reasons other than faithfulness to the gospel (1:16), or as divine judgment, a sign of the errors of Paul's message and ministry. Perhaps, too, they saw it as an opportunity to preach their particular version of the gospel and to throw around their own apostolic weight, now that Paul was out of the picture. Paul felt that at least some of them were deliberately trying to hurt him and his reputation (1:17).

Surprisingly, perhaps, Paul rejoices even in this aspect of his circumstances (1:18a). The motives for their preaching, their criticisms of the imprisoned apostle — none of this matters to Paul, who is glad simply that his arrest has somehow led to more people proclaiming and hearing the gospel of Christ. What is particularly astounding about Paul's attitude is that the behavior of these people seems blatantly to contradict the very gospel he and they proclaim, the gospel the Philippians sing (2:6-11). This is made explicit, perhaps, in 2:22, where Paul contrasts Timothy with just about everyone else, for "all of them are seeking their own interests" (2:21), which violates the gospel at its very core (2:3-5).

THE FUTURE OF THE IMPRISONMENT (1:18b-26)

Paul's words about his indifference to impure motives, and about the present impact of his imprisonment on the gospel and on others, turn now into a moving meditation on his own future. It is linked to what immediately precedes it by the mention of rejoicing (1:18a, 18b), but its actual subject matter is first announced in 1:19 and then, forming an *inclusio*, repeated in 1:25-26. The subject, of course, is Paul's fate. It is clear that he expects deliverance, as both bookends of the *inclusio* indicate and as 2:24 assumes. In between the bookends we find a tremendous example of Paul's own candid introspection and spiritual discernment — his theologizing, so to speak. Paul may be borrowing a rhetorical device called *synkrisis*, the weighing of alternatives, to do this theologizing.

Paul is certain that the Philippians' prayers and the activity of Christ's Spirit (1:19) will result in his release. If he is in prison on serious charges, as it would appear, he may be facing the death penalty. Has he had a dream or other divine revelation about his future? There is no evidence of this. Has he decided to back down, to compromise his confession in order to insure his release and the continuation of his missionary work elsewhere? If this thought ever crossed

Paul's mind (or the Philippians'), the apostle quickly banishes it in 1:20, where he affirms his commitment to speaking boldly, avoiding the shame of denying Christ, and thereby exalting Christ by living or, if necessary, by dying.

The temptation for Paul, in fact, is not to pursue release from jail at any cost in order to continue living. Rather, the temptation is to pursue death — to let go of the desire to be released. This may be a bit perplexing to modern readers, so it deserves careful attention.

Paul clearly believes that the purpose of life is to "exalt" (NRSV) or "magnify" (NAB) Christ in his "body" — in the concreteness of bodily existence (1:20; cf. Rom. 12:1-2). To him, life is all about Christ (1:20), about living worthily of the gospel (1:27). His motto (1:21) is "living is Christ" (NRSV), or "to live is Christ" (NIV). This can be accomplished in how one lives and in how one dies, "by life or by death" (1:20) — and thus even in *whether* one lives or dies. For Paul (and for all believers), however, life in this present age is not the ultimate goal; "dying is gain" (1:21) because dying means "depart[ing] and be[ing] with Christ" (1:23). This hope permeates all of Paul's letters.[12]

In prison, therefore, facing the possibility of death, Paul is 'betwixt and between.' Does he want to remain "in the flesh," i.e., alive and in Christ but not "with Christ" in the presence of God? Or does he want to "depart," to die, which is "far better" (1:23)? "I do not know which I prefer," the NRSV has him saying (1:22). This makes it sound as if Paul cannot decide whether he would prefer to accept a martyr's death or to gain release, either by the sheer grace of God working through the pagan courts or authorities, or by extraordinary human effort (such as playing his 'Roman citizen' card).

This scenario is complicated by the verb Paul uses at the end of 1:22 (*hairēsomai*), which the NIV and NAB render "choose" rather than "prefer" (NRSV). In what sense might Paul have a choice? Could it mean that Paul is contemplating suicide? Though such a suggestion sounds preposterous, if not 'heretical,' to many, in the ancient world causing one's own death was often deemed a noble deed, as the examples of Socrates and even Jesus himself (see, e.g., John 10:17-18; Gal. 1:4; 2:20) attest. Even prisoners, such as gladiators, would sometimes attempt suicide (and succeed) to avoid the shame of the death penalty and to exercise control over their own death. The philosopher Seneca, Paul's contemporary, even advocates the position that life can be lived for others, but death is done only for oneself (*Epistle* 70.11-12).

For Paul, any desire to take his own life would stem not from the desire to avoid shame or to live the end of his life for himself, but rather from the glorious goal of being with Christ. Whether Paul was contemplating active suicide or a more passive death (e.g., by not resisting the Roman authorities), unless his

12. E.g., 1 Thess. 4:13-18; 1 Cor. 15; 2 Cor. 4:16–5:10.

words are hyperbolic (as some think), he really is "hard pressed" (1:23) between the choice of life and the choice of death. He experiences a complex and intense set of feelings, which are on display in this passage, especially in 1:20-24. In the end Paul opts for life. He is so certain that this is the right and necessary choice that he becomes absolutely convinced that he will be released.

Why is he so certain on these two points? Because dying would be better for him but worse for the Philippians. If Paul chooses to stay in the flesh, he will be able to engage in "fruitful labor" (1:22) and will be of ongoing benefit to the church at Philippi ("for you," 1:24; "for your progress and joy in faith," 1:25). In other words, for Paul to desire and choose life, rather than death, is to act in Christlike love, emptying himself of selfish interest and acting for the welfare of others. This is what the first part of the hymn (2:6-8) and its accompanying interpretation (2:3-4) are all about, as we will see momentarily. Paul struggles with, but eventually embodies, his own gospel in choosing life over death for the good of that gospel and the Philippians. Ironically, he embraces the death of Christ most faithfully in this circumstance by choosing *not* to die, even as a martyr. Whether or not his perplexity is real, his perspective is cruciform.

1:27–2:18. A LIFE WORTHY OF THE HYMN

Having shown the Philippians his own struggle and decision in their behalf, Paul can now move on with integrity and rhetorical power to urge them to behave similarly within their fellowship. (Paul uses a similar strategy in 1 Corinthians 8:1–11:1.) It is not that the Philippians, or Paul for that matter, can accomplish the salvation of the world with their cruciform actions, for only God in Christ can do that. Rather, because both Paul and the Philippians are citizens of the empire where Christ is Lord, and because they live in this Lord Christ, they must be shaped by him — by the hymnic narrative of his obedient self-emptying. Such an existence is *possible* in Christ because of God's activity in their midst, and it is *necessary* for a unified witness in the world that opposes Paul, the gospel, and the Philippian believers.

UNITY IN SUFFERING FOR CHRIST (1:27-30)

Paul begins and ends this section of the letter (1:27–2:18) on the theme of unity for the sake of witness in suffering (1:27-30 and 2:14-18). The Philippians have opponents (1:28) and are suffering for Christ (1:29). This occasion provides Paul with the opportunity to issue a fundamental exhortation and one of the

Philippi: Capstones of columns along the city streets were
inscribed in Latin, a sign of the city's devotion to Rome.

governing metaphors of the letter: he calls the Philippians to live out their lives
as citizens (*politeuesthe,* related to *polis,* 'city,' as noted above)[13] in a manner
worthy of the gospel of Christ, the gospel that will be rehearsed in 2:6-11. To be
worthy of citizenship is to bring honor rather than shame to the city, its rulers,
and its traditions.

"Worthy of" the gospel in this context can only mean 'consistent with' it,
whether or not Paul is physically present (1:27; cf. 2:12). The gospel to which
Paul refers is the good news that the crucified Jesus — not the Roman emperor
— is Lord (2:11). To be a citizen in the realm of Jesus' lordship is to honor God
by bending the knee to Jesus and living obediently as his servant, as Paul has attempted to do (1:30; cf. 2:12). When the Philippians live in this way, they will,
Paul claims, stand firm and united, "striving side by side with one mind for the
faith of the gospel" (1:27; cf. 4:1, 3), unintimidated by opposition (1:28). In other
words, unity for Paul is derivative, a by-product of faithfully embodying the
truth that Jesus is Lord, even in the face of opposition.

Paul puts the most positive spin possible on the Philippians' experience of
persecution: it is evidence of their (future) salvation and their opponents' de-

---

13. NRSV (like most translations) has the bland "live your life."

struction (1:28; cf. 2 Cor. 2:16; 2 Thess. 1:5-10);[14] it creates a bond with Paul (1:30); and it is a gift from God — the gracious privilege (*echaristhē,* related to *charis,* 'grace') not only of believing in but also of suffering for Christ (1:28-29). Both Paul and the Philippians are involved in a "struggle" (1:30; *agōna,* 'athletic contest'),[15] though it is radically different from the contests held in honor of the emperor.

UNITY WITHIN THROUGH THE MIND OF CHRIST (2:1-5)

The theme of unity continues in 2:1-4, focused this time on the internal relationships among the saints. These verses function as both a preface to and an interpretation of the Christ hymn in 2:6-11, with 2:5 acting as the bridge that connects the two passages.

This passage divides neatly into several components: a series of four suppositions about life in Christ (2:1), a request to be of one mind or disposition (2:2a), and a series of phrases describing the nature of that one mind in terms of unity and humble, others-oriented love rather than conceited self-interest (2:2b-4). (English translations generally segment 2:2-4 into several sentences, though there is only one long Greek sentence.) Paul brings together numerous expressions to make one main point: unity through love is the one disposition, the disposition of Christ (2:5), that is needed in the church.

The four phrases that constitute 2:1, beginning with the word "if," are not possibilities but realities. Paul means to say, '*Since* these conditions do in fact exist in Christ [i.e., in the church]. . . .' The phrases are various ways of expressing Paul's conviction that a community in Christ is infused with deep love and compassion, generated by the Spirit, that create a common bond of mutual concern and encouragement (2:1, *paraklēsis*). This normal work of the Spirit in the body of Christ is the basis for Paul's exhortation to the Philippians (2:2-4) to cooperate with the Spirit (cf. 2:12-13) by being unified in love, which will "complete" the joy Paul already has vis-à-vis this community (2:2).

The substance of Paul's exhortation in 2:2-4 is that the Philippians "be of the same mind" (2:2), or perhaps better, 'possess the same disposition.' This disposition is then spelled out in some detail before being linked directly to Christ in 2:5-11. In both 2:2 (twice) and 2:5 Paul uses the key verb *phroneō,* and in 4:2 he combines these two verses in urging Euodia and Syntyche "to be of the same mind in the Lord." It would be difficult for Paul to have stressed unity more

14. Another possible (but less likely) interpretation of 1:28 is that the persecution is a sign to the persecutors of the Philippian believers' (eventual) destruction, but it is a sign to the believers of their (eventual) salvation.

15. Cf. 2:16; 3:13-14; 4:3.

than he does in 2:2: one mind, love, and soul.[16] Although there are echoes of Hellenistic friendship language here, Paul's overall emphasis is on the unique common life created by Christ and the Spirit.

Paul does not leave the call to oneness in love in the theoretical stratosphere but gives it concreteness by presenting two sets of radically opposite behaviors (2:3-4):

v. 3   Do nothing from selfish ambition or conceit,
            but
        in humility regard others as better than yourselves.

v. 4   Let each of you look not to your own interests,
            but
        to the interests of others.

The structure and language of these verses is parallel to 2:6-8, where it is said that Christ

v. 6   did not regard equality with God as something to be exploited
        [i.e., for his own advantage]
            but
vv. 7-8 emptied himself, taking the form of a slave . . . [and] humbled
        himself.

Other Pauline texts embody this 'not *y* but *z* pattern,' similarly pitting interest in others against selfish concern as the fundamental character of love, *agapē* (see, e.g., 1 Cor. 10:24, 33; 13:5), and connecting this understanding to the example of Christ (e.g., 1 Cor. 11:1; Rom. 15:1-3; and of course Phil. 2:6-8). To possess the mind or disposition that Paul wants the Philippians to have, then, involves not merely attitudes but actions, and actions of a rather radical sort. Just as Christ chose between self-interest and self-emptying/self-humbling, so too the Philippians must choose between selfish ambition and high regard for others, between empty self-glory and humility (note the verbal links to 2:7-8), between their own interests and those of others.[17]

16. NRSV's "being in full accord" (2:2) renders *sympsychoi,* something like 'soul mates,' "being one in spirit" (NIV), or "united in heart" (NAB).

17. The radical contrast depicted in the hymn suggests strongly that this must be maintained in the translation of 2:4, as the NRSV cited above does ("look not to your own interests, but to the interests of others") but the NIV does not: "look not *only* to your own interests, but *also* to the interests of others" (emphasis added). The word "only" does not appear in the Greek text, and the word translated "also" should be rendered 'rather.'

In 2:5 Paul makes it clear that the parallels between 2:6-8 and 2:1-4 are not accidental. The action-oriented disposition he has been urging is indeed connected to Christ. But in what way? Much ink has been spilled over the translation and interpretation of this verse, which connects the exhortation to the hymn text (which is introduced with the linking word "who," referring back to Christ Jesus). Space permits only the mention of the two basic options and an alternative to both that may make more sense of this text in both its immediate and its larger Pauline contexts.

Option 1 (majority opinion)
Let the same mind be in you that was in Christ Jesus, [who . . .] (NRSV)
Your attitude should be the same as that of Christ Jesus: [Who . . .] (NIV)

Option 2 (minority opinion)
Let the same mind be in you that you have in Christ Jesus, [who . . .] (NRSV mg.)
Have among yourselves the same attitude that is also yours in Christ Jesus, [Who . . .] (NAB)

Option 3
Let this mind be in your fellowship [lit. 'in you,' plural], which is also [a fellowship] in Christ Jesus, [who . . .] (author's translation)[18]

This alternative translation is meant to convey the sense that Paul's main point in 2:5 is the necessary correspondence between the pattern of Christ's story, as narrated in the hymn, and the pattern of life of those who are "in" this Christ (see also "in Christ" in 2:1). Option 3 preserves the insight of option 1 that Paul is making a plea to cultivate a Christlike disposition, not telling them (rather nonsensically) to 'have what they have' (option 2, wrongly). It also retains the insight of option 2 that the phrase "in Christ Jesus" is a typical Pauline reference to the community, not to something that was supposedly "in" Christ the individual (option 1, wrongly).[19]

Whether option 1 or 3 is correct (and perhaps even option 2), 2:5 shows that Paul wants to draw a parallel between the attitude and behavior he expects of the Philippians who live in Christ and the attitude and behavior he finds in Christ himself.

---

18. More literally, 'Let this mind be in you, i.e. in Christ Jesus, who . . . ,' meaning 'Cultivate the preceding disposition [see 2:1-4] in your community, which is in fact an "in-Christ" community, and that disposition can be seen in the following story of Christ, who. . . .'

19. For further discussion, see my *Cruciformity*, pp. 40-43.

THE HYMNIC STORY OF CHRIST (2:6-11)

No passage in Paul, and perhaps no passage in the entire Bible, has received more scholarly attention than Philippians 2:6-11. Space does not permit a review of all the issues and perspectives that this attention has generated, but a few introductory words are necessary to supplement those already offered above.

Scholarly Trends and the Hymn's Background

Scholarship in the first two-thirds of the twentieth century focused primarily on issues of form, philology, and background: What kind of text is this? What do all the unusual words mean? What are the religious and literary influences on the text? Much work focused on the text in isolation, as an example of early (pre-Pauline) Christian theology in the form of a hymn or hymn fragment, and not on how Paul used this hymn in the letter. The poetic structure and unusual vocabulary of the text were two of the main factors leading to the general scholarly opinion that it is a pre-Pauline hymn that Paul modified a bit (e.g., with the addition of the line "even death on a cross" in 2:8) — though there were endless proposals dividing the poem into lines and stanzas (strophes).

More recent studies have shown that the structure, thought, and vocabulary of the text could very well have come from Paul, who draws on many of the text's words and images. Thus there is a growing number of scholars today who doubt that the text is a pre-Pauline hymn inserted into the letter. In the view of this writer, although Paul did not originally compose the text, he turns it into his master story. The primary argument for the pre-Pauline character of the text is the fact that Paul does in fact interpret it so creatively. The text does not explicitly say what Paul makes it say, for apart from its context in Philippians the text speaks solely of Christ in relation to God — not to humanity — as a self-humbling, obedient servant. Thus it is most likely that Paul found this early poetic piece being sung in churches he knew, perhaps in Jerusalem or Antioch, early in his apostolic life. Attracted to its simplicity and yet also its profundity and power, he found that it encapsulated not only the story of Christ but also his own story, and the story he hoped his churches would narrate in their life together.

A word about the background of this story is in order. Earlier claims that it reflects a Gnostic redeemer myth are now dismissed. But scholars disagree on the primary religious context out of which the text emerges and to which it alludes. Three main suggestions have been made: (1) the fourth servant hymn of Isaiah 40–55, with Christ being depicted as the suffering servant of 52:13–53:12; (2) the Adam story (Gen. 1–3), with Christ being contrasted with Adam's disobedience and selfish exploitation of his status as God's image; (3) the emperor cult, with Christ being contrasted with power-seeking emperors and the false claims (e.g., to divinity and lordship) made by them and their admirers. There is no reason why all these stories cannot have informed the writing, use, and hearing of this text. In my view, the deliberate allusions to the suffering servant are most prominent, such that the text is really a hymn that merges the very early Christian preaching with the fourth Isaianic servant hymn. But there may well have been an allusion to Adam, either intended or heard. And at least for Paul, writing to the Philippians, there can be little doubt that he intends the hymn to be heard as giving honor to the one true Lord — not the emperor — who is equal to God.

In essence, then, the text portrays Christ, in contrast to the self-exalting behavior of Adam and of Roman emperors, as the fulfillment of the Isaianic servant of God, the one who was equal to God but willingly became a human being and suffered on the cross. He was consequently exalted by God to the position of Lord, sharing in the honor due God alone, and not Caesar. This is, in Philippians, the gospel to which Paul repeatedly refers. It is to this story that he and the Philippians bear witness in preaching, singing, living, and suffering.

As noted earlier, the text itself clearly falls into two main parts, or dramatic 'acts,' 2:6-8 and 2:9-11, the division indicated by the "therefore" of 2:9 (cf. Isa. 53:12). These two main divisions may be referred to as Christ's humiliation (cf. Isa. 52:14–53:9) and his exaltation (cf. Isa. 52:13; 53:10-12). The narrative pattern of humiliation-exaltation later becomes the pattern for believers, too (3:10-11), as the existential structure of hope. The first part of the hymn has Christ as the sole subject of each verb, while the second part shifts the subject first to God, responding to Christ's acts (2:9), and then to all creation (2:10-11), responding to God's response to Christ's acts.[20]

Humiliation (2:6-8)

The primary acts of Christ enumerated in 2:6-8 (and indicated in Greek by the only main verbs in these verses) are three in number: "did not regard" . . . "emptied himself" . . . "humbled himself." This text states that Christ made a decision *not* to do one thing but rather (the first word of 2:7) to do something else. That something else came in two parallel but distinct stages, consisting of two radically self-involving, self-giving actions: incarnation ("emptied himself") and death ("humbled himself"). The other phrases in 2:6-8 (all indicated in Greek with participles) amplify the meaning of these main actions.

---

20. For a graphic display of the text of 2:6-11, see the chart in chap. 4, p. 103.

Despite a long history of various interpretations for 2:6, it is now generally agreed that the text refers to something ("the form of God," i.e., 'equality with God') that the preincarnate Christ had but chose not to exploit for his own advantage. (Such appears to be the sense of the unusual Greek word *harpagmos*; older translations have various vague renderings using the phrase "to be grasped.") Because the sense of the text is that Christ chose not to exploit something he could have exploited, the first phrase of the verse should be translated "though he was in the form of God" (NRSV, NAB) rather than the less clear "being in the form of God" (NIV mg.).

Similarly, despite years of speculation about what Christ emptied himself of according to 2:7 (divinity, power, some divine attribute, etc.), it is generally agreed that the self-emptying (*kenōsis*, from the Greek verb used here) is metaphorical, pointing to the complete self-lowering that becoming human involved for one equal to God. This is confirmed by the three subsequent phrases: "taking the form of a slave, being born in human likeness. And being found in human form." (The phrase "form of God" in 2:6 is in deliberate contrast to "form of a slave" here.) The last of these phrases is probably to be taken with the main verb in 2:8, "humbled himself," which is further explained as 'becoming' (in the Greek) "obedient to the point of death — even death on a cross." An echo of Isaiah 53:12 — "he poured out himself to death" — is probably to be heard here.

What 2:6-8 offers, then, is an interpretation of Christ's incarnation ("emptied himself," etc.) and death ("humbled himself," etc.) as a pattern of non-self-centered, self-giving obedience, in basic continuity with the narrative of Isaiah's suffering servant. The addition of a certain status ("in the form of God") that is renounced makes the pattern of self-humbling obedience all the more radical. This pattern may be represented as follows —

although *x*, not *y* but *z* —

where *x* represents a status possessed, *y* a selfish action not taken, and *z* alternative, selfless action (self-emptying and self-humbling). There are echoes of this pattern elsewhere in Paul. This full pattern appears also in abbreviated form as 'not *y* but *z*,' as we have just seen in 2:3-4.[21]

Like the humiliation-exaltation pattern, Paul will use the pattern from 2:6-8 — in fact, he has already repeatedly used it — to describe the norm for life in

21. For 'although *x*, not *y* but *z*,' see 1 Thess. 2:7-8 and 1 Cor. 9 (esp. v. 19) in reference to Paul. For the abbreviated pattern 'not *y* but *z*,' see Rom. 15:1-3 in reference to both Christ and believers. Paul also uses other abbreviated forms of this pattern. For 'although *x*, *z*,' see 2 Cor. 8:9 in reference to Christ. For simply '*z*,' see Gal. 1:4 and 2:20 in reference to Christ, and 2 Cor. 12:15 in reference to Paul.

Christ.[22] The clearest example is the parallel between 2:6-8 and 2:3-4, noted above. From its use in 2:3-4, elsewhere in Philippians, and in other letters, we see that Paul clearly intends his readers to interpret this pattern as the pattern of cruciform love, found first in Christ — even though the word 'love' does not appear in 2:6-11.

Furthermore, by introducing the word "obedient" in 2:8, the text stresses the slave/servant image (2:7) and interprets Christ's death as his (faithful) obedience, probably in contrast to Adam's disobedience (cf. Rom. 5:12-21, esp. 5:19). It also allows Paul to refer back to the obedience of believers (2:12) and, later, to the faithfulness of Christ (3:9). In other words, Paul interprets Christ's death not only as an act of love but as an act of (voluntary! cf. 2:6) obedience, and he expects such voluntary obedience to be the pattern of believers' existence, too.

Exaltation (2:9-11)

In 2:9-11 the hymn outlines the two-stage response to Christ's voluntary, obedient death: exaltation by God and acclamation by creation. The word "therefore" stresses God's exaltation as a direct consequence of Christ's obedience (an implicit promise for believers, too). There is a clear echo here of the hymn of the suffering servant:

> See, my servant shall prosper;
>> he shall be exalted and lifted up,
>> and shall be very high. (Isa. 52:13)

> Therefore I will allot him a portion with the great,
>> and he shall divide the spoil with the strong;
> because he poured out himself to death. (Isa. 53:12)

In these texts God rewards and exalts the servant for fulfilling his mission in dying. Some have wondered whether God exalts Christ to a position 'higher' than or otherwise different from the "equality with God" he possessed according to 2:6. That is unlikely; the consequential action of exaltation (the typical biblical reward for the humble) is rather the alternative to whatever divine action would have been appropriate had the incarnate Christ disobeyed the Father.

In any event, what follows Christ's exaltation is expressed in language taken directly from Isaiah 45:23, where the Lord (YHWH) proclaims:

> By myself I have sworn,
>> from my mouth has gone forth in righteousness

22. Phil. 1:21-26; 2:3-4, 20-21, 26-27.

a word that shall not return:
"To me every knee shall bow,
    every tongue shall swear."

This text appears within one of the most powerful expositions of Hebrew monotheism in the Bible (Isa. 45), in which the Lord God of Israel (YHWH) calls all
other gods false, claiming for himself alone all honor and praise. For the writer of
the hymn text, for the early Christians, and for Paul, transferring this text and its
confession of lordship to Jesus was an unprecedented and probably blasphemous
move, from a Jewish perspective. God's exaltation of Jesus is expressed in the giving of the name — the divine name "Lord" (Gk. *kyrios*) — to Jesus (2:9). Henceforth Jesus shares the name, the character, and the honor due to God alone. The
universal acclamation of Jesus' lordship, the adoration of him on bended knee
(2:10) does not, however, steal the thunder from God the Father. In fact, the hymn
says, quite the opposite is true; the universal confession of "Jesus Christ is Lord"
(2:11) — which was likely said already in many early churches (see, e.g., 1 Cor. 12:3)
— is done *"to the glory of God the Father"* (2:11, emphasis added).

THE FAITHFUL WITNESS OF THE
COMMUNITY AND OF PAUL (2:12-18)

As mentioned in the discussion of 1:27-30, 2:12-18 contains echoes of that passage as well as 2:1-5 and 2:6-11, suggesting that Paul's overriding concern in all of
1:27–2:18 is the unity and integrity of the community in the face of opposition.

Paul explicitly connects this section to the preceding hymn with the linking word "therefore" and the mention of obedience (2:12). Although the NRSV
has Paul say "just as you have always obeyed me" (2:12), the Greek text lacks the
word 'me.' The obedience is more general — to the gospel, to God, or to Christ
the Lord. In other words, Paul says the Philippians have so far been faithful and
obedient, like Christ (2:8), whether Paul was present or not (cf. 1:27), and they
should now continue faithfully. This is the meaning of the (plural) imperative
"work out your own salvation with fear and trembling" (2:12), also an echo of
Paul's earlier words (1:28). This obedient embodiment of the Philippians'
Christlike disposition is necessary to insure their final salvation. It is possible
because God is at work 'among you' or 'in your fellowship' (as in 2:5, and better
than the "in you" found in most translations) both to desire and to accomplish
the will of God (2:13).

Paul then returns to the theme of unity and mutual concern — no mur-
muring or arguing (2:14) — as necessary for a corporate witness with integrity
"in the midst of a crooked and perverse generation" (2:15; cf. Deut. 32:5). (One

is reminded of John 17, in which unity for the sake of mission is also the theme.) The mission of the Philippian church is to "shine like stars in the world," which is likely an allusion to the Isaianic theme of being a light to the Gentiles/nations (e.g., Isa. 49:6; 55:4-5), and which appears also in the Gospel tradition (Matt. 5:14). Paul will judge his own success as an apostle — and be judged by Christ, he infers — on the basis of the Philippians' (and others') faithfulness in "holding fast to" (NRSV; or perhaps 'holding forth') the "word of life" — the gospel preserved in the hymn (2:16). As long as the Philippians remain faithful to the hymn, Paul rejoices at his part in the offering of their faith as a sacrifice to God (2:17-18). He sees himself (either because of his ministry in general, his suffering in particular, or — some argue — his possible martyrdom) as a libation — an outpouring of wine or oil on a sacrificial fire. That is, Paul and the Philippians share together in the common experience of faithful obedience to God that includes suffering (cf. 1:29-30), but suffering with joy. In other words, Paul and the Philippians continue the story of the faithful suffering of Jesus, the servant of God, narrated in the hymn.

2:19-30. TWO LIVING EXAMPLES OF THE HYMN

After portraying Christ as the paradigmatic servant to be imitated and the exalted Lord to be obeyed, and then pointing out the necessity of sharing together in the cruciform life, Paul provides two examples of that life, namely, Timothy and Epaphroditus. He does this while accomplishing the more mundane task of discussing his (non)travel plans — the sending of envoys until he can return to Philippi himself.

TIMOTHY (2:19-24)

Paul's words about Timothy (2:19-24) reveal his deep esteem for his younger assistant. Awaiting his own fate and then an eventual visit to Philippi, Paul hopes soon to send Timothy to obtain a positive update on the church's faithfulness in the gospel (2:19, 23-24). Paul characterizes Timothy in the words of selfless, Christlike love he has used in 2:1-4: "concerned for your welfare" (2:20), not seeking his own interests (2:21). The interesting opposition of "their own interests" and "those of Jesus Christ" in 2:21 suggests that Paul closely identifies concern for the interests of others and concern for the interests of Christ. Like Timothy, Paul implies, those who wish to serve Christ the Lord must do so by serving others, even as Timothy has served with Paul (2:22).

439

EPAPHRODITUS (2:25-30)

Even closer to home is Epaphroditus, who had brought Paul the Philippians' gift (4:18) and whom Paul esteems deeply, too (2:25-30). Epaphroditus receives five titles: Paul's brother, coworker, and cosoldier; the Philippians' messenger (*apostolos*, 'emissary') and minister to Paul's need. The ministry of Epaphroditus is also described in Paul-like and especially Christlike terms. Like Paul, he has been "longing for" the Philippians (2:26; cf. 1:8), and like Christ, his ministry "for the work of Christ" (2:30) took him to the point (in this case the 'brink') of death — *mechri thanatou* (2:30, as in 2:8; cf. 2:27). He risked his life — though precisely how he did so is unclear, as is the relationship (if any) of this event to his near-fatal illness (2:26-27); the two references to Epaphroditus's brush with death may or may not refer to the same episode. Whatever exactly transpired, Paul of course rejoiced at his friend's recovery from illness and either is sending him (with the letter) or will send him so that the Philippians will be relieved, too (2:28). More importantly, Paul urges the Philippians to welcome him and to honor any and all such paradigms of Christlike, cruciform love (2:29).

Summary of Philippians 1-2

We find in Philippians 1-2 the consistent theme of Christlike (cruciform) suffering and love as the hallmark of life in Christ, whether in the life of Paul, the Philippians as a church, or Timothy and Epaphroditus. Some specific dimensions of this life that Paul stresses are the following:

- Suffering for Christ/the gospel is an occasion for joy and for confidence that God will complete the work of faith begun in the church. In fact, suffering for Christ/the gospel can actually advance the gospel.
- Believers live to magnify Christ in life or death, and should view death as a departure to be with Christ.
- Paul's gospel (as summarized in his master story, the hymn in Phil. 2:6-11) depicts Christ as the preincarnate one who did not exploit his status of equality with God but emptied and humbled himself in incarnation and death.
- The gospel also proclaims God's exaltation of the crucified Christ to the position of Lord.
- As citizens of God's imperial city, believers honor Christ as Lord, seeking to live worthily of the gospel by embodying the selfless, other-regarding love of Christ in their fellowship.
- The unity such love creates bonds believers together in faithful witness to a hostile world.

- The church should both honor and emulate those who faithfully embody the pattern of Christ's love.

3:1–4:1. THE HYMN AND THE ENEMIES OF THE CROSS

Philippians 3 is well known for its extended Pauline autobiographical remarks in the context of warning the Philippians about "the dogs" (3:2). Those who find parts of several letters in Philippians often point to the apparent beginning of the end in 3:1, followed by the unexpectedly long speech from 3:2 to 3:21 (or 4:1). But however we explain the oddity that is 3:1, the remainder of chapter 3 is clearly related to all of chapters 1–2 and especially to 2:6-11. As in the first two chapters, also in chapter 3 Paul depicts life in Christ as one shaped by the narrative of Christ found in the hymn. Now, however, the emphasis is not on love but on faith and hope.

As Philippians has already indicated (1:15-18), and some of Paul's other letters confirm (e.g., Gal. 1:7-9; 2 Cor. 10–13), Paul had 'rivals' — other missionaries whose methods and/or message differed from his. Paul tolerated some of these preachers, but others he did not, for to him they preached another gospel that was in reality no gospel at all. The preachers who most provoked his ire were those fellow Jewish believers who tried to supplement the gospel of the crucified Christ and his Spirit with a requirement that Gentiles adhere to Jewish law, especially circumcision (see especially Galatians and perhaps also Colossians). Of all the possible candidates for those under attack in Philippians 3, this kind of teacher is the most likely.[23] Those who read Paul's invectives today must especially remember three things: that name-calling was a normal part of ancient rhetoric; that Paul is criticizing specific people, not all Jews or Judaism per se; and that Paul's positive affirmations about life in Christ constitute the focus and most important aspect of the chapter.

TRANSITION (3:1)

There is no completely satisfactory explanation for the combination of elements in this verse — the word "finally," the phrase "rejoice in the Lord," and

---

23. An older view is that Paul is opposing Gnostic believers. Some scholars have found evidence of several opponents, including not only 'Judaizers' (as some have inaccurately called them) and Gnostics, but also 'perfectionists' (see 3:12) and 'antinomians' (see 3:18-19). But the unified polemic of 3:1–4:1 argues against multiple opponents.

the sentence about writing "the same things" as a safeguard for the Philippians
— and their connection to what follows. It may be that the word translated "finally" should be rendered 'And now for the one remaining subject,' or 'once
again': "rejoice in the Lord." The appearance of the theme of joy should not surprise us, and it may be that Paul believes the best antidote to the problem he is
about to describe is the prescription he has dispensed all along: joy in suffering
faithfully for Christ, no matter what the opposition may be.

KNOWING CHRIST: THE LIFE OF FAITH (3:2-11)

It is not certain whether any "dogs" had already arrived on the Philippians' front
steps, so to speak, or whether Paul is simply warning them about possible trouble (note "beware" three times in 3:2). His three labels — dogs, evil workers,
those who mutilate the flesh (lit. "the mutilation," as in NAB) — suggest, respectively, their uncleanness, their negative impact, and their wrong focus on circumcision. Paul's insults also reveal his fluency in irony: Jews (and some Jewish
believers?) sometimes referred to Gentiles as dogs and accused them of doing
evil, while the word "mutilation" *(katatomē)* is a play on words with "circumcision" *(peritomē)*. Paul claims in 3:3 that "we" are in fact "the circumcision" (cf.
Rom. 2:25-29), the "we" being those in relationship with God (the Father),
Christ, and the Spirit (3:3) apart from confidence in the flesh — i.e., in circumcision or any other supposed human (especially ethnic or nationalistic) grounds
for confidence before God. Paul and the Philippians "boast" in Christ Jesus and,
he implies, in Christ's cross (cf. 1 Cor. 1:31; Gal. 2:15-21; 5:2-12).

Paul categorically rejects the "flesh" — human achievement and status —
as grounds for confidence before God even for those (like himself) who might
possess such achievements and status (3:4). In a rare display of his former nationalistic status and pride, Paul portrays himself in quasi-Christlike fashion as
one who had possessed a certain status, come to regard that status differently,
and demonstrated his new perception through a decision to take on suffering.
It is a version of the 'although *x*, not *y* but *z*' pattern of 2:6-8. (The qualifier
'quasi-' is necessary because there are clear differences between Christ's story
and Paul's, though each is exemplary in different ways.) In these verses, then,
Paul narrates his own self-emptying, his cruciform death to the old self and resurrection to a new life, his cruciform conversion. In a word, he narrates his
coming to faith.

In 3:5-6 Paul tries to show that he was about as righteous by human standards, about as fully a member of the covenant, as one could possibly be: a
properly circumcised Israelite of excellent stock (tribe of Benjamin), with close
ties to the land and language of Israel ("a Hebrew born of Hebrews"), commit-

ted to promoting and righteously observing the Law as a Pharisee, so zealous for Israel's purity as to persecute the wayward movement called "the church" (cf. Gal. 1:13-14).

The following verses (3:7-11) narrate Paul's radical change in perspective (note "regard" or "consider," as in 2:6, three times: 3:7, 8 [twice]) that has come since he encountered Christ. Told in economic terms, the story is one of 'gains' (the religious and social benefits derived from his reasons for confidence in the flesh) now being perceived as "loss," and indeed of "all things" being equated with loss compared to the one asset of 'gaining' or 'knowing' Christ (3:8). These losses are not all matters of perception, however; Paul has in fact lost "all things" (3:8); he has forfeited any gain associated with his various achievements, associations, and other status indicators. These he now regards as "rubbish" (3:8) — better translated 'dung.'

Paul now reveals the core of his own spirituality: to know Christ (3:8, 10) and to be found in him (3:9). The latter phrase Paul links with the term "righteousness," or being in proper relationship to God. He has abandoned the former way, deriving from (his version of) compliance with the Law, which he says was in fact his own righteousness. He now has a new righteousness, whose source is not the Law but either "faith in Christ" (NRSV, NIV, NAB) or "the faith of Christ" (NRSV mg.). Space does not permit a full discussion of the extended debate over this phrase, so it will have to suffice to say that a growing number of scholars — perhaps now the majority — prefer the reading "the faith of Christ" (as also in parallel passages in Rom. 3 and Gal. 2 and 3). If this reading is correct, it means that for Paul the faith(fulness) or obedience of Christ expressed in his death (2:8), rather than circumcision or Law keeping, is the basis of membership in God's covenant people. Those who have faith (3:9) in the gospel are thereby "found in him [Christ]" and participate in his life-giving death and all its benefits.

Which leads to the other phrase, "knowing Christ." Paul explains what he means by this in 3:10-11. It is to share in Christ's death and resurrection, the former now, the latter later, corresponding to the humiliation-exaltation pattern of 2:6-11. The "power of his resurrection" will be experienced by Paul (and all believers) as "the resurrection from the dead" (3:11), but only if ("if somehow") they participate in his sufferings and death now (cf. Rom. 8:17). (Yet even now that power may be experienced as the strength to endure suffering; see 4:13.) This may take the specific form of literal sufferings and/or the more general form of conformity to his death — following the pattern of selfless, cruciform love. Such a life of death is, in fact, the life of faith, the faith of the gospel (1:27), the gospel of Christ's obedient faith and self-giving love that culminated in his resurrection and exaltation by God.

PURSUING CHRIST: THE LIFE OF HOPE (3:12–4:1)

Contrary perhaps to his own former sense of having 'arrived,' and contrary perhaps also to the claims of his rivals, Paul feels compelled to insist that the resurrection of the dead (and the state of completion or perfection [3:12, *teteleiōmai;* NRSV, "reached the goal"] it brings) is still a hope, not something he and the Philippians have already attained (3:12). Playing with forms of the verb 'obtain' and images from athletics, however, Paul insists (speaking representatively for all believers) that his current objective is to move ahead toward the final goal, "to make it my own, because Christ Jesus has made me his own" (3:12). The precise goal or "prize" (3:14) has been debated, but in context it should be understood as the promise of resurrection and exaltation that is the culmination of God's call in Christ, subsequent to the present life of cruciformity. Paul assumes that all the truly complete or "mature" (NRSV and NIV in 3:15, rendering *teleioi;* NAB, "'perfectly mature'") — perhaps a term used by his rivals — will adopt this Christ-centered disposition (the verb *phroneō* is used twice) and hold on to the message of righteousness based on Christ's death and the pattern of death followed by resurrection (3:15-16). To lose this would be to lose that which already has been gained — the knowledge of Christ and participation in him.

The thought that some Philippians might not "hold fast to what we have attained" prompts Paul to issue a plea that they become "[fellow] imitators" *(symmimētai)* of himself and others (e.g., Timothy and Epaphroditus) like him (3:17). Paul may actually mean to say 'fellow imitators *of Christ* [which does not explicitly appear in the text] with me,' for that is not only the sense of the unusual word he uses but also the point he makes elsewhere (1 Cor. 11:1). This kind of imitation means centering on the cross, unlike those "enemies of the cross" (3:18) against whom Paul now rails. Whether these "enemies" are the "dogs" of 3:2, the persecutors of the church, former believers who have returned to idolatry and immorality ("belly . . . shame," 3:19), or all of the above, Paul's point is clear: believers must always be friends with the cross. They must identify with the message and the reality of the crucified Christ.

For it is this crucified Christ, and none other, who is the Lord and coming Savior (3:20). He is now exalted to heaven, from which place he will return and in which is located believers' "citizenship" or, better, "commonwealth" (NRSV mg.; Gk. *politeuma*). They are not citizens of the empire and culture of Rome, which pretends to offer the world a Savior and Lord in the person of the emperor. They are not a colony of the powerful. They are part of the colony of heaven, of the true Lord, and so their current status is to be a body characterized by 'humiliation,' as was that of their Lord while on earth (2:6-8). But that situation will change, as the pattern of Christ's humiliation-exaltation narrated in the hymn will become the pattern of believers, too. Their Savior will transform them with his divine power, so that their bodies will share his glory (cf. 1 Cor. 15:42-54).

Such a message — of humiliation followed by glory — motivates Paul to endure his imprisonment and to urge his beloved family in Christ at Philippi to "stand firm . . . in this way" (4:1) — the way of the cross.

4:2-9. EXHORTATIONS TO PERFORM THE HYMN

The final portion of Paul's letter (4:2-23) consists of a series of exhortations and greetings surrounding an extended word of thanks for the Philippians' financial support of Paul. Before acknowledging their gift in 4:10-20, Paul offers some final words of counsel in 4:2-9 that, in various ways, sum up the themes of the letter.

HARMONY: EUODIA AND SYNTYCHE (4:2-3)

Not much is known of the two women Paul names in these verses, except that he views them as his costrugglers (using the athletic image once again) and coworkers in the gospel. With Clement (4:3), they may be among the church's overseers/bishops and deacons/ministers (1:1). The names of all three are of Gentile origin. The women have obviously come to some sort of unhealthy disagreement, and Paul views either their mutual treatment or the resulting situation (or both) as less than Christlike. Though not something that would endanger their salvation — their names are still written in the book of life (a common biblical image for the roster of the elect, as well as a civic term for the citizens of a city) — the affair calls forth Paul's serious attention. He urges each of the women individually to "be of the same mind [*to auto phronein*] in the Lord" (4:2), language lifted from the general exhortation to a Christlike disposition of humility, love, and unity in 2:1-5 (*to auto phronein*, 2:2; in Christ [Jesus], 2:1, 5). Thus the women are not merely to agree artificially but to exhibit cruciform love. Paul also asks his "loyal companion" (*gnēsie syzyge*) — probably a reference to the whole church, but possibly a mistranslation of the proper name Syzygus — to assist in their reconciliation. Strife among leaders is a matter of concern for the entire church.

JOY AND PEACE (4:4-7)

Paul continues with general exhortations concerning joy, so prominent a theme in the letter, and peace. For an imprisoned apostle and a persecuted church, the two belong together. "Rejoice" (twice spoken) is an appropriate biblical imperative for those whose confidence is "in the Lord," no matter the circumstances — and thus "always" (4:4). The assurance of the presence and/or soon return of the Lord (who "is near," 4:5) allows believers to deal both externally with others and internally with themselves and their own fears.

Believers' relations with others — everyone, including persecutors — are to be characterized by gentleness (4:5). Though Paul uses an unusual word, the idea reflects his conviction that such treatment of others is the cruciform way of Christ (2 Cor. 10:1) and the fruit of the Spirit (Gal. 5:22-23); anything else (such as anger or retaliation) would contradict the gospel they believe in and sing. Believers' internal life is to be characterized by a suprarational peace that comes from God to those who are in Christ (4:6) and who deal with their anxiety as Paul has already demonstrated — with prayers of supplication and thanksgiving (1:3-11). Those who live faithfully according to the gospel may put their bodies at risk, but God protects their hearts and minds.

In order not to trivialize these admonitions and 'promises,' contemporary readers of this passage must be careful to remember the circumstances in which Paul was writing these words and the Philippians were hearing them. It was a time of suffering, and the temptations to mistreatment of others and to fear were great.

GOODNESS (4:8-9)

Finally (though, once again, not quite), Paul composes a short call to noble and virtuous thoughts (4:8; "true . . . honorable," etc.) that catches anyone familiar with ancient literature a bit off guard. After all of Paul's words implying criticism of pagan Roman values, here he writes like a good Roman Stoic. Two points about this apparent anomaly should be made. First, Paul is not suddenly putting his stamp of approval on *all* pagan values but only on what he considers the *highest and best* in pagan thought and culture. Second, the addition of 4:9 interprets the call to embody the highest pagan virtues as fundamentally a call to follow the example of Paul and, therefore, of Christ. To the extent that these universally acknowledged virtues are found in and defined by Paul as Christ's representative, their divine origin is to be recognized, and their adoption in mind and life will ensure the presence of the God of peace (4:9) and thus the peace of God (4:7).

4:10-20. THE FELLOWSHIP OF THE HYMN

As noted in the introductory remarks, some interpreters of Philippians believe the letter really boils down to finances. It has always struck readers as odd, however, that Paul's thanksgiving for the monetary gift appears so late in the letter. As noted earlier, this oddity has led some to posit a separate letter of thanks, now incorporated into the conglomerate we call 'the letter to the Philippians.' But recent study of ancient social conventions surrounding friendship, patronage, and gift giving suggests that Paul was following the etiquette of his day in postponing the issue of money until the end. Moreover, it is likely that Paul, though grateful, was never completely comfortable with financial support for his ministry, preferring for a variety of reasons to support himself. Most importantly, however, the postponement of this topic until the end signals that for Paul the issue of money was only one dimension of the "partnership [*koinōnia*] in the gospel" (1:5 NIV) that he and the Philippians shared. Nonetheless, Paul cannot help but give thanks, and to connect both his circumstances and the gift to the hymn of the cross.

PAUL'S CRUCIFORM CONTENTMENT (4:10-14)

Paul's words of thanks do not begin, as some have thought, with a subtle reprimand for the Philippians' delay in their concern, but with genuine thanks that their uninterrupted concern could again find concrete expression (4:10). Their temporary lack of opportunity was likely due, not to poverty, but to an intensifying of persecution (cf. 2 Cor. 8:1-5), an affliction that perhaps has decreased but not ceased. In fact, Paul proceeds to explain quite eloquently that he has learned, through the ups and downs of his ministry, the secret of contentment in any and all circumstances (4:11-12); he can thus harbor no resentment.

Despite the use of another Stoic term (*autarkēs*, 4:11), meaning "content" (NRSV, NIV) or "self-sufficient" (NAB), Paul is not adopting a traditional Stoic attitude of apathy toward, and self-reliance in, bad circumstances. Rather, these times of abasement (*tapeinousthai*, an echo of the verb "humbled himself" in 2:8) and abundance, of hunger and of plenty, have been Paul's teachers. He has learned to identify with the suffering Christ narrated in the hymn and to rely on the power of Another (4:13, probably meaning specifically Christ the Lord — i.e., "the power of his resurrection," 3:10). These lessons have not, however, made the apostle indifferent to assistance (4:15).

Philippi: **Remains of the agora**

THE PHILIPPIANS' CRUCIFORM GIFT (4:15-20)

Paul continues his expression of deep gratitude for the Philippians' gift, but he does so cautiously lest he be thought greedy. Ultimately his words are as much words of commendation and blessing as they are thanks. After reminding the Philippians of their lone and repeated support of him in the early days of his ministry, even as early as his visit to Thessalonica immediately after his time in Philippi (4:15-16; cf. Acts 17:1), Paul tells them that his appreciation for these past and present gifts is really for the benefit it accrues to them, not him (4:17). Nevertheless, their gift, brought by Epaphroditus, has lifted him into a period of (relative) abundance (4:18).

Though clearly grateful, Paul does not stress the relationship the gift might create between himself and the Philippians, but the relationship between the Philippians and God that it symbolizes. It is a sacrificial offering to God more than a gift to Paul (4:18). It is one important dimension of their life of faith that, in its entirety, is a sacrificial offering to God (2:17). For this reason it is God and not Paul who rewards their Christlike, faithful, sacrificial giving (4:19; cf. 2 Cor. 8:1-5, where the context stresses the Macedonians' cruciform generosity even more explicitly). Paul's role is simply to promise God's blessing and provision (4:19) and to offer glory to "our God and Father" (4:20; cf. 2:11).

As in considering the first part of chapter 4, so also modern readers must be careful not to domesticate this passage, and miss its power, either.[24]

4:21-23. GREETINGS AND BENEDICTION

Paul concludes his letter quickly with a personal greeting to "every saint" (cf. 1:4, 7-8) and a pair of greetings from the fellow believers with him (in jail or visiting) and from all the others, "especially those of the emperor's household." (This does not necessarily mean that Paul was in Rome, for the imperial household — the network of managers and workers that functioned as a 'civil service' — included those who served the emperor in the provinces.) His last words are a typical Pauline benediction (4:23).

Summary of Philippians 3–4

We may summarize these two chapters in the following way:

- Paul maintains that the cross alone (understood as the faith of Christ) together with the response of faith alone, and no ethnic, national, or other human achievements or status indicators, is the basis for membership in God's people.
- Believers are to pursue the call of God and the knowledge of Christ, which consists of living a pattern of humiliation/suffering followed by resurrection/glory, like that of Christ.
- The church exists as a colony of heaven, not of Rome, waiting for the final appearance of the true Savior-Lord, who is Jesus, not the emperor.
- Believers are called to rejoice and be content in all circumstances, showing the gentleness of Christ and experiencing the presence, peace, and power of God through prayer and the development of a Christlike mind.
- Financial support of gospel workers like Paul is above all an offering to God.

To summarize the letter as a whole, we may say that Paul desires that the hymnic story (2:6-11) that he and the Philippians use to proclaim the exalted crucified Jesus as Lord is also the story of their lives as citizens of a

---

24. For instance, the motto of a Christian high school's track team, "I can do all things through Christ which strengtheneth me," may be true, but does it take Paul's claims in context with sufficient seriousness?

counterimperial society. As such, that story they sing must constantly form and re-form their common life.

THE STORY IN FRONT OF THE LETTER

Some Readings of Philippians

"Throughout the letter Paul bears witness to his joy in them [the Philippians] and praises their obedience and faith. He is, however, concerned that they, like all who are subject to human conceits, might become elated as though they were already worthy. So he tells them openly, speaking of his own person, that something is still wanting for perfect righteousness. He urges them to good works. If he who is adorned with dignity confesses that he is still wanting in perfection, they would understand how much more they must work to acquire the blessings of righteousness."

> Ambrosiaster (late fourth century), quoted in Mark J. Edwards, ed., *Galatians, Ephesians, Philippians,* vol. 8 in *Ancient Christian Commentary on Scripture,* ed. Thomas C. Oden (Downers Grove, Ill.: InterVarsity, 1999), p. 272

"What greater mercy is there than this, which caused to descend from heaven the maker of heaven; which reclothed with an earthly body the one who formed the earth; which made equal to us the one who, from eternity, is the equal of the Father; which imposed 'the form of a servant' on the Master of the world — such that the Bread itself was hungry, Fullness itself was thirsty, Power itself was made weak, Health itself was wounded, and Life itself was mortal? And that so that our hunger would be satisfied, so that our dryness would be watered, our weakness supported, our love ignited. What greater mercy than that which presents to us the Creator created; the Master made a slave; the Redeemer sold; the One who exalts, humbled; the One who raises the dead, killed?"

> Augustine, *Sermon 207,* cited in Albert Verwilghen, *Christologie et Spiritualité selon Saint Augustin* (Paris: Beauchesne, 1985), pp. 287-88 (my translation)

"Important as this passage [Phil. 2:6-11] has been in the history of Christian thought, a still greater significance attaches to the epistle in the history of Christian spirituality. The springs and aspirations of the Christian life, its hopes and its resources, are here unfolded for us in a manner that has contributed mightily to the whole shape and character of Christian piety from the beginning and which has lost none of its compelling instructiveness for us in our time."

> F. W. Beare, *The Epistle to the Philippians,* Black's New Testament Commentaries (London: Black, 1959), p. 33

"I find Philippians to belong with the earlier letters and to be eccentric, displaying Paul's theology at perhaps its least noble. In it, after appearances to the contrary, Paul is primarily preoccupied with himself and not yet at all aware of the present fact of unconditional grace. Rather, as in 1 and 2 Thessalonians and 1 Corinthians, he still looks to a future *parousia,* the Day of Christ, for the solution of all practical human difficulties (see 1:6, 10; 2:16; 3:20-21; 4:5b). . . . Paul's self-concern intrudes embarrassingly soon — concern with his ministry (v. 5 [of chap. 1]) and especially with his own present adversity. . . . I propose that it is this predicament that really preoccupies him as he addresses a letter to his mostly loyal followers in Philippi — indeed, it has chiefly occasioned the letter. We need hardly fault him for this concentration of his attention on himself. But the urgency, desperation, and chaos of his changing responses to these circumstances patiently belie a widely prevailing view of Paul as the great other-directed hero of the nascent Christian movement. . . . Yes, Philippians is surely Paul's most self-centered letter, the most subtly arrogant of all — before God and the world. . . . But it is not to be discounted, certainly not ignored. Within it are passages of great power and truth. That is due to the grace of which Paul is not yet truly aware."

> Robert T. Fortna, "Philippians: Paul's Most Egocentric Letter," in *The Conversation Continues: Studies in Paul and John in Honor of J. Louis Martyn,* ed. Robert T. Fortna and Beverly R. Gaventa (Nashville: Abingdon, 1990), pp. 220-34, here 221, 230

"Since the writing of Philippians, the Christian community has been inspired not only by the words of the apostle, but by the example of the imprisoned leader who speaks with such affection, hope, and faith. Perhaps one of the most beautiful and well-known of Paul's letters, Philippians represents a reflection on the meaning of fidelity in the midst of trial. . . . The christological hymn of Philippians 2 not only inspired the Philippians to greater unity but continues to invite believers of every age to imitate Christ. . . . We are indebted to both Paul and the Philippians for preserving this masterpiece of reflection in Christian suffering and hope."

> Mary Ann Getty, "Philippians Reading Guide," in *The Catholic Study Bible,* gen. ed. Donald Senior (New York: Oxford University Press, 1990), pp. RG514-18, here RG517-18

"[Philippians'] most comprehensive purpose is the shaping of a Christian *phronēsis,* a practical moral reasoning that is 'conformed to his [Christ's] death' in hope of his resurrection."

Wayne A. Meeks, "The Man from Heaven in Paul's Letter to the Philippians," in *The Future of Early Christianity: Essays in Honor of Helmut Koester,* ed. Birger Pearson (Minneapolis: Fortress, 1991), p. 333

QUESTIONS FOR REFLECTION

1. To what degree does the contemporary church see itself as a 'colony of heaven' or 'counterimperial community'? What are the possible strengths and weaknesses of such images? What kinds of conflicts could or should arise when churches and Christians see themselves as servants of the Lord Jesus and not of any other power or 'lord'?
2. What insights about the nature of the term 'fellowship' *(koinōnia)* does this letter offer?
3. It was the church father Tertullian who said, "The blood of the saints is the seed of the church." What is the connection in Paul's mind and experience between suffering for the gospel and its advancement in the world? Does this connection exist today?
4. What challenges to our conceptions of Christian unity, integrity, and witness does Philippians present the contemporary church?
5. Philippians 2:6-11 depicts love and power in 'downwardly mobile' terms. To what current circumstances in corporate or individual Christian life might this text speak? Is there anything potentially problematic with this pervasive Pauline attitude?
6. What is the relevance, if any, of Paul's concerns about those who wish to supplement or supplant the cross, and thus become its enemies? What does it mean today to be friends of the cross?
7. What embryonic aspects of a theology of finances might be discernible in the letter to the Philippians?
8. How appropriate is it to apply affirmations of God's peace, power, and blessing (e.g., 4:4-7, 11-13, 19), made in a context of suffering and difficulty, to our contemporary situation?
9. How do you respond to the interpretations of Philippians quoted above?
10. In sum, what does this letter urge the church to believe, to hope for, and to do?

FOR FURTHER READING AND STUDY

General

Bockmuehl, Markus. *The Epistle to the Philippians*. Black's New Testament Commentary. Peabody, Mass.: Hendrickson, 1998. A commentary that pays special attention to the political character of Paul's language.

Fowl, Stephen E. *Philippians*. Grand Rapids: Eerdmans, forthcoming. A careful theological interpretation of the letter.

Hooker, Morna D. "Philippians." In *The New Interpreter's Bible*, edited by Leander E. Keck et al., 11:467-549. Nashville: Abingdon, 2000. An analysis of the letter's practical apostolic aims as well as its theology and ethics.

Martin, Ralph P. *Philippians*. New Century Bible. London: Oliphants, 1976. A commentary by one of the letter's leading interpreters, with special attention to the hymn and Paul's opponents.

Osiek, Carolyn. *Philippians, Philemon*. Abingdon New Testament Commentaries. Nashville: Abingdon, 2000. A sociorhetorical interpretation with special attention to the role of women.

Witherington, Ben, III. *Friendship and Finances in Philippi*. Valley Forge, Pa.: Trinity Press International, 1994. A brief, insightful commentary on Philippians as a 'family letter,' highlighting the concerns named in the title.

Technical

Fee, Gordon D. *Paul's Letter to the Philippians*. New International Commentary on the New Testament. Grand Rapids: Eerdmans, 1995. A scholarly but very readable interpretation focusing on Paul's call to righteousness or Christlikeness.

Hawthorne, Gerald. *Philippians*. Word Biblical Commentary 43. Waco, Tex.: Word, 1983. A very helpful commentary on the Greek text, stressing the letter's multiple purposes.

Martin, Ralph P., and Brian J. Dodd, eds. *Where Christology Began: Essays on Philippians 2*. Louisville: Westminster John Knox, 1998. An excellent collection of essays on many facets of this extraordinarily important chapter (esp. 2:6-11).

O'Brien, Peter T. *The Epistle to the Philippians*. New International Greek Testament Commentary. Grand Rapids: Eerdmans, 1991. A detailed commentary emphasizing the letter's concerns about perseverance and unity.

CHAPTER 14

PHILEMON

The Cross and the Status Quo

Perhaps this is the reason he was separated from you for a while, so that you might have him back forever, no longer as a slave but more than a slave, a beloved brother.

Philem. 15-16

Paul's letter to Philemon is a brief but fascinating, complex, and dramatic document. Though only twenty-five verses and 335 Greek words in length, it has spawned a variety of competing interpretations and produced a flood of articles and commentaries, among which is a recent work more than five hundred pages in length — nearly two pages for each word!

On one level this letter is about early Christianity and slavery.[1] At another level it is about a triadic relationship among three first-century believers who are connected to one another in very interesting ways, one of whom happens to be an apostle, one a slave owner, and one a slave. Most profoundly, however, the letter to Philemon is about the essential gospel requirement that faith express itself in cruciform love. Such faith and love challenge the status quo, even in the supposedly stable Roman household. The subtitle of this chapter — "The Cross and the Status Quo" — indicates, therefore, that this brief letter goes to the very heart of Paul's gospel. For although the death of Christ on the cross is never explicitly mentioned in Philemon, it is the subtext of the entire document, offering both Paul and Philemon a pattern for life in Christ.

---

1. For a brief discussion of slavery in the Roman world, see chap. 1, under "Paul's Mediterranean Culture."

THE STORY BEHIND THE LETTER

Behind this short letter of appeal (see v. 10) lies a fairly complicated series of events and an equally intricate network of relationships. This situation can be compared to a drama with a cast of characters performing in several acts, the last act of which is yet to be written. Unfortunately, not all scenes in this multi-act play are completely and indisputably discernible to the modern reader. Of particular importance in this regard is the basic plot. The traditional interpretation — that Onesimus was a runaway slave who had stolen from his master Philemon — has come under widespread criticism, as we will see.

The drama is set in two locations — the house of Philemon, almost certainly in Colossae (see Col. 4:9),[2] and the unknown place of Paul's imprisonment (Rome? Philippi? Caesarea Maritima? Ephesus?). Since Colossae is only about 120 miles east of Ephesus, imprisonment in Ephesus might make the most sense of the letter's various details. This location cannot, however, be established with any degree of certainty, and Rome, a frequent destination for runaway slaves, is a viable option.

We begin our analysis of the drama with a brief survey of the characters, introduced in order of appearance in the letter.

THE CHARACTERS

Paul, the principal author, identifies himself as "a prisoner of" (NAB, "for") Christ Jesus (v. 1).[3] He may be in a Roman jail awaiting trial or under house arrest. Paul does not explicitly invoke the title 'apostle,' perhaps since he did not found the church in Colossae (Col. 1:3-8), though his apostolic status may well be implied in verses 8-9 and 21. He does, however, call himself an "old man" (v. 9, meaning in his fifties), if that is here the best translation of the Greek word *presbytēs* (some have suggested "ambassador"). Wherever Paul is, he knows Philemon and a few other members of the Colossian church that meets in Philemon's house (vv. 1-2). He esteems Philemon as his "beloved" *(agapētos)*[4]

2. Col. 4:9 identifies Onesimus — and thus, implicitly, his master Philemon — as being from Colossae. See also the names associated with the two documents in Col. 1:7, 4:7-17, and Philem. 1-2, 10, 23-24. There is, however, scholarly dispute about the reliability of any connections between the letters to Philemon and to the Colossians because the authorship and date of the latter document are in question. In this chapter I assume the conclusions of the next chapter, namely, that Colossians is from the time of Paul, not later. On this issue, and on the city of Colossae, see the introduction to Colossians in the next chapter.

3. Cf. vv. 9, 10, 13, 23.

4. So NAB, meaning 'beloved brother in the Lord.' NRSV and NIV have the weaker "dear friend"; cf. vv. 7, 20.

and as a "co-worker" (v. 1; cf. v. 17). It is virtually certain that Paul was responsible for Philemon's conversion to Christ (v. 19b). While imprisoned, Paul has fathered at least one other spiritual child, Onesimus (v. 10), Philemon's slave.

Timothy, the letter's cosender, plays no explicit role in the drama, but he was likely known and respected in Colossae since he is also named as the coauthor of the letter to the Colossians (Col. 1:1). He is identified only as a "brother" (v. 1), but his name adds authority to the letter's request.

Philemon, the letter's chief (but not sole) addressee, is sufficiently well-to-do to host a house church (v. 2). In addition to being Paul's convert (v. 19b), brother (vv. 7, 20), and coworker (v. 1), he has a reputation for love and faith (v. 5), and he has been a source of encouragement to Paul (v. 7).

Apphia, Archippus, and the church in Philemon's house are the corecipients of the letter. Speculation about this "sister" and this "fellow soldier" (v. 2), respectively, includes the suggestion that they are Philemon's wife and son, but this thesis is not widely accepted. (Even far less probable is the occasional suggestion that Archippus, not Philemon, is the owner of Onesimus.) It is likely, however, that they are also, like Philemon, prominent members of the Colossian church; in Colossians Archippus is told to complete his assigned task in the Lord (Col. 4:17). In any event, what is important is that Paul's letter to Philemon is also a letter to the entire church. Paul wants Philemon, as a believer and especially as a church leader, to know that the subject of this letter is not a personal matter. The corecipients are witnesses to Paul's request, as they will be also to Philemon's decision.

"God our Father and the Lord Jesus Christ" are not mere formalities belonging to the opening and closing benedictions (vv. 3, 25). They are always for Paul a real presence, and he wants Philemon and the entire church to be reminded of it.

Onesimus was a common name in antiquity (especially for slaves) that means 'useful, profitable, beneficial.' He is first introduced almost halfway through the letter as Paul's "child," someone Paul has led to faith in the gospel (v. 10). Of course, Onesimus was first Philemon's slave (v. 16), but even that is now up for grabs as Onesimus has become a believer and thus Philemon's *brother* (v. 16).[5] Moreover, he has been of comfort and service ("useful") to Paul in prison (vv. 11-13). Apparently Onesimus has done something to displease and perhaps wrong Philemon (vv. 11, 18), becoming temporarily "useless" (v. 11). Exactly what Onesimus did is unclear, but now, Paul claims, he is somehow once again useful also to Philemon (v. 11).

Not only the *character* Onesimus but also the *name* Onesimus is impor-

---

5. The very recent view that Philemon and Onesimus were actually *blood* brothers has won almost no acceptance.

tant in this letter. Paul's rhetorical creativity leads him to a series of wordplays with the slave's name in verses 11 and 20. The text says Onesimus ('Useful') was once "useless" (*achrēston*, v. 11) to Philemon but is now "useful" (*euchrēston*, v. 11) to him and to Paul. The two Greek words Paul uses also sound very much like forms of the word 'Christ' *(christos)*. The word *achrēston* would suggest 'without Christ,' while the word *euchrēston* would suggest 'good in Christ,' the pair of words drawing a parallel between the man's 'usefulness' and his relationship to Christ. The puns conclude in verse 20, where Paul requests a "benefit" (NAB, "profit"; Gk. *onaimēn*, like the name *Onesimos*) from Philemon.

The final members of the cast, serving also (like the church) as witnesses to Philemon's decision about Onesimus, from a distance, are five people who are or have been with Paul and who greet Philemon and his church (vv. 23-24): *Epaphras* (also imprisoned), *Mark, Aristarchus* (later imprisoned with Paul, according to Col. 4:10), *Demas,* and *Luke.* The same five greet the Colossian church at the end of the letter to the Colossians (4:10-14), where Onesimus's name also reappears (Col. 4:9). Epaphras, mentioned first, is of special importance as a native Colossian and the "minister of Christ" (Col. 1:7) who founded the Colossian church (Col. 1:7-8; 4:12).

THE DRAMA

As we have already indicated, some details of the drama in which these characters participate cannot be discerned with certainty. However, the following sequence of four dramatic acts, broadly outlined, seems fairly clear:

Act 1: **The (Relatively) Distant Past**
    Scene 1: Epaphras founds the church in Colossae.
    Scene 2: Philemon, perhaps while traveling on business, encounters Paul (somewhere other than in Colossae)[6] and believes the gospel.
    Scene 3: A church in Colossae begins to meet in Philemon's house.
Act 2: **The Immediate Past**
    Scene 1: Paul, along with Epaphras, is imprisoned.
    Scene 2: Onesimus, Philemon's slave, leaves his master's household and Colossae.
    Scene 3: Onesimus encounters Paul in prison, believes the gospel, and begins assisting Paul in some way.

---

6. Assuming that Paul did not found the church at Colossae and had not visited it: Col. 1:6-7; 2:1.

Scene 4: Paul receives news of Philemon's love and faith, as well as either direct or indirect expressions of love from him that have encouraged fellow believers.

Act 3: The Present

Scene 1: Paul writes to Philemon, appealing to him to welcome Onesimus back as he would welcome Paul himself, as a brother rather than a slave, and to forgive any perceived debt or wrong.

Scene 2: Paul sends the letter (and probably Onesimus with it) to Philemon, perhaps (though this is less certain) accompanied by someone to read and interpret the letter to the church.

Act 4: The Future (as yet unwritten)

Scene 1: The letter arrives in Colossae and is read to the church.

Scene 2: Philemon ponders a critical and difficult request, and finally makes a decision.

Scene 3: Paul arrives at Philemon's house.

Since the place of writing is not certain, we cannot date this sequence of events with precision. Act 3 (the writing of the letter itself) should probably be dated in the middle to late 50s, unless it occurred during Paul's Roman imprisonment in the early 60s.

SOME QUESTIONS

Despite the relative certainty of the script of the letter to Philemon just outlined, the letter does raise numerous difficult questions. Several of those questions, and some of the proposed answers, will now be briefly summarized before a tentative reconstruction answering the questions is offered under the next heading.

1. *Why did Onesimus leave Philemon?* (a) The traditional answer has been that Onesimus was a fugitive who had stolen from, and/or otherwise materially harmed, Philemon. This would make Onesimus a criminal whose return by whoever found him was mandated by law, and whose severe punishment by the owner was permitted and expected. A variation of this thesis would be to consider Onesimus a runaway but not a thief. (b) A more recent, and now widely accepted, suggestion is that, following a serious dispute with Philemon, perhaps over issues of financial management, Onesimus followed the legal custom of the day and sought mediation

through a friend of his master — Paul. (c) Yet another proposal is that Onesimus was actually sent to Paul, as a representative of Philemon and/or the church in his house, to provide some assistance to the imprisoned apostle. (d) A less likely scenario is that Onesimus had been imprisoned, at the instigation of Philemon, and then escaped. (Of these four options, the first two are the most plausible.)

2. *How and why did Onesimus encounter Paul?* This question is obviously related to the preceding one. (a) One option is that their meeting was a chance encounter, either because Onesimus ended up in prison with Paul (an unlikely happenstance for a Roman citizen — on the assumption that Paul was one — and a common slave) or found his way into a circle of believers associated with Paul, who then introduced him to the apostle. (b) If Onesimus was not a fugitive, he may have been sent to Paul either as part of his service to Philemon or to seek out Paul's mediation. (c) It is also possible that Onesimus deliberately sought out Paul on his own, perhaps knowing of him through his master.

3. *What is the debt, if any, Onesimus owes Philemon?* Is it (a) the value of stolen property? (b) the value of missed or inadequate work, either before or during the absence? or (c) nothing at all — only a hypothetical debt that is mentioned as part of Paul's rhetorical strategy?

4. *What is Paul's goal?* (a) It is possible that Paul's primary goal is simply to have Philemon take the fugitive Onesimus back without punishing him, forgiving any wrong and treating him from now on as a fellow believer. This interpretation focuses on verses 15-18. (b) It is also possible that Paul wants Philemon actually to release Onesimus from slavery (manumit him) for life in the Colossian church as a freed person. This view centers on verses 16 and 21. (c) It has also been suggested that Paul's ultimate agenda is for Philemon to release Onesimus (granting him either actual or virtual freedom) so that he may return to Paul's side. This perspective concentrates on verses 11-14 and 21.

This last, and perhaps most difficult and important, question takes us into the story within the letter itself: Paul's rhetorical goal in writing.

THE STORY WITHIN THE LETTER

The letter itself is a rhetorical gem. Within it Paul deftly constructs a triadic relationship (consisting of himself, Philemon, and Onesimus) that is in turn part of a wider network of relationships among the three principals and the believers named at both ends of the correspondence, and between the three and their Lord. The rhetorical goals of the letter grow out of the relationships constructed in the text.

PERSONAL RELATIONSHIPS IN PHILEMON

The letter to Philemon is full of titles, adjectives, and images that reveal the apostle at work establishing a complex network of intimate bonds in Christ. We may look at these in pairs; in the triad of Paul, Philemon, and Onesimus; and in the wider arena.

Paul and Philemon are, in many respects, equals: brothers in Christ (vv. 1, 7, 20), coworkers and partners (vv. 1, 17) who are capable of assisting one another in mutually beneficial ways (vv. 7, 13, 19, 20). At the same time, however, Paul is an apostle and Philemon is not — even if Paul does not mention this difference specifically. Moreover, Philemon is also Paul's debtor, owing him his own "self" (v. 19) — that is, his life in Christ. In other words, Philemon is not only Paul's spiritual *brother* but also his spiritual *son*.

Paul and Onesimus also have this father-child relationship (v. 10). Since they are both believers, they are also brothers, even if Paul does not say so explicitly. In addition, Onesimus has performed useful service to Paul and could do so in the future (vv. 11, 13). Paul also cares deeply — very deeply — for Onesimus, who practically *is* Paul, or at least his "heart."[7] Thus Onesimus is Paul's brother, his son, his helper, and his 'self.'

Philemon and Onesimus have a relationship of master-slave "in the flesh" (v. 16). But now they are also brothers "in the Lord" with the same spiritual father, Paul, and the same heavenly Father and Lord, too. So now Onesimus is "no longer" a slave but a "beloved" or "dear" (v. 16, *agapētos*) brother, both in the flesh (in the public sphere, apart from spiritual considerations) and in the Lord (v. 16). Onesimus and Philemon are in the same relationship of mutual brotherly love as are Philemon and Paul. Furthermore, for whatever reason, Onesimus had become useless to Philemon, but he is now useful to him in a brand-new way (v. 11). What does this mean? In context it likely means that Onesimus can be useful to Philemon as a substitute for him in service to Paul (v. 13). Thus Onesimus is no longer Philemon's slave but his brother and potential proxy — his 'self.'

What does all this mean for the three principal characters together? First, it means that Philemon and Onesimus are the sons of one spiritual father, Paul, and thus each other's brother:

---

7. See vv. 12, 20; cf. v. 17. The term *ta splanchna* (heart) in vv. 12 and 20 is literally 'bowels' — the seat of the self's deepest emotions.

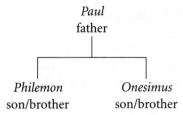

Second, it means that Philemon and Onesimus are equally Paul's apostolic helpers in his imprisonment, Onesimus now to take Philemon's place:

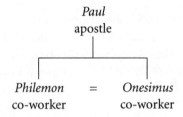

Third, it means that Onesimus functions as both Paul ("my heart") and as Philemon ("in your place"):

$$Paul \quad = \quad Onesimus$$
Paul's heart
$$Onesimus \quad = \quad Philemon$$
Philemon's proxy

Furthermore, in relation to God they are all three 'sons,' 'brothers,' and 'slaves' together in Christ, having the same Father and Lord:

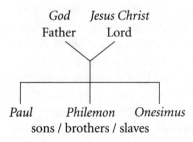

Finally, this last relationship they share with all believers, particularly those mentioned at the beginning and end of the letter, who are the witnesses to the entire multidimensional reality.

RELATIONSHIPS, RHETORIC, AND STORY

Considering this network of relationships, what can we now suggest, by way of reconstruction, about the story within and behind the letter?

There is no hard evidence that Philemon was a runaway who had stolen from his master (though this possibility cannot be completely dismissed). Paul's offer of compensation seems deliberately open-ended ("if," v. 18) as part of his rhetorical and apostolic agendas: to absorb another's 'sin' as an act of love, and to make Philemon more easily able to comply. It seems probable, however, that Philemon had become very displeased with Onesimus and that he considered him "useless" (v. 11). Furthermore, it seems highly unlikely that Onesimus just 'stumbled upon' Paul, whom his master happens to know and through whom he too became a believer. Their encounter is much more likely to have been arranged. Thus the scenario that best fits the textual evidence we have is that Onesimus deliberately sought out Paul, whether or not at Philemon's command, in order to rectify a serious breach in the slave-master relationship. Although Philemon may not have been considering corporal punishment of Onesimus at any point (though again, this cannot be altogether ruled out), and in fact may have effectively sent Onesimus to Paul instead of punishing the slave, he had found him to be useless, and that is the primary *presenting* issue at stake: the uselessness or usefulness of Onesimus.

Paul's spiritual 'fathering' of Onesimus altered the situation in ways that neither Onesimus nor Philemon could have expected. The goal of Paul's construction of relationships through the letter (act 3 in the dramatic sequence) in light of recent events (act 2) seems to be to convince Philemon that he is bound to express his faith in love by (1) welcoming Onesimus as a brother; (2) releasing him from slavery and from any debt; and ultimately (3) blessing his return to Paul as his personal substitute — as an equal, not a slave. Although Paul desires to have Onesimus back, however, it appears from the letter that only the first two are absolutely necessary. The third goal is the "even more than I say" of verse 21.[8] How Philemon will respond, and what else will happen, is the unwritten act 4.

The *underlying* issue, then, involves the challenge of the gospel to the status quo of relationships. Specifically, although the word 'cross' does not appear in the text, this letter expresses Paul's apostolic embodiment of the cross — by acting in love through persuasion rather than exercising his apostolic right through a command (vv. 8-9) — so that Philemon in turn will embody the cross of faith and love by voluntarily welcoming and honoring his new brother in Christ.

The letter itself does not, of course, follow point by point the sequence of

---

8. Some interpreters would reverse (2) and (3), arguing that Paul's first goal is obtaining Onesimus and that the "even more" is his liberation.

the story. Rather, Paul uses a variety of epistolary and rhetorical devices to win Philemon's consent. A brief outline of the letter follows:

Vv. 1-3   Opening
Vv. 4-7   Thanksgiving and Petition
Vv. 8-22   Paul's Appeals
     Vv. 8-17   Reconstructing Relationships
     Vv. 18-22   Paul's IOU and Coming Visit
Vv. 23-25 Greetings and Benediction

It appears that Paul's requests were understood and heeded by Philemon, and that Onesimus became a distinguished worker in the church (see Col. 4:9). The name Onesimus was later adopted by numerous Christian leaders, including perhaps the early-second-century bishop of Ephesus (see Ignatius of Antioch, *To the Ephesians* 1–6) — unless, as some have thought, Onesimus of Colossae himself was that bishop. (This is possible but not likely.)

VV. 1-3. OPENING

Paul identifies himself not as Christ's apostle but as his prisoner; no other letter opening marks Paul as such.[9] Having his trusted coworker Timothy as a cosender (as in Colossians, Philippians, and 1 and 2 Thessalonians) not only expresses Paul's colleague's support of the letter's requests, but also gives Paul occasion to introduce the familial language ("brother") that is so important to this letter.

Paul and Timothy write both to Philemon and to the church that meets in his house ("your" is singular, v. 2), including especially two apparent leaders in the church, Apphia and Archippus. The situation this letter will address is not a private matter, and Philemon's response to the letter's appeals will be made in the company of — and perhaps with input from — his fellow believers. The motif of family intimacy continues in the designations "beloved" (NAB, rightly, against NRSV/NIV, "dear friend") given to Philemon and "sister" given to Apphia. Furthermore, the theme of partnership with Paul (cf. Phil. 1:5) is introduced in the epithets assigned to both Philemon ("co-worker") and Archippus

---

9. Not even the other 'prison' letters: Colossians ("apostle," 1:1), Ephesians ("apostle," 1:1), and Philippians ("servant/slave," 1:1). The term "prisoner" *(desmios)* does, however, also surface as a Pauline self-designation in Ephesians (3:1; 4:1) and 2 Timothy (1:8), and it reappears in Philemon in v. 9.

("fellow soldier"). As Paul and Timothy greet Philemon and the church in typical Pauline fashion (v. 3), they have (not so subtly) issued a reminder that 'we are family, and we are in this together, especially when I am imprisoned.'

Despite the presence of Timothy and the church in the opening, the bulk of the letter continues formally as a personal request from Paul ("I") to Philemon ("you" singular) — until the closing benediction (v. 25).

VV. 4-7. THANKSGIVING AND PETITION

In normal Pauline fashion the letter continues with a thanksgiving, this time combined with a petition, that highlights the letter's theme. Paul's constant gratitude to God when he remembers Philemon in his prayers (v. 4) is due to his hearing of Philemon's "love for all the saints" and "faith toward the Lord Jesus" (v. 5). These words — "love" and "faith," which are repeated in reverse order in verses 6-7 — are fundamental to Paul's understanding of the essence of life in Christ (cf. Gal. 5:6).

Expecting "faith" to precede "love," the reader is jolted and becomes aware that Paul's emphasis is on Philemon's love, which both begins (v. 5) and ends (v. 7) this short prayer. Unfortunately, Paul does not identify the source of his knowledge (general reputation? Onesimus?) or the exact form of Philemon's expressions of love, but these acts of kindness have "refreshed" the hearts of the saints and therefore given Paul much joy and encouragement (cf. 2 Cor. 7:4). Paul will use the same Greek expression *(anapauein ta splanchna)* in verse 20: "Refresh my heart in Christ." The point of including the brief narrative of Philemon's deeds of love is clearly to encourage him to act lovingly once again.

This love, however, does not exist in a vacuum; it has derived, and must derive, from faith. The phrase "faith toward the Lord Jesus" — rather than toward God (1 Thess. 1:8) — probably means *faithfulness* toward Christ (rather than belief in him), which in turn for Paul means living according to Christ's own faithfulness and love revealed in the cross (cf. Gal. 2:19-20). This connection of faith and love explains verse 6: Philemon's faith will be "effective" (NRSV, NAB) or "active" (NIV) as it continues to express itself in love (cf. Gal. 5:6, with similar terminology). It is this "sharing" *(koinōnia)* of faith through love that leads to knowledge of all the "good" that can be had (NIV) or done (NRSV) in (or perhaps "for") Christ (v. 6).

This 'prayer' is really more a narrative description *(narratio)* of Paul's prayer and experience in light of Philemon's love. It is addressed, therefore, to God only indirectly (v. 4) and to "his brother" Philemon directly (v. 7) — continuing the family theme.

VV. 8-22. PAUL'S APPEALS

At this point in reading or hearing the letter, Philemon may be wondering, 'What's going on?' He probably had no idea that any appeal was coming until the "therefore" (NIV, NAB) of verse 8. Imagine the shock when he learns that his "useless" slave Onesimus has become a believer and has been helping the apostle Paul (vv. 10-13)!

The appeals that follow the prayer and constitute the body of the letter are offered on the basis of the personal relationships discussed above. Five explicit or implicit appeals can be discerned in verses 8-22:

1. that Philemon welcome Onesimus back as a brother — as he would welcome Paul himself — rather than as a slave (vv. 12, 15-17);
2. that Philemon release Onesimus from slavery (v. 16);
3. that Philemon transfer any debts from Onesimus to Paul, and then forgive Paul (vv. 18-19);
4. that Philemon do "even more" (v. 21; probably meaning, in light of vv. 13-14, to send Onesimus back to Paul); and
5. that Philemon prepare a guest room for Paul (v. 22).

RECONSTRUCTING RELATIONSHIPS (VV. 8-17)

In light of Philemon's history of faith expressing itself in love ("for this reason," v. 8), Paul says he will appeal "on the basis of love" (v. 9) rather than order Philemon to do his "duty" (v. 8; 'What duty?' Philemon is no doubt asking). The Greek syntax suggests specifically that Paul's decision not to issue a command is an expression of his apostolic love; out of love for Philemon he has conceded an apostolic right (to command) and decided instead lovingly to "urge" him (NAB, translating *parakalō*, v. 9). In this decision Paul himself is imitating Christ by denying himself the use of a certain status and power, thereby embodying the pattern 'although *x*, not *y* but *z*.' The text echoes similar refusals to use apostolic privilege (1 Thess. 2:7; 2 Thess. 3:7-9; 1 Cor. 9, esp. v. 19), all of which in turn are based on texts about Christ's self-denial (e.g., Phil. 2:6-8; 2 Cor. 8:9). Thus Paul sets himself up as an example of forgoing the exercise of rights, setting the stage for a request that Philemon do the same. He does so (v. 9) as Christ's prisoner and as an old(er) man (or perhaps an ambassador [NRSV mg.]).

In verse 10 Paul finally mentions the name Onesimus — the other principal subject of the letter. Now the triadic relationship — Paul, Philemon, Onesimus — is constructed, or reconstructed (on the assumption that

Philemon knew Onesimus had gone to Paul), in surprising terms. Paul says he is appealing for his "child," Philemon's slave Onesimus, for somehow the imprisoned Paul has shared the gospel with Onesimus, who has believed and become Paul's "child."

The formerly "useless" slave (as Paul thought Philemon viewed him) has become useful to both Paul and Philemon (v. 11). This usefulness is explained in verse 13: Onesimus rendered service to Paul, and he did so as Philemon's proxy. The precise character of this service is not named, but it must have been sufficiently significant to tempt Paul to keep another man's slave. Onesimus has become so dear to Paul that the apostle calls him "my own heart" (*splanchna*, v. 12). He is therefore returning his "heart" to Philemon so that Philemon would feel no compulsion to allow Onesimus to stay with Paul but would voluntarily consent to such an arrangement (v. 14). Whatever feelings of ill will Philemon had toward Onesimus must have dissipated — or at least this result must have been Paul's hope — at the thought that Onesimus was now so dear to Paul. And for Philemon not to send Onesimus back to Paul seems now almost impossible.

Yet Paul's first concern does not appear to be regaining Onesimus as his assistant. Rather, he wants Philemon to welcome Onesimus back as a brother rather than as a slave: "*no longer* as a slave" (v. 16, emphasis added). Paul implies, in fact, that whatever the human cause of Onesimus's departure from Philemon, God's providence was at work ("Perhaps this is the reason he was separated from you," v. 15). This is Paul's most basic conviction: that Onesimus was separated from Philemon in order to become a believer and brother. His postconversion location is therefore not the primary issue; perhaps it is to be with Philemon, even "forever" (v. 15), but it must be under brand-new conditions (v. 16). Philemon's welcome, therefore, must not merely be a change of attitude but an actual and permanent change in the character of the relationship; Onesimus is now a brother 'spiritually' ("in the Lord," v. 16) and 'socially' (NRSV: "in the flesh"; NAB, NIV: "as a man"). Here is a concrete example of Paul's dictum in Galatians 3:28: "There is no longer Jew or Greek, there is no longer slave or free, there is no longer male and female; for all of you are one in Christ Jesus." Philemon the master cannot merely treat his slave well now; he must recognize that he and Onesimus are brothers and that he must welcome him as he would his partner — and brother — Paul (v. 17). This is his "duty" (v. 8).[10]

---

10. There has been considerable discussion about the possible conflict between Paul's desire to have Onesimus released and his (debated) words about slaves in 1 Cor. 7:21-24. If in 1 Corinthians he counsels slaves to seek freedom, then there is obviously no conflict with this letter; if not, then there may be deep conflict. It must be remembered, however, that Paul ad-

PAUL'S IOU AND COMING VISIT (VV. 18-22)

But what about any debts Onesimus might owe his master and now brother? Paul extends an IOU to Philemon in his own hand (vv. 18-19a) before reminding him of the incredible debt — his very self — that Philemon owes the apostle (v. 19). Paul is again willing to be lovingly Christlike, but this oblique reference to Philemon's own conversion suggests that, for Paul, the talk of debt — and even more so of punishment, if any were contemplated — in this situation is truly inappropriate for Philemon.

Despite Paul's emphasis on reconciliation between Onesimus and Philemon, he does feel that Onesimus belongs, not with Philemon, but with himself, and he hopes Philemon will 'benefit' him "in the Lord" and "refresh [his] heart" (v. 20) by obeying and by even doing more than Paul explicitly asks in verses 15-17. Paul, in other words, hopes Philemon will express his faithfulness — his "obedience" — to Christ in an act of love (cf. vv. 5, 7) by welcoming Onesimus and then releasing him from all debts and from slavery in order that Paul may have him for gospel service.

This goal leads to Paul's last request — that Philemon prepare a guest room (v. 22). Paul makes this request in confidence that he will be released from imprisonment and as an added 'incentive' for Philemon. Perhaps Paul hopes to pick up Onesimus when he comes.

VV. 23-25. GREETINGS AND BENEDICTION

As noted above, Paul's final greetings broaden the context within which his appeals are issued — and therefore their authority. The mention of Epaphras, the evangelist from and to Colossae, is especially significant in this regard.

Paul's final benediction forms, with verse 3, a pair of bookends (a rhetorical *inclusio*) for the letter. The appeal Paul makes, as well as the decision Philemon will make, are grounded in the grace of the Lord Jesus Christ, who though rich became poor, and who though equal to God became a slave (2 Cor. 8:9; Phil. 2:6-8).

All the other rhetorical resources Paul brings to bear on the situation (and on Philemon) — the presence of witnesses, the appeal to reputation and past

---

dresses *slaves* in 1 Corinthians and a *master* here in Philemon. The obligation of a master to grant freedom and the obligation of a slave to pursue it, or not, may be grounded in different theological convictions (e.g., eschatological patience in the case of slaves, cruciform love in the case of masters).

action, the (re)construction of personal relationships in Christ, wordplays and images — serve the greatest warrant for Paul's request, which is love — Philemon's, Paul's, and above all, Christ's.

In the end, then, is Philemon compelled to comply? On the one hand the answer is no, because Paul never does order — even if he does practically intimidate — Philemon. On the other hand the answer is yes, but only in the sense that Paul knows, and believes that Philemon also knows, that "Christ's love compels us" (2 Cor. 5:14 NIV) to make certain choices. Philemon's freedom is preserved, yet it is a freedom that empties itself in love for others, especially those of lesser status (cf. Phil. 2:6-11; 1 Cor. 8:1–11:1; Rom. 15:1-3).

Summary of Philemon

Paul's brief but compelling letter to Philemon expresses a number of Pauline themes for a particular situation:

- Faith must express itself in deeds of love — Christlike, sacrificial, cruciform love.
- In Christ all believers are brothers and sisters, no matter what their position or status in the church or in the world.
- The cross subverts the status quo, reconstructing relationships not only in the church, but also in the world.

It seems clear that Paul wants Philemon to release Onesimus from slavery and any debt, and then to Paul's gospel service. In view of other texts, it is difficult to know with certainty, however, whether Paul opposed all slavery in principle, opposed only certain kinds or instances of slave-master relationships, or had ambiguous feelings about slavery as a 'social institution' or about slavery within the church.

THE STORY IN FRONT OF THE LETTER

Some Readings of Philemon

"This epistle gives us a masterful and tender illustration of Christian love. For here we see how St. Paul takes the part of poor Onesimus and, to the best of his ability, advocates his cause with his master. He acts exactly as if he were himself Onesimus, who had done wrong. Yet he does this not with force or compulsion, as lay within his rights; but he empties himself of his rights in order to compel Philemon also to waive his rights. What Christ has done for us with God the Father, that St. Paul does also for Onesimus with Philemon. For Christ emptied himself of his rights (Phil. 2:7) and overcame the Father with love and humility, so that the Father had to put away his wrath and rights, and receive us into favor for the sake of Christ, whoso earnestly advocates our cause and heartily takes our part. For we are all his Onesimus's if we believe."

> Martin Luther, "Preface to the Epistle of Saint Paul to
> Philemon, 1546 (1522)," in *Luther's Works*, ed. E. Theodore
> Bachmann, American ed. (Philadelphia: Fortress, 1960), 35:390

"I was preaching to a large congregation on the *Epistle of Philemon:* and when I insisted upon fidelity and obedience as Christian virtues in servants and upon the authority of Paul, condemned the practice of *running away,* one half of my audience deliberately rose up and walked off with themselves, and those that remained looked any thing but satisfied, either with the preacher or his doctrine. After dismission, there was no small stir among them; some solemnly declared 'that there was no such an Epistle in the Bible'; others, 'that they did not care if they ever heard me preach again!'"

> Rev. Charles Colcock Jones, white Methodist missionary to
> slaves, quoted in Albert J. Raboteau, *Slave Religion: The "Invisi-
> ble Institution" in the Antebellum South* (New York: Oxford
> University Press, 1978), p. 294

"[Philemon] finds that 'being in Christ' makes a totalistic claim upon him from which there are no exceptions. *If he is to remain in the service of Christ the Lord, he cannot be 'in Christ' only when he is 'in church.'*"

> Norman R. Petersen, *Rediscovering Paul: Philemon and the So-
> ciology of Paul's Narrative World* (Philadelphia: Fortress, 1985),
> p. 269

QUESTIONS FOR REFLECTION

1. What do you think motivated the early church to preserve and canonize the letter to Philemon? What contributions to the canon does this letter make? What would the church be lacking if Philemon had not been preserved and canonized?

2. In what sense does Philemon provide, or not provide, insight into the practice of pastoral care and spiritual direction in Christian decision making?

3. Are there contemporary status quo relationships that are analogous to the slave-master relationship and in need of scrutiny in light of the gospel?
4. What theological themes are present within, or underneath, this letter that ought to be part of contemporary discussions about the character of relationships within the church?
5. What do you think of the interpretations of Philemon quoted above?
6. In sum, what does this letter urge the church to believe, to hope for, and to do?

FOR FURTHER READING AND STUDY

General

Felder, Cain. "Philemon." In *The New Interpreter's Bible*, edited by Leander E. Keck et al., 11:881-905. Nashville: Abingdon, 2000. A brief commentary with reflections, stressing the class-transcending, reconciling power of the gospel.

Martin, Ralph P. *Ephesians, Colossians, and Philemon.* Interpretation. Atlanta: John Knox, 1991. A brief exposition especially for preachers.

Osiek, Carolyn. *Philippians, Philemon.* Abingdon New Testament Commentaries. Nashville: Abingdon, 2000. A brief sociorhetorical analysis, inconclusive about Paul's ultimate agenda.

Wright, N. T. *The Epistles of Paul to the Colossians and Philemon.* Tyndale New Testament Commentaries. Grand Rapids: Eerdmans, 1986. A brief but helpful exposition.

Technical

Barth, Markus, and Helmut Blanke. *The Letter to Philemon.* Eerdmans Critical Commentary. Grand Rapids: Eerdmans, 2000. An amazingly detailed analysis of the text.

Dunn, James D. G. *The Epistles to the Colossians and to Philemon.* New International Greek Testament Commentary. Grand Rapids: Eerdmans, 1996. A careful analysis of the Greek text.

Fitzmyer, Joseph A. *The Letter to Philemon: A New Translation with Introduction and Commentary.* Anchor Bible 34C. New York: Doubleday, 2000. A commentary with introduction, critical notes, and extensive biography espousing a perspective similar to the one found in this chapter.

Petersen, Norman R. *Rediscovering Paul: Philemon and the Sociology of Paul's Narrative World.* Philadelphia: Fortress, 1985. A landmark reading of the narrative and social worlds of the letter to Philemon.

CHAPTER 15

COLOSSIANS

The Cosmic Crucified Christ
as the Wisdom of God

God's mystery, that is, Christ himself, in whom are hidden all the trea-
sures of wisdom and knowledge.

Col. 2:2-3

The letter to the Colossians has an air of majesty about it. It exalts Christ as the cosmic sovereign, the preexistent Wisdom of God whose death has liberated those who believe from the hostile powers of the universe and whose resurrection has raised them to sit with him above the defeated powers. This cosmic experience, however, inspires a down-to-earth spirituality that, according to the letter, surpasses misguided attempts to renew humanity through a 'philosophy' and its extreme ascetic practices that do not recognize the reality and power of Christ's death and resurrection. Colossians is an extended commentary on Paul's claim that Christ is the wisdom and power of God (1 Cor. 1:18-25).

Before looking at the letter itself, we will consider some dimensions of the story behind and within the letter, concluding with a discussion of the letter's authorship, for not everyone is convinced that Paul is the actual author.

THE STORY BEHIND THE LETTER

Colossians — like Galatians, but with less anger and invective — appears to have been written for one purpose: to convince its recipients that Christ is sufficient for their spiritual liberation and life. They should therefore resist the temptation to engage in practices that purport to supplement, but actually supplant (as far as Paul is concerned), their participation in Christ's death and resurrection. This is not to say that the letters to Colossae and to Galatia address exactly the same problem, or that they address similar problems in the same way. But their common singularity of purpose is striking. As with Galatians (in fact, even more so), much ink has been spilled in the attempt to reconstruct the specifics of the situation presupposed in Colossians. Something of a consensus about the symptoms of the illness has emerged, but there are many diagnoses of the underlying disease.

THE CITY AND ITS COMMUNITY OF BELIEVERS

In the Roman period Colossae was a city of moderate importance. It was located in the region of Phrygia and in the Roman province of Asia, about 120 miles east of the provincial capital of Ephesus and not far from the more prominent cities of Laodicea and Hierapolis. What significance it had derived from its location in the fertile Lycus River valley and on a trade route that connected Ephesus and the Aegean Sea, to the west, with the provincial capital of Pisidia (Antioch) and points beyond, to the east.[1]

Not a Roman colony, Colossae was populated primarily by Phrygian natives and by Greeks. In addition, according to the Jewish historian Josephus (*Jewish Antiquities* 12.149), the regions of Phrygia and Lydia had many Jews whose ancestors had been brought there from Babylonia and Mesopotamia by Antiochus III in about 200 B.C. The city was therefore part of an area in which Judaism flourished alongside local religions and the standard pagan cults of the empire. The possibility of religious syncretism — the fusion of beliefs and practices from diverse traditions — was perhaps even stronger here than elsewhere in Paul's polytheistic world.

The church in Colossae was almost certainly not founded by Paul (see 2:1) or the letter's cosender, Timothy, but by their "beloved fellow servant" *(syndoulou)* Epaphras, himself a Colossian (1:7-8; 4:12; Philem. 23). There were certainly Gentiles in the church (1:27), and they may have been in the majority, but there is also every reason to suspect that there were Jewish believers in the community; it was a multiethnic church (3:11). From its inception the church was a growing, flourishing body (1:4-8).

---

1. The Roman city of Colossae was probably destroyed by an earthquake in the early 60s and never rebuilt. All that remains of Colossae is a pair of large, unexcavated mounds, or tells. Lying on top of these hills are fragments of pottery, and at their base one sees portions of a few ancient columns. In the side of one the shape of a small theater, perhaps the *bouleutērion,* can be discerned.

Western Asia Minor

A PHILOSOPHY OF SELF-ABASEMENT

The first purpose of this letter, as noted above, is to warn against a certain "philosophy" that is opposed to Christ (2:8). (The second is to provide the properly grounded alternative.) Traditionally this philosophy has been called the 'Colossian heresy.' Although a few scholars have suggested that the letter is a preemptive strike, most believe the heresy or philosophy is already present at Colossae. As we will see below, the religious environment that generated this philosophy has been warmly debated, but even among those who disagree

Colossae: Remains of the unexcavated ancient city lie buried
beneath two large mounds, or tells.

about the origins of the philosophy there is a fair amount of agreement about
its general shape.

The letter itself, especially in 2:16-23, suggests the following elements of
the philosophy:

- observation of Jewish diet and holidays (2:16)
- self-abasement/extreme asceticism, probably including fasting and perhaps other disciplines (2:18, 21, 23)
- "worship of angels," which may mean worship or veneration *of* angels, or
  participation *with* the angels at worship (2:18)
- visionary experiences (2:18)
- interest in the "elemental spirits of the universe," the forces that rule the
  cosmos and human life (2:8)

The advocates of this philosophy seem to have been grounded in a philosophical and religious dualism that identified God and "the flesh" — normal bodily
existence — as being at odds. The purpose of worship, they would have
thought, was to escape the flesh and enter the "heavenly realms." The means to,
or prerequisite for, this heavenly entry was observance of appointed fasts and
other means of detachment from the flesh (the evil body) that supposedly sup-

pressed its urges. In addition, it seems likely that these mystical ascetics, as we will call them, required the circumcision of Gentiles (cf. 2:11-23). The entire experience may have led to ascetic 'competition' and pride (2:18).

What kind of religious worldview would have led to this lifestyle? The answer is that many could have. It was fashionable among some scholars of an earlier generation to call the Colossian philosophy 'Gnosticism.' But since this term is used to describe a later dualistic religious worldview with complicated accounts of levels of heavenly emanations, the most we can say is that in Colossae there was an incipient Gnosticism. Within the Pauline teachings themselves there was apparently enough talk against "the flesh" and in favor of charismatic experience that some believers could overemphasize these dimensions of experience in Christ (e.g., at Corinth). And we know from Galatians that the idea of requiring Gentile believers to practice circumcision and other Jewish symbolic boundary markers was 'in the air.'

Other possible sources that have been suggested are the mystery cults and various forms of Judaism itself. In fact, a few scholars have suggested that the mystical ascetics were not (Christian) heretics at all but simply Jews, representing some form of hellenized Diaspora Judaism, perhaps an early mystical *(Merkabah)* Judaism, as briefly described in chapter 1. Though it is true that all the distinctive features of the mystical ascetics (except probably the worship of angels, if that is what is referred to) could be purely Jewish, the majority of interpreters have called the Colossian philosophy syncretistic, arguing that it blends elements of certain pagan religions and philosophies, Judaism, and 'Christianity.' By syncretistic, we should not understand an official or formal appropriation of various religions but rather a popular blending of seemingly congruous elements. Although we cannot be certain, the assumption made here is that the mystical ascetics were (Christian) believers who were convinced that certain practices — especially extreme ascetic disciplines — known among their fellow Jews and pagans would allow them to suppress their fleshly desires and thus more fully encounter God/Christ in the presence of the various hostile and benevolent powers of the universe.

THE STORY WITHIN THE LETTER

The letter to the Colossians is directed to those under the influence, or possible influence, of such syncretistic, heavenly minded ascetics. In a daring move the letter's author takes up the language of a hymn or poem quoted in 1:15-20 and, most likely, the vocabulary of those he seeks to condemn, asserting that believers are *already* raised with Christ to the highest heights and that the powers of the universe they either fear or seek (or both) have been defeated by Christ's cross and superseded by his resurrection. This 'heavenly' life of believers, however, is not one of extreme ascetic practices and visions but of ongoing death to the old self in order to be renewed in the new self. This is accomplished not by extraordinary external measures but by the indwelling presence of Christ, who as divine Wisdom (whose story is narrated in the hymn or poem) was God's agent of both creation and reconciliation and who now, exalted and preeminent, empowers the community with faith, hope, and love.

In essence, then, Colossians tells a story of Christ's wisdom, power, and sufficiency. Nothing reveals more of God than does Christ, nothing is more powerful than the exalted crucified Christ, and nothing more is needed than Christ. He is, however, experienced by participation in his death and resurrection, not by any other means — not by adherence to the Law, not by fasting, not by visions.

PAUL AS AUTHOR?

This daring story of Christ and believers strikes nearly all readers of Paul as somewhat different from the stories to which they have become accustomed in the undisputed letters. Interpreters have perceived differences in both form (style, vocabulary) and substance (theology). Are these differences due to Paul's adapting to a new kind of threat to the gospel, or are they the mark of another hand — or both?

With respect to style and vocabulary, Colossians exhibits certain syntactical patterns and a number of terms that are not found in the undisputed Pauline letters but are found especially in Ephesians (for the relationship between these two letters, see the chapter on Ephesians). To a reader of Greek, the letter does not 'feel' like the Paul we know from, say, Romans and 1 Corinthians.

As for substance, many interpreters have argued that Colossians differs from the undisputed letters in its (1) Christology, (2) ecclesiology, (3) eschatology, and (4) ethics — a rather comprehensive list of key theological topics. In sum, these interpreters perceive a distinctive emphasis on (1) the cosmic Christ; (2) the church as a cosmic or universal, rather than a local, entity; (3) a 'realized' eschatology such that resurrection is a present rather than a future experience; and (4) a patriarchal ethic (preserved in the 'household code' of 3:18–4:1).

Space does not permit a full exploration of each of these topics. However, the supposed differences are sometimes misread or exaggerated. For instance:

1. The preexistent, cosmic Christ of Colossians is still the crucified Christ (1:20, 24; 2:14), and the crucified Christ of the undisputed letters is the

preexistent and exalted "Lord" (e.g., Phil. 2:6-11), a term that identifies him in significant ways with the sovereign creator God of the universe. The identity of the crucified Messiah with the exalted Lord is a hallmark of Paul's experience and theology. Furthermore, according to both Colossians and the undisputed letters, God was in Christ reconciling the world to himself (2 Cor. 5:19; cf. Col. 1:19-20).

2. In Colossians the 'cosmic' church remains a local entity that meets in houses (4:16), with identifiable leaders (1:7; 4:7-17), while throughout the undisputed letters one of Paul's goals is to get individual churches to see themselves as part of an empirewide network with mutual relations and responsibilities (e.g., the collection for Jerusalem).

3. The so-called realized eschatology of Colossians has much more of a future dimension than that term would suggest (1:5, 23, 27; 3:4, 6, 10, 24), while the undisputed letters have more emphasis on the present tense — the experience of the Spirit (e.g., Gal. 5; Rom. 8; cf. Col. 1:8), the new life as simultaneously resurrection from the dead and ongoing death (Rom. 6:4, 11, 13; 12:1-2; Gal. 2:19-21; cf. Col. 3:1-7), and ongoing transformation into glory (2 Cor. 3:18; cf. Col. 3:10) — than many of Paul's interpreters have wanted to admit.

4. As we will see in the discussion of 3:18–4:1, the social and literary contexts of the household code reveal that this text is far more radical than a superficial reading might suggest. The Pauline conviction that in Christ there is neither Gentile nor Jew, male nor female, slave nor free (Gal. 3:28; cf. Col. 3:11) is alive and well in Colossians.

With respect to the first three points, some have said that the *temporal* (or horizontal, or eschatological) emphasis of the undisputed letters has become a *spatial* (or vertical, or 'heavenly') emphasis in Colossians. Although there is some truth to this observation, in Colossians life 'in heaven' is still life on earth and life lived in hope; the resurrection life is still the cruciform life. What we have in Colossians, then, is much more continuity with the undisputed letters than is often recognized.

Nonetheless, it cannot be denied that there are differences in style and theological emphasis in Colossians. Although Paul himself could have authored a letter with such differences, it is likely that he did not actually pen or dictate Colossians word for word. But it is so close to Paul that it must have been written by someone who knew his mind quite well. This person might have been a 'disciple' or coworker writing after Paul's death, but then the personal references at the beginning and the end of the letter would be artificial devices intended to lend authority to the letter; this is possible but does not seem probable in this instance. More likely, as others have suggested, Paul's imprisonment (in chains, 4:18) required him to ask an assistant to write the letter after he gave general directions. As many scholars have suggested, this person may have been Timothy, the formal cosender (1:1). It could also have been Epaphras, the Colossian evangelist (1:7). Another possible writer is Tychicus, who serves as the reporter on Paul's condition and apparently also as the letter bearer (4:7-9). Since Tychicus fulfills a similar function in the delivery of the letter to the Ephesians (Eph. 6:21-22), his role in penning both Colossians and Ephesians would explain, in part, their similarity. (See also the introductory remarks on Ephesians.)

If written during Paul's lifetime, Colossians was composed in the middle to late 50s (possibly from Ephesus) or, more likely, in the early 60s (from Rome), following Philemon and preceding Ephesians (no matter who wrote Ephesians). If written after Paul's death, it was probably penned very soon afterward. (A frequently cited scholarly dictum is 'If by Paul, as late as possible; if after Paul, as early as possible.') In any case, the letter unfolds as follows:

1:1-2	Opening	
1:3-23	Liturgical Introduction: Christ Preeminent	
	1:3-8	Thanksgiving
	1:9-14	Intercession
	1:15-20	Hymn
	1:21-23	Exhortation
1:24–2:5	Narrative Introduction: Paul's Ministry	
2:6-23	Life in Christ as Freedom from the Powers	
	2:6-8	Christ, Not 'Philosophy'
	2:9-15	The Experience of Christ
	2:16-23	The Error of the Philosophy
3:1–4:6	The Shape of Life in Christ	
	3:1-4	Introduction
	3:5-17	Renewal in Christ
	3:18–4:1	Relationships in the Household
	4:2-6	General Exhortations
4:7-18	Greetings and Benediction	

1:1-2. OPENING

Paul's salutation contains a few elements of importance for the letter. Writing to people who have generally not met him face-to-face, he identifies himself as an apostle "by the will of God" to give his letter appropriate weight at Colossae.

The letter's cosender, Timothy,[2] is a "brother" (1:1) of the same status as all the Colossians (1:2). The recipients themselves are designated as "holy and faithful" (NIV, rightly) "brothers and sisters" (NRSV). They are set apart for God and faithful to the gospel of God in Christ; these phrases suggest Paul's confidence in the Colossians' willingness to resist the 'philosophy' that is being bandied about in Colossae. The wish for grace and peace is standard in Paul's letters.

1:3-23. LITURGICAL INTRODUCTION: CHRIST PREEMINENT

It has often been observed that Colossians has a 'liturgical' air about it, a sense of majesty and worship. This is fostered in large measure by the first part of the letter, in which prayers of thanks and petition (1:3-14) precede the letter's centerpiece, which is the poem or hymn contained in 1:15-20. The hymn is followed by a summary exhortation deriving from it.

THANKSGIVING (1:3-8)

The constant thanks Paul and Timothy give to God (1:3) is for the Colossians' faith, hope, and love (1:4-5a), a triad we find elsewhere in Paul.[3] Christ Jesus is not named as the object of faith but as its location or sphere, "in Christ" (1:4), just as the Spirit is identified as the sphere (1:8) in which their love for one another (1:4) takes place. The reality of the Colossians' being "in Christ" (as well as Christ's being in them, 1:27) is the heart of believers' spirituality according to the letter; the phrase "in Christ" (or "in him/whom") appears fourteen times. This 'mutual indwelling' of Christ and believers is a hallmark of Pauline spirituality in the undisputed letters, too (see, e.g., Rom. 8:1-17).

Paul and Timothy remind the Colossians that their present experience of faith and love is grounded in the future — in a hope "laid up for you in heaven" — about which they heard in the past (1:5-6). This strong eschatological emphasis inaugurates one of the themes of Colossians, and its connection to the "gospel" hints at another. The gospel of God's grace, which was planted on behalf of Paul by Epaphras in Colossae and which has blossomed among the Colossians and throughout the world (1:6-7), is twice linked to the word "truth" (1:5, 6). It is

2. Also the (or a) cosender of 2 Corinthians, Philippians, 1 and 2 Thessalonians, and Philemon.

3. 1 Cor. 13:13; Gal. 5:5-6; 1 Thess. 1:3; 5:8.

this gospel alone, and no other message — especially not the one preached by the mystical ascetics — that is the truth worthy of the Colossians' adherence.

INTERCESSION (1:9-14)

Paul and Timothy now shift from thanksgiving to petition, revealing the content of their regular intercessory prayer for the Colossians. In essence, their prayer is for full knowledge of God's will through spiritual wisdom and understanding (1:9), which all points ahead to the "fullness" of wisdom celebrated in the hymn, namely, Christ himself. Thus the prayer, despite its allusions to scriptural texts and Jewish wisdom themes, is implicitly christocentric from the very start; one knows God by knowing the Son. By 1:13 this implicit Christocentrism has become explicit ("the kingdom of his [God's] beloved Son").

Although English translations convey the substance of the prayer in similar language, they vary in nuances about the interrelationships among its various dimensions. The Greek suggests the following. The basic content of the prayer — fullness, knowledge of God's will, wisdom, understanding (1:9) — derives from the Wisdom tradition. In line with this Jewish tradition, knowledge of God is not merely an intellectual enterprise but has a practical and ethical — a covenantal — purpose: to live (literally 'walk' for NRSV's "lead lives," 1:10) worthily of the Lord, which means doing his pleasure. According to these verses, this kind of life has four basic aspects:

- bearing fruit in every good work (1:10)
- growing in the knowledge of God (1:10)
- being strengthened for suffering (1:11; implied by the combination of references to endurance [*hypomonē*], patience [*makrothymia*], and joy [*chara*])
- giving thanks to God the Father (1:12)

Of particular note is the source of strength for suffering, God's glorious might (1:11), which hints at God's sovereignty over all hostile powers.

The prayer ends with a series of phrases describing the Father's salvific activity that serves as a transition into the poem/hymn. This divine action has past, present, and future dimensions (1:12-14). In the past God rescued (NAB, "delivered") us from the power of darkness so that we now live in his beloved Son's kingdom, or sphere of power (1:13).[4] In him believers have redemption, or

---

4. The unusual language of the "Son's" kingdom only makes explicit what Paul's language of Jesus' lordship implies; cf. 1 Cor. 15:24-28.

liberation from the darkness and forgiveness of sins (1:14). However, this liberation out of the darkness and into the light is not yet complete, and believers will one day receive the "inheritance" due the saints (1:12).

HYMN (1:15-20)

The closing words of the petitionary prayer in 1:9-14 prepare us for the words in praise of what God has done in Christ. As noted above, many think these verses constitute an early Christian hymn, or at least a poem, full of poetic imagery and 'thought rhyme.' The text appears to be divisible into two stanzas. These stanzas tell the story of creation and of reconciliation through Christ, respectively, and thus the hymn (as we will call it) is a narrative hymn, similar in general character to Philippians 2:6-11.

Background and Form

The background of this hymn is the Wisdom tradition, especially the Jewish conviction that wisdom had played a role in creation and does (or will) again play a role in re-creation. This tradition comes to greatest expression in the canonical book of Proverbs and the deuterocanonical book of the Wisdom of Solomon. A few excerpts are in order, but readers are especially encouraged to consult the entirety of Proverbs 8 and Wisdom of Solomon 7:22–8:1.

> The LORD by wisdom founded the earth;
>   by understanding he established the heavens. (Prov. 3:19)

> The LORD created me at the beginning of his work,
>   the first of his acts of long ago.
> Ages ago I was set up,
>   at the first, before the beginning of the earth. . . .
> When he established the heavens, I was there. (Prov. 8:22-23, 27a)

> Wisdom, the fashioner of all things, taught me. . . .
> For she is a breath of the power of God,
> and a pure emanation of the glory of the Almighty;
> therefore nothing defiled gains entrance into her.
> For she is a reflection of eternal light,
> a spotless mirror of the working of God,
> and an image of his goodness.
> Although she is but one, she can do all things,

and while remaining in herself, she renews all things;
in every generation she passes into holy souls
and makes them friends of God, and prophets;
for God loves nothing so much as the person who lives with wisdom.
(Wisd. of Sol. 7:22, 25-28 NRSV)

Wisdom is here portrayed not only as the agent of creation and of human renewal, but also as the reflection or image of God. All these themes are found in the Colossians hymn.

There has been considerable debate about the precise point of transition between the first and second stanzas of the hymn, but it is likely that the end of the first is 1:17 ("He . . . is before all things . . .") and the beginning of the second is parallel to it in 1:18 ("He is the head . . ."). Each stanza is dominated by the image of the firstborn (*prōtotokos*, 1:15, 18), the privileged child in Jewish tradition, the one who would receive a double portion of the father's inheritance (Deut. 21:15-17) and the one through whom subsequent generations received their family heritage and status. This image points (even if confusingly) to Christ's supremacy in both creation and re-creation (resurrection). In each stanza the assertion that Christ is the "firstborn" is followed by the justification of that assertion — "for in him . . ." (1:16, 19). The 'in Christ' language now refers, not to the location of believers, but to the locus of God the Father's activity.

The Two Stanzas

The first stanza (1:15-17) begins by claiming for Christ the attributes of wisdom — and more: being the preexistent image of the invisible God (1:15) in whom the entire creation was made (1:16). Although the term "firstborn" might imply that Christ is also a created being (as wisdom was probably thought to be), 1:16 asserts just the opposite: all things in heaven and earth that were created, were created "in" and "through" Christ. Moreover — and this goes beyond the Wisdom tradition — they were created *for* Christ (also 1:16). Christ existed before all things, and all things continue to "hold together" in him (1:17). Among "all things" are the various powers of the universe, whether in the heavens (plural in Greek because there were multiple levels of heaven in Jewish thought) or on earth, and whether visible or invisible. This is a direct reference both to the hostile powers that may be intimidating certain believers and to the angelic powers who may be tantalizing them. The presence of the long list shifts the focus from a general affirmation about Christ's supremacy in creation to a specific claim about his supremacy to the powers.

The second stanza (1:18-20) begins by formally echoing the end of the first stanza yet shifting the focus from creation to re-creation. Christ is the head of his body, the church, where the new creation is constituted (cf. 2:10-11). Now the image of firstborn includes the Pauline idea of Christ as the first of many children who share, or will share, the family's inheritance of resurrection and glory (1:18; cf. Rom. 8:29). Yet as the family's firstborn and therefore its head (according to Jewish tradition), Christ receives the place of preeminence (1:18) that makes him distinct from his body (the church), as he was also distinct from the creation.

The reason for this distinction is Christ's uniqueness as the place of God's indwelling (1:19) and the means of God's reconciliation (1:20): incarnation — to use a later term already implied elsewhere in Paul[5] — and cross. Wisdom was thought to indwell (Wisd. of Sol. 1:4) and renew (7:27) human beings; now, Paul says, Christ is worthy of all honor because God has fully indwelt him; Christ is God, and wisdom, incarnate. The use of the term "fullness" may stem from claims in Colossae that there is some font of divine wisdom other than Christ — the Law perhaps, or angels. The prayer of 1:9 for divine wisdom can be answered only in reference to Christ, the very seat of divine wisdom.

Furthermore, because the wisdom of God is Christ crucified (cf. 1 Cor. 1:23-24), incarnation is inseparable from crucifixion. The purpose of incarnation was reconciliation, or making peace (cf. 2 Cor. 5:19; Rom. 5:6-8). This reconciliation is cosmic in scope, including the "all things" (1:20) of the creation (1:16; cf. Rom. 8:18-25). The implication is clearly that the universe — including the powers mentioned in 1:16 — is estranged from God, and that Christ's sacrificial death (his "blood," 1:20) not only provides forgiveness for sins (1:14), but also liberates humanity from the hostile forces of the universe (1:13) and even somehow restores those powers (eventually?), with all things, to their divinely created purpose (1:20). The combination of forgiveness and liberation from powers is another hallmark of Paul's convictions (cf. Rom. 3:21-26).

Paul's vision is a grand and sweeping one, a narrative of creation and re-creation. He tells this story not to inform the Colossians, but to remind them of their involvement in it. Modern reflection on this hymnic text has inspired Christians to take the universal lordship of Christ and the cosmic scope of salvation seriously. But it has also generated questions about the precise meaning of this universality.

EXHORTATION (1:21-23)

The hymn is now applied to the Colossians; they are the beneficiaries of Christ's reconciliation (1:22), having been alienated from God, as evidenced in

5. E.g., Gal. 4:4; 2 Cor. 8:9; Phil. 2:6-8.

evil deeds (1:21), which are the opposite of God's will (1:9). Reconciliation with God has a purpose: the undoing of the way of life characteristic of those who are not reconciled, so that Christ may one day present believers as "holy and blameless and irreproachable" (1:22; cf. 1 Thess. 3:13; 5:23). This entails responsibility by the Colossians and all believers: faithfulness to the hope of the gospel that Paul preaches (1:23) — and that of course focuses on Christ the firstborn, the source of all wisdom and hope. The community must, in other words, embody the hymn it sings.

1:24–2:5. NARRATIVE INTRODUCTION: PAUL'S MINISTRY

The mention of Paul as a gospel minister at the end of 1:23 provides a segue from the liturgical introduction into a narrative summary of his ministry. This is for the benefit of the letter's recipients and to further establish the appropriateness of the present communication to them.

The passage begins with the common Pauline combination of suffering and joy,[6] and it continues immediately with the idea of Paul's "completing what is lacking in Christ's afflictions" (1:24). In the context of this letter that exalts the completeness of Christ's person and work, this claim cannot mean that Christ's passion was somehow deficient. Rather, it suggests that because Christ's suffering and death were definitive of God's self-revelation and activity in the world, they must be continued in the life of the apostle (cf. 2 Cor. 1:5). Just as Paul constantly reminds his readers that Christ (suffered and) died for them, he now reminds them that *he* suffers for them, for Christ's body. His role of suffering servant is complemented by his preaching and teaching ministry (1:25) in which he participates in the full revelation of God's mystery to those who believe the message (God's "saints"), especially among the Gentiles (1:26-27).

The essential content of that mystery, that "word of God" (1:25), is "Christ in you, the hope of glory" (1:27). This motto deftly combines present reality with future hope. In so doing, it summarizes the thrust of the entire letter: the indwelling of God's wisdom (Christ) enables believers to walk in a way that pleases God and ensures their future inheritance (cf. 1:9-10, 22-23). For this reason Paul proclaims Christ as the source of wisdom and the means to maturity (NRSV) or perfection (NAB, NIV) — completeness (1:28). To this Paul devotes himself tirelessly while recognizing Christ himself as the true source of his strength (1:29–2:1; cf. 1:11; Phil. 2:12-13; 4:13).

6. Explicitly or implicitly in Rom. 5:2-5; 2 Cor. 6:8-10; Phil. 1:12-18; 4:4-6; 1 Thess. 5:16-18.

This brief self-description evolves into a warning and a transition to the discussion of the 'philosophy' as Paul states the goals of his ministry more specifically to those he has never met face-to-face (the Colossians, Laodiceans, and others). Paul desires united communities characterized by love (2:2) and faith — i.e., in this context, full understanding of Christ as the wisdom of God (2:2-3), "in whom are hidden all the treasures of wisdom and knowledge" (2:3). In the specific context of the Colossians, Paul is concerned about "plausible" (NRSV), "specious" (NAB), or "fine-sounding" (NIV) arguments that, as we will see, challenge the sufficiency of Christ. Present in spirit with them, he rejoices in advance in the firmness of their faith (2:5).

2:6-23. LIFE IN CHRIST AS FREEDOM FROM THE POWERS

The concrete goal of Paul's letter now comes to the fore: to persuade the Colossians to remain firm in Christ and to dissuade them from embracing the deceitful philosophy (as Paul sees it) of the mystical ascetics. Paul's rhetorical strategy is to contrast the emptiness of the practices associated with the philosophy with the "fullness" of Christ and of the Colossians' experience in him.

CHRIST, NOT 'PHILOSOPHY' (2:6-8)

The first few verses set out the theme, positively and negatively, of this section, and in fact of the entire letter. Positively, inasmuch as the Colossians have received Christ the Lord (2:6) through faith (cf. 2:5), they are now to 'walk' (most translations have "live") in him. This means both stability and growth, as the metaphors "rooted . . . built up . . . established" suggest, as well as a constant spirit of thanksgiving (2:7). Negatively, they are not to be seduced and captured by any supposed alternative or supplement to Christ that is ultimately only an empty, deceitful philosophy (worldview and practices) stemming from human tradition and, worse, from the (hostile) elemental powers of the universe (cf. 2:8; Gal. 4:8-9), not from God's revelation in Christ. That which is not Christ is human at best, demonic at worst; in any event, it is not the gospel.

THE EXPERIENCE OF CHRIST (2:9-15)

The reason for this double admonition is now given: the sufficiency of Christ. Echoing the hymn of 1:15-20, Paul asserts that because Christ is the fullness of

God, believers have come to fullness in him (2:9-10). They have no need to fear or worship any 'powers' because Christ — through whom all powers were created, and who on the cross disarmed and defeated the hostile ones (1:16; 2:15) — is the head (sovereign) not only over his church, but also over all the powers (2:10). Believers share in the victory of Christ's cross. This is an experience of *Christus victor.*

This share in Christ's victory is portrayed in three images: circumcision, burial and resurrection, and debt forgiveness (2:11-14a). The circumcision that Paul describes is spiritual, not physical (2:11; cf. Rom. 2:26-29), removing not a piece of flesh but "the body of the flesh" — the inner anti-God force that manifests itself in trespasses (2:13). This spiritual circumcision is equated with, or perhaps assumed to lead to, the public act of baptism, in which believers' faith allowed them to move from death in trespasses, through burial, and into new life — resurrection (2:12-13). At this time their trespasses were forgiven (2:13b), a reality expressed in the last metaphor of debt forgiveness (2:14). The human situation outside of Christ, then, was one of guilt, death, and hostility to God.

Two allusions to the Jewishness of the mystical ascetics' message likely appear in these verses. First, Paul implies that their focus on circumcision is misguided; baptism into Christ (a spiritual circumcision spawned by faith) replaces circumcision and accomplishes what circumcision did not. Second, Paul implies that the Law did not help the human predicament but exacerbated it by demonstrating human failure. Thus to turn to physical circumcision and the Law — that is, to symbols of Jewish identity that do not release Gentiles from spiritual death — would be a grave error.

This passage ends with a brief but significant twofold depiction of the cross as God's act of victory. First, God erased "the record that stood against us" — the enemy of guilt derived from the accusations made by the Law; that record was nailed to the cross (2:14). Second, God "disarmed the rulers and authorities" (2:15); that is, in the cross God has defeated the very cosmic powers that hold humanity in the grip of fear. As in 2 Corinthians 2:14, the image here also includes a triumphal procession, in which the military victor made a "public spectacle" (2:15 NIV) of the defeated enemies. Together these two parts of the *Christus victor* (or better, here, *Deus victor*) image convey liberation from guilt and fear, in whatever ancient or modern forms they present themselves. The hostile powers of guilt and fear (as well as other cosmic forces and personal demons) are revealed for what they truly are for those who are in Christ and who benefit from his death: power*less.*

THE ERROR OF THE PHILOSOPHY (2:16-23)

The specifics of this kind of error in Colossae are now described and addressed. As in 2:6-8, Paul names both what to avoid and what to embrace.

As noted in the introductory remarks, to be avoided are:

- the observance of (Jewish) diet and calendar laws as a requisite and symbol of covenant membership (2:16; cf., e.g., Ezek. 45:17)
- "self-abasement" (probably meaning fasting) and other required ascetic practices (2:18, 22)
- "worship of angels," meaning either angel veneration or, less likely, worship in the company of angels (2:18)
- fixation on visions (2:18)

Believers have died with Christ to the "elemental spirits of the universe" (2:20), including the angels and other powers associated with them, so to pay them homage by venerating them directly or by submitting to the human traditions they have inspired (2:22; cf. 2:8) would be an anachronism (cf. 3:7). The ascetic or 'unworldly' regulations and experiences rooted in preoccupation with these "elemental spirits" are in fact actually quite worldly (2:20), completely human (2:22; cf. Mark 7:1-22), unable to promote true wisdom and piety (2:23), and ultimately ineffective in treating the root human problem of the "flesh" (NAB, rendering *sarx* in 2:23).[7] Moreover, they lead to judgmentalism and arrogance (2:16, 18) about who is truly 'in' and truly 'spiritual' or 'wise.'

If this all sounds merely like name-calling, we must press on to the real issue: all of these supposed means to wisdom and practices of piety take the focus off Christ as the true source of wisdom and growth in God (2:19). To be embraced, then, on the other hand, is simply Christ, and Christ alone (2:19). He is the "head" (= Lord; 2:19; cf. 1:18) and the substance, the reality, to which all Jewish symbols ultimately point (2:17). Moreover, no spiritual experience is needed except the experience of receiving Christ the Lord (2:6), of dying with Christ in victory over the elemental spirits (2:20), and then continuing to 'walk' in him (2:6).

Summary of Colossians 1–2

- Christ, as the preexistent image and wisdom of God, in whom the fullness of God dwelled, is the mediator of both creation and redemption; in his death

---

7. NRSV, "self-indulgence"; NIV, "sensual indulgence."

God defeated the hostile powers of the cosmos and effected a reconciliation that affects the entire creation.

- Believers have received this Christ as Lord, sharing in his death and resurrection, and have thereby been seated with him in the heavenly places above the defeated powers, yet their task is to grow in him and 'walk' in him in this world.
- The church is not to be misled by any kind of empty 'philosophy' that purports to supplant or supplement Christ by offering wisdom, knowledge, self-discipline, or any other spiritual experience outside of him.
- Specifically, the church is to avoid the syncretistic mysticism and extreme asceticism that certain teachers are advocating.

3:1–4:6. THE SHAPE OF LIFE IN CHRIST

If embracing Jewish symbols of covenant membership, extreme asceticism, angel veneration, and visions does not constitute true wisdom and piety, then what does? The answer to this question occupies the remainder of the letter (3:1–4:6) until the final greetings and wishes. In sum, Paul's answer seeks to address the same concerns that might lead to the practices of the mystical ascetics. It is to have a resurrection experience of Christ that is, paradoxically, also a death experience that deals with the sources of human sin and embodies the virtues of Christ on the cross. It is to express covenant membership, not in symbolic ritual boundary markers like calendar observance and self-abasement, but in substantive ethical ones like compassion and humility. It is not to refrain from living in the body and the world by escaping from its realities and into heaven, with its various cosmic powers, but to live a life of heavenly inspired thanksgiving and praise here and now, in the body and in the world.

INTRODUCTION (3:1-4)

Paul begins with a brief meditation on the central experience of believers: their resurrection to new life with Christ (3:1). They have been raised as high as possible: "above," that is, with Christ at the right hand of God — the seat of power (3:2). This focus on the 'vertical' dimension of believing existence likely stems from the mystical ascetics' preoccupation with heavenly powers and with visions. Believers do not need these things. Indeed, such things are ultimately (ironically) earthly and very human (2:20-22), and believers are to set their minds on things above (3:2), for they have died and their true life is hidden with Christ, ready to be revealed on a future day of glory (3:3-4).

Such language to describe the early Christian experience has struck many people as expressing a realized eschatology of present glory and success, and it is one of the chief reasons they wish to distance Paul from Colossians. However, the resurrection experience narrated here is hardly literal or triumphalist. Believers are certainly not yet in heaven but must await a coming day of glory. Neither have they 'arrived' spiritually. The first four verses of chapter 3 cannot be separated from what follows them. That is, identification with the *exalted, cosmic* Christ means also identification with the *humble, crucified* Christ. Believers' death (3:3) is not completed but continues, for resurrection means death (3:5). This is consistent with the example of the apostle, whose own resurrection with Christ entailed suffering (1:24). This paradoxical dimension of the resurrection experience is unpacked in the following verses.

RENEWAL IN CHRIST (3:5-17)

Paul continues with a summary exhortation, "Put to death . . ." (3:5), providing a list of two kinds of sins, related to sex (3:5) and to speech (3:8), that believers must rid their lives of (3:8). The meaning of the vivid metaphor "put to death" is thus clear from the more mundane language of 3:8. Paul calls for radical surgery ('kill off') instead of a set of regulations ('don't touch'). It is important, therefore, not to think of this exhortation merely as a different kind of asceticism. Rather, Paul grounds the command to avoid certain practices in the grand scheme of humanity's re-creation in Christ (3:11) that plays itself out in the radical transformation of each and every believer (3:7, 9). Believers have "stripped off" the old self and "clothed" themselves with the new (3:9-10), and cannot therefore live anachronistically.[8] If this is a reference to baptism, it is not concerned with the ritual itself but with its subsequent change in lifestyle.

The two lists of sins each include the thought life (e.g., impurity, passion, lust, anger, wrath, malice) as well as actions (e.g., fornication/sexual immorality, slander, abusive language, lying). But why the focus on sexual sins and sins of speech? Perhaps because these are 'ordinary' passions that destroy households and communities but are largely unchecked by ascetic disciplines. What might alter such behaviors is participation in the divine work of restoring creation to its intended harmony. That work has begun now in the community called the church, in which the person and presence of Christ, God's wisdom for the world's creation and re-creation, unites all who are being renewed in

---

8. Cf. Rom. 6:1-14; 13:14; Gal. 3:27.

him (3:11; cf. Gal. 3:28). Of particular importance for Colossians is the double emphasis on Jew-Gentile unity, and the focus on slave-free equality. (Scythians were a northern tribal people viewed as especially barbarian.)

This renewal of humanity, depicted in images of creation, is now also expressed in terms of covenant (3:12). Believers are God's beloved "chosen ones," set apart, like Israel, to live in distinction from those who do not know God (3:12). Continuing with the language of both covenant and clothing (new creation), Paul calls the Colossians to traits that are particularly appropriate for those associated with Christ: compassion, kindness, humility, meekness, and patience (3:12); mutual forbearance and forgiveness (3:13; cf. Eph. 4:32); and above all love, the force that unifies these traits and those that embody them (3:14). These virtues constitute the ongoing experience of the cross, not merely as 'death' to the old way of life but as the positive shape of the new.

Three final general admonitions about life together conclude this section of Paul's description of renewal in Christ. First is an exhortation to allow Christ's peace — the source of reconciliation — to rule in his body (3:15). Second is an exhortation to allow Christ's word and wisdom to permeate the community through mutual instruction and grateful songs (such as 1:15-20?) of praise (3:16; cf. Eph. 5:19). Finally, there appears a broad Pauline slogan about doing everything in a manner consistent with Christ and honoring to God (3:17; cf. 1 Cor. 10:31; Eph. 5:20). This 'whatever you do' principle provides a natural segue into the following provisions for conduct in the household.

RELATIONSHIPS IN THE HOUSEHOLD (3:18–4:1)

In various ancient pagan and Jewish texts we find admonitions to fathers and others about appropriate behavior within the household, so it is not surprising to find similar texts in early Christian literature; this one happens to be the earliest Christian specimen that has been preserved.

Perhaps the Philemon-Onesimus incident led Paul to two conclusions: (1) that *despite* the equality of slave and free in Christ (3:11; cf. Gal. 3:28), it would be impossible (for many reasons) for every household effectively to disintegrate through the manumission of all slaves; and (2) *because* of this equality of slave and free in Christ but in view of the impossibility of universal liberation, special guidelines were needed for the mutual treatment of believing masters — plus the master's wife and children — and believing slaves in the same household so that they would live together as a household in Christ, a kind of 'domestic church.' Paul's primary interest, then, is not in the preservation of the Greco-Roman patriarchal household but in the application of appropriate 'in

Christ,' or christocentric, norms to an institution that was a given of life in the world — the household, which often included slaves.

At the same time, this 'household code' focuses in a distinct way on one individual, the male head of household, or paterfamilias. It is he who is addressed three times: about his relations with his wife, his children, and his slaves. The paterfamilias was in fact an institution within an institution. In the Roman world the members of his household — his wife, children, and slaves — were his property, and he could (in theory, and often in practice) dispose of them as he saw fit, having even the power of life and death over them. This passage in Colossians subverts and transforms the power *(patria potestas)* of the paterfamilias.

In 3:18–4:1 this conversion of the household into a domestic church and the simultaneous transformation of the power of the paterfamilias take place in three important ways, as seen in the existential, literary, and cultural contexts of the code.

- First, the duties of the various members of the household are explicitly situated within the reality of life in Christ. The repeated mention of the Lord's name in 3:18–4:1 is not a series of religious platitudes. This aspect of the text reminds the household members that they are to embody the admonition of 3:17 in the household and to keep the teachings and example of Jesus ever in mind. They can certainly begin to do this with the several allusions to Christ's ministry in 3:12-16 (e.g., meekness, forgiveness) and with the general shape of life in Christ depicted throughout chapter 3. Even the master (the paterfamilias) must recall that he is accountable to a higher Master (4:1). This is the significance of the *existential* context of the code.
- Second, the exhortations in 3:18–4:1 follow the more general exhortations about life in Christ in 3:1-17 and are presented as a subset of those more general imperatives. Since the code is clearly written for a household of believers accountable to the same Lord, all members of the household are first of all expected to live by the general precepts; the code is an application of, not an alternative to, 3:1-17. *Consequently, 3:18–4:1 cannot be properly interpreted in any way that would contradict the general principles of life in Christ articulated in 3:1-17.* For example, the believing paterfamilias cannot act with impurity, greed, anger, or filthy or abusive language toward his wife, children, or slaves. He must be gentle toward his wife, kind toward his slaves, and patient with his children. He has the 'patriarchal' duty of establishing a household marked by love, humility, forgiveness, and the mutual edification of its members. He will have to learn Christ not merely from his cultural peers or 'superiors,' but even from his cultural 'subordinates.' This is the significance of the *literary* context of the code.

- Third, the code focuses on the duties, rather than the rights, of the members of the household, including especially the paterfamilias. In this respect this household code provides an alternative to any legal code that would do just the opposite. The paterfamilias, in fact, has no explicit rights granted him. To be sure, others have duties to him, but if they fail to comply, he has no right to punish or kill them. He has only the duty to be patient with them and forgive them — to live a cruciform life before them! He, like all the members of the household, has the responsibility of being a sort of Christ to his neighbors. This is the significance of the *cultural* context of the code.

Therefore, to summarize, the household code does not *underwrite* a patriarchal system but rather *rewrites* it in the context of life in Christ. It is not an example of 'baptizing the status quo,' as some have charged. Nor is it an example of Paul's potentially revolutionary ethic being tamed. It is, on the contrary, no less revolutionary than any other occasion in which people are called to a cruciform life in Christ.

A believing wife is to be subject to her husband (there was no other option), but only in a way appropriate to a person (and a couple) in Christ (3:18). The paterfamilias, in his role as husband, is to exhibit Christlike agape and not harshness (3:19 NRSV, NAB). Children of a believing household are to obey their parents (not just their father) "in everything," a scriptural commandment that endures in Christ (3:20). But even the "everything" of this requirement is implicitly nuanced by the larger context. The paterfamilias as father, in turn, may not use his authority to harass and exasperate his children, for that would have detrimental effects on their maturation as believers (3:21).

Slaves are given the longest set of instructions (3:22-25), but the point is simple: obey and work for their masters as if serving their true Master, for the Lord Christ is in fact the one who truly receives their honor and recognizes their integrity. As believers, they are accountable to their ultimate Lord for any wrong done, even to a master (3:25). The paterfamilias, as slave owner, is reminded that he, too, has the same Lord in heaven and is expected to treat slaves justly and fairly (4:1). This pair of admonitions within the household code puts flesh and blood (though some would say not enough) on the statement of equality in 3:11. *Since the slave and the master are both slaves of the one true Master, neither is really (despite Roman law) the owner or property of the other.*

GENERAL EXHORTATIONS (4:2-6)

Paul concludes this part of the letter by tying together his own story with that of the Colossians. He does this by adding some further general exhortations.

The major focus is on the Colossians' responsibility toward those who have not yet believed the gospel.

A general call to prayer with thanksgiving (4:2) turns quickly into a request for prayer for Paul's evangelistic mission, Paul desiring that they pray for both opportunity and clarity (4:3-4). But the Colossians cannot rely on Paul alone to spread "the mystery of Christ." They must embody the gospel in their conduct and speech, demonstrating its wisdom and grace (4:5-6). This requires not only being prepared to answer inquiries (4:6), but also taking initiative whenever possible (4:5).

4:7-18. GREETINGS AND BENEDICTION

Colossians concludes with a set of greetings in which eleven people associated with Paul are named. Those who believe the letter to be pseudonymous understand this list to be an artificial device designed to lend it authority and credibility. Though it is true that a number of the people mentioned here are regular characters in the disputed letters and Acts, that is no reason to dismiss the genuineness of their association with Paul in connection with the Colossians.

The first two people mentioned, Tychicus and Onesimus, will bring greetings from Paul as they go to Colossae, apparently bearing his letter to the church (4:7-9). As noted in the introduction, Tychicus fulfills a similar role in Ephesians and may be responsible for some aspects of the two letters' style and content (Eph. 6:21-22).[9] Paul's description of him (4:7) reveals much about his understanding of ministry: "a beloved brother, a faithful minister [*diakonos*], and a fellow servant" (lit. "coslave," *syndoulos,* the same title given to Epaphras in 1:7). Interestingly, Onesimus, the onetime slave from Colossae, is described in similar language — "faithful and beloved brother" — but without the epithet 'slave.' Perhaps we should conclude that the letter to Philemon and the church at his house was successful, and Onesimus has been freed for service with Paul. He returns to his hometown of Colossae with a new identity in the Lord.

Greetings, with short glosses, follow from three more of Paul's fellow laborers, Aristarchus (also in prison), Mark (who may be coming on some mission), and Jesus (called Justus), who are identified as his sole Jewish coworkers (4:10-11) — perhaps to reinforce the appropriateness of his gospel for those with Jewish heritage or inclination. Epaphras, the evangelist from and to the Colossians, is mentioned as one who vigorously intercedes for the churches ("wrestling in his prayers," 4:12) he has founded in Colossae (1:7-8) and, proba-

---

9. Tychicus also appears in Acts 20:4; 2 Tim. 4:12; and Titus 3:12.

bly, also in nearby Laodicea and Hierapolis (4:13). All these men save Justus are named also in Philemon 23-24, with Epaphras (not Aristarchus) in prison with Paul at that time. Similarly, Luke and Demas, also mentioned in Philemon 24, send greetings (4:14).

Paul's own greetings are sent to the believers in Laodicea, some at least of whom assemble in the house of a woman called Nympha, and to whom he has written a letter (4:15-16). The contents of that letter — unknown to us, despite the existence of a later (fourth or fifth century?) apocryphal *Letter to the Laodiceans* — and of the letter to the Colossians were sufficiently general or sufficiently important to be shared between the cities (4:16). Paul's ongoing relationship with the believers in Colossae is further indicated by his message for Archippus, one of the named corecipients of the letter to Philemon (Philem. 2), to complete an unspecified task (4:17).

Finally, Paul somehow takes up the pen, despite being in chains — no doubt after leaving the actual writing of the letter to a secretary (Tychicus?) — to authenticate the letter and to send his word of grace (4:18), ending the letter on the note with which he began it (1:2, 6). It is a fitting summary of his message — the fullness of the grace of God in Christ.

Summary of Colossians 3–4

- Believers, having been "raised with Christ" and having "put on Christ," constitute the new humanity being re-created in the image of the Creator.
- Believers' resurrection life is, paradoxically, a death experience: death to the old self and its sins associated with sex and speech, and embodiment of the Lord's cruciform compassion, humility, forgiveness, and peace.
- Within this context, all members of the household — with special emphasis on the paterfamilias — are to exercise their domestic responsibilities in a manner consistent with Christ and in dedication to their common Lord.
- All believers have a measure of responsibility to spread the gospel.

THE STORY IN FRONT OF THE LETTER

Some Readings of Colossians

"With a feeling of great temerity I asked her [my grandmother] one day why it was that she would not let me read any of the Pauline letters [aloud to her]. What she told me I shall never forget. 'During the days of slavery,' she said, 'the master's minister would occasionally hold services for the slaves. Old man McGhee was so mean that he would not let a Negro minister preach to his slaves. Always the white minister used as his text something from Paul. At least three or four times a year he used as a text: "Slaves, be obedient to them that are your masters . . . as unto Christ." Then he would go on to show how, if we were good and happy slaves, God would bless us. I promised my Maker that if I ever learned to read and if freedom ever came, I would not read that part of the Bible.'"

The grandmother of Howard Thurman, quoted in his *Jesus and the Disinherited* (Nashville: Abingdon, 1949; repr. Boston: Beacon, 1996), pp. 30-31

"The concrete evidence of this triumph [Christ's triumph over the powers] is that at the cross Christ has 'disarmed' the Powers. The weapon from which they heretofore derived their strength is struck out of their hands. This weapon was the power of illusion, their ability to convince [people] that they were the divine regents of the world, ultimate certainty and ultimate direction, ultimate happiness and the ultimate duty for small dependent humanity. Since Christ we know that this is illusion. We are called to a higher destiny: we have higher orders to follow and we stand under a greater protector. No powers can separate us from God's love in Christ. Unmasked, revealed in their true nature, they have lost their mighty grip on [people]. The cross has disarmed them: wherever it is preached, the unmasking and the disarming of the powers takes place."

Hendrikus Berkhof, *Christ and the Powers* (Scottdale, Pa.: Herald, 1962), p. 31

"[A]lthough Colossians offers many apparently clear-cut answers to religious questions, its overall message is marked by considerable openness and an evident intent to stimulate rather than to cut off questioning. It offers bold assertions, for example, about Christ's relation to God the Father and to the cosmos, but it does not go too far in defining those relationships. . . . Colossians insists that all wisdom is hidden in Christ, but its author does not claim to provide an exhaustive exploration of the mystery."

David M. Hay, *Colossians*, Abingdon New Testament Commentaries (Nashville: Abingdon, 2000), pp. 34-35

QUESTIONS FOR REFLECTION

1. In what ways, if any, is the sufficiency of Christ as God's agent of creation and reconciliation challenged today? How does, and how should, the church respond to these challenges?
2. How might the opening hymn of Colossians, as well as the letter as a whole, prompt Christians today to understand and act on the universal lordship of Christ and the cosmic scope of his reconciling work?
3. In what ways do people today experience the universe as either a safe or a hostile place, and to what benevolent and/or malevolent power(s) do they ascribe their good or bad fortunes? How might the letter to the Colossians offer helpful perspectives on the nature and potency of these powers, and on an appropriate attitude toward them?
4. What kinds of supplemental — but ultimately inappropriate — spiritual practices and experiences do people sometimes attempt to impose on Christians today? What might be their motivations? What is the appeal of such experiences?
5. Does Paul's rejection of 'philosophy' render all intellectual and/or nontheological study pointless, or even harmful? What kind of attitude toward culture might this notion, in the context of all of Colossians, foster?
6. What kind of perspectives on spiritual disciplines such as fasting might the critique of extreme asceticism in Colossians generate?
7. What significance do (or could) the metaphors 'being raised with Christ' and 'putting on Christ' have for the contemporary church? Why is it important to keep these metaphors connected to the cross?
8. What are the contemporary sins associated with sex and speech that modern believers must 'put to death'?
9. How might the gospel as it is related in Colossians impact family life in our day?
10. What is the church's responsibility in assisting its members to be prepared to share their faith with others?
11. How do you respond to the interpretations of Colossians quoted above?
12. In sum, what does this letter urge the church to believe, to hope for, and to do?

FOR FURTHER READING AND STUDY

General

Hay, David M. *Colossians.* Abingdon New Testament Commentaries. Nashville: Abingdon, 2000. A careful, accessible commentary stressing the theological message of the text and its ancient Jewish and non-Jewish parallels.

Lincoln, Andrew T. "Colossians." In *The New Interpreter's Bible,* edited by Leander E. Keck et al., 11:551-669. Nashville: Abingdon, 2000. An insightful analysis focusing on the theme of wisdom in Christ over against the teachings of visionary ascetics.

MacDonald, Margaret Y. *Colossians and Ephesians.* Sacra Pagina. Collegeville, Minn.: Liturgical Press, 2000. An interpretation arguing that Paul is not the author, that the philosophy is syncretistic, and that baptism is a central issue.

Martin, Ralph P. *Ephesians, Colossians, and Philemon.* Interpretation. Atlanta: John Knox, 1991. A brief commentary for preachers and teachers, assuming Paul as the likely author.

Wright, N. T. *The Epistles of Paul to the Colossians and Philemon.* Tyndale New Testament Commentaries. Grand Rapids: Eerdmans, 1986. A readable exposition that argues for Pauline authorship and the letter's opposition to Gentile believers turning to Judaism.

Technical

Dunn, James D. G. *The Epistles to the Colossians and to Philemon.* New International Greek Testament Commentary. Grand Rapids: Eerdmans, 1996. A careful work whose author believes that Paul probably instructed Timothy to write the letter and that the 'philosophy' represents the teachings of the local synagogue(s).

Lohse, Eduard. *Colossians and Philemon.* Hermeneia. Philadelphia: Fortress, 1971. A detailed commentary arguing that in this letter a member of the Pauline school expressed his opposition to syncretism.

Schweizer, Eduard. *The Letter to the Colossians: A Commentary.* Translated by A. Chester. Minneapolis: Augsburg, 1982. An influential analysis with attention to both the letter's theology and the history of its interpretation on the assumption of Timothy's authorship for the imprisoned Paul.

CHAPTER 16

EPHESIANS

Walking Worthily of the
Cosmic Crucified Christ

For we are what he has made us, created in Christ Jesus for good works,
which God prepared beforehand to be our way of life.

Eph. 2:10

The document called the letter (or epistle) of Paul to the Ephesians is a liturgical celebration of God's eternal purpose in Christ and an exhortation to the church — the present manifestation of the divine purpose — to embody that purpose in daily life. As in Colossians, but even more explicitly, this purpose and its embodiment are focused on the cross of Christ, who is now exalted to the "heavenly places." Also as in the case of Colossians, but even more so, the authenticity and character of this letter are disputed. We should not, however, permit disputes about authorship to prevent us from engaging Ephesians itself. To do so would be a regrettable mistake, for Ephesians is a rich, even if sometimes difficult, document.

THE STORY BEHIND THE LETTER

Although the emphasis of this book is on the theological message of each letter, we of course cannot avoid paying some attention to the kinds of questions that are related to issues of the document's authenticity and character. Was Ephesians written to the church in Ephesus? Is it a letter? Was it written by Paul?

498

A LETTER TO THE EPHESIANS?

The truth of the matter is that we do not know much about the story behind the letter to the Ephesians. In fact, the earliest and best New Testament manuscripts omit the phrase "in Ephesus" from 1:1.[1] It is quite possible, then, that this document was intended as a circular letter and that believers in Ephesus, if they received it at all, were not the only intended audience.

The contents of Ephesians seem to support such a theory. There is very little hint of any specific situations being addressed, or of one concrete community being envisioned. Although there are exhortations to beware of doctrinal error (e.g., 4:14; 5:6), these seem quite general, and it is much more difficult to reconstruct an 'Ephesian philosophy/heresy' like the 'Colossian philosophy/heresy' (though some have discerned Gnostic or anti-Gnostic themes in the letter). Moreover, the theological affirmations and ethical exhortations have a generic air about them. Unlike Romans, about which the same might be said for chapters 1–8 (or 1–11) but not 12–16, Ephesians does not move from the general to the specific.

Furthermore, the text assumes that the recipients have not had, or at least may not have had, direct contact with Paul (1:15; 3:2), certainly suggesting a place other than Ephesus (where Paul spent considerable time). It is likely, however, whether or not 1:1 originally contained the words "in Ephesus," that this 'circular' letter became associated with Ephesus because it was intended to circulate throughout the province of Asia, of which Ephesus was the capital and the epicenter from which Paul's gospel spread throughout the province (cf. Acts 19:10). Of course, not everyone who had heard Paul's gospel would have had direct (or even once-removed) contact with him, which would explain the feeling of distance between writer and readers in Ephesians. In light of this probable connection between the letter and the city, and because of the importance of Ephesus in Paul's ministry, a brief note about the city is in order.

THE CITY OF EPHESUS

Ephesus was a large (with maybe a quarter-million inhabitants), spectacular city whose expansive, partially reconstructed ruins are perhaps the most fascinating — and among the most visited — of all ancient cities in the Mediterranean basin. Originally a Greek colony, it eventually became the capital of the Roman province of Asia, with a thriving harbor (which later disappeared, due to silting, and essentially ended the life of the city) and a strategic location on overland

---

1. For example, the phrase is absent from p[46] and B (Vaticanus).

Ephesus: The huge agora near the harbor

land trade routes. Among its distinguished structures at the time of Paul were an acoustically magnificent theater; a stadium; two large agoras; impressive gates and a basilica (used for trading and banking) dedicated to Augustus; temples to Apollo, Rome/Julius, and either Augustus or Isis; a *pyrtaneion* (from Gk. *pyr,* 'fire'), where priestesses of Artemis guarded the city's sacred eternal flame; and of course, a temple to Artemis/Diana (the Artemision), one of the seven wonders of the ancient world. Four times the size of the Parthenon in Athens, the Artemision was dedicated to the Greek god of chastity, fertility, and hunting who had been transformed in Ephesus ("Artemis of the Ephesians," Acts 19:28, 34) into the heir of the Anatolian mother-goddess tradition (e.g., Cybele). Artemis was the mother and soul of all aspects of life in and around Ephesus. According to Acts 19, Paul's gospel and the worship of Artemis came into serious conflict. Although Artemis dominated Ephesian life, other forms of religious devotion (including magic) existed in Ephesus. Attempts to identify traces of peculiarly Ephesian religious issues in the letter have not, however, been widely accepted.

No matter what its precise relation to this letter, Ephesus was a strategic city in Paul's ministry, functioning for him in Asia as Corinth did in Achaia.[2] It remained an important center of the early church, prompting letters from John

2. Cf. Acts 18:19-21; 19:1–20:1; 20:16-38; 1 Cor. 15:32; 16:8-9; 2 Cor. 1:8-9.

Ephesus: Approaching the city from the harbor, one saw the spectacular theater, dating from Hellenistic times. After first-century A.D. renovations, it could hold nearly 25,000 people.

(Rev. 2:1-7) in the late first century and from Ignatius, bishop of Antioch *(To the Ephesians)*, in the early second century, and later becoming the site of church councils.

A LETTER FROM PAUL?

The significance of Ephesus to Paul's ministry makes it peculiar that no letter of definite Ephesian destination has been preserved. Not only has the likely circular, generic character of Ephesians led some to disassociate it from Ephesus, but its character as a letter — specifically as a letter from Paul — has also been seriously questioned. Many scholars have suggested categorizing it as a speech, essay, or homily (perhaps a baptismal homily) rather than a letter. But since it has an epistolary beginning and ending, and since all Pauline letters have something of a speechlike character, it is best to call Ephesians a letter whose precise occasion and audience cannot be determined with certainty.

What is quite likely about the story behind the letter, however, is that it is modeled on Colossians. The structure, vocabulary, and theology of Ephesians' six chapters are similar to — though not identical with — the shorter letter. Approximately half of Ephesians has parallel material in Colossians (some exact or nearly so), and, like Colossians, Ephesians contains material that sounds 'liturgical' — that is, taken from early Christian worship and catechesis. Scholars who find Colossians to be written by someone other than Paul will obviously conclude that Paul did not write Ephesians either, pointing to the distinctive features of the two letters and concluding that Ephesians is the work of a later disciple of Paul, writing after the apostle's death sometime in the last third of the first century. Others who find Colossians plausibly to be from Paul's own hand will often still attribute Ephesians to a later disciple of Paul, writing after the apostle's death. Perhaps 20 to 30 percent of New Testament scholars think that Paul actually wrote Ephesians.

Something of a middle ground between authorship by Paul and by a later disciple may, however, be proposed. As in Philippians and Colossians (as well as Philemon), the text of Ephesians has Paul in prison (3:1, 13; 4:1; 6:20). As we will see below, Ephesians has echoes not only of Colossians but also of Philippians that may be due to the circumstances of captivity. Moreover, such a predicament would likely have necessitated more assistance from a secretary, or amanuensis, than letters written in freedom. Interestingly, both Colossians (4:7-9, 16) and Ephesians (6:21-22) endorse Paul's coworker Tychicus as the bearer of news about Paul and, implicitly, of the letters. Is the appearance of Tychicus in Ephesians to be explained as imitation of Colossians, or is it possible that Tychicus is not only the messenger but also the distinctive voice that appears in both these letters? If so, then Ephesians was written after Colossians but during Paul's lifetime, sometime in the early 60s. In the commentary below I refer to Paul as the writer, since he is either the real (as I am prone to believe) or fictive (implied) author of the text.

THE STORY WITHIN THE LETTER

Ephesians definitely has a distinctive voice. But its peculiarity has sometimes been overemphasized. Ephesians, like Colossians but even more so, is said to possess a realized eschatology/soteriology and an exalted Christology and ecclesiology that differ substantially from the undisputed Pauline letters. Two of the common assertions about these differences, together with brief comments, follow:

- *In Ephesians, many contend, salvation is presented as an event in the past tense ("saved"; 2:5, 8) that has created a present experience of resurrection with Christ with little emphasis on a future hope, expressed in un-Pauline and unusual phrases like "[God] raised us up with him [Christ] and seated us with him in the heavenly places" (2:6).* These supposedly radical differences from the authentic Paul depend in part on a misreading of the undisputed letters and in part on a misreading of Ephesians. Though it is true that Paul prefers the term 'justified' or 'reconciled' when speaking of the believer's past experience (e.g., Rom. 5:1-11) and generally reserves 'salvation' language for the future, he does say "in hope we were saved" (Rom. 8:24).

Moreover, contrary to the opinion of many scholars, in reflecting on baptism Paul does speak of a resurrection to new life (Rom. 6:4, 11, 13). This resurrection to new life is to a life of cruciform self-offering to God and love for others, according to Romans; being seated "with him in the heavenly places" (Eph. 2:6) likewise involves a cruciform lifestyle (e.g., 5:1-2). The trajectory from "[raised] in newness of life . . . alive to God in Christ Jesus" (Rom. 6:4, 11) to "raised with Christ . . . your life is hidden with Christ in God" (Col. 3:1, 3) to Ephesians 2:6 is not as radical a development as some have suggested. As in Philippians 3:7-11, in Ephesians the power of resurrection is experienced as the power to be conformed to the cross in suffering and in selfless love. Furthermore, there is a stronger future eschatology in Ephesians than is often recognized (1:9-14, 21; 4:13, 30). The lack of an explicit reference to Christ's return (contrast Col. 3:4) should not be exaggerated, especially in light of phrases like "set our hope on Christ" (1:12), "the age to come" (1:21), and "the day of redemption" (4:30).

• *Also, many claim, Ephesians has a cosmic Christology and ecclesiology in which Christ is the cosmic Lord who begins to usurp some of God's role in salvation (cf. Eph. 2:16 with 2 Cor. 5:19 and even Col. 1:20, on reconciliation; cf. Eph. 4:7-11 with 1 Cor. 12:28 on granting gifts/offices). Christ is designated as the "head" (Eph. 4:15; contrast 1 Cor. 12) of his body, which is the cosmic or universal church, not the local church. The church, not the world, is the ultimate goal of salvation/reconciliation.* Space does not permit a full response, but a few remarks are essential. First, most of the earliest Christian liturgical and theological traditions have Christ 'usurping' God's titles (Lord, Savior) and role in salvation. This is the problem inherent in 'christological monotheism'; Philippians 2:6-11 (cf. Isa. 45:23) is a perfect example. The initiative in, agent of, and goal of salvation and all its benefits is always God for Paul, but sometimes the roles of Father, Son, and Spirit are not drawn with clear lines (e.g., in 1 Cor. 12:11 the Spirit, not the Father or the Son, gives gifts).

Next, it is hardly an unexpected or inappropriate shift in imagery to have Christ the Lord called the "head" of the church; in fact, what is more puzzling is that the image did not move in that direction already in 1 Corinthians. And finally, it is simply untrue that the church is not 'local' in Ephesians. The distinctiveness of Ephesians is in placing the local church, with all its activities and gifted members (stressed in chap. 4 and, indeed, all of chaps. 4–6), within the context of a more fully articulated vision of the universal church, to which certain texts in undisputed letters, as well as Paul's collection for Jerusalem, already point. Although the church as Christ's (universal) body is currently the "fullness of him [Christ]" (1:23), God's plan does not end in the church, for all creation will eventually be "gather[ed] up" in Christ (1:10; cf. Rom. 8:18-25).

These comments cannot, of course, answer all the interpretations of Ephesians that contribute to its supposed distance from the authentic Paul. Ephesians does indeed portray an exalted Christ and an exalted church (no one can dispute that), but these emphases can be explained from within the circumstances and trajectory of the major Prison Epistles: Philippians, Colossians, and Ephesians. As Philippians itself already demonstrates, Paul's Prison Epistles reveal a heavy emphasis on Christ as Lord over against any and all powers — especially imperial powers in Philippians. A corresponding emphasis on the church as a distinct, counterimperial, countercultural entity appears in Philippians. These themes are not absent from other and earlier letters, but they are more pronounced in Philippians, and they are so, perhaps, because Paul is facing the spectacle of anti-Christ power as he writes. The powers depicted in Colossians and Ephesians are more cosmic but no less threatening, at least not to the ancients. Furthermore, there are at least implicitly anti-imperial texts in Ephesians (e.g., the portrayal of Christ as the great, universal unifier and peacemaker).

Ephesians, then, announces the story of this cosmic salvation of God in Christ known in the church. It is the eternal purpose (3:11), plan (*oikonomia*; 1:10; 3:9), and "mystery" (*mystērion*; 1:9; 3:3, 4, 5, 9; 6:19) of God. The first half of the letter (chaps. 1–3) focuses on this plan of God to unify all things in Christ, a plan effected by Christ's death and demonstrated in the salvation and unification of Jews and Gentiles, especially through the ministry of Paul. The second half (chaps. 4–6) offers counsel on the contours of a corresponding countercultural, Christlike cruciform lifestyle that is lived, in anticipation of the completion of God's story, as a kind of warfare against the spiritual forces that oppose the Spirit-empowered church in the world. Thus the letter connects the grace of being in Christ, and therefore incorporated into God's great plan, to the responsibilities associated with being in him. (Similar letter structures appear in Colossians [chaps. 1–2, chaps. 3–4] and Romans [chaps. 1–11, chaps. 12–16].)

The letter unfolds according to the following structure:

1:1-2   **Opening**
1:3–3:21   **God's Eternal Plan in Christ**
      1:3-14   Blessing for Heavenly Blessings in Christ
      1:15-23   Prayer for Enlightenment
      2:1-10   God's Grace in Christ
      2:11-22   The Unity of Jew and Gentile in Christ
      3:1-13   Paul's Role in God's Plan
      3:14-21   Paul's Second Prayer for His Readers
4:1–6:20   **Life in Christ: Worthy of God's Calling, Empowered by the Spirit**
      4:1-16   The Unity and Maturity of the Church
      4:17–6:9   Learning and Living Christ
            4:17-24   No Longer Like the Gentiles
            4:25–5:2   Loving Speech and Action
            5:3-14   Countercultural Sexual Purity
            5:15–6:9   Community Life
                  5:15-21   Community and Trinity
                  5:22–6:9   Life in Christ in the Household
      6:10-20   Spiritual Warfare
6:21-24   **Final Matters**

Summaries of chapters 1–3 and 4–6 follow the commentary on those sections of the letter.

1:1-2. OPENING

The letter begins in rather typical Pauline fashion, but a few details are worth noting. The wording here is very similar to the opening of Colossians, including the adjective "faithful" (Colossians has "faithful brothers [and sisters]"), a word which appears in the greeting only in these two letters. The addition of "in Christ Jesus" to "faithful" (cf. Col. 1:2, "in Christ") is especially appropriate given the letter's strong emphasis on being in Christ.[3] Unlike Colossians, however, Ephesians names no cosender and (in the original manuscript) probably no specific city of destination. Also, Ephesians quite interestingly adds "the Lord Jesus Christ" to the "God our Father" of Colossians as the source of grace and peace.

3. Eph. 1:3-14; 4:1, 17, 21; 5:8; 6:1, 10, 21.

1:3–3:21. GOD'S ETERNAL PLAN IN CHRIST

The first half of Ephesians is celebratory and even liturgical in tone, beginning with a Jewish-style blessing of God (1:3-14), followed by an intercessory prayer (1:15-23), and concluding with another intercessory prayer (3:14-21). The intervening theological (2:1-22) and autobiographical (3:1-13) material serves to link both the addressees and the author to the grace of God being celebrated.

BLESSING FOR HEAVENLY BLESSINGS IN CHRIST (1:3-14)

Ephesians 1:3-14 is one long, complex, remarkable sentence in Greek. It has the form of a Jewish prayer of praise, or blessing (*berakah;* cf. 2 Cor. 1:3-7), and is also similar to the public orations ancients gave in honor of great benefactors (cf. 2 Cor. 1:3-4). The blessings of God in Christ that are listed in these verses include:

- election (1:4)
- adoption (1:5)
- grace (1:6)
- redemption/forgiveness (1:7-8a)
- revelation (1:8b-10)
- inheritance/hope (1:11-12)
- the Holy Spirit (1:13-14)

This list is itself quite remarkable, stressing the wealth of God's grace in the past, present, and future (cf. Rom. 5:1-11) with a variety of striking biblical terms and provocative metaphors, many of which appear in other Pauline letters but seldom in such quantity in one place.

This breadth explains the phrase "every spiritual blessing" (1:3), though "in the heavenly places" — a unique phrase for 'in heaven' — needs a brief comment. Its usage in Ephesians suggests, not that believers are somehow transported to heaven and out of the struggles of this world (in fact, "the spiritual forces of evil" are also "in the heavenly places" [6:12]), but rather that by being in Christ they share in the powerful grace of God that is at work ultimately to defeat the cosmic forces of evil.

The first blessing, election (1:4), is of course a biblical term that is now used for God's call in Christ of Gentiles as well as Jews, as chapters 2 and 3 will especially stress. The phrase "before the foundation of the world" indicates that this is not some divine afterthought but part of an 'eternal purpose' (1:11). The church's election, like Israel's, is not to some place of privilege without responsibility but to a covenant, to a countercultural ('holy,' 'distinctive') life characterized by love. It must be "blameless," a word associated with integrity in witness as well as accountability on the day of judgment (5:27; Phil. 2:15; Col. 1:22).

The next blessings, adoption and grace (1:5-6), are additional biblical terms related to election ("destined us," 1:5). Scripture calls God's people "the children of Israel," with God as their father who blesses and protects them. The grace experienced first by Israel in the exodus has now been granted to Jew and Gentile alike "in the Beloved" (1:6). This unique way of referring to Christ likely implies his sonship to God (cf. 4:13) and anticipates the next verse (cf. Rom. 8:3, 32). In return for this gracious gift of adoption, Israel — and now the church — owes God the honor due a father (thus the call to holiness in 1:4 and to imitation of God and Christ in 5:1-2).

The specifics of this divine grace, with an emphasis on both present reality and future hope, are now spelled out in the following blessings. The first of these is "redemption" (1:7-8a), a metaphor from the realm of slavery defined here (and similarly in Rom. 3:24-26) as forgiveness. Although redemption as forgiveness is a present possession, the totality of salvation it is not yet possessed in full (cf. 1:14; 4:30). The next blessing (1:8b-10) is the revelation of "the mystery of his will," to be accomplished in Christ, which is to "gather up" or unify the whole creation in Christ. This is a distinctive mark of Ephesians, though there are echoes in Romans 8. This gathering up will transpire in the "fullness of time," a reference to the future (unlike the similar phrase in Gal. 4:4, which refers to the past).

The next benefit is that those in Christ are and will be part of this unfolding mystery, having already received an "inheritance" (as God's children, based on the death of Christ) that guarantees their place (1:11). This inheritance is not fully realized, however, and thus generates the blessing of hope (1:12) marked by a life of praise in the present. The gift of the Holy Spirit is the final blessing mentioned (1:13-14) and is characterized in two images connecting present and future. As God's "seal," the Spirit marks and protects believers as God's possession. As "the pledge (*arrabōn*, as in 2 Cor. 1:22; 5:5) of our inheritance," the Spirit is the "deposit" (NIV) or "first installment" (NAB) of future redemption. The experience of redemption is real, but not yet complete.

Both the form and the content of this entire passage urge believers to offer praise to God (1:6, 12, 14) for these gracious and lavish blessings, which are for the church a participation in the trinitarian work of grace offered by the Father, in Christ, via the Spirit.[4]

---

4. As in earlier chapters, trinitarian language is used here in recognition that although Paul does not have a fully developed theology of the Trinity, such language is nonetheless appropriate.

PRAYER FOR ENLIGHTENMENT (1:15-23)

The prayer that follows the blessing grows directly out of it; it is, in effect, a prayer that the letter's recipients may fully experience the reality to which the *berakah* bears witness. Like the blessing, this prayer is (probably) one long sentence in Greek.

After a brief mention of the recipients' covenant faithfulness (1:15, faith and love, the 'vertical' and 'horizontal' dimensions of the covenant; cf. Gal. 5:6), Paul states that he offers constant prayers of thanksgiving and intercession for them (1:16).[5] The remainder of the passage (1:17-23) articulates the content of the prayer, which is trinitarian in both substance and structure.

The first part of the prayer (1:17) invokes the triune God as the source of the believers' spiritual experience, which is summarized here as "know[ing] him [God]." Mention of God the Father and of Jesus suggests that the "spirit of wisdom and revelation" (cf. 1:8b-9) is the Holy Spirit named in 1:13. Characterized as those with the "eyes of your heart enlightened" (1:18), the letter's recipients are not being invited to some secret knowledge and mystery but one that is a very public, even cosmic, reality, the lordship of Christ, described in verses 20-23. To be "enlightened" about this is not merely to have access to information but to participate fully in the gracious redemption in Christ described in 1:3-14. It is knowledge (1:18, "to know") in the 'biblical' sense of experience. Specifically, this means an experience of hope (1:18; cf. 1:12), of a lavish inheritance experienced both now and later (1:18; cf. 1:7, 11, 14), and immeasurable power (1:19). As in the prayer of blessing, these dimensions of knowing God are all interconnected as blessings of God the Father, in Christ, via the Spirit.

The mention of power appears to be a new element, one that receives rather extensive elaboration as the divine power that raised and exalted Christ (1:20-23). It is likely, however, that the reference to power as "power for us" (1:19) is an allusion to the presence of the Spirit (cf. 3:16). This power is said to be the same as that which raised Christ and seated him at God's right hand (cf. Ps. 110) "in the heavenly places" (1:20), which is also where believers have been seated with Christ (2:6). Though Christ (and thus also believers) is seated above every power (1:21), believers still fight against such cosmic powers (6:12).[6] They do so in the strength of the Spirit (6:17-18) with the whole "armor of God" (6:13). Thus to share in Christ's heavenly reign over all powers means, ironically, to live on earth and do combat with those powers in the power of the Spirit.

Christ's past resurrection and exaltation by God (1:20) have resulted in

---

5. Cf. Col. 1:3-5; 1 Thess. 1:2-3; 2 Thess. 1:3; Phil. 1:3-5.
6. See the previous chapter on Colossians for a brief discussion of the identity of these powers.

Christ's present rule over all powers (cf. 1 Cor. 15:24-28; Col. 2:10, 15). Although it sounds as if this lordship means that the powers have no power at all, 6:12 speaks against that reading. Rather, we should understand that Christ's rule is both present and future ("in this age but also in the age to come," 1:21), and that his power over powers in the present means he protects the church, by the power of the Spirit, from these cosmic forces of evil even as the church battles them. Thus, the text says, God has made him the head over all things "for the church" (1:22). The church, indeed, is Christ's body, and in that sense a cosmic reality that shares in Christ's lordship (1:23) — but only as described above. This is no triumphalism, as some have said. There is still evil in the world, and there is still a future in God's plan. For the present the church is the fullness of Christ. The gathering up of "all things" in him (1:10) awaits the future.

GOD'S GRACE IN CHRIST (2:1-10)

Having praised God for the riches of grace bestowed in Christ, and having prayed for the recipients of his letter to have a full experience of that grace, Paul proceeds to 'unpack' the substance of this grace more fully. Ephesians 2:1-10 elaborates on the notion of the church as the fullness of Christ (1:23), sharing in the power of his resurrection in new life. The corollary reality of Christ's fullness as restoration to unity will be explored in the following passage, 2:11-22. By any account, Ephesians 2:1-10 — though another long (and awkward) Greek sentence — is a magnificent summary of the "word of truth, the gospel of your salvation" (1:13) preached by Paul. Combined with 2:11-22 (which is parallel in structure to 2:1-10), it has the semblance of an extended commentary on Galatians 5:6 and 6:15: "For in Christ Jesus neither circumcision nor uncircumcision counts for anything; the only thing that counts is faith working through love"; "For neither circumcision nor uncircumcision is anything; but a new creation is everything!"

The gist of this passage is that although the Gentiles were dead because of the sins in which they once "lived" or "walked" (2:1, 3),[7] God in grace made them (like Paul) alive with Christ (2:4-9), a new creation in Christ destined to walk now in good deeds (2:10). The extended description of walking in sin (2:2-3) interrupts the syntax of the sentence (leading to the partial repetition of 2:1 in 2:5), but it serves to heighten the contrast between humanity's sin and God's intervening grace, and between the former and present 'walk' of the letter's recipients. Indeed, the Jewish metaphor of life as a 'walk' (2:1, 3, 10, translating the Greek verb *peripateō*) becomes the dominant metaphor for life in Christ in the remainder of Ephesians (4:1, 17; 5:2, 8, 15), though it is missed in most modern translations.

---

7. NRSV, NAB, and NIV all use forms of the verb 'live'; KJV rightly uses "walked."

The first three verses (2:1-3, with 2:5a) describe the former situation of the author and recipients, and the status of all nonbelievers, as one of death (2:1, 5) and disobedience (2:2). Although the text does not portray sin (singular) as a power to which humans are enslaved (as does Romans), it does suggest that humans not in Christ are in a state of obeisance and even slavery to the "flesh" (2:3) and especially to the "ruler of the power of the air" (2:2). This is likely a reference to the devil (4:27; 6:11; cf. "god of this world/age" in 2 Cor. 4:4) and to the very cosmic forces under his command over which Christ is now Lord but which still exercise power during this "present darkness" (6:12). Moreover, the results of this condition are the same as those in Romans and elsewhere: not only death and disobedience, but also divine wrath (2:3).[8]

In great contrast to this tragic human condition comes the life-giving grace of God: "But God . . ." (2:4)! This God of abundant mercy and love (as already introduced in 1:3-14) performed one mighty act: he coenlivened, coraised, and coexalted us with Christ (2:5-6), Paul exclaims. That is to say, God brought us from death to life (cf. Rom. 6:4, 11, 13). Lest this image be thought to avoid the cross, the previous usage of the term "redemption" as "the forgiveness of our trespasses" (1:7) indicates that this experience of God's love and of resurrection is part of an entire experience of forgiveness for the trespasses and sins that necessitated a resurrection from death in the first place (2:1). Moreover, the new life to which believers are raised is one of conformity to the love of God expressed in Christ's death (5:1-2, 21-33). Though the stress is on resurrection, it is still a resurrection requiring a kind of death. Being seated with Christ "in the heavenly places" simply means being "in Christ Jesus" (2:6), i.e., in his church, where God's love and power are experienced. The whole nature of this experience is theocentric — to show forth forever the luxuriousness of God's grace (2:7).

It is indeed by this grace that Paul and his audience "have been saved" (2:5, 8). Although spoken in the past tense, this salvation, as we have seen, still has a future dimension. Faith is the means ("through faith") by which human beings appropriate this salvation (2:8). "This" — the entire experience of salvation understood as redemption, resurrection, and new life — is completely a divine gift, not merited, earned, or accomplished in any way whatsoever by human effort and deeds, as 2:8-9 emphasizes. (The word "this" is a neuter pronoun in Greek, referring to the whole matter being discussed and not, for instance, to "faith," which is a feminine noun and cannot be the referent of the neuter "this.")

This text does not in the least minimize the role of "works" or deeds. In fact, it stresses them in an extraordinary way, for in verse 10 Paul says the very *purpose* of this resurrection experience, or (new) creation in Christ, is to walk in (NAB, "live in"; NIV, "do") good works, which God has prepared (cf. 2 Cor. 5:15; Rom. 6)

---

8. Cf. Eph. 5:6; Col. 3:6; Rom. 1:32; 2:5-16; 5:9; 6:16-23; 1 Thess. 1:10; 2:16; 5:9.

"to be our way of life" (NRSV). Even the forgiveness of sins is not the (sole) purpose of Christ's death and our resurrection; forgiveness without new life is no redemption! The question, then, is not *whether* deeds matter, but rather *how* — not as the *cause* of salvation but as its *purpose* and proper *result*. As Galatians 5:6 also suggests, what is absolutely essential is faith expressing itself in deeds of love (cf. Eph. 4:1-3; 4:31–5:2). A Jewish covenant theologian could have it no other way.

THE UNITY OF JEW AND GENTILE IN CHRIST (2:11-22)

In this passage Paul takes the experience described in 2:1-10 and puts it into a larger context — God's unification of Gentiles and Jews in Christ. The structure of this passage is parallel to that of 2:1-10, as the following chart shows:

Parallels between Ephesians 2:1-10 and 2:11-22

	2:1-10	2:11-22
Gentile predicament	2:1-3 — You were dead . . . children of wrath. . . .	2:11-12 — You Gentiles by birth . . . were at that time without Christ . . . aliens from the commonwealth of Israel. . . .
God's intervention	2:4-9 — But God . . . made us alive . . . by grace you have been saved through faith.	2:13-18 — But now in Christ Jesus you . . . have been brought near by the blood of Christ . . . he has made both groups into one.
New creation	2:10 — created in Christ Jesus for good works.	2:19-22 — So then you are no longer strangers and aliens, but . . . members of the household of God . . . a dwelling place for God. (cf. "one new humanity," 2:15)

The first two verses (2:11-12) remind the letter's recipients that as Gentiles outside of Christ, the Jewish Messiah, they were previously "the uncircumcision," 'not Israel,' so to speak (cf. Hos. 1:9, 10; 2:23). None of the special benefits of Israel, God's vehicle for the salvation of the world, were theirs: aliens to Israel and strangers to all God's covenants, they were without hope and, despite their gods, without (the one true) God.

God's grace has brought those who were distant from God and Israel into a relationship with God and into membership in God's "new humanity" (2:15). Though rooted in Israel's story, this divine intervention does not involve a covenant based on physical circumcision; Gentiles are not becoming Jews. Rather, God in Christ has made peace, creating one group of two (2:14). This divine act

Ephesus: Arches like this one, together with temples and other
monuments, were dedicated to Augustus, as the creator
of peace and unity throughout the empire.

of peacemaking and reconciliation took place on the cross (2:13). Christ is "our"
peace, because his death eliminated the two items that separated Jews and
Gentiles: the "dividing wall" (2:14), a reference to the wall in the Jerusalem temple separating the Court of the Gentiles from the main temple precincts where
Jews could freely go; and "the law with its commandments and ordinances"
(2:15). This is not so much a criticism of the Law in itself, as if it had no value,
but of its divisive functions, symbolized by circumcision (2:11). In the new hu-

manity, the text implies, both Gentiles and Jews in Christ have equal access to God and live in a covenantal relationship in which all perform the same kinds of good deeds in love that God has prepared for them.

The cross of Christ, then, is the means of a two-dimensional peace: vertically it effects reconciliation with God for each group (2:16; cf. 2 Cor. 5:19), and horizontally it eradicates the hostility between the two groups of people into which the world might be divided, Jews and Gentiles (2:14, 16). As Paul sees the human condition, all people are in need of this reconciliation, even the Jews like himself who had "the covenants of promise" mentioned in 2:12 (2:17; cf. Rom. 1:18–3:20). The outcome is access to the triune God — in Christ, through the Spirit, to the Father (2:18).

The corporate result of this reconciling grace has already been mentioned in several ways; in 2:19 Paul returns to the conditions mentioned in 2:11-12 and says they have been reversed. Gentiles are no longer strangers and aliens but members of God's commonwealth, God's household. This is a household built on the apostles and prophets, the latter being perhaps Israel's prophets, but more likely the churches' (cf. 3:5; 4:11), with Christ as the cornerstone (NRSV, NIV) or (less likely) keystone (NRSV mg.; cf. NAB, "capstone"). (The shift in image from 1 Corinthians 3:11, where Christ is the only foundation, is frequently overexaggerated. Christ's role is not here lessened but given added prominence as the singular stone that defines the entire structure.) Continuing the image of a building, 2:21-22 depicts the church as God's temple, a work in progress by and for, once again, the triune God — in Christ, by the Spirit (cf. NIV, NAB, and NRSV mg. versus NRSV, "spiritually"), for God.

Contrary to the comments made by many interpreters, this passage does not necessarily reflect a time in which tensions between Gentile and Jewish believers (such as those seen in Galatians) have been resolved and there is one big happy Jewish and Christian church. Though it is true that this new humanity is presented in the indicative mood here as a present reality, that is precisely the kind of reality that requires special gratitude by Gentiles (so also Rom. 9–11) and ongoing efforts toward the realization of unity by all (Eph. 4–6 and most of the Pauline letters). The reality depicted in Ephesians is not substantively different from — and carries no less of a corollary exhortation than — the assertion in Galatians 3:28 that there is "no longer Jew or Greek."

PAUL'S ROLE IN GOD'S PLAN (3:1-13)

After presenting the reconciling, unifying plan of God, Paul now moves on to inform (or remind) the recipients of his letter about his own role in this plan. The passage appears to be based in part on Colossians 1:23b-28.

In 3:1-6 Paul's identity is established: prisoner for (or "of") Jesus for the sake of "you" Gentiles (3:1), graced (3:2, meaning 'called to be an apostle' — one of those mentioned in 3:5 — again for "you" [Gentiles]), and recipient of revelation.[9] This status Paul had already summarized "in a few words" (3:3) in the first line of the letter, and the mystery (3:3, 4, 5; cf. 1:9) has been the subject of his prayer and discourse thus far. As noted in the introductory remarks, the lack of familiarity between writer and recipients seen in 3:2 has been explained in several different ways.

Whether or not Paul wrote these verses, they concur with the undisputed letters but bear their own peculiar mark in the context of this letter: the repeated use of the word "mystery" — meaning 'unveiled secret' — to describe God's plan. This plan, once unknown to humans, has been revealed to apostles and prophets like Paul (3:5). In 3:6 a summary statement of this plan — the inclusion of the Gentiles — uses three words, all beginning with the prefix 'co-' (Gk. *syn-*) and all echoing the first two chapters, to stress the equality of Gentiles and Jews in Christ: "fellow heirs, members of the same body . . . sharers in the promise."

The subsequent verses continue to identify Paul and his mission, but actually function primarily once again to summarize and stress the content of the divine grace and wisdom. Paul is now presented as one who has become a "servant" (3:7, *diakonos*; cf. Col. 1:7, 23, 25; 1 Cor. 3:5; 2 Cor. 3:6; 11:23) of the gospel, which was an act of divine grace and power (3:7) even though Paul, as "the very least of all the saints," was unworthy (3:8; cf. 1 Cor. 15:8-10). Reiterating the content of the gospel, the following verses emphasize God's boundless grace in Christ (3:8); the plan as the activity of God the creator and thus, implicitly, recreator (3:9); the church as the vehicle of the proclamation of the gospel (God's "wisdom"), even to the cosmic powers (3:10); and the eternal and christocentric character of this plan (3:11).

A transitional phrase highlighting the confidence before God that believers now have in Christ (3:12) leads to the mention of Paul's prayer that the letter's recipients not be discouraged at his sufferings "for you" (3:13; cf. 3:1). They are the fruit of his God-ordained mission to the Gentiles, and therefore not something to be ashamed of but to honor and glory in.

PAUL'S SECOND PRAYER FOR HIS READERS (3:14-21)

The mention of prayer at the end of 3:13 leads to a longer prayer text in 3:14-21, the second such intercessory prayer in Ephesians 1–3 (cf. 1:15-23). Paul addresses

9. Cf. esp. Rom. 1:1-6; 1 Cor. 9:1-2; Gal. 1:1, 11-24.

his prayer (3:14) to the Father *(pater)* as the one source (and thus, implicitly, unifier) of every human family and nation *(familia, patria)*. Concluding the intercession is a doxology (3:20-21).

The intercessory prayer Paul offers grows out of, and is an integral part of, his ministry set forth in 3:1-13 ("for this reason," 3:14). Once again it is one long, complex sentence in Greek. The specific intercessions appear to be four in number, presented in two pairs, though they are closely interrelated:

- Spirit-empowered strength in the inner being (3:16)
- the indwelling of Christ through faith and love (3:17)
- power to comprehend the extent of Christ's love (3:18)
- knowledge of Christ's love (3:19)

The first request is for God to grant an inner power, through the Spirit, from the abundant resources of divine glory, an echo of the request made in 1:19. The second request is parallel: that Christ may dwell in the recipients' hearts. As elsewhere in Paul (cf. esp. Rom. 8:1-11), there is in Ephesians an interchangeability concerning the believers' existential relationship with Christ and with the Spirit. The Spirit is in them (3:16, the inner being), and they are in the Spirit (6:18); they are also in Christ (1:4, 7, etc.), and he in them (3:17). The indwelling of Christ mentioned here occurs through faith and in conjunction with love, an echo of the description of the recipients in 1:15. As always, Paul refuses to separate faith and love, and especially in thinking of the indwelling Christ (cf. Gal. 2:20 NRSV mg.; 5:6): "It is no longer I who live, but it is Christ who lives in me. And the life I now live in the flesh I live by the faith of the Son of God, who loved me and gave himself for me."

The third and fourth requests are also closely connected: to "comprehend" or grasp *(katalabesthai)* the extent of, and to know *(gnōnai)*, Christ's love (3:18-19). (Paul uses the same two verbs in Philippians 3:10, 12 to describe knowing Christ and his power and apprehending the goal of conformity to Christ, for which Christ has apprehended him.) This love is truly beyond measurement (3:18) and knowledge (3:19), yet it is the essence of life in Christ. Knowing Christ's power and fullness (3:19; cf. 1:23) is possible only by knowing and sharing his self-sacrificial love (5:1).

These requests for power and love give rise to a trinitarian doxology (3:20-21), praising the God who, through "the power at work within us" (the Spirit in the inner person, the indwelling Christ), exceeds our imaginations and thus deserves eternal praise in the church — that is (rather than "and"), in Christ Jesus.

Summary of Ephesians 1–3

In the first three chapters of Ephesians the following major themes develop:
- God has an eternal plan, a mystery, which has now been revealed: to gather up all things in Christ.
- This plan springs from the depths of God's bounteous grace and has begun to unfold in the death of Christ, through which God reconciles people to himself and to one another — as seen especially in the uniting of Jews and Gentiles in the church as the new humanity.
- God has raised and exalted Christ, seating him above all cosmic powers and making him the head of his body, the church.
- In Christ, Jews and Gentiles alike have every possible spiritual blessing, being raised with Christ, becoming members of God's household, and growing together as a holy temple characterized by covenant faith and good deeds of love.
- Paul's particular mission is to bring this mystery, this gospel, to the Gentiles, and to suffer and pray on their behalf.

4:1–6:20. LIFE IN CHRIST: WORTHY OF GOD'S CALLING, EMPOWERED BY THE SPIRIT

The first half of Ephesians has concluded with a beautiful prayer and an inspiring doxology, each reflecting the incredible "mystery" of God's plan in Christ. Although there have been hints along the way about the meaning of this great plan for the daily life of believers — good deeds, love, unity, peace — this appropriate lifestyle has not been discussed in any detail. Now, however, the logical consequences — "therefore" (4:1) — of this gospel of the crucified, exalted, cosmic Christ must be explored. This is summarized in the *propositio* of the last three chapters (4:1-3): to "walk"[10] worthily of this great calling in unity and love. In fact, this is likely the thesis of the entire letter.

THE UNITY AND MATURITY OF THE CHURCH (4:1-16)

The first part of chapter 4 carefully links the exhortations that follow in chapters 4 through 6 with the liturgical celebrations and theological reflections that

---

10. KJV, as in chap. 2 and in both chap. 4 and chap. 5; NRSV, "lead a life" (NAB, NIV similarly).

have characterized the first half of the letter. Special emphasis is then placed on the unity of the church, and especially on the role of diverse gifts in contributing to its unity and maturity.

As noted above, the first three verses introduce not only this passage but the remainder of the letter, and function as a summary of the message of the entire document. Paul writes as a prisoner "in the Lord" — still part of the one body of Christ (4:1). His counsel from prison can be condensed into one phrase: 'to walk worthy of your calling' (4:1).[11] Three key words stand out in this 'walk': "love" (4:2), "unity" (4:3), and "peace" (4:3). Several aspects of what love entails are listed in verse 2, and these will be developed beginning at 4:25. For now the focus is on mature unity. But even in this passage, love is the key to the exercise of gifts that will produce growth toward that end (4:15, 16). This passage is therefore rightly compared not only with 1 Corinthians 12 (one body with diverse members and gifts), but to all of 1 Corinthians 12–14, in which gifts must be exercised in love for the edification of the body of Christ.

Before speaking of gifts, which will be the means to unity, Paul provides the theological basis of this unity in the so-called seven unities of the church (4:4-6). These unities, which have all been previously mentioned in the letter, are:

- one *body* — the body of Christ, the church (1:23; 3:6; 4:12, 16; 5:23, 30)
- one *Spirit* — the power at work within the church (1:20; 3:16, 20)
- one *hope* — the inheritance and redemption promised to those in Christ (1:11-14, 18; 3:6)
- one *Lord* — Jesus, sovereign in the cosmos and in the church (2:20-22; there are twenty-three occurrences of "Lord" in Ephesians)
- one *faith* — the mystery of the gospel of salvation, now revealed (1:13)
- one *baptism* — though not previously mentioned explicitly, the means of incorporation into the church (rather than circumcision) for Jews and Gentiles, in which those dead in sins are raised to new life (2:1-6, 11)
- one *God and Father of all* — the God and Father of Jesus and of all believers (1:2, 3, 17; 2:18; 3:14; 5:20; 6:23)

This sevenfold theological and experiential basis of unity provides the framework within which gifts and ministry are to be lovingly exercised for the unifying and maturing of the one body of Christ (4:7-16). As in 1 Corinthians 12, diversity in gifts is also essential to unity in Ephesians. Paul first discusses the source of the gifts given to the church (4:7-10). Then, in another long, complex Greek sentence (4:11-16), he presents some types of gifts (4:11) and elaborates on their purpose (4:12-16).

11. Cf. Col. 1:10; Phil. 1:27; 1 Thess. 2:12.

Like 1 Corinthians (12:7, 11), Ephesians affirms that *all* believers (4:7) have been granted a gift that issues from "grace." Unlike 1 Corinthians, however, Ephesians attributes this benevolent giving to Christ himself (4:7-11; cf. God and the Spirit, 1 Cor. 12:11, 18, 28). No doubt this shift is due to the centrality in this letter of Christ's exaltation (1:20-22) and his position as "head" of the church (4:15; 5:23). This is documented here by an exegesis of Psalm 68:18, in which the enemies of the Lord acknowledge God's sovereignty by giving — not receiving — gifts. However, in light of God's gracious reconciliation of the "children of wrath" (2:3) in Christ, and because God has made Christ "head over all things for the church" (1:22), the Lord is now Christ, and he is not the receiver but the giver of gifts (4:8). A parenthetical explanation of Christ's 'ascension' — the psalm implies also a descent either to or, less likely, beneath the earth (cf. 1 Pet. 3:19) — serves primarily to repeat the letter's stress on Christ's cosmic sovereignty (1:10, 22).

The gifts listed (4:11) are either four or five in number and are clearly meant to be representative, not exhaustive, with emphasis on those gifted for preaching and teaching the gospel. Apostles and prophets have already been mentioned as the church's foundation (2:20) and as the recipients of the divine mystery (3:5). Evangelists, pastors (lit. 'shepherds'), and teachers (or perhaps, grammatically, one office, 'shepherd-teachers') would appear to be leaders who are the indirect recipients of revelation, in contrast to someone like Paul.

All these individuals have one primary task: it is not to do all the church's ministry, but rather to "equip the saints" — all members of the community — for the work of ministry, for the edification of Christ's body (4:12). Ministry, then, is the work of all believers; leaders are equippers. A definition of 'edification' is then provided: unity in faith and knowledge of the Son of God, which is Christlike maturity (4:13). In view of 3:17-19 it is tempting to connect the knowledge of Christ mentioned here with love, which would mean that Paul measures maturity, not surprisingly, in terms of faith and love.

But maturity in Christ, the text suggests, is not merely about virtue but also about knowledge, about doctrine and theology. Verse 14 depicts a state of believing existence that is the opposite of maturity; the imaginative imagery of being blown to and fro in the wind is a warning against doctrine inspired by deceit. This may be a generic word of caution, or it may envisage a particular group that is, in Paul's eyes, deliberately misleading people. In either case, the antidote, and the way to maturity, is "speaking the truth in love" (4:15), a phrase pregnant in meaning that communicates, in Ephesians, one of the fundamental obligations of believers to one another (cf. also 4:25). For this letter, of course, the truth is "in Jesus," as 4:21 will say. Truth is ultimately the revelation of God's eternal plan in Christ, as this letter has repeatedly emphasized.

Maturity in Christ, then, is a comprehensive ("in every way," 4:15), communal experience. Returning to the body imagery, the text concludes with the image of an immature body developing into the maturity already possessed by its head (Christ), as each part works together for the edification of the entire body (4:16; cf. 1 Cor. 12:14-26). All such activity can be summarized in one word: "love" (the last word of 4:16 in the Greek text), for as 1 Corinthians puts it, "love builds up" (8:1; cf. 14:4-5) and is the chief mark of believers' maturity (13:11).

LEARNING AND LIVING CHRIST (4:17–6:9)

Much of the remainder of Ephesians is a series of exhortations on various aspects of the process of maturing in Christ. Two themes in 4:17–5:21 deserve special mention: the note of contrast between believers' former and present lives, and the emphasis on speech. The following section, the so-called household table (5:22–6:9), must be seen, on grammatical and contextual grounds, as a subset of the more general exhortations.

No Longer Like the Gentiles (4:17-24)

Conversion, by definition, means change — change in belief, belonging, and behavior. It is sometimes called secondary socialization, or resocialization. One of the persistent themes in the entire New Testament is the need for believers to be different from their old selves and from their nonbelieving neighbors. (This particular passage has echoes of similar material especially in Colossians and Romans, all of which may point to common patterns of early Christian instruction.) In 4:17 Paul offers an oath of sorts about the necessity of this transformation: "you must no longer live ['walk'] as the Gentiles live ['walk']" (cf. 1 Thess. 4:5; 5:4-8). A standard pattern of 'old . . . new' (4:22; cf. Col. 3:9-10; Rom. 6:6) and 'once . . . now' (4:22; cf. 5:8; Col. 3:7-8) likely developed before Paul and may well have been used in the context of baptism as well as ongoing community formation.

The description of how nonbelieving Gentiles 'walk' (4:17; "live" in most translations) is certainly not attractive (4:17-20). It contains echoes of Romans 1:18-32, focusing on the Gentiles' darkened, futile, ignorant minds (4:18-19; cf. Rom. 1:21-22, 28); their hard hearts (4:19; cf. Rom. 1:24; 2:5); and their immorality (4:19; cf. Rom. 1:24-32).[12] Special emphasis is placed on sexual immorality

---

12. Interestingly, Ephesians clarifies the thrice-repeated phrase in Rom. 1, "God gave them up" (1:24, 26, 28), putting the blame squarely at the feet of the Gentiles who "abandoned themselves" to immorality (4:19).

(4:19), which was constantly a concern in the early churches (cf., e.g., 1 Cor. 6:12-20; 1 Thess. 4:3-5).

This is not, of course, how the letter's recipients "learned Christ" (4:20). In a feint of disbelief (discernible only in the Greek text) that actually functions to express his certainty about what they have learned, Paul raises the irrational possibility that they have heard and learned otherwise (4:21). But of course, they have learned Christ as the transformer of human life. They were taught to put away the old life, the old self, and to put on the new self *(kainon anthrōpon),* like a change of clothing from old to brand-new (4:22, 24; cf. Rom. 13:12, 14), including a renewed mind (4:23; cf. Rom. 12:1-2). This is a (re-)creation in God's image (4:24), part and parcel of being the "new humanity" *(kainon anthrōpon,* 2:15; cf. Col. 3:9-10; 2 Cor. 5:17). It is the complete renewal of mind and life.

Loving Speech and Action (4:25–5:2)

Having made the case for the necessity of moral transformation, Paul moves on to describe the new life in Christ, doing so here and in the next passage by way of contrast, 'don't do this, but do this' (antithesis), corresponding to the old self/new self and nonbelievers/believers pattern enunciated in the previous verses. As noted earlier, there is a remarkable emphasis on speech in these verses, which is clearly seen as an occasion to impart either grace or its opposite. Speech is therefore seen as an act, as much as stealing is an act, and there are inappropriate acts to avoid and appropriate ones to practice. The general warrant for doing these appropriate acts is, of course, being a new person in Christ. But also connected to each prohibition and admonition is a reason. The following chart summarizes these three aspects of this passage:

Moral Transformation in Ephesians 4:25–5:2

Text	Prohibition	Admonition	Rationale
4:25	Falsehood	Speaking the truth (cf. 4:15, adding "in love")	Members of one another (e.g., as one body; cf. 4:4, 16)
4:26-27	Prolonged anger	Quick resolution of conflict and anger	Prevent opportunities for the devil
4:28	Stealing (directed at thieves)	Manual labor	Honesty; assist the needy

Text	Prohibition	Admonition	Rationale
4:29-30	Evil talk	Edifying talk	Impart grace to others; avoid grieving the Holy Spirit
4:31-32	Bitterness, wrath, anger, wrangling, slander, malice	Kindness, tenderheartedness, forgiveness	The experience of forgiveness by God in Christ

The final verses of this passage (5:1-2) continue the notion of the imitation of God in Christ begun at the end of 4:32. Introduced by "therefore," they are probably to be understood not merely as part of the alternative to wrath and anger but more broadly as a summary of the kind of love that undergirds all the appropriate behaviors listed in this passage. In fact, the admonition to "live [lit. 'walk'] in love" (5:2) adequately summarizes the ethic of Ephesians and of Paul generally. It means to be imitators of God, to love as a result of being loved by God, and to offer oneself to others sacrificially as Christ himself did (cf. Gal. 2:20). This is an ethic for all believers, at all times. It will reappear in 5:25.

Countercultural Sexual Purity (5:3-14)

The reference to sexual immorality in 4:19 now reappears and is addressed at some length, incorporating issues of thought, speech, and action. The discussion is set, once again, in the context of believers' distinctiveness vis-à-vis their nonbelieving peers.

The passage begins with a ban on speech about sexual immorality, and on speech laced with inappropriate sexual content (5:3-4). Prohibited first of all is talk about sexual immorality generally (so NIV and NAB, translating *porneia;* NRSV, "fornication"), impurity, and lust ("greed" in NRSV, NIV, and NAB, like NRSV's "greedy" in 4:19 and 5:5, is too general in context). To discuss such things is to behave like nonbelievers, not like people who are different ("saints"). To engage in levity about sex or vulgarity is to dishonor God the creator, and should be replaced with thanksgiving (5:4). The seriousness of this matter is presented next (5:5), presumably on the assumption that speech itself is an act that puts the speaker/doer at risk for his or her inheritance in Christ and that may lead to other acts (cf. 1 Cor. 5:9-11; 6:9-11). These kinds of sexually immoral acts — which amount to idolatry (5:5), as Jews were prone to say — are characteristic of pagans, not saints.

It seems to have been a temptation for the early Christians (and they are certainly not alone) to return to their earlier habits in this area of sexual thought, speech, and behavior. The text warns against "empty words" — spoken by whom? — that might entice the letter's recipients into laxity in this area (5:6). But God's wrath is not to be taken lightly (5:6), and the need for avoiding the blatantly sexually immoral is stressed (5:7), as it is in 1 Corinthians 5:11, where it specifies the avoidance of immoral *believers*. It is likely, then, that the scenario is similar here: self-styled believers trying to convince other believers that pagan sexual practices do not harm their status in Christ.

This would lend especially weighty force to the theme of 'then and now' that reappears in 5:8-14 (cf. 4:17-24). It is a reminder that the past is past, that to live like pagans is to live anachronistically, to live outside Christ. The inappropriateness of this kind of life is highlighted by the apocalyptic language of darkness and light (5:8-14; cf. 1 Thess. 5:4-11). Believers are to walk (NRSV, etc., "live") as what they are, children of light (5:8), doing what is good, seeking the Lord's will (5:9-10). Rather than participating in shameful "works of darkness," they are (as light) to expose such works (5:11-13) — not to point fingers at people, but to name immoral activities for what they truly are.

This section concludes with a quotation, perhaps from a baptismal liturgy or a hymn (5:14b). It summarizes the point of the entire passage and of 4:17-24 as well. Christ, imaged here as a light (cf. John 8:12; 9:5; etc.), has shone on those who are now believers. Through faith in the gospel, and in baptism, they have awakened from their sleep of death that was the fruit of their sins and trespasses, sexual and otherwise (cf. 2:2, 5). Those who have been thus raised from the dead have encountered the light that is Christ (5:13) and been transformed into light (5:14). Their task now is to live as light (cf. Matt. 5:14; Phil. 2:15) and to bear witness against evil and to Christ the Light.

Community Life (5:15–6:9)

The general exhortations to the letter's recipients are now drawing to a conclusion, and summary words are offered about the community's life with God, which are then applied to relationships within the household of believers.

Community and Trinity (5:15-21)

The notion of walking (5:15; NRSV, etc., "live") makes its final appearance, together with the either-or theme, now in terms of wisdom and foolishness (5:15, 17). Walking carefully or wisely is defined in apocalyptic terms as having an awareness of the evil character of the present time and, therefore, making good use of it (5:16) — that is, understanding and doing the Lord's will (5:17; cf. 5:10).

(The actual term for using the time — *exagorazomenoi ton kairon* — has to do with 'buying' or perhaps 'redeeming' it, meaning "making the most of every [NAB "the"] opportunity," as NIV puts it.)

The theme of being not foolish but wise continues with the admonition to be filled with the Spirit instead of getting drunk with wine (5:18). This metaphor and contrast seem to come out of the blue. Although there may be some connection to the Acts story of the effects of the Spirit being mistaken for drunkenness (Acts 2:1-13), it is more likely that the foolishness of drunkenness is linked to pagans' "shameful" nocturnal activities that were just mentioned (5:12).

In any case, being filled with the Spirit is presented both as an admonition for all believers and as a continual rather than a once-for-all experience. What being "filled with the Spirit" means in this context is depicted very clearly in a series of participial ('-ing') phrases in 5:19-21 that elucidate the main verb, "be filled," 5:18. These are as follows, translated rather woodenly:

- *speaking* to one another with psalms, hymns, and spiritual songs (5:19a)
- *singing* and *making music* to the Lord in your hearts (5:19b)
- *giving thanks* at all times and for all things in the name of our Lord Jesus Christ to God the Father (5:20)
- *being subject* to one another in the fear/reverence of Christ (5:21)[13]

These four parts of the text form a kind of *abb'a'* (chiastic) parallel pattern, with a focus on relations to one another *(a, a')* and with God *(b, b')*. Though it is difficult to know for certain whether the first two items (5:19) are meant to be distinguished, they seem different, the first referring to music intended to inspire and edify others, the second to music offered as praise to God. Perpetual thanksgiving is a hallmark of Pauline spirituality (5:4; cf. Col. 3:17; 1 Thess. 5:16-18). Being subject (NAB, "subordinate") to one another (NIV, "submit to one another") is not clearly defined, but is reminiscent of passages such as Philippians 2:1-4: "Let each of you look not to your own interests, but to the interests of others" (v. 4). It may be intended here to summarize 4:25–5:2, which, like Philippians 2:1-4, links concern with others to imitation of the Lord.

Such mutual submission is done as a gesture of honor to Christ, who gave himself in love (5:2, 25). It is a general requirement for any and all who are in Christ, and it is proof of the Spirit's fullness in the believer's and community's

---

13. Unfortunately, few translations reveal the participial form of the verb in 5:21 (e.g., 'being subject'), which is crucial to seeing both the inseparability of the various aspects of the fullness of the Spirit noted here and the duties of husbands and wives as a subset of the general admonition to mutual submission in the community. The NRSV, NIV, and NAB all render 5:21 as a new sentence with an independent imperative verb, though the KJV rightly has "submitting."

life. Life in the Spirit — life with God the Father, life in Christ — requires mutual edification (5:19a) and cruciform love (5:21) as much as it does praise (5:19b) and thanksgiving to God (5:20). This is the community that speaks the truth, and builds itself up, in love (4:15-16), in communion with the triune God of love.

Life in Christ in the Household (5:22–6:9)

Because this section of Ephesians, the 'household table' or 'household code,' is so important and yet so controversial, it is absolutely crucial that the remarks about 5:18-21 be kept in mind from the outset. The household code is not an attempt to impose pagan, patriarchal values onto an otherwise Christian value system. Rather, it is an attempt to apply the notion of mutual submission, of mutual cruciformity or Christlike love, to an inherently patriarchal structure. The result, though perhaps not sufficiently radical for some, is nonetheless revolutionary, challenging the assumptions that every adult Gentile male would have brought to family life.

The household table (drawing on Col. 3:18–4:1 or a common antecedent) divides into three sections, but in each section one figure reappears — the male head of household. He is the husband (5:22-33), the father (6:1-4), and the master (6:5-8). By law and custom the ancient male owned all the members of his household as pieces of his personal property. This did not mean that no men had respect for their wives, children, or slaves, but it did place them in a fundamental position of power, with all kinds of rights but few enforceable duties vis-à-vis their household members. In Christ, however, says Ephesians, that has changed dramatically.

The first relationship to be affected is husband and wife. It is often argued that the woman is given an inferior place: she alone is told to "be subject" (vv. 22, 24), and in fact subject "in everything" (v. 24). Moreover, the husband is explicitly called "the head of the wife just as Christ is the head of the church" (v. 23), and the wife (at least implicitly) his body (vv. 28-29), suggesting that the husband alone has the Christlike role of head and savior. Although on first reading this interpretation has some obvious points in its favor, it must be rejected.

The principal verbs used to describe marital responsibility — "be subject" (vv. 22, 24), "respect" (v. 33), and "love [as Christ loved the church by giving himself up for her]" (vv. 25, 28, 33) — are drawn directly from the general, fundamental injunctions to all believers stated in 5:2 (sacrificial love) and 5:21 (mutual subjection, respect). The wife's subjection to her husband is simply one aspect of her general obligation to all believers (5:21). In fact, the grammar of the text requires us to see things this way, for there is no verb in the Greek text of

5:22; it is supplied in English translation, but in reality the whole of 5:22 is, both linguistically and materially, a continuation of the thought expressed in 5:21. Subjection to one's husband is a subset of the general community practice of subjection. *The woman's husband therefore has the same obligation (subjection) to her, inasmuch as they are members of the believing community.*

Requiring the man to show his wife Christlike love (5:25) is, therefore, another way of saying that he should be subject to her — absolutely self-sacrificial. In spite of the husband's being called "the head of the wife," he is not being granted any kind of cosmic power over his wife. The only admonition he receives is to be self-giving and self-sacrificing; to interpret this as a 'power trip' would be to misread everything Ephesians says about believers being called to love and gentleness. Furthermore, inasmuch as the wife is a believer, she too shares the common obligation of believers to love others, including her spouse, with Christlike love.

Part of the difficulty in reading this passage is that, by his own admission, Paul is blending ethics and Christology (5:32). The talk of a husband sanctifying, cleansing, presenting his wife (5:26-27), and of loving his wife like his own body (5:28-29) must not be overemphasized. Its primary focus is Christ and the church; the marriage parallel is not perfect. Taken metaphorically, the language is intended to show the need for mutual care because of the unity of persons that marriage creates (cf. esp. v. 31, quoting Gen. 2:24). Neither the language of 'submitting to one's head' nor 'caring for one's own body' expresses patriarchal or patronizing values; rather, such language undermines those values.

The text therefore assumes, but also subverts, the hierarchy of the husband-wife relationship through the image of "head" and "body." In Paul's view this image primarily conveys, not the husband's authority and the wife's submission, but the intimate unity between the head and the body that makes them one flesh (5:31, quoting Gen. 2:24). Thus the head's duty is not to govern but to nourish, and to do so sacrificially. The radical image of headship here is of a crucified Lord — power in weakness and self-giving love, which can be reciprocated.

Mutual submission, and therefore respect and love, also exists in the father-child relationship (6:1-4). The biblical expectation of children's obedience is reaffirmed, and its corollary promise noted (6:1-3). At the same time, fathers are to exercise their paternal obligations of discipline and instruction in ways that are consistent with "the Lord" (6:4b) — that is, with the kind love of God in Christ. Otherwise they will treat their children harshly, as they used to do, and thereby provoke them to anger (6:4a).

Similarly, there exists mutuality in the master-slave relationship (6:5-9). The slaves' obedience to the master is to be done as service to Christ and God, not as to humans (6:6-7). This is predicated not on the pagan principle of patriarchy, but on the biblical principles of goodness and impartiality (6:8-9). The Lord expects his people always to do good, judging and rewarding slave and free alike on precisely the same terms (6:8).

For this reason, almost incredibly, the text requires masters to "do the same [things] to them" (6:9). While a master cannot perhaps "obey" his slaves, he can — and, as a believer, now must! — treat them with respect and even love. Restraint from threats is only the tip of the iceberg. To do "the same" means that the master is called to treat his slaves like Christ, seeking God's will and Christ's pleasure in his treatment of slaves. This may not be a summons to dismantle slavery, but it is a radical restructuring of relationships within that system.

SPIRITUAL WARFARE (6:10-20)

The letter's final admonition is a summons to participate with divinely provided power, and with prayer, in a battle. The first part of the admonition is the creative use of an image — that of a soldier and his armor (6:11-17). The second part is a fourfold request for prayer, especially for the advance of the gospel. In summary, the text calls believers to "be strong" and to "pray."

The strength of which the text speaks is not normal human strength but that received in and from the Lord; it is divine "armor," and it must be donned by all believers, not a select few (6:10-11). The battle to be fought is an apocalyptic one, not against humans but against the devil and the cosmic powers of evil (6:11-12). The struggle is present already, but it may also be on the increase as the "evil day" — perhaps a final cosmic battle — draws nearer (6:13). Since Ephesians presents Christ as Lord over all the powers in the universe (1:20-22), it seems likely that here Paul envisages an ongoing battle that will culminate in the future in the final submission of all God's enemies, an integral part of the 'gathering up' of all things in Christ (1:10). Those who participate in the warfare must not allow themselves to be defeated but must "stand firm" (6:13). In light of both the description of the armor for battle and the requests for prayer, it is clear that the warfare being described here is the advance of the gospel.

The elements of the believers' armor are the following:

- belt = the truth (6:14)
- breastplate = righteousness (6:14)
- shoes = preparedness to proclaim the gospel of peace (6:15)
- shield = faith (6:16)
- helmet = salvation (6:17)
- sword = word of God (6:17)

Ephesus: **Relief of a gladiator, whose armor was like a soldier's**

The text is a deliberate echo of several biblical texts in which various divine qualities are portrayed as God's own armor or as that of God's king or servant.[14] Thus to take up this armor is to take up God's cause and do battle in God's cosmic campaign to spread righteousness throughout the world. It is probably beyond the author's intent for readers to press the details of this military image. The realities to which the various parts of the armor refer are the realities of the gospel as preached by Paul and experienced among the letter's re-

14. E.g., Isa. 11:5; 49:2; 52:7; 59:15b-17; Wisd. of Sol. 5:17-20.

cipients, according to Ephesians. The only new element not previously encountered in the letter is the Spirit's sword, "the word of God," which is most likely the gospel, not the Scriptures. This gospel is the force, or the weapon, of the Spirit against any and all powers that are opposed to God and humanity.

For this reason, then, the description of the believers' warfare with the gospel in hand leads to the requests for prayer in 6:18-20. These requests move from the general to the specific — pray always (6:18a), pray for all the saints (6:18b), pray for me (Paul — twice, 6:19-20). Paul's specific prayer for himself as an "ambassador in chains" is that he will speak with boldness. No doubt, in view of 6:10-17, he hopes others will join the battle and declare the "mystery of the gospel" (6:19) with equal or greater boldness.

6:21-24. FINAL MATTERS

Paul begins the conclusion of the letter with a word about its bearer, Tychicus, whom Paul commends as a brother and faithful minister, and whom he sends to inform and encourage the recipients about his situation in prison (6:21-22). He then offers words of peace, love, faith, and grace to all, adding a phrase peculiar to Ephesians, "with all who have an undying love" for Christ (6:24).

Summary of Ephesians 4–6

Ephesians 4–6 provides the Pauline imperatives that flow logically from the mystery of the gospel outlined in the first three chapters. These imperatives can be summarized as follows:

- Believers are to walk worthily of their calling, in a way that is clearly distinct from that of their pagan past and their peers.
- As members of the body of Christ, all believers are ministers and have a gift of grace for the unification, maturation, and edification of the whole body; of particular importance are those gifted to equip the entire church for ministry by teaching and preaching.
- Especially emphasized are the virtues of kind, forgiving behavior and speech, and sexual purity in thought, speech, and action.
- Underlying all the imperatives is a general call to the imitation of God's kindness as demonstrated in Christ's sacrificial death.
- This call is to be expressed in a lifestyle of mutual submission (cruciform care for the other) both within the church in general and within the believing household in particular.

• The church participates in a spiritual battle with cosmic forces, its weapons being those characteristics of life associated with the gospel.

THE STORY IN FRONT OF THE LETTER

Some Readings of Ephesians

"[T]he Epistle itself is full of sublime conceptions and doctrines. . . . It abounds with sentiments of overwhelming loftiness and grandeur. Thoughts which he [Paul] scarcely so much as utters anywhere else, he here plainly declares."

> John Chrysostom (d. 407), introduction to his *Homilies on the Epistle of St. Paul the Apostle to the Ephesians* in *A Select Library of the Nicene and Post-Nicene Fathers,* edited by Philip Schaff (New York: Scribner's, 1905; orig. 1889), 13:49

"[Ephesians is] the crown of the Pauline writings."

> C. H. Dodd, quoted in C. L. Mitton, *Ephesians,* New Century Bible Commentary (Grand Rapids: Eerdmans, 1976), p. 2

"Whether one concludes that the letter was written by the apostle Paul or at a later time by one of his close followers, one cannot deny the power of the Christian witness contained in it and the consummate way in which, without slavishly quoting from the apostle's letters, it represents the heart and core of Paul's proclamation of the gospel of Jesus Christ to Gentiles."

> Paul J. Achtemeier, Joel B. Green, and Marianne Meye Thompson, *Introducing the New Testament: Its Literature and Theology* (Grand Rapids: Eerdmans, 2001), p. 389

"Ephesians is sometimes criticized for its 'cosmic' and overly 'realized' eschatology, which pictures the recipients already raised up with Christ in the heavenly places (cf. 2:5-6), thereby leaving the reality of life on earth far behind. But it should be clear especially from chapters 4–6 that Ephesians is still very much in touch with the realities of this world. We should assess the language of 'realized' eschatology more in terms of its rhetorical effect than in view of its literal content. As the author works to open the Ephesians to a renewed imagination, he makes claims that blur the distinctions between future and present, and [between] heaven and earth. Ephesians is more interested in transformed imagination than theological precision. The statements that ring of 'realized' eschatology work powerfully to underline the then/now contrast that is so prominent in [chap. 2]. The writer is not attempting to produce a sober, balanced theological statement, but to lift us into a time and place where we can see the world differently. With good reason [New Testament scholar] Nils Dahl has affirmed that Ephesians was, and is perhaps still today, one of the most influential statements of Christian thought and spirituality."

Stanley P. Saunders, "Learning Christ: Eschatology and Spiritual Formation in New Testament Christianity," *Interpretation* 56 (2002): 155-67, here 166

QUESTIONS FOR REFLECTION

1. What are some of the strengths, as well as some of the possible dangers, of a theology and spirituality that stress present resurrection and exaltation with Christ? What, if anything, does Ephesians offer to help keep such dangers in check?
2. What might the first half of Ephesians 2 contribute to the centuries-old debate about 'faith and works'?
3. What major divisions among people are found today within society and the church? How might the divine plan for unity among Gentiles and Jews speak to these divisions?
4. What can Ephesians contribute to our contemporary attempts to define ministry in general, and lay ministry in particular?
5. Why is speech a matter for theological and spiritual consideration as it is, prominently, in Ephesians? Is there a need in the contemporary church for more careful attention to the theology and practice of speech?
6. In what areas of life does the church need to be more (or less) distinct from its 'pagan' culture?
7. In your experience, how has the household table (5:22–6:9) been used and abused in discussions of marriage and family life? How would the interpretation offered here — that the household table is about the application of cruciform mutual submission to all household relationships — affect contemporary discussions of marriage, 'family values,' and family life?
8. What value might the image of 'spiritual' or 'cosmic' warfare have for the church today?
9. How do you respond to the interpretations of Ephesians quoted above?
10. In sum, what does this letter urge the church to believe, to hope for, and to do?

FOR FURTHER READING AND STUDY

General

Martin, Ralph P. *Ephesians, Colossians, and Philemon*. Atlanta: John Knox, 1991. A general commentary on the text as an encyclical letter by one of Paul's disciples.

O'Brien, Peter T. *The Letter to the Ephesians*. Pillar NT Commentary. Grand Rapids: Eerdmans, 1999. An interpretation arguing for Pauline authorship and showing continuities with the undisputed letters and Colossians.

Perkins, Pheme. "Ephesians." In *The New Interpreter's Bible*, edited by Leander E. Keck et al., 11:349-466. Nashville: Abingdon, 2000. A theological and sociological reading of the letter, arguing for pseudonymity and highlighting developments from the undisputed letters and Colossians.

―――. *Ephesians*. Abingdon New Testament Commentaries. Nashville: Abingdon, 1997. See previous annotation.

Technical

Barth, Markus. *Ephesians*. Anchor Bible 34, 34A. 2 vols. New York: Doubleday, 1974. A classic commentary that defends Pauline authorship of the letter and Paul's use of liturgical sources.

Best, Ernest. *A Critical and Exegetical Commentary on Ephesians*. International Critical Commentary. Edinburgh: T. & T. Clark, 1998. A detailed commentary that sees the author as part of the 'Pauline school.'

Lincoln, Andrew T. *Ephesians*. Word Biblical Commentary 42. Dallas: Word, 1990. A thorough, insightful commentary on the supposition of authorship by an heir of the Pauline tradition.

CHAPTER 17

2 TIMOTHY

Suffering Rather than Shame

Do not be ashamed, then, of the testimony about our Lord or of me his prisoner, but join with me in suffering for the gospel, relying on the power of God.

2 Tim. 1:8

Paul's second letter to Timothy, if actually written by the apostle, was his last letter to anyone that has been preserved. It breathes the air of both death and victory at the end of Paul's earthly life as the need for faithfulness in the ongoing proclamation of the gospel, even in the face of suffering, is set forth. For various reasons this letter has greater claims to authenticity than 1 Timothy, which is why we are considering it out of its canonical and numerical sequence.

PREFACE: THE PASTORAL EPISTLES

Since the early eighteenth century, three of the Pauline letters — 1 and 2 Timothy and Titus — have been known as the Pastoral Epistles or Letters (the Pastorals for short). These letters are addressed to two of Paul's closest associates.[1]

---

1. On Timothy see Acts 16:1-10; 17:10-15; 18:1-5; 19:21-22; 20:1-6; Rom. 16:21; 1 Cor. 4:14-17; 16:10-11; 2 Cor. 1:1, 15-22; Phil. 1:1; 2:19-24; 1 Thess. 1:1; 3:1-10; and Philem. 1; also Col. 1:1 and 2 Thess. 1:1. On Titus see 2 Cor. 2:12-13; 7:5-16; 8:1-6, 16-24; 12:14-18; and Gal. 2:1-3. Interestingly, already in the thirteenth century Thomas Aquinas had called the letters to these colleagues of Paul 'pastoral.'

Since we suggested in chapter 3 that all of Paul's letters are pastoral in nature, some explanation is in order. When we say that Paul's letters have a pastoral character, we mean they are a tool of his own pastoral ministry, a means of apostleship by proxy. The term 'the Pastoral Epistles' or 'the Pastoral Letters' derives from the fact that in these three letters Paul is writing to individuals about how *they* should exercise their pastoral ministry as leaders of the church, about the need for and qualifications of *other* church leaders ('shepherds' or 'pastors,' from the Latin *pastor*, 'shepherd'), and about the ordering of life in the church. Indeed, the purpose of these letters was described as 'for ordering church discipline' as early as the late second century in the first preserved list of the New Testament canon (the Muratorian Canon).

This grouping of the three letters under one heading has some liabilities, however. Although the three letters have something of a common vocabulary and style, 2 Timothy is quite distinct in both form and substance from 1 Timothy and Titus: it has no extended job descriptions for church leaders, designations of various offices, or rules for church order. Rather, it is a very personal letter of farewell wishes and instructions to a cherished younger colleague. Thus we must exercise extreme caution in associating 2 Timothy with 1 Timothy and Titus, for their differences are at least as important as their similarities.

Important similarities do, however, exist. In fact, it is the family resemblances among the three letters that have led most scholars not only to group them together, but also to argue for their non-Pauline authorship and their late date — anywhere from shortly after the death of the apostle to the middle of the second century. (Most scholars would lean toward the end of the first or the beginning of the second century.) These conclusions are based on perceived differences in vocabulary, style, theology, 'polity' (approach to ministry and church life), and apparent historical situation vis-à-vis the undisputed letters.

The various pieces of evidence for this conclusion will not be examined here. Rather we will briefly consider the options available to us in light of both the general observations already made and the understanding of authorship as a 'spectrum' discussed in chapter 3. It is possible that Paul himself wrote, perhaps with the assistance of colleagues, all three letters. If he did so, we must still account for the significant differences from the undisputed letters, probably as developments in his thinking that occurred as he matured (or, some would say, deteriorated) toward the end of his ministry and life. We must probably also account for the situation of the letters by positing an extension of his activity after the events suggested by both the undisputed letters and the book of Acts, which leaves Paul in Rome under house arrest, bearing bold witness to the gospel for one last period of time (so it would seem) before his death (Acts 28:16-31).

It is also possible — and, for most biblical scholars, virtually certain —

that Paul wrote none of the three letters. If he did not, we must account for their particular contents and attempt to situate them in their appropriate time period and social location. If Paul did not write the Pastoral Epistles, it has been suggested, the author (sometimes called 'the Pastor') would have been appealing to Paul's persona, authority, and teaching to fend off perceived heretics and to establish doctrinal and behavioral order within the churches he addressed.

A 'compromise' position would be to hold that the basic contents of 2 Timothy come from the time of Paul and represent his thought accurately, while 1 Timothy and Titus are from a later time and represent a development from Paul himself. This is the perspective adopted in this text. This position may take two basic forms on the genuineness of 2 Timothy: either that Paul authorized the production of this letter near the end of his life, or that the letter preserves genuine fragments of letters from Paul's last days that were later edited into the letter form we now possess. In either case, this proposal must of course still wrestle with all the similarities and differences in the Pastorals, as well as the questions of time and place and purpose, previously noted. In sum, the compromise position adopted in this book may be stated as follows: *2 Timothy faithfully preserves the spirit, though not necessarily the letter, of the apostle Paul, while 1 Timothy and Titus preserve the letter, though not necessarily the spirit, of 2 Timothy.*

A final word of caution and invitation may be in order. As noted briefly in chapter 3, the Pastoral Epistles have often been accused of a kind of subversion of Paul and of the freedom and spontaneity he supposedly brought to the church and the world. The (generally pejorative) term 'early Catholicism' — the beginnings of the institutionalization of creed and ministry — was coined to describe the (implicitly negative) developments from the genuine Paul to 'the Pastor.' Among the typical criticisms of the Pastorals are the following:

- The new faith and gospel have become static, definable, and containable, like a "deposit" (see, e.g., 2 Tim. 1:12-14).
- Believing existence has become accommodationist, bourgeois, and patriarchal — a baptized version of Roman status-quo piety and virtue.
- The church has become routinized and institutionalized in its leadership and ministry.
- The church has, in sum, settled down for the long haul, with no sense of newness, distinction from its host culture, or eschatological urgency.

All these developments, it is often said, are in contrast to the dynamic versions of faith, the gospel, life in Christ, and the church that we find in the genuine Pauline letters.

In reading and assessing the Pastorals, however, we must be careful that our own biases, shaped especially by the values of modern, 'progressive' churches and democracies, do not impede our hearing, understanding, and even learning from the voices of Scripture that may at first rub against our modern or postmodern sensibilities. Nor may we assume uncritically that the 'genuine Paul' was the forerunner of those ecclesiastical and political bodies.

Furthermore, we must not fail to appreciate some of the clear high points of the Pastorals, no matter who wrote them. These might include:

- the emphasis on the inseparability of belief and practice;
- the call for the integrity of the church's ministers before both internal and external publics;
- the stress on holding to the fundamental convictions of the faith despite attacks from within or outside of the church; and
- the theme of modeling and mentoring as integral to the health of the church.

We turn now to 2 Timothy itself.

THE STORY BEHIND THE LETTER

One's view of the story behind this letter depends, of course, on when one believes it was written (during or after Paul's lifetime) and by whom (Paul, an associate, or someone writing in his name). Nevertheless, a partial reconstruction of the story without a decision on authorship issues is possible, as we will see.

A LETTER FROM PAUL?

The majority of scholars rejects the Pauline authorship of 2 Timothy, though a growing minority wishes to make the case that it was by Paul. Yet another group believes that although the letter postdates Paul, it preserves some authentic fragments from the apostle.

One important but infrequently mentioned argument for the letter's authenticity is the abundance of personal and place names on the one hand, but the general lack of references to the other letters or to specific incidents in Acts on the other. The presence of many personal names and details about the persons named is often used to support pseudonymity (the names allegedly being devices to trick the reader), but only at the expense of the integrity of the letter's author — a serious charge to bring against someone responsible for a letter so zealous for the truth.

Furthermore, it is difficult to imagine a later writer deliberately fabricating a series of references to specific people and places without also adding to the plausibility of the letter (as the work of the apostle) by including references to events known to the churches through earlier, genuine Pauline letters or through Acts.[2] But that is precisely what has happened if the letter is pseudonymous; there is no explicit connection whatsoever to any events narrated or implied in the other letters or Acts, yet surely these documents were already in circulation by the time a pseudonymous writer would have taken up the pen in Paul's name. If the letter is a forgery, why is it not a credible one?

Another piece of evidence is the depth of emotion expressed in the letter; Paul the apostle feels abandoned and without hope of deliverance (4:6-18). Despite these feelings — which seem unlikely candidates for creation by a supposedly later 'disciple' of the apostle — the Paul of 2 Timothy remains steadfast and trusting in the face of likely death.

Finally, we must stress that the dominant theme of 2 Timothy is what we have called cruciformity. This is indeed the spirit of Paul, even if expressed in new language. These differences in language between 2 Timothy and the undisputed letters may well be the result of the work of an amanuensis, or secretary. It is even possible that this assistant was Luke (4:11).

PAUL THE FAITHFUL HERALD IN PRISON

Whether by Paul or not, the letter presents the apostle as one who "suffer[s] hardship, even to the point of being chained like a criminal" (2:9), perhaps (though not necessarily) in Rome (1:17). Scholars are undecided, if a Roman imprisonment is in view, whether the letter reflects Paul's thoughts after the first phase of a Roman imprisonment while awaiting the next phase, or during a second Roman imprisonment (see 4:16-18). If Rome was not the location, the best alternative is Caesarea (see Acts 20 and 23).

Paul's frequent imprisonments seem to have been a constant source of embarrassment, or shame, to some early believers. The letter recognizes this reality, exhorting Timothy to imitate Paul's other colleague, Onesiphorus (1:16), in not being "ashamed . . . of the testimony about our Lord or of me [Paul] his prisoner" (1:8). Perhaps, under the influence of the false teachers to which the letter refers, Timothy had become ashamed of the gospel, or Paul, or both (1:6-7).

Whether the words of Paul or another, 2 Timothy depicts the imprisoned apostle as the model of teaching and suffering (3:10-12) — a source of honor rather than shame. He is presented as the one about to depart (4:6-8),

2. For the personal and place names in 2 Timothy, see 1:5, 15-18; 2:17; 3:11; 4:9-15, 19-21.

which raises the question, Who will carry the Pauline message and ministry forward after Paul's death? Just as Paul's imprisonment has not enchained the gospel, neither can (or will) the end of his earthly life mean the end of his gospel.

The need for the continuation of Paul's gospel is all the more pressing, according to 2 Timothy, because of the arrival of false teachers in Ephesus (the most likely destination of the letter) or wherever else the letter was intended to be sent (2:14–3:9; 3:13; 4:3-4). According to the letter, these teachers are dangerous frauds who are both deceived and deceiving, gangrene in the church's body (2:17). They signal the presence of the last days. Substantively (apart from this general polemic), the letter contends that these teachers claim "that the resurrection has already taken place" (2:18).

Paul becomes, in this situation, the bearer of truth over against the errors of the false teachers. He is the model for all believers, but especially for teachers, combining the roles of teaching the truth and suffering for it (e.g., 2:2-3; 3:10-12). As teacher, Paul is faithful to the gospel, not distorting or misusing it as the false teachers do. As one who suffers for the truth, Paul is furthermore paradigmatic for all who live (3:12) and teach (1:8, 12; 2:8-9; 3:11) faithfully. The call to Timothy is to teach and suffer in similar fashion (4:5).

THE STORY WITHIN THE LETTER

2 Timothy is a call to faithful ministry understood as teaching the Pauline gospel without compromise or shame — and even suffering for it. In essence it is a call to the imitation of Paul as both pastor/teacher and martyr; he is the pattern for both.[3] Though in the letter's narrative world Paul has not yet been killed, he has been constantly persecuted and is soon to die. Timothy is being called to 'take up the mantle.'

Some have suggested that 2 Timothy is Paul's 'last will and testament' or that it has the features of a 'farewell discourse.' One great commentator several centuries ago called it 'Paul's swan song' (Bengel). While there is no doubt some truth in these suggestions, the letter is much more of a personal charge or 'parenesis' (exhortation) than anything else. The theme of the letter, then, is the charge to guard and suffer for the truth of the gospel in imitation of Paul.[4] This is presented early in the letter: "Do not be ashamed, then, of the testimony about our Lord or of me his prisoner, but join with me in suffering for the gos-

---

3. As pastor/teacher: 1:5-8, 11-14; 2:1-2, 7, 14-16; as martyr: 1:8, 12, 15-18; 2:8-10; 3:11-12; 4:6-18.
4. See esp. 1:8, 11-14; 2:1-3; 3:10-14; 4:1-5.

pel, relying on the power of God. . . . Hold to the standard of sound teaching that you have heard from me, in the faith and love that are in Christ Jesus. Guard the good treasure entrusted to you, with the help of the Holy Spirit living in us" (1:8, 13-14). Timothy — and all ministers of the gospel, the letter implies — must continue Paul's ministry of word and witness and do so à la Paul: with a willingness to suffer rather than be ashamed of the gospel. As we have seen in other letters, such Spirit-empowered cruciform ministry will be both effective and rewarded (2:1-13; 4:8).

The letter unfolds as follows:

1:1-2	Opening	
1:3-18	The Gospel and Its Trusted Heralds	
	1:3-5	Paul's Memories and Thanksgiving
	1:6-14	Passing the Torch: Initial Exhortation
	1:15-18	Examples of Support and of Shame
2:1-26	Images of Timothy's Charge	
	2:1-7	Teacher, Soldier, Athlete, Farmer
	2:8-13	Evangelical Memory and Endurance
	2:14-19	An Unashamed Worker
	2:20-26	The Lord's Servant
3:1–4:8	The Charge to Timothy in Its Eschatological Context	
	3:1-9	The Advent of False Teachers as Eschatological Sign
	3:10–4:8	The Charge to Steadfastness
		3:10-17 Paul the Example, Scripture the Norm
		4:1-5 The Charge Itself
		4:6-8 Paul's Present, Past, and Future
4:9-22	Final Words	
	4:9-18	Memories, Requests, and Hopes
	4:19-22	Greetings and Benediction

1:1-2. OPENING

The letter begins with a statement of the origin and purpose of Paul's apostleship. Echoing the opening words of other Pauline letters (1 and 2 Corinthians, Galatians, Ephesians, Colossians), the first words claim that Paul's apostleship is by the will of God. Its purpose, presented in language distinctive to 2 Timothy, is to spread the reality of "life and immortality" through the gospel (cf. 1:10) — a formulation appropriate for a letter that suggests the imminence of death. Also distinctive is the addition of "mercy," found otherwise only in 1 Timothy, to the standard opening wish for grace and peace.[5] Timothy is addressed as Paul's "beloved child," the adjective "beloved" being often applied to Paul's converts and colleagues.

1:3-18. THE GOSPEL AND ITS TRUSTED HERALDS

The body of the letter opens with memories of the past and a challenge for the future.

PAUL'S MEMORIES AND THANKSGIVING (1:3-5)

The brief thanksgiving serves to reconnect Paul with his "beloved child" Timothy and to link their past to the exhortations to come. Like Paul himself (1:3), Timothy is carrying on a family tradition (cf. Acts 16:1) by being in covenantal relationship with God, possessing the same dynamic and life-giving faith his mother and grandmother had (1:5). When Paul prays, the memories of Timothy's faith and of his tears (perhaps at the most recent parting of the two men) fill him with joy.

PASSING THE TORCH: INITIAL EXHORTATION (1:6-14)

The reminders of Timothy's close relationship with Paul lead to the premise of all that follows: not only has Timothy received a living faith transmitted through his family, but he has also received a special gift from God, transmitted through Paul by the laying on of hands (1:6; cf. 1 Tim. 4:14). Although the laying on of hands likely took place in the context of the church's worship, it should not be interpreted anachronistically in terms of later understandings of 'ordination.' The gift given to Timothy is the call to participate in the same Spirit-empowered ministry that Paul has exercised (1:7). The basic meaning of the laying on of hands, then, is the continuity of the Spirit's activity and acknowledgment of Timothy's gift as both a bequest and a partnership. Henceforth Timothy could share in the character of Paul's ministry, and he must carry it on when Paul is gone. To insure the continuity in Timothy's (and thus Paul's) ministry, Timothy must "rekindle" (NAB/NIV, "stir/fan into flame") the gift (*cha-*

---

5. These observations about the opening immediately raise, but of course cannot settle, the question of authorship. They do, however, suggest a relationship between 1 and 2 Timothy.

risma, 1:6). Already we hear, implicitly, that this will be no easy task, yet there is no excuse for timidity (NIV) or cowardice (NRSV, NAB), because the Spirit (rather than simply "spirit") given by God engenders three things: (1) the power to endure suffering, (2) love (perhaps to provide the necessary motivation for suffering), and (3) self-discipline for the dangers ahead.

The presence and power of God's Spirit become the basis for Paul's exhortation to Timothy to join him in testimony to the gospel and in the suffering that will accompany that witness (1:8). Suffering must replace shame. Timothy must be willing to identify both with the Lord (Jesus) and with Paul. There follows a brief rehearsal of this Pauline gospel that stresses God's grace in calling and saving those who believe it (1:9-10). The use of salvation language in the past tense ("saved," 1:9), coupled with the rejection of 'works' as the basis of that salvation, is similar to Ephesians 2:8 and Titus 3:5, which are often thought to be pseudonymous. But the text also recalls Romans (esp. 3:28 and 8:24-30) and Galatians (e.g., 2:16); the notion, and perhaps even the wording, is clearly the apostle's.

What is more unusual, however, is the way this salvation is described: God's eternal grace in Christ has been "revealed through the appearing [*epiphaneia;* NAB, 'appearance'] of our Savior Christ Jesus, who abolished death and brought life and immortality to light through the gospel" (1:10).[6] As noted above, the language of death and life/immortality makes sense in a kind of last testament. The use of the word "appearing," however, might be thought to express a purely 'incarnational' theology somewhat at odds with the Pauline gospel's emphasis on Christ's death. It is clear from Galatians 4:4-5 and Philippians 2:6-8, however, that for Paul joint emphasis on both Christ's 'incarnation' and his death was possible. Moreover, elsewhere in 2 Timothy (esp. 2:11) the death of Jesus is essential both to salvation and to the spirituality of apostolic suffering that pervades the letter.

From the description of the gospel the text moves to a description of its apostle, revealing the letter's theme: the apostolic call to costly faithfulness to the gospel. Paul's three-part title of "herald . . . apostle . . . teacher" is connected with suffering (1:11-12).[7] Throughout the undisputed letters, as well as

---

6. *Epiphaneia* recurs as a reference to the *second* coming in 4:1, 8 and in 1 Tim. 6:14. See also 2 Thess. 2:8 and cf. Acts 2:20. In antiquity the word meant an act of divine intervention, not just revelation. It could also refer to the (divine) emperor's appearing.

7. The only other occurrence of this trio of titles in the Pauline letters is 1 Tim. 2:7, and nowhere besides these two texts does Paul refer to himself as a "herald" (*kēryx;* NAB, "preacher") or "teacher" (*didaskalos*). However, the verb forms of these two nouns, especially "herald" (*kēryssō*, 'proclaim,' 'preach'), are used to characterize his ministry even in the undisputed letters (Rom. 10:8; 1 Cor. 1:23; 9:27; 15:11; 2 Cor. 1:19; 4:5; 11:4; Gal. 2:2; cf. *didaskō*, 'teach,' in 1 Cor. 4:17, as well as in the disputed texts 2 Thess. 2:15 and Col. 1:28).

Colossians and Ephesians, this conjunction is evident; suffering is constitutive of Paul's apostleship. Paul's suffering does not cause him shame, however, because he maintains an eschatological perspective, trusting in God's protective power (1:12; cf. 1:1, 10). It is not completely clear whether this protection is meant to refer to that which Paul has entrusted to God (so NRSV, NIV) or, more likely, to that which God has entrusted to Paul (so NAB, NRSV mg.). The image is of valuables being entrusted by a voyager to a friend for safekeeping.

The content of the trust is somewhat clearer than the question of who is trusting and who is being trusted: it is the gospel (or the traditions associated with it), which is now also in Timothy's care (1:13-14; cf. 1 Tim. 6:20). This gospel is characterized as "sound" teaching or words, those that reflect and embody the fundamental covenantal features of faith and love that characterize Christ and therefore also the gospel (1:13; cf. 1 Tim. 1:14). It is further characterized twice as a "good deposit/treasure" (NIV/NRSV) or "rich trust" (NAB), indicating not its static character but its immense value (1:14; Gk. *parathēkē*, used also in 1:12). This call to faithful perseverance is possible only by the power of the (uncowardly) Spirit (1:14; cf. 1:7).

EXAMPLES OF SUPPORT AND OF SHAME (1:15-18)

Having issued Timothy his initial charge, the apostle now briefly recounts examples and counterexamples of that charge before developing the exhortation more fully. On the one hand there is the positive example of Onesiphorus (1:16-18), who often attended to Paul in prison in Rome and "was not ashamed" of the jailed apostle. He also performed some ministry in Ephesus (1:18), perhaps also while Paul was jailed. Now near Timothy (4:19), Onesiphorus receives Paul's blessing and eschatological best wishes (1:16, 18). On the other hand is the negative example of "all who are in Asia," including two otherwise unknown men (1:15; cf. 4:10-11). If the claim is hyperbolic, it serves the purpose of the letter: to encourage faithfulness to, rather than shame about, the apostle and his gospel.

2:1-26. IMAGES OF TIMOTHY'S CHARGE

The initial exhortation given to Timothy is now developed through a series of images that depict his charge — costly faithfulness — as a natural outgrowth of the gospel.

TEACHER, SOLDIER, ATHLETE, FARMER (2:1-7)

The first images are prefaced by two general admonitions (2:1-2): first, to be strong in the grace that is in Christ (perhaps a reference to the Spirit as in 1:7, 14); and second, to prepare other faithful teachers of the gospel. The three images that follow would apply explicitly to Timothy and implicitly to all other teachers or proclaimers of the gospel. All three were commonly used of teachers in antiquity.

First, like a soldier, Timothy is to accept the suffering that accompanies his battle for the gospel, aiming only to please his commander (or recruiter) and not be tempted or distracted by outside activities (2:3-4). Like an athlete, he must follow the demanding rules of the competition if he wants to receive the (eschatological) crown of victory (2:5). And like a persistent farmer, he will share in the first (eschatological) fruits of his labor. Unlike 1 Corinthians 9:7, none of these images is used to justify the financial support of those who minister. Rather, together they seem intended to suggest (2:7) that all preachers are called to faithful endurance, which will ultimately be rewarded — as the gospel demonstrates. The minister of the gospel must suffer hardships single-mindedly like a soldier, unflinchingly like an athlete, and unceasingly like a farmer.

EVANGELICAL MEMORY AND ENDURANCE (2:8-13)

The call to costly faithfulness and its reward is grounded, for Paul, in the gospel. Timothy must constantly "remember" the focus of this gospel, which is Jesus, who is the (implicitly, crucified) Messiah (Christ, descendant of David) raised by God from the dead (2:8; cf. Rom. 1:3-4). The story of Jesus is the ground of Timothy's hope in the midst of faithful suffering. For this gospel of Jesus' death and resurrection Paul suffers and is even now chained, though — he announces with vivid imagery — the gospel is *not* chained (2:9). The example of Paul's own endurance in suffering is of course meant to encourage Timothy. But Paul's suffering is not first of all an example, and it is not here primarily a 'means' to his own salvation, in spite of 2:11 (cf. Rom. 8:17). Rather, it is an integral part of his ministry to others in order to guarantee *their* eternal glory (2:10). The premise behind this claim seems to be that ministerial faithlessness in the face of suffering could inspire others to abandon the faith and thus lose their future salvation.

This claim leads to the citation of a "saying" (2:11) of some kind, perhaps part of a hymn or creed. Rhetorically structured like Hebrew poetry, the text is a series of four 'if . . . then' assertions. The first two (2:11a-12a: "died . . . live"; "endure . . . reign") are parallel and synonymous, expressing the pattern of suffering followed by glory. The second two (2:12b-13) are antithetical to the first pair, expressing the consequences of avoiding costly faithfulness ("deny . . . are faithless/unfaithful"). Though these texts are parallel, they are not synonymous. The first (2:12b) conveys the fate of the unfaithful denier (cf. Matt. 10:33; Mark 8:38), while the second (2:13) reaffirms the unchanging character of Christ without reversing the claims of the previous verse. In other words, Christ's faithfulness does *not* mean that human faithlessness is somehow less serious than denying Christ.

AN UNASHAMED WORKER (2:14-19)

The shift in tone from 2:13 to 2:14-19 at first appears dramatic: from words that deny Christ to mere "wrangling" (2:14). But the evangelical reminder in 2:8-13 serves as a notice about the importance of words; the preacher is a worker in words, a wordsmith, so to speak. Gospel workers have a responsibility not to participate in, or to perpetuate, worthless and spiritually dangerous word wrestling (2:14, 16; cf. 1 Tim. 6:20) — perhaps a reference to unknown 'controversies' apparently sparked by some false teachers (2:23). Such activity is akin to the spread of gangrene in the body (2:17). Ministers, therefore, are to teach "the word of truth" — the gospel — rightly and faithfully, to avoid infecting the community and experiencing shame before God.

A serious example of this kind of bad teaching — which seems to be more than just word wrangling — is then offered: certain teachers are claiming that the resurrection (of the dead) has already occurred, and this is having deleterious effects on some (2:18). It appears that similar viewpoints, examples of 'overrealized eschatology,' emerged now and again in the early churches, at Thessalonica, for example (2 Thess. 2:2), and perhaps at Corinth (1 Cor. 4:8; 15:12). The Pauline response to that position is always that the new life is characterized in the present by suffering, and the resurrection glory promised to the faithful is still future. That answer is implied here by the context (2:8-13) and is presumed to be obvious. The more pressing concern is the problem of the teachers themselves. Two brief allusions to Scripture (2:19) are meant to identify these teachers as something other than the Lord's spokespersons and to summon them to repentance.

THE LORD'S SERVANT (2:20-26)

Timothy, in contrast to such propagators of error, is called upon to be a true servant of the Lord, an "apt" (NRSV) teacher (2:24; cf. 1 Tim. 3:2). The role of servant is depicted in the image of household utensils, some of which are golden and silver and made for special use, while others are wooden and clay for ordinary (lit. 'dishonorable') use (2:20). This image represents the contrast between faithful and unfaithful teachers; the former are 'cleansed' from the errors that stain the latter, and they are therefore useful (2:21; cf. Philem. 11). This means that Timothy (and, implicitly, the colleagues he trains) must leave behind youthful vice in order to pursue godly virtue (2:22; cf. 1 Tim. 4:12; 6:11) and forsake quarrels in order to teach the truth — even to the false teachers (2:23-26). For even they could possibly repent from the demonic trap (cf. 1 Tim. 3:7) that has held them in their erroneous ways (2:25-26).

3:1–4:8. THE CHARGE TO TIMOTHY IN ITS ESCHATOLOGICAL CONTEXT

After presenting the series of images for Timothy's charge in chapter 2, centered on the *content* of the gospel message (2:8-13), the letter moves on to reemphasize the character of this charge by placing it in its eschatological *context*. The section 3:1–4:8 begins on the note of the "last days" (3:1) and concludes with a reference to the Lord's "appearing" (*epiphaneia*, 4:8). References to both of these rhetorical bookends appear also in the middle of the passage (3:13; 4:1-3). The sober, suffering "work of an evangelist" (4:5), including opposition to false teachers, to which Timothy is called takes place within this eschatological frame of reference.

THE ADVENT OF FALSE TEACHERS AS ESCHATOLOGICAL SIGN (3:1-9)

This section does not begin with a prediction about the evil associated with some future "last days" (3:1), but rather with the identification of the current crisis (note the present-tense verbs in 3:5-8) as a sign that *these* days are indeed the last days. The appearance of the false teachers described in 2:14-25 is understood, in common with much apocalyptic thought, as proof that the time just before the end of this age will be characterized by dangerous and misleading religious guides (see, e.g., 1 Tim. 4:1-3; Mark 13:3-6, 21-23).

The negative description of people in nearly twenty phrases (3:2-4) is similar to Paul's characterization of (especially Gentile) humanity in Romans 1:18-32, and is the stock of Jewish wisdom and apocalyptic thinking. The significant feature here is that these people are not 'out there' but 'in here' — in the church itself. They are "holding to the outward form of godliness [NAB: making 'a pretense of religion'] but denying its power" (3:5), people "of corrupt mind and counterfeit faith . . . [who] oppose the truth" (3:8). In the general context of 2 Timothy, these accusations refer to teachers who have distorted the gospel message itself (2:18), that "treasure" or "deposit" entrusted to Timothy (1:14), and have simultaneously introduced an ethic that is inconsistent with the true gospel (2:16, 19). In other words, they lack both faith and love (1:13); they do not know the "truth" (2:25), "truth" clearly referring to both the creedal and moral dimensions of the gospel.

Apparently these teachers are having special success among certain women[8] whose own ability to learn the truth in this Pauline sense is questionable (3:6-7). Timothy is not to associate with these false teachers (3:5), despite whatever pretense of divine power — like Jannes and Jambres (3:8), the two magicians of Pharaoh, according to Jewish tradition — they might have. The "folly" of these teachers will eventually reveal itself (3:9).

THE CHARGE TO STEADFASTNESS (3:10–4:8)

"Steadfastness" (Gk. *hypomonē*, 3:10) is not a term we use much in contemporary English, but it serves well to summarize what Timothy is called to in these verses: a hope-filled faithfulness to the gospel in spite of opposition and suffering. His example, of course, is Paul.

Paul the Example, Scripture the Norm (3:10-17)

The charge opens with an introductory description of the qualities of Paul's ministry that Timothy has observed and (it is implied) should himself imitate. These qualities include not only the content of his teaching but also the conduct of his life (3:10). The main focus is clearly on the cost of ministry — the realities of "patience" and "steadfastness" in the face of "persecutions" and "suffering" — and on the "faith" and "love" (cf. 1:13) that empowered Paul to accept the cost (3:10). The events of persecution recalled took place in and around Timothy's hometown of Lystra (Acts 16:1; 13:44–14:20).

This brief summary yields the following all-important conclusion: "all who want to live a godly life in Christ Jesus will be persecuted" (3:12). This verse serves as a succinct summary of Paul's vision of the manner and consequences

---

8. NIV, "weak-willed women," is far preferable to NRSV, "silly women"; the word is descriptive of a particular group of women, not all women in general.

of life in Christ. Though so far God has delivered Paul from his persecutors (3:11), for all faithful believers persecution is inevitable — and so also, at least for Paul, is martyrdom (4:6).

Opposition will come from both "wicked" people (outsiders?) and impostors (insiders), and will increase (3:13), as one would expect in the last days. The charge to Timothy, and to all ministers he teaches (2:2), is steadfastness in the gospel as preached and lived not only by Paul, but also by Timothy's own mother and grandmother (3:14-15; cf. 1:5). Both he and they have pointed Timothy to the Scriptures of Israel as the divine testimony to salvation in Christ (3:15). As God's inspired (NIV, "God-breathed," *theopneustos*) word, these Scriptures are useful for both the formation ("teaching . . . training in righteousness") and reformation ("reproof . . . correction") of character, equipping believers for all the good works to which God calls them (3:16-17). Timothy must now "continue" in the Scriptures (3:14).

The Charge Itself (4:1-5)

These introductory words, combining the two features of faithfulness and suffering, lead to Paul's solemn, eschatological charge to Timothy, given in the presence of God and Christ and "in view of his [Christ's] appearing and his kingdom" (4:1). In two words, the charge is to 'preach' and 'teach' (4:2). This ministry of proclamation and education must take place at all times (4:2), whether "favorable or unfavorable" (NRSV), "in season and out of season" (NIV). This steady, faithful ministry is all the more crucial now that the time is coming — and is already here! (3:1-8) — when people will have "itching ears" and prefer self-selected and self-satisfying myths rather than "truth" and "sound doctrine" (4:3-4). Titillating preaching, the text suggests, does not produce the spiritual health of mind and heart that generates the faith and love required by the gospel.

In contrast to such prostitutes of the truth, Timothy has a mission of costly faithfulness, outlined in three specific imperatives and one general summary exhortation (4:5):

- be sober[9] (an eschatological call to adherence to the truth and to alertness; cf. 1 Thess. 5:6-8)
- endure suffering
- spread the gospel (the work of an evangelist)
- perform your ministry fully

9. The NAB ("be self-possessed in all circumstances") and the NIV ("keep your head in all situations") miss the clear eschatological context and image.

Paul's Present, Past, and Future (4:6-8)

The charge now comes full circle with a return to the ministry of Paul himself. The moving words of 4:6-8 are offered by one who views his present circumstances in light of both his past and his future. There are clear echoes of the letter to the Philippians, also written from prison with the threat of death hovering overhead. According to 4:6, Paul knows that his "departure" (cf. Phil 1:23) is at hand and that his death will be, as his life of suffering has been, a kind of "libation," or drink offering (cf. Phil. 2:17). Turning from cultic to athletic imagery, he claims to have "fought the good fight" (NAB, "competed well") and "finished the race" (4:7). Interpreting these images, Paul says he has "kept the faith" — which, ironically, really means he has given it away, whole, intact, and therefore sound. He has already done what Timothy, and all other ministers of the gospel, must now do.

Continuing the athletic imagery and looking ahead to the future, Paul expresses confidence that the Lord will reward his costly faithfulness with the "crown of righteousness" (4:8). This will be the gift given at the appearing of Christ to all who have so "longed for" that day that they have offered their lives for the spread of the gospel. Thus the promise of God from Scripture, that the righteous who suffer will one day be vindicated, sustains Paul in his hour of death, as it had no doubt sustained him throughout his cruciform ministry.

4:9-22. FINAL WORDS

Second Timothy concludes with additional personal words that suggest that Paul's recent experience has been anything but pleasant from a human perspective, yet he maintains hope in Timothy and, more importantly, in God. The effect of these final words is the creation of empathy for Paul and for the important role that Timothy and others — in contrast to certain other Pauline colleagues — can and indeed must play in the preservation of the Pauline gospel.

MEMORIES, REQUESTS, AND HOPES (4:9-18)

The theme of this section is Paul's experience of abandonment. He urges Timothy to meet up with Mark and to come to him, bringing Paul's cloak, books, and parchments, because aside from Luke, he is alone (4:9, 11, 13; cf. 4:21). One colleague, Demas, has left Paul, perhaps out of fear ("in love with this present

547

world," 4:10), while two others, Titus and the otherwise unknown Crescens (4:10), have moved on for unstated reasons, and Paul has sent Tychicus to Ephesus (4:12). At the same time, Alexander, perhaps Paul's onetime defender at Ephesus (Acts 19:33), has opposed and perhaps betrayed the Pauline team's work.[10]

To make things worse, the text claims, Paul had no supporters at an earlier trial (or earlier portion of the current proceedings), and yet he forgives those who deserted him (4:16). Whatever happened, and wherever it occurred (in Rome or elsewhere), Paul attributes to the Lord's (Jesus') presence and power his temporary stay of execution in order to continue evangelizing the Gentiles, especially during the trial itself (4:17). This leads Paul, in 4:18, to express confidence and praise in the Lord's ability to rescue him from every evil attack (even if he in fact dies after the next proceedings) in the sense of bringing the apostle to Christ's "heavenly kingdom" (cf. 4:1).

GREETINGS AND BENEDICTION (4:19-22)

The greetings to Paul's longtime coworkers Prisca and Aquila, and to the household of one Onesiphorus who had stood by him in his imprisonment (1:16), are joined with words expressing a further sense of aloneness, as Paul has left behind two more friends in other cities (4:20). Yet even before Timothy arrives, Paul is not truly without some support in addition to Luke. Though not present with him, there are four (otherwise unknown) believers still in contact (4:21), and they send greetings on behalf of others, too.

The final blessing ("with your spirit") is reminiscent of those in Galatians 6:18, Philippians 4:23, and Philemon 25, and unlike those in 1 Timothy 6:21 and Titus 3:15.

Summary of 2 Timothy

Second Timothy is a charge to steadfastness, or costly faithfulness to the gospel. It claims that:

- Timothy's ministry is a gift from God, empowered by the Spirit, that needs to be rekindled and then exercised without fear.
- The gospel is a sacred trust that must be treated with care as Timothy preaches and teaches its interrelated doctrinal and moral dimensions.

---

10. Demas, Luke, and Mark all appear also at the end of Colossians (4:10, 14) and of Philemon (24), additional Pauline Captivity Letters.

- The presence of false or 'unsound' teachers is a characteristic of the 'last days' in which the gospel is currently being proclaimed.
- Those who preach and live the gospel faithfully will suffer persecution, as Paul has done with faith, love, and enduring hope.

THE STORY IN FRONT OF THE LETTER

Some Readings of 2 Timothy

"This letter is Paul's testament and swan song."

> Johannes Albrecht Bengel (d. 1752), *Gnomon Novi Testamenti* (London: Nutt, Williams, and Norgate, 1855), p. 837

"In 2 Timothy suffering becomes almost the principal sign of a Christian. And suffering is at least one of the things that connects the believer with Christ. Perhaps the imagery is focused best in 2 Timothy 2:11: 'If we have died with him, we will also live with him.' Second Timothy can be read effectively as a meditation on the cross."

> Lewis R. Donelson, *Colossians, Ephesians, 1 and 2 Timothy, and Titus*, Westminster Bible Companion (Louisville: Westminster John Knox, 1996), p. 120

QUESTIONS FOR REFLECTION

1. Which of the images used to describe the ministry of Timothy or Paul speak most forcefully in the present context?
2. Is the claim that "all who want to live a godly life in Christ Jesus will be persecuted" (3:12) still true? If not, why not? If so, what does it mean for the contemporary church, and especially for contemporary ministry? What does it mean for churches and individuals who have not had to suffer for their faith?
3. Is the notion of 'unsound' or 'false' teachers still a valid one in the church? What are the key features of 'unsound' teaching according to 2 Timothy? of 'sound' teaching?
4. How do you respond to the interpretations of 2 Timothy quoted above?
5. In sum, what does this letter urge the church to believe, to hope for, and to do?

FOR FURTHER READING AND STUDY

Note: many of the following works treat all three of the Pastorals.

General

Bassler, Jouette. *1 Timothy, 2 Timothy, Titus.* Abingdon NT Commentary. Nashville: Abingdon, 1996. An exposition based on the assumption of the letters' pseudonymity.

Dunn, James D. G. "1 and 2 Timothy and Titus." In *The New Interpreter's Bible,* edited by Leander E. Keck et al., 11:773-880. Nashville: Abingdon, 2000. An appreciative commentary on the letters' historical and contemporary message within the framework of a balanced approach to the question of authorship.

Harding, Mark. *What Are They Saying about the Pastoral Epistles?* Mahwah, N.J.: Paulist, 2001. A concise overview of recent trends in the study of 1 and 2 Timothy and Titus.

Johnson, Luke Timothy. *Letters to Paul's Delegates: 1 Timothy, 2 Timothy, Titus.* Valley Forge, Pa.: Trinity Press International, 1996. A commentary that defends Pauline authorship and focuses on the social context of the letters.

Young, Frances. *The Theology of the Pastoral Epistles.* Cambridge: Cambridge University Press, 1994. An overview by a specialist in patristics.

Technical

Dibelius, Martin, and Hans Conzelmann. *The Pastoral Epistles.* Hermeneia. Philadelphia: Fortress, 1972. A commentary that denies Pauline authorship and focuses on parallels in other texts from the ancient world.

Johnson, Luke Timothy. *The First and Second Letters to Timothy: A New Translation with Introduction and Commentary.* Anchor Bible 35A. New York: Doubleday, 2000. A thorough and insightful analysis on the assumption of Pauline authorship.

Mounce, William D. *Pastoral Epistles.* Word Biblical Commentary 46. Nashville: Nelson, 2000. A detailed analysis of the Greek text, building on a comprehensive argument for Pauline authorship with Luke as secretary.

Quinn, Jerome D., and William C. Wacker. *The First and Second Letters to Timothy.* Grand Rapids: Eerdmans, 2000. A thorough analysis of every aspect of these two letters, on the assumption of pseudonymity.

CHAPTER 18

1 TIMOTHY

*Proper Order and Conduct
in God's Household*

*I am writing these instructions to you so that . . . you may know how
one ought to behave in the household of God, which is the church of the
living God, the pillar and bulwark of the truth.*

1 Tim. 3:14-15

The document known as Paul's first letter to Timothy is a text that many modern interpreters love to hate. It bears, for them, all the negative characteristics of 'subapostolic' Christianity or 'early Catholicism' against which the contemporary church needs to struggle: ecclesial hierarchy, oppression of women, and a general unhealthy accommodation to culture.

It will not suffice, however, to dismiss a canonical text so quickly. The interpreter's task is both to try to understand this document on its own terms in its own context and, without ignoring its possible limitations, to allow it to speak in unexpected ways to our own situations. This strategy seems especially appropriate for a text with the theme of "know[ing] how one ought to behave in the household of God, which is the church of the living God, the pillar and bulwark of the truth" (3:15). Though this chapter focuses on the first part of the task (understanding 1 Timothy in its own context), the questions at the end of the chapter allow for consideration of the second part (engaging it today).

THE STORY BEHIND THE LETTER

First Timothy purports to be a letter from Paul to his close associate and dear child in faith and ministry, Timothy (see biblical references in n. 1 of the previous chapter, p. 532). The letter suggests that Paul and Timothy had been together in Ephesus and that Paul, upon departing Ephesus for Macedonia, left the youthful (4:12) Timothy in Ephesus to teach, combat false teaching, and help the Ephesian church to order its common life (1:3-7; 3:14-15; 4:11-16; 6:2b, 20-21). This was not to be a permanent appointment as 'pastor,' however, but a temporary supervisory role in Paul's stead (4:13) for a church that had a number of regular leaders.

This role of Timothy as proxy for Paul "until I [Paul] arrive" (4:13) reveals what those who argue both for and against Pauline authorship should agree upon: 1 Timothy is a charge to order the faith and life of the church in continuity with Paul during a period of his absence. The question of whether the content of this charge is actually faithful to the apostle raises the question of authorship.

A LETTER FROM PAUL?

The vast majority of scholars rejects Pauline authorship of this letter, dating it to the late first or early second century. The primary reasons for this opinion are perceived differences between 1 Timothy and the undisputed letters. Specifically, these alleged differences include:

- *vocabulary and style* — the presence of a significant number of words and expressions that are absent from the uncontested letters, and the absence or redefinition of key Pauline terms
- *ecclesiology* — a vision of a structured church with defined leadership roles or 'offices' that is unknown in the undisputed letters, but is similar to that suggested by church documents from the late first and early second centuries
- *Christology* — an understanding of Jesus focused on his being "Savior" and on his future *epiphaneia,* or "appearance," a vocabulary unknown in the undisputed letters
- *spirituality* — an undefined (or missing) connection between theological pronouncements and ethical injunctions, a very un-Pauline approach
- *attitude toward women* — a restrictive view of women's activity and place in the church, in contrast to genuine Pauline theology and practice (e.g., Gal. 3:28; Rom. 16; and even 1 Cor. 11:2-16)

To this common list we might add the fact that 1 Timothy speaks very little about the Pauline spirituality of conformity to Christ crucified (the sole place being 6:11-13, and that only implicitly).

Resolving the questions raised by these and related observations is no easy task. Some of the observations may be inaccurate or incomplete. For instance, we cannot really compare the offices of 1 Timothy to the supposed lack of offices in the undisputed letters since both 1 Corinthians 12 and Philippians 1:1 name leadership roles without describing their duties or qualifications. Furthermore, some scholars have suggested that the probable configuration of ministries or 'offices' in 1 Timothy — overseer(s), elders, and deacons (Gk. *episkopos/episkopoi, presbyteroi,* and *diakonoi*) — is parallel to the arrangement of leadership in the Jewish synagogue (and maybe also the pagan collegium, or 'club') at the time of Paul himself.

As for the letter's attitude toward women, it is not unambiguously negative. Despite the restriction on teaching (2:12), the letter may acknowledge the presence of females in the office of deacons (3:11), and it clearly recognizes a role, and perhaps a formal ministry or office, for certain widows (5:3-16). It is also possible that the restrictive attitude toward teaching, if generated by unusual circumstances, might not fully contradict the undisputed letters, which are not monolithic in their own approach. Similarly, the Christology and spirituality of the letter might be dictated by pressing needs unknown in other letters, but not necessarily yielding incompatible approaches. As for the vocabulary and style, the differences could be explained by developments in Paul himself, by the role of a secretary, or by the nature of the letter and the background of its addressee (a coworker, not a community).

None of these explanations is foolproof. Thus it is probably best to remain agnostic about the letter's origin, admitting the possibility of either Pauline or post-Pauline authorship. In either case, 1 Timothy is likely indebted to 2 Timothy for some of its vocabulary and theology, though on the whole, as noted in the previous chapter, 1 Timothy preserves more of the letter than the spirit of 2 Timothy.

SITUATION AND THEME

As noted above, the theme of 1 Timothy is right conduct in the church as God's "household" *(oikos),* the "pillar and bulwark of the truth" (3:15). The letter's emphasis on the ordering of belief, behavior, and leadership that flows from this governing metaphor for the church is due in large measure to the presence of false or 'unhealthy' teachers and to a related concern for the reputation of the church and its leaders. The precise character of the teachers is difficult to determine — and there may be more than one group — but there are at least Jewish (1:3-11) and ascetic (4:3) strains present, and perhaps proto-Gnostic ones as well (6:20).[1]

Much of the doctrinal and ethical truth affirmed in opposition to these teachers is preserved in pithy statements and in liturgical fragments quoted in the letter. There is little sustained argument, though there is a fairly robust account of the virtues and good deeds expected of church leaders and of all believers. The language used to express these virtues and good deeds appears to combine elements of Jewish, pagan, and distinctively Christian morality in ways that differ somewhat from the strategies of the undisputed letters. It should also be noted that although the cruciform character of Paul's spirituality is not explicitly present, it is perhaps implied in 6:11-13, as noted above.

Whether written by Paul, a colleague, or a 'disciple' — and whatever the precise circumstances of its composition — 1 Timothy is a charge to teach the truth of God revealed in Christ, to connect this teaching to right living, and to make certain that church 'offices' (which are assumed already to exist) are filled by people of integrity. This is behavior appropriate to God's household. There is no reason to question the letter's placing of this particular divine household in Ephesus (1:3), even if Paul is not the author.

THE STORY WITHIN THE LETTER

The letter unfolds as follows:

1:1-2	**Opening**
1:3-20	**A Charge to Combat False Teaching**
2:1-15	**Prayer and Teaching in the Assembly**
	2:1-7 The Community's Prayer and Witness
	2:8-15 Husbands and Wives at Worship
3:1-13	**Qualifications of Overseers and Deacons**
	3:1-7 Overseers/Bishops
	3:8-13 Deacons
3:14–4:16	**Instructions regarding Timothy's Own Ministry**
	3:14-16 The Theme of the Charge
	4:1-5 Responding to the Ascetic Error
	4:6-16 A General Charge

---

1. The Gnostic movement, probably originating in the middle to late second century, taught that special knowledge (gnōsis) is the means to salvation.

5:1–6:2a   Charges regarding Various Church Groups
    5:1-2   The Church as Family
    5:3-16   Widows
    5:17-25   Elders
    6:1-2a   Slaves
6:2b-19   Concluding Exhortations
    6:2b-10   False Teachers
    6:11-16   The Faithful Fight
    6:17-19   A Word for the Wealthy
6:20-21   Summary Charge and Benediction

1:1-2. OPENING

The letter opens in a traditional format but with some unusual features for a Pauline letter. The characterization of Paul's apostleship ("by [the] command . . .") in 1:1 is found elsewhere only in Titus 1:3; the identification of God as "our Savior" appears only in 1 Timothy (also 2:3; 4:10) and Titus (2:10; 3:4);[2] and the epithet "our hope" is applied to Christ only here and in Colossians 1:27, though Titus 1:2-3 also associates Christ with hope.[3] This distinctive three-part opening phrase, referring to Paul, God, and Christ, establishes Paul as the divinely willed proclaimer of salvation and hope. To carry on the Pauline mandate is to bear an awesome responsibility.

The text suggests in 1:2 that Timothy, as a "true" (NIV, NAB) or "loyal" (NRSV) child in faith (or "the faith," NRSV, NIV), is prepared to carry out that responsibility with the grace, mercy, and peace that come jointly (like Paul's commission) from both God the Father and Christ Jesus "our" Lord. Similar language appears only in the opening of 2 Timothy and Titus.[4]

1:3-20. A CHARGE TO COMBAT FALSE TEACHING

The traditional place for a thanksgiving is occupied with a word of thanks (1:12-17) enveloped in a charge to fight against false teaching (1:3-11, 18-20). This chi-

---

2. Elsewhere in the New Testament God, rather than Christ, is called Savior only in Luke 1:47 and Jude 25. It is implied also in 2 Tim. 1:9 and Titus 3:5.

3. See also Titus 2:13; 3:7.

4. "Grace, mercy, and peace" only in 2 Tim. 1:2; "loyal [NIV, NAB: "true"] child" only in Titus 1:4; "beloved child" in 2 Tim. 1:2.

astic structure suggests that the first way Timothy can exercise his role as Paul's "child" is by protecting from corruption the gospel of salvation and hope that Paul first experienced and then proclaimed.

Paul urges Timothy to remain in Ephesus, where he had apparently stationed him as his delegate before leaving for Macedonia (cf., possibly, Acts 19:22 and 20:1). Perhaps now the various problems at Ephesus had discouraged Timothy (and/or others). Timothy's job (1:3) is to halt the spread of "different" (NRSV) — that is, "false" (NIV, NAB) — teaching (Gk. *heterodidaskalein*). The precise character of this false teaching is not clear, but it seems to be a movement centered in speculation (1:4) about the Jewish law (1:7-10) that is preoccupied with "myths and endless genealogies" (1:4).

This "meaningless talk" (1:6) is contrasted with "sound" — that is, 'healthy' — teaching (1:10).[5] The fundamental feature of sound teaching is that its aim *(telos)* is the conjunction of belief and behavior, the creation of a community whose faith issues in love (1:5). Though "love" is connected here with "a pure heart" and "a good conscience," the point is essentially the same as Galatians 5:6: "faith working through love." This is "divine training" (NRSV) or "the plan of God" (NAB) known by faith (1:4).

We can assume, therefore, that however the false teachers are using the Law in their teaching, it is not to promote love. It is possible then, that these teachers are Jewish believers trying to persuade the church under Timothy's care to engage in intense interpretation of Jewish Law and in the application of its minutiae to the regulation of individual and communal life. Paul counters (1:8-9) that the Law is not intended for the "innocent" (NRSV) or "righteous" (NAB, NIV) — that is, believers — but for those who break it in various ways (1:8-10). Paul is not saying that the Law has no relevance for believers, as if they can now avoid its ethical demands and do whatever they please, but rather that its focus is on covenant stipulations and not on speculation regarding minutiae. The problem with the false teachers is not that they heed the Law, but rather that instead of using the plain covenant demands of the Law to demonstrate to nonbelievers their need for transformation, they are using it with believers to promote speculation about its obscurities.

In this situation, it is fair to indicate that the Law is not "laid down" (1:9) for believers in that sense. Any "legitimate" (cf. NRSV, 1:8) use of the Law focuses on "sound teaching": the fundamental connection between law and gospel, between the good news and the divinely given moral Law it was intended to empower people to fulfill (cf. Rom. 8:3-4).

The power of this gospel to transform human life could find no greater witness than Paul's own conversion and appointment to Christ's service, which

5. See also 1 Tim. 6:3; 2 Tim. 1:13; 4:3; Titus 1:9, 13; 2:1, 2.

is narrated, and linked with liturgical texts, in 1:12-17. Paul thanks Christ himself for empowering him (1:12) to be trusted with the gospel (1:11) and appointed to his ministry (*diakonia*, 1:12). This occurred despite Paul's having been a blasphemer, persecutor, and "man of violence" (NRSV) who acted without knowledge or faith (1:13).[6]

The abundant grace of Christ has altered all that, and now Paul lives in Christ, sharing in Christ's faith and love (cf. 1:5). His transformation illustrates the truthfulness of a liturgical proclamation cited in 1:15 — that Christ came to save (i.e., transform) sinners; Paul is an example to all of the power of Christ's mercy (1:16). For this the apostle bursts into praise in another liturgical text that connects his transformation also to the "only God" (i.e., God the Father; cf. 1:2), who is the "King of the ages" (1:17).

This narrative of Paul's transformation into a person of faith and love sets the stage for a return to the charge to Timothy (1:18-20). Timothy is to be guided and inspired in his spiritual battle by certain prophecies once uttered about him (1:18). These may well have revealed his own call to continue the Pauline mission, which he must do by imitating Paul's own commitment to both appropriate belief and appropriate behavior — "faith and a good conscience" (1:19). This echo of 1:5 and 1:14 suggests that Paul is not interested in the vagaries of an introspective 'clean conscience' but in the practical demonstration of love — broadly understood as right covenantal relations with others — that is consistent with both the Law and the gospel.

Those who reject the ethical implications of faith — like Hymenaeus and Alexander (1:20; cf. 2 Tim. 2:17; 4:14) — have blasphemously "made a shipwreck of their faith" (NAB) and have been (temporarily?) separated from the community. Timothy's job is to make sure this happens to no one else.

2:1-15. PRAYER AND TEACHING IN THE ASSEMBLY

The mention of two men's separation from the community leads next to a brief — but controversial — discussion of the assembled community's worship, which includes both prayer and instruction.

---

6. Cf. Gal. 1:1-17, where Paul says that God set him apart and then transformed him through a revelation of Christ.

THE COMMUNITY'S PRAYER AND WITNESS (2:1-7)

The first set of instructions is about intercession and witness, which both men and women, it appears, are called to do (2:1-7). The instructions begin with a call for intercession and thanksgiving for all people and for political authorities (2:1-2). The goal of this prayer is to enable the community to live in peace, probably a reference to the possibility of unofficial and official persecution (2:2). The tranquil language of 2:2, then, does not promote a bourgeois ethic, as some have suggested, arguing that terms like "godliness" (NRSV) or "devotion" (NAB; *eusebeia*) reveal accommodation to the Roman status quo. Rather, the hope of this letter is that neighbors and public officials will be drawn to — rather than opposed to — the believers' lifestyle and thus come to salvation (2:3-4). The witness of the community cannot have been so completely Roman or bourgeois as some have suggested if it was necessary to pray that people not disturb them.

The missionary motivation for the community's prayer leads next to the citation of another liturgical fragment emphasizing the uniqueness of God the Savior and Christ the mediator (2:5-6a). The text focuses on Christ's mediatorial role in both incarnation and death, a death understood in sacrificial terms ("ransom"). Reminding the readers of his own missionary call (2:7), Paul implies that they share in his mission by testifying to the neighbors and authorities for whom they pray. Since Christ's death has just been described (2:6) as a "testimony" (NIV, NAB; *martyrion*), the text implies that the church's faithful witness is also a continuation of Jesus' testimony, which was likewise to political authorities (cf. 6:13).

HUSBANDS AND WIVES AT WORSHIP (2:8-15)

The remaining verses about prayer (2:8-10) and the instructions about teaching and learning (2:11-15) are thornier because of the controversial attitudes toward women embodied in them. Several important questions surface in a close reading of this text:

- Does it distinguish between men and women generally, or between husbands and wives specifically?
- Does it exhort women to pray or simply to dress modestly?
- *Why* does it say whatever it actually says?
- Does it express anything positive about women, or is it irredeemably patriarchal and chauvinist?

We shall attempt to answer these questions more or less in order, noting up front that there is a very wide range of interpretive options, many dependent on reconstructions of the social setting supposedly reflected in this text.

In Greek the words for 'man' and 'woman' may also mean 'husband' and 'wife,' depending on context. Here the context (the mention of childbirth in 2:15) suggests the latter pair of translations.[7] The text affirms the standard ancient view that wives should not teach their husbands (2:11-12). It does so, however, in light of the Genesis stories of creation and 'fall' (2:13-14). Eve, created after Adam, set a bad precedent by misteaching her husband, the text avers, yet all is not lost for her descendants. A wife (singular in the text) is expected to learn and is not excluded from salvation as long as she bears children and "they" exhibit faith and love — the basic requirements of all believers (1:5) — along with holiness and modesty (2:15). To whom does the "they" refer? Is it a grammatical slip meant to refer to 'a wife' (i.e., 'all wives'), or does it refer to the children, making the wife's salvation contingent on her faithfulness in raising her children as believers? If the latter interpretation is correct, then wives are in fact expected to teach — though their spiritual pupils are their children rather than their spouses.

The reference to childbearing may allude to a Jewish tradition that Eve's seduction was sexual, which would explain the reference to modesty (2:9 and perhaps also 2:15). The point would be that a daughter of Eve will be saved if she avoids sexual sin and practices holiness, symbolized by raising believing children with her husband rather than dressing seductively at the church's gatherings. The first of the references to modesty (2:9) appears in connection with "good works" (2:10) as the proper attire at the assembly (2:9-10). The criticism of extravagant jewelry and dress may simply allude to a traditional ethical maxim, or it may imply the presence of wealthy women who are coming to the assembly inappropriately dressed.

It is not clear from the Greek text of 2:9 whether wives (or women) are being exhorted to pray (like men/husbands), or just to adorn themselves with modesty and good deeds, as most translations imply. The context, however, suggests that husbands and wives are each being given particular guidelines for their behavior at prayer in the context of public worship: males without aggression (2:8), females without sensuality.

If this analysis is correct, it means that wives may pray with, but not teach, their husbands at worship. This prohibition may be due not so much to theological principles as to circumstances in which (especially wealthy?) women were captivated by false teachers. If this is the case, then the theological principles used are intended for specific, rather than general, application. In any

---

7. The interpretation of the childbirth as a reference to Jesus' birth (the incarnation) has no contextual support.

event, both males and females are expected to worship and learn together and to express their faith through good deeds of holiness and love, which is the theme of the first part of the letter. In this sense, husbands and wives have a certain equality in spite of their differences. This call to faith expressed in love blunts, at least to some degree, the patriarchy many find in the text.

3:1-13. QUALIFICATIONS OF OVERSEERS AND DEACONS

As noted in the introduction, 1 Timothy seems to know of at least three church 'offices.' Two are discussed in 3:1-13. These are the "overseer" (NIV, NRSV note) or "bishop" (NRSV, NAB, NIV note; Gk. *episkopos*) and the "deacon" *(diakonos)* — including perhaps female deacons. (The third office, "elder" [*presbyteros*], is discussed in 5:17-25.) We can only offer educated guesses about their roles based on the words used for the offices and on the qualifications themselves.[8]

OVERSEERS/BISHOPS (3:1-7)

The "bishop" or "overseer" *(episkopos)* is a noble position that can be properly sought (3:1). An overseer must possess integrity, self-control (no successive marriages or, less likely, polygamy), dignity, hospitality, and teaching skill, and he (women need not apply) must not be aggressive or greedy (3:2-3). Furthermore, he must manage his own household well (3:4-5), be sufficiently mature in the faith to avoid pride and its consequences (3:6), and have a good reputation outside the church (3:7). These qualifications suggest administrative, teaching, and perhaps 'public relations' responsibilities. The use of the singular noun *episkopos* should not be anachronistically taken to mean that a whole city had one bishop. Rather, the text suggests that each household church had one overseer, like the 'president' of a synagogue or collegium. Perhaps the churches met in the houses of the overseers.

DEACONS (3:8-13)

Deacons *(diakonoi)* must also be persons of good character who are not greedy (3:8) but are known as people of faith and love (3:9, referring to their con-

---

8. The "sure" (NRSV) or "trustworthy" (NAB, NIV) saying referenced in 3:1 may be the following sentence(s) about overseers or the preceding sentence(s) about wives.

science; cf. 1:5). They, too, must exercise self-control and manage their households well (3:12). This suggests internal responsibilities of serving in capacities other than teaching. Interestingly, deacons are to be tested (or examined) in some fashion, probably on belief and behavior, before being appointed (3:10).

The reference to "women" in 3:11 may be to the deacons' wives (so NIV) or, more likely, to female deacons, since they are expected to be "serious" (NRSV) or "dignified" (NAB) like their male counterparts (3:11; cf. 3:8).[9]

3:14–4:16. INSTRUCTIONS REGARDING TIMOTHY'S OWN MINISTRY

This section of instructions occurs mainly, though not exclusively, in the second-person singular as direct address to Timothy. It consists of three parts: a general thematic instruction (3:14-16), a warning about a particular false teaching (4:1-5), and a set of general admonitions about exercising the ministry (4:6-16).

THE THEME OF THE CHARGE (3:14-16)

As noted in the introduction, 3:15 constitutes the basic theme of 1 Timothy: "how . . . to behave in the household of God." These instructions, meant as a temporary stand-in for Paul's own teaching ministry in person (3:14), are said to be essential to the church's essence as the "pillar and bulwark" (NRSV) of the truth (3:15).

This claim leads immediately into the recitation of another liturgical piece, probably a creed or hymn, in 3:16. This carefully structured confession of faith summarizes Paul's gospel in three pairs of phrases, totaling six affirmations. These are not arranged chronologically, but rhetorically, depending on pairs of opposites to give structure to the text:

> revealed in *flesh* — vindicated in *spirit*
> seen by *angels* — proclaimed among *Gentiles*
> believed in throughout the *world* — taken up in *glory*

The three sets of pairs share a this-worldly/otherworldly schema that indicates the divine-human interaction that the gospel ("the mystery of our religion,"

---

9. The NRSV and NAB are both vague ("women"), but the NRSV indicates both interpretive options in a note.

NRSV, 3:16) proclaims. Jesus is indeed the mediator between heaven and earth (cf. 2:5). The church is therefore obligated to order its life in ways that witness to the truth of that gospel of Christ's incarnation, vindication, and exaltation.

RESPONDING TO THE ASCETIC ERROR (4:1-5)

Among the false teachers was a strain of asceticism that forbade marriage and insisted on some form of food abstinence, perhaps vegetarianism (4:3). Similar early Christian asceticism is attested in 1 Corinthians 7 and Romans 14.

The response to this asceticism is first to connect it with the expected apostasy of the "later" (NRSV, NIV) or "last" (NAB) times. The polemic against the ascetic teachers (4:1-2) implies a demonically inspired problem of conscience, or disjunction between proper theology and ethics. Therefore the second part of the response is to link marriage and eating to the doctrine of creation (4:3b-5), a distinctly Jewish move that demonstrates the right use of Scripture (1:8). For believers, God's word pronounces the created order good (cf. Gen. 1), and they respond with a word of thanks.

A GENERAL CHARGE (4:6-16)

In contrast to the various false teachers, Timothy is called to be a good servant or minister *(diakonos)* of Christ, one who avoids the false teachers' obsession with myths (4:7a; cf. 1:4) but pursues "sound teaching" (4:6; cf. 1:10), teaching that connects doctrine to "godliness," as a faithful saying or proverb reminds the writer and reader (4:7b-9). The true toil of any minister — Paul, Timothy, or others — is to teach for godliness, for transformation rather than speculation, a task grounded in the hope of future salvation (4:9-10).

For the young Timothy this charge means, in concrete terms, living as an example of sound teaching — doctrine that results in a life of faith, love, and general integrity (4:11-12). Such integrity will demonstrate that sound teaching is independent of age (4:12, 15). Timothy is to exercise, and not neglect, the gift given to him. He will do this by reading (i.e., reading Scripture), exhorting (ethical instruction), and teaching (doctrinal instruction) in Paul's absence (4:13-14). The salvation he and his hearers hope for (4:10, 16) depends, in some measure, on the integrity of his life and teaching (4:16) — an awesome responsibility.

5:1–6:2a. CHARGES REGARDING
VARIOUS CHURCH GROUPS

The next part of the letter considers the responsibilities to and of various groups in the church.

THE CHURCH AS FAMILY (5:1-2)

A general admonition to treat others as blood relatives (creating what sociologists call a 'fictive' or 'alternative' family) begins the section. This reminds Timothy as a 'minister' that he has a deep kinship with those he serves, and that such a kinship requires love and integrity.

WIDOWS (5:3-16)

This fascinating passage is the only extended one in the New Testament that deals directly with the place of widows in the early church.[10] There is some debate about whether the text deals with the treatment of just one group of widows — those, according to 5:9, to be "put on the list" (NRSV, NIV) or "enrolled" (NAB) — or also with widows in general (5:3-8). There is also debate about the precise role of the enrolled widows. Do they constitute an 'office' or 'order' like that of the deacons and elders? That is, do they exercise an official ministry, or are they simply expected to do good deeds for the church in gratitude for the church's financial support?

We can answer these questions in part, at least, by looking at how the passage begins and ends: with the question of which widows are *really* widows (5:3, 5, 16). The NIV translates "real widows" as those "who are really in need," which is partly correct. Jewish and early Christian practice assumed that widows (and orphans) were objects of special divine concern.[11] The limited funds of the early churches raised the practical question of how that divine concern was to be expressed. Were there limits on whom the church should help? The entire discussion in 5:3-16, then, addresses the practical question: Which widows should *the community* support financially? The qualifications for 'true widowhood' are meant primarily to answer this question.

---

10. Cf. Acts 6:1-3. Widows are also mentioned in Mark 12:40, 42-43; Luke 2:37; 4:25-26; 7:12; 18:3; 20:47; 21:2-3; Acts 9:39-41; 1 Cor. 7:8; James 1:27; Rev. 18:7.

11. In addition to the New Testament texts cited in the previous note, see Deut. 10:18; 24:19-21; 27:19; Ps. 146:9; Isa. 1:17; Jer. 7:6. The theme continues in early Christian literature after the New Testament, too.

The first and chief qualification is being left alone and thus without financial support (5:5), which means not only that a woman has no husband but also that she has no family at all. If she has surviving family members, it is their duty to care for her (5:4, 8, 16). For them not to do so — assuming they are believers — would be to deny the faith (which here is clearly continuing Jewish custom) and to do less than what even pagans routinely did (5:8).

The second qualification is devotion to God rather than pleasure (5:6). There may be a hint here that some widows were women of means who were rather self-indulgent. This is no doubt related to the third qualification: age. The true widow must be at least sixty and married only once (5:9). The concern is apparently with women who have demonstrated, or might demonstrate, unhealthy sensuality in their widowed state.

With respect to older widows, the specific concern seems to be related to yet a fourth qualification — devotion to the church — as demonstrated in good works such as hospitality, raising children (including orphans?), and so on (5:10). Although the text does not state explicitly that enrolled widows must continue to render such service, it is likely that they did. In fact, it appears that widows who wished to be enrolled made a pledge to remain single and continue in good works of service to and on behalf of the community (5:12).

The concern about younger women and sensuality, if they were enrolled as widows, is that they would be unable to keep such a pledge; they would go house to house engaging in gossip rather than good deeds (5:13), and would want to marry (5:11). This would obviously be bad PR for the church; hence the advice is not to enroll them as widows but to encourage them to marry (5:14). If this advice sounds prejudiced and sexist, its bias is apparently not unfounded (5:15).

In conclusion, we can say that although the 'true widow' may not have been an office like overseer or deacon, being enrolled as such a widow probably carried with its privileges some responsibilities, perhaps including going "house to house" (5:13) to help the afflicted within the church.

ELDERS (5:17-25)

The next group to be considered in the letter, and probably the third 'office' described, has also generated some controversy. The Greek word *presbyteroi*, "elders" (NRSV, NIV) or "presbyters" (NAB), appears to refer to a group of remunerated men who, though not necessarily elderly, command the respect of the church and lead it ("direct the affairs of the church," NIV, 5:17). The same responsibility (and corresponding Greek term) appears in Romans 12:8 and 1 Thessalonians 5:12, as well as in this letter at 3:4, concerning bishops/overseers.

Some, but not all, elders preach and teach (5:17). Elders who excel should receive a double wage (5:17), as Scripture infers (5:18).[12] As a body, the elders ordain others to ministry by the laying on of hands (4:14).

But is this group the same as the "bishops" or "overseers" described in 3:1-7? Scholarly opinion is divided. Although Titus 1:5-7 may use the terms "elder/presbyter" and "overseer/bishop" interchangeably (or nearly so), the evidence in 1 Timothy is inconclusive.[13] It is likely, however, that two distinct but somewhat overlapping offices are in view. Whatever the precise structure, the functions of administration, education, and ordination (or laying on of hands) are executed by a body, not by one person.

Along with the good elders, there were apparently some bad ones. Instructions for dealing with them include: (1) the use of multiple witnesses (5:19), as required by Deuteronomy 19:15; (2) public rebuke of the unrepentant (5:20); and (3) impartiality (5:21). The existence of such problem leaders offers opportunity for an admonition not to 'ordain' (lay hands on) people too hastily, and not to imitate sinners, even if they happen to be ordained (5:22). A final proverbial word about the eventual public character of both evil and good deeds (5:24-25) is preceded by a curious piece of advice to Timothy (5:23). It is perhaps intended as an antidote not only to stomach ailments, but also to ascetical elders.

SLAVES (6:1-2a)

A brief word to believers who are slaves concludes this section of exhortations to specific groups in the church.[14] Unlike Colossians and Ephesians, however, there is no corresponding admonition to masters. Rather, slaves are told to be respectful to all masters, whether (implicitly) nonbelievers (6:1) or (explicitly) believers (6:2a). In the former case, the motive is once again to protect the church from bad relations with — and possible danger from — the world outside the church (6:1). In the latter instance, the motive is to serve fellow beloved believers, not allowing their status in the Lord as "brothers" to be an excuse for less respect or service (6:2a).

Whether this perspective is consonant with, or contradictory to, other Pauline texts on slaves and masters (e.g., Philemon; Col. 3:22–4:1; Eph. 6:5-9) is

12. See Deut. 25:4; 1 Cor. 9:9; Luke 10:7.
13. Overseers/bishops must be able to teach (3:2), but that does not mean that all actually do. If some do not teach, then the two groups may be the same. If all overseers actually teach, then the group of presbyters is distinct.
14. A word about the wealthy appears in 6:17-19.

debated. But the text cannot be interpreted as providing support for oppressive masters. That would hardly be consistent with the letter's call to love and good deeds, or with the kind of family relationship articulated in 5:1-2. This text applies to all relationships in the community, even that of master-slave. The text seeks to prevent slaves from taking advantage of that relationship.

6:2b-19. CONCLUDING EXHORTATIONS

The final section of this letter consists of a collection of exhortations, many proverbial in character, that further develop two earlier themes (false teachers and Timothy's duties) and underscore the apparently vexing problem of greed in the community.

FALSE TEACHERS (6:2b-10)

This passage suspects that the false teachers have two problems: their doctrine itself and their motives. Appropriate doctrine is once again characterized as both faithful to Christ and connected to ethics (promoting "godliness," *eusebeia*, 6:3) rather than promoting controversy (6:2b-5; cf. 1:3-7; 4:6-16). The negative effects of such teaching are listed and traced to a combination of arrogance, ignorance, and greed (6:4-5).

The explicit attention given to money in these concluding admonitions, together with the implicit concern voiced elsewhere, suggests that the accusation of greed is not merely polemical. "Religion" (NAB) or "godliness" (NRSV, NIV) — *eusebeia* — is not a means to financial gain (6:5), but only to an eternal reward in the future (so 4:8) and to contentment in the present (6:6-8; cf. Phil. 4:11). Believers should be reminded of the ancient wisdom that human beings enter and depart this world empty-handed (6:7; cf. Job 1:21), and that the love of money (not money itself) leads to all kinds of evils, including departure from the faith (6:9-10). This haunting reminder is likely intended as both a criticism of certain teachers and a warning to all.

THE FAITHFUL FIGHT (6:11-16)

The next set of admonitions pertains to and summarizes Timothy's ministry. He is to pursue the moral and spiritual virtues that have been the theme of this letter (godliness, faith, love, etc.; 6:11), and to "fight the good fight of the faith"

(NRSV, NIV; NAB, "compete well for the faith"), a summary of his vocation as Paul's delegate (6:12a; cf. 1:18) and something Paul himself has done (2 Tim. 4:7). Performing such a faithful ministry is Timothy's way of taking hold of the eternal life to which he was called and which he confessed publicly (6:12b) — either when he was baptized or, more likely, when he received the laying on of hands (cf. 4:14).

The next part of the summary charge (6:13-16) has a solemn, liturgical character. The text may in fact represent a portion of an early 'ordination' rite in which the presence of God and Christ is invoked (6:13; the passing on of the Spirit may be implied by 4:14; cf. 2 Tim. 1:6-7). The reference to Christ's "good [NAB, 'noble') confession" is a call to faithfulness even when it is dangerous, and a reminder of the inevitability of suffering (6:13). This is all placed in an eschatological framework (6:14-15a, using *epiphaneia* to refer to Jesus' return) that concludes with a burst of praise (6:15b-16).

A WORD FOR THE WEALTHY (6:17-19)

The letter's final set of instructions concerns the wealthy in the church. They are not to be proud of their riches or trust in them, but are to trust in God the generous provider (6:17). Moreover, the wealthy must be rich in good works and must share generously (6:18). This alone is their proper treasure and guarantee of *true* life in the future (6:19), an echo of Jesus' words (e.g., Matt. 6:19-21; Luke 12:13-21).

6:20-21. SUMMARY CHARGE AND BENEDICTION

In one last admonition to Timothy (6:20-21a), the theme of this letter is summed up: "guard what has been entrusted to you" *(tēn parathēkēn),* that is, by maintaining the truth of Paul's gospel and turning away from "so-called knowledge" (NAB). There is a real danger of deviation from this gospel, with the possibility of "ruin and destruction" (6:9). It is doubtful that we should read this admonition, therefore, as 'conservative.' Rather, it is radical in the first sense of that word: a charge to preserve, and even suffer for, the original message — the truth embodied in Jesus, the truth to which Jesus himself bore witness and for which he suffered and died.

In this light the letter concludes briefly but poignantly with a blessing of grace — for Timothy and all concerned (6:21b, "you" plural).

Summary of 1 Timothy

First Timothy is a charge to ensure that the church's corporate life embodies certain key elements.

- As God's "household," the church must order its worship, doctrine, and life in accord with the principles of Paul's gospel preserved in the church's liturgical fragments.
- Sound or healthy doctrine is concerned with spiritual transformation and ethical conduct, not with speculation of various sorts.
- Teaching that is preoccupied with the minutiae of Jewish Law and genealogies, various aspects of "knowledge," or ascetic beliefs and practices is unsound (unhealthy) because it is not consonant with the gospel and does not lead to greater virtue.
- Church leaders (overseers, deacons, elders, and, less formally, widows) are servants who must be people of mature faith, proven character, and good reputation in the broader community who also possess the requisite gifts and/or experience for teaching, administration, and good works.
- Although women (wives) must not teach their husbands in the context of public worship, they are expected to learn and pray, to live godly lives, and to teach their children faithfully; moreover, some of them likely serve as deacons, and some of the older widows are formally enrolled, a status that likely involves a kind of diaconal ministry, too.

THE STORY IN FRONT OF THE LETTER

Some Readings of 1 Timothy and the Pastorals Generally

"In contrast to these two giants [Paul and John], the author of the Pastorals, and indeed most other later New Testament writers, seem without originality — sincere and devoted, it is true, but without fresh ideas. Our author is best described as a priest devoted to transmitting that which he has received, not a prophet or creative spirit illuminating the Christian faith with his own genius, not restating it or reinterpreting it to include whatever of value there may have been in the presentation of the heretics. He is a churchman, fanatically loyal, intense, intolerant, yet able in administration. Concerned that the church shall be respected in its pagan environment, that is, concerned with what we should call public relations, he advocates virtues which are as pagan as they are Christian. They represent what we should call a common-sense, middle-of-the-road, conservative point of view — the point of view of church which will minimize the difference between itself and the world so that it may the more easily win the world."

> Fred D. Gealy, "The First and Second Epistles to Timothy and the Epistle to Titus," in *The Interpreter's Bible*, ed. George A. Buttrick et al. (New York and Nashville: Abingdon, 1955), 11:343-551, here 373

"In one form or another, these questions [addressed in the Pastoral Epistles] — of identity and authority — always face the church on earth. One use of the Pastoral Epistles is to stop us [from] ignoring them out of mere impatience and because we feel that Christians have paid them enough attention in the past. In the end, the questions had better be answered than banished from sight."

> J. L. Houlden, *The Pastoral Epistles*, Pelican New Testament Commentaries (New York: Penguin Books, 1976), p. 18

"The Pastoral Epistles have been accused of surrendering the great visions of the kingdom in the teachings of Jesus and the mystical ethics of Paul for mundane, un-heroic, bourgeois morality. This is true only in the sense that ordinary Christians with ordinary responsibilities find an ethic that speaks to them. The heroism that emerges is a quiet one, found in the midst of maintaining other duties. Christian virtue is found in the turmoil of ordinary life, not in the pristine order of an other-worldly sect. Christianity is moving into the mainstream of the Greek and Roman world. And the question will always be, What was gained and lost in that transition?"

> Lewis R. Donelson, *Colossians, Ephesians, 1 and 2 Timothy, and Titus*, Westminster Bible Companion (Louisville: Westminster John Knox, 1996), p. 120

"[T]heology and ethics are thoroughly integrated in the Pastorals — evident, not least, in the flow of argument in several passages (e.g., 1 Tim. 2:1-6; 4:3-5; Titus 2:1-15; 3:1-7). Theology was not a mere clinging to old formulae; it issued directly in practical corollaries for living. Nor were ethics simply a nervous conformity to bourgeois ideals; their rationale was deeply rooted in the gospel. The importance of this observation for churches of all time can hardly be overemphasized."

> James D. G. Dunn, "1 and 2 Timothy and Titus," in *The New Interpreter's Bible*, ed. Leander E. Keck et al. (Nashville: Abingdon, 2000), 11:773-880, here 784-85

QUESTIONS FOR REFLECTION

1. Are there modern parallels to the unhealthy pursuit of speculation and matters of minutiae in the study of theology and the teaching of doctrine that is criticized in this letter? What contribution to 'sound' teaching might 1 Timothy make to the contemporary church? In what ways, if any, might its own teaching seem 'unsound'?
2. What is the most appropriate way to engage the attitude toward women expressed in 2:8-15?
3. How might the qualities required of overseers, bishops, and widows provide guidance for church leadership today? Are any of the requirements out of date or otherwise inappropriate?
4. Which aspects of 1 Timothy's ministerial charge to Timothy should be (a) appropriated, (b) modified, or (c) rejected today?
5. How do you respond to the interpretations of 1 Timothy, and the Pastorals generally, quoted above?
6. In sum, what does this letter urge the church to believe, to hope for, and to do?

FOR FURTHER READING AND STUDY

See the suggestions on the Pastorals as a whole at the end of the previous chapter.

CHAPTER 19

TITUS

Ordering Church Life and Leadership
between the Epiphanies

*For the grace of God has appeared, bringing salvation to all, training us
to renounce impiety and worldly passions, and in the present age to live
lives that are self-controlled, upright, and godly, while we wait for the
blessed hope and the manifestation of the glory of our great God and
Savior, Jesus Christ.*

Titus 2:11-13

Even more than the other Pastoral Epistles, the letter to Titus unfairly suffers
from neglect by some and disparagement by others. Although it does not exhibit the passion of 2 Timothy or contain the controversies associated with
parts of 1 Timothy, this letter is not a bland post-Pauline diet that deserves the
canonical marginalization it has experienced.

Rather, the letter to Titus is an attempt to articulate a Pauline vision of
faith, love, self-control, and hope — in a word, "godliness" *(eusebeia)* — lived
in the real world between the first and second comings of Christ. Each of these
two comings is understood as an appearing or 'epiphany' (Gk. *epiphaneia*): a
divine manifestation of grace and salvation.[1]

---

1. The letter uses the noun *epiphaneia* itself only once, of the second coming (2:13), but it
also twice uses the related verb *epiphanein* of the first coming (2:11; 3:4). Translations use "appeared" for the verb and "appearing" (NIV), "appearance" (NAB), or "manifestation" (NRSV)
for the noun.

THE STORY BEHIND THE LETTER

As noted in previous chapters, the letter to Titus is routinely dismissed as a pseudonymous work by a 'disciple' of the apostle. The major arguments for this perspective need not be rehearsed here, since they are the same as those noted for 1 and 2 Timothy. One additional problem should be mentioned, however: apart from this letter, the New Testament provides no evidence that Paul ever visited Crete, yet 1:5 states he left Titus there to "put in order what remained to be done" and to "appoint elders in every town."

Though it is obviously impossible to confirm or refute the historical situation affirmed in this verse, that is the story the reader is asked to imagine. Paul the great missionary is leaving his trusted coworker Titus to order the life and leadership of the Pauline churches on Crete, a large island in the Mediterranean due south of the Aegean Sea that separates Greece from Asia Minor. The 'historical Titus,' according to Galatians and 2 Corinthians, was a Gentile convert whom Paul showcased as proof that the Jerusalem leaders did not require Gentiles to be circumcised (Gal. 2:1-3). Titus took on an especially significant diplomatic role in Paul's relationship with the Corinthian believers (2 Cor. 2:13; 7:6, 13-16), above all (appropriately) concerning the collection for the poor believers in Jerusalem (2 Cor. 8:6, 16, 23; 12:18). Titus was clearly one of Paul's most cherished and trusted associates: a brother, partner, and coworker (2 Cor. 2:13; 8:23).

As Paul's delegate, then, Titus (whether the historical figure or a literary device) receives in this letter instructions from Paul regarding church leadership, opposition to false teachers and their controversies, and the general conduct of believers in the world. The themes of sound doctrine and good works, known from 1 Timothy, reappear. These topics and themes are all set in the context of the two epiphanies that frame life in the present age (2:11-14).

The charge of fostering a 'bourgeois' or 'conservative' ethic has been leveled against Titus as it has also against 1 Timothy. Whether by Paul himself or (as seems more likely) a later author indebted to Paul, this letter does not deserve these labels without serious qualifications. In addition to comments made in previous contexts, we may make the following brief observations. Although it is true that Titus affirms what might be called 'traditional civic virtues,' the letter does not affirm *all* such pagan 'virtues.' This document rejects certain forms of thinking and behavior that characterize outsiders and that *formerly* characterized the believers in the towns of Crete (or elsewhere). The *eusebeia* ('godliness, piety, devotion') of this letter is not the religious and patriotic allegiance to Roman gods, emperors, and values that its Latin equivalent, *pietas,* denotes and demands. Titus is hardly a defense of the Roman status quo.

The letter to Titus engages, in other words, in a theological sifting of 'traditional civic virtues' in order to discover which ones are sufficiently compatible with the gospel and can be appropriated or transformed into a life of faith, love, and hope lived between the epiphanies. The explicitly covenantal character of the ethics of this letter must not be overlooked (2:14). The letter to Titus is not intended to form communities of secluded believers but of believers who exist as God's people within the realities of the Roman Empire.

THE STORY WITHIN THE LETTER

The letter unfolds as follows:

1:1-4   **Opening**
1:5-16   **Appointing Leaders and Opposing False Teachers**
           1:5-9   Elders/Overseers
           1:10-16   False Teachers
2:1–3:11   **Ordering the Community's Life**
           2:1   The General Charge to Titus
           2:2-10   Instructions for Specific Groups
           2:11–3:11   The Ministry of Titus and Its Evangelical Basis
3:12-15   **Greetings and Final Charge**

1:1-4. OPENING

The opening of Titus echoes the openings of 1 Thessalonians, 1 Timothy, and Romans in significant ways. Paul is God's servant/slave and Christ's apostle (1:1). His mission has a threefold emphasis: faith, "truth that is in accordance with godliness," and "the hope of eternal life" (1:1-2). This is a version of the Pauline triad of faith, love, and hope (cf. 1 Thess. 1:3). The themes of divine promise (1:2-3; cf. 2 Tim. 1:1) and command/commission (1:3; cf. Rom. 1:1-6) are important throughout the Pauline corpus. The designation of both God and Jesus as "Savior" (1:3, 4) is not an example of theological confusion but an affirmation of the participation of both God and Christ in the entire scheme of salvation (cf. 2:11, 13; 3:4, 6; 1 Tim. 1:1, where God also is named as Savior). Like Timothy (1 Tim. 1:2), Titus is Paul's "loyal" (NRSV) or "true" (NIV) child (1:4), and thus a suitable channel of God's work in the world.

1:5-16. APPOINTING LEADERS
AND OPPOSING FALSE TEACHERS

The first part of the letter deals with the good and the bad in the towns of Crete, namely, the need to appoint good leader-teachers (1:5b-9) and to oppose bad leader-teachers (1:10-16). These tasks are essential parts of the general charge given to Titus to "put in order" (NRSV), "set right" (NAB), or even "straighten out" (NIV) the situation on Crete as Paul left it (1:5a).

ELDERS/OVERSEERS (1:5-9)

The titles given to the leaders Titus is to appoint are those used for the two offices named in 1 Timothy, elders/presbyters (*presbyteroi*, 1:5) and overseer/bishop (*episkopos*, 1:7; the singular noun, in context, does not suggest just one overseer). Translations represent these terms in various ways: the NRSV uses "elders" and "bishop" (with a note: "or *an overseer*"); the NIV has "elder" and "overseer" (with a note: "traditionally *bishop*"); and the NAB uses "presbyters" and "bishop."

In 1 Timothy the two terms appear to refer to different functions; here, however, they seem to be used interchangeably. The qualities required for such leaders are also reminiscent of 1 Timothy: the possession of good moral character, 'family values' (one marriage, believing children), a humble and calm personality, self-control, a good reputation, the gift of hospitality, obvious devotion to God (1:6-8). These leaders are not to be rebellious or greedy — traits associated with false teachers (1:6, 7). Rather, elders/overseers are teachers (not just administrators) who must know the truth of the gospel in order both to preach it soundly and to refute error resolutely (1:9).

FALSE TEACHERS (1:10-16)

The mention of those who contradict or oppose the truth provides a natural segue into a discussion of the character of such teachers in contradistinction to the nature of good church leaders. It is quite possible that the name-calling that appears in these verses is exaggerated. (The anti-Cretan epithet from the Cretan Epimenides [ca. 600 B.C.] in 1:12 might upset some of those who aren't false teachers!) Nevertheless, we can discern several traits of the opponents: there are some who are Gentiles and some who are Jews (1:10); they differ from Paul and Titus in their interpretation of the gospel (erroneously and deceitfully, from the writer's perspective; 1:10-11); they are disrupting families (1:11); and they likely charge for their services (1:11).

It is also probable that, like the false teachers implied in 1 Timothy, these people are infatuated with speculative Jewish mythology (1:14a) and have ascetic tendencies (1:14b-15a). The job of Titus is not to destroy these people but to refute their ideas so that they can become "sound in the faith" (1:13). Until such time, they are hypocritical and despicable excuses for messengers of the truth (1:15b-16).

2:1–3:11. ORDERING THE COMMUNITY'S LIFE

Similar to 1 Timothy 5:1–6:2a and to much of 1 Timothy generally, the next section of the letter gives instructions for Titus, including admonitions applicable to specific groups.

THE GENERAL CHARGE TO TITUS (2:1)

In stark contrast to the work of those who teach unsound doctrine and thereby reject the truth, Titus is charged to "teach what is consistent with sound doctrine" (2:1). Above all, as in 1 Timothy, this means teaching doctrine in a way that is not speculative or ascetic but transformative for life in the world, promoting values consistent with the gospel.

INSTRUCTIONS FOR SPECIFIC GROUPS (2:2-10)

Despite the variety in the instructions to specific groups, there is a general four-dimensional theme: the need for (a) virtue (especially self-control, including freedom from addiction and promiscuity) and (b) good instruction for (c) the benefit of the community itself and (d) its reputation in the community.

Titus is to teach older men (2:2) to have some of the virtues (including self-control) associated with overseers in 1 Timothy 3:2, together with an interesting variation on the Pauline triad of faith, love, and hope (here "endurance," *hypomonē*). We may conclude that at least some of the church's leadership is drawn from this group. But in a very important sense older women are also leaders. They are to be virtuous themselves (including, like overseers in 1 Tim. 3:3, freedom from alcohol addiction) and to teach what is good to younger women (2:3). The content of this teaching — the expectations of younger women — is 'traditional' instruction for married women: faithful devotion to husband and children, including self-control, chastity, and submission to their husbands, as a form of witness to the world (2:4-5). Similarly, younger men are to be self-controlled, exemplary in good works, and sound teachers, again to protect the community's reputation (2:6-8). Some of them are clearly also community leaders and are generally expected to be like the overseers in 1 Timothy 3:1-7.

Why slaves alone are addressed (2:9-10) and not also masters is unclear, but the rationale for slaves' obedience given here is once again its testimonial value. By obedience, respect, honesty, and faithfulness, slaves become an "ornament" (NRSV) to the "doctrine" of God's salvation (2:10).

THE MINISTRY OF TITUS AND ITS
EVANGELICAL BASIS (2:11–3:11)

The preceding series of admonitions that Titus is expected to pass on as part of his ministry had a consistent theme, as noted above. The letter now locates the basis for this work in a pair of brief expositions of the gospel (2:11-14; 3:4-8a), which prepare the way also for more general admonitions intended for Titus to deliver to the entire community (2:15–3:3; 3:8b-11).

The letter refers to the 'Christ event' (as some modern interpreters clumsily call it) more eloquently as the appearance of the salvific grace of God (2:11-12), which educates *(paideuousa)* people to live in righteousness and godliness *(dikaiōs kai eusebōs)*. As noted in the introduction to this chapter, this refers to the first appearance or epiphany of the Savior — meaning God/Christ, not the emperor. Some interpreters have understood the strong ethical emphasis in these verses and throughout the passage as a late, un-Pauline, moralistic interpretation of the gospel. Nothing could be further from the truth. In all his letters Paul insists (as a good Jew) that the purpose of election, redemption, and justification is to die to sin and the flesh in order to serve God and others. Paul likewise insists that this life of faith and love is lived in hope between Christ's first and second comings (death/resurrection and parousia).

The same structure of existence is described here: liberation from "worldly passions" for a godly life during the present age (2:11-12) in hope of the final revelation of salvation, here called the "appearing" (NIV; NAB, "appearance") or "manifestation" (NRSV; Gk. *epiphaneia*) of the "glory of our great God and Savior, Jesus Christ" (2:13). The attribution of the title "God" to Jesus has sparked debate since it occurs rarely in the New Testament.[2] But it is a logical move to make for people who have already attributed the divine titles

2. It is possible, though not likely, that the text means to say "our great God and our Savior, Jesus Christ," distinguishing between God and Christ.

"Lord" (elsewhere in the New Testament) and "Savior" (here) to Jesus, and for a writer who from the beginning of the letter expresses his conviction that both God the Father and Jesus should be called "Savior" (1:3-4). The salvific role of Jesus is then described as a self-giving death for redemption, purification, and creation of a covenant people "zealous for good deeds" (2:14; cf. 2 Cor. 5:15; Gal. 5:6; Exod. 19:5).

The obligation of Titus is to preach this gospel and its corollary ethic with authority (2:15). This ethic is summarized in 3:1-2 as one of submission to authorities, obedience, gentleness, good will to others, and general goodness. That this is no bland ethic is clear from the following verse (3:3), in which the previous, contrasting lives of the community's members are described, lives characterized by disobedience and various evils.

There follows another rich summary of the Pauline gospel of merciful liberation, narrated again in terms of an *epiphaneia* (3:4-7). This description of the trinitarian act of salvation contains many traditional Pauline terms, but also some new language, especially the words "the goodness [*chrēstotēs*] and loving kindness [*philanthrōpia*] of God our Savior" (3:4 NRSV; NAB: "kindness and generous love"; NIV: "kindness and love"). The emphasis on grace and mercy, plus the role of the Spirit in making people heirs of eternal life, is especially reminiscent of both Galatians and Romans. This eloquent précis of the Pauline gospel, which may have been used in liturgy, is called a sure or trustworthy saying (3:8a).

The concluding words to Titus repeat a key theme of this letter and of 1 Timothy: that true doctrine has nothing to do with speculation, controversies, or genealogies, but only with that which promotes good deeds (3:8b-9). Titus is to warn those who think and act otherwise two times, and then disassociate himself from them (3:10-11) — which would signal to others their error.

3:12-15. GREETINGS AND FINAL CHARGE

The letter concludes in typical Pauline fashion, though two of the people mentioned (Artemas, Zenas) and the city named (Nicopolis, on the coast of western Greece) appear nowhere else in the letters or Acts. The theme of the letter — the need for "good works" — reappears in 3:14, and the letter ends on a word of greeting and benediction.

Summary of Titus

The letter urges Titus to order the leadership and life of the communities on the island of Crete according to the Pauline gospel.

- Life in the present age is to be lived with an eye on the past and future epiphanies of Christ as God's grace and salvation.
- Titus is to appoint qualified overseers/elders who will teach sound doctrine, and to oppose false teachers.
- Titus is to admonish the church as a whole regarding its need for (a) virtue (especially self-control, including freedom from addiction and promiscuity) and (b) good instruction for (c) the benefit of the community itself and (d) its reputation in the community.

THE STORY IN FRONT OF THE LETTER

A Reading of Titus

"The Epistle to Titus is short, but it is a kind of epitome and summary of other, wordier epistles. We should be imbued with the attitudes that are taught in it. Paul is the sort of teacher who is engaged most of all in these two topics, either teaching or exhorting. Moreover, he never exhorts in such a way that he fails to mingle didactic, that is, doctrinal, instruction with it. And so while this whole epistle is obviously a hortatory one, yet he writes in such a way that he superbly mingles doctrine with exhortation, and in double measure. He is a true teacher, one who both teaches and exhorts. By his teaching he sets down what is to be done. Thus by doctrine he builds up faith, by exhortation he builds up life. He begins with exhortation, yet he mingles instruction with it. Therefore this is a hortatory epistle, yet not exclusively so."

Martin Luther, foreword to *Lectures on Titus*, 1527
(in Jaroslav Pelikan, ed., *Luther's Works*, vol. 29
[St. Louis: Concordia, 1956])

QUESTIONS FOR REFLECTION

1. Is the contemporary church called to engage in "a theological sifting of 'traditional civic virtues' in order to discover which ones are sufficiently

compatible with the gospel and can be appropriated or transformed into a life of faith, love, and hope lived between the epiphanies"? If so, which main cultural values might survive — and which might not survive — such a sifting, and why?

2. What significance should be attached today to the theological notion of Christ's two epiphanies?

3. What are the potential benefits and liabilities in considering the possible effects (both positive and negative) on the outside world as a major factor in the ordering of the church's life and worship?

4. How do you respond to the interpretation of Titus quoted above?

5. In sum, what does this letter urge the church to believe, to hope for, and to do?

FOR FURTHER READING AND STUDY

See also the suggestions on the Pastorals as a whole in chapter 17 on 2 Timothy.

Technical

Quinn, Jerome D. *The Letter to Titus: A New Translation with Notes and Commentary and an Introduction to Titus, I and II Timothy, the Pastoral Epistles.* Anchor Bible 35. New York: Doubleday, 1990. A detailed analysis, on the assumption of pseudonymity, that argues for Titus as the first of the Pastoral Epistles.

CHAPTER 20

EPILOGUE

Paul Our Contemporary

*When Paul was absent, he wrote you letters, and if you study them care-
fully, you will be able to be built up into the faith that has been given to
you, "which is the mother of us all" [Gal. 4:26], if hope follows, and if
love for God and Christ and for neighbor leads the way.*

Polycarp, Bishop of Smyrna,
Letter to the Philippians 3.2-3, ca. 115

Polycarp of Smyrna (located in western Asia Minor) was a courageous Christian bishop and martyr who, three or four decades after writing these words,
was burned at the stake by Roman authorities for refusing to confess Caesar as
Lord. He was 86 years old. Polycarp's description of Paul's epistolary ministry
to the Christians in Philippi — both those addressed in the middle of the first
century and those living several generations later — serves as a provocative
summary of our own encounter with Paul in this book.

Polycarp's words, especially interpreted in light of his final fate, tell us
several things about the apostle: he really is our contemporary, our pastor-
theologian, who teaches us about the inseparability of faith, hope, and love,
and about the meaning of that most basic Christian confession: "Jesus is
Lord." In fact, Polycarp's life and death remind all Christians that the wisest
readings of Paul's letters, whether in the first century, the second century, or
later, always involve participation in a story, the story of God's revelation and
redemption in the exalted crucified Messiah Jesus. That is, the ultimate goal of
the interpretation of Paul's letters is not merely to understand them, but to live

them, to continue their story, especially in challenging times such as those faced by Christians in the first part of the 21st century. In this epilogue, we briefly consider that goal.

PAUL, OUR CONTEMPORARY

Polycarp tells the Christians at Philippi that the apostle Paul's letters, written many years earlier, still speak today. His voice is not silent, for he is their — and our — contemporary. This claim, as Polycarp recognizes, does not mean that Paul's voice is always clear, or that the contemporary appropriation of Paul is facile. On the contrary, the interpretation of Paul requires careful study, and it requires that this diligent exegesis take place in the Christian community. Polycarp, like Paul, addresses the Philippians and us in the second-person-plural: "if you [*all, together*] study them carefully...." The mention of multiple letters may refer to more than one epistle addressed to the Philippians or, more likely, to Polycarp's conviction that the entire Pauline corpus is ultimately addressed to the entire church of all places and times.

To be sure, not everyone has found Paul to be a welcome contemporary voice, or even a past voice worthy of their attention. Over the centuries, and in our own day, there have been plenty of critics who have found Paul, or some of the letters ascribed to him, to be so seriously mistaken on one or more significant matters that they have dismissed him as hopelessly patriarchal, or arrogant, or conservative, or antinomian, or anti-Judaic, or "Puritanical," or homophobic, or whatever. Some have even felt that Christianity would be better off without Paul or his letters. Still others have concluded, and in some measure rightly so, that Paul needs liberating — not so much from his own errors, but from centuries of misinterpretation.[1]

The seriousness of these difficulties should not be underestimated. Yet Paul continues to speak, and people continue to listen. It is in part the constellation of problems in Paul that keeps drawing readers back to his correspondence, even when they do not fully understand it or agree with it. There is an enduring quality to his letters, a timeless religious and intellectual depth that has seldom, if ever, been matched in the history of letter writing, or of Christianity. That is why the interpretation of his tiny literary corpus continues to preoccupy some of the sharpest minds in both academic and ecclesial circles. Many of his issues are also our issues: unity and diversity in the church, ethnic

---

1. See, for example, Neil Elliott, *Liberating Paul: The Justice of God and the Politics of the Apostle* (Maryknoll, N.Y.: Orbis, 1994).

reconciliation, appropriate embodied sexuality, the challenge of counter-cultural living ("holiness") in a hostile culture, love for enemies in a dangerous world, hope in the face of suffering and death, and so on. Letters written *to* the Philippians, the Corinthians, the Romans, and others were written also *for* us, as Polycarp knew.

This is not to diminish the reality of the 'particularity' of Paul's letters, or to suggest that there exists no gap between him and us, between his times and ours. Quite the contrary. We must certainly acknowledge the specificity of Paul's letters, but that is in part what is so attractive about them: they were addressed to real people in real-life situations. We identify with them because we find ourselves to be similar people in similar situations. We can and must, therefore, employ our God-given, Spirit-empowered, disciplined-but-creative imaginations to discern analogies between Paul's stories and our own. Thus the Christian theological principle of *particularity* (manifested also in the incarnation) and the Christian ethical principle of *analogical thinking* (rooted in the conclusion of the parable of the Good Samaritan: "go and do likewise") combine to provide both the challenge and the promise of interpreting Paul in the church today.

PAUL, PASTOR-THEOLOGIAN

For Christians, then, Paul is not simply a riddle to solve, an opponent to take down, or even a great intellect to admire. He comes to us, through his letters, as our teacher and spiritual guide, as a conduit of the Word of God. What is remarkable about Paul — and Polycarp realizes this as well — is that his intellectually challenging letters are the work of a pastor, one whose goal is the edification of the church. His writing is that of a pastor-theologian whose task of teaching doctrine has a pastoral purpose: the formation of better Christian people and communities.

It is no accident, therefore, that theologian Ellen Charry borrows from Paul for the title of her insightful book, *By the Renewing of Your Minds: The Pastoral Function of Christian Doctrine,* a study of theologians who practiced theology pastorally.[2] The first theologian she considers is Paul. As Charry points out in her introduction, Paul's famous words at the beginning of Romans 12 succinctly summarize the apostle's approach to the task of theology:

---

2. Ellen T. Charry, *By the Renewing of Your Minds: The Pastoral Function of Christian Doctrine* (New York: Oxford, 1997).

> I appeal to you, therefore, brothers and sisters, by the mercies of God, to present your bodies as a living sacrifice, holy and acceptable to God, which is your spiritual [or "reasonable"] worship. Do not be conformed to this world [or "age"], but be transformed by the renewing of your minds, so that you may discern what is the will of God — what is good and acceptable and perfect. (Rom. 12:1-2)

For Paul, the task of theological teaching and reflection is transformative of both mind and life, of both individuals and communities. True theology is also doxological, because when the will of God is embodied in transformed people, God is truly honored and glorified. True theology is the work of a pastor who has a shepherd's heart as well as an academic's mind.

Paul constantly displays his commitment to this kind of understanding of theology. For him, every practical problem in the church has a theological cause and solution, and every theological assertion has practical consequences. No matter is too mundane for an appeal to the cross, the resurrection, the parousia and judgment, the unity and character of the church, the covenant faithfulness of God, the lordship of Jesus, or another of Paul's central theological convictions. The divisions at Corinth, for instance, or the debates about circumcision in Galatia, bring out a host of theological assertions that underlie and underline Paul's concrete exhortations.

THE INSEPARABILITY OF FAITH, HOPE, AND LOVE

If good theology is ordered to pastoral ends, what are those ends for Paul? The trinitarian spirituality we have found in Paul suggests that we could answer generally with something like "communion with God the Father; Jesus the Son, Messiah, and Lord; and the (Holy) Spirit of God and the Son." More concretely, throughout this book we have seen that the famous Pauline triad of faith, hope, and love permeates his letters. Polycarp noticed this as well, speaking vividly of the interconnectedness of these three 'theological virtues,' as the Christian tradition has come to call them. We have attempted to indicate the centrality of these virtues to Paul, and to a theologically oriented reading of his letters, by concluding each of the chapters on the thirteen letters with the question for reflection and discussion, "In sum, what does this letter urge the church to believe, to hope for, and to do [i.e., in love]?"

It is not the purpose of this brief epilogue to answer that question in detail or depth; hopefully, readers have begun to do that for themselves while reading this text. Furthermore, I have attempted to address these topics of faith, hope, and love (together with power) elsewhere, in a comprehensive study of Paul's spirituality.[3] But two major points for us today must be stressed: first, that Paul does in fact see this triad as a unity, and second, that Paul understands and experiences this triad only in light of the cross.

THE UNITY OF FAITH, HOPE, AND LOVE

Theological debates about Paul have centered on justification by faith and the role of "good works" for half a millennium. Those debates have been rekindled, supposedly settled, and rekindled once again during the last half-century of unprecedented discoveries and debate about Judaism in Paul's day, on the one hand, and unprecedented ecumenical and interfaith dialogue, on the other. In 1999, when Roman Catholics and Lutherans came to agreement — actually a kind of unity in diversity — about the 'doctrine' of justification, there was great rejoicing in many (though not all) circles.[4] The upshot of their agreement can be stated in two claims: that for Paul and for the Christian church, justification is solely by divine grace, and that the evidence of justification is the manifestation of good works. Put differently, justification by faith and a life of neighbor-love are inseparable, as Polycarp had already discerned in his own reading of Paul.

In the opinion of some observers, including the present writer, the Catholic-Lutheran accord would be articulated somewhat differently, and strengthened, by an even closer reading of Paul. As we have seen in this book, for Paul, justification is the establishment of right covenantal relations with the God of Israel, who now calls all the world to be part of the divinely initiated covenant that requires and offers love for God and for others — a covenant with inseparable 'vertical' and 'horizontal' dimensions. That covenant was displayed and fulfilled in Christ's one act of covenant faithfulness on the cross, an event that was simultaneously an expression of his faithful obedience to God (i.e., love for God) and of his self-giving devotion to others (i.e., love for neighbor). To respond to and participate in the cross of Christ is, therefore, to enter into a covenantal relationship with both God and humans in which there can be no vertical relationship (what Paul usually calls "faith") without a corollary horizontal relationship (what Paul normally calls "love"). Those who try to have one without the other have not understood what Paul is all about or, as far

3. Michael J. Gorman, *Cruciformity: Paul's Narrative Spirituality of the Cross* (Grand Rapids: Eerdmans, 2001).

4. *Joint Declaration on the Doctrine of Justification,* available in several formats and editions.

as Paul is concerned, what God is all about. There is, for Paul, as for Dietrich Bonhoeffer, no such thing as "cheap grace."

If faith and love are inextricably intertwined, what about hope? In a world full of hostile powers and other kinds of dangers, hope can either be in short supply or it can be cheap, but Paul will have it neither way. For him, hope is the future tense of faith, the assurance that what God has done in Christ's death and resurrection — for us, for all of humanity, and indeed for the entire cosmos — will be brought to completion. It cannot be thwarted by any power, human or demonic, that may seem to be victorious at the moment. Hope that is rooted in anything other than this kind of faith is vacuous and, indeed, dangerous. In its most distorted forms, hope that is not rooted in faith can lead to idolatrous expressions of trust in powers other than God, and can at the same time lead also to acts of hatred, even to crimes against humanity, rather than to deeds of love. The twentieth century was home to far too many perversions of hope.

THE CRUCIFORM CHARACTER OF FAITH, HOPE, AND LOVE

The second main point we need to make about the unity of faith, hope, and love is that this triad makes sense for Paul and for us only when perceived through the lens of the cross. Faith, hope, and love are first of all aspects of the cross of Christ, and therefore also dimensions of our response to, and participation in, that cross.

For many Christians, the death of Christ remains primarily a transaction between God and humanity in which Christ is a willing but largely passive figure. In such a scenario, Christ's cross does not define either his or our humanity. The cross is seen as the *source* of our salvation, but not as the *shape* of it. For Paul, however, Christ's cross is both the source *and* the shape of our salvation. When we respond to the gospel, we embrace the cross not only as gift but also as demand. To borrow the language of Jesus, we 'take up the cross,' beginning a life that can be best described with one word: *cruciform* — cross-shaped. Our devotion to God, our love for others, and our hope for the future are all grounded in and shaped by the cross.

In such a cruciform spirituality, sacrifice, difficulty, and suffering are not to be seen as intruders, but as part and parcel of the arrangement, sustained by the presence of the Spirit as the foretaste and guarantee of a future resurrection similar to Christ's. Neither, however, are such experiences ends in themselves. Cruciformity, in harmony with the cross itself, always has a goal, such as reconciliation, or the good of another, or the welfare of a community. To live in Christ in this way is to be working "with the grain of the universe," to use the words of the late John Howard Yoder.[5] For that reason, it brings more joy and happiness than any of the cheap, triumphalistic spiritualities currently on the market.

Much more can and should be said about this important aspect of Paul's contemporary voice, but space permits only a reminder that the topic may be explored in depth elsewhere.[6]

JESUS IS LORD

Both Paul and his early interpreter Polycarp understood the mystery of cruciform yet joyful existence. They understood it, at least in part, because they grasped the meaning of the confession "Jesus is Lord." Or rather, perhaps, because they were grasped by it.

Unfortunately, the significance of the claim that Jesus is Lord has not always captured the church's imagination as it did in the time of the Roman Empire. As we have seen at several junctures in this book, this confession reveals the 'political' as well as the 'religious' dimension of early Christianity. Because these two dimensions of human life were inextricably interconnected in antiquity, early Christianity did not wonder *whether* politics and religion were related, but rather *whose* politics would affect religion, and vice versa. For Paul and the early church, the answer was the religion and politics of the exalted crucified Messiah Jesus. These were, of course, one reality.

We have suggested, therefore, that it is more appropriate to speak of the *theopolitical* character of Paul's gospel (see chapter 4). To confess Jesus as Lord was, for Paul, a theopolitical confession. It meant that Jesus embodied the God of Israel's rightful claim to universal sovereignty and acclamation, and that all other pretenders to the place that is rightfully God's alone were to be rejected. Such pretenders would obviously include the deities of Paul's polytheistic world. Paul said that people who acknowledged Jesus as Lord had turned their backs on the pagan gods and turned to the one, true, living God (1 Thess. 1:9-10).

---

5. John Howard Yoder, "Armaments and Eschatology," *Studies in Christian Ethics* 1 (1988): 58. The phrase has been made known to a wider audience by Stanley Hauerwas; see, for example, his published 2001 Gifford Lectures: *With the Grain of the Universe: The Church's Witness and Natural Theology* (Grand Rapids: Brazos, 2001).

6. See Gorman, *Cruciformity*. On the centrality of the cross today, see also Douglas John Hall, *The Cross in Our Context: Jesus and the Suffering World* (Minneapolis: Augsburg Fortress, 2003).

LORDS AND GODS

Our world is hardly lacking for so-called "gods and lords" (1 Cor. 8:5) that pretend to be viable alternatives to Jesus as Lord. As N. T. Wright (among others) reminds us, our supposedly "secular" Western cultures are, in fact, quite religious; they are pagan.[7]

This does not mean that there is a temple to Artemis or Isis on every corner — though some ancient pagan deities actually have staged a comeback in certain circles. More often, however, our pagan deities, like many of old, are cultural values that have been idolized and thus effectively deified. This contemporary competition for the Christian gospel might include the pagan deities of Lust, Pleasure, Choice; Pride, Athletic Prowess, Popularity; Power, Ambition, Greed; Violence, Hatred, Revenge; and some of the reigning ideologies or "-isms" of our day: Racism, Nationalism, Militarism. Need anyone doubt that Western society is religious, indeed polytheistic?

These deities demand people's allegiance, their sacrifices of time and energy and money, and their singleness of purpose. They determine their adherents' goals and the means to reach them. Ethics — the lifestyle required by the deities — then becomes merely a means to achieve the ends demanded by the deities. These impersonations of morality de-humanize relationships, sexuality, and even life itself.

In this context, Paul's gospel of the lordship of Jesus means that people today, no less than the Thessalonians or Corinthians of the apostle's own day, need to turn from idols, and from their idolatrous ethics that exchange virtue for vice, to serve the living and true God. They must present their minds and bodies as a living sacrifice to the God known most fully in the Son of God. They must, that is, live lives determined by Jesus the Lord, and not by any deities seeking to displace his sovereignty.

PRINCIPALITIES AND POWERS

It was not, and is not, only the reality of traditional deities that challenges the lordship of Jesus for Christians. It was, and is, also the existence of political rulers and systems — "the principalities and the powers" (Col. 2:15, NAB) — whose ambitions and actions contradict the character and kingship of God. In a word: if Jesus is Lord, he is Lord because of divine appointment, and if Jesus is Lord, Caesar is not — even if he claims a divinely appointed sovereignty.

---

7. N. T. Wright, *What Saint Paul Really Said: Was Paul of Tarsus the Real Founder of Christianity?* (Grand Rapids: Eerdmans, 1997), pp. 153-57.

Polycarp knew this well. When arrested and threatened with execution, he was asked simply to pledge his allegiance to sovereign Caesar by confessing that "Caesar is Lord." "Just a few words — what harm can they do?" his Roman tempters asked (*Martyrdom of Polycarp* 8). But Polycarp, like Paul, had been apprehended by Jesus Christ and could not betray the one who had been so faithful to him for 86 years. He refused to comply, and he died a martyr (*Martyrdom of Polycarp* 9-16).

Few Christians in Western churches today currently face the possibility of such dramatic encounters with the civil authorities. But that may be in part because Western Christians have failed to hear the radical theopolitical claims of Paul's gospel. The notion that Paul's gospel could challenge the 'principalities and powers' of the modern world has often been buried, if not lost, amid the ruins of Christendom: civil religion, nationalism, and personal pieties that never challenge any status quo — religious, cultural, or political.

For example, we might do well in the West to imagine that Jesus bears the title of "Governor," "Prime Minister," "President," or, perhaps more to the point (especially for Americans), "Commander-in-Chief." Not that any of these titles corresponds precisely to "Lord" or adequately conveys the estimation of Jesus that modern Christians ought to have of him. But such titles do suggest that to confess Jesus always involves a theopolitical claim and a challenge to the political status quo. American Christians, in particular, need to reflect on the significance of the confession that it is Jesus, and not any human being, who is ultimately their "commander-in-chief" and thus the one who determines the kind of "warfare" (spiritual) they are to conduct in this life (see, e.g., 2 Cor. 10:1-6; Eph. 6:10-20).

Paul thus challenges our allegiances to both paganism and politics in the process of renewing our individual and corporate minds. But Paul has been domesticated, fitted into our preconceptions about ultimate reality and ultimate values. Yet the gospel of Jesus Christ that Paul preached cannot be domesticated for long, because it is the "power of God for salvation" (Rom. 1:16), and its power is unleashed in the world in ways that liberate human beings from everything and anything that is contrary to the character and story of God unveiled in the exalted crucified Messiah. What may be in short supply today is a group of interpreters of Paul — communities of Christians — so fully apprehended by Jesus that they will tell the story of his lordship with their lips and with their lives. But for those of us who believe in the power of Paul's gospel, even that lacuna in the world is not a permanent state of affairs, and it neither can nor will prevent the gospel from being effective in the world.

PERFORMING THE STORY:
THE NATURE OF CHRISTIAN WITNESS

That leads us, finally, to what may be the most basic need in the Christian churches today with respect to the study of Paul: it is the need for communities that do not merely *read* Paul's letters but *live* them, embody them, "perform" them. The ultimate goal of all biblical interpretation is for the readers to become a living exegesis of the texts they read.[8] As the very format of chapters seven to nineteen in this book has suggested, Paul intended the Story and the stories he told — the stories behind and within the letters — to continue into the future: "the story in front of the letter." The future of those stories is our present. Nearly nineteen centuries ago, the future of the same stories was Polycarp's present.

When the Roman soldiers who came to arrest Polycarp arrived at the house where the bishop was staying, they were met with a simple but powerful performance of the gospel that Paul had preached and Polycarp had extolled in his letter to the Philippians: Polycarp made a meal for the soldiers (*Martyrdom of Polycarp* 7). To those who were about to facilitate his death, Polycarp bore faithful witness by offering hospitality — cruciform hospitality. To the powerful who made painfully clear his own weakness, Polycarp manifested the power of the gospel and its Pauline promises: "Whenever I am weak, then I am strong"; "I can do all things through the one who makes me strong" (2 Cor. 12:10; Phil. 4:13).

Like Jesus and like Paul, Polycarp knew that the cross called for a certain life-story, one described, for example, by the beatitudes (*Letter of Polycarp* 2). Polycarp also knew that the story was not his alone to live. He did not live or die alone but in the company of other story-tellers (*Martyrdom of Polycarp* 19). They were martyrs — 'witnesses' — whose lives and deaths had been "conformed to the gospel" (*Martyrdom of Polycarp* 1.1). They had exhibited the basic early Christian virtue of faithful, patient endurance in suffering (Greek *hypomonē*). Interestingly, in his letter to the Philippians, Polycarp had repeatedly urged the Philippians to practice this virtue, citing Paul (*Letter of Polycarp* 9) as a model. Ultimately, however, Polycarp and his companions were conformed not to Paul, but to Christ. Paul himself had already told the Corinthians, one hundred years earlier, that that is the way it should be (1 Cor. 11:1). Such conformity, inasmuch as it was and is an expression of Christian faithfulness, constitutes also truly an act of witness, of evangelism. Evangelism or witness-

---

8. See, among others, Nicholas Lash, "Performing the Scriptures," pp. 37-46 in *Theology on the Way to Emmaus* (London: S.C.M., 1986); Michael J. Gorman, *Elements of Biblical Exegesis: A Basic Guide for Students and Ministers* (Peabody, Mass.: Hendrickson, 2001), pp. 123-33.

bearing in the manner of Paul (or Polycarp) is not a marketing strategy designed to gain more members; it is the faithful, cross-centered proclamation — in word and deed — of the gospel.

PAUL'S INVITATION TO US

Paul our contemporary invites us, too, to hear the call and promise of the gospel. He calls us not merely as readers, or as individuals, but as *communities of performers.* He calls us to a dying with Christ that may not be literal but will nonetheless be costly, and he promises — or rather God promises through him — the joy of new life in the present as well as the certain hope of resurrection in the future.

The apostle of the crucified Lord invites us, like the Thessalonians, to incarnate a hope that engenders holiness and goodness; like the Galatians, to become communities of the cross and Spirit that welcome persons from every gender, race, and socio-economic condition; like the Corinthians, to embody a love that is willing to go to the cross for the good of those persons or an entire community; like the Philippians, to live with other believers in unity and humility in the face of opponents both internal and external; like the Romans, to construct communities that offer self-giving worship to God and cruciform hospitality to friends who differ and to enemies who dominate; like the Colossians and Ephesians, to allow our relationships to be re-formed by the power of the gospel of Christ's cosmic lordship; and, like Philemon, Timothy, and Titus, to give leadership to communities by evangelical example. Paul invites us, in sum, to cruciform faith, hope, and love. These three, proclaimed in word and deed, constitute in and through us the power of the gospel, which is the power of the cross, in the world.

QUESTIONS FOR REFLECTION AND DISCUSSION

1. What are some of the issues discussed in Paul's letters that seem most contemporary? most foreign or irrelevant? With respect to the latter group, is it still possible to find contemporary analogies to these issues, or to any of the principles they embody?
2. What are the theological, spiritual, and moral consequences of seeing the cross as the source but not the shape of our salvation? of disjoining faith and love?
3. In what concrete ways is the gospel of Jesus' lordship challenged by today's lords, gods, principalities, and powers?
4. What kinds of practices either hinder or assist the church in becoming a

transformed, cruciform community able to discern and do the will of God?

5. How, in sum, might the recovery of Paul's gospel and letters assist in the renewal of the church, within a post-Christian culture, so that it might embody a life of faith, hope, and love in witness to the lordship of Jesus?

FOR FURTHER READING AND STUDY

Babcock, William S., ed. *Paul and the Legacies of Paul.* Dallas: Southern University Methodist Press, 1990. A series of essays by distinguished scholars of early Christianity on the influence of Paul on Christian theology and practice from the late first to the fifth century.

Bonhoeffer, Dietrich. *The Cost of Discipleship.* Rev. ed. Trans. R. H. Fuller. New York: Macmillan, 1959 [and other editions]. The classic work of the German pastor-martyr who used the Gospels and Pauline letters to demonstrate the costly grace of discipleship over against the cheap grace of a supposedly Christian cultural and religious establishment.

Braxton, Brad R. *No Longer Slaves: Galatians and African American Experience.* Collegeville, Minn.: Liturgical, 2002. An examination of Paul's letter, informed by the experience of African Americans, as an instrument of cultural, ethnic, and racial liberation and reconciliation, both then and now.

Charry, Ellen T. *By the Renewing of Your Minds: The Pastoral Function of Christian Doctrine.* New York: Oxford, 1997. A study of theologians, beginning with Paul (chapter 2), who have understood the task of theology as intellectual and moral formation.

Gorman, Michael J. *Cruciformity: Paul's Narrative Spirituality of the Cross.* Grand Rapids: Eerdmans, 2001. An analysis of Paul's trinitarian, cross-centered spirituality, with a concluding chapter that specifically focuses on Paul's contemporary relevance, developing some of the themes briefly discussed in this epilogue.

Gross, Nancy Lammers. *If You Cannot Preach Like Paul.* Grand Rapids: Eerdmans, 2002. An approach to preaching Paul as a conversation with the apostle in which sermons must engage both head and heart to achieve their pastoral function.

Hall, Douglas John. *The Cross in Our Context: Jesus and the Suffering World.* Minneapolis: Augsburg Fortress, 2003. A digest of Hall's three-volume theology, provocatively demonstrating the centrality of the cross for contemporary discipleship.

Harink, Douglas. *Paul among the Postliberals: Pauline Theology beyond Christendom and Modernity.* Grand Rapids: Brazos, 2003. An insightful exploration of the appearance of Pauline themes in theologians such as Yoder and Hauerwas, and of the relevance of Paul, as understood by recent interpreters, for the church today.

Matera, Frank J. *Strategies for Preaching Paul.* Collegeville, Minn.: Liturgical, 2001. An exposition of Paul's letters, organized according to the lectionary (years A, B, and C), offering three strategies for competent preaching: analysis of the context, exegesis of the text itself, and consideration of its theological themes.

Meeks, Wayne A., ed. *The Writings of St. Paul.* New York: Norton, 1972. A collection of theological and critical interpretations of Paul from the early church until the middle of the 20th century.

Thompson, James W. *Preaching Like Paul: Homiletical Wisdom for Today.* Louisville: Westminster John Knox, 2001. A stimulating analysis of Paul's preaching (revealed in his letters) as a model for pastoral preaching that is community-forming, rather than individualistic and therapeutic, for a post-Christian culture.

Scripture Index

including the apocryphal/deuterocanonical books

Note: **Boldfaced** page numbers correspond to headings that are part of "The Story within the Letter" of chapters seven to nineteen (e.g., Romans 8:18-39). The index does *not* include page references for specific verses that are a subset of such a passage (e.g., Romans 8:21) when those verses are discussed within the boldfaced pages, but only when those verses are cited elsewhere. (E.g., because Romans 8:18-39 has a boldfaced entry for pages **376-78**, the entry for 8:21 will refer the reader only to pages other than 376-78, such as 129.)

Genesis					Numbers	
1–3	434	17:15–18:15	213		25:6-13	26n.16, 196
1	280, 562	21	212		25:7-9	54
1:27	365	21:8-14	381		25:10-13	55
2–3	372	21:10	214		25:11	54
2:15-17	366, 373	22	361, 378n.19		25:13	54
2:16	373					
2:24	525	**Exodus**			**Deuteronomy**	
3	105	12	247		4:24	262
3:1-5	366	12:40	208		5	396n.36
3:1-24	373	16:18	316		5:9	262
3:6	373	19:5	577		6:4	104, 257
3:13	373	20	396n.36		6:15	262
3:17b-19	377	32:1-20	299		10:12-22	356
3:19	366	32:25-29	54n.8		10:16	356
6:1-4	266	32:30-34	380		10:17	354, 356
12:3	207	33:19	381		10:18	563n.11
15–17	360	34:29-35	299, 300		13:1-5	247n.4
15:6	207, 360				17:1-7	55, 247n.4
16–18	212				17:6	360
16:2	213	**Leviticus**			17:8-13	247n.4
17	207	18:1-3	158		19:15	331, 360, 565
17:1-8	362	18:24-30	158		19:15-21	247n.4
17:5	360, 361	19:18	218		21:15-17	482
17:9-14	207	20:11	247		21:18-21	247n.4

21:23	55, 207, 207n.13, 208, 208n.14	68:18	518	1:9	382	
22:20-24	247n.4	69	401	1:12-17	20n.10	
22:30	247	69:9	401	1:17	563n.11	
24:7	247n.4	69:22 (LXX)	385	2:10-21	173	
24:19-21	563n.11	80:8-19	386n.28	4:2	386n.28	
25:4	258, 565n.12	81:11-12	353	5:1-7	386n.28	
27:19	563n.11	92:12-14	386n.28	8:14	383n.23	
27:20	247	106:30-31	54	10:20-23	382	
27:26	207n.13	110	508	11:5	527n.14	
28:58-59	207n.13	111:9 (LXX)	317	11:10	401	
30	219	112:9	317	27:2-6	386n.28	
30:1-5	384	117:1	401	27:9	385	
30:15	219	142:2 (LXX)	203	28:16	383n.23, 384	
32:5	438	143:2	203	29:14	241	
32:16-21	262	146:9	563n.11	29:16	381	
32:21	384			40–66	64, 64n.18, 65, 106, 307	
32:35	393	**Proverbs**		40–55	58n.12, 64n.18, 65, 422, 434	
32:43	401	3:19	481	40:1-2	64	
		8	481	40:9	106n.9	
1 Kings		8:22-23	481	42:1-9	64	
16:31-34	55	8:27a	481	42:6-7	64	
17–19	26n.16, 197	11:24-25	317	42:9-10	64	
17:1-7	55n.9	20:22	393	43:1-7	64	
18:4	55	22:8-9	317	43:8-13	64	
18:13	55	24:12	354	43:10-13	64	
18:17-40	55	25:21-22	393	43:14-21	64	
19:10	55			44:6-20	64	
		Wisdom		44:21-28	64	
2 Chronicles		1:4	483	45	438	
19:7	354	5:17-20	527n.14	45:1-8	64	
		6:1-21	395n.34	45:5–46:13	64	
1 Maccabees		6:3	395n.34	45:22-23	104	
2:23-26	26n.16, 197	6:4-5	395n.34	45:23	65, 118, 136, 503	
2:23-28	55	7:22	481-82	49	58n.12	
		7:22–8:1	481	49:1-6	64	
Job		7:25-28	481-82	49:1b-2a	197	
1:21	566	7:27	483	49:2	527n.14	
		11–19	352	49:3	197	
Psalms		13–14	352	49:5-6	58	
14	357			49:6	58, 64, 439	
18:49	401	**Sirach**		49:6b	197	
28:4	354	48:1-2	197	50:4-11	64	
32:1-2	111	48:1-4	55	51:4	64	
44:22	378n.18	48:1-12a	26n.16	51:5	64	
53	357			51:12-16	64	
62:12	354	**Isaiah**				
		1–39	58n.12, 64n.18			

52:1-12	64	4:4	356	**Malachi**	
52:7	64, 106n.9, 384,	7:6	563n.11	1:3	381
	527n.14	9:23-24	241, 321		
52:7-10	64, 106-7, 384	11:16-17	386n.28	**Matthew**	
52:13	435, 437	18:6	381	5:14	439
52:13–53:12	64, 105, 422,	31:31-34	133, 356, 375	5:31-32	253
	434	31:32	299	6:19-21	567
52:14–53:9	435	31:33-34	299	9:13	20n.10
52:15 (LXX)	401	46–51	58	10:10	258
53:10-12	435			10:33	543
53:12	435, 436, 437	**Ezekiel**		12:7	20n.10
54:1-17	64	1	27	16:19	296
55:4-5	439	19:10-14	386n.28	19:3-9	253
55:5	64	36:22-32	207n.12	21:42	383n.23
55:10	317	36:26-27	299	24:43	162
55:11	98, 349	36:26-28	375		
56–66	64n.18	45:17	487	**Mark**	
56:1-8	64			7:1-22	487
57:14-21	64	**Daniel**		8:38	543
59:15b-17	527n.14	7–12	22	10:2-12	253
59:15b-21	64	7:13	160	12:28-31	218
59:17	527n.14	11:36	176	12:31	396n.35
59:20-21	385			12:40	563n.10
60:1-3	64	**Hosea**		12:42-43	563n.10
60:1-22	64	1:9	511	13	22
60:6	106n.9	1:10	382, 511	13:3-6	544
60:21	386n.28	2:23	382, 511	13:14-23	176
61:1	64	6:6	20n.10	13:21-23	544
61:1-2	106n.9	10:1	386n.28	13:22	175n.3, 176
61:1-3	64	10:12 (LXX)	317	14:36	118
61:1-11	64			15:21	404
61:3	386n.28	**Joel**			
62:2	64	2:28-29	207n.12	**Luke**	
65:1	384	2:32	384	1:47	555n.2
65:1-2	64			1:68-75	351
65:2	385	**Amos**		2:37	563n.10
65:17	222	1:2–2:3	355	4:25-26	563n.10
65:17-25	64			6:27-36	393
65:17a	129	**Micah**		6:28	393
66:20-23	64	6:6-8	20n.10	6:38	317
66:22	64, 129			7:12	563n.10
		Habakkuk		10:7	563n.10
Jeremiah		2:4	207n.12, 350	12:13-21	567
1:4-8	58			16:18	253
1:5	197	**Zechariah**		18:3	563n.10
2	353	9:14	160, 281	20:47	563n.10
2:21	386n.28			21:2-3	563n.10

22:15-20	269	14:1-7	185	17:10-15	532n.1
23:32-43	393	14:1-20	67	17:14-15	67, 147
		14:8-20	185	18–20	288
John		14:20-21	185	18	45, 234
8:12	522	14:21-23	185	18:1	150
9:5	522	15	45n.4, 187, 198,	18:1-3	403
10:17-18	428		199nn.7, 8	18:1-4	67, 230
15:1-11	386n.28	15:1	185	18:1-5	532n.1
17	439	15:1-29	185, 198	18:2	340
		15:1-39	67	18:2-3	67
Acts		15:5	185	18:5	67, 293
2:1-13	523	15:12	69	18:5-6	230
2:10	340	15:19-20	199n.8	18:5-17	177
2:20	540n.6	15:22-41	67	18:7	21
4:11	383n.23	15:24	185	18:7-8	231
4:36	199n.7	15:28-29	199n.8	18:11	43, 230
6:1-3	563n.10	15:36–18:22	48	18:12	232
7:54–8:3	54n.7	16	49, 414	18:12-17	42, 232
8:1	54	16:1	539, 545	18:17	67, 231, 239
8:1-3	44	16:1-3	67, 147	18:18-28	67
9	45, 56n.10	16:1-5	185, 415	18:19-21	500n.2
9:1-2	44, 54, 54n.7	16:1-10	532n.1	18:23	43, 186
9:1-31	56, 196n.3	16:4-5	185	18:23–21:16	49
9:2	56	16:6	43, 186	18:24–19:1	234
9:4	59	16:11	415	19	45, 500
9:11	50	16:11-15	414, 415	19:1–20:1	500n.2
9:23-25	327	16:11-40	148	19:8	43, 45
9:27	67	16:12	413	19:10	499
9:30	45	16:13	414	19:21-22	532n.1
9:39-41	563n.10	16:14	21	19:22	67, 293, 340n.1,
10	45, 45	16:16	414		556
10:2	21	16:16-18	414	19:28	500
11:22-30	67	16:16-24	417	19:33	548
11:26	40	16:16-32	67	19:34	500
11:27-30	45, 45n.4, 198	16:16-39	415	20	536
12:25	67	16:19	415	20:1	556
13–14	188, 199n.7, 206	16:25	415	20:1-2	151n.1
13	51, 51n.16	16:25-34	415	20:1-3	340n.1
13:1-12	67	16:37	50	20:1-6	532n.1
13:6	30	16:40	414, 415	20:2	288
13:13-51	184	17:1	448	20:4	67, 493n.9
13:16	21	17:1-9	18, 147	20:13	34
13:39	184	17:1-15	67	20:16-38	500n.2
13:39-40	184	17:2	150	20:31	43, 45
13:42-50	67	17:4	148	21:15–28:31	49
13:44-51	185	17:6-7	150	21:27-36	45, 403n.40
13:44–14:20	545	17:6b-7	148	21:39	50

22	45, 56n.10	1:16	63, 98, 112, 344, 383, 588	3:5	173n.1
22:1-21	56, 196n.3			3:6	84n.8
22:2	51	1:16-17	62, 102, 134, 343, 344, **348-51**, 358, 365, 382, 395	3:8	368, 370
22:3	50, 52			3:9	84n.8, 134, 344, 355, 369, 372, 373
22:4-5	54n.7				
22:7	51n.6, 59	1:17	348, 358, 379, 536	3:9-20	86, **357-58**
22:27-28	50	1:18	173n.1, 367, 361, 388, 396	3:19-20	355
23	536			3:21	363
23:1-11	24n.14	1:18-32	21, **352-54**, 354, 364, 370, 519, 544	3:21-26	102, 111, 134-35, 201, 307, 350, **358-59**, 366, 368, 483
23:6	51, 53, 60n.16				
23:12-35	403n.40	1:18–3:20	133, **352-58**, 358, 359, 373, 513		
23:23–26:32	418			3:21-31	111, 122, **358-60**, 360
23:27	50	1:18–4:25	**351-62**		
25:1-5	403n.40	1:21	390	3:22	102, 344
26	21, 40n.1, 45, 56n.10	1:21-22	519	3:23	113, 365, 373, 381
		1:22	360	3:24	369, 372
26:2-23	56, 196n.3	1:23	376	3:24-25a	100
26:4	52	1:24	390, 519, 519n.12	3:24-26	507
26:5	53	1:24-32	519	3:27	365
26:9-11	54n.7	1:26	519n.12	3:27-31	**360**
26:10	54	1:28	519, 519n.12	3:28	540
26:11	54	1:30	360	3:28-30	138, 344
26:14	51n.6, 59	1:32	510n.8	3:29	135, 344
26:28	40n.1	2–3	21	3:29-30	349, 384n.26
28	40n.1, 45	2	84	3:29-30a	133
28:16-31	**417, 533**	2:1-5	355	4	359
		2:1-16	**354-55**, 356, 360	4:1-25	**360-62**
Romans		2:4ff.	355	4:6-9	365
1–11	84, 499, 504	2:4-11	393	4:7-8	111
1–8	342, 499	2:5	173n.1, 354, 519	4:12-25	381n.21
1–4	343	2:5-16	510n.8	4:15	366
1	519n.12	2:6-16	355	4:24-25	100, 111
1:1-4	99, 348	2:7	376n.14	5–8	343, 363, 379, 390, 409
1:1-5	**346-48**	2:8	173n.1		
1:1-6	514n.9, 573	2:9-10	344	5	370
1:1-7	82, **346-47**	2:9-11	344	5:1	374
1:2	106	2:9-13	133	5:1-2a	138
1:3	348	2:17	354, 360	5:1-2	113
1:3-4	86, 99, 542	2:17–3:8	**355-56**	5:1-5	112, 122n.9, 216n.17
1:5	62, 122, 217n.18, 343, 349, 384, 402, 406	2:25-29	375, 442		
		2:26-29	486	5:1-8	322
		2:28-29	361, 381, 387	5:1-11	101n.4, 111, 118, 201, 306, **364-66**, 503, 506
1:7	117n.4	3	443		
1:8-15	340, **348**	3:1-9	379		
1:9	126	3:2	349	5:1–8:39	**363-78**
1:10-14	402	3:3-4a	134	5:2	346, 358, 381
1:11-13	402	3:4	84n.8	5:2-5	484n.6

5:3-4	376	6:20-23	112	8:18-39	376-78
5:3-5	123, 393	6:22	122, 372, 391	8:19-25	123
5:5	118, 124	6:23	123, 375	8:21	129
5:5-8	211	6:23a	354	8:22-23	129
5:6-8	112, 117, 119, 124,	7	120n.7, 375	8:23	129
	393, 483	7:4	372	8:24	503
5:6-11	112	7:7	84n.8	8:24-30	540
5:8	118, 135	7:7-12	368	8:28	123
5:9	173n.1, 510n.8	7:7-25	**371-73**	8:28-39	112
5:9-10	201	7:7–8:39	371, **371-78**	8:29	120, 123, 300, 390,
5:12-14	372	7:13	84n.8		483
5:12-20	370	7:17	120	8:30	381
5:12-21	111, 135, 300, 350,	7:24	375	8:31	110
	366-68, 368, 369,	8	206n.11, 347, 364,	8:31-39	365
	371, 373, 437		365, 369, 373, 477,	8:32	100, 507
5:15	135		507	8:34	366
5:18-19	122n.10	8:1	120n.6, 372	8:35	71n.24
5:19	359, 370, 437	8:1-11	515	8:37	393
5:20	117, 356, 368, 373	8:1-17	**374-76**, 479	9–16	342
5:20-21	358	8:1-27	112	9–11	86, 106, 342, 343,
5:20b	117, 368	8:1-39	**374-78**		344, 349, 356, 364,
5:21	60, 84, 85, 121	8:3	136, 507		387, 389, 390, 401,
6	368, 373, 391, 392,	8:3-4	218, 371, 383, 396,		409, 513
	510		556	9:1-5	63, **380**, 383
6:1-2	86, 119, 121, 356	8:3-17	397	9:1-29	**380-82**
6:1-11	112, 117, 306	8:3a	134	9:1–11:36	**379-89**
6:1-14	204, 489	8:3b-4	139	9:4	376
6:1-23	84n.8, 350, 371	8:4	372	9:4-5	349, 356
6:1–7:6	**368-71**	8:8-9	372	9:6-7	387
6:2	372	8:9	118, 301, 322	9:6-29	**381-82**, 382
6:3	397	8:9b	124	9:7-29	382
6:4	391, 477, 503, 510	8:9-10	125	9:14	84n.8
6:6	358, 372, 391, 519	8:9-11	139, 372	9:24	344
6:10-11	399	8:10	120	9:25-26	384
6:11	112, 119, 120n.6,	8:10-11	301	9:27-29	385
	122, 138, 358, 372,	8:11	118	9:30	384
	391, 477, 503, 510	8:12-17	119	9:30–10:4	**382-83**
6:12	372	8:12-39	113	9:30–10:21	**382-85**
6:12-23	111, 122, 373	8:13	372	9:31-33	385
6:13	122, 391, 477, 503,	8:13b	375	9:32-33	385
	510	8:14	118	9:33	384
6:15	84n.8, 356	8:15	86, 118, 119, 211	10	381n.21
6:16	372	8:17	119, 123, 174n.2,	10:1-21	112
6:16-23	510n.8		376, 377, 443, 542	10:2-3	55
6:18	372	8:18	123, 381	10:4	137, 388n.30
6:19	372, 391	8:18-21	143	10:5-13	369
6:20	372	8:18-25	112, 162, 483, 504	10:5-17	122, 387

10:5-21	**383-85**	12:18	394	16:3	67
10:8	540n.7	13	409	16:3-4	340
10:8-13	110	13:1-7	89, **394-96**	16:5	340
10:9	100, 102	13:7	396	16:19	402
10:11	383	13:8	400n.37	16:20	117n.4
10:12	344	13:8-10	218, 394, **396-97**	16:21	67, 532n.1
11:1	84n.8	13:11-14	394, 396, **397**	16:22	87
11:1-5	382	13:12	520	16:23	340n.1
11:1-24	**385-86**	13:13-14	338	16:25(24)-27	**406**
11:1-36	**385-89**	13:14	120, 209, 489, 520	16:26	122, 343, 347, 384,
11:11	84n.8, 383	14-15	342, 344, 354n.9		402
11:12	387, 388	14	341, 397, 562		
11:13	62	14:1	391	**1 Corinthians**	
11:15	387	14:1-23	**399-400**	1-4	245
11:16	388	14:1-15:13	342, 344, 380,	1:1	67
11:20	384		391, 393, 396, **397-**	1:1-9	**239**
11:23	387		**401**, 401, 402	1:2	231, 243, 424
11:25-36	**387-89**	14:10-12	352	1:3	117n.4
11:26	385	14:17	401	1:4-9	82
11:29	391	14:22-23	391	1:7	315
11:30-32	389	15-16	343	1:7-8	237
11:31	384	15	341	1:8	236
11:33-36	380, 385, 387, 389	15:1	400, 432	1:9	68, 237, 261, 288
12-16	406, 499, 504	15:1-3	105n.8, 397,	1:10	236
12-15	342, 343, 364, 375,		436n.21, 468	1:10-17	**240**
	396	15:1-13	**400-401**	1:10-4:21	**239-45**
12	219, 582	15:3	397	1:11	236
12:1	112, 380	15:5	332	1:12	234
12:1-2	370, **390-91**, 394,	15:7-13	399	1:13	243
	397, 402, 428, 477,	15:8-9	338	1:13-14	234
	520, 582-83	15:9	380	1:14	340n.1
12:1-13:14	**390-97**	15:14-21	69	1:16	231, 312
12:1-15:13	**389-401**, 390	15:14-33	340, **401-3**	1:18	298, 306, 349
12:3-8	125	15:16	118	1:18-25	84, 119, 301, 325,
12:3-13	394	15:18	69		471
12:3-21	127, **391-94**	15:20	321, 398	1:18-2:5	**240-42**, 242, 270
12:8	564	15:22-29	312n.10	1:21b-24	349
12:9-13	396	15:22-33	289, 342	1:22-25	135
12:9-21	124	15:25-26	340n.1	1:23	208, 540n.7
12:10	126	15:26	312, 313, 317	1:23-24	227, 483
12:14	86, 394, 395	15:27	313	1:24	237, 319
12:14-21	127, 396	15:31	312	1:26	231
12:15	220	16	127, 340, 403-6,	1:26-28	405
12:15-16	394		552	1:26-31	268, 272
12:17	86	16:1-2	340n.1, 424	1:30	112, 120n.6
12:17-20	395	16:1-23	**403-6**	1:31	243, 295, 321, 442
12:17-21	394	16:1-27	**403-6**	1:31b	349

2:1-5	52, 84, 290, 323	5:7	399	8:5	27, 587
2:6–3:4	**242-43**	5:9	92, 288, 289, 310	8:6	133
2:2	99, 102, 227, 237,	5:9-11	521	8:9	258
	245, 284, 291, 319	5:9-13	235	8:11	248, 260
2:9	123n.11	5:11	522	8:12	268
2:16	78	5:12-13	248	9	84, 105n.8, 155,
3	277	6	246		155n.5, 178, 256,
3:1-3	77	6:1	274		277, 290, 323,
3:1-4	375	6:1-11	235, **248-49**, 277		436n.21, 465
3:4-5	234	6:7-9	274	9:1	56, 61
3:4-6	234	6:9-10	219, 247, 249	9:1-2	57n.11, 514n.9
3:5	240, 514	6:9-11	142, 521	9:1-12a	68
3:5-9	240, 302	6:11	118	9:1-12	61
3:5–4:13	**243-45**	6:12	236	9:1-27	**258-61**
3:9	240	6:12-18a	250-51	9:2-12	155
3:9-17	112	6:12-20	235, 247, **249-52**,	9:6	67
3:10-15	61, 305		276, 277, 370, 520	9:7	542
3:11	513	6:15	84n.8	9:9	565n.12
3:16	118, 124, 127, 252,	6:18	262	9:12b	62, 68
	310, 391	6:18b-20	250-51	9:12c	69
3:16-17	255	6:19-20	111, 207, 400	9:13-14	68
3:21-23	302	7	246, 277, 562	9:14	261
3:22	234	7:1	236	9:15	68
4	277	7:1-40	235, **252-54**	9:15-18	324
4:1	240, 302	7:8	563n.10	9:18	68
4:1-5	61, 305	7:10	78, 86	9:19	178n.6, 323,
4:6	234, 236	7:12	78		436n.21, 465
4:8	278, 543	7:17-20	62	9:19a	68
4:8-13	71n.24	7:21-24	466n.10	9:19b	69
4:9-13	62	7:22-23	400	9:19-23	62, 63, 212, 348
4:10	325	7:39	158	9:21	140
4:12-13	127, 248	7:39-40	254	9:27	540n.7
4:14-17	293, 532n.1	7:40	78	10	266
4:14-20	61	8–14	246, 255, 256	10:1–11:1	261-63
4:14-21	61, **245**, 319, 331	8–13	390	10:3-4	269
4:17	67, 236, 540n.7	8–10	256, 310	10:3-5	269
4:18	236	8	256, 262, 400	10:11	137
4:19	236	8:1	123, 218, 396, 519	10:15	325
5-7	246, 255	8:1-3	275	10:16-21	269
5	246	8:1-13	235, **257**, 276	10:23	236, 251
5:1-5	61	8:1–11:1	217, 256, **256-64**,	10:23-24	274
5:1-8	235		247, 277, 398, 429,	10:23-30	256
5:1-13	**246-48**, 277, 296		468	10:23–11:1	105n.8
5:1–7:40	238, **246-54**	8:1–14:40	**255-76**	10:24	237, 432
5:2	236	8:1b	274	10:25	232
5:3-5	178	8:3	117, 123n.11, 211	10:26	257
5:6-8	217	8:4b-6	104	10:31	399, 490

10:33	237, 432
10:33–11:1	274, 400
11–14	231, 277
11:1	69, 78, 121, 178n.5, 237, 432, 444, 589
11:2	268
11:2-16	**264-66**, 272, 552
11:5	272, 276
11:17-34	70, 124, 235, **266-70**, 270, 277
11:20	262
11:23-26	86, 265
11:25	138
12–14	267, 517
12–13	275
12	70, 125, 127, 128, 219, 237, 251, 268, 270, 391, 503, 517, 553
12:1-3	275
12:1-7	124
12:1-31	112, **270-73**
12:1–14:40	235, **270-76**
12:2	231
12:3	100, 102, 118, 136, 384, 438
12:4-6	118, 139
12:7	126, 518
12:9	391
12:11	126, 503, 518
12:12	142
12:12-26	124
12:13	62, 118
12:14-26	519
12:18	518
12:22-24	237
12:22-26	393
12:28	57n.11, 61, 275, 391, 518
12:28-29	391n.31
12:30-31	391
12:31	275
13	84, 237, 248, 252, 256, 269, 273, 277
13:1-3	125
13:1-13	**273-75**
13:4	236

13:4-7	262
13:5	123, 248, 432
13:6	248
13:11	519
13:13	117n.4, 122, 154, 216n.17, 479n.3
14	253, 274
14:1	270, 391n.31
14:1-5	126
14:1-40	**275-76**
14:4-5	273, 519
14:14	126
14:18	125, 126
14:23	231
14:31	392
14:33	266
14:33b-35	89
14:33b-36	89
14:34b-36	272
14:40	266
15	62, 99, 102, 123, 237, 282, 428n.12
15:1	101
15:1-2	112
15:1-11	**278**
15:1-58	112, **277-82**
15:3	111
15:3ff.	86, 89, 105
15:3-5	269
15:3-7	265
15:3-8	101-2
15:3-10	57n.11
15:5-8	56
15:7-11	61
15:8	58
15:8-10	514
15:9	44, 54n.7, 59
15:9-10	59, 117
15:11	540n.7
15:12	236, 543
15:12-34	**279-80**
15:14	278
15:17	111
15:19	303
15:20	142, 348
15:20-28	143
15:24-28	480n.4, 509

15:26	281
15:28	142
15:32	86, 282, 294, 418, 500n.2
15:35-50	**280-81**
15:42-54	445
15:51-57	**281**
15:52	160
15:58	278, **281-82**
16:1	312n.10
16:1-4	402
16:1-24	**282-83**
16:3-4	312
16:8	236
16:8-9	500n.2
16:10	67
16:10-11	236, 245, 293, 532n.1
16:12	234, 236
16:14	237, 275
16:15	231
16:17	236
16:19	67
16:21	87n.10, 179
16:22	86, 275
16:23	117n.4
16:24	275

2 Corinthians

1–9	288n.1, 289, 291
1–8	289
1–7	288, 288n.1, 289, 290, 291, 311, 319
1:1	67, 82, 424, 532n.1
1:1-2	**293**
1:1–2:13	309
1:2	117n.4
1:2a	82
1:3-4	506
1:3-7	311, 333, 506
1:3-11	**294**, 332
1:3–2:13	**293-97**
1:3–7:16	**293-311**
1:5	484
1:5-6	71
1:6	303
1:8	418

1:8-9	500n.2	4:5	102, 308, 540n.7	7:13-14	199n.7
1:8-11	326, 327	4:6	323	7:13-16	572
1:12	298	4:7-12	71, 71n.24, 298,	8–9	288, 291, 317, 402
1:12-14	298		308, 325, 330	8	288n.1, 289, 291,
1:12–2:4	**295-96**	4:10	300, 308		316, 319
1:12–2:13	**294-97**	4:16–5:10	112, 428n.12	8:1-2	289
1:15-22	532n.1	4:17	376	8:1-5	447, 448
1:15–2:13	295	5:5	141, 507	8:1-6	417, 532n.1
1:16	312n.10	5:11	310	8:1-15	124
1:17	329	5:11-21	101n.4	8:1-24	**314-16**
1:18-22	332	5:11–6:10	**305-8**	8:1–9:15	**312-17**
1:19	67, 540n.7	5:14	314, 315, 324, 332,	8:2	417
1:20	137		468	8:3-4	333
1:21	120n.6	5:14b	136	8:6	67, 199n.7, 572
1:22	124, 299, 304, 377,	5:15	122, 163, 304, 399,	8:6-7	289
	507		577	8:7	291
1:23	383	5:16	329	8:9	105, 105n.8, 117,
2:1	289	5:16-18	123		308, 323, 331, 333,
2:3-4	289	5:16-21	61		401, 436n.21, 465,
2:5	289	5:17	112, 120n.6, 128,		467
2:5-11	289, 309		138, 222, 333, 358,	8:10	316
2:5-13	**296-97**		520	8:10-12	289
2:9	311	5:18-19	111	8:11	289
2:10	303	5:18-21	111	8:16	199n.7, 572
2:12-13	311, 532n.1	5:19	105, 136, 314, 477,	8:16-24	289, 532n.1
2:13	67, 199n.7, 309,		483, 503, 513	8:23	199n.7, 572
	572	5:19a	128	8:24	291
2:14	308, 317, 486	5:21	207, 315, 375	9	288n.1, 289, 291,
2:14-15	298	6:1-2	291		319
2:14-17	**298**, 301	6:3	316	9:1-15	**316-17**
2:14–6:10	**297-308**	6:3-10	71n.24	9:2	289
2:15	306	6:4-10	302	9:3	289
2:16	431	6:5	124	9:4-5	289
2:17	120n.6	6:8-10	484n.6	9:5	291
3	86	6:11-13	291, **309**	9:8-10	331
3:1-11	307	6:11–7:16	305, **308-11**	9:13	291, 333
3:1-18	**298-301**	6:14–7:1	288, 289, 289n.2,	9:14	333
3:3	118		**309-11**	10–13	183, 288, 288n.1,
3:6	133, 303, 514	7:1	291		289, 290, 291, 310,
3:9	307, 307n.9	7:2-16	**311**		311, 333, 441
3:12–4:6	113	7:4	464	10:1	126, 220, 446
3:17	118	7:5	288n.1	10:1-6	**319-20**, 588
3:18	304, 477	7:5-16	289, 297, 532n.1	10:1–13:13	292, **318-33**
4:1–5:10	**301-5**	7:6	67, 199n.7, 289,	10:2	329
4:3	306		572	10:3	329
4:3-4	306	7:8	92, 289	10:5	323
4:4	300, 510	7:13	289	10:7-18	**320-21**

10:10	52, 84, 290, 290n.3
10:12	290n.3
10:18	290n.3
11:1-4	**321-22**
11:1-15	**321-24**
11:1–12:13	321
11:4	290, 310, 540n.7
11:5	290, 324
11:5-11	**322-24**
11:6	290, 290n.3
11:7	322, 330
11:7-11	85, 290, 326
11:9	331
11:12-15	**324**
11:13	290
11:13-15	310, 318, 324
11:14	322
11:15	290
11:16	321
11:16-21a	**325-26**
11:16–12:10	**324-30**
11:18	290n.3, 329
11:21b-33	**326-27**
11:22	290
11:23	290, 330, 514
11:23-28	71
11:23-29	197n.6, 302
11:23-33	71n.24
11:24	54, 63, 197n.6, 222
11:25	51n.5, 66, 85
11:26	66
11:27	124
11:28	297
12:1	290n.3
12:1-4	27
12:1-10	125, **327-30**, 330
12:5	326
12:7	188
12:9-10	303, 327, 333
12:10	71, 71n.24, 287, 326, 589
12:11	290
12:11-12	290n.3
12:11-13	**330**
12:11–13:10	61
12:12	62, 69, 328, 330, 402

12:13	326
12:14-18	532n.1
12:14–13:13	292, **330-33**
12:15	71, 123, 330, 436n.21
12:18	67, 199n.7, 572
12:19	291, 320, 330
13:1-4	319
13:1-10	320
13:5	291, 324
13:13	118, 139

Galatians

1–4	215
1–2	192, 205
1	61, 198
1:1	99, 195, 514n.9
1:1-5	82, **194-95**
1:1-10	192
1:1-17	557n.6
1:2	184
1:3	117n.4
1:4	100, 109, 111, 192, 195, 204, 209, 215, 217, 222, 358, 428, 436n.21
1:6	191
1:6-7	191
1:6-8	188
1:6-10	82, **195-96**
1:6–2:21	**195-204**
1:7	191
1:7-9	441
1:8-9	191
1:10	222
1:11	78
1:11-12	99
1:11-17	557
1:11-24	**196-98**, 514n.9
1:13	54, 206
1:13-14	44, 53, 54n.7, 144n.5, 217, 383, 443
1:14	53, 54, 372
1:15	57, 58, 59, 117
1:15-16	45
1:16	56, 58

1:17	45
1:18-19	45
1:21	45
2	45n.4, 62, 84, 443
2:1	67, 312
2:1-2	62
2:1-3	532n.1, 572
2:1-10	45, 187, 189, **198-99**
2:1-13	67
2:1-21	206
2:2	45n.4, 540n.7
2:3-5	189
2:4	189, 217
2:4-5	196
2:5	191, 217n.18
2:8	62
2:9	62, 321
2:10	282, 312, 313
2:11-14	189, 196, 198, **200**
2:12	189
2:14	189, 191, 217n.18
2:15	196
2:15-20	369
2:15-21	111, 119, 122, 194, **200-204**, 209, 442
2:16	195, 369, 540
2:17	84n.8
2:19	121, 222
2:19-20	110, 119, 140, 211, 306, 391, 464
2:19-21	306
2:19b-20	115
2:20	100, 112, 120, 121, 122n.10, 123, 136, 194, 195, 197, 215, 216, 218, 218n.19, 220, 273, 436n.21, 515, 521
2:21	191
3–4	192, 214
3	67, 84, 86, 443
3:1	85, 188, 191, 195
3:1-5	69, 70, 124, 187, 188, 189, **206**, 211, 322, 365
3:1–4:31	**205-14**

SCRIPTURE INDEX

3:1–5:1	300	4:8-9	187, 210n.15, 217, 485	5:19-21a	220
3:2	195			5:19-21	397
3:3-5	330	4:8-20	210, **211-12**	5:19-23	86
3:4	188, 191	4:9	117, 210, 216	5:21	220
3:5	188, 189	4:9-10	189	5:22	218, 273, 396
3:6-9	349	4:11	191	5:22-23	125, 446
3:6-14	**206-8**	4:12-15	188	5:22-24	370
3:8	106, 133	4:12-20	77, 191	5:23b	371
3:10	189	4:13	187, 188, 218n.19	5:24	119, 121, 204, 222
3:12	189	4:15	188, 190	5:25	188, 204
3:13	217, 380	4:17	189	6	194
3:13-14	141	4:18-20	191	6:1-10	**220-21**
3:14	189, 208, 211	4:19	62	6:2	140, 218, 400
3:14-29	106	4:19-20	61	6:5	178
3:15-29	**208-10**	4:21-31	86, **212-14**	6:9	179
3:21	84n.8	5–6	192, 194, 215, 222	6:10	124, 393n.33
3:21-22	134	5	194, 477	6:11	87n.10, 179, 215
3:22	210, 217	5:1	205, 217	6:11-18	192, 214, **221-22**
3:23	212n.16	5:1-12	**215-17**	6:12	187, 188, 191, 192, 206, 217
3:23-25	300	5:1-15	125		
3:23-29	211	5:1–6:10	**214-21**	6:12-13	189
3:24	216	5:2	191	6:13	191, 218
3:25	212n.16	5:2-4	189	6:14	84n.8, 119, 191
3:26	120n.6, 204	5:2-12	189, 442	6:14b	204
3:26-27	203	5:4	191	6:15	129, 210, 253, 307, 358, 509
3:26-28	272	5:5	122, 201, 211, 221		
3:27	120, 188, 369, 376, 397, 489	5:5-6	140, 210, 275, 479n.3	6:15-16	62
				6:16	112, 127, 385
3:27-28	86	5:6	62, 119, 120n.6, 121, 123, 140, 183, 218, 220, 222, 253, 464, 508, 509, 511, 515, 555	6:17	188, 191, 197, 197n.6, 206
3:28	62, 63, 120n.6, 127, 203, 222, 266, 405, 466, 477, 490, 513, 552			6:18	117n.4, 548
				Ephesians	
4	210	5:7	188	1–3	514, 516
4:1-7	**210-11**	5:9	189	1:1	463n.9, 499
4:1-11	111	5:10	188, 191, 214	1:1-2	**505**
4:3	211	5:11	53, 191, 383	1:2	117n.4, 517
4:4	106, 124, 136, 212n.16, 347, 507	5:12	188, 189, 191	1:3	295, 517
		5:13-15	**217-18**	1:3-14	100n.3, 294, **506-7**, 510
4:4-5	100, 117, 540	5:13–6:5	375		
4:4-6	118, 375	5:13–6:10	127, 188	1:3–3:21	**506-15**
4:4-7	119	5:14	396	1:4	515
4:5	212n.16, 217	5:16	125, 217	1:7	508, 510, 515
4:6	86, 118, 119, 120, 124, 125, 139, 188, 204, 301, 322, 376	5:16-25	204	1:8b-9	508
		5:16-26	188, 210, 218, **218-20**, 221, 375	1:9	504, 514
				1:9-14	503
4:6-7	188	5:18	212n.16, 217	1:10	504, 509, 518, 526

1:11	508	3:14	517	5:20	490, 517
1:11-14	517	3:14-21	**514-15**	5:21	524, 525
1:12	503, 508	3:16	508, 517	5:21-33	510
1:13	508, 509	3:17-19	518	5:21–6:9	70
1:13-14	505n.3, 508	3:20	517	5:22-32	322
1:14	296, 508	4–6	504, 513, 516, 529	5:22–6:9	**524-26**, 530
1:15	499, 515	4	219, 504	5:23	517, 518
1:15-23	**508-9**, 514	4:1	463n.9, 502,	5:25	521, 523
1:17	517		505n.3	5:27	507
1:18	517	4:1-3	511	5:30	517
1:19	517	4:1-16	**516-19**	6:1	505n.3
1:20-22	518, 526	4:1–6:20	**516-28**	6:5-9	565
1:21	210n.15, 503	4:4	520	6:10	505n.3
1:22	518	4:7-11	503	6:10-20	**526-28**, 588
1:23	504, 509, 515, 517	4:7-16	125	6:11	510
2	530	4:11	513	6:12	210n.15, 506, 508,
2:1-3	511	4:13	503		509, 510
2:1-6	517	4:14	499	6:13	508
2:1-10	**509-11**, 511	4:15	296, 503, 520	6:17-18	508
2:2	522	4:15-16	524	6:18	515
2:3	518	4:16	520	6:19	504
2:4-9	511	4:17	505n.3, 509	6:20	502
2:5	502, 522	4:17-24	**519-20**, 522	6:21	505n.3
2:5-6	529	4:17–6:9	**519-26**	6:21-22	478, 493, 502
2:6	502, 503, 508	4:19	521	6:21-24	**528**
2:8	502, 540	4:21	505n.3	6:23	517
2:10	498, 511	4:24	209	6:24	117n.4
2:11	517	4:25	517, 518		
2:11-22	203n.10, 509,	4:25–5:2	**520-21**, 523	**Philippians**	
	511-13	4:27	510	1–2	440, 441
2:14	203n.10	4:30	503, 507	1	418
2:15	520	4:31–5:2	511	1:1	67, 120n.6, 417,
2:16	503	4:32	490		420, 445, 463n.9,
2:18	517	5:1	515		532n.1, 553
2:20	518	5:1-2	503	1:1-2	**424**
2:20-22	517	5:2	509, 523, 524	1:2	117n.4
3:1	463n.9, 502	5:3-14	**521-22**	1:3-4	126
3:1-13	**513-14**, 515	5:4	523	1:3-5	508n.5
3:2	499	5:6	499, 510n.8	1:3-11	**425-26**, 446
3:3	504	5:8	505n.3, 509, 519	1:4	449
3:4	504	5:10	522	1:5	417, 447, 451, 463
3:5	504, 513, 518	5:12	523	1:6	174, 419, 451
3:6	517	5:15	509	1:7	417, 422n.5
3:9	504	5:15-21	**522-24**	1:7-8	449
3:10	210n.15	5:15–6:9	**522-26**	1:8	440
3:11	504	5:18-21	524	1:10	419, 451
3:13	502, 514	5:19	490	1:11	421

1:12-14	71, 417	2:4	123n.12, 237,	2:19-24	**439**, 532n.1
1:12-18	484n.6		401n.38, 523	2:19-30	**439-40**
1:12-18a	**426-27**	2:5	125, 421, 422n.5,	2:20	420
1:12-26	**426-29**		423, 424, 438, 445	2:20-21	424, 437n.22
1:13	417, 424	2:5-7a	412	2:21	420, 427
1:15-18	441	2:5-11	431	2:22	420, 424, 427
1:17	417	2:6	18, 136, 401, 419-	2:23-26	424
1:18	417n.3		20, 432, 437, 443	2:24	417, 427
1:18a	427	2:6a	68, 103, 260	2:25	420
1:18b	427	2:6b	68, 103, 260	2:25-30	417, 418, **440**
1:18-19	126	2:6-8	122n.10, 155,	2:26-27	437n.22
1:18b-26	**427-29**		155n.5, 218, 260,	2:28	417n.3
1:19	417		315, 323, 422, 425,	2:29	417n.3
1:20-21	421		429, 432, 433, **435-**	2:30	421
1:21-26	437n.22		**37**, 442, 444, 465,	3-4	449
1:23	547		467, 540	3:1	417n.3, **441-42**
1:23-26	417	2:6-11	68, 86, 89, 99n.2,	3:1–4:1	**418**, 441-45
1:25	417n.3		103-5, 315, 347,	3:2	444
1:26-27	440		412, 412n.1, 419-23,	3:2-11	196, 201, **442-43**
1:27	127, 419, 428, 438,		425, 427, 430, 431,	3:3	385
	443, 517n.11		**434-38**, 438, 440,	3:3-6	53
1:27-30	**429-31**, 438		441, 443, 449, 450,	3:3-11	45
1:27–2:4	418		452, 468, 477, 481,	3:4-6	372
1:27–2:5	105n.8		503	3:5	50, 51, 53
1:27–2:18	429, **429-39**	2:7	260, 302, 419, 420,	3:6	44, 53, 54, 54n.7,
1:28	173n.1, 174, 298,		424, 469		383
	417, 438	2:7-8	69, 103, 237, 432	3:7	420
1:28-29	418	2:7d-8	100	3:7-11	503
1:28-30	417	2:8	122, 260, 421, 440,	3:7-14	123
1:29	329, 421, 425		443, 447	3:8	420
1:29-30	415, 439	2:9	103, 421, 422	3:8-9	420
1:30	417	2:9-11	65, 118, 136, **437**	3:9	138, 437
2	259-60, 418, 451	2:10-11	103, 421, 422	3:10	374, 419, 421, 447,
2:1	120n.6, 424, 425,	2:11	102, 384, 424, 426,		515
	445		430, 448	3:10-11	141, 143, 174n.2,
2:1-4	126, 425, 439, 523	2:12	420, 421, 430, 437		435
2:1-5	121, 391, 393, 419,	2:12-13	431, 484	3:11	112
	431-33, 438, 445	2:12-16	127	3:12	420, 515
2:1-8	140	2:12-18	**438-39**	3:12-21	113
2:1-11	140, 390, 400	2:13	174	3:12–4:1	**444-45**
2:2	332, 401n.38,	2:14-18	429	3:13-14	431n.15
	417n.3, 422n.5,	2:15	507	3:15	422n.5
	424, 445	2:16	420, 431n.15, 451	3:18	324, 421
2:3	420, 421	2:17	417n.3, 448, 547	3:19	421, 422n.5
2:3-4	420, 429, 436, 437,	2:18	417n.3	3:20	108n.10, 127, 142,
	437n.22	2:19	67		419
2:3-5	427	2:19-21	303	3:20-21	112, 451

3:21	112, 374, 420, 421
4:1	417n.3, 430
4:2	120n.6, 332, 415n.2, 422n.5, 424, 431
4:2-3	415, 418, 424, **445**
4:2-9	**445-46**
4:2-23	445
4:3	421, 430, 431n.15
4:4	120n.6, 417n.3
4:4-6	484n.6
4:4-7	126, **446**, 452
4:5b	451
4:7	120n.6, 446
4:8-9	**446**
4:10	417n.3, 422n.5
4:10-14	**447**
4:10-20	417, 418, 445, **447-49**
4:11	86, 566
4:11-13	452
4:12	421
4:13	330, 443, 484, 589
4:15	447
4:15-20	**448-49**
4:18	417, 440
4:19	120n.6, 421, 452
4:20	421
4:21	424
4:21-22	417
4:21-23	**449-50**
4:22	426
4:23	117n.4, 548

Colossians

1–2	487-88, 504
1	475
1:1	67, 456, 463n.9, 478, 532n.1
1:1-2	**478-79**
1:2	117n.4, 494, 505
1:3-5	508n.5
1:3-8	455, **479-80**
1:3-23	**479-84**
1:4-5	122n.9
1:4-8	472
1:5	477

1:6	494
1:6-7	457n.6
1:7	455n.2, 457, 477, 478, 493, 514
1:7-8	457, 472, 493
1:8	477
1:9	484
1:9-10	484
1:9-14	**480-81**, 481
1:10	517n.11
1:11	484
1:13	483
1:14	483
1:15-20	100n.3, 475, **481-83**, 485, 490
1:16	210n.15, 483, 486
1:18	487
1:19-20	477
1:20	476, 503
1:21-23	**483-84**
1:22	507
1:22-23	484
1:23	477, 484, 514
1:23b-28	513
1:24	489
1:24–2:5	**484-85**
1:25	514
1:27	477, 479, 555
1:28	540n.7
2:1	457n.6, 472
2:2-3	471
2:4	476
2:5	485
2:6	487
2:6-8	**485**, 487
2:6-23	**485-87**
2:8	210n.15, 473, 474, 475, 487
2:9-15	**485-86**
2:10	509
2:10-11	483
2:11-23	475
2:14	476
2:15	509, 587
2:16	474
2:16-23	474, **487**
2:18	474

2:20	210n.15
2:20-22	488
2:21	474
2:23	474
3–4	494, 504
3	491
3:1	503
3:1-4	**488-89**
3:1-7	477
3:1-17	491
3:1–4:6	**488-93**
3:3	503
3:4	477, 503
3:5	489
3:5-17	**489-90**
3:6	477, 510n.8
3:7	487
3:7-8	519
3:9-10	519, 520
3:10	477
3:11	62, 272, 472, 477, 490, 492
3:12-16	491
3:17	491, 523
3:18–4:1	70, 476, 477, **490-92**, 524
3:22–4:1	565
3:24	477
4:2-6	**492-93**
4:7-9	478, 502
4:7-17	455n.2, 477
4:7-18	**493-94**
4:9	455, 455n.2, 457, 463
4:10	457, 548
4:10-14	457
4:12	457, 472
4:14	548
4:16	92, 477, 502
4:17	456
4:18	87n.10, 117n.4, 179, 478

1 Thessalonians

1–3	151, 156
1:1	67, 117n.4, **152**, 532n.1

1:1-5	118	3:10	150	5:12-28	158, **163-64**
1:2	126	3:10-13	150	5:14	159, 170
1:2-3	141, 508n.5	3:11	152	5:14-15	159
1:2-10	**153-54**	3:11-13	163	5:14-18	142
1:2–3:13	**153-56**	3:11-15	172	5:15	124, 159, 393n.33
1:3	122n.9, 150, 171,	3:12	173	5:16-18	126, 484n.6
	174, 216n.17, 275,	3:13	112, 146, 151, 160,	5:16-19	118
	479n.3, 573		484	5:19	152
1:3-8	173	4–5	151, 164	5:21-22	392
1:5	154	4:1	159, 173	5:23	151, 484
1:5-6	152	4:1-3a	**157-58**	5:23-24	239
1:6	150, 174n.2, 177	4:1-8	112, 125	5:27	92
1:7-9	150	4:1-12	**157-59**	5:28	117n.4
1:8	464	4:1–5:11	**157-63**		
1:9	122, 147, 397	4:3	151, 163	**2 Thessalonians**	
1:9-10	152, 157, 175, 586	4:3-5	142	1:1	67, 177, 532n.1
1:9b-10	100	4:3b-8	**158-59**	1:1-2	**172**
1:10	112, 155, 159, 160	4:6	155	1:2	117n.4
	173n.1, 510n.8	4:7	163	1:3	172, 177
2	150	4:8	152	1:3-4	**173**
2:1-2	415	4:9-12	**159**	1:3-12	**173-74**
2:1-12	62, 85, 150, **154-55**	4:10	171	1:4	169
2:2	148, 150, 540n.7	4:10-12	179	1:5-10	**173-74**, 431
2:6-8	155n.5	4:13	162	1:11	173, 177
2:7	61, 62, 77, 465	4:13-18	77, 150, **160-61**,	1:11-12	172, **174**
2:7-8	105n.8, 153,		162, 169, 174n.2,	1:12	177
	436n.21		175n.3, 428n.12	2:1-3a	**175**
2:7-9	178	4:13–5:11	77, 158, **159-63**	2:1–3:5	**174-77**
2:7b-12	61	4:14	153	2:2	92, 167, 169, 170,
2:9	67, 69, 150, 178	4:14-17	303		171, 179, 543
2:12	517n.11	4:15	175n.3	2:3b-12	**175-77**
2:13-16	**155**	4:15-17	86	2:8	540n.6
2:14	120n.6, 150	4:16	281	2:9-12	177
2:14-16	89, 177	4:16-17	143	2:13	98, 172, 173
2:15	153	4:17	163, 175n.3	2:13–3:5	**177**
2:16	173n.1, 510n.8	4:18	77, 159	2:15	171, 540n.7
2:17-20	150	5:1-11	77, **162-63**, 169	2:16	172
2:17–3:13	**156**	5:3a	164	3:5	172
2:18	348	5:4-11	397	3:6	171, 179
2:18–3:5	152	5:6-8	546	3:6-9	171
3:1-10	532n.1	5:8	122n.9, 153, 154,	3:6-10	**178**
3:2	67		216n.17, 275,	3:6-15	170, 177, **178-79**
3:3	150		479n.3	3:7-9	465
3:4	150	5:9	112, 173n.1, 510n.8	3:8	69
3:6	150	5:11	77, 159	3:11-15	**178-79**
3:6-10	150	5:12	564	3:12	178
3:8	120n.6, 177	5:12-22	83, 392	3:14-15	171, 179